A Reader's Guide
to the Great Religions

SECOND EDITION

EDITED BY

Charles J. Adams

THE FREE PRESS
A Division of Macmillan Publishing Co., Inc.
NEW YORK

Collier Macmillan Publishers
LONDON

The Free Press
A Division of Macmillan Publishing Co., Inc.
866 Third Avenue, New York, N.Y. 10022

Collier Macmillan Canada, Ltd.

Library of Congress Catalog Card Number: 76–10496

Printed in the United States of America

printing number

1 2 3 4 5 6 7 8 9 10

Library of Congress Cataloging in Publication Data

Adams, Charles J   ed.
    A reader's guide to the great religions.

    Includes indexes.
    1. Religions--Bibliography. I. Title.
Z7833.A35 1977   [BL80.2]   016.2   76-10496
ISBN 0-02-900240-0

Contents

Contents

List of Contributors

CHARLES J. ADAMS, Professor and Director of the Institute of Islamic Studies, McGill University.

SEYMOUR CAIN, Senior Editor for Religion, Fifteenth Edition, *Encyclopaedia Britannica*.

W.A.C.H. DOBSON, Profesor of Chinese, Department of East Asian Studies, University of Toronto.

KENDALL W. FOLKERT, Assistant Professor of Religion, Central Michigan University.

JUDAH GOLDIN, Professor of Postbiblical Hebrew Literature, University of Pennsylvania.

NORVIN J. HEIN, Professor of Comparative Religion, Yale University.

JOSEPH M. KITAGAWA, Professor of the History of Religions and Dean of the Divinity School, University of Chicago.

CHARLES H. LONG, William Rand Kenan, Jr., Professor of History of Religions, University of North Carolina.

WILLARD G. OXTOBY, Professor, Trinity College, University of Toronto.

JAROSLAV PELIKAN, Dean of the Graduate School and Sterling Professor of History and Religious Studies, Yale University.

FRANK E. REYNOLDS, Associate Professor of Buddhist Studies, Department of Asian Languages and Civilizations, University of Chicago.

KHUSHWANT SINGH, Editor in Chief, *The Illustrated Weekly of India.*

JUAN ADOLFO VÁZQUEZ, Professor, Department of Hispanic Languages and Literatures, University of Pittsburgh.

H.H. WALSH, former Professor of Church History, McGill University.

Preface to the Second Edition

The reception accorded the first edition of this volume has been a source of gratification to all who have had a part in it. Bibliographical guidance apparently fills a felt need for many persons, and it is with the hope that this need may be more satisfactorily met that the second edition is offered to the public.

The objectives and principles that have governed the preparation of the second edition are identical with those exemplified in the first, as set out in its Preface. The principal differences between the two editions are the following: (1) the second edition has been painstakingly revised and brought up to date; (2) the lacunae noted in the first edition have been filled; and (3) new chapters have been added to make the treatment fuller and more comprehensive. The result is a thoroughly reworked and much larger book; we hope that it will also be a more useful one. There has also been an attempt to hold down the size of the volume by a greater resort to the use of abbreviations, shortened forms of publishers' names, elimination of subtitles, elimination of unnecessary series identifications, and so forth. In each case, however, enough information has been provided to permit easy location or identification of the publication in question.

Acknowledgments and expressions of gratitude are due to many persons for their assistance with the work on this volume. Professors Willem Bijlefeld and Donald P. Little of the Institute of Islamic Studies have contributed generously with suggestions and criticisms. Miss Salwa Ferahian of the Institute's Library and Mrs. Norma Babikian have rendered invaluable help in confirming bibliographical details. The editor's capable secretaries, Mrs. Eve Law and Mrs. Christine Korah, have been responsible for the preparation of the manuscript, for much of the bibliographical work, and for preparing the indexes. Finally, gratitude is due to Joanna Adams, the editor's wife, for active help, and especially for her support, encouragement and patience in the course of a gruelling task.

CHARLES J. ADAMS

Preface to the First Edition

The purpose of this volume is to give bibliographical guidance to persons who, for whatever reason, are interested in learning more of the world's great religious traditions. Its preparation was undertaken at the initiative of the Free Press, who published a somewhat similar work on the social sciences in 1959. Believing that there is a widespread need felt for a sound guide to literature about religions, the Free Press commissioned the editor to embark on the present volume. The book is presented to the public with the hope that it may prove a useful and trustworthy guide.

Among the North American public, interest in religions, especially in the religious traditions alien to the West, has experienced a tremendous upsurge in the years since World War II. Expressions of this lively new interest, to mention only two of them, may be seen in the numerous publications on religions crowding the shelves of our bookshops and in the growing trend of universities, state institutions not excepted, to include courses on religion in their curricula. In universities such as Princeton and Syracuse, where courses in religion have been offered for some time, the appeal of the subject for undergraduates is astonishingly strong and consistent. At any given time a sizeable fraction of the students in these universities follows one or another course in religion. This development is more striking for having occurred at a time when the humanities generally are on the decline in the universities and when science has achieved new and unprecedented prestige.

The situation is no different with the educated public outside the universities. If one requires evidence to support this assertion, it is amply available in the sales of books on religion to a vast group of general readers. There is today an active market for books on religion, and it shows signs of becoming stronger still. In response to the demand, publishers are offering a flood of books on religion, both new works and reprints of former ones. In paperback editions alone it is now possible to build up an extensive and respectable library on the great religious traditions. So numerous are these publications and so rich the resources they offer that one is often left in puzzled bewilderment about which among them to choose. In these circumstances it seems appropriate and useful that a volume such as this, giving bibliographical advice of trained specialists in religious studies, should be made available.

Although the purpose of this work is bibliographical, it is much more than a bare list of books. In form it is a series of essays. The authors of its various chapters have endeavored not only to state what should be read in their respective fields but have also been conscious of the need to explain why these particular recommendations have been made. Sometimes by relating a book to a general framework within which the religious tradition of their particular interest may be studied, and at other times by exhibiting the role of a work in the history of scholarly thought, or by some similar device, they have sought to show to the user of this volume why those writings recommended to him have been chosen. Where it has seemed appropriate to offer comments or criticism directed at the literature cited, this has been done. It is hoped that the result is a volume that will be of greater utility to those who employ it than would a mere list of titles.

While preparing this volume, the contributors have had in mind the needs of several classes of people. Perhaps the largest and most difficult to define group are the "general readers," members of the educated segment of the public whose interest may have been drawn to some aspect of religious studies and who may wish direction in the choice of reading materials. Another considerable group are graduate students in the history of religions, who may, by use of this volume, move toward a comprehensive overview of their field of study and the bibliographical resources requisite for a balanced grasp of it. The authors have been mindful, too, of the needs of librarians. In the smaller colleges and public libraries especially, librarians have long needed a reliable guide for the formation of an adequate collection on religion. Accordingly, the authors have attempted to list works that they consider sound and which, taken together, constitute a solid foundation for more advanced study into the life of the various religious traditions represented. Lastly, the authors have sought to provide assistance to the sizeable group of college instructors who in recent days have found themselves chosen to meet the demand upon the colleges for courses in religion. In a great number of cases these men are without professional training in the history of religions and are compelled to teach religion courses only because there is no one else to teach them. Many experience difficulty in finding out trustworthy bibliographical resources for their own and their students' purposes.

To sum up, then, this volume is intended for a broad range of people with serious interest in religion who may stand to benefit from the considered opinions of specialists on the literature of the religious field. So far as specialists are concerned, they do not require a bibliographical guide of this level within their own fields, but the volume may prove of use to the scholar who wishes a quick survey of the fields of his colleagues.

It should not be necessary to emphasize that a comprehensive bibliography on the subjects covered in this *Reader's Guide* would be all but impossible to compile. To consider in comprehensive fashion only one of the great traditions dealt with here—Christianity, for example—would be the work of a lifetime for a large group of people. Entire libraries of works on Christianity have been written through the centuries of its history, and the same is no less true of others of the religious traditions. For a student of one of the great religious traditions, the problem is not so much to discover sufficient materials for his work as it is to discriminate among the superabundance available on every hand. The purpose of this *Reader's Guide* is precisely to aid in the process of discrimination by suggesting a selection of works that appear to its authors to be the best or most useful or most typical of their kind. Doubtless in many instances there is room for disagreement with the selection made; any accomplished scholar in the fields concerned would be able to name dozens of books that might be added to the list of those recommended here or substituted for some of them. Selection, however, has been unavoidable, and it is, indeed, on the selective quality of this bibliographical guide that its value should be judged.

Some words are in order about the principles of selection employed in this volume. The general criterion that has determined whether a given title should be included or not has been one of utility. If a work has qualities that make it especially valuable for the persons whom the volume seeks to serve, it has been included, no matter whether it is published as a separate book or in the pages of a journal. Literary quality and readibility are among the factors considered in judging utility. The endeavor to list useful materials has meant that the authors have sometimes passed over the most erudite and technical or the latest works in their fields to suggest reading that may be more readily understandable or more immediately relevant. It is not uncommonly the case that books which are most helpful to the sophisticated scholar are of only limited use to one who lacks a background in depth in the subject matter concerned. As this work is not intended primarily for specialists, their needs and interests have been subordinated to those of the groups mentioned above.

As a secondary criterion, the authors have also considered the availability of the reading materials they are suggesting. If a work, despite its quality and usefulness, is unlikely to be obtainable in a first-class library or purchasable in the book market, there has seemed less urgency in listing it in these pages. There are, however, many exceptions to this rule. Books are often mentioned whose sheer importance demands their inclusion apart from questions of availability. In the chapters that concern the religions of the Far East especially, a number of titles published by relatively obscure firms in various parts of the Orient are cited. The consideration reigning there has been twofold: (1) that Western readers should to some degree be aware of publications on these subjects in the non-Western world and (2) that many of these publications are still available in the book market in the Orient, though unlikely to find their way into the hands of a Western bookseller. Awareness of its existence may be encouragement to some to exploit this body of literature.

One of the most important principles of selection used here will strike the reader immediately—namely, the heavy preference for works in English. As this *Reader's Guide* will be presented to an English-reading public, it is natural that the major part of the literature discussed should be in that language. There is no lack of works in English on the great religious traditions, but the effort to restrict the *Reader's Guide* even largely to English has imposed a considerable limitation upon its contributors. In many, if not most, fields in the study of religions, Europeans have been both the pioneers and the principal investigators, and any survey of literature on religions must take account of the enormous volume of work in European languages. Many European language works have, consequently, been included here, but there has been a conscious effort to restrict their number to those of outstanding quality or of particular influence in the history of scholarship. Where books exist both in the original language and in translation, preference has been given to the translation.

Much the same considerations apply to works in the languages of the Orient. If French and German pose difficulties for a large number of English readers, the problem is incalculably greater with such tongues as Japanese, Chinese, and Sanskrit. Works in these languages will prove of use only to specialists and a favored few others, and for this reason they have been rigorously excluded. As an implication of this policy, it follows that the citation of original materials from Oriental religions has necessarily had to be limited to those documents rendered into English.

One of the difficult problems of selection has been to decide on the proportion of secondary to primary works cited. The advantages of exposing the student of Hinduism, to take an example, to a variety of the original and formative documents of that religious tradition are too obvious to require comment. Such primary documents, however, are not always capable of being understood by the uninitiated, and for this reason a well-rounded bibliographical guide requires the inclusion of large numbers of secondary and interpretive works. It has proved impossible to formulate an adequate general rule on this point, and the proportion of primary to secondary sources has been left to the discretion of contributors.

The bibliographical information given concerning each title mentioned is sufficient in the editor's opinion to allow easy identification and location of the work. For books, place and date of publication and the publisher's name normally have been given, though there are some exceptions. In a few instances the publisher's address is included as well. The latter measure was thought necessary for Oriental books that would be impossible to procure without this information. In the case of works that are well known and that have been through numerous editions—St. Augustine's *City of God,* for example—it has not been thought necessary to give data about one particular edition unless there is special reason for preferring one above the others. The edition of a book cited is normally the one that the contributor considers either the most useful or the most readily available. No attempt has been made to reconstruct the publishing history of the numerous works cited in the *Reader's Guide;* to have done so would have made the volume many times its length without a commensurate increase in its value. For periodicals the information given includes title of the article, title of the journal, volume number, number, date, and the page upon which the article begins.

Attached to several of the chapters of the *Reader's Guide* are appendices that list, largely without comment, the principal reference works and principal journals in the fields concerned. It was felt that this information would be particularly appreciated by librarians and more advanced students. In the chapter on Christianity similar information has been included in the text of the article rather than being confined to an appendix. The chapter on primitive religions has, as well, a special appendix, prepared by the editor, in order to extend the suggestions made there concerning the history of the study of religion in the West.* For many persons the history of scholarship in an area of study offers the best way of coming to terms with the area. Furthermore, this brief appendix has afforded the opportunity to cite some of the literature bearing on the broad problems of the origin and nature of religion.

The editor's contribution to this volume, apart from the chapter which he has written, has consisted in (1) laying out the plan for the volume and attempting to maintain some unity of viewpoint in its various chapters and (2) verifying the accuracy of the bibliographical information given. The latter has been a difficult and demanding task, and if, in spite of the efforts made, errors yet remain, the editor acknowledges his responsibility for all such shortcomings. The content and method of treatment of each chapter in the volume have been solely due to the contributors. The editor would

* In the second edition this appendix has been expanded and placed at the end of the volume.

like especially to emphasize that he has not attempted to impose upon the contributors any firm conception of the nature of religion that would guide their work or orient their points of view. Each has been given perfect freedom to explore the nature of the religious tradition with which his studies are concerned. If, as appears to be the case, it is impossible to abstract from the finished volume a clear and satisfying definition of religion that covers all the traditions dealt with, this fact may be one of the volume's genuine contributions. At the least it appears to bear out the conclusions of an important recent work in the religious field where it is argued that the concept "religion" has outlived its usefulness and should be abandoned (see Wilfred C. Smith, *The Meaning and End of Religion* [N.Y., The Macmillan Co., 1963]).

The title chosen for this volume represents a compromise by the editor and was agreed upon only after the expenditure of much effort to find a more satisfactory one. Application of the terms "religion" and "religions" to such diverse phenomena as the cults of noncivilizational peoples in the more remote regions of the earth, on the one hand, and to the highly sophisticated, articulate, and self-conscious piety of the great traditions of India, China, and the Middle East, on the other, implies a closeness of connection between the two that is much too simple if it can be accepted at all. A similar problem presents itself when one begins to consider in detail the historical manifestation of any single one of the traditions treated in the chapters of this volume. No one of them is monolithic and simple; rather each is multiform, complex, and always changing. To the thoughtful observer this state of affairs must suggest at least a question concerning the validity of a terminology that seems to imply that each tradition is a recognizable entity with a clear identity of its own. Moreover, there is reason for challenging the use of the adjective "great" in the title in view of the inclusion of a chapter on primitive religions. Objections on this point could, perhaps, be met by an argument designed to show that the so-called primitive religions are, indeed, a "great" tradition in virtue of the very extent of their spread through time and space and the numbers of persons who have been affected by them. Finally, the clarity of the title is compromised by the method of organizing the material of the volume as a whole. One of the chapters deals with a most diffuse group of phenomena that have been designated by the abstraction "primitive religions." Another group of chapters takes distinct religious traditions and treats of them separately and to some extent in relation with one another. Yet a third group of chapters, those dealing with the religions of China and Japan, have been conceived and organized in geographical terms. Although any usefulness this volume may have will not be materially affected by the felicitousness of the title chosen for it, it seems better to acknowledge these reservations about the adequacy of the title from the beginning.

Unfortunately, another acknowledgment of deficiency in this work is also called for. Within the scope of the chapters as they have been planned, there have been at least three omissions of quite major importance. No treatment is given in these pages to the Buddhist tradition in its Chinese context, to the later history of the Jewish community from the Middle Ages to the present time, to the minor religious communities of India, such as the Sikhs and the Jains. It is unnecessary to trouble the reader with the reasons for the inability to cover these important areas of study; the editor wishes only to call attention to these lacunae and to acknowledge his responsibility for them. If ever it should be possible to revise this volume, attention would be given to filling these unfortunate gaps.

Finally, it is the editor's pleasant task to thank those who have assisted in this project. Thanks go first of all to Professor James Luther Adams of Harvard University for having suggested this piece of work to the editor and suggesting the editor's name to the Free Press. Secondly, recognition is due to Mr. John Christopher Kyle of Montreal who labored faithfully in the arduous task of confirming bibliographical details. The editor's secretaries, Mrs. Jean Kerr, Mrs. Madeleine Widawska and Miss Eve Yuile, of Montreal, are due a large measure of gratitude for their willingness, patience and careful work in the preparation of the manuscript. Finally, the editor would like to acknowledge the assistance of the Committee on Research of the Faculty of Graduate Studies and Research, McGill University, in the form of a grant of money to employ help in confirming bibliographical details.

CHARLES J. ADAMS

Montreal

March, 1965

Primitive Religion

Charles H. Long

I. INTRODUCTION: THEORETICAL CONSIDERATIONS

Primitive religions do not constitute self-conscious authentic religious historical traditions in the same manner as Christianity, Hinduism, Buddhism, and so on. In other words there are no people who refer to themselves as practitioners of primitive religions. Primitive religion is thus a phrase referring to a constructed Western mode of categorizing certain kinds of cultural historical religious traditions. As such the phrase itself raises a constitutive methodological issue. It is as much a cultural methodological category of the modern West as it is a way of describing certain kinds of religious data.

The phrase "primitive religion" is defined within the disciplines of anthropology, ethnology, and the history of religions. To a certain extent each discipline has roots in the world view of the Enlightenment. While these disciplines have added much to the meaning of the phrase in terms of method and content, they have also accepted explicitly and implicitly some of the more philosophically oriented definitions of the past in their formulations of the meaning of primitive religion. This is true especially in their understanding of the term "primitive."

Arthur O. Lovejoy and George Boas in their book, *A Documentary His-*

tory of Primitivism and Related Ideas (Baltimore, Johns Hopkins Univ. Press, 1935), have examined some of the meanings of "primitivism" in classical antiquity. They have classified these meanings into two general categories, "chronological" and "cultural."

> Chronological primitivism is one of the many answers which may be and have been given to the question: What is the temporal distribution of good, or value, in the history of mankind, or more generally, in the entire history of the world? It is, in short, a kind of philosophy of history, a theory, or a customary assumption, as to the time—past or present or future—at which the most excellent condition of human life, or the best state of the world in general, must be supposed to occur (p. 1).

> Cultural primitivism is the discontent of the civilized with civilization or with some conspicuous characteristic feature of it. It is the belief of men living in the relatively highly involved and complex cultural condition that a life far simpler and less sophisticated in some or all respects is a more desirable life (p. 7).

One can see the above interests reflected in the philosophical, historical and systematic studies of the Enlightenment. A very good description and analysis of the historical study of religion in the Enlightenment is Frank E. Manuel's *The Eighteenth Century Confronts the Gods* (Cambridge, Harvard Univ. Press, 1959).

Though many of the Enlightenment thinkers tended to regard primitivism in either its chronological or cultural sense, they were confronted with new problems. Since many thinkers of this period had dissociated themselves from the Church, they were unable to regard the witness of the Bible as a norm for the study of man's history. Secondly, they were confronted with empirical data concerning the religions and cultures of the high civilizations such as India, China, and Greece. In addition, they had to come to terms with the reports of explorers, missionaries, and traders regarding those cultures that were neither a part of the Western heritage nor members of one of the centers of high civilization, such as the cultures of the Americas, Oceania, Polynesia, Melanesia, and sub-Saharan Africa.

The immediate reaction to these new data was to apply a variation of chronological or cultural primitivism in a modified form with either "nature" or "reason" as a norm. If "reason" were the norm, the "primitives" were understood as an example of the earliest and most rudimentary instance of this human capacity. History showed a development from the lowest stage to the highest and most refined exemplification of reason in its Enlightenment expression. If "nature" were the norm, the "primitives" might be seen as an example of the naturalness and innocence which originally belonged to human beings. The history of human beings was thus interpreted as a degeneration of their natural freedom and innocence. The most religious form was often equated with the most primitive and vice versa.

(2)

These predominantly philosophical explanations regarding the cultures of "extracivilizational" man receded into the background as historical scholarship slowly came to terms with the reports and descriptions of primitive man. To a great extent many of the philosophical implications of Enlightenment thinking remained, but as time went on, these philosophical doctrines could not be offered as a total explanation of the historical phenomena. Ernst Cassirer has written that after David Hume's critique of deism in his *Dialogues Concerning Natural Religion* (many editions), every conception of religion had to be based on history; see Ernst Cassirer, *The Philosophy of the Enlightenment* (Princeton, Princeton Univ. Press, 1951), 182.

From this developing historical consciousness the disciplines of anthropology, ethnology, and history of religions emerged. Each of them attempted to base its understanding as far as possible on an analysis of the empirical data, and each wished to arrive at some judgment on the meaning and nature of the human as expressed in these extracivilizational cultures. Their common interest in religion resulted from the fact that this dimension of life seemed to be the most pervasive and highly elaborated form in the cultures under discussion. It was thus considered to be the most important form of human life in these cultures and the form most amenable to examination and analysis. The confusion surrounding the term "primitive" has been noted with increasing intensity over the last several years; Francis L. K. Hsu's article "Rethinking the Concept 'Primitive' " in *Current Anthropology* 5 (1964), 169–78, traces the term in the discipline of anthropology and lists the several different ways it has been used by modern anthropologists. He concludes that the term is empirically, theoretically and practically obsolescent. He feels that the insistent use of the concept by anthropologists reveals the reluctance on their part to examine their own societies and cultures. However, he also thinks, "whatever the reason, the continued use of and preoccupation with the concept 'primitive' (through such efforts as redefinition or substitution), will hamper the further progress of our science" (p. 78).

Stanley Diamond has undertaken a philosophical analysis of the term "primitive" in his *In Search of the Primitive* (New Brunswick, N.J., Transaction Books, 1974). Diamond thinks that the term is legitimate descriptively and critically and wishes to reinstitute the integrity of the concept. One of the chapters, "The Search for the Primitive," has been republished in Ashley Montagu's *The Concept of the Primitive* (N.Y., Free Press, 1968). Montagu's book adopts a critical stance toward the concept primitive with chapters by: Ashley Montagu, Catherine H. Berndt, Sol Tax, Catherine George, Marshall Sahlins, Edward P. Dozier, and Jules Henry. Jules Henry's chapter is entitled, "The Term 'Primitive' in Kierkegaard and Heidegger." This usage of the term in a non-anthropological and non-ethnographical manner had already been pointed to in the realm of literature by Lois Whitney in her work, *Primitivism and the Idea of Progress in the Eighteenth Century* (Baltimore, Johns Hopkins Univ. Press, 1934).

It is obvious from reading the critical materials dealing with the concept "primitive" that the term is used in contrast to the concept of "civilization." Emile Benveniste has pointed out in his *Problems in General Linguistics* (Coral Gables, Univ. of Miami Press, 1971) that the term "civilization" came into usage in the French language in 1756 with the publication of Marquis de Mirabeau's *L'Ami des hommes ou traité de la population*. He thinks from the evidence at hand that the term came into English around 1772 and is first mentioned in Boswell's *Life of Johnson*. Taking the two terms primitive and civilization together, we must conclude that the new meaning and ambiguity surrounding these terms became a part of Western languages in the latter part of the eighteenth century. A similar ambiguity surrounds another term often used in conjunction with primitive as its correlate, viz: tribe. Maurice Godelier in his article "The Concept of Tribe: Crisis of a Concept or Crisis of the Empirical Foundations of Anthropology?" in *Diogenes* 81 (1973), 1–25, has discussed the history of the concept of tribe in modern anthropology from Lewis Morgan's *Systems of Consanguinity, an Affinity of the Human Family* (Smithsonian Institution, Contributions to Knowledge, vol. 17, article 2, Washington, D.C., Government Printing Office, 1871) to contemporary anthropological theorists. His essay reveals the ambiguity surrounding the term and the kinds of problems the term attempts to resolve regarding the nature of social relationships. He feels that it is time to develop a new concept to deal with the multifarious meanings which the term "tribe" had intended to clarify.

The ambiguity surrounding the terms "primitive" and "tribe" refers not simply to inability to give language its proper referent; it points as well to a fundamental ambiguity lying at the center of the methodological foundations of the disciplines that use these concepts.

The prestige and excitement evoked by Claude Lévi-Strauss may be attributed to the fact that he has made this ambiguity the fundamental methodological problem of the discipline of anthropology. Especially in *Totemism* (Boston, Beacon Press, 1963) and *The Savage Mind* (Chicago, Univ. of Chicago Press, 1966) he moved the discussion away from the context of history, which had become the locus for the distinction between the primitive and the civilized and the distinction between the tribe and the nation-state, to a discussion of the modes of thought which distinguish the human species from other species. His diary-novel-fieldwork report-methodological treatise, *Tristes Tropiques* (New York, Atheneum, 1974) places Lévi-Strauss the anthropologist in an exotic non-Western culture as a context for the contemplation of this methodological issue.

The first text of modern anthropology was E. B. Tylor's two-volume work entitled *Primitive Culture,* first published in 1871. It is available now through Harper Torchbooks (N.Y., Harper & Brothers, 1958). The first volume was entitled *The Origins of Culture,* the second volume *Religion in Primitive Culture.* Thus, we see from the very beginning that there was a wedding of the terms primitive and religion. The very fact that Tylor undertook a "scientific" study of culture and religion meant that the definition of religion could no longer be controlled by the theological categories of the Western religious tradition, and thus the term religion came to exhibit the same ambiguity as the previous terms primitive, civilization, and tribe. Wilfred Cantwell Smith in his *The Meaning and End of Religion* (N.Y., New American Library, 1964) has pointed out that the Western usage of the term "religion" may be inadequate for the understanding of other religious traditions. Other historians of religions have been aware of the same problem. Joachim Wach attempted to deal with this issue from within the context of a general hermeneutical theory. In his posthumous work, *The Comparative Study of Religion* (N.Y., Columbia Univ. Press, 1958), he presents some of the problems and resolutions raised by the terms "history" and "religion" in the discipline of the history of religion. Wach defines religion in *Types of Religious Experience* (Chicago, Univ. of Chicago Press, 1951) as "a response to what is experienced as ultimate reality" (p. 32).

G. Van der Leeuw working as a phenomenologist of religion in *Religion in Essence and Manifestation,* 2 vols. (N.Y. and Evanston, Harper & Row, 1963) refers to the experience of power in the form of the natural and social worlds as the origin of the religious sentiment. This approach is reminiscent of Rudolf Otto's earlier phenomenological text *The Idea of the Holy,* 2nd ed. (London, Oxford Univ. Press, 1958) where Otto undertakes to define and understand religion at the level of its origin, at the level at which it has not yet become formalized into rational concepts. In other words Otto wishes to understand religion experientially, in its non-rational *form.* To the extent that historians of religion have sought to define religion without making use of the rational concepts of theology, they have found themselves employing terms which were either abstract, e.g., Joachim Wach's notion of ultimate reality, or so radically concrete as not to seem amenable to the rational theologies and philosophies of the West, e.g., Van de Leeuw's notion of power or Rudolf Otto's notion of religious experience expressing itself in the modalities of *mysterium tremendum et fascinans.*

Mircea Eliade is aware of the constitutive issues surrounding the problem of a definition of religion, but he has laid down a new starting point for the question. He eschews the epistemological problems evoked by the hermeneutical approaches of Rudolf Otto and Joachim Wach, and he does not wish to involve himself in philosophical questions regarding the meaning of the phenomenon as G. Van der Leeuw has done. This new starting point is expressed precisely by Georges Dumézil in his introduction to Mircea Eliade's *Traité d'histoire des religions,* 2nd ed. (Paris, Payot,

1964), where he says, "In short it is under the sign of the *logos* and not that of *mana* that research takes place today" (p. 5).* This methodological approach by Eliade is an expression of what Paul Ricouer has called the first naiveté. Eliade attempts first of all to describe the forms of the world, especially the natural forms of the world as they become a basis for orientation, language, and imaginative symbolic structures for the human consciousness. We see this best in his *Patterns in Comparative Religion* (N.Y., World Publishing, 1972) wherein the formation of human consciousness as a religious consciousness is always correlated with a "natural" form of the world.

In spite of the differences of methodological perception among historians of religion all theoretical orientations in the discipline have always tended to give prestige to the data of archaic and primitive cultures. From the side of those scholars whose primary interest lay in religion, the data pool tended to move toward *primitive cultures* in the same manner in which those interested in a definition of culture derived their data from the *religious practices* of the cultures under discussion.

Given the state of thought in anthropology and the history of religions, it would be very difficult and not within the province of this essay to attempt to resolve the problems presented by the term "primitive" on the one hand and "religion" on the other; nor can we resolve the even more difficult issue involved in the combination of the terms. It is the intent of this essay to present materials which will allow the reader to continue this theoretical inquiry on the basis of the data already generated by these terms taken separately and in combination.

E. E. Evans-Pritchard's *Theories of Primitive Religion* (Oxford, Clarendon Press, 1965) has already begun a theoretical typological analysis of various theories of primitive religion. This book is a good starting place for a reconstitution of the question regarding primitive religion.

II. SOURCES OF RELIGIOUS SENTIMENT IN PRIMITIVE SOCIETIES

In light of the theoretical issues surrounding the terms "primitive" and "religion" we do well to see how many of the same kinds of issues have been raised concerning the nature of religious experience in primitive cultures. It is often presumed by anthropologists and historians of religion that insight into the religious experience of those cultures outside of the great civilizational complexes (the modern primitives) might provide an entrée into the meaning of the earliest and first form of religion. Thus E. B. Tylor, the father of modern anthropology, in *Religion in Primitive Culture,* vol.

* Editor's translation.

II of *Primitive Culture* (London, 1872; N.Y., Harper Torchbooks, 1958) set forth as a minimum definition of religion the notion of "Animism."

> It seems best to fall back at once on this essential source, and simply to claim as a minimum definition of Religion, the belief in Spiritual Beings. . . . I propose under the name of Animism to investigate the deeplying doctrine of Spiritual Beings, which embodies the very essence of Spiritualistic as opposed to Materialistic philosophy (p. 8).

Tylor arrived at his notion of Animism from a study of the religious sentiment in the societies of early man. Tylor's general theory of cultural and religious development gained wide acceptance. Though he adhered to a form of progressive evolutionism in his understanding of religion, his work was characterized by a careful analysis of empirical data from the societies under discussion.

The problem raised by Tylor's definition of Animism was directly related to the question of the origin of religion. While the empirical method of analysis of historical materials was given an impetus by Tylor's work, he was accused of being intellectualistic or too philosophical in his discussion of the origin of religion. A contemporary critic of Tylor writes:

> The most significant point in Tylor's interpretation of religion in primitive culture is that he bases religious belief upon a psychological delusion and mistaken logical inference. Primitive man is said to confuse subjective and objective reality, ideal and real objects. (David Bidney, "The Concept of Value in Modern Anthropology" in *Anthropology Today*, A. L. Kroeber, ed. [Chicago, Univ. of Chicago Press, 1953], 682–99.)

Paul Radin, who wrote the introduction to the paperback edition of Tylor's *Primitive Culture* (N.Y., Harper Torchbook, 1958), defends Tylor from the charge of intellectualism by showing that intellectualism and mysticism were compatible from the point of view of Tylor's Quakerism (p. xi).

The most telling criticisms of Tylor's conception of the origin of religion came, however, from the data of field-work studies of primitives such as R. H. Codrington's *The Melanesians* (Oxford, Clarendon Press, 1891); W. E. Gudgeon's "Maori Religion," *Journal of the Polynesian Society,* XIV (1905), 107–30; and Baldwin Spencer and F. J. Gillen, *The Native Tribes of Central Australia* (London, Macmillan, 1904).

The works relating to Melanesia and Polynesia presented for the first time a description of *mana* as a basic religious concept, and the works devoted to the Australians brought to light the importance of *totemism* as a religious reality among primitives. In *The Melanesians,* Codrington describes *mana* as follows:

> The Melanesian mind is entirely possessed by the belief in a supernatural power or influence, called almost universally "mana." . . . But this power, though itself impersonal, is always connected with some person

who directs it; all spirits have it, ghosts generally, some men (pp. 118–19).

Words describing the same type of religious phenomenon were subsequently discovered in other primitive societies. J. N. B. Hewitt's article, "Orenda and a Definition of Religion," *American Anthropologist*, n.s., IV, 1 (1902), 33–46, is a discussion of this phenomenon among the Iroquois Indians. Paul Radin analyzes the phenomenon among various American Indians in "Religion of the North American Indians," *Journal of American Folklore*, XXVII (1914), 335–73. This phenomenon—described as *mana, wakanda, orenda,* etc.—led some interpreters to see in it a new and basic source of the religious sentiment in primitive societies. Thus, before man formed a conception of Spiritual Beings (Tylor), he experienced emotionally an impersonal and dynamic power. The experience of this power was the primal religious experience. An interpretation of the religious sentiment along these lines may be seen in R. R. Marett's *The Threshold of Religion* (London, Methuen, 1909); *Faith, Hope, and Charity in Primitive Religion* (Oxford, Clarendon Press, 1932); *Sacraments of Simple Folk* (Oxford, Clarendon Press, 1933); and *Head, Heart, and Hands in Human Evolution* (London, Hutchinson, 1935).

The notion of *mana* and related terms led to the religious theory of dynamism or pre-animism. This theory sets forth the belief that the earliest and most basic religious experience came as a response on the emotional level (feeling) to the object of religion. This object of religion is defined as the power of life.

Vestiges of this theory may be seen in Rudolf Otto's nonrational interpretation of religious experience, *The Idea of the Holy* (many editions), chaps. 1–3, 15, and 16. In chapter 15, entitled "Its Earliest Manifestations," Otto discusses the notions of *orenda* and *mana* in relationship to his theory of religious experience. G. van der Leeuw devotes the first three chapters of his *Religion in Essence and Manifestation* (London, George Allen & Unwin, 1938) to the notions of *mana* and analogous terms.

Totemism, which was first brought to the attention of the Western world by the investigations of Baldwin Spencer, F. J. Gillen, A. Howitt, and others, also raised the problem of the origin of the religious sentiment. Totemism describes the relationship between some human group and some natural object, such as a plant, animal, or stone. Generally speaking, the group will not marry within its totemic group nor eat the animal or plant with which it is associated. The fact that members of a totem group married outside the group led Sir James Frazer to an investigation of totemism along these lines in *Totemism and Exogamy* (London, Macmillan, 1910). Earlier Andrew Lang had conceived of totemism as an early method of giving names among the primitives, *Secret of the Totem* (London, Longmans, Green, 1905). The most elaborate theoretical work on totemism is

Émile Durkheim's *Elementary Forms of the Religious Life* (rep., Chicago, Free Press, 1947). Building his views upon the investigations of the Australian aborigines by Spencer and Gillen, Durkheim understood totemism to be the basis of Australian religious life and culture. He thought also that the Australian aborigines represented the most primitive form of culture. Their religion, it would follow, represents the earliest form of religion. For Durkheim, the totemic symbol was an expression of the cohesion or integration of the social group. Religion thus consisted in the worship by the social group of a symbol of itself.

Good critical analyses of the totemistic theories of Andrew Lang, James Frazer and Émile Durkheim may be read in two writings of Alexander Goldenweiser: "Totemism: An Essay on Religion and Society," in V. F. Calverton, ed., *The Making of Man* (N.Y., Modern Library, 1931) and chap. 16, "Theories of Early Mentality," in his book *Early Civilization* (N.Y., Alfred A. Knopf, 1922).

The most trenchant and brilliant critique of totemistic theory is contained in *Totemism* (Boston, Beacon Press, 1963) by Claude Lévi-Strauss. In this critique Lévi-Strauss sets forth the notion that totemism is fundamentally a *mode of thought* rather than a *sui generis* form of the religious experience.

Closely related to the notion of *mana* is *tabu* or *taboo*. This word found its way into Western language through its inclusion in a description of Captain James Cook's third voyage around the world. Cook stated (regarding the natives of Atui):

> The people of Atooi, again, inter both their common dead and human sacrifices, as at Tongataboo; but they resemble those of Otaheite in the slovenly state of their religious places, and in offering vegetables and animals to their gods. The *taboo* also prevails in Atooi in its full extent, and seemingly with more rigour than at Tongataboo. For the people here always asked, with great eagerness and signs of fear to offend, whether any particular thing, which they desired to see, or we were unwilling to shew, was *taboo,* or, as they pronounced the word *tafoo?**

"Taboo" became an important term in the interpretation of religion because of its interdictory connotation. It was thought to provide an understanding for the separation of the sacred from the profane—a separation which lies at the heart of every religion.

* Part III, section xii: A voyage to the Pacific Ocean, undertaken by the Command of his Majesty, for making Discoveries in the Northern Hemisphere; to determine the Position and Extent of the West Side of North America, its Distance from Asia, and the Practicability of a Northern Passage to Europe. Performed under the Direction of Captains Cook, Clerke, and Gore in his Majesty's Ships, the Resolution and the Discovery, in the years 1776, 1777, 1778, 1779 and 1780. (Found in *A General History and Collections of Voyages and Travels,* ed. by Robert Kerr [Edinburgh, W. Blackwood & Sons, 1811–17], XVI, 192–93.)

The history of the discussion of this term may be observed in the following literature: James G. Frazer, "Tabu," *Encyclopaedia Britannica* XXI (14th ed.); and *Taboo and Perils of the Soul* (London, Macmillan, 1911). Generally speaking, Frazer saw the origin of taboo in animistic religion. Though it later acquired moral and legal dimensions, such dimensions were due to the evil ambitions of priests and rulers. A. van Gennep in his *Tabou et totemisme à Madagascar* (Paris, Leroux, 1904) understands taboo to be primarily concerned with the passage of something in or out of the body. Taboo in this sense has to do primarily with the orifices of the body. Rudolf Lehmann in his analysis of taboo in *Die polynesischen Tabusitten* (Leipzig, Voigtlander, 1930) divides taboos into three main types: (1) sociological taboos, (2) personal taboos, and (3) bodily taboos. Hutton Webster's *Taboo; A Sociological Study* (London, Oxford Univ. Press, 1942) attacks the problem from a sociological point of view. Sigmund Freud in *Totem and Taboo* (N.Y., Moffat, Yard, 1918) attempts to deal psychologically with the meaning of taboo as a method of understanding the origin of religion. Finally, the history of the interpretation of taboo in the disciplines of history of religions, psychology, and the social sciences is set out in Franz Steiner's *Taboo* (N.Y., Philosophical Library, 1956).

Another theory concerning the origin of the religious sentiment among primitives is Sir James Frazer's theory of magic. His major work is the twelve-volume edition of *The Golden Bough: A Study in Comparative Religion* (London, Macmillan, 1911–15), which probably had greater influence on the social sciences and humanities than any comparable work in the modern period. Frazer brings together a vast amount of data from a wide variety of cultures. His comparative historical method is not carefully worked out, but his twelve volumes constitute a mine of historical detail. The volumes carry the following titles: *The Magic Art*, 2 vols.; *Balder the Beautiful*, 2 vols.; *Adonis, Attis, Osiris*, 2 vols.; *The Scapegoat*, 2 vols.; *Taboo and the Perils of the Soul*, 1 vol.; *Spirit of the Corn and of the Wild*, 2 vols.; *The Divine God*, 1 vol.; and a *Bibliography and General Index*. His discussion of the origin of religion is found in *The Magic Art*. Magic, for Frazer, is a stage of human consciousness prior to and inferior to religion. It may develop into religion, but it is distinct from the religious sentiment. A great deal of what is called "primitive religion" is thus classified as magic by Frazer.

A more recent discussion of the relationship between magic and religion is Bronislaw Malinowski's *Magic, Science, and Religion* (Boston, Beacon Press, 1948). Malinowski separates these as specific functions in primitive society, but he believes that they coexist in an interrelated manner in primitive cultures.

The above theories of the primitive religious sentiment emphasize either a type of mind or a kind of emotion. Lucien Lévy-Bruhl attempted to avoid the dangers of either extreme by combining the mental and emotional fa tors in his theory of religious origins. For Lévy-Bruhl primitives perceive reality in terms of what he calls "a law of mystical participation." This led to his theory of prelogical mentality. His theory is worked out in *Primitive Mentality* (London, George Allen & Unwin, 1923); *Primitives and the Supernatural* (N.Y., E. P. Dutton, 1935); and *How Natives Think* (London, George Allen & Unwin, 1926). Some of his theories are modified in *Les Carnets* (Paris, Presses universitaires de France, 1949), published posthumously.

By and large, all of the theories mentioned up to this point have explicitly or implicitly depended on some form of progressivistic evolutionism. This evolutionism caused them to insist on the movement from the simple to the complex and to interpret the higher form as a growth from a lower and simpler form. Andrew Lang in his *The Making of Religion* (London, Longmans, Green, 1898) offered a criticism of this trend by pointing out that many primitive peoples believed in a "high god." He continued this same criticism in *Magic and Religion* (London, Longmans, Green, 1901). Support for Lang's general theory of primitive monotheism may be found in the work of Fr. Wilhelm Schmidt, *Der Ursprung der Gottesidee*, 12 vols. (Munster, Aschendorff, 1926–55), and *The Origin and Growth of Religion* (London, Methuen, 1931). An informative summary of the problem of primitive monotheism is given by Paul Radin in *Monotheism Among Primitive Peoples* (London, George Allen & Unwin, 1924).

All the above theories regarding the nature of religious experience in primitive cultures, with the exception of those of Claude Lévi-Strauss, were based upon the inner subjectivity of the experiencer. For this reason words such as "belief in" and "faith" tend to loom large in these interpretations. We see a transition from these modes of understanding in a work such as G. Van der Leeuw's *Religion in Essence and Manifestation,* 2 vols. (N.Y., and Evanston, Harper & Row, 1963). Though Van der Leeuw's work is permeated by a general theory of "religious dynamism," he does relate every mode of the religious consciousness and behavior to an objective form of the world, whether this form be a structure of nature or of human community. This kind of transition is completed in the work of Mircea Eliade. In a certain sense Eliade moves towards the objectivity and neo-positivism of Lévi-Strauss, but instead of understanding the human consciousness as a purely intellectual structure, Eliade tends to see human consciousness as a locus for the intellectual and imaginative ordering of the world. Especially in his *Patterns in Comparative Religion* (N.Y., World Publishing, 1972) he, in very much the same vein as G. Van der Leeuw, accounts for the modalities of the religious consciousness by showing how it is related to forms in the natural order, sky, earth, stones, water, for example. The narration of this relationship is not accompanied by a sophisticated epistemological theory; rather, Eliade is at pains in almost every chapter to point out the *force of passivity* of the forms of nature as constitutive of the imaginative and intellectual structures of human consciousness.

Within such a context Eliade is able to give a meaning to history as the temporal-spatial location in which certain manifestations of the sacred occur. In this manner he gives a positive evaluation of history without slipping into the progressivistic and evolutionistic ideologies of history that characterized his predecessors in anthropology and the history of religions. See his *The Sacred and the Profane* (N.Y., Harcourt, Brace, 1959); and *The Myth of the Eternal Return* (N.Y., Pantheon Books, 1954), republished as *The Myth of the Eternal Return* (Princeton, Princeton Univ. Press, 1971).

It is the religious orientation which makes life "real" for the primitive man. For Eliade sacredness is being. Orientation in a "real world" necessarily involves a transcendent dimension. Reality for the world of man is insured because he believes in events which happened outside of history *in illo tempore*. The myth is the intense religious expression of this meaning. The creative acts of man are imitations of the creative acts and models of mythic time.

Joseph Campbell, another contemporary historian of religions, interprets the origin of the religious sentiment in psychical-historical and social-historical terms. The history of the psychic structure reveals the manner by which the psyche has responded to the human condition—birth, death, gravitational force, etc. The history of man's social life reveals his discovery of and adjustment to his natural environment. These two types of responses are discussed in *The Masks of God* (N.Y., Viking Press, 1959).

III. THE CULTURAL STRATA OF PRIMITIVE RELIGION

In his abridgement of James Frazer's *Golden Bough*, entitled *The New Golden Bough* (N.Y., Criterion Books, 1959), Theodore Gaster remarks of Frazer's method: "[Frazer] pays far too little regard to the necessity of a cultural stratification tending to place all 'savage' customs and beliefs on a single vague level of 'the primitive'" (p. xviii). To be sure, some investigators had recognized stages of human culture prior to the advent of the great ancient civilizations. This level of cultural stratification is recognized by Tylor and Durkheim, but neither of them made it a basic ingredient in his methodology. Indeed, they could not fully appropriate their insight until the sciences of prehistory and archeology had developed more precise methods.

The research in these areas resulted in the recognition of the historical past of the "modern primitives." For a general orientation to prehistoric cultures the following works of V. G. Childe provide an excellent introduction: *The Dawn of European Civilization* (London, Alfred A. Knopf, 1925); *New Light on the Most Ancient East* (London, Kegan Paul, Trench, Trubner, 1934); *Man Makes Himself* (London, C. A. Watts, 1936); *What Happened in History* (Middlesex, Penguin Books, 1943); and *Social Evolution* (London, C. A. Watts, 1951). Childe's works emphasize the role of technological development as the basic innovating element in culture. Other works in prehistory presenting a more general or eclectic point of view are Robert Braidwood's *Prehistoric Men* (Chicago, Chicago Natural History Museum, 1948) and Carleton Coon's *The Story of Man* (London, Alfred A. Knopf, 1950).

The above general works on prehistory concentrate their attention on the history of physical utilitarian artifacts. Insight into the spiritual horizon of prehistoric man was gained from a study and analysis of his artistic forms. Analysis and interpretation of prehistoric art in France and Spain may be found in H. Breuil, *Four Hundred Centuries of Cave Art* (Montignac, Centre d'études et de documentation préhistoriques, 1952); H. Breuil and H. Obermaier, *The Cave of Altamira* (Madrid, Tip. de Archivos, 1935); and H. Breuil, M. C. Burkitt, and M. Polleck, *Rock Paintings of Southern Andalusia* (Oxford, Clarendon Press, 1929). An example of the prehistoric art of a modern primitive culture is Charles Mountford's *Arnhem Land Expedition,* vol. I, *Art, Myth, and Symbolism* (Melbourne, Melbourne Univ. Press, 1956).

On the basis of archeological methods we are able to classify the cultural history and religion of primitives into three periods: Paleolithic, high Paleolithic and Neolithic.

Listed below are texts dealing with an overall synthetic view of the cultures of the lithic periods. Grahame Clark's, *World Prehistory, An Outline,* (Cambridge, University Press, 1962) is probably the best text in this area. Though dealing in a minimal manner with religion, Richard B. Lee and Irven Devore, eds., *Man the Hunter,* (Chicago, Aldine, 1968), gives us a thorough analysis of all other aspects of historical and modern hunting societies. Elman R. Service, *The Hunters,* (Englewood Cliffs, N.J., Prentice-Hall, 1966) is a compact intensive discussion of the major aspects of hunting societies. His chapter on ideology (chapter 5) touches on religion. Paul Shepard's *The Tender Carnivore and the Sacred Game,* (N.Y., Charles Scribner's Sons, 1973) could almost be called a "theology of hunting cultures," for in this work Shepard weaves together economic, social and ecological dimensions to set forth the ultimate nature of the values in these societies. Wilhelm Kopper's study, *Primitive Man and His World Picture,* (London and N.Y., Sheed and Ward, 1952), portrays the religious values expressed in the world-view of hunting societies and early agriculturalists. Karl J. Narr's article, "Approaches to the Religion of Early

Paleolithic Man," *History of Religions: An International Journal for Comparative Historical Studies,* IV, 1 (Chicago, 1965), is an analytical essay laying the basis for religious values in Paleolithic cultures. Fritz Kern's *The Wildbooters,* (Edinburgh and London, Oliver and Boyd, 1960), is a comprehensive work dealing with modern hunting cultures. Kern coined the term, "wildbooter" to designate those food gathering and hunting communities which represent the earliest cultures in the history of man.

A more detailed analysis of the development of Paleolithic cultures and the interrelations of biological, social, technical, and aesthetic religious values in these cultures may be found in the following volumes by André Leroi-Gourhan: *L'Homme et la matière. Evolution et techniques,* I (Paris, Albin Michel, 1971); *Milieu et techniques. Evolution et techniques,* II (Paris, Albin Michel, 1950); *Le Geste et la parole.* I, *Technique et langage* (Paris, Albin Michel, 1964); and *Le Geste et la parole.* II, *La Mémoire et les rythmes* (Paris, Albin Michel, 1965). Leroi-Gourhan devoted an entire text to the study of prehistoric religion. This is *Les Religions de la préhistoire* (Paris, Presses universitaires de France, 1971). The basis for his discussion lies in the analysis of burial sites, bones, and the art of prehistoric societies. He has written a very large handsomely illustrated text on European prehistoric art, *The Art of Prehistoric Man in Western Europe,* (London, Thames and Hudson, 1968). In contrast to an earlier work such as Johannes Maringer's *The Gods of Prehistoric Man* (N.Y., Alfred A. Knopf, 1960), whose hermeneutical method is based on a general theory of religious epistemology, André Leroi-Gourhan works in a more empirical manner with his material, making use of a structural methodology in his analysis of the artifacts. We observe this same kind of orientation in method in *The Roots of Civilization* (N.Y., McGraw-Hill, 1972), by Alexander Marshack. This fascinating text describes how the author, working from the engravings on prehistoric bones, developed the concept of a notational system which reveals the cognitive and imaginative structures of prehistoric cultures.

Karl Butzer in his *Environment and Archeology* (Chicago and N.Y., Aldine Atherton, 1971) discusses the methodological implications of the similarities and differences between prehistoric cultures and "modern primitives," in the following comment,

> No modern "primitive" group provides an accurate picture of pre-historic populations. In particular, the technological traits vary strongly between dispersed groups of a similar economic level, emphasizing their acculturation to nearby higher cultures. But certain aspects of the economic and social structure may provide a fair analogy to prehistoric communities (p. 406).

This statement emphasizes the structural analogy between prehistoric and modern "primitive" cultures, but shows equally the historical differences between them.

It is generally assumed that the great change from hunting-gathering cultures to cultures of the civilizational kind occurred in the late Neolithic period with the domestication of plants and animals. This is the basis for cultures of the civilizational type, but such changes do not always lead to civilizational cultures. Butzer's work is a thorough study of the transition from hunter-gatherers to agricultural societies; his work represents an ecological approach to prehistory. A similar work is edited by Peter J. Ucko and G. W. Dimbleby. This work, *The Domestication and Exploitation of Plants and Animals* (Chicago, Aldine, 1969), discusses the transition to agriculture in various parts of the world. The religious meaning of this transition is taken up by Joseph Campbell, *The Masks of God* (N.Y., Viking Press, 1959), especially in Part Two, "The Mythology of Primitive Planters"; Part Three, "The Mythology of Primitive Hunters"; and Part Four, "The Archaeology of Myth." Mircea Eliade takes up the same issue in his article "Sources and Changes in the History of Religion," in *City Invincible* (Chicago, Univ. of Chicago Press, 1960), 351ff.

Certain sites called ceremonial centers constitute the first stage of urbanization and sedentary existence in many cultures of the world. The most thorough discussion of the origin and development of the ceremonial center is found in Paul Wheatley, *The Pivot of the Four Quarters* (Chicago, Aldine, 1971). See especially chapter 3, "The Nature of the Ceremonial Center."

A. E. Jensen believes that there was a religious historical stage between the Paleolithic and the Neolithic. This is the religion of the cultures in which the planting and tending of plants is practiced but the cultivation of cereal grains has not been discovered. See his *Das religiöse Weltbild einer frühen Kultur* (Stuttgart, A. Schröder, 1948) and *Myth and Cult among Primitive People* (Chicago, Univ. of Chicago Press, 1963). Jensen develops the idea of a god or goddess who is sacrificed. Out of the parts of the deity's cut-up body, the trees and cultivated plants grow. To myths and religion of such a kind Jensen gives the name *Dema* type. Both the mythical type and the historical implications arising from it are discussed in Jensen's *Hainuwele; Volkerzählungen von der Molukkeninsel Ceram* (Frankfurt-am-Main, V. Klostermann, 1939).

With the coming of agriculture, a new and powerful religious force was released in human culture. The most important new religious forms developed in this period are the cult of the great mother and megalithic religion. E. O. James devotes a volume, *The Cult of the Mother-Goddess* (London, Thames & Hudson, 1959) to this topic. A psychological interpretation of this cult along Jungian lines is Erich Neumann's *The Great Mother* (N.Y., Pantheon Books, 1955). The term "megalithic" is derived from the Greek "megas," great, and "lithos," stone. This religious form centered around ancestor worship and veneration of the dead. The dead were understood as powerful fertility symbols in the womb of the earth.

Great stone monuments were erected on the site of the grave or served as tombs for the dead. Sibylle von Cles-Reden's book, *The Realm of the Great Goddess* (Englewood Cliffs, N.J., Prentice-Hall, 1962) deals with the relationship of the great mother cult to megalithic religion. Three works, though restricted to a specific geographical interpretation of megalithic culture, are quite informative. They are G. E. Daniel, *The Megalith Builders of Western Europe* (London, F. A. Praeger, 1958–59); John Layard, *Stone Men of Malekula* (London, Chatto & Windus, 1942); and Alphonse Riesenfeld, *The Megalithic Culture of Melanesia* (Leiden, E. J. Brill, 1950).

Too often, modern cultures which are not historically traceable to the civilizational complexes of the Ancient Near East, India, and China are thought to possess no history. Listed below are works on "prehistory" from some of these cultures.

A. Africa

An overall popular survey of African history, culture, and religion is found in *The Horizon History of Africa* (N.Y., American Heritage, 1971). Basil Davidson's *The African Genius* (Boston & Toronto, Little Brown, 1969) is a similar text but has the advantage of single authorship. Margaret Shinnie's work is devoted to a study of *Ancient African Kingdoms* (N.Y. and Toronto, New American Library, 1970). The ancient kingdom of Ife in Nigeria is dealt with in an article, "Ancient Ife, An Ethnological Summary," in *Odù*, 8:21–35 (October 1960), by William Fagg and Frank Willett. A full length study of Ife may be found in Frank Willett's, *Ife in the History of West African Sculpture* (N.Y., McGraw-Hill, 1967). A description of these cultures as well as the common elements among them are dealt with in Jacques Maquet, *Civilizations of Black Africa,* (N.Y., Oxford Univ. Press, 1972), and *Africanity: The Cultural Unity of Black Africa* (N.Y., Oxford Univ. Press, 1972).

The general problems relating to hominoid origins in Africa and the lithic ages are discussed in the work ed. by Walter W. Bishop and J. Desmond Clark, *Background to Evolution in Africa* (Chicago, Univ. of Chicago Press, 1967). The following texts contain descriptions of African cultures, their histories, and the various methods employed in the reconstruction of African history: George P. Murdock, *Africa, Its People and Their Culture History* (N.Y., McGraw-Hill, 1959); Creighton Gabel and Norman R. Bennett, eds., *Reconstructing African Culture History* (Boston, Boston Univ. Press, 1967); Daniel F. McCall, *Africa in Time Perspective* (Boston, Boston Univ. Press, 1964); J. D. Fage and R. A. Oliver, *Papers in African Prehistory* (Cambridge, University Press, 1970); and Jan Vansina, *Oral Tradition; A Study in Historical Methodology* (Chicago, Aldine, 1965). General problems of archeology, prehistory, and oral tradition are presented in R. A. Hamilton, ed., *History and Archeology in Africa* (London, London Univ., 1955). Over all problems of prehistcry in Africa are treated in H. Alimen, *The Prehistory of Africa,* tr. by A. H. Broadrick (London, Hutchinson, 1957); H. Breuil, "L'Afrique préhistorique," *Cahier d'Art,* 5 (1930); L. S. B. Leakey, *Stone Age Africa* (London, Oxford Univ. Press, 1936) and his *Adam's Ancestors* (London, Methuen, 1934). The works of A. J. Arkell provide a good orientation to the prehistory of the Anglo-Egyptian Sudan: *The Old Stone Age in Anglo-Egyptian Sudan* (London, Oxford Univ. Press, 1949) and *A History of the Sudan from the Earliest Times to 1821* (London, Athlone Press, 1955).

For the prehistory of South Africa see M. C. Burkitt, *South Africa's Past in Stone and Paint* (Cambridge, Cambridge Univ. Press, 1928); G. Caton Thompson, *The Zimbabwe Culture* (Oxford, Clarendon Press, 1931); and John D. Clark, *The Stone Age Cultures of Northern Rhodesia,* South Africa Archaeological Society (Claremont, Cape, 1950). For East Africa see J. D. Clark, *The Prehistoric Cultures of the Horn of Africa* (Cambridge, Cambridge Univ. Museum, 1954) and Sonia Cole, *Early Man in East Africa* (London, Macmillan, 1958). Walter B. Cline traces the history of metallurgy in Africa in *Mining and Metallurgy in Negro Africa,* General Series in Anthropology, No. 5 (Menasha, Wisc., G. Banta, 1937). For the origin of certain cultural techniques in Africa see H. Epstein, *The Origin of the Domestic Animals of Africa,* 2 vols. (N.Y. and London, Africana, 1971), and R. L. Shinnie, ed., *The African Iron Age* (N.Y. and London, Oxford Univ. Press, 1971).

The following works deal more specifically with the history of religion in Africa: Jalmar and Ione Rudner, *The Hunter and His Art* (Cape Town, C. Struik, 1970); Gilbert Charles-Picard, *Les Religions de l'Afrique antique* (Paris, Plon, 1954); and T. O. Ranger and Isaria Kimambo, eds., *The Historical Study of African Religion* (Berkeley, Univ. of California Press, 1972).

B. The Americas

The aboriginal cultures of the Americas comprise several types of cultures and civilizations.

One of the earliest general and comprehensive studies of American Indians was H. R. Schoolcraft's *Information Respecting the History, Conditions and Prospects of the Indian Tribes of the United States,* 6 vols. (Philadelphia, J. B. Lippincott, 1851–57). A selective bibliography in this area would include Louis A. Brennan, *No Stone Unturned* (N.Y., Random House, 1959); Samuel G. Goodrich, *History of the Indians of North and South America* (Boston, Rand, 1855); Frank C. Hibben, *Treasure in the Dust* (Philadelphia, J. B. Lippincott, 1951); George E.

Hyde, *Indians of the High Plains from Prehistoric Period to the Coming of Europeans* (Oklahoma, Univ. of Oklahoma Press, 1959); Diamond Jenness, *The American Aborigines, Their Origin and Antiquity* (Toronto, Univ. of Toronto Press, 1933); Alfred L. Kroeber, *Native Culture of the South-West* (Berkeley, Univ. of California Press, 1928); Stephen D. Peet, *Prehistoric America,* 5 vols. (Chicago, Office of the American Antiquarian, 1890–1905); and *Essays in Historical Anthropology of North America* (Washington, D.C., Smithsonian Institution, 1940).

Edward Sapir's article, "Time Perspective in Aboriginal Culture. A Study in Method," *Geological Survey of Canada Memoir 90,* Anthropological Series 13 (Ottawa, 1916) is an attempt to provide a cultural time strata method for North American aboriginal cultures. Clark Wissler's two texts provide introductions to North American cultures; they are *The Relation of Nature to Man in Aboriginal America* (N.Y., Oxford Univ. Press, 1926) and *The American Indian* (N.Y., Oxford Univ. Press, 1938). The latest and most comprehensive sourcebook is edited by Roger Owen, James J. F. Deety, and Anthony D. Fisher, *The North American Indian: A Sourcebook* (N.Y., Macmillan, 1967). Similar texts are Robert F. Spencer, J. D. Jennings, et al., *The Nature Americans* (N.Y., Harper & Row, 1967); and Ruth M. Underhill, *Red Man's Religion* (Chicago, Univ. of Chicago Press, 1965).

For the other Americas the reader is referred to the comprehensive bibliography covering all the Americas by Juan Comas, *Bibliografía Selectiva de las Culturas Indígenas de America* (Mexico City, Comisión de Historia, Instituto Pan Americano de Geografía e Historia, 1953). A good introductory book to Mesoamerican and South American indigenous religions in *Pre-Columbian American Religions* (N.Y., Holt, Rinehart and Winston, 1969) by Walter Krickeberg, Hermann Trimborn, Werner Müller, and Otto Zerries.

C. Oceania and Australia

We have already referred to the works of Layard and Riesenfeld. In addition, the prehistory of this area is dealt with in Walter Iven's *Melanesians of the Solomon Islands* (London, Kegan Paul, Trench, Trubner, 1927) and *Island Builders of the Pacific.* (London, Seeley, Service, 1930). John White's *The Ancient History of the Maori,* 4 vols. (Wellington, G. Didsbury, 1887–90) is almost a classic in this field. H. G. Quaritch Wales' *Prehistory and Religion in South-east Asia* (London, B. Quaritch, 1957) shows the historical relationship between Southeast Asia and India in prehistoric times.

Douglas Oliver's three-volume work, *Ancient Tahitian Society* (Honolulu, Univ. Press of Hawaii, 1974) is the latest comprehensive study of Tahiti. Volume three contains a very extensive bibliography. W. E. H.

Stanner and Helen Sheils edited a group of papers, *Australian Aboriginal Studies* (Melbourne, Oxford Univ. Press, 1963); these papers cover all the important aspects of Australian aboriginal history and culture. The Festschrift for Professor A. P. Elkin, ed. by Ronald and Catherine Berndt, entitled *Aboriginal Man in Australia* (Sydney, Angus and Robertson, 1965) is again a treatment of the various aspects of Australian aboriginal cultures. It contains a complete bibliography of the works of A. P. Elkin.

The above sections dealing with the cultural strata or prehistory of three broad geographical areas represent a compromise in two senses. They are a compromise first in terms of data, for all areas of the world possess such cultural strata or prehistory. This fact is overlooked by the conventional methods of history where the concentration of data and method falls upon the civilizational or post-neolithic stages of these cultures. While such data should legitimately have been included in a section such as this one, to do so would have occasioned a theoretical discussion going beyond the limits of this essay. Some of the problems of method alluded to here are discussed in the first section of this essay.

The second compromise has to do with the post-neolithic cultures of the Americas. The bibliography by Juan Comas mentioned above covers the ancient civilizations of Meso- and South America. At the present time these cultures are hardly ever discussed historically or structurally within the context of similar cultural situations; they are either omitted or discussed separately. I have mentioned the ambiguity surrounding the term "primitive," but given this ambiguity, it is difficult to understand why mention should be made of these cultures in an essay dealing with primitive religion. And yet clarity regarding the usage of the term "primitive" might have the salutary repercussions of defining a more authentic methodology for the understanding and proper integration of religious cultural studies.

IV. MYTH IN PRIMITIVE RELIGION

Many of the works in section II of this essay contain chapters on the interpretation of myths. In this section we shall present (a) additional theoretical works in the area of myth, (b) compilations of myths of many types from all parts of the world, and (c) studies which deal with a particular type or structure in the myth.

A. Theoretical works

Ernst Cassirer has dealt with the problem of myth from a philosophical point of view more thoroughly than any other contemporary philosopher. Within his philosophy of symbolic forms, he was able to present a profound interpretation of myth in *Language and Myth* (N.Y. and London, Harper & Brothers, 1946); *The Philosophy of Symbolic Forms:* vol. II, *Mythical Thought* (New Haven, Yale Univ. Press, 1953); and *An Essay on Man* (New Haven, Yale Univ. Press, 1944). His orientation was taken over and expanded by Susanne Langer in *Philosophy in a New Key* (Cambridge, Harvard Univ. Press, 1942); and *Feeling and Form* (N.Y., Charles Scribner's Sons, 1953). See also the two symposia on myth: *Myth: A Symposium,* ed. by T. A. Sebeok (Philadelphia, American Folklore Society, 1955); and *Myth and Mythmaking,* ed. by Henry Murray (N.Y., George Braziller, 1960).

Psychological and psychoanalytic interpretations of myths have, since the work of Freud, opened up a whole new area of mythological interpretation. Geza Roheim interpreted Australian myths psychoanalytically in *Australian Totemism: A Psychoanalytic Study in Anthropology* (London, George Allen & Unwin, 1925) and *The External Ones of the Dream* (N.Y., International Universities Press, 1945). Bronislaw Malinowski applied psychology in his study of myth in *Myth in Primitive Psychology* (N.Y., W. W. Norton, 1926). Carl G. Jung and Carl Kerenyi have developed a new methodological approach in terms of Jungian psychological principles in *Essays on a Science of Mythology* (N.Y., Pantheon Books, 1949).

The relevance of the study of myth in classical and Indo-European cultures for the general understanding of myth is dealt with in C. Scott Littleton's *The New Comparative Mythology* (Berkeley, Univ. of California Press, 1973) and G. S. Kirk's *Myth: Its Meaning and Functions in Ancient and Other Cultures* (Cambridge, University Press, 1971).

Mircea Eliade's contribution to the field is the development of an historical approach to myth. Some comments about his interpretation have already been made above. Eliade believes the cosmogonic myth to be the basic myth in every culture. See his "The Prestige of the Cosmogonic Myth," *Diogenes,* 23 (Fall, 1958), 18ff. Since all myths express some dimension of creativity, they all recall the first creation as described in the cosmogonic myth. The yearning for paradise is understood by Eliade as the religious desire of primitive man to live again in that time before creation *in illo tempore.* This is the substance of his article "The Yearning for Paradise in Primitive Tradition," *Diogenes,* 3 (Summer, 1943), 18ff., also reprinted in *Daedalus,* LXXXVIII, 2 (1959), 255–66. He presents a general theory for the interpretation of myths and other religious symbols in "Remarks on Religious Symbolism" in *The History of Religions: Essays in Methodology,* ed. by M. Eliade and J. M. Kitagawa (Chicago, Univ. of Chicago Press, 1959).

Raffaele Pettazzoni, especially in his essays "Myths of Beginning and Creation Myths" and "The Truth of Myth" in his *Essays on the History of Religions* (Leiden, E. J. Brill, 1954) explicates a theory of myth which is similar in intention to that of Eliade. For Pettazzoni myths are true stories. They tell the story of a people and demonstrate the manner by which reality is accessible to them. Eric Dardel has analyzed the conception of myth underlying the researches of Maurice Leenhardt in "The Mythic," *Diogenes,* 7 (Summer, 1954), 33–51.

Claude Lévi-Strauss has revived and added intellectual excitement to the study of myth in particular and religion in general. Setting himself squarely against a phenomenological hermeneutics—see his "The Bear and the Barber," *Journal of the Royal Anthropological Society,* vol. 93 (London, 1963)—he develops an interpretive method that draws heavily on insights from structural linguistics. Reference is made to his *Savage Mind* in the first section of this essay; this work, along with his *Structural Anthropology* (N.Y., Basic Books, 1963), especially Part Three, "Magic and Religion," reveals the bases for his interpretation of myth. He has followed through with a four-volume work which he calls an "Introduction to a Science of Mythology." The title of volume one is *The Raw and the Cooked* (N.Y., Harper & Row, 1964); volume two, *From Honey to Ashes* (N.Y., Harper & Row, 1966). The other volumes, *L'Origine des manières de table* (Paris, Librairie Plon, 1968) and *L'Homme nu* (Paris, Librairie Plon, 1971), have not yet been translated into English.

B. Compilations of myths

The most ambitious effort in the compilation of mythological materials from all over the world is probably *The Mythology of All Races,* ed. by John A. MacCulloch and Louis H. Gray, 13 vols. (Boston, Archaeological Institute of America, Marshall Jones Co., 1916–32). The volumes are: vol. 1, *Greek and Roman* by William S. Fox; vol. 2, *Eddic* by John A. MacCulloch; vol. 3, *Celtic, Slavic* by John A. MacCulloch and Jan Machal; vol. 4, *Finno Ugric, Siberian* by Uno Holmberg; vol. 5, *Semitic* by Stephen H. Langdon; vol. 6, *Indian, Iranian* by A. Berriedale Keith; vol. 7, *Armenian, African* by Mardires Ananikian and Alice Werner; vol. 8, *Chinese, Japanese* by John Ferguson and Masaharu Anesaki; vol. 9, *Oceanic* by Roland B. Dixon; vol. 10, *North American* by H. B. Alexander; vol. 11, *Latin American* by H. B. Alexander; vol. 12, *Egypt, Far East* by W. Max Müller, and vol. 13, *Index.*

Alexander Krappe's books *Mythologie universelle* (Paris, Payot, 1930) and *La Genèse des mythes* (Paris, Payot, 1938) give a broad coverage of myths but in typological categories. Another compilation of myths in typological terms is *La Naissance du monde,* ed. by Anne Marie Esnoul, Paul Garelli, et al. (Paris, Éditions du Seuil, 1959).

Mircea Eliade's one-volume text, *From Primitives to Zen* (N.Y., Harper & Row, 1967), though not devoted entirely to myths, contains myths from several different cultures. This work has been divided into four separate paperbacks with the following titles: *Gods, Goddesses and Myths of Creation,* Part One; *Man and the Sacred,* Part Two; *Death, Afterlife, and Eschatology,* Part Three; and *From Medicine Men to Mohammed,* Part Four. (All these volumes were published by Harper and Row, N.Y., 1974.) Charles H. Long's *Alpha: The Myths of Creation* (N.Y., George Braziller, 1963) treats cosmogonic myths along structural and morphological lines.

Regional compilations and interpretations of myth are as follows:

AFRICA   Hans Abrahamsson in *The Origin of Death* (Uppsala, Studia Ethnographica Uppsaliensa 3, 1951) discusses myths of this type in Africa. Hermann Baumann deals with myths of beginning and end in Africa in *Schöpfung und Urzeit des Menschen im Mythus der afrikanischen Völker* (Berlin, Andrews & Steiner, 1936). H. Tegnaeus interprets myths of the hero in Africa in *Le Héros civilisateur* (Stockholm, Studia Ethnographica Uppsaliensa 2, 1950)

Daryll Forde, ed., *African Worlds: Studies in the Cosmological Ideas and Social Values of African Peoples* (London, Oxford Univ. Press, 1954) is a good introduction to the mythological world view of several African societies. Geoffrey Parrinder's *West African Religion* (London, Epworth Press, 1949) describes the relationship of myth to the total religious system of West African peoples. Melville Herskovits' works do the same for Dahomey in *Outline of Dahomean Religious Belief,* American Anthropological Association, Memoir 41 (1933) and *Dahomey: An Ancient West African Kingdom,* 2 vols. (N.Y., J. J. Augustin, 1938). Eva Meyerowitz presents an interesting study in *The Sacred State of the Akan* (London, Faber & Faber, 1951) and *Akan Traditions of Origin* (London, Faber & Faber, 1952). By an analysis of the myths of a West African society (the Akan), she attempts to arrive at an understanding of their historical past. Marcel Griaule relates the religious masks to the mythological forms of the Dogon people of West Africa in *Masques Dogon* (Paris, Institut d'enthnologie, 1938), and in his *Conversation with Ogotemmêli* (London, Oxford Univ. Press, 1972) he recognizes a highly developed systematic interpretation of Dogon mythology.

NORTH AMERICAN ABORIGINES   General interpretations of North American aboriginal myths may be found in *Creation Myths of Primitive America* (Boston, Little, Brown, 1898) by Jeremiah Curtin and *The World's Rim* by H. B. Alexander (Lincoln, Nebr., Univ. of Nebraska Press, 1953). Ake Hultkrantz takes over a Greek mythological theme in his study of shamanistic elements in American Indian myths, *The North American Indian Orpheus Tradition* (Ethnographical Museum of Stockholm, 1957). For the New England Indians, John N. B. Hewitt's *Iroquoian Cosmology* (Washington, U.S. Bureau of America Ethnology, 1928) and John M. Cooper's *The Algonquin Supreme Being*

(Washington, Catholic Univ. of America Press, 1934) present very good materials. For a broad coverage of the myths of the Algonquin and Iroquois, Charles G. Leland, *The Algonquin Legends of New England* (N.Y., Houghton Mifflin, 1884); and E. A. Smith, "Myths of the Iroquois" in *Annual Report of the American Bureau of Ethnology* (Washington, 1883) are still the best studies.

Ruth Benedict's *Zuñi Mythology* (N.Y., Columbia Univ. Press, 1935) and Ruth Bunzel's article, "Zuñi Origin Myths" in the *47th Annual Report of the United States Bureau of American Ethnology* (Washington, 1929–30), 547–609, are classics in this area. A more thorough study of Zuñi religion and mythology is Matilda Stevenson, "The Zuñi Indians: Their Mythology, Esoteric Fraternities and Ceremonies" in *United States Bureau of American Ethnology Annual Report,* XXIII (Washington, 1904). A comparable work dealing with the mythology and religion of the Pueblos is Elsie C. Parsons, *Pueblo Indian Religion,* 2 vols. (Chicago, Univ. of Chicago Press, 1939). A. L. Kroeber has recorded the myths of the California Indians in his articles, "Indian Myths of South Central California" and "The Religion of the Indians of California" in IV, 4 and 6, respectively, of the *University of California Publications in American Archaeology and Ethnology.*

Comparable research has not been done on the indigenous societies of South America. For a general orientation to the myths and religion of this area, there are the following: Paul Radin, *Indians of South America* (N.Y., Doubleday, 1942); Julian Steward, ed., *Handbook of South American Indians* (Washington, D.C., U.S. Government Printing Office, 1946–59), and Alfred Métraux, *Myths of the Toba and Pilagá Indians of Gran Chaco* (Philadelphia, American Folklore Society, 1946). See also Rafael Karsten, *The Civilization of the South American Indians with Special Reference to Magic and Religion* (N.Y., Alfred A. Knopf, 1926).

POLYNESIA AND AUSTRALIA   One of the best introductions to Polynesian mythology is R. W. Williamson's *Religion and Cosmic Beliefs of Central Polynesia,* 2 vols. (Cambridge, Cambridge Univ. Press, 1933); and his *Religion and Social Organization in Central Polynesia* (Cambridge, Cambridge Univ. Press, 1937). Elsdon Best's articles in the *Dominion Museum Bulletin* have for over two generations been excellent: "Some Aspects of Maori Myth and Religion," *Dominion Museum Bulletin Memoirs,* 1 (1922); and "Maori Religion and Mythology part I," *Dominion Museum Bulletin* 10 (1924). Valuable studies have come from the Bernice P. Bishop Museum. They include Katherine Luomala's study of the Polynesian trickster, "Maui-of-a-Thousand-Tricks: His Oceanic and European Biographers," *Bernice P. Bishop Museum Bulletin,* 198 (1949) and her "Specialized Studies in Polynesian Anthropology," *Bernice P. Bishop Museum Bulletin,* 193 (1947). J. F. Stimson's valuable "Tuamotuan Religion" *Bernice P. Bishop Museum Bulletin,* 103 (1933) as well as E. S. C. Handy's "Polynesian Religion" *Bernice P. Bishop Museum Bulletin,* 34 (1927) are among the early systematic studies of Polynesian myths and rituals.

The following works will provide the reader with both a geographical and phenomenological range of Polynesian mythological and religious meanings: W. W. Gill, *Myths and Songs from the South Pacific* (London, H. S. King, 1876); W. E. Gudgeon, "Maori Religion," *Polynesian Society Journal,* XIV (1905); Hare Hongi, "A Maori Cosmogony," *Polynesian Society Journal,* XVI (1907); S. M. Kama Kau, "Ancient Hawaiian Religious Beliefs and Ceremonies" (Honolulu, Hawaiian Annual for 1911); W. H. R. Rivers, "Sun, Cult and Megaliths in Oceania," *American Anthropologist* 17 (1913); Robert von Heine-Geldern, "Die Megalithen Südostasiens und ihre Bedeutung für die Klarung der Megalithenfrage in Europa und Polynesien," *Anthropos* 23 (1928); S. Czarnowsky, "Le Kiev créateur des cosmogonies polynésiennes," *Actes du Vême Congrès Internationale d'Histoire des Religions* (Lund, Gleerup, 1930); Ralph Piddington, "Religion and Life in Polynesia," *Religions. The Journal of the Society for the Study of Religions* 25 (1938); Alfred Métraux, "Easter Island and Melanesia, A Critical Study," *Mankind* 2 (1938); J. C. Anderson "Maori Religion," *Polynesian Society Journal* XLIX (1940); Raymond Firth, *The Work of the Gods in Tikopia,* 2 vols. (London, London School of Economics and Political Science Monographs on Social Anthropology, 1940); K. D. Mellen, *The Gods Depart* (N.Y., Hastings House, 1956).

Very good Australian mythological accounts are given in the works cited above by F. J. Gillen and W. B. Spencer. In addition to these, one should consult the works of Professor A. P. Elkin, especially his introductory text, *The Australian Aborigines* (N.Y., Doubleday, 1964). This work contains an excellent bibliography. In addition see C. P. Mountford, *The Aborigines and Their Country* (Kent Town, Rigby, 1969); Ainslie Roberts and C. P. Mountford, *The Dreamtime* (Adelaide, Rigby, 1965); and W. E. H. Stanner, "On Aboriginal Religion," *Oceania,* XXX, 2 and 4; XXXII, 2; and T. G. H. Strehlow, *Aranda Traditions* (Melbourne, Melbourne Univ. Press, 1947).

The most recent and prolific scholars of Australian culture and religion have been Ronald M. and Catherine H. Berndt. First of all mention may be made of works completed separately: R. M. Berndt, *Djanggawul* (London, Routledge & Kegan Paul, 1952); and *Kunapipi* (Melbourne, Cheshire, 1951). These are interpretations of two myth-ritual cycles. Catherine H. Berndt's *Women's Changing Ceremonies in Northern Australia* (Paris, Hermann, 1950) is one of the few studies of women's rites among the Australians. Finally, R. M. and C. H. Berndt's *The World of the First Australians* (Chicago, Univ. of Chicago Press, 1964) is the best and most comprehensive text. It deals with all of the major forms of Australian life and contains a very good bibliography. Two more recent works, Nancy D. Munn's *Walbiri Iconography* (Ithaca, Cornell Univ. Press, 1973) and Mircea Eliade's *Australian Religions* (Ithaca, Cornell Univ. Press, 1973) provide the reader with other perspectives on this much studied area of religious phenomena.

C. Studies of types of myths

Joseph Campbell deals with the specific mythological form of the hero in *The Hero with a Thousand Faces* (N.Y., Pantheon Books, 1949). The hero myth in various cultural areas is discussed by D. G. Brinton in *American Hero-Myths* (Philadelphia, H. C. Watts, 1882), and H. Tegnaeus deals with the hero in African myths in his *Le Héros civilisateur* (Stockholm, Studia Ethnographica Uppsaliensa 2, 1950). Ugo Bianchi's *Il Dualismo Religioso* (Rome, "L'Erma" di Bretschneider, 1958) is an interpretation of dualisms in myth; Paul Radin's *The Trickster* (London, Routledge & Kegan Paul, 1955) is a study of the trickster-hero-twin in American Indian myths.

V. TYPES OF RELIGIOUS PERSONAGES

The best introductory discussions of this aspect of the religious life are found in Chapter 8, "Types of Religious Authority" of Joachim Wach's *Sociology of Religion* (Chicago, Univ. of Chicago Press, 1944, and several reprints) and Part II, "The Subject of Religion" of G. Van der Leeuw's *Religion in Essence and Manifestation* (London, George Allen & Unwin, 1938). Wach builds on and extends Max Weber's notion of *charisma* as a basis for defining religious types. Van der Leeuw sees specific types of religious men in relationship to their apprehension or possession of power.

A. The primitive "philosopher" and the shaman

As an argument against the view that primitive man possesses an un-developed mind, Paul Radin wrote *Primitive Man as Philosopher* (N.Y., D. Appleton, 1927). A work along similar lines is A. P. Elkin's *Aboriginal Men of High Degree* (Sydney, Australasian Co., 1946). These studies show that primitive men do not have an underdeveloped intellect, but, as C. Lévi-Strauss has said, the difference lies "not in the quality of the intellectual process, but in the nature of the things to which it is applied." (*Structural Anthropology* [N.Y., Basic Books, 1963] p. 230.) Lévi-Strauss' theoretical imaginative discussion of "bricolage" and the "bricoleur" offers new possibilities for the understanding of the thinker in these cultures. (See his *Savage Mind* mentioned above.)

Closely related to these "aboriginal men of high degree" is the shaman. The shaman may function as a magician or priest, but the basic element in his makeup is his ability to have an ecstatic experience. We are here following Mircea Eliade's interpretation of shamanism. He has written a definitive book on this subject: *Le Chamanisme et les techniques archaïques de l'extase* (Paris, Payot, 1951). In his article "Recent Works on Shamanism: A Review Article," *History of Religions: A Journal for Comparative Historical Studies,* I, 2 (1961), 152ff., Eliade discusses the most recent literature on this subject. In delineating the specific shamanistic religious type, he says:

> This is why we thought it useful to limit the term "shaman" to those among the various "specialists of the sacred" (medicine men, magicians, contemplative, inspired, and possessed people, etc.) who know how to employ ecstasy for the benefit of the community. Ecstasy always involves a trance, whether "symbolic" or pretended or real, and the trance is interpreted as a temporary abandonment of the body by the soul of the shaman. During ecstasy, the soul of the shaman is thought to ascend to Heaven, to descend to the other world (to the nether world) or to travel far away in space (pp. 153–54).

Andreas Lommel in his *Shamanism* (N.Y., McGraw-Hill, 1967) relates the shaman of modern hunting cultures to prehistoric paintings and undertakes to identify the beginning of art in the shamanistic vision. Joseph Campbell in *The Masks of God* has seen the origin of shamanism in the paleolithic stage of hunting culture (pp. 229–81). Eliade seems to confirm this belief and cites other authors in support of Campbell's position. See "Prehistory of Shamanism" in Eliade's article on shamanism (pp. 182ff.). A critical discussion of Eliade's view concerning shamanism may be found in Alois Closs, "Das Religiöse in Schamanismus," *Kairos,* II (1960), 29.

Eliade states that though shamanism is a specifically Siberian phenomenon, vestiges and traces of it are found throughout the world, with the possible exception of Africa (p. 153). Thus any study of the primitive religions of Oceania, the Americas, the circum-polar peoples, or Asians will in some measure show signs of shamanism.

An enlarged and revised English version of Eliade's *Le Chamanisme et les techniques archaïques de l'extase* was published in 1964 under the title *Shamanism: Archaic Techniques of Ecstasy,* tr. by Willard R. Trask (N.Y., Bollingen Foundation, 1964). This work is a comprehensive study from the viewpoint of an historian of religion. It also contains a complete bibliography.

B. Medicine men, kings, and priests

The shaman is a medicine man or priest, but, as Eliade states, all medicine men and priests are not shamans. As the phrase implies, the medicine man is concerned with healing. Healing is not limited to physical ailments, and even when it is, the cause of the ailment is not understood simply as an organic disorder. The medicine man may be at the same time a priest or king. If he is a priest, he has the power to act on behalf of all the people in a formalized cult. Such a role may also be combined with kingship. The king, if he is a holy man, is a symbol of an ancestral cult and may or may not have priestly powers.

Though the phenomenon represented by the term "medicine man" is almost universal among primitives, the specific term is of North American origin, and any general study of a primitive society will devote a chapter or two to its description.

The interrelatedness of healing and religion among American Indians is dealt with by John R. Swanton in his article "Religious Beliefs and Medicinal Practices of the Creek Indians," *U.S. Bureau of American Ethnology*, 42nd Annual Report (Washington, 1928). The relationship of the medicinal practices and the cultural role of the medicine man is the subject of W. T. Corlett's *The Medicine-man of the American Indian and His Cultural Background* (Illinois, Charles C. Thomas, 1935). Charles M. Barbeau's *Medicine-men on the North Pacific Coast* (Ottawa, Department of Northern Affairs & National Resources, 1958) demonstrates how closely medicine men are related to shamans, and Samuel Barret describes the actual practice of medicine men in his *Pomo Bear Doctors* (Berkeley, Univ. of California Press, 1917). A sociological analysis of this same problem is undertaken by John J. Maddox in *The Medicine-man* (N.Y., Macmillan, 1923). The combination of the magician and medicine man may be seen in Sir Richard Winstedt's *The Malay Magician* (London, Routledge & Kegan Paul, 1951).

Studies dealing with primitive medicine are found in Erwin Acker-knecht's "Psychopathology, Primitive Medicine, and Primitive Culture," *Bulletin of the History of Medicine*, XIV (1943), 30–67; and his "Natural Diseases and Rational Treatment in Primitive Medicine," *Bulletin of the History of Medicine*, XIX (1946), 467–97; and also in M. Bartels, *Die Medizin der Naturvölker* (Leipzig, T. Grieben, 1893). Both interpretations emphasize the magical element in medicinal practices of the primitives. This mixture of magic and medicine among primitive and archaic peoples is treated by Jean Filliozat in *Magie et médecine* (Paris, Presses universitaires de France, 1943). A study of examples of the use and function of negative magic or witchcraft in primitive societies is Peter H. Buck's *Regional Diversity in the Elaboration of Sorcery in Polynesia* (New Haven, Yale Univ. Press, 1936). For this same phenomenon in Africa the reader may consult E. E. Evans-Pritchard, *Witchcraft, Oracles, and Magic among the Azande* (Oxford, Clarendon Press, 1937); Pierre Fontaine, *La Magie chez les noirs* (Paris, Dervy, 1949); and Frederick Kiagh, *Witchcraft and Magic of Africa* (London, R. Lesley, 1947).

Among modern primitives, the Africans still seem to possess the exemplary form of the priest-king or divine kingship. A summary discussion of divine kingship in Africa is found in V. van Bulck's "La Place du roi divin dans cercles culturels d'Afrique noire" in *The Sacral Kingship* (Leiden, E. J. Brill, 1959), 98. Other articles relating to the religious role of kingship in this same volume are Paul Radin's "The Sacral Chief among American Indians," 83, and Patrick Akoi's "Divine Kingship and Its Participation in Ashanti," 135. The sociological and religious aspects of kingship are described by Olof Pettersson in *Chiefs and Gods; Religious and Social Elements in South Eastern Bantu Kingship* (Lund, C. W. K. Gleerup, 1953). The same aspects of the problem of kingship in Africa are the subject of Tor Irstam's *The King of Ganda* (Lund, H. Ohlssons Boktr., 1944). Percival Hadfield in *Traits of Divine Kingship in Africa* (London, C. A. Watts, 1949) and Eva Meyerowitz in *Divine Kingship in Ghana and Ancient Egypt* (London, Faber & Faber, 1960) attempted to find the origin of kingship in Africa. Luc de Heusch in *Essais sur le symbolisme de l'inceste royal en Afrique* (Brussels, Institut de sociologie Solvay, 1958) shows the social and mythological relationship of incest to the notion of kingship.

VI. RITUALS AND CULTS

The relationship of ritual and ceremonials to myth, religious symbols, and sociological forms has always posed a problem for historians and sociologists of religion. Theodor Gaster's discussion of ancient Near Eastern religion in *Thespis; Ritual, Myth, and Drama in the Ancient Near East* (N.Y., Henry Schuman, 1950) has a great deal to say concerning this problem in all archaic and primitive cultures. For Gaster all seasonal rituals express two elements: Kenosis, or emptying, and Plerosis, or filling (p. 4). The reality which is subject to this emptying and filling is denominated by Gaster as the *topocosm* (p. 4). *Topocosm* is a comprehensive term for the human community and all animate elements in a particular place. The essence of the *topocosm* is that it possesses a twofold character, at once real and punctual and ideal and durative, the former aspect being necessarily merged in the latter as a movement is merged in time (p. 5). Myth provides the necessary relation between the punctual and the durative transcendent dimension of reality. In Gaster's interpretation, myth is not an outgrowth of ritual but a parallel aspect of it.

Clyde Kluckhohn takes up this same problem in his important article "Myths and Rituals: A General Theory," *Harvard Theological Review,* XXXV (January, 1942), 45ff. Kluckhohn dismisses as unfounded any general theory of the priority of myth over ritual or vice versa. He maintains that one can find either type of priority by examining the empirical evidence. Myth and ritual are for him interdependent since they refer to a common psychological basis.

Ritual is an obsessive repetitive activity—often a symbolic dramatization of the fundamental "needs" of the society whether "economic," "biological," "social," or "sexual." Mythology is the rationalization of these same needs, whether they are all expressed in overt ceremonial or not (p. 29).

Jean Cazeneuve in *Les Rites et la condition humaine* (Paris, Presses universitaires de France, 1958) interprets rituals as arising out of the need of man to live in a sacred world. "But if religion tends to sacralize the human condition by making it depend upon an archetype that transcends it, by the same token religion transfigures it in conserving it" (p. 439). "Religion, through its rites affirms both this transcendence and the possibility for man to participate in its sacred archetypes" (p. 442).

It is possible to classify rituals into historical-cultural types. We could thus speak of those rituals common to paleolithic hunters and nomads, those common to the upper paleolithic period, and finally those which presuppose a neolithic background. This typology of rituals is carried out in Joseph Campbell's *The Masks of God*. During the paleolithic period the rituals were related to the animal as a symbol of sacrality.

The upper paleolithic period is represented by the rituals of those who tend and cultivate plants but who have not discovered agriculture. A. E. Jensen's work cited above deals with these types of rituals. In addition to the sacrificial ritual which involves the killing of a person or animal, the religious meaning of cannibalism in this cultural stage was explicated by E. Volhard in *Kannibalismus* (Stuttgart, Strecker und Schröder, 1939).

With the coming of the neolithic age we find rituals which are related to seasonal changes and fertility. The model for these rituals is the sowing, tending, and reaping of cereal grains. In these rituals sacrifices are performed to insure the fertility of the soil; and the earth, symbolized as a great mother, appears as one of the dominant symbols. We hardly, if ever, find pure types of any of these rituals. In every case new elements and survivals from the past occur. We are able to infer certain meanings from the archeological finds of paleolithic times; Johannes Maringer in his book *The Gods of Prehistoric Man* makes inferences regarding the religious rituals of paleolithic man. The Australian aborigines represent a mixture of old paleolithic and late paleolithic religious ritual. The emphasis on totemism and the sexual connotations of the *Kunapipi* and *Djanggawal* ceremonies confirm this observation.

An interpretation and historical comparative study of the corn-mother symbolism is given by G. Hatt in "Corn Mother in Indonesia and America," *Anthropos,* XLVI (1951), 853ff. H. Baumann traces the historical and cultural meaning of the myths which have reference to androgyny and hermaphroditism in his *Das doppelte Geschlecht* (Berlin, D. Reimer,

1955). He shows that these myths and their rituals are historically related to agricultural matriarchal societies.

The early neolithic rituals developed into the great rituals and sacrifices which we associate with the ancient Near East, India, and China. The rituals of the southwestern American Indians and the New England agricultural Indians and the great rituals of the Mayas and Aztecs are also related to this neolithic structure. The Plains Indians of North America practiced an older ritual form which probably had its origin in late paleolithic times. Examples of this ritual may be seen in Ralph Linton's account of *The Sacrifice to the Morning Star by the Skidi Pawnee* (Chicago, Field Museum of Natural History, 1922) and, by the same author, *The Thunder Ceremony of the Pawnee* (Chicago, Field Museum of Natural History, 1922). In both of these accounts three symbols are dominant: first, sky symbolism; second, the identity of human being with an animal; and, third, the sacrifice of the human for the increase of fertility. For an overall view of aboriginal American rituals see Paul Radin's *The Road of Life and Death, A Ritual Drama of the American Indian* (N.Y., Pantheon Books, 1945).

General cultural interpretations may be found as follows: for Melanesia, Michael R. Allen, *Male Cults and Secret Initiations in Melanesia* (Melbourne, Melbourne Univ. Press, 1967); and Raymond Firth, *Tikopia Ritual and Belief* (London, George Allen and Unwin, 1967); for New Guinea, Roy A. Rappaport, *Pigs for the Ancestors* (New Haven, Yale Univ. Press, 1968); and for Africa, Victor Turner, *The Drums of Affliction* (Oxford, Clarendon Press, 1968), and *The Forest of Symbols* (Ithaca, N.Y., Cornell Univ. Press, 1967).

For a description and interpretation of a variety of rituals and cults see the following: John Middleton, ed., *Magic, Witchcraft, and Curing* (N.Y., Natural History Press, 1967), and *Gods and Rituals: Readings in Religious Belief and Practice* (N.Y., Natural History Press, 1967). See also J. S. La Fontaine, ed., *The Interpretation of Ritual* (London, Tavistock, 1972) and Frank Wilbur Young, *Initiation Ceremonies* (Indianapolis, Bobbs-Merrill, 1965).

G. van Gennep, tr. by Monika B. Vizedom and Gabrielle L. Caffee, in *Rites of Passage* (Chicago, Univ. of Chicago Press, 1960), states a position which has become a watershed for all dicussions of initiation rituals. It is his belief that rites of initiation are ritual forms related to the movement from one status to another. The passage across is considered dangerous. The ritual protects and "carries the novice across the passage." Victor Turner's *The Ritual Process Structure and Anti-Structure* (Chicago, Aldine, 1969) extends this analysis by dealing more precisely with what G. van Gennep had called the "liminal phase" of the rites of passage. For Turner,

> Liminal entities are neither here nor there; they are betwixt and between the positions assigned and arrayed by law, custom, convention, and cere-

monial. As such, their ambiguous and indeterminate attributes are expressed by a rich variety of symbols in the many societies that ritualize social and cultural transitions (p. 95).

Herein lies the genius of Turner's work; he opens up an entirely new understanding of ritual. This analysis of the ritual process is continued in Turner's, *Dramas, Fields, and Metaphors, Symbolic Action in Human Society* (Ithaca, Cornell Univ. Press, 1974).

Mircea Eliade in *Birth and Rebirth* (N.Y., Harper & Brothers, 1958) extends van Gennep's understanding of initiation by concentrating on the process of passage itself. He sees initiation as a paradigmatic gesture which imitates the cosmogony. The novice is "reborn" in the initiation rite. To be reborn, he must return to chaos or "die" to his old mode of being. This initiatory death is the new and indispensable element in initiation (pp. xiii–xiv). Bruno Bettelheim in *Symbolic Wounds* (Glencoe, Free Press, 1954) applies a psychological methodology to arrive at his understanding of this phenomenon. On the basis of the initiation rites of the Australian aborigines, he sees initiation rites rooted in the antagonism of the sexes He interprets the mutilation of the penis which takes place during the course of these rites as the expression of the desire of the male to be androgynous— that is, able to bring forth a new human being.

Dominique Zahan's *Sociétés d'initiation bambara: le N'Dome, le Korè* (Paris, Mouton, 1960) is the first volume of a projected study of the six initiation societies of the Bambara, a West African culture. It is interesting because of its description of initiation rites which, in addition to covering the lifespan from childhood to manhood, form a mythological-theological drama. R. Thurnwald's "Primitive Initiations and Wiedergeburtriten," *Eranos-Jahrbuch,* VII (1940), takes up the meaning of the rebirth motif in initiation.

In addition to initiations related to the "rites of passage" are those initiatory rites by which one enters a secret society. Wach defines the secret society as a group which is open to membership on the basis of a special experience (*Sociology of Religion,* p. 114). Eliade deals with initiation rites of secret societies in chaps. III, "From Tribal Rites to Secret Cults," and IV, "Individual Initiations and Secret Societies," in his *Birth and Rebirth.* A general discussion of the character and nature of secret societies is presented in Wach's *Sociology of Religion,* chap. V, section 2, "The Secret Society." Hutton Webster's study, *Primitive Secret Societies* (N.Y., Macmillan, 1908) emphasizes the social and political role of secret societies in the evolution of culture.

An overall view of African secret societies is found in W. D. Hambly's *Source Book for African Anthropology,* Field Museum of Natural History, vol. XXVI (Chicago, 1937), 498ff. Specific studies of African secret societies are offered in George Harley's *Notes on the Mano in Liberia*

(Cambridge, Harvard Univ. Press, 1941) and F. W. Butt-Thompson's *West African Secret Societies* (London, H. F. & G. Witherby, 1929).

Information concerning North American Indian secret societies may be found in R. H. Lowie, *Indians of the Plains,* American Museum of Natural History, Anthropological Handbooks, No. 1 (N.Y., McGraw-Hill, 1954); Reo F. Fortune, "Omaha Secret Societies," *Columbia University Contributions to Anthropology,* No. 14 (1932), and George Boas, "The Social Organizations and Secret Societies of the Kwakiutl Indians," *U.S. National Museum Annual Report for the Year 1895* (Washington, D.C., Smithsonian Institution, 1897).

Secret societies of Oceania are described in Gunnar Landtman, *The Kiwai Papuans of British New Guinea* (London, Macmillan, 1927); D. F. Thomason, "The Hero Cult, Initiation and Totemism on Cape York," *Journal of the Royal Anthropological Institute,* LXIII (1933), 453–537; and R. Piddington, "Karadjeri Initiation," *Oceania,* III (1932–33), 46–86.

VII. CARGO-CULTS AND THE IMPACT OF MODERNIZATION

The term "cargo-cult" refers to a prophetic and millenarian religious phenomenon common among modern primitives. The origin of the phrase may be found in F. E. Williams, *The Vailala Madness and the Destruction of Native Ceremonies in the Gulf District,* Papuan Anthropology Reports, no. 4 (Port Moresby, 1923). Concerning the cults, Williams reports:

> Perhaps one of the most fundamental ideas was that of the ancestors, or more usually the deceased relatives, of the people who were shortly to return to visit them. They were expected in a large steamer which was to be loaded with cases of gifts—tobacco, calico, knives, axes, food stuffs and the like. . . . A feature of interest and importance is that in some places the returning ancestors or relatives were expected to be white and indeed some white men were actually claimed by the natives to be their deceased relatives (pp. 14–15).

Kenelm Burridge in his excellent description of one of these cults and cult leaders in *Mambu: A Melanesian Millennium* (London, Methuen, 1960), gives us a more general definition of the cargo-cults. He says,

> Cargo movements, often described as millenarian, messianic, or nativistic movements, and also Cargo cults, are serious enterprises of the *genre* of popular revolutionary activities. Mystical, combining political-economic problems with expressions of racial tension, Cargo cults compare most directly with the Ghost-dance cults of North America and the prophetist movement among African peoples. Typically, participants in a Cargo cult engage in a number of strange and exotic rites and ceremonies the purpose of which is, apparently, to gain possession of Euro-

pean manufactured goods such as axes, knives, aspirins, china plates, razor blades, colored beads, guns, bolts of cloth, hydrogen peroxide, rice, tinned food, and other goods to be found in a general department store. These goods are known as "cargo" or in the Pidgin English rendering Kago (pp. xv–xvi).

With the coming of the Westerners, the old traditional ways were seriously undermined. The cargo-cult ideology represents the longing of the primitives for a return and a renewal of their spiritual and cultural life. This longing for a return to paradise is found among all modern primitive peoples. Many of the prophetic elements among modern primitives appear within the context of this cargo-cult mentality.

The phenomenon of cargo-cults has loomed so large in the history of religions and anthropology that I. C. Jarvie has spoken of it as constituting a "revolution" in anthropology. See his *The Revolution in Anthropology* (Chicago, Henry Regnery, 1967). In this work we find a trenchant analysis of most of the theories of cargo-cults.

Vittorio Lanternari in his article "Messianism: Its Historical Origin and Morphology," *History of Religions,* II, 1 (1962), 52ff., and in his full length study, *The Religions of the Oppressed* (N.Y., Alfred A. Knopf, 1963), sees in these movements the dialectic relationship between "myth" and history, a dialectic which is present in all prophetic movements. Mircea Eliade has dealt with this topic in his article "Dimensions religieuses du renouvellement cosmique," *Eranos-Jahrbuch,* XXVIII (1959), 24ff. This article also appears as "Renouvellement cosmique et eschatologie" in his *Mephistopheles et L'Androgyne* (Paris, Gallimard, 1962). Eliade pays special attention to the religious symbols of return to primordial time and the paradisal elements which are present in the cargo-cult. By way of contrast, one could say that Eliade's interpretation emphasizes the mythological motifs and symbols, whereas Lanternari's essay emphasizes the historical causal elements in the cults. These works are highly instructive for those interested in general religious interpretation of this phenomenon. Robert Lowie discusses the meaning of primitive messianism in "Primitive Messianism and an Ethnological Problem," *Diogenes,* 19 (1957), 62–72.

We are in debt to Weston La Barre for his excellent bibliographical essay "Materials for a Study of Crisis Cults: A Bibliographical Essay," *Current Anthropology,* XII, 1, (February, 1971) 3–44. This essay deals with the history of interpretation of this phenomenon, presents the pertinent literature in an exhaustive bibliography, and also gives La Barre's conclusions. La Barre's study of this religious behavior is taken up again in *The Ghost Dance* (N.Y., Doubleday, 1970).

Other studies of a theoretical kind may be seen in Peter Worsley, *The Trumpet Shall Sound: A Study of Cargo Cults in Melanesia* (London, Macgibbon & Kee, 1957) and Kenelm Burridge, *New Heaven, New Earth* (N.Y., Schocken Books, 1969). Bryan Wilson's *Magic and the Millennium*

(N.Y., Harper & Row, 1973) is a full-length study of these movements all over the world. His bibliography is excellent.

Messianism appeared among the North American Indians during the latter part of the nineteenth and early twentieth centuries. A rich body of literature describes and documents this movement. A general book showing the relationship between American Indian nationalism and its religious expression in the peyote cult is *The Peyote Religion* by J. S. Slotkin (Glencoe, Free Press, 1956). Peyote is a drug derived from a type of cactus plant; it is chewed during the worship of this Indian group. Slotkin's book is heavily documented.

Another aspect of this phenomenon among the American Indians goes by the name of "ghost dance" or "hand dance." The dances were ritualistic militant movements which looked forward to the overthrow of the dominant white culture by a Messiah who was to re-establish the old Indian way of life. Some representative literature dealing with this aspect of Indian cargo-cults is: James Mooney, "The Ghost-Dance Religion and the Sioux Outbreak in 1890" *Annual Report of U.S. Bureau of American Ethnology,* No. 14 (Washington, D.C., 1896); C. DuBois, *The 1870 Ghost Dance,* Univ. of California Records (Berkeley, 1939); Leslie Spier, *The Prophet Dance of the Northwest and Its Derivatives,* General Series in Anthropology, No. 1 (Menasha, Wisc., G. Banta, 1935); Nat P. Phister, "The Indian Messiah," *American Anthropologist,* IV (1891), 105–08.

For this phenomenon in Oceania, see Ida Lesson's *Bibliography of Cargo Cults and Other Nativistic Movements in the South Pacific* (Sydney, South Pacific Commission Technical Paper, No. 30, 1952).

For Africa, see G. Balandier's "Messianismes et nationalismes en Afrique noire," *Cahiers internationaux de sociologie,* XIV (1953), 41ff.; E. Andersson, *Messianic Popular Movements in the Lower Congo* (Uppsala, Almquist & Wiksells, 1958); H. von Sicard, *Ngoma Lungundu* (Uppsala, Almquist & Wiksells, 1952); and Bengt Sundkler, *Bantu Prophets in South Africa* (London, Lutterworth Press, 1948).

APPENDIX

I. General works on primitive religion

A section of most textbooks on the history of religion or comparative religion is almost always devoted to an interpretation of primitive religion. For example, see John Murphy, *The Origins and History of Religions* (Manchester, Manchester Univ., Press, 1949); John B. Noss, *Man's Religions,* 4th ed. (N.Y., Macmillan, 1969); and Winston King, *Introduction to Religion* (N.Y., Harper & Brothers, 1954).

In addition to this type of text, there are other texts devoted exclusively to a study of primitive religion. Alexander Goldenweiser's *Early Civilization* (N.Y., Alfred A. Knopf, 1922) is a critical theoretical work. In it Goldenweiser examines the various theories of primitive mentality and the origin of religion. William J. Goode's *Religion among the Primitives* (Glencoe, Free Press, 1951) is a sociologically oriented study of primitive religion, as is Edward Norbeck, *Religion in Primitive Society* (N.Y., Harper & Brothers, 1961). Paul Radin, *Primitive Religion, Its Nature and Origin* (N.Y., Viking Press, 1937), Robert Lowie, *Primitive Religion* (N.Y., Boni & Liveright, 1924), and Wilson Wallis, *Religion in Primitive Society* (N.Y., F. S. Crofts, 1939) combine historical, sociological, and phenomenological dimensions in their treatments. I consider them the most adequate texts. Catherine H. and Ronald Berndt's *The Barbarians* (Harmondsworth, Penguin Books, 1973) raises some of the issues noted in the first section of this essay regarding primitive religion.

Two other works should be mentioned: *Primitive Heritage,* ed. by Margaret Mead and Nicholas Calas (N.Y., Random House, 1953), and *Reader in Comparative Religion,* ed. by William A. Lessa and Evon Z. Vogt (Evanston, Row, Peterson, 1958). Edited texts of this type enable a teacher to cover several dimensions of the topic with the aid of primary source material. Furthermore, a teacher using such an edited text is not forced to accept completely the method and point of view of a textbook or to spend a great deal of time qualifying it. The opportunity for developing his own approach is made available.

A final word concerning the art forms of primitive cultures is in order. There is no separate section dealing with this topic since many works already mentioned contain a section on art. While the books listed below (with the exception of Andreas Lommel, *Masks: Their Meaning and Function* [N.Y., McGraw-Hill, 1972]) concentrate on African cultures, they are placed here primarily for the theoretical considerations put forth. Robert F. Thompson, *African Art in Motion* (Berkeley, Univ. of California Press, 1974), and Robert P. Armstrong, *The Affecting Presence* (Urbana, Univ. of Illinois Press, 1971), develop a philosophical anthropology in their approach to art forms. Daniel Biebuyck, *Tradition and Creativity in Tribal Art* (Berkeley, Univ. of California Press, 1969), gives us a history of the interpretation of primitive art, devoting several chapters to particular cultures as well as opening up the problems of creativity and style. J. H. Kwabena Nketia, *The Music of Africa* (N.Y., W. W. Norton, 1974) is the best text on African music. Frank Willett, *Ife in the History of West African Sculpture* (N.Y., McGraw-Hill, 1967), traces the history and influence of an artistic style in West Africa.

II. Periodicals relevant to primitive religion

American Anthropologist
Annual Reports of Smithsonian Institution
Anthropological Quarterly
Anthropos
Archiv für Religionswissenschaft
Archiv für Völkerkunde
Arctic Anthropology
Bantu Studies
Bernice P. Bishop Museum Bulletin
Bulletin de l'Institut Français d'Afrique Noire

Bulletin de l'Institut Français d'Afrique Noire, Série B
Bulletin de la Société d'Anthropologie de Paris
Bulletin de la Société de Géographie
Bulletin de la Société Royale Belge de Géographie
Bulletin de la Société des Recherches Congolaises
Carnegie Institution Publications
Eranos-Jahrbuch
Ethnos
Études de sociologie et d'ethnologie juridiques
Field Museum of Natural History Anthropological Series
Folk-Lore
Folklore Fellows Communications
General Series in Anthropology
Harvard African Studies
History of Religions. An International Journal for Comparative Historical Studies
Internationales Archiv für Ethnographie
Journal de la Société des Africanistes
Journal of American Folklore
Journal of the American Oriental Society
Journal of the American Society for Semitic Languages
Journal of Polynesian Society
Journal of the Royal Anthropological Institute
Journal of the Royal Asiatic Society
L'année sociologique
Man
Mana
Mémoires de l'Institut d'Études Centrafricaines
Mémoires de l'Institut Français d'Afrique Noire
Mémoires de l'Institut Français d'Afrique Noire, Centre du Cameroun, Série Populations
Mitteilungen der Anthropologischen Gesellschaft in Wien
Oceania
Orientalia
Papers of the Peabody Museum of American Archaeology and Ethnology, Harvard University
Préhistoire
Publications of U.S. Bureau of American Ethnology
Revue d'anthropologie
Revue archéologique
Revue d'ethnographie et de sociologie
Revue d'ethnographie et des traditions populaires
Revue de l'histoire des religions
Revue des études ethnographiques et sociologiques
Revue des sciences religieuses
Rhodes-Livingstone Journal
Rhodes-Livingstone Papers
Royal Anthropological Institute Occasional Papers
Southwestern Journal of Anthropology
Studien zur Völkerkunde
University of California Publications in American Archaeology and Ethnology (UCAAE)

III. Bibliographies covering the geographical areas of primitive religions

A. Africa

W. D. Hambly, *Source Book for African Anthropology*: Field Museum of Natural History Anthropological Series, 26, part 2 (Chicago, 1937).

———, *Bibliography of African Anthropology, 1937–49*, Chicago Museum of Natural History, Fieldiana, XXXVII, 2 (1952).

Evans Levin, *Annotated Bibliography of Recent Publications on Africa South of the Sahara*, Royal Empire Society (London, 1943).

Twentieth Century Fund, *Selected Annotated Bibliography of Tropical Africa*. Compiled by the International African Institute under the Direction of Professor Daryll Forde (N.Y., 1956).

U.S. Library of Congress, European Affairs Division, *Introduction to Africa: A Selective Guide to Background Reading*. Prepared by Helen F. Conover (Washington, D.C., 1952).

U.S. Library of Congress, General Reference and Bibliographic Division, *Africa South of the Sahara, A Selected Annotated List of Writings, 1951–56*. Compiled by Helen F. Conover (Washington, D.C., 1957).

H. A. Wieschhoff, *Anthropological Bibliography of Negro Africa* (New Haven, American Oriental Society, 1948).

B. North America

F. W. Hodge, ed., *Handbook of American Indians North of Mexico*, 2 vols., Bureau of American Ethnology Bulletin 30 (Washington, D.C., 1907–10).

Clyde Kluckhohn and Katherine Spenser, *A Bibliography of the Navaho Indians* (N.Y., J. J. Augustin, 1940).

A. L. Kroeber, *Handbook of the Indians of the Southwest*, Univ. of California Publications in American Archaeology and Ethnology, XXIII, 9 (Berkeley, 1929).

———, *Cultural and Natural Areas of Native North America*, Univ. of California Publications in American Archaeology and Ethnology, XXXVIII (Berkeley, 1939).

———, *Handbook of the Indians of California*, Bureau of American Ethnology Bulletin 78 (Washington, D.C., 1925).

George P. Murdock, *Ethnolographic Bibliography of North America*, 1st ed. (New Haven, Yale Univ. Press, 1941).

C. South America

George P. Murdock, *Outline of South American Cultures* (New Haven, Human Relations Area Files, 1951).

Julian H. Steward, ed., *Handbook of South American Indians*, 6 vols. (Washington, D.C., U.S. Government Printing Office, 1946–50).

Juan Comas, *Bibliografía Selectiva de las Culturas Indígenas de America*. Mexico City, Comisión de Historia, Instituto Pan Americano de Geografía e Historia, 1953).

D. Oceania

A. P. Elkin, Social Anthropology in Melanesia; *A Review of Research* (London, Oxford Univ. Press, 1953).

Léonce A. N. H. Jore, *Essai de bibliographie du Pacifique* (Paris, Éditions Duchartre, 1931).

Clyde R. H. Taylor, *A Pacific Bibliography* (Wellington, Polynesian Society, 1951).

E. General

John G. Barrow, *A Bibliography of Bibliographies in Religion* (Ann Arbor, Mich., Univ. of Michigan Press, 1955).

Katherine Smith Diehl, *Religions, Mythologies, Folklores: An Annotated Bibliography* (New Brunswick, N.J., Scarecrow Press, 1956).

II

The Ancient World

Willard G. Oxtoby

This chapter treats literature on the religions of the Middle Eastern and Mediterranean world from the dawn of recorded history to the spread of Judaism, Christianity, and Islam. After some general works in the first section, Babylonia and Egypt will appear in the second, Greece and Rome in the third, Iran in the fourth, and the Arabian and European perimeter in the fifth.

The Christian West has referred to the ancient religions of these areas as "pagan." Etymologically, that word, from the same root as "peasant," means "rural," its connotation rooted in the historical situation of Roman imperial times when old cults survived in the countryside after the cities had been won over to newer movements and creeds such as Christianity. Likewise, in northern Europe, the word "heathen," associated with the heath or waste land, refers to the faith and practice of folk living in backward areas.

What is important about the notion of paganism for our endeavor in this chapter is that each of the three major monotheistic faiths—Judaism, Christianity, and Islam—has traditionally seen itself as standing in sharp contrast with its ancient environment. What went on in Canaan was idola-

(39)

try to the Hebrews; the cults of Greece and Rome were error to the Christians; and the era before Muhammad is seen by Muslims as one of ignorance or barbarism. In modern times it may be a subtle and debatable question whether monotheistic faith necessarily requires so negative a judgment of other people's cultural riches and religious insights; but classically, it is clear, these three traditions have stressed their discontinuity from what preceded them.

Thus it is that, for example, while South and East Asian legends and folk religion are treated as part of their major religious traditions, the religions of the ancient world west of India constitute an entity apart. Religion in this ancient world stands alongside the great religions as an identifiable set of regional cults and cultures, though by no means as one single system. We study this group as we study the other great religions: out of an interest in them for their own sake, out of an interest in the range and variety of man's religiousness, and out of an interest in their historical relationships with our own culture.

I. ANCIENT RELIGION IN OVERVIEW

Because of the wide range of primary-source languages involved, it is inevitable that practically all the comprehensive works on the religions of the ancient world should be composite, consisting of essays by specialists in different literatures on the one hand, or of efforts by generalists using translated sources on the other. In the first type of effort, a committee undertaking may lack unity of theme and treatment, while in the second, a broad theory may sweep too much specific variation under the rug. The breadth-and-depth problem is perennial and may never be solved to the satisfaction of all, but a number of overall efforts nevertheless deserve the reader's attention.

The most authoritative and up-to-date multi-author survey in English is C. Jouco Bleeker and Geo. Widengren, eds., *Historia Religionum: Handbook for the History of Religions,* 2 vols. (Leiden, E. J. Brill, 1969–71). Unlike many survey texts dealing only with the principal living religions, the first volume of this work is devoted to "Religions of the Past." The editors have instructed each contributor to include in his treatment some history of the study of the religion assigned him, a feature which along with the volume's length and detail lifts the book above the usual introductory level. It is thus a more substantial summation of scholarship than Vergilius Ferm, ed., *Forgotten Religions* (also reissued as *Ancient Religions*) (N.Y., Philosophical Library, 1950). Readers who wish an introductory orientation to individual religions such as is offered within the average composite volume should not overlook the coverage of the material in the fifteenth edition of the *Encyclopaedia Britannica* (Chicago, Encyclopaedia Britannica, 1974). Users of the new *Britannica* for bibliographical leads should beware of spelling: diacritics such as umlauts are consistently omitted from authors' surnames in its articles' bibliographies.

A single-author survey of ancient religion is offered by Edwin O. James, *The Ancient Gods* (London, Weidenfeld and Nicolson, 1960). As in many of his other works, James organizes his treatment thematically, under such headings as cosmology, the mother goddess, sacral kingship, seasonal festivals, and the cult of the dead. Although James does mention contrasts between one ancient culture and another, the critical reader will be tempted to wonder whether similarities are being stressed at the expense of idiosyncratic or unique developments, and whether he is at the mercy of the author's selection of categories. If a category coincides with the reader's interest, however, such works can be a useful starting point. Alongside James' comparative contributions may be mentioned those of Samuel G. F. Brandon, such as *Creation Legends of the Ancient Near East* (London, Hodder and Stoughton, 1963).

British studies in comparative religion owe much to the momentum generated at the turn of the century by James G. Frazer, a classical scholar who sought anthropological explanations for ancient religious practices, and amassed in *The Golden Bough,* 3rd ed., 12 vols. (London, Macmillan, 1911–36), a prodigious corpus of material on ritual, especially ritual killing of kings, and the theme of death and rebirth, coupled with a theoretical interpretation of the relation of ritual to myth and to magic. Into the general influence and significance of Frazer's work for theories of religion we cannot go here; for a spread of opinion about Frazer see Edmund R. Leach, "Golden Bough or Gilded Twig?" and Herbert Weisiger, "The Branch That Grew Full Straight," in *Daedalus,* XC (1961), 371–87 and 388–99. But both for classical and for Near Eastern religions Frazer's work spurred the "Myth and Ritual" school, influential between the two world wars. Rather than viewing myths simply as literary creations or as speculative explanations of origins, this school stressed the ritual re-enactment of myth as functioning to maintain the order of things. A useful review of this subject is S. G. F. Brandon's chapter, "The Myth and Ritual Position Critically Considered," in Samuel H. Hooke, ed., *Myth, Ritual, and Kingship: Essays on the Theory and Practice of Kingship in the Ancient Near East and in Israel* (Oxford, Clarendon Press, 1958), 261–91.

Interest in myth has not abated. Works on mythology aimed at the popular market appear constantly, often with large page formats and copious illustrations. Two works, however, which stand apart from such a genre in different ways, deserve mention. The symposium *Mythologies of the Ancient World,* ed. by Samuel N. Kramer (Garden City, Doubleday, 1961), combines general interest with scholarly accuracy, and does not try to force an overall theory on diverse cultures. The thirteen volumes of *The*

Mythology of All Races, ed. by Louis H. Gray and John A. MacCulloch (Boston, Archaeological Institute of America, Marshall Jones Co., 1916–32), include syntheses that remain useful particularly for Europe's ancient religions.

Certain reference sources in fields bordering on religion which will orient the student to the world of antiquity are mentioned below, at the beginning of the Greek and Roman section.

II. THE NEAR EAST BEFORE THE PERSIAN CONQUEST

Before modern times the two mountains of Sinai and Olympus could have been said to symbolize the monotheistic and the pagan origins of Western culture. In the nineteenth and twentieth centuries, however, recorded history going back about twenty centuries earlier has been pieced together from the two valleys of Mesopotamia and Egypt. Their history may now be found in many treatments; perhaps the most straightforward and up-to-date is William W. Hallo and W. Kelly Simpson, *The Ancient Near East: A History* (N.Y., Harcourt Brace Jovanovich, 1971). Other convenient introductions to the culture, with emphasis on its religious aspects, are two books of Sabatino Moscati, *The Face of the Ancient Orient* (London, Vallentine, Mitchell, 1960) and *Ancient Semitic Civilizations* (London, Elek Books, 1957). Also, one usable survey specifically of religions, which covers ancient southwestern Asia but not Egypt, is Helmer Ringgren, *Religions of the Ancient Near East* (London, Society for Propagating Christian Knowledge [hereafter SPCK], 1973).

The standard collection of ancient sources in translation is James B. Pritchard, ed., *Ancient Near Eastern Texts Relating to the Old Testament,* 3rd ed. (Princeton, Princeton Univ. Press, 1969), an indispensable source of mythic, hymnic, and didactic religious literature as well as of historical and legal texts. Much of what is needed for an understanding of ancient Israel's neighbors on their own terms is included; mention of the Old Testament in the title should not be taken by the reader as a serious restriction on the scope of the book. A companion volume, also edited by Pritchard, is *The Ancient Near East in Pictures Relating to the Old Testament,* 2nd ed. (Princeton, Princeton Univ. Press, 1969); it includes temples and images of gods as well as, of course, more seemingly secular aspects of life such as costumes and warfare. Pritchard also has a shorter volume of selections from the two, *The Ancient Near East: An Anthology of Texts and Pictures* (Princeton, Princeton Univ. Press, 1958), suitable as a textbook in a course; but the serious student will find that *ANET,* as the full volume of texts is designated, is the source to which the most references are made.

A number of specific topics cut across the religions of the ancient Near East. On the notion of kingship, for example, a work which makes principal use of Mesopotamian materials and their relationships to ancient Israel is Cyril J. Gadd, *Ideas of Divine Rule in the Ancient East* (London, Oxford Univ. Press for the British Academy, 1948), while Henri Frankfort works with a major emphasis on Egyptian materials in *Kingship and the Gods: A Study of Ancient Near Eastern Religion as the Integration of Society and Nature* (Chicago, Univ. of Chicago Press, 1948). Another topic of interest is the interpretation of history; a general symposium on the subject is Robert C. Dentan, ed., *The Idea of History in the Ancient Near East,* American Oriental Series, 38 (New Haven, Yale Univ. Press, 1955); and a specific address to theological views of history as the locus of revelation is Bertil Albrektson, *History and the Gods: An Essay on the Idea of Historical Events as Divine Manifestations in the Ancient Near East and in Israel,* Collectanea biblica, Old Testament series, 1 (Lund, C. W. K. Gleerup, 1967). That the Near East shared much with ancient Israel has of course been a fruitful hypothesis for a century; one expression of it out of many which could be cited is Morton Smith, "The Common Theology of the Ancient Near East," *Journal of Biblical Literature,* LXXI (1952), 135–47.

By all odds, though, the most widely influential Near Eastern thematic discussion in the past generation has been the symposium involving Henri Frankfort and other scholars at the University of Chicago, *The Intellectual Adventure of Ancient Man: An Essay on Speculative Thought in the Ancient Near East* (Chicago, Univ. of Chicago Press, 1946), most of it reprinted by Penguin Books under the title *Before Philosophy.* One of its central claims is that ancient thought was "mythopoeic," that is, myth-making: man personified the forces of nature, saw the cosmos as governed like his own cities by a council of gods, and so on. The authors have pushed their stimulating thesis so as to suggest that mythopoeic thought excluded the possibility of critical rational inference, a point challenged by Samuel N. Kramer in his review of the book in *Journal of Cuneiform Studies,* II (1948), 39–70. Kramer mentions such genres as mathematical and administrative texts to make a case for non-mythopoeic Near Eastern man as well.

A. Mesopotamia

We must suppose that religious and political institutions were established in the Tigris-Euphrates valley well before 3000 B.C. and the dawn of writing, but without written documents from earlier eras we are barred from detailed knowledge of them. From the invention of writing, however, to the fall of the late Babylonian empire in 538 B.C., we are tempted to see

Mesopotamian religion as a continuity—as a stable system pervading the area, whether under Sumerian or Babylonian or Assyrian rule. In effect, like a football substitution, one local god replaces another, but the rules and strategy of the game remain. What makes it hard to offer any alternative view is, of course, the still fragmentary nature of our evidence for many things. In discussing religion in *Ancient Mesopotamia: Portrait of a Dead Civilization* (Chicago, Univ. of Chicago Press, 1964), A. Leo Oppenheim reflects on the impossibility of writing a history of the development of Mesopotamian religion. Oppenheim's book, a fine introduction to the culture in general, offers a direct and reliable point of entry to the religion.

Other general discussions of Mesopotamian religion tend to force a choice between readability and reliability. Samuel H. Hooke surveys *Babylonian and Assyrian Religion* (London, Hutchinson's University Library, 1953) but stresses patterns emphasized by the myth-and-ritual school at the expense of other features of the religion. Georges Contenau, in *Everyday Life in Babylon and Assyria* (London, Edward Arnold, 1954), is easy reading and gives strong emphasis to thought and religion, but does not take into account Sumerian and older Babylonian material as much as the Assyrian and late Babylonian. On the other hand, Willem H. P. Römer, "Religion of Ancient Mesopotamia," in Bleeker and Widengren, eds., *Historia Religionum* (Leiden, E. J. Brill, 1969–71), vol. I, 115–94, offers a technical, well-documented review of the current state of scholarship for the reader who already has some acquaintance with the subject. And there are two fine essays by Thorkild Jacobsen whose subtlety and authority are best appreciated by a reader with some prior background: "Ancient Mesopotamian Religion: The Central Concerns," *Proceedings of the American Philosophical Society,* CVII (1963), 473–84; and "Formative Tendencies in Sumerian Religion," in G. Ernest Wright, ed., *The Bible and the Ancient Near East: Essays in Honor of William Foxwell Albright* (Garden City, Doubleday, 1961), 267–78. Both of these are accessible in Jacobsen's volume of reissued essays, *Toward the Image of Tammuz* (Cambridge, Harvard Univ. Press, 1970).

A principal feature of interest in Mesopotamian religion is its myths. The third-millennium-B.C. Sumerian literature containing them is the oldest, and the various publications of Sumerologist Samuel N. Kramer are the principal means of access to them in English. His standard general treatment is *Sumerian Mythology,* rev. ed. (N.Y., Harper & Row, 1961). One of the main narratives of Mesopotamia is the Gilgamesh Epic, containing the account of a flood similar to the Noah story in the Bible. A brief illustrated account of this document is Edmond Sollberger, *The Babylonian Legend of the Flood* (London, Trustees of the British Museum, 1962). The Babylonian account of the creation of the world, with the slaying of a primeval chaos-monster, is studied by Alexander Heidel, *The Babylonian Genesis,* 2nd ed. (Chicago, Univ. of Chicago Press, 1951). An older study which explored the annual ritual renewal of the creation at the new year is Svend A. Pallis, *The Babylonian Akîtu Festival,* Det kongelige Danske Videnskabernes Selskab, historisk-filologiske Meddedelser, 12:1 (Copenhagen, Bianco Lunos Bogtrykkerei, 1926).

Wilfred G. Lambert discusses "Myth and Ritual as Conceived by the Babylonians" in *Journal of Semitic Studies,* XIII (1968), 104–12. For his study of another Mesopotamian genre, more reflective and sometimes worldly in its outlook, see *Babylonian Wisdom Literature* (Oxford, Clarendon Press, 1960). On the practice of divination, an important subject, much of the literature is in French, but one work in English is A. Leo Oppenheim, *The Interpretation of Dreams in the Ancient Near East, with a Translation of an Assyrian Dream Book,* Transactions, n.s., 46:3 (Philadelphia, American Philosophical Society, 1956). Among the discussions of Mesopotamian symbolism are those of Elizabeth Douglas Van Buren, *Symbols of the Gods in Mesopotamian Art,* Analecta Orientalia, 23 (Rome, Pontifical Biblical Institute, 1945), and "The Dragon in Ancient Mesopotamia," *Orientalia,* n.s. XV (1946), 1–45, and XVI (1947), 251–54. While somewhat uncritical in their conception of what constitutes proof of association or identification, her works do provide a repertory of information about religion in representational art.

B. Egypt

There is a particular romance surrounding the subject of ancient Egypt. While the Rosicrucians and the Mormons may have indulged a fascination with ancient Egyptian culture more than most others have, a curiosity about Egypt grips practically everybody to at least some degree. Partly responsible may be the remarkable state of preservation of very old Egyptian reliefs and paintings, some of them looking as though, like their forged copies, they had been made yesterday. Part of the fascination must also be due to the combination of pictorial and abstract symbolism in the hieroglyphic writing. In any event, books on ancient Egypt, often lavishly illustrated, appear regularly in the market place.

Under such circumstances it seems ironic that the best introduction to Egyptian religion is one without a single illustration at all. It is Jaroslav Černý, *Ancient Egyptian Religion* (London, Hutchinson's University Library, 1952), a well-organized book which moves from a discussion of the gods and their character to man's moral and ritual obligations, and includes a chapter on the importation of foreign gods and the decline of the old religion in the later centuries of ancient Egypt.

With Černý at hand, one hardly needs any other introduction, but there are others available: Henri Frankfort's *Ancient Egyptian Religion: An Interpretation* (N.Y., Columbia Univ. Press, 1949), a short statement about religion as a part of the ancient Egyptian way of social and personal life; Siegfried Morenz, *Egyptian Religion* (London, Methuen, 1973), a full-length introduction translated from a German series, which also gives play to the role of religion in the life of the individual; James H. Breasted, *The Development of Religion and Thought in Ancient Egypt* (N.Y., Charles Scribner's Sons, 1912), an old classic which pioneered a developmental approach to the material; and Samuel A. B. Mercer, *The Religion of Ancient Egypt* (London, Luzac, 1949), a full-length work whose first half inventories the deities one by one and whose second half looks at different topics of faith and practice. Finally, an introduction to many aspects of the religion may be gained from Serge Sauneron, *The Priests of Ancient Egypt,* Evergreen Profile Books, 12 (N.Y., Grove Press, 1960).

From an introduction one might be well advised to proceed to a further study specifically of the Egyptian myths. One of the best treatments is Rudolf Anthes, "Mythology of Ancient Egypt," in Samuel N. Kramer, ed., *Mythologies of the Ancient World* (Garden City, Doubleday, 1961), 15–92. Anthes is also the author of a good article, "Egyptian Theology in the Third Millennium B.C.," *Journal of Near Eastern Studies,* XVIII (1959), 169–212. Anthes' work is both lucid and authoritative. The most significant and probably the most interesting myth is that of Osiris, whose death and rebirth are, of course, linked to the seasonal cycle. Despite mention of Osiris in Egyptian texts of the older periods, it is only in Greek times that we find the myth as an extended narrative; hence there are subtle problems of detail for research. A recent study based on an assembly of all the material is John Gwyn Griffiths, *The Origins of Osiris,* Münchner ägyptologische Studien, 9 (Berlin, Bruno Hessling, 1966).

For a reference book there is nothing in English whose scope quite matches the alphabetically arranged work of Hans Bonnet, *Reallexikon der ägyptischen Religionsgeschichte* (Berlin, W. de Gruyter, 1952). On the various gods there is the useful book of Alan W. Shorter, *The Egyptian Gods: A Handbook* (London, Kegan Paul, Trench, Trübner, 1937). The gods are listed, and their functions described, in the illustrated work of Veronica Ions, *Egyptian Mythology* (London, Paul Hamlyn, 1965).

The main sources for the older periods of Egyptian religion are available in translations by Raymond O. Faulkner, *The Ancient Egyptian Pyramid Texts* (Oxford, Clarendon Press, 1969), and *The Ancient Egyptian Coffin Texts* (Warminster, England, Aris & Phillips, 1973). For a subsequent period the standard complete translation of the Book of the Dead is still that of E. A. Wallis Budge, *The Book of the Dead,* 2nd ed. (London, Kegan Paul, Trench, Trübner, 1923). Sources in classical authors for the history of Egyptian religion after the middle of the first millennium B.C. are collected but not translated in Theodor Hopfner, *Fontes historiae religionis aegyptiacae,* 5 parts, Fontes historiae religionum, 2 (Bonn, A. Marcus and E. Weber, 1922–25).

An episode of lasting fascination is the career of the maverick fourteenth-century-B.C. pharaoh Akhenaton, who tried to obliterate all mention of Amon and the other gods and to suppress the powerful Amon priesthood. The extent to which Akhenaton's struggles were more than simply political and represent the birth of an explicit monotheism is a problem for interpretation, as is the extent to which the new naturalism in the artistic style of the period can be said to embody a philosophical outlook; and for students of religious history there is the question of how far Akhenaton's religious views extended in space and time. The critical arguments of John A. Wilson in his superb survey *The Burden of Egypt* (also published as *The Culture of Ancient Egypt*) (Chicago, Univ. of Chicago Press, 1951), 206–35, are fundamental reading for a review of these problems. More recently, Cyril Aldred has given attention to the art-historical and other questions in *Akhenaton, Pharoah of Egypt: A New Study* (London, Thames & Hudson, 1968).

In certain areas the definitive works are in French or German. The classic on magic, an important feature of Egyptian religion, is François (František) Lexa, *La Magie dans l'Égypte antique de l'ancien empire jusqu'à l'époque copte,* 3 vols. (Paris, Paul Geuthner, 1925). The definitive syntheses both on the gods and on life beyond death are by the careful scholar Hermann Kees, *Der Götterglaube im alten Ägypten,* 2nd ed. (Berlin, Akademie-Verlag, 1956), and *Totenglauben und Jenseitsvorstellungen der alten Ägypter,* 2nd ed. (Berlin, Akademie-Verlag, 1956). However, for a review of the fascination which ancient Egypt has held for later civilizations we may turn to a virtually unique, unchallenged work in English: Erik Iversen, *The Myth of Egypt and Its Hieroglyphs in European Tradition* (Copenhagen, G. E. C. Gad, 1961).

C. Asia Minor

The principal culture of ancient Asia Minor (Anatolia) and northern Mesopotamia in the second millennium B.C., vying for power with Egypt and Babylonia, was the kingdom of the Hittites. Little known prior to modern archeological discovery, they are now represented by their texts and monuments and by a certain amount of scholarly literature. The best short introduction to their religion is Hans G. Güterbock, "Hittite Religion," in Vergilius Ferm, ed., *Forgotten Religions* (reissued as *Ancient Religions*) (N.Y., Philosophical Library, 1950), 81–109. Güterbock stresses the influence of the Hurrians, an earlier north Mesopotamian people, on the Hittites, and distinguishes between originally Anatolian myths such as the Telepinu myth and myths of Hurrian origin such as the Kumarbi myth. Extracts of these myths are given in Güterbock's chapter "Hittite Mythology," in Samuel N. Kramer, ed., *Mythologies of the Ancient World* (Garden City, Doubleday, 1961), 139–79. Güterbock argues, moreover, that Hittites must have transmitted the Hurrian myths to the Aegean, because of parallels in the Greek author Hesiod; see his article "The Hittite Version of the Hurrian Kumarbi Myths: Oriental Forerunners of Hesiod," *American Journal of Archaeology,* LII (1948), 123–34.

Some work by other authors is available in English. Giuseppe Furlani, whose book on Hittite religion in Italian appeared in 1936, is the author of "The Basic Aspect of Hittite Religion," *Harvard Theological Review,* XXXI (1938), 231–62. The standard general discussion of Hittite history in English, Oliver R. Gurney, *The Hittites,* 3rd ed. (Harmondsworth, Penguin Books, 1961), includes a chapter on religion. And a good survey of iconographic detail is available in Ekrem Akurgal, *The Art of the Hittites,* with photographs by Max Hirmer (London, Thames & Hudson, 1962).

The classic survey of Hittite culture in all its historical, literary, and religious aspects is in German, unmatched in English: Albrecht Goetze, *Kleinasien,* 2nd ed. (Münich, C. H. Beck, 1957). An alphabetically arranged reference source is Einar von Schuler, "Kleinasien: Die Mythologie der Hethiter und Hurriter," in Hans W. Haussig, ed., *Wörterbuch der Mythologie,* 1. Abteilung, I. Band (Stuttgart, Ernst Klett, 1965), 141–215.

D. The Levant

Toward the end of the second millennium B.C., when the Hebrews were becoming sedentarized in the territory we know as Palestine, the two principal populations of the area were the Arameans of inland Syria and the Canaanites of the Syro-Phoenician coast. Earlier in this century knowledge of both peoples was derived largely from assorted inscriptions, reliefs, and figurines, and from their mention in the Bible. Our knowledge of Canaanite religion has developed abundantly since the discovery in 1929 of extensive mythological texts as Ras Shamra, the Syrian coastal site of the ancient city Ugarit.

Few available works introduce the reader to everything from the Canaanite-Aramean world of the mid-second millennium B.C. to the late Phoenician world of the late first, since many scholars, approaching the subject from an interest in the Old Testament, tend not to follow the Phoenician narrative after the time of Elijah's contest with the priests of Baal. One concise overall survey, however, is Helmer Ringgren, "The Religion of Ancient Syria," in Bleeker and Widengren, eds., *Historia Religionum,* vol. I, 195–222. Ringgren sketches the roles of the different deities mainly on the basis of the Ugaritic material. A fuller overall survey, with detailed references to the scholarly literature, is Hartmut Gese, in Gese et al., *Die Religionen Altsyriens, Altarabiens, und der Mandäer* (Stuttgart, W. Kohlhammer, 1970), 1–232.

For an authoritative brief statement on Canaanite culture, in any presentation of which, of course, the Ugaritic myths figure importantly, the reader may consult William F. Albright, "The Role of the Canaanites in the History of Civilization," in G. Ernest Wright, ed., *The Bible and the Ancient Near East: Essays in Honor of William Foxwell Albright* (Garden City, Doubleday, 1961), 328–62. Albright, a very versatile student of the archeological and historical background of the Old Testament, writes from an intimate knowledge of a variety of sources. Another general work for Canaanite material culture as well as intellectual culture is John Gray, *The Canaanites* (London, Thames & Hudson, 1964).

Besides H. Louis Ginsberg's translation of the Ugaritic myths in Pritchard, ed., *ANET*, 3rd ed., 129–55, there are Cyrus H. Gordon, *Ugaritic Literature: A Comprehensive Translation of the Poetic and Prose Texts* (Rome, Pontifical Biblical Institute, 1949), and Godfrey R. Driver, *Canaanite Myths and Legends* (Edinburgh, T. & T. Clark, 1956). Driver's translation is more recent than the others, has taken them into account, and gives the original text on the facing page; but all three suffer from archaisms in English.

A general picture of the Ugaritic pantheon is given by Mitchell J. Dahood, "Ancient Semitic Deities in Syria and Palestine," in Sabatino Moscati, ed., *Le antiche divinità semitiche* (Rome, Centro di Studi Semitici, Università di Roma, 1958), 65–94. Unmatched by anything in English as an alphabetically arranged reference work is Marvin H. Pope and Wolfgang Röllig, "Syrien: Die Mythologie der Ugariter und Phönizier," in Hans W. Haussig, ed., *Wörterbuch der Mythologie* (Stuttgart, Ernst Klett, 1965), 217–32.

The Phoenicians continued to flourish in what today is Lebanon down to the time of Alexander the Great, and the Phoenician (hence the name "Punic") settlement at Carthage in North Africa lasted until it was destroyed by the Romans in 146 B.C. Donald Harden, in *The Phoenicians* (London, Thames & Hudson, 1962), gives an appreciative sketch of the role of these people in both the eastern and western Mediterranean, with attention mainly to their material culture. His thirty-page chapter on religion surveys the results of temple and tomb excavations in both Phoenicia and Carthage for a composite picture.

Over the past two generations most of the scholarship on Phoenicia and Carthage has been produced by the French, because of the modern involvement of France as the ruling power both in Syria-Lebanon and in Tunisia. Readers of French interested in the east may therefore consult the archeologically informed treatment of religion in Georges Contenau, *La Civilisation phénicienne* (Paris, Payot, 1949), 79–117, and the study by Robert du Mesnil du Buisson, "Origine et évolution du panthéon de Tyr," *Revue de l'histoire des religions,* CLXIV (1963), 133–63. French is indispensable for a study of religion in Carthage, for which the classic is Stéphane Gsell, *Histoire ancienne de l'Afrique du Nord,* 8 vols. (Paris, Hachette, 1921–28), particularly vol. IV, 221–469. A very good shorter study for the acculturation of Phoenician religion in its North African environment is Gilbert Charles-Picard, *Les Religions de l'Afrique antique* (Paris, Librairie Plon, 1954), and a recent work tracing that legacy is Robert du Mesnil du Buisson, *Études sur les dieux phéniciens hérités par l'Empire romain* (Leiden, E. J. Brill, 1970). Even for the Arameans, in the earlier biblical milieu, French scholarship has produced a synthesis not duplicated in English: André Dupont-Sommer, *Les Araméens* (Paris, A. Maisonneuve, 1949).

III. THE GREEK AND ROMAN WORLD

It would be impractical in these pages to press a separation between Greece and Rome very far, for such a separation cannot be made neatly. Much that is Roman has its roots in that which is Greek, from the second century B.C. onwards, just as much of modern American culture has its antecedents and contacts in Britain. The Greek myths were assimilated in Republican Rome, and the cults of the Greek-speaking eastern Mediterranean spread throughout the Roman Empire. Rather than a geographical division, therefore, we shall follow a chronological division, looking at Greece and Rome in their archaic or domestic periods first, followed by the "common market" of the Empire. Even this division will, however, be bridged by various general and thematic works.

Many features of Greek and of Roman religion are familiar to us in the modern West, often through classical allusions in literature. But for all readers, experts on the classics or otherwise, the introductions to Greek and to Roman religion by Herbert J. Rose are highly recommended reading. The beginner will appreciate their clarity and comprehensiveness, while the advanced student of the classics will admire Rose's selection of themes and materials. The two books were originally published as *Ancient Greek Religion* (London, Hutchinson's University Library, 1946) and *Ancient Roman Religion* (London, Hutchinson's University Library, 1948). Rose is in command of major lines of historical development in antiquity and is also interested in later survivals of ancient religion. Reissued under the title *Religion in Greece and Rome* (N.Y., Harper & Brothers, 1959), the whole is greater than the sum of its two parts to the extent of a six-page preface in which Rose contrasts the Greek and Roman cultural temperaments and reflects on their interaction to form one culture in later antiquity.

Space limitations permit mention of only a few works in fields other than religion offering general background for the classical world. The primary sources and secondary resources for ancient history are discussed in a handbook by Hermann Bengtson, *Introduction to Ancient History,* a *vade mecum* for students through several German editions before its translation into English (Berkeley, Univ. of California Press, 1970). A quick and convenient source for dynasties, dates, and major political events is William L. Langer, ed., *An Encyclopedia of World History,* 5th ed. (Boston, Houghton Mifflin, 1972). The most extensive encyclopedia for classical studies is *Paulys Real-Encyclopädie der klassischen Altertumswissenschaft,* ed. Georg Wissowa, 34 vols. (Stuttgart, J. B. Metzlerscher & Alfred Druckenmüller, 1894–1972), in many ways as useful for its authoritative command of broad topics as for its specific detail on precise ones. Bibliographical aid for frequently cited separate titles may be drawn from J[ohn] *A. Nairn's Classical Hand List,* 3rd ed. (Oxford, B. H. Blackwell, 1953) and, for hard-to-trace articles in anniversary volumes, Dorothy Rounds, *Articles on Antiquity in Festschriften: The Ancient Near East, the Old Testament, Greece, Rome, Roman Law, Byzantium* (Cambridge, Harvard Univ. Press, 1962).

A. Ancient Greece

The reader who has gained an orientation to Greek religion from H. J. Rose's work already mentioned may wish to fill in further details and perspectives from overall surveys. For the period down to the fifth century William K. C. Guthrie's *The Greeks and Their Gods* (London, Methuen, 1962) is a thoughtful book which can be understood by the beginner but appreciated by the specialist on re-reading; Guthrie's use of quotations from ancient sources is apt, and his representation of the views of modern interpreters perceptive. An older classic which carries the narrative on into the Hellenistic age and which gave currency to the phrase "failure of nerve" as a characterization of that era is Gilbert Murray's *Five Stages of Greek Religion,* 3rd ed. (Boston, Beacon Press, 1951). And while most of the best writing on Greek religion is the work of classical historians, the brief treatment of one specialist in the history of religions may be suggested: Raffaele Pettazzoni, "Introduction to the History of Greek Religion," in Pettazzoni, *Essays on the History of Religions* (Leiden, E. J. Brill, 1954), 68–80.

By all odds the dominant figure in twentieth-century study of Greek religion has been Martin P. Nilsson. In every major area of the subject his writings are definitive. Nilsson's *A History of Greek Religion,* 2nd ed. (Oxford, Clarendon Press, 1959), will offer a concise statement of his emphases, while his two-volume German synthesis, *Geschichte der griechischen Religion,* 2nd ed. (München, C. H. Beck, 1955), the second volume dealing with the Hellenistic and Roman imperial era, is the most definitive treatment available in any language. Nilsson's contribution included the use of archeological materials such as figurines, burials, and altars to relate the cults of the familiar Greek gods to antecedents in Crete and the Aegean in the second millennium B.C., in *The Minoan-Mycenaean Religion and the Origins of Greek Religion* (Lund, C. W. K. Gleerup, 1927). Another major area of his work was the application of anthropological considerations to sketch the religious life of the common man alongside the literary and intellectual picture available from the texts: *Greek Popular Religion* (reissued as *Greek Folk Religion*) (N.Y., Columbia Univ. Press, 1940).

On the subject of Minoan and Mycenean religion, the French survey by Charles Picard, *Les Religions préhelleniques (Crète et Mycènes)* Paris, Presses universitaires de France, 1948), gives copious references to older scholarly literature in an "État des questions" section at the end of each chapter. Against the continuity emphasized by Nilsson, Emily T. Vermeule, in "Mythology in Mycenean Art," *Classical Journal,* LIV (1958–59), 97–108, sees, however, a break between the older Helladic era and the Hellenic in the absence of any representations of heroes on pottery from the older period. Literary continuities between the ancient Near East and the Aegean implying a Near Eastern source from themes in Greek myth or epic have been the subject of various speculations, for example, Cyrus H. Gordon, "Homer and Bible: The Origin and Character of East Mediterranean Literature," *Hebrew Union College Annual,* XXVI (1955), 43–108. The perennial question of when a parallel proves an influence remains to haunt Gordon's work. A more subtle and more multi-faceted investigation of possible Near Eastern sources, looking to various literatures in Asia Minor, Mesopotamia, and Egypt, is Peter Walcot, *Hesiod and the Near East* (Cardiff, Univ. of Wales Press, 1966).

The average person probably associates Greek religion dominantly, if not exclusively, with the myths. "Myth," after all, is a word of Greek derivation meaning "saying" or "story," and it was within ancient times that the critically minded who did not share in other persons' sense of participation in the narratives already began to give the word "myth" its connotation of falsehood or fancy. The best comprehensive introduction to the subject is Herbert J. Rose, *A Handbook of Greek Mythology Including Its Extension to Rome,* 6th ed. (London, Methuen, 1960), in which the grouping of topics runs from myths of creation, to the Olympian gods, to the epics, to local and regional stories and to Italy. Robert Graves, *The Greek Myths,* 2 vols. (Harmondsworth, Penguin Books, 1957), provides a good introductory discussion of the nature of myth as well as fluent translations. A more extended discussion by a classicist of myth as a genre is Geoffrey S. Kirk, *Myth: Its Meaning and Functions in Ancient and Other Cultures* (Cambridge, University Press, 1970). The standard exhaustive encyclopedia on the subject remains Wilhelm H. Roscher, *Ausführliches Lexikon der griechischen und römischen Mythologie,* 6 vols. (Leipzig, B. G. Teubner, 1884–1937), which includes as a supplementary volume a history of the study of Greek religion, Otto Gruppe, *Geschichte der klassischen Mythologie und Religionsgeschichte während des Mittelalters im Abendland und während der Neuzeit* (Leipzig, B. G. Teubner, 1921). An authoritative and useful more recent reference source is Pierre Grimal, *Dictionnaire de la mythologie grecque et romaine,* 3rd ed. (Paris, Presses universitaires de France, 1963).

Greek philosophy has a religious dimension in that the goal of reflection is the contemplation of reality, a point stated in Plato and later claimed as experience by Plotinus. In the fine selections drawn from Hellenic literature and philosophy by Francis M. Cornford, *Greek Religious Thought from Homer to the Age of Alexander* (London, J. M. Dent and Sons, 1923) it will be clear to the reader that the intellectual boundaries which have come to demarcate theology as a domain separate from poetry or literature were yet to be drawn. An impressive study in the history of ideas which ranges across several genres of Greek literature is Bruno Snell, *The Discovery of the Mind: The Greek Origins of European Thought* (Oxford, Basil Blackwell, 1953); in it such themes as myth, virtue, and logic are interrelated and contrasted, and Snell's narrative concludes with the "discovery of Arcadia" as a "spiritual landscape" in Virgil's *Eclogues* in the first century B.C. Donald B. King offers a typology of roles for religion as a norm in "The Appeal to Religion in Greek Rhetoric," *Classical Journal,* L (1954–55), 363–71. Jean Rudhart, focusing on the vocabulary of classical texts, explores the semantic ranges of key Greek terms in *Notions fondamentales de la pensée religieuse et actes constitutifs du culte dans la Grèce classique* (Geneva, Librairie E. Droz, 1958). Rudhart devotes significant attention to methodological considerations and to theories of religion not only in that work but also in "Sur la possibilité de comprendre une religion antique," *Numen,* XI (1964), 189–211.

Much of the reading which the serious student will undertake will involve him in the study of particular cults, on which the literature is vast and only part of which can be mentioned here. A comprehensive older work is Lewis R. Farnell, *The Cults of the Greek States,* 5 vols. (Oxford, Clarendon Press, 1896–1909). William K. C. Guthrie, *Orpheus and Greek Religion: A Study of the Orphic Movement,* 2nd ed. (London, Methuen, 1952), is what its title implies. Walter F. Otto, *Dionysus: Myth and Cult* (Bloomington, Indiana Univ. Press, 1965), writes a conscious assumption of the reality of Dionysus for purposes of empathetic description. George E. Mylonas, *Eleusis and the Eleusinian Mysteries* (Princeton, Princeton Univ. Press, 1961), weaves a variety of evidence together into a good synthesis. Emma J. Edelstein and Ludwig Edelstein, *Asclepius: A Collection and Interpretation of the Testimonies,* 2 vols. (Baltimore, Johns Hopkins Press, 1945), illustrate this deity credited with healing from the fifth century on into the Hellenistic era. William R. Halliday discusses *Greek Divination: A Study of Its Methods and Principles* (London, Macmillan, 1913), still authoritative; Herbert W. Parke discusses *Greek*

Oracles (London, Hutchinson, 1967); and Ludwig Drees, *Olympia: Gods, Artists, and Athletes* (London, Pall Mall Press, 1968), provides a readable account of the Olympic festival.

The nature of the individual and the destiny of man constitute the focal point of quite a few works. A nimble and succinct survey of Greek, Roman, Hellenistic, and early Christian material is W. F. Jackson Knight, *Elysion: On Ancient Greek and Roman Beliefs Concerning a Life after Death* (London, Rider, 1970). An older classic is Lewis R. Farnell, *Greek Hero Cults and Ideas of Immortality* (Oxford, Clarendon Press, 1921). Drawing on a range of Greek literature, William C. Greene explores divinity and destiny in a broad and erudite work, *Moira: Fate, Good, and Evil in Greek Thought* (Cambridge, Harvard Univ. Press, 1944). One influence of Edwin Rohde's classic study, *Psyche: The Cult of Souls and Belief in Immortality among the Greeks* (London, Kegan Paul, Trench, Trübner, 1925), on three generations of classicists has been to direct attention to a dimension of intense individual feeling in Greek religion which modern emphasis on Greek rationality has sometimes tended to obscure. Rohde's hints have been picked up and developed by a classical scholar who is also psychologically sophisticated, Eric R. Dodds, *The Greeks and the Irrational* (Berkeley, Univ. of California Press, 1951).

Jungian psychological theory tends to influence the selection and interpretation of material in the many works of Carl (Károly) Kerényi, whose most general treatment is *The Religion of the Greeks and Romans* (London, Thames & Hudson, 1962). The influence of James Frazer's anthropological approach to myth and ritual may be seen in Jane E. Harrison's works, such as *Prolegomena to the Study of Greek Religion,* 3rd ed. (Cambridge, University Press, 1922). Survivals of ancient Greek religion in Greek folkways may be seen in Philip P. Argenti and Herbert J. Rose, *The Folk-lore of Chios,* 2 vols. (Cambridge, University Press, 1949). An application of sociological insights is Svend Ranulf, *The Jealousy of the Gods and Criminal Law at Athens,* 2 vols. (London, Williams & Norgate, 1933–34). And an historical classic from a century ago is Numa D. Fustel de Coulanges, *The Ancient City: A Study on the Religion, Laws and Institutions of Greece and Rome* (Boston, Lee and Shepard, 1874). This book's emphasis on the connections between religious and social forms had an important influence in developing the sociological thought of Émile Durkheim.

B. Ancient Rome

Following on H. J. Rose's introduction to Roman religion mentioned earlier, one of the most useful brief pictures of Roman religion is Robert M. Ogilvie, *The Romans and Their Gods in the Age of Augustus* (London, Chatto & Windus, 1969), organized to treat such topics as prayer, sacrifice, divination, the priests, and rituals of the religious year. A more detailed, standard work whose range includes many of the same topics and whose detail gives a view of the historical development of Roman religion is W. Warde Fowler, *The Religious Experience of the Roman People from the Earliest Times to the Age of Augustus* (London, Macmillan, 1911). Along with a discussion of the older institutions of the state cult and household piety, their transformation by Greek philosophy and by the cults of the eastern Mediterranean forms part of the treatment in Cyril Bailey, *Phases in the Religion of Ancient Rome* (Berkeley, Univ. of California Press, 1932).

A good anthology of translated materials from classical sources is Frederick C. Grant, ed., *Ancient Roman Religion* (N.Y., Liberal Arts Press, 1957). Helpful as a review of half a century's scholarship is Herbert J. Rose, "Roman Religion 1910–1960," *Journal of Roman Studies,* L (1960), 161–72.

The Etruscan archeological and epigraphical remains are our earliest evidence for religion in the region of Rome. A readable introduction to Etruscan material culture and to the enigma of the Etruscan language may be gained from Raymond Bloch, *The Etruscans* (London, Thames & Hudson, 1958) or Bloch's work *The Origins of Rome* (London, Thames & Hudson, 1966). Another good survey, which gives initial emphasis to religion, is Otto-Wilhelm von Vacano, *The Etruscans in the Ancient World* (London, Edward Arnold, 1960).

It may well be, however, that the Romans did not acquire the main features of their religion from the Etruscans but rather drew on an Indo-European heritage. Such is the position of the comparative Indo-European philologist Georges Dumézil, who therefore puts the Etruscans at the end of his treatment rather than at the beginning: *Archaic Roman Religion, with an Appendix on the Religion of the Etruscans,* 2 vols. (Chicago, Univ. of Chicago Press, 1970). No serious student of ancient religions will ignore Dumézil's writings. Particularly in such earlier works as *L'Idéologie tripartie des indo-européens* (Brussels, Latomus, 1958) and *Les Dieux des indo-européens* (Paris, Presses universitaires de France, 1952), he has employed a structuralist theoretical position. His view of three social classes or functions (kings and priests, warriors, farmers) represented all the way from Rome to India in triads of deities such as Jupiter-Mars-Quirinus, has occasioned lively criticism. Some have held that not all Indo-European evidence fits his procrustean theory, and others have argued that the theory proves little since non-Indo-European evidence fits it just as well; for an entertaining example of the latter, see John Brough, "The Tripartite Ideology of the Indo-Europeans: An Experiment in Method," *Bulletin of the School of Oriental and African Studies,* University of London, XXII (1959), 69–85, and Dumézil's rejoinder, "L'Idéologie tripartie des indo-européens et la Bible," *Kratylos,* IV (1959),

97–118. A full, methodologically sophisticated discussion of Dumézil's position is C. Scott Littleton, *The New Comparative Mythology: An Anthropological Assessment of the Theories of Georges Dumézil* (Berkeley, Univ. of California Press, 1966).

In treatments of religion in the period of the Roman Republic attention has characteristically been devoted to the importation of the Greek myths and the functional identifications made between deities bearing Greek and Latin names. One book, however, concentrating on such characteristically Roman narratives as the founding of Rome is Michael Grant, *Roman Myths* (London, Weidenfeld & Nicolson, 1971); Grant devotes considerable attention to the political function of statements of origins of the Roman order. The way in which the Roman narrative is related to Greek traditions in Virgil's *Aeneid* is a subject which comes in for authoritative discussion from Cyril Bailey, *Religion in Virgil* (Oxford, Clarendon Press, 1935). And in a good article, "The Roman Nobility and the Religion of the Republican State," *Journal of Religious History,* IV (1966–67), H. D. Jocelyn discusses Greek perceptions of Republican Rome, and a credulous or accepting tendency of Roman piety in contrast with Greek intellectuals' critiques of traditional religion as fraud and deceit.

C. The Hellenistic and Roman Imperial World

The imperial tradition we associate with Rome lasted longer than many of us in the West have been schooled to think; borrowed by Arabic, for example, the word "Roman" means Byzantine and applies to the Greek-speaking Christian world centered on Constantinople, whose succession of emperors extended until the fifteenth century. Looking at the eastern Mediterranean, we should perhaps also push our beginning point earlier, for the idea of empire probably owes as much to Alexander the Great as it does to Julius Caesar. The salient fact is that from Alexander to Constantine and beyond, the Mediterranean was a huge cosmopolitan civilization. For three or four centuries of that time it was actually governed from Rome, but over a much longer period the Greek-speaking east was the major source of economic and of cultural strength. Thus, for the purposes of our inquiry, Hellenistic religion—Greek religion after Alexander—is inseparable from the religion of the Roman Empire. A glimpse of what the world looked like to a person living in this age may be gained from a pair of books: John Ferguson, *The Heritage of Hellenism* (London, Thames & Hudson, 1973), and Peter Brown, *The World of Late Antiquity: From Marcus Aurelius to Muhammad* (London, Thames & Hudson, 1971). Brown in particular has accomplished a remarkable synthesis for a period on which it has not been too often attempted.

It was characteristic of the religions which spread in this era that membership in them was not automatic by heredity or residence but rather called for the individual to undertake a process of instruction and initiation. The aim of spiritual rebirth through such a process is the theme of Harold R. Willoughby, *Pagan Regeneration: A Study of Mystery Initiations in the Graeco-Roman World* (Chicago, Univ. of Chicago Press, 1929), a well-written survey of the major cults, enumerating several in turn, and a good first step in the reader's initiation to the subject.

Thus initiated, the reader should proceed before long to the classic study by Arthur D. Nock, *Conversion: The Old and the New in Religion from Alexander the Great to Augustine of Hippo* (Oxford, Clarendon Press, 1933), which draws on specific details from the different cults to form a general assessment of their appeal. Nock's work is an enviable example of breadth of scope combined with depth of mastery of detail. The recent and readable book by John Ferguson, *The Religions of the Roman Empire* (London, Thames & Hudson, 1970), is likewise organized thematically. An older work, still influential, is Franz Cumont, *The Oriental Religions in Roman Paganism* (Chicago, Open Court Publishing Co., 1911), in which he refers to the sum of these influences as an ensemble of beliefs about which a consensus emerged in the Roman Empire—that is, that "paganism," while diverse, is nonetheless an identifiable tradition. The fourth French edition of this work (Paris, Paul Geuthner, 1929), containing expanded documentation in its notes, is frequently cited in scholarly contexts. Another French work which has remained useful is Jules Toutain, *Les Cultes païens de l'empire romain,* 3 vols. (Paris, E. Leroux, 1907–20).

The most useful anthology of translated source materials is Frederick C. Grant, ed., *Hellenistic Religions: The Age of Syncretism* (N.Y., Liberal Arts Press, 1953). Its introduction includes a concise explanation of the term "syncretism" and the phenomenon in antiquity for whose description the term is employed. Three other anthologies contain useful material and are tangential to the Hellenistic cults in different ways. In Edwyn R. Bevan, *Later Greek Religion* (London, J. M. Dent & Sons, 1927), the religious concerns of philosophers, particularly the Stoics and Neoplatonists, dominate the material selected. C. Kingsley Barrett, ed., *The New Testament Background* (London, SPCK, 1956), includes a considerable amount of Hellenistic Jewish religious material, and selects some of the non-Jewish material to illustrate Roman government and ancient literary genres of a secular character. A third, Ernest Barker, ed., *From Alexander to Constantine: Passages and Documents Illustrating the History of Social and Political Ideas, 336* B.C.–A.D. *337* (Oxford, Clarendon Press, 1956), shows the setting of Hellenistic religion far more than it discusses religion itself. A good anthology specifically on Hellenistic religions, but in the classical language, is Nicola Turchi, ed., *Fontes historiae mysteriorum aevi hellenistici* (Rome, Libreria di Cultura, 1923).

A discussion of trends in scholarship in the field, together with a bibliography, is Raffaele Pettazzoni, "Les Mystères grecs et les religions à mystères d'antiquité: Recherches récents et problèmes nouveaux," *Cahiers d'histoire mondiale,* II (1954–55), 303–12 and 661–67. Bibliographical aids may also be drawn from the valuable manual by Karl Prümm, *Religionsgeschichtliches Handbuch für den Raum der altchristlichen Umwelt* (Rome, Pontifical Biblical Institute, 1954).

Mention can be given here of only a sampling of works on specific cults or specific regions, on which there is an abundant literature in several languages. Martin P. Nilsson, in *The Dionysiac Mysteries of the Hellenistic and Roman Age* (Lund, C. W. K. Gleerup, 1957), traces an earlier Hellenic tradition into the period under discussion. Maarten J. Vermaseren, in *The Legend of Attis in Greek and Roman Art* (Leiden, E. J. Brill, 1966), integrates iconographic evidence with points known from literature. Reginald E. Witt, *Isis in the Graeco-Roman World* (London, Thames & Hudson, 1971), is an account of this Egyptian deity's influence in a variety of regions, while H. Idris Bell, *Cults and Creeds in Graeco-Roman Egypt* (Liverpool, University Press, 1953), sketches the interaction of diverse influences within Egypt. Samuel K. Eddy, *The King Is Dead: Studies in the Near Eastern Resistance to Hellenism, 334–331* B.C. (Lincoln, Univ. of Nebraska Press, 1961), sees religion as part of regional identities and therefore a factor in political opposition to Seleucid rule. Eve Harris and John R. Harris, *The Oriental Cults in Roman Britain* (Leiden, E. J. Brill, 1965), devote attention to Mithraism, on which tradition see also the literature discussed under Iranian religion in a later section of this chapter. In Lily Ross Taylor, *The Divinity of the Roman Emperor* (Middletown, American Philosophical Association, 1931), Hellenistic influences as well as older Roman traditions can be traced.

The role of magicians and diviners in the Hellenistic and Roman world is important for a view of popular religion. An admirably well-informed and well-written overall picture is provided in the third and fourth chapters of Ramsay MacMullen, *Enemies of the Roman Order: Treason, Unrest, and Alienation in the Empire* (Cambridge, Harvard Univ. Press, 1966), 95–162. Aretalogies, the biographical genre on heroic and wonder-working figures, are discussed and anthologized by Moses Hadas and Morton Smith, *Heroes and Gods: Spiritual Biographies in Antiquity* (N.Y., Harper & Row, 1965); in it the wonders ascribed to Moses and Jesus are compared with the marvels recounted in the lives of Pythagoras and of Apollonius of Tyana. Franz Cumont's concise synthesis, *Astrology and Religion among the Greeks and Romans* (N.Y., G. P. Putnam's Sons, 1912), is still read; and an important research study is Hans Lewy, *The Chaldean Oracles and Theurgy: Mysticism, Magic and Platonism in the Later Roman Empire* (Cairo, Institut Français d'Archéologie Orientale, 1956).

Doubtless the ultimate threat from which the individual sought to be protected by ritual or reflection was death. An up-to-date review of Roman customs is Jocelyn M. C. Toynbee, *Death and Burial in the Roman World* (London, Thames & Hudson, 1971), while an older work which still rewards the reader is Eugénie Strong, *Apotheosis and After Life* (London, Constable, 1915). A work of Franz Cumont which weaves the Greek and Oriental traditions into a single synthesis is *After Life in Roman Paganism* (New Haven, Yale Univ. Press, 1922).

As we have already hinted when mentioning Edwyn Bevan's *Later Greek Religion,* personal religion in the intellectual circles of the Hellenistic and Roman world cannot be discussed without reference to the ethical teachings of Stoic philosophy and the mystical and metaphysical contributions of Neoplatonism. Thus André-Jean Festugière, in *Personal Religion among the Greeks* (Berkeley, Univ. of California Press, 1954), discusses goals of piety common to both cults and philosophies. A classic study of Neoplatonism is William R. Inge, *The Philosophy of Plotinus* 2 vols. (London, Longmans, Green, 1918), and a successful effort to situate this teaching in the context of movements which we more commonly call religious is Édouard Krakowski, *Plotin et le paganisme religieux* (Paris, Les Éditions Denoël et Steele, 1933).

It was in such a milieu that Christianity spread, and the reader may refer to many studies by historians of Christianity for accounts of its struggle with other teachings for the allegiance of the empire. But a superb treatment of the passage from one order to another which should be read as much for its subtle appraisal of the Hellenistic and Roman world as of Christendom is Charles N. Cochrane, *Christianity and Classical Culture,* rev. ed. (London, Oxford Univ. Press, 1944). Also worth especial note is Eric R. Dodds, *Pagan and Christian in an Age of Anxiety,* (Cambridge, University Press, 1965), a psychologically sensitive work already becoming a classic, which among other things, proposes a three-phase historical division of the dialogue of paganism with Christianity. And a first-rate article by Arthur D. Nock, "Hellenistic Mysteries and Christian Sacraments," *Mnemosyne,* 4th series, V (1952), 177–213, explores the appropriation of the word and concept "mystery" into the vocabulary of Christian discussion of sacraments. Roelof van den Broek also documents contacts between paganism and Christianity in *The Myth of the Phoenix according to Classical and Early Christian Traditions* (Leiden, E. J. Brill, 1972).

The pagan past lives on. Morton W. Bloomfield, for example, in a tidbit of an article "The Origin of the Concept of the Seven Cardinal Sins," *Harvard Theological Review,* XXXIV (1941), 121–28, argues for an Hellenistic astrological origin of the church's list of seven, corresponding to seven planets and aerial demons. And in a veritable feast of scholarship in the history of art, Jean Seznec illustrates Europe's continuing affection for the religious tradition of pagan antiquity: *The Survival of the Pagan*

Gods: The Mythological Tradition and Its Place in Renaissance Humanism and Art (N.Y., Pantheon Books, 1953).

D. Gnosticism

By "Gnosticism" most scholars mean a mythical account of the fallen nature of the world and the path to its redemption which flourished as a secret teaching in ancient Jewish and Christian circles. Two other traditions whose central teaching derives from Christian Gnosticism but whose communal identity, cultus, and organization may be called distinct from Christianity are the Mandaean, mentioned at the end of this section, and the Manichaean, discussed later under Iran.

Gnosticism was known chiefly through the arguments of its Jewish and Christian opponents until the ancient Coptic manuscripts from Nag Hammadi in upper Egypt came to light in 1945. A revival and overhaul of Gnostic studies has resulted during the past generation, enlisting considerable attention from students of Christian origins. The resulting literature is already vast, and growing exponentially.

Andrew K. Helmbold provides a simple introduction to the circumstances of the discovery and the character of the manuscripts, *The Nag Hammadi Gnostic Texts and the Bible* (Grand Rapids, Baker Book House, 1967). Good alternatives are Willem C. van Unnik, *Newly Discovered Gnostic Writings: A Preliminary Survey of the Nag-Hammadi Find* (London, SCM Press, 1960), slightly fuller in its description of the literature, and Jean Doresse, *The Secret Books of the Egyptian Gnostics: An Introduction to the Coptic Gnostic Manuscripts Discovered at Chenoboskion* (London, Hollis & Carter, 1960), decidedly fuller.

A basic discussion of Gnosticism as a system of thought is the well-written, philosophically perceptive book of Hans Jonas, *The Gnostic Religion,* 2nd ed. (Boston, Beacon Press, 1963). Jonas' use of Mesopotamian and Mediterranean material to build a composite picture is open to challenge from historians who wish to keep different Gnostic sub-traditions separate, but no student can afford to ignore it. Another authoritative sketch of the system in its Hellenistic context is Arthur D. Nock, "Gnosticism," *Harvard Theological Review,* LVII (1964), 255–79. The beginning reader will find a good selection of texts in translation in Robert M. Grant, ed., *Gnosticism: A Source Book of Heretical Writings from the Early Christian Period* (N.Y., Harper & Brothers, 1961). A more extensive anthology is appearing, Werner Foerster, ed., *Gnosis: A Selection of Gnostic Texts* (London, Oxford Univ. Press, 1972–   ).

Access to recent scholarship on Gnosticism is available through review articles. The most useful are James M. Robinson, "The Coptic Gnostic Library Today," *New Testament Studies,* XIV (1967–68), 356–401; and Kurt Rudolph, "Gnosis und Gnostizismus, ein Forschungsbericht," distributed in seven installments through *Theologische Rundschau*, XXXIV–XXXVIII (1969–73). An exhaustive bibliography is provided by David M. Scholer, *Nag Hammadi Bibliography 1948–1969* (Leiden, E. J. Brill, 1971), and supplements include Scholer, "Bibliographica Gnostica, Supplementum I," *Novum Testamentum*, XIII (1971), 322–36. The Swiss psychologist Carl Jung and his circle have had a particular interest in the structure and influence of Gnostic ideas; for this particular line see Gilles Quispel, "C. G. Jung und die Gnosis," *Eranos-Jahrbuch*, XXXVII (1968), 277–98.

A particularly engrossing problem is the histôrical origin of Gnostic ideas. One lucid introduction to aspects of this topic is Robert McL. Wilson, *The Gnostic Problem: A Study of the Relations between Hellenistic Judaism and the Gnostic Heresy* (London, A. R. Mowbray, 1958). Arguments for an Iranian source for Gnosticism continue to be pressed by such scholars as Geo. Widengren, "Der iranische Hintergrund der Gnosis," *Zeitschrift für Religions- und Geistesgeschichte*, IV (1952), 97–114. Gnostic origins proved to be a virtually ideal subject for an international conference, and the papers, in several languages, were published: Ugo Bianchi, ed., *Le origini dello Gnosticismo* (Leiden, E. J. Brill, 1967), supplemented by *Studi di storia religioso della tarda antichità, pubblicati dalla cattedra di storia delle religioni dell'Università di Messina* (Messina, 1968). A useful review of the issues is offered by George W. MacRae, "Gnosis in Messina," *Catholic Biblical Quarterly*, XXVIII (1966), 322–33.

The Mandaeans are a community, now numbering only five thousand, in southern Mesopotamia, in whose religion Gnosticism survives to the present day; *mandā* is a Semitic vocabulary equivalent to the Greek word *gnōsis*, "revealed knowledge." Because the Mandaeans practice baptism they were called "Christians of St. John" by Portuguese missionaries in the seventeenth century, but their religion is better viewed as an ancient syncretism than as a Christian sect. In her ethnographic account of the community, *The Mandaeans of Iraq and Iran: Their Cults, Customs, Magic Legends, and Folklore* (Oxford, Clarendon Press, 1937), Ethel S. (Stevens) Drower attempts to relate the Mandaean ceremonies to other Near Eastern ritual usage such as the Zoroastrian. Lady Drower has also translated a number of Mandaean texts, published as separate monographs. The two most substantial Mandaean documents are the pair translated into German by Mark Lidzbarski, *Ginza, der Schatz, oder das Grosse Buch der Mandäer* (Göttingen, Vandenhoeck & Ruprecht, 1925), and *Das Johannesbuch der Mandäer*, 2 vols. (Giessen, A. Töpelmann, 1905–15).

The most authoritative recent synthesis on Mandaean religion is also in German, Kurt Rudolph, "Die Religion der Mandäer," in Hartmut Gese et al., *Die Religionen Altsyriens, Altarabiens und der Mandäer* (Stuttgart, W. Kohlhammer, 1970), 403–69. Rudolph is the author of two earlier major monographic studies on the Mandaeans as well. An English-language review of research is Edwin M. Yamauchi, "The Present Status of Mandaean Studies," *Journal of Near Eastern Studies,* XXV (1966), 88–96.

IV. IRAN

The spectacular festivities at Persepolis in the autumn of 1971, attended by heads of state from around the world, celebrated the 2,500th anniversary of Cyrus the Great's founding of the Persian Empire. But while some other strands in Iranian culture continue through the two and a half millennia, the religious is broken at the midpoint with the displacement of Zoroastrianism by Islam. Still, many Iranian Muslims today regard their ancient past with a patriotic affection like that of the West for the glories of ancient Rome. Consequently, the amount of Iranian scholarship on the pre-Islamic period is increasing; but the bulk of important work to date remains in the languages of western Europe.

The Iranian historical framework necessary for any view of the development of Zoroastrianism can be picked up in a straightforward summary from Roman Ghirshman, *Iran: From the Earliest Times to the Islamic Conquest* (Harmondsworth, Penguin Books, 1954). Richer in detail but requiring more patient reading is Richard N. Frye, *The Heritage of Persia* (London, Weidenfeld and Nicolson, 1963). The student will find the historical associations of particular locations described by Robert North, *Guide to Biblical Iran* (Rome, Pontifical Biblical Institute, 1956).

For some aspects of ancient Iranian studies, reference resources are underdeveloped since relatively few scholars have been working in this field. However, elusive articles in anniversary volumes, often hard to trace when they are varyingly and incompletely cited, are now accessible through Willard G. Oxtoby, *Ancient Iran and Zoroastrianism in Festschriften: An Index* (Waterloo, Council on the Study of Religion, 1973). This volume also contains on pp. 205–07 a bibliography of indices to *Festschriften* in various fields.

A. Zoroastrianism

The tradition which bears the name of Zarathushtra (Zoroaster, as the Greeks called him) involves both South Asian and Near Eastern studies. Zoroaster preached his message in a milieu similar to that of the Indian Vedas; the religion became established in the Near Eastern environment of Mesopotamia and Iran during the twelve centuries before Islam; and for the last twelve centuries since the Islamization of Iran a small remnant have kept the faith, the majority of whom, known as Parsis (i.e., "Persians"), live in western India.

An overview of so checkered a history is no easy task. Robert C. Zaehner, in the intermediate-level survey which he edited, *The Concise Encyclopedia of Living Faiths* (London, Hutchinson, 1959), provides a ten-page summary of Zoroastrian teachings which is both simple and reliable. His book-length synthesis, however, *The Dawn and Twilight of Zoroastrianism* (London, Weidenfeld and Nicolson, 1961), takes the beginner into intricate historical arguments which do not always reflect the consensus of scholarship; in it, however, as some have remarked, the twilight section is better than the dawn.

The most lucid summations of European scholarship on the tradition as a whole have come from the pen of Jacques Duchesne-Guillemin. His chapter in Bleeker and Widengren, eds., *Historia Religionum,* vol. I, 323–76, is first-rate. For a fuller survey see Duchesne-Guillemin's *Religion of Ancient Iran* (Bombay, K. M. JamaspAsa, 1973), the best balanced book on the subject in English. It is distinctly preferable to his *Symbols and Values in Zoroastrianism* (N.Y., Harper and Row, 1966), written originally to fit a German series on religious symbolism.

A history of the interpretation of the subject is Jacques Duchesne-Guillemin's *The Western Response to Zoroaster* (Oxford, Clarendon Press, 1958). With admirable erudition, the author locates different theories from the seventeenth century onward in the context of European intellectual fashions as well as of linguistic and archeological discovery. Recent trends are discussed by Gherardo Gnoli, "Problems and Prospects of the Studies on Persian Religion," in Ugo Bianchi et al., eds., *Problems and Methods of the History of Religions* (Leiden, E. J. Brill, 1972), 67–101.

Much of the pre-Islamic Iranian literature which survives is religious in character, since it was such literature which the Zoroastrian community sought to preserve. The most convenient survey of it is the chapter by Otakar Klíma in Jan Rypka, *History of Iranian Literature* (Dordrecht, D. Reidel, 1968), 3–65. Alongside this the reader may use the chapters in English by Ilya Gershevitch and Mary Boyce in *Handbuch der Orientalistik,* I. Abteilung, IV. Band ("Iranistik"), 2. Abschnitt ("Literatur"), Lieferung 1 (Leiden, E. J. Brill, 1968), 1–30 and 31–66. Still useful for full detail are Karl F. Geldner, "Avesta Literature," in *Avesta, Pahlavi, and Ancient Persian Studies in Honour of the Late shams-ul-ulama dastur Peshotanji Behramji Sanjana, M.A., Ph.D.* (Strasbourg, Karl J. Trübner, 1904), 1–82, and Edward W. West, "Pahlavi Literature," in Wilhelm Geiger and Ernst Kuhn, eds., *Grundriss der iranischen Philologie* (Strasbourg, Karl J. Trübner, 1885–1904), vol. II, 77–129.

The scriptural passages most highly prized by the Zoroastrian tradition are the Gāthās, poetic hymns which, it is widely agreed, are the words of the prophet himself, found in the Yasna section of the Avesta. An accessible rendering of them is the translation, via French, by Jacques Duchesne-Guillemin, *The Hymns of Zarathustra* (London, John Murray, 1952). An anthology of key passages from the later Pahlavi literature is Robert C. Zaehner, *The Teachings of the Magi: A Compendium of Zoroastrian Beliefs* (London, George Allen & Unwin, 1956). Translations of Zoroastrian scriptures *in extenso* will be found in the *Sacred Books of the East* (hereafter *SBE*) (Oxford, Clarendon Press, 1879–1910), the *Avesta* (then called "Zend-Avesta") by James Darmesteter and Lawrence H. Mills (volumes 4, 23, and 31) and the Pahlavi texts by Edward W. West (vols. 5, 18, 24, 37, and 47). These translations are stilted and cumbersome and employ antiquated transliterations of proper names, but have not been superseded in English.

The figure of Zoroaster in traditional and legendary accounts is sketched by A. V. Williams Jackson, *Zoroaster: The Prophet of Ancient Iran* (N.Y., Columbia Univ. Press, 1898). Modern scholarship has preferred to clear the slate of tradition and to reconstruct the prophet's biography by analogy with other discoveries; thus, Henrik S. Nyberg, in *Die Religionen des alten Iran* (Leipzig, J. C. Hinrichs, 1938), saw Zoroaster as comparable to a Central Asian shaman, while Ernst Herzfeld, in *Zoroaster and His World,* 2 vols. (Princeton, Princeton Univ. Press, 1947), thought he had seen in archeological excavations in southwestern Iran the steps the prophet had trod. Both these extremes are reduced to absurdity by Walter B. Henning in *Zoroaster: Politician or Witch Doctor?* (London, Oxford Univ. Press, 1951), one of the most readable and entertaining pieces of scholarly disputation in the field.

The influence of Zoroaster's reforms on the religion of the Achaemenid empire is very much a matter of conjecture and inference. One important view to consider is a distinction between the prophet's religion and the more or less syncretized Achaemenid official cult which claimed its legitimation from him, in Ilya Gershevitch, *The Avestan Hymn to Mithra* (Cambridge, University Press, 1959), 1–22. To decide what Achaemenid religion actually was, the historian must reconcile the stipulation of observances in the Iranian literature with the practices reported by Greek and Roman writers. These were published in the classical languages by Carl Clemen in *Fontes historiae religionis persicae* (Bonn, A. Marcus and E. Weber, 1920) and may be found in translation in W. Sherwood Fox and R. E. K. Pemberton, trs., "Passages in Greek and Latin Literature Relating to Zoroastrianism Translated into English," *Journal of the K. R. Cama Oriental Institute,* no. 14 (1929), 1–145, and also issued separately as that institute's Publication no. 4. The problems raised by the reports of classical authors are discussed succinctly in a set of lectures by Émile Benveniste, *The Persian Religion according to the Chief Greek Texts* (Paris, Paul Geuthner, 1929).

However uncertain the pattern and practice of Zoroastrianism in Achaemenid times, it is clear that after the establishment of the faith as the official religion of the Sasanians in the third century A.D. an explicit set of doctrines and institutions was elaborated. An old work which has not been replaced as a statement of Zoroastrian religion in systematic terms is Louis C. Casartelli, *The Philosophy of the Mazdayasnian Religion under the Sassanids* (Bombay, Jehangir Bejanji Karani, 1889). One of the features most characteristic of the religion in this period was a dualism of good and evil, pitting Ahura Mazdā (or Ohrmazd), the Wise Lord, against the demonic Angra Mainyu (or Ahriman). A good treatment specifically of Zoroastrian dualism is Jacques Duchesne-Guillemin, *Ormazd et Ahriman: L'Aventure dualiste dans l'antiquité* (Paris, Presses universitaires de France, 1953). Zoroastrian dualism contrasts with Gnostic and Manichaean dualism in that the material world is not in itself evil but is simply the scene of the divine–demonic struggle. For a comparison of various types of dualism the books of Simone Pétrement, in French, are valuable; a digest of her views is now available in English in her article "Dualism in Philosophy and Religion," in Philip P. Wiener, ed., *Dictionary of the History of Ideas* (N.Y., Charles Scribner's Sons, 1973), vol. II, 38–44. A Sasanian Zoroastrian effort to subsume both the good and evil powers under one principle by tracing their birth to an anterior parent, Zurvān, infinite Time, was branded heretical. The detailed study of this by Robert C. Zaehner, *Zurvan: A Zoroastrian Dilemma* (Oxford, Clarendon Press, 1955), is recommended to the serious student as a highly technical work but an important one.

Another problem of interest is what influence Zoroastrianism may have had in the shaping of post-exilic Jewish or early Christian thought on such topics as creation and judgment, angels and demons, and heaven and hell. A suggestive article by Morton Smith, "II Isaiah and the Persians," *Journal of the American Oriental Society,* LXXXIII (1963), 415–21, drawing textual parallels between the Avesta and the Bible, will whet one's appetite for the subject. The state of the discussion is explored by David Winston, "The Iranian Component in the Bible, Apocrypha, and Qumran: A Review of the Evidence," *History of Religions,* V (1965–66), 183–216. Winston concentrates on the period prior to the New Testament; for suggestions of contact at a later time see John R. Hinnells, "Zoroastrian Savior Imagery and Its Influence on the New Testament," *Numen,* XVI (1969), 161–85.

On Iranian myth and legend, the summary by John R. Hinnells, *Persian Mythology* (London, Hamlyn, 1973), is part of a pictorial series and offers a well-chosen range of illustrations not conveniently available elsewhere. An older discussion still worth consulting is the treatment of Iranian mythology by Albert J. Carnoy in *The Mythology of All Races,* vol. VI, 253–351. The recollection of ancient tradition in Islamic Iran may be seen notably in the great tenth-century epic by Ferdowsi. An abridged translation is Reuben Levy, *The Epic of the Kings: Shah-nama, the National Epic of Persia* (Chicago, Univ. of Chicago Press, 1967), while a full translation is by Arthur G. Warner and Edmond Warner, *The Sháhnáma of Firdausí,* 9 vols. (London, Kegan Paul, Trench, Trübner, 1905–25).

For most of the present century, historians of religion have treated Zoroastrianism as a nearly dead religion, its history since the Islamic conquest of Iran being one of stagnation or decline. A fine description of Zoroastrianism as a living religion is given by Mary Boyce in Bleeker and Widengren, eds., *Historia Religionum,* vol. II, 211–36. A major source for medieval Zoroastrian history and practice is the correspondence between the Iranian and Indian communities, some of which has been studied and published by Bamanji N. Dhabhar in *The Persian Rivayats of Hormazyar Framarz and Others* (Bombay, K. R. Cama Oriental Institute, 1932). A rich source for the condition of the community at the turn of the century is Kharsedji N. Seervai and Bamanji B. Patel, "Gujarát Pársis: From Their Earliest Settlement to the Present Time (A.D. 1898)," *Gazetteer of the Bombay Presidency,* IX (1899), 183–254 and 277–88. Prior to Mary Boyce's efforts the two principal books on Parsi history were Dosabhai F. Karaka, *History of the Parsis: Including Their Manners, Customs, Religion, and Present Position,* 2 vols. (London, Macmillan, 1884), and the work of Delphine Menant, expanded by Murzban M. Murzban, *The Parsis in India,* 2 vols. (Bombay, M. M. Murzban, 1917).

Central to Zoroastrian worship are a number of traditional prayers repeated in the Avestan language. A facing-page translation with word-by-word interpretations intended for Zoroastrians' own instruction is Framroz Rustomjee, *Daily Prayers of the Zoroastrians (in English)* (Colombo, the author, 1959). The prolific scholar Jivanji J. Modi, who wrote articles on Zoroastrian ceremonies for James Hastings' *Encyclopaedia of Religion and Ethics,* expanded his material to form *The Religious Ceremonies and Customs of the Parsees,* 3rd ed. (Bombay, Jehangir B. Karani, 1938). Open to the latest findings of Western scholarship, Modi drew heavily on archeological and anthropological discoveries for explanations of the significance of Parsi practices. Likewise appreciative of the values of the Western world was Rustom P. Masani, whose book *The Religion of the Good Life: Zoroastrianism* (London, George Allen and Unwin, 1938), is probably the most felicitous available statement of the meaning of the religion by one of its adherents.

B. Mithraism

Mithra is an Indo-Iranian deity whose cult flourished in Iran, particularly during the era when the Parthians were the principal eastern rivals of Rome. From there it spread through the Roman Empire, notably but by no means exclusively in military garrisons and cities along the northern European frontiers. As a result of this history, the literature on Mithraism is of two kinds: one which treats the Indo-Iranian Mithra, and another which treats Mithraism as one of the cults of the Roman Empire. The amount of scholarly endeavor in the second of these categories has been by far the more ample.

Literature on the Iranian Mithra is, by and large, quite technical. An exception for readers who can use French is the basic overview of the cult of Mithra in Iran provided by Henri-Charles Puech in André Aymard et al., *La Civilisation iranienne (Perse, Afghanistan, Iran extérieur)* (Paris, Payot, 1952), 102–111. One of the main historical problems regarding the worship of Mithra in Iran is how it was harmonized with the Zoroastrian tradition; see Mary Boyce, "On Mithra's Part in Zoroastrianism," *Bulletin of the School of Oriental and African Studies,* University of London, XXXII (1969), 10–34, and Ilya Gershevitch, *The Avestan Hymn to Mithra* (Cambridge, University Press, 1959). Also important for piecing together the history of Mithra in Iran is Mary Boyce, "On Mithra in the Manichaean Pantheon," in Walter B. Henning, ed., *A Locust's Leg: Studies in Honour of S. H. Taqizadeh* (London, Lund Humphries, 1962), 44–54.

For an introduction to Mithraism as it developed in the Roman Empire the reader has a choice of two concise books: Maarten J. Vermaseren, *Mithras, the Secret God* (London, Chatto & Windus, 1963), and Franz Cumont, *The Mysteries of Mithra,* 2nd ed. (Chicago, Open Court, 1910). Each covers the diffusion, the rituals, and the iconography of the tradition; Vermaseren has the benefit of more recent information but has a more miscellaneous chapter structure. A third survey, Esmé Wynne-Tyson, *Mithras: The Fellow in the Cap* (London, Rider, 1958), is written with a strong interest in comparisons with early Christianity.

Our knowledge of Mithraism is based in part on characterizations of it by outsiders, and in part on inscriptional and archeological remains. Some of the texts will be found in Alfred S. Geden, *Select Passages Illustrating Mithraism* (London, SPCK, 1925). Research on Mithraism was massively influenced by Franz Cumont, whose major work on the subject was *Textes et monuments figurés relatifs aux mystères de Mithra,* 2 vols. (Brussels, H. Lamartin, 1894–1900). While Cumont's researches have dominated the field for at least a generation, there are indications of new diversity and enthusiasm in the papers of a 1971 conference, John R. Hinnells, ed., *Mithraic Studies* (Manchester, Manchester Univ. Press, 1973).

Like the other mystery religions of the Hellenistic world, the cult of Mithra focused on the cycle of death and rebirth. Mithra's miraculous birth was celebrated on December 25, at the midwinter solstice (and various reliefs, incidentally, depict shepherds present at the birth). Uniformly, every Mithraic sanctuary would devote one wall to a representation of Mithra's most outstanding feat, the slaying of the bull—a death from which comes fresh life, as details of these scenes indicate, showing other animals consuming the bull's blood or ears of grain springing from it. One example of a Mithraic sanctuary, particularly interesting because of its location in proximity to the Parthian empire, was at the frontier town of Dura-Europos, on the Euphrates river; see "The Mithraeum," in Michael I. Rostovtzeff et al., ed., *The Excavations at Dura-Europos Conducted by Yale University and the French Academy of Inscriptions and Letters: Preliminary Report of the Seventh and Eighth Seasons 1933–34 and 1934–35* (New Haven, Yale Univ. Press, 1939), 62–134. A volume which draws together and interprets the iconographic material from sundry locations is LeRoy A. Campbell, *Mithraic Iconography and Ideology* (Leiden, E. J. Brill, 1968).

A question which will engage students of Mithraism is that of accounting for its appeal to particular groups in society. For this, see R. L. Gordon, "Mithraism and Roman Society: Social Factors in the Explanation of Religious Change in the Roman Empire," *Religion,* II (1972), 92–121; also Samuel Laeuchli, "Urban Mithraism," *The Biblical Archaeologist,* XXXI (1968), 73–99.

C. Manichaeism

Mani, who lived in Mesopotamia in the third century A.D., preached an essentially Gnostic message seeking redemption from bondage to cosmic forces of evil. We treat Manichaeism as a religion separate in its own right because Mani and his followers maintained an organization as a distinct community both in doctrine and discipline. Indeed, Wilfred C. Smith, in *The Meaning and End of Religion* (N.Y., Macmillan, 1963), chapter 4, suggests that Mani was the first person anywhere to set out self-consciously to "found" a "religion."

Manichaeism as an entity means different things to different people. A lucid brief account of Mani's teaching as a system of east Mediterranean Gnostic thought is given by Hans in *The Gnostic Religion,* 2nd ed. (Boston, Beacon Press, 1963), chap. 9. Another short sketch of the religion, viewed from the western Mediterranean as background for a chapter on Augustine's polemic against the Manichees, is Gerald Bonner, *St Augustine of Hippo: Life and Controversies* (London, SCM Press, 1963), 157–92. Geo. Widengren, in his book *Mani and Manichaeism* (London, Weidenfeld and Nicolson, 1965), stresses the Iranian connections of the religion. In a sense each of these introductions provides part of the picture, and they can be read together and contrasted with profit. The best and most comprehensive single introduction in any language is Henri-Charles Puech, *Le Manichéisme: Son fondateur, sa doctrine* (Paris, Civilisations du Sud, 1949), echoed in his entry on Manichaeism in Puech, ed., *Histoire des religions,* Encyclopédie de la Pléiade, 29, 34 (Paris, Gallimard, 1970–72), vol. II, 523–645. One work of Puech's which is in English is his article "The Concept of Redemption in Manichaeism," in Joseph Campbell, ed., *The Mystic Vision, Papers from the Eranos Yearbooks,* 6 (Princeton, Princeton Univ. Press, 1968), 247–314.

For centuries after the Church Fathers, Manichaeism was viewed as a Christian heresy. In the nineteenth century, Western scholars reading medieval Arabic sources discovered that the Muslims did not regard Manichaeism as Christian at all, and a phase of its study began in which Manichaeism was now considered as an independent Eastern religion. During the first decades of the twentieth century, the discovery of Manichaean texts in central Asia and in Egypt provided a view of the religion from its own sources for the first time. This history of scholarship through the nineteenth century is treated in detail by Julien Ries, "Introduction aux études manichéennes: Quatre siècles de recherches," *Ephemerides Theologicae Lovanienses,* XXXIII (1957), 453–82, and XXXV (1959), 362–409 (also reissued as 'Analecta lovaniensia biblica et orientalia,' ser. III, fasc. 7 and 11). Twentieth-century research can be traced in the bibliography of Jes P. Asmussen, *Xuāstvānīft: Studies in Manichaeism,* Acta Theologica Danica, 7 (Copenhagen, Munksgaard, 1965), 265–87.

The reader seriously interested in Manichaeism will soon learn that the principal documents of this tradition are scattered through a variety of languages and that few are available in English translation. Many of the chief passages discussing Manichaeism are published in Greek or Latin, together with extracts in German from documents in Near Eastern languages, in Alfred Adam, ed., *Texte zum Manichäismus* (Berlin, Walter de Gruyter, 1954). A description in English of "The Manichaean Literature in Middle Iranian," by Mary Boyce, is in *Handbuch der Orientalistik,* I. Abteilung, IV. Band ("Iranistik"), 2. Abschnitt ("Literatur"), Lieferung 1 (Leiden, E. J. Brill, 1968), 67–76.

On the biography of Mani the best book is in German, Otakar Klíma, *Manis Zeit und Leben* (Prague, Československa akademie věd, 1962). Unfortunately, the work in English by Lodewijk J. R. Ort, *Mani: A Religio-Historical Description of His Personality* (Leiden, E. J. Brill, 1967), cannot be recommended to the unwary reader.

In the east, the Manichaeans came into contact with central Asian Buddhism, and pressed on toward China. See Otto J. Maenchen-Helfen, "Manichaeans in Siberia," in Walter J. Fischel, ed., *Semitic and Oriental Studies Presented to William Popper* (Berkeley, Univ. of California Press, 1951), 311–26; and Thomas A. Bisson, "Some Chinese Records of Manichaeism in China," *The Chinese Recorder,* LX (1929), 415–28. Bisson's article, relying heavily on the work of Édouard Chavannes and Paul Pelliot, indicates that Manichaeism entered China as early as the seventh century and remained there for over a thousand years.

Manichaeism's spread in the Mediterranean world is more familiar to Westerners, and better documented in English. An important article is Peter

Brown, "The Diffusion of Manichaeism in the Roman Empire," *Journal of Roman Studies,* LIX (1969), 92–103. Brown contends that Manichaeism failed both in the Roman world and in Persia in the fifth and sixth centuries because its cosmopolitanism and its missionary emphasis were out of place in a time of shrinking political, commercial, and doctrinal horizons.

Yet in medieval Europe there continued to appear dualistic movements whose Christian opponents termed them Manichaean and wheeled out against them the arsenal of argument built up by Augustine and other Church Fathers. An attractive book which ties together the Paulicians of Asia Minor, the Bogomils of the Balkans, and the Albigensians (or Cathars) of southern France into one package is Steven Runciman, *The Medieval Manichee: A Study of the Christian Dualist Heresy* (Cambridge, University Press, 1947). Runciman speaks of an overall dualist tradition as Gnostic in origin but not carrying Mani's specific elaboration of it. There remains the historical question of how much which is dualistic in form is Manichaean in origin. Dimitri Obolensky, in *The Bogomils: A Study in Balkan Neo-Manichaeism* (Cambridge, University Press, 1949), holds that Bogomilism may be traced through Paulicianism to a Manichaean origin. Nina Garsoian holds otherwise, finding very little explicit Manichaean influence, in *The Paulician Heresy: A Study of the Origin and Development of Paulicianism in Asia Minor and the Eastern Provinces of the Byzantine Empire* (The Hague, Mouton, 1967). A good introduction to problems of historical transmission to the Albigensians in the western Mediterranean will be found in the early chapters of Jeffery B. Russell, *Dissent and Reform in the Early Middle Ages* (Berkeley, Univ. of California Press, 1965).

V. THE PERIMETER

In this section we shall attempt a brief view of some additional regions, contiguous to the major Near Eastern and Mediterranean civilizations before Islam. To group these regions together is not to imply that they had any significant interaction with one another; rather, each was independently in contact with the Persian or Greek or Roman world. In such contact during antiquity, moreover, the outlying areas tended more to be the recipients of cultural influences than contributors influencing the major central civilizations. Indeed, what appears as an exception, the rise of Islam—the remarkable spread in the central area accomplished by a new religio-political order originating on the periphery—marks as effective an end to the world of antiquity as any single event one might choose.

A. Arabia

Despite the fact that classical Islam dismissed previous Arabian civilization as ignorance or barbarism, ancient Arabia had enjoyed a prosperous urban culture for more than a thousand years, particularly in the spice-rich Yemen. Modern knowledge of that culture is based partly on the fragmentary archeological and inscriptional remains, partly on survivals of custom to the present among the bedouin, partly on occasional mention of Arabia in other ancient literatures, and partly on subsequent discussions of the age of "ignorance" by Muslims. As the last of these sources is covered under Islam in this Guide, the reader should consult that chapter as well for key items.

Giorgio Levi della Vida, "Pre-Islamic Arabia," in Nabih A. Faris, ed., *The Arab Heritage* (Princeton, Princeton Univ. Press, 1944), 25–57, reflects in a manner which the beginner will appreciate on the problems of reconstructing a history from such sources. For the latter part of the pre-Islamic era, contacts with the Byzantines provide somewhat fuller documentation for the historian, and this material figures importantly in the work of Irfan Shahid, who is able in his chapter "Pre-Islamic Arabia," in Peter M. Holt, ed., *The Cambridge History of Islam,* vol. I (Cambridge, University Press, 1970), 3–29, to put some emphasis on the displacement of the older cults by Christianity and Judaism during the last pre-Islamic centuries. A full synthesis of ancient Arabian history has still to be written, though Albert Dietrich, "Geschichte Arabiens vor dem Islam," *Handbuch der Orientalistik,* I. Abteilung, II. Band ("Keilschriftforschung und alte Geschichte Vorderasiens"), 4. Abschnitt ("Orientalische Geschichte von Kyros bis Mohammed"), Lieferung 2 (Leiden, E. J. Brill, 1966), 291–336, does offer a somewhat fuller outline than can be had in English. The culture of the Ethiopians, who were involved with Arabia in early Christian times, may be appreciated in John Doresse's readable *Ethiopia* (London, Elek Books, 1959), 13–89.

On Arabian religion as such the standard treatments are likewise in languages other than English. Two which cover the entire peninsula are Gonzague E. Ryckmans, "Les Religions arabes préislamiques," in Matthieu M. Gorce and Raoul Mortier, eds., *Histoire générale des religions* (Paris, Librairie Aristide Quillet, 1944–51), vol. IV, 307–32 and 526–34, also issued separately in the series 'Bibliothèque du Muséon,' 26 (Louvain, Publications universitaires, 1951); and Maria Höfner, "Die vorislamischen Religionen Arabiens," in Hartmut Gese et al., *Die Religionen Altsyriens, Altarabiens und der Mandäer* (Stuttgart, W. Kohlhammer, 1970), 233–402. Ryckman's principal specialty is northern Arabia, and Höfner's is southern; and within each of their surveys the two regions are discussed separately.

Reconstructions of Arabian religion for this ancient period amount principally to a catalogue of the different deities named in inscriptions and of the kinds of guardianship sought from them. For southern Arabia this is true of the two works already named and also of Albert Jamme, "La Religion sud-arabe préislamique," in Maurice Brillant and René Aigrain, eds., *Histoire des religions* (Paris, Bloud et Gay, 1953–56), vol. IV, 201–237. (A brief synopsis in English of Jamme's presentation may be found in the *New Catholic Encyclopedia* [N.Y., McGraw-Hill, 1967] s.v. "Arabia.") Such discussions are methodologically passive, often bringing together material from different times and places into a composite picture, leaving little room for change through time and minimizing local variation. But the anthropologically based contributions of Walter Dostal, "The Evolution of Bedouin Life," and Joseph Henninger, "La Religion bedouine préislamique," in Francesco Gabrieli, ed., *L'antica società beduina* (Rome, Centro di Studi Semitici, Istituto di Studi Orientali, Università di Roma, 1959), 11–34 and 115–40, do offer a gratifyingly more explicit sense of method and inference.

The best, and almost the only, general studies of north Arabian religion are in French. An authoritative source is Jean Starcky, "Palmyréniens, nabatéens et arabes du nord avant l'Islam," in Brillant and Aigrain, eds., *Histoire des religions* (Paris, Bloud et Gay, 1953–56), vol. IV, 239–307, with again a short English article by the same author on the same subject in the *New Catholic Encyclopedia* (*op. cit.*) s.v. "Arabia." The Syrian-Transjordanian desert fringe was for centuries a zone of contact where men who bore Arabic names built cities in Hellenistic architectural styles astride the caravan routes, and worshipped both Arabian and Hellenistic and older Semitic deities. An overview of the cultural setting of these cities can be had from Michael I. Rostovtzeff, *Caravan Cities* (Oxford, Clarendon Press, 1932), and an important synthesis with sections on religious developments in the region is the work of René Dussaud, *La Pénétration des arabes en Syrie avant l'Islam* (Paris, Paul Geuthner, 1955).

It was also through northern Arabia that Judaism and Christianity made their influence felt in the peninsula, though this process does not eliminate the possibility of an indigenous pre-Islamic Arabian monotheism as well. Hebrew contacts are discussed in an older work still serviceable as an introduction to the main types of problems, James A. Montgomery, *Arabia and the Bible* (Philadelphia, Univ. of Pennsylvania Press, 1934). For Christian contacts, one may consult technical studies by Irfan Shahid and Jacques Ryckmans, "Le Christianisme en Arabie du Sud préislamique," *Atti del convegno internazionale sul tema: L'Oriente cristiano nella storia della civiltà* (Rome, Accademia Nazionale dei Lincei, 1964), 413–53. On the enigmatic "ḥanīfs," pre-Islamic Arabian monotheists who in rejecting the old pagan polytheism also seem to have set the stage for Islam, see W. Montgomery Watt, *Muḥammad at Mecca* (Oxford, Clarendon

Press, 1953), excursus C; and Nabih A. Faris and Harold W. Glidden, "The Development of the Meaning of Koranic *ḥanīf*," *Journal of the Palestine Oriental Society,* XIX (1939–40), 1–13.

B. Southwestern Asia and Eastern Europe

Several histories of Armenia and the Caucasus include discussions of local religion before the coming of Christianity to these areas. Charles Burney and David M. Lang treat ancient paganism in their book *The Peoples of the Hills: Ancient Ararat and the Caucasus* (London, Weidenfeld and Nicolson, 1971), 214–25. Chapters 1–4, by Adrian David H. Bivar, in Gavin R. G. Hambly, ed., *Central Asia* (N.Y., Delacorte Press, 1969), likewise include a consideration of the religion of the region. Similarly, on Armenia, one may consult Vahan M. Kurkjian, *A History of Armenia* (N.Y., Armenian General Benevolent Union of America, 1964), 300–10. But for longer treatments there is little available in English to update the work of Mardiros H. Ananikian, "Armenian Mythology," in *The Mythology of All Races,* vol. VII, 1–100. Readers using French may see Georges Charachidze, *Le Système religieux de la Géorgie païenne: Analyse structurale d'une civilisation* (Paris, F. Maspero, 1968).

A starting point in English regarding the religions of the Slavic peoples is the writing of Marija Gimbutas, a student of European prehistory. She deals with religion in her book *The Slavs* (London, Thames & Hudson, 1971) and in "Ancient Slavic Religion: A Synopsis," in *To Honor Roman Jakobson* (The Hague, Mouton, 1967), vol. I, 738–59. Alternatively, one may consult Adolf Stender-Petersen, "Russian Paganism," in his *Russian Studies* (Copenhagen, Universitetsforlaget i Aarhus, 1956), 44–53. The best balanced longer treatment of Slavic religion, containing a good discussion of earlier European scholarly literature on the subject, is in French: Boris O. Unbegaun, "La Religion des anciens slaves," in Albert Grenier et al., *Les Religions étrusque et romaine, les religions des celtes, des germains et des anciens slaves* (Paris, Presses universitaires de France, 1948), 387–445. One of the older issues on which Unbegaun remains noncommittal is whether Slavic religion was Indo-European in origin, as scholars such as Alexander Brückner and Vittore Pisani had been contending, or had specific parallels to Iran, as Roman Jakobson subsequently argued. Unbegaun prefers not to postulate a common Slavic pantheon of great antiquity, but simply to describe the religious patterns of the Slavs at the time when the medieval documentary sources discuss them.

Those sources, in their original languages, are collected by Karl H. Meyer, *Fontes historiae religionis slavicae* (Berlin, W. de Gruyter, 1931). A folkloric source on which an older study is available in English is William R. S. Ralston, *The Songs of the Russian People: As Illustrative of Slavonic Mythology and Russian Social Life,* 2nd ed. (London, Ellis &

Green, 1872). Other studies in English involving survivals in regions of Slavic influence include Mircea Eliade, *Zalmoxis, the Vanishing God: Comparative Studies in the Religions and Folklore of Dacia and Eastern Europe* (Chicago, Univ. of Chicago Press, 1972), and V. I. Sanarov, "Elements of Ancient Belief in Gypsy Religion," *Soviet Anthropology and Archeology,* VIII (1969–70), 187–213.

If one is to look for Indo-European origins of the religions of eastern Europe, then Hungarian traditions might offer a point of comparison, inasmuch as their language does not belong to the Indo-European family. Most of the scholarship on ancient Hungarian religion, however, is in Hungarian and therefore inaccessible to most readers. Two works in German which provide a point of entry into the subject, however, are George Vernadsky and Michael de Ferdinandy, *Studien zu ungarischen Frühgeschichte* (Munich, R. Oldenbourg, 1957), and de Ferdinandy, "Die Mythologie der Ungarn," in Hans W. Haussig, ed., *Wörterbuch der Mythologie,* 1. Abteilung, II. Band (Stuttgart, Ernst Klett, 1973), 209–59. The same scarcity of English material holds for Albania; see Maximilian Lambertz, "Die Mythologie der Albaner," *ibid.,* 455–509.

The Baltic peoples occupied Latvia, Lithuania, and East Prussia. For an introductory sketch of their religion, see the prehistorian Marija Gimbutas, *The Balts* (London, Thames & Hudson, 1963), 179–204. Baltic religion personified the forces of the heavens, of fate, and of the earth on which agricultural fertility depended. The leading recent authority on it has been Haralds Biezais, whose principal books are in German but who has described "Baltic Religion" in the *Encyclopaedia Britannica,* 15th ed. (1974). Biezais reviews the historical sources and trends of scholarship in the field in "Die Religionsquellen der baltischen Völker und die Ergebnisse der bisherigen Forschungen" in the Scandinavian periodical *Arv,* IX (1953), 65–128. With Jonas Balys he has also provided a reference work in "Baltische Mythologie," in Hans W. Haussig, ed., *Wörterbuch der Mythologie* (*op. cit.*), 373–454.

C. Northern Europe

The Finns, the Estonians, and the Lapps all belong to the Ural-Altaic language group, and a study in English is available as an entrée to the religion of each. For the Finns and the group in general, time has not erased the usefulness of Uno Holmberg-Harva's extensive survey, "Finno-Ugric Mythology," in *The Mythology of All Races,* vol. IV, 1–295. Ivar Paulson, the author of a more recent synthesis in German, *Die Religionen der finnischen Völker* (Stuttgart, W. Kohlhammer, 1962), has had a work on the Estonians translated into English: *The Old Estonian Folk Religion* (Bloomington, Indiana Univ., 1971). For the Lapps, an article in English is Christiaan Nooteboom, "Sketch of the Former Religious Concepts of the Asele Lapps (the Southern Lapps)," in the Dutch anthropological periodical *Bijdragen tot de taal-, land- en volkenkunde,* CXVII (1961), 118–40. A reference work with alphabetical entries for individual figures is Lauri Honko, "Finnische Mythologie," in Hans W. Haussig, ed., *Wörterbuch der Mythologie (op. cit.),* 261–371.

Since the Germanic-speaking language group includes the Anglo-Saxons as well as the Germans and the Scandinavians, there has never been any lack of interest in the mythology and religion of northern Europe among scholars writing in English. Both in Britain and on the Continent, the study of northern European literary traditions and myths began to develop in the eighteenth century before the major growth of comparative philology and comparative religion in the nineteenth. To this in time was added the study of local legal custom and the significant interest in folklore spurred by the Grimm brothers; the work of Jakob Grimm, *Teutonic Mythology,* 4 vols. (London, G. Bell and Sons, 1883–88), remains a classic. In the twentieth century, archeological excavations have offered new data, and the social sciences have provided new avenues of theory for the exploration of Germanic religion.

The most readable point of entry to the subject in general is Hilda R. Ellis Davidson, *Gods and Myths of Northern Europe* (Harmondsworth, Penguin Books, 1964); an older, also readable, introduction is John A. MacCulloch, *The Celtic and Scandinavian Religions* (London, Hutchinson's University Library, 1948). Scandinavia is the principal focus of this field, rather than Britain or Germany, because the Christianization of Scandinavia took place later, and the mythology was preserved longer there, to be recorded by such Christian writers as the twelfth-century Danish historian Saxo Grammaticus and the thirteenth-century Icelandic poet Snorri Sturluson. Thus Hilda R. Ellis Davidson's *Pagan Scandinavia* (London, Thames & Hudson, 1967) provides a picture of what is central to Germanic religion; thus, also, E. O. Gabriel Turville-Petre's book *Myth and Religion of the North* (London, Weidenfeld and Nicolson, 1964), the fullest and most authoritative up-to-date account in English, is primarily a discussion of the Norse gods and heroes and their functions as based on the myths. This book also provides good bibliographical leads for further reading. Problems of approach and method are reviewed by Peter Buchholz, "Perspectives for Historical Research in Germanic Religion," *History of Religions,* VIII (1968–69), 111–38. The standard work in German for the serious student is Jan de Vries, *Altgermanische Religionsgeschichte,* 2nd ed. (Berlin, W. de Gruyter, 1956). Before leaving the subject we should mention also, for classical sources in the original languages, Carl Clemen, *Fontes historiae religionis germanicae,* 3 parts (Berlin, W. de Gruyter, 1928).

The Celts occupied Gaul and the British Isles in antiquity, and we owe our knowledge of them and their religion to two principal types of evidence:

the discussion of the customs of Gaul in such Latin writers as Julius Caesar, and the Celtic epic tradition preserved in medieval Ireland. Many details vary; the task of harmonizing Irish epic and Gaulish custom is not easy, and there may indeed have been considerable variation between island and mainland culture. The possibility of introducing the hypothetical Indo-European pantheon as a touchstone of what is fundamental to Celtic religion has appealed to some, such as Jan de Vries, *Keltische Religion* (Stuttgart, W. Kohlhammer, 1961; French translation, *La Religion des celtes* [Paris, Payot, 1963]). Many scholars, however, have taken the Irish epic, despite the medieval date of its compilation, as the most authentic available reflection of basic forms of Celtic religion; where it departs from the system of Indo-European deities, the argument goes, it may reflect an even older or more local sense of spirits and powers in nature. Such a view is held, for example, by Marie-Louise Sjoestedt-Jonval, in *Gods and Heroes of the Celts* (London, Methuen, 1949), a fine treatment of the mythology and perhaps the best introduction to a study of the religion in general. Another straightforward, concise work by an older scholar is John A. MacCulloch, *The Celtic and Scandinavian Religions* (London, Hutchinson's University Library, 1948). A good, handsomely illustrated treatment of the mythology is Proinsias MacCana, *Celtic Mythology* (London, Hamlyn, 1970). Probably the most reliable avenue to more advanced work on the religion is the fine survey in French by Joseph Vendryès, in Albert Grenier et al., *Les Religions étrusque et romaine, les religions des celtes, des germains et des anciens slaves* (*op. cit.*), 239–320.

An aspect of Celtic religion of particular fascination is its priestly intellectual class, the Druids, the group most frequently associated with sacrificial killings and other rituals conducted in open-air forest settings. An issue among scholars has been whether Roman opposition to the Druids was political, holding them to be disloyal; or cultural, holding their practices to be savage. Hugh Last, "Rome and the Druids: A Note," *Journal of Roman Studies,* XXXIX (1949), 1–5, sees a Roman opposition to savagery, while Nora K. Chadwick, *The Druids* (Cardiff, Univ. of Wales Press, 1966), stresses Roman political concern over Druid organization and discpline. Chadwick's is a scholarly but concise work; also useful, particularly for a history of interpretations of these practitioners, is Stuart Piggott, *The Druids* (London, Thames & Hudson, 1968).

It is by no means certain that the impressive circle of Stonehenge in southern England should be assigned any identifiable religious significance, let alone associated with the Druids in particular. Like the pyramids of Egypt, Stonehenge has come in for a full share of fanciful interpretations. An introductory book on the site is Richard J. C. Atkinson, *Stonehenge* (Harmondsworth, Penguin Books, 1960), and for scores of similar locations in the British isles the properties of such circles for astronomical observation are carefully measured by Alexander Thom in a technical study, *Megalithic Sites in Britain* (Oxford, Clarendon Press, 1967).

Two remaining items fall outside the categories we have so far treated: virtually the only authoritative work on Basque religion, José M. de Barandiarán, *Mitología vasca* (Madrid, Ediciones Minotauro, 1960), and a study of ritual survivals even if not of personal ones, Maurice Broëns, "The Resurgence of Pre-Indo-European Elements in the Western Medieval Cult of the Dead," *Diogenes*, no. 30 (1960), 75–103. Our circuit of ancient religions thus ends at the shores of the Atlantic, a once peripheral region with relatively little economic, technological, or cultural power which has come in modern times to be the center of gravity of civilization, the same as the Mediterranean was in antiquity.

III

The Religions of Mexico and of Central and South America

Juan Adolfo Vázquez

I n the American continent there is an area called Nuclear America which includes a large part of Mexico, all of central America and the Andean countries including northwest Argentina and the upper half of Chile. This area has been inhabited for several thousand years and has seen the rise of a number of civilizations, the most famous of which are the Maya, the Aztec and the Inca. The Aztec and the Inca were latecomers, having developed only shortly before they fell totally under Spanish sway. The Maya, like the forerunners of the Aztec in Mexico and of the Inca in Peru, attained their prime between the fourth and the tenth centuries A.D. They still subsist as Indian folk societies in southern Mexico, Yucatan, Guatemala and its eastern neighboring states. Most of the Indian population of Mexico, Central America and the Andes have retained pre-Hispanic beliefs and practices to this day, although acculturation in some areas is very heavy.

In Mexico, Central America and notably in South America there have been also many other Indian societies. They are sometimes called, rather misleadingly, "marginal tribes." Although they never reached the status of civilization, they are important for the study of comparative religion, especially for their mythology and shamanism. It is among some of these tribes still existing in South America that we can find examples of aboriginal beliefs and cults without mixture of modern Western thought and practice.

Pre-Columbian American Religions by Walter Krickeberg et al., trans. by Stanley Davis (N.Y., Holt, Rinehart and Winston, 1969), offers a general introduction to our subject. There are chapters by Walter Krickeberg on "Mesoamerica," Hermann Trimborn on "South America and the Andean Civilizations," and Otto Zerries on "Primitive South America and the West Indies." (There is also a chapter on "North America" by Werner Müller.)

I. MESOAMERICA

The concept of Mesoamerica was established by Paul Kirchhoff in his paper "Mesoamerica: Its Geographic Limits, Ethnic Composition and Cultural Characteristics," later translated and included in Sol Tax, ed., *Heritage of Conquest* (Glencoe, Ill., Free Press, 1952; rep. N.Y., Cooper Square Publishers, 1968). It covers, roughly, the area between the Tropic of Cancer and the 85th meridian, including a large part of Mexico, all of Guatemala and neighboring places of the Maya. According to Kirchhoff, the distinctive religious features of Mesoamerica are: an original ritual and divinatory calendar of great mathematical accuracy determining fifty-two-year cosmic periods at the end of which there were special ceremonies; religious centers with elaborate pyramidal temples; certain forms of self-sacrifice and human sacrifice; a mythological pantheon where the Rain God and the Civilizing God, called by different names at different places, were prominent though by no means the only ones. Another original accomplishment was the codices or colored manuscripts, painted on especially prepared paper or leather. The contents of these screenfold books was religious or historical or both.

The question whether there is in Mesoamerica one religion or many was discussed in Alfonso Caso in his paper "¿Religión o religiones mesoamericanas?" *Verhandlungen des XXXVIII. internationalen Amerikanistenkongresses,* Band III (München, Klaus Renner, 1971) 189–200. Caso deals briefly with the idea of a High God who transforms himself into a creative couple, also conceived as foodgiving lords bearing twin gods. There are also stratified world layers with four cardinal directions and one central point, combined with certain colors and other characteristics which are often met with outside Mesoamerica. Human sacrifice, religious games, divination, ritual use of drugs, belief in a magic relationship between men and animals (tonalism, nagualism) are also touched upon. After a more detailed consideration of the Mesoamerican pantheon and the *tonalpo-hualli* or ritual calender of 260 days resulting from a combination of twenty day signs and thirteen numbers, Caso concludes that there is one, not many Mesoamerican religions.

Under the same title as Caso's paper, in the same volume of the "Proceedings of the 38th Congress of Americanists" (pp. 201–06), Wigberto Jiménez Moreno stresses rather the internal differences of Mesoamerica, comparing it with the Fertile Crescent in the Near East where an observer might conclude there is but a single religion that includes Zoroastrianism, Judaism, Christianity, and Islam. In brief, notwithstanding some common traits, there are several Mesoamerican religions that were never completely integrated by the Aztecs.

Among the papers of the Twelfth Symposium of the Mexican Anthropological Society, devoted to Mesoamerican religions, there are quite a few interesting contributions. See Jaime Litvak King and Noemi Castillo Tejero, eds., *Religión en Mesoamerica* (México, Sociedad Méxicana de Antropología, 1972).

On survivals of hunters' religions in Mesoamerica: Josef Haeckel, "Der 'Herr der Tiere' im Glauben der Indianer Mesoamerikas," *Mitteilungen aus dem Museum für Völkerkunde in Hamburg,* XXV, 60–69 (Hamburg, Ludwig Appel, 1959). See also Otto Zerries, "Wildgeister und Jagdritual in Zentral-amerika," in the same volume, 144–50.

II. THE RELIGIONS OF MEXICO

The Formative or Pre-Classic period of the major Mexican cultures lasted from some time in the second millennium B.C. till the early centuries A.D. The belief in fertility goddesses and the presence of shamans can be conjectured from extant figurines. Tlatilco, in the Valley of Mexico, conquered much later by the Aztecs, is one of the best known places of that period. During the mid-centuries of the first millennium B.C. Tlatilco was under the influence of the Olmecs, usually considered as the creators of the first Mesoamerican civilization. They may have introduced into Tlatilco the cult of the plumed serpent which would become the symbol of the most important civilizing god in the Mesoamerican pantheon. The Olmecs, carvers of giant heads in stone, had a major ceremonial center at La Venta,

Tabasco, near the Gulf of Mexico, but expanded in several directions from Western Mexico to El Salvador. The Olmecs made little statuettes in jade, a stone which, as elsewhere, had sacred significance among Mesoamerican cultures. The Olmecs also buried elaborate stylized were-jaguar masks made of mosaic. The best treatment of the Olmec civilization, including a discussion of its religion, is Ignacio Bernal's *The Olmec World*, trans. by Doris Heyden and Fernando Horcasitas (Berkeley, Univ. of California Press, 1969). A shorter, more popular, and very well illustrated exposition is given by Michael D. Coe in *America's First Civilization* (N.Y., American Heritage; Toronto, McClelland & Stewart, 1968). On Tlatilco and the Olmecs see also Michael D. Coe's *The Jaguar's Children* (N.Y., Museum of Primitive Art, 1965).

In the Valley of Mexico the first great civilization was developed in Teotihuacan during the Classic period. Its contributions to art are among the finest in Mesoamerica. Religion was organized around cults of the Rain God Tlaloc, who was probably the favorite deity with the peasants, and the Feathered Serpent God Quetzalcoatl, who seems to have been an hierophany revered as the teacher of fine arts and crafts and a rigorous spiritual life. The religious significance of Teotihuacan's art and architecture has been studied by Laurette Sejourné in her books *Un Palacio en la Ciudad de los Dioses* (México, Instituto Nacional de Antropología e Historia, 1959) and *El Universo de Quetzalcoatl* (México, Fondo de Cultura Económica, 1962). The last mentioned book is an outstanding essay in interpretation of religious symbolism.

By the tenth century A.D. the remnants of the Teotihuacan civilization became the foundations of new developments. They were later taken over and modified by the militaristic Toltecs of Tula who passed them on to the smaller warring kingdoms of the Central Valley. The Aztecs were finally heirs to this double tradition of deep-seated mysticism and intolerant despotic aggression. Laurette Sejourné's *Burning Water; Thought and Religion in Ancient Mexico* (London, Thames & Hudson, 1957) is the main study, giving a fresh interpretation of the facts known through the codices and dirt archeology. Other works on Aztec religion are Lewis Spence, *The Gods of Mexico* (London, T. F. Unwin, 1922), Alfonso Caso, *The Aztecs: People of the Sun* (Norman, Univ. of Oklahoma Press, 1958), Cottie Arthur Burland, *The Gods of Mexico* (London, Eyre & Spottiswoode, 1967). A useful synthesis of the religion of the late Pre-Hispanic central Mexican Nahua-speaking peoples is given by Henry B. Nicholson in his article "Religion in Pre-Hispanic Central Mexico," in *Handbook of Middle American Indians,* ed. by Robert Wauchope, vol. X, *Archeology of Northern Mesoamerica,* part I, ed. Gordon Eckholm and Ignacio Bernal (Austin, Univ. of Texas Press, 1971) 395–446. The religious significance of a great work of art is analyzed by Justino Fernández in his book *Coatlicue* (México, Universidad Nacional Autónoma de

México, 2nd ed., 1959). Religion in connection with the Aztec system of higher education and philosophy is presented by Miguel León-Portilla in *Aztec Thought and Culture,* trans. by J. F. Davis (Norman, Univ. of Oklahoma Press, 1963). For Aztec symbolism of the four cosmic directions, the colors, the creation of the world and man, see Eduard Seler, "Mythus und Religion der alten Mexikaner," in *Gesammelte Abhandlungen zur amerikanischen Sprach- und Alterthumskunde,* 5 vols. (Berlin, A. Asher, 1902–23), vol. IV, 3–167; Jacques Soustelle, *La Pensée cosmologique des anciens mexicains* (Paris, Hermann, 1940) and Hermann Beyer, *Mito y Simbolismo del México Antiquo* ed. by Carmen Cook de Leonard (México, Sociedad Alemana de Mexicanistas, 1965). Religious symbolism in Aztec poetry has been studied by Irene Nicholson in *Firefly in the Night* (London, Faber & Faber, 1959) and Miguel León-Portilla in *Trece Poetas del Mundo Azteca* (México, Universidad Nacional Autónoma de México, 1967). The Mexican calendar, of recognized religious significance, has been the subject of many studies. Among them: Eduard Seler, *The Tonalamatl of the Aubin Collection,* ed. by A. H. Keane (London, no publisher indicated, printed by Hazell, Watson & Viney, 1900–01), George Clapp Vaillant, *A Sacred Almanac of the Aztecs* (N.Y., American Museum of Natural History, 1940).

For a detailed account of ancient historical and religious documents the reader should consult the anthology of sources and studies edited by Miguel León-Portilla: *De Teotihuacán a los Aztecas* (México, Universidad Nacional Autónoma de México, 1971), especially the sections devoted to myth and ritual (pp. 471–508) and to modern interpretations (pp. 509–590). The early history of the Aztecs, their mythical predecessors and historical rivals, is told in the Nahua texts variously known as *Codex Chimalpopoca, Annals of Cuauhtitlan,* and *History of the Reigns of Colhuacan and of Mexico.* Excerpts from this work have been published in Miguel León-Portilla's *Pre-Columbian Literatures of Mexico,* English trans. by Grace Lobanov and M. León-Portilla (Norman, Univ. of Oklahoma Press, 1969). Walter Lehmann's edition of the text with an annotated German translation, *Die Geschichte der Königsreiche von Colhuacan und Mexiko* (Stuttgart and Berlin, W. Kohlhammer, 1938) supersedes earlier editions. The best single source for ancient Mexican religions, however, is the compilation made in the late sixteenth century by Fray Bernardino de Sahagún with the assistance of native informants: *General History of the Things of New Spain,* trans. and ed. by A. J. O. Anderson and Charles E. Dibble (Sante Fe, School of American Research, to be completed in 13 volumes, 1950–   2nd. rev. ed. of Book II, 1970). Another early source is the *Tratado de los Ritos y Ceremonias y Dioses que en su Gentilidad Usaban los Indios de esta Neuva España,* to be found in pp. 85–113 of the so-called *Manuscrit Tovar: Origines et croyances des Indiens du Méxique,* Spanish text and French translation by Jacques La Faye (Graz, Akademische Druck- u. Verlagsanstalt, 1972). Among the important sixteenth-century sources special mention should be made of Fray Diego de Durán's *Book of the Gods and Rites and the Ancient Calendar,* trans. and ed. by Fernando Horcasitas & Doris Heyden (Norman, Univ. of Oklahoma Press, 1971), based on native manuscripts now lost. Fray Juan de Torquemada's *Monarquía Indiana* is a lengthy compilation drawing valuable references to the religious life of the Indians largely from early Spanish sources. First published in Seville, 1615, there is a reprint of the 1723 (third) edition (México, S. Chávez Hayhoe, 1943).

III. THE MAYA

Unlike the Aztecs, the Maya never established anything like a militaristic administration over Mesoamerica. Their refined civilization was unsurpassed, and some of their contributions rank with the highest among the civilizations of the world. While many traits of the Maya religion can also be found elsewhere in Mesoamerica, certain remarkable characteristics stand out, notably the phenomenal development in mathematical calculation and astronomical knowledge, both of astrological and ritual import, and a complex artistic style representing the major deities in stone carvings, mural paintings and codices. Human sacrifice, where it was practiced, never went to the extremes of Aztec terrorism.

The best general introduction to Maya religion is to be found in Ferdinand Anton's *Das Pantheon der Maya* (Graz, Akademische Druck- u. Verlagsanstalt, 1963), 2nd section, 31–224. The first section includes a discussion of the sources, while the third presents the Maya pantheon according to the traditions of a dozen different Maya peoples or places. Ancient Maya cosmology is the subject of Miguel León-Portilla's *Time and Reality in the Thought of the Maya,* trans. by Charles L. Boilés and Fernando Horcasitas (Boston, Beacon Press, 1973). The modern counterpart is presented in an appendix to the same volume by Alfonso Villa-Rojas: "The Concepts of Space and Time Among the Contemporary Maya" (p. 113–59).

A recent discovery of the Lacandon sacred traditions called *The Book of Chan K'in* has led to a comparison with the *Popul Vuh* and speculations about the older Maya world view. See R. B. Bruce S., Carlos Robles U., and Enriqueta Ramos Chao, *Los lacandones. 2. Cosmovision maya* (México, Instituto Nacional de Antropología e Historia, 1971).

The written traditions of the Maya of Yucatan are recorded in *The Book of Chilam Balam of Chumayel,* trans. by Ralph L. Roys (Washington, D.C., Carnegie Institution, 1933). Similar traditions are recorded in *The Book of the Jaguar Priest,* a translation of the *Book of Chilam Balam of Tizimin,* with commentary by Maud Worcester Makemson (N.Y., Henry Schuman, 1951). Less esoteric than the Balam (or Jaguar Priest) books is *The Annals of the Cakchiquels,* tr. from the Cakchiquel Maya by Adrián Recinos and Delia Goetz (Norman, Univ. of Oklahoma Press, 1953), very valuable for the mythology and early history of the Cakchiquels of the Guatemala Highlands. The most important literary source for the reconstruction of Maya religious thought, however, is the *Popol Vuh; the Sacred Book of the Ancient Quiché Maya,* English translation by Delia Goetz and Sylvanus Morley from the Spanish translation of Adrián Recinos (Norman, Univ. of Oklahoma Press, 1950), originally in the Quiché language of the Maya family spoken in Guatemala. This famous book is also very valuable for Maya mythology.

No Spanish chronicler did for the Maya what Sahagún did for the Aztecs. The best single early source is, however, Diego de Landàs' *Relación de las Cosas de Yucatán* (1566), of which there is an English translation, copiously annotated by Alfred M. Tozzer, and published under the original Spanish title (Cambridge, Peabody Museum, 1941), an indispensable work. Worth mentioning also is Diego López de Cogolludo's *Historia de Yucatán* (1688) based on earlier documents and reprinted several times, the latest including Walter Lehmann's marginal notes (Graz, Akademische Druck-u. Verlagsanstalt, 1971, 2 vols.). The fourth book of Cogolludo's *Historia* contains a report on the Indians' religion by Pedro Sánchez de Aguilar.

For modern general surveys of Maya culture see Sylvanus Griswold Morley, *The Ancient Maya,* 3rd ed., rev. by George W. Brainerd (Stanford, Stanford Univ. Press, 1956) and John Eric Sidney Thompson, *The Rise and Fall of Maya Civilization,* 2nd ed. enl. (Norman, Univ. of Oklahoma Press, 1966). The latter is particularly relevant for an understanding of the role of religion in the Maya view of life. A shorter exposition is to be found in Alberto Ruz Lhuillier's *La Civilisation des anciens Mayas* (México, Instituto Nacional de Antropología e Historia, 1970).

There are many studies of Maya communities showing survivals of old religious patterns until today. One of the more thorough analyses of this deep-rooted syncretism is Evon Zartman Vogt's *Zinacantán: A Maya Community in the Highlands of Chiapas* (Cambridge, Harvard Univ. Press, 1969).

On the religion of other Mexican Indians in modern times, see Alain Ichon, *La Religion des Totonaques de la Sierra* (Paris, Centre National de la Recherche Scientifique, 1969), and the classic books of Karl S. Lumholtz, *Symbolism of the Huichol Indians* (N.Y., American Museum of Natural History, 1900), *Unknown Mexico* (N.Y., C. Scribner's Sons, 1902, 2 vols.) and *New Trails in Mexico* (N.Y., C. Scribner's Sons, 1912). Another classic study of western Mexico, containing important documents in the native Cora language with a German translation, is Theodor Preuss' *Die Nayarit-Expedition* (Leipzig, B. G. Teubner, 1912).

IV. THE MESOAMERICAN CODICES

One of the great original contributions of the ancient Mesoamerican civilizations to world art, science and religion was their codices, folded strips of brightly painted pictures and hieroglyphs. Comparatively few have survived the zeal of the Spanish invaders. Three of them originated in the Maya area of Yucatán, their contents being astronomical and ritual. Some proceed from the Mixtec-Zapotec area, mainly in the state of Oaxaca, including perhaps the famous codex Borgia group, of great worth for religious studies. The largest number of codices, however, stems from the Central Valley of Mexico and other areas of Aztec predominance. Many of them show Spanish influence, significant for our understanding of the social, economic and political background of the Indies at the time of the Conquest, but generally speaking, they are less interesting than codices from the other areas for the study of the history of religions.

A handy list of the Mesoamerican codices was prepared by Miguel León-Portilla and Salvador Mateos-Higuera: *Catálogo de los códices indígenas del México antiguo* (México, Secretaría de Hacienda, 1957). For a short introduction to the subject see Cottie Arthur Burland, *Magic Books from Mexico* (Harmondsworth, Penguin Books, 1953). A better introduction in a larger format and with more adequate color plates is Hans Biedermann's *Altmexikos heilige Bücher* (Graz, Akademische Druck- u. Verlagsanstalt, 1971) presenting examples from different areas, mostly Pre-Hispanic. A useful "reader" for students of the Mexican codices, giving prominence to the Borgia group, has been prepared by Karl A. Nowotny: *Tlacuilolli* (Berlin, Gebr. Mann, 1961). The plates are very good halftones.

A large number of codices has been reproduced in facsimiles of varying quality, mostly in small editions now hard to come by. The most ambitious and successful project, now well under way, is sponsored by Akademische Druck- und Verlagsanstalt of Graz, Austria, in the series "Codices Selecti, Group C: Manuscripts from Foreign Cultures." Among the codices already published in this series the more relevant ones for religious studies are: *Codex Vindobonensis Mexicanus I,* ed. with an introduction in English by Otto Adelhofer (1963); *Codex Laud,* ed. with an introduction in English by Cottie Arthur Burland (1966); *Codex Cospi* or *Codex Copianus,* ed. with an introduction in German by Karl A. Nowotny (1968); *Codex Magliabecchiano (Anon. Vida de los Yndios),* ed. with an introduction in German by F. Anders (1970); *Codex Fejérváry-Mayer,* ed. with an introduction in English by Cottie Arthur Burland (1971); *Codex Vaticanus B,* ed. with an introduction in German by F. Anders (1972). As a rule the introductions to the above-mentioned codices do not deal with their symbolic contents but concentrate on the physical aspects of the codex in hand. On the other hand, the complete colored manuscript is reproduced with a very high degree of technical accuracy.

Most of the codices have been commented upon by different scholars. Lord Kingsborough, in his nine extra-large folio volumes titled *Antiquities of Mexico* (London, various publishers, 1830–48), appended to the hand-painted reproductions of Augustine Aglio some useful materials from the Spanish chroniclers and also his own, now outdated, commentaries. A new edition of this work, in smaller format, includes modern explanations in Spanish by José Corona Núñez: *Antigüedades de México,* 4 vols. (México, Secretaría de Hacienda, 1964–   ). The commentaries of Eduard Seler on some of the codices remain unsurpassed. His edition of the *Codex Borgia,* 3 vols. (Berlin, Druck von Gebr. Unger, 1904–09) has been translated into Spanish and the plates reproduced in color: *Comentarios al Codice Borgia,* 3 vols. (México, Fondo de Cultura Económica, 1963). Two others have been translated into English: *Codex Fejérváry-Mayer,* 2 vols. (Berlin, published at the expense of the Duke of Loubat, 1901–02) and *Codex Vaticanus no. 3773,* 2 vols. (Berlin, published at the expense of the Duke of Loubat, 1902).

V. THE ANDES

Between the Maya in Central America and the northern outposts of the Inca empire in Ecuador there was a group of Chibcha-speaking peoples who originated somewhere in the Colombian Andes. The most advanced of them all were the Muisca of the Bogotá plateau. Among the earlier civilizations, the most impressive for its stone statues of anthropomorphic and zoomorphic beings is San Agustín, which developed during a millennium and a half but had already disappeared when the Spanish arrived. The first full-length, fundamental study, with a discussion of its probable religion, is K. Th. Preuss' *Monumentale vorgeschichtliche Kunst,* 2 vols. (Göttingen, Vandenhoeck & Ruprecht, 1929). An up-to-date résumé of what is known about this mysterious culture can be read in Gerardo Reichel-Dolmatoff's *San Agustin: A Culture of Colombia* (London, Thames & Hudson, 1972), including a chapter on "The World of the Jaguar Monster," 83–114.

In the Central Andes some great civilizations had already existed, and a number of cultures were still alive when the Quechua-speaking Incas (like the Nahua-speaking Aztecs in Mesoamerica) overran and conquered many of their neighbors, establishing one of the more tightly organized empires in the world. But Peru had no Sahagún, and modern archeological investigation in general, and research into the ancient religions in particular, have proceeded here at a slower pace than in Mesoamerica. There is still the possibility of obtaining a clearer picture of the many hierophanies worshipped by the older civilizations upon which the Incas superimposed their own cult of the Sun and the Inca King. Among the early Spanish sources, some important writings were translated by Sir Clements Robert Markham in *Narratives of the Rites and Laws of the Incas* (London, Haykluyt Society, 1873); including Cristoval de Molina, *An Account of the Fables and Rites of the Yncas;* Juan de Santa Cruz Pachacuti-Yamqui Salcamayhua, *An Account of the Antiquities of Peru;* and Francisco de Ávila, *A Narrative of the Errors, False Gods and Other Superstitious and Diabolical Rites* [. . .] *of Huarochiri.* Another early source is Father Pablo José de Arriaga, *The Extirpation of Idolatry in Peru,* tr. and ed. by L. Clark Keating (Lexington, Univ. of Kentucky Press, 1968). As some of the titles indicate, these studies were not carried out by dispassionate observers of the indigenous religions; and where that may have been the case, the writers had to present their subject in an unfavorable light to escape suspicion of infidelity. The critical reader, of course, will be able to sieve the facts.

Of the native sources, best known is the Inca Garcilaso de la Vega's *Royal Commentaries and General History of Peru,* 2 vols., a classic of Spanish Golden Age prose which can now be read in the translation of Harold V. Livermore (Austin, Univ. of Texas Press, 1966). Although the Inca was a devout Christian living in Spain when he wrote his *Commentaries,* they still are worth reading for their wealth of information and the charm of the exposition. The least acculturated Indian source, written in barbarous Spanish heavily interlarded with sentences in Quechua, is Felipe Huamán Poma de Ayala's *Nueva Coronica y Buen Gobierno* (Paris, Institut d'Ethnologie, facsimile ed., 1936), including valuable pen-drawings by the author. The last two mentioned sources contain not only materials of religious interest but also information on many aspects of the cultural life of the Incas that represented old traditions in the period shortly after the Spanish conquest. The best short modern accounts of Inca religion in its general historical context are: John Howland Rowe, "Inca culture at the Time of the Spanish Conquest," in *Handbook of South American Indians,* 7 vols. ed. by Julian H. Steward, Bulletin 143, Bureau of American Ethnology, vol. 2, *The Andean Civilizations,* 183–338 (Washington, D.C., Smithsonian Institution, 1946) and Burr Cartwright Brundage, *Empire of the Inca* (Norman, Univ. of Oklahoma Press, 1963), especially chaps. three and four ("Basic Forms of Peruvian Religion" and "Peruvian Myths of Creation"). By the same author, *Lords of Cuzco* (same publisher, 1967) brings the account to the last days of the Inca empire. Rowe and Brundage cover practically all the relevant sources. On the other hand, a longer analysis and transcription of early sources of Peruvian religion and mythology are given by Julio C. Tello in his article "Wira Kocha," *Inca,* vol. I, 93–320 and 583–606 (Lima, 1923), and by Luis

E. Valcárcel in the chapter of his *Historia del Perú antiguo* (Lima, Juan Mejía Baca, 1964) on religion, magic and myth (vol. II, 11–522).

The renowned Temple of the Sun at Cuzco has been studied by Robert Lehmann-Nitsche in his *Coricancha, Revista del Museo de La Plata,* v. XXX, 1–260 (La Plata, 1928), the main points of which are reproduced in his lecture *Coricancha* (La Plata, Universidad Nacional de La Plata, 1929). See also Samuel Kirkland Lothrop, *Inca Treasure as Depicted by Spanish Historians* (Los Angeles, Southwest Museum, Frederick Webb Hodge Anniversary Publication Fund, vol. 2, 1938).

Although for some time in contact with the Incas, the Araucanians of south Central Chile still retain beliefs and practices which are seemingly older. See Fray Félix José de Augusta, *Lecturas Araucanas,* 2nd, ed., rev. (Padre Las Casas, Imprenta y Editiorial "San Francisco," 1934), Louis C. Faron, *Hawks of the Sun* (Pittsburgh, Univ. of Pittsburgh Press, 1964). For the religion of the Araucanians in Andean Argentina: Rodolfo M. Casamiquela, *Estudio del Nillatún y la Religión Araucana* (Bahía Blanca, Universidad Nacional del Sur, 1964).

VI. BEYOND THE ANDES

There is no overall detailed exposition of the South American "primitive" religions, but a few good books and articles are available. The posthumous edition of some studies by Alfred Métraux under the title of *Religions et magies indiennes d'Amérique du Sud* (Paris, Gallimard, 1967) includes papers on shamanism in the Guiana, Amazonia, Gran Chaco and Araucania, besides others on rites of the Tupinanba of Brazil, the Bolivian Uros, etc. See also by the same author: *La Religion des Tupinanba et ses rapports avec celle des autres tribus Tupi-Guarani,* Bibliothèque de l'École des Hautes Études, Sciences religieuses, vol. 45 (Paris, Leroux, 1928); "Le Chamanisme chez les indiens de l'Amérique sudtropicale," *Acta Americana,* vol. II, 197–219, 320–41 (Mexico, 1944); and his survey of "Religion and Shamanism" in *Handbook of South American Indians,* ed. by Julian H. Steward, Bulletin 143, Bureau of American Ethnology, vol. V, *The Comparative Ethnography of South American Indians,* 559–99 (Washington, D.C., Smithsonian Institution, 1949). The classic study on Animism in Guiana is Walter E. Roth's *An Inquiry into Animism and Folklore of the Guiana Indians,* contained in the 30th Annual Report of the Bureau of American Ethnology (Washington, D.C., Smithsonian Institution, 1915). Nature spirits are also studied by Rafael Karsten in *The Civilization of the South American Indians* (N.Y., Knopf, 1926) and in his posthumous book: *Studies in the Religion of the South American Indians East of the Andes,* ed. by Arne Runeberg and Michael Webster (Helsinki, Societas Scientiarum Fennica, 1964). The fundamental study of the subject is Otto Zerries' *Wild- und Buschgeister in Südamerika* (Wiesbaden, Franz Steiner, 1954). Additional references by Zerries in "Wildbeuter und Jägertum in Südamerika—Ein Überblick," *Paideuma,* VIII, 2, 98–114 (Wiesbaden, 1962). On the High Gods see: Mircea Eliade, "South American High Gods" in *History of Religions,* VIII, 338–54, and X, 234–66 (Chicago, 1969 and 1971).

VII. MYTHOLOGY

To *The Mythology of All Races,* edited by Louis Herbert Gray and J. A. MacCulloch, Hartley Burr Alexander contributed vol. XI: *Latin America* (N.Y., Cooper Square, rep. 1964). Myths are here mostly retold, including short quotations from the sources. The bibliography is good up to 1920, the date of the first edition. The best general anthology of Latin American Indian myths is in Raffaele Pettazzoni's *Miti e Legende,* vol. IV, *America Centrale e Meridionale* (Torino, Unione Tipografico-Editrice Torinese, 1959). Texts retold by chroniclers and historians or collected and translated by modern anthropologists have been retranslated save a few cases of materials originally in Italian. On South American mythology the pioneer study of Paul Ehrenreich, *Die Mythen und Legenden der südamerikanischen Urvölker und ihre Beziehungen zu denen Nordamerikas und der alten Welt, Zeitschrift für Ethnologie,* vol. 37, Supplement (Berlin, 1905) is still suggestive. Robert Lehmann-Nitsche contributed a large number of articles under the general title of *Mitología sudamericana, Revista del Museo de La Plata,* from vol. 24, 28–62 (La Plata, 1918) to vol. I (n.s.) 27–33 (1937). See also his *Studien zur südamerikanischen Mythologie, die ätiologische Motive* (Hamburg, Friederichsen, de Gruyter, 1939). Among the shorter, well illustrated mythologies published by Paul Hamlyn, two deal with Latin America: Irene Nicholson, *Mexican and Central American Mythology* (London, 1967) and Harold Osborne, *South American Mythology* (Feltham, 1968).

SOME BIBLIOGRAPHIES

Baldus, Herbert, *Bibliografía Crítica da Etnologia Brasileiia* (São Paulo, 1954; Neudeln/Liechtenstein, Kraus Reprint, 1968–70, 2 vols.)

Bernal, Ignacio, *Bibliografía de Arqueología y Etnografía. Mesoamerica y Norte de México, 1514–1960.* (México, Instituto Nacional de Antropología e Historia, 1962).

Catálogos de la Biblioteca Nacional de Antropología e Historia [of Mexico] (Boston, G. K. Hall, 1972) 10 vols.

Steward, Julian H., ed., *Handbook of South American Indians* (N.Y., Cooper Square Publishers, repr. 1963, Bureau of American Ethnology, Bulletin 43) 7 vols.

IV

The Religions of China

(excepting Buddhism)

W. A. C. H. Dobson

The study of Chinese religion in any systematic and scholarly sense is in its infancy. Much of what has been written in the West in the past has been from the hands of Christian apologists. It is rarely objective and often ill-informed. I have, in the following pages, suggested readings and sources which the student might find helpful in beginning a study of Chinese religion. Much of the basic source material, however, remains as yet untranslated.

I. INTRODUCTION: RELIGION AND RELIGIONS IN CHINA

What we call "religions" the Chinese call *chiao,* "teachings" or, more precisely, "disciplines." Confronted with proselytizing religions from outside of the Chinese tradition—for example, Buddhism (*Fo-chiao*), Islam (*Hui-hui-chiao*), or Christianity (*Chi-tu-chiao* or *T'ien-chu-chiao*)—the Chinese have apposed, as their own indigenous counterparts, Confucianism (*Ju-chiao*) and Taoism (*Tao-chiao*).[1] In this sense, therefore, we may speak of Confucianism and Taoism as religions of China.

But to confine inquiry to the religious aspects of Confucianism and Taoism is to ignore many expressions of Chinese religious thought and feeling, whether of a "higher" or of a "lower" kind, which do not specifically relate to either of these two philosophical systems. There are, or have been, religious elements present in many facets of family and social organization, in the cults and practices of economic and other groups, in political theory and action at almost all levels from local to national government. The multiplicity and variety of temples and shrines in every city and village across the land and the presence in countless households of the domestic gods and their altars provide tangible evidence of those elements.[2]

When Buddhism came to China in the beginning of the Christian era, it brought with it the notion of religion as a formally organized institution. Taoism, in a riposte to Buddhism, evolved similar institutions, acquiring, as Buddhism already possessed, a priestly order and a hierarchy, temples and monasteries, and a sacred canon. But Confucianism, too, as the philosophy of a dominant governing class, became institutionalized in official rites and ceremonies and in the imperial sacrifices and, in aspects such as these, served as part of the apparatus of government. Confucianism became the state cult. But both Confucianism and Taoism in their origins were simply philosophical systems followed by "schools" and individuals and were neither institutionalized nor particularly "religious."

The study of Chinese religion, by Western scholars at least, has been colored in the past by attempts to find parallels in Chinese experience for Western religious history; such as, for example, social or political dominance by a religious doctrine, struggles between church and state or wars between states in the cause of religion, and theological disputations in which doctrinal boundaries are sharply defined. When closely comparable aspects were not found, the conclusion was rashly drawn that the Chinese were not "religious." Such studies came at a time when Chinese thought was, as it were, joining the mainstream of world thought, with its drift toward secularization. This accounts, in part at least, for the comparative thinness of modern literature in Western languages on Chinese religion written from a systematic and scientific viewpoint.

1. See, for example, P. A. Cohen, "The Anti-Christian Tradition in China," *Journal of Asian Studies,* XX, 2 (1961), 169–80.
2. The reader might like to compare W. E. Soothill, *The Three Religions of China* (Oxford, H. Milford, 1923)—a Western missionary's view of Chinese religions, with C. K. Yang, *Religion in Chinese Society* (Berkeley, Univ. of California Press, 1961) —a study of Chinese religion as actually encountered in contemporary Chinese society.

As a general introduction, see W. A. C. H. Dobson, "Religion in China," in Geoffrey Parrinder, ed., *Man and his Gods: Encyclopedia of the World's Religions* (Feltham, Hamlyn, 1973); Laurence G. Thompson, *Chinese Religion: An Introduction* (Belmont, Cal., Dickenson, 1969); and D. Howard Smith, *Chinese Religions* (N.Y., Holt, Rinehart and Winston, 1968). C. K. Yang's *Religion in Chinese Society* (Berkeley, Univ. of California Press, 1961) gives an excellent account of indigenous religion as it functions in Chinese society; E. R. and K. Hughes, *Religion in China* (London, N.Y., Hutchinson's Univ. Library, 1950), provides a brief history of religions both Chinese and foreign in China; and Y. C. Yang, *China's Religious Heritage* (Nashville, Abingdon-Cokesbury, 1943) is a study of Confucianism, Buddhism, Taoism, and Christianity from a Chinese Christian's viewpoint. For a more detailed bibliography, see under "Religion," chap. 13, T'ung-li Yüan, *China in Western Literature* (New Haven, Yale Univ. Press, 1958).

II. AUGURY AND SACRIFICE, 14TH–7TH CENTURIES B.C.

In the prephilosophic age—the period of augury and sacrifice—the "old religion"—untouched by refinements of certain of its features by the philosophers and unchallenged by religious influence from beyond China—held full sway.

A. The world of divination
(Shang dynasty, 16th–11th centuries B.C.)

Chinese recorded history begins with the Shang dynasty. Its records are the Oracle Bones discovered at the end of the nineteenth century and, since then, our principal source for the history of the Shang. The Oracle Bones, of which some hundred thousand have been recovered, are requests engraved on bone and shell made to the spirits for guidance. They are thus essentially religious in nature. The diviner interpreted the response as either "auspicious" or "inauspicious." From our reading of these inscriptions, we gain a picture of a society regulated in almost every aspect of life by divination and governed by considerations of good or bad luck. The "powers" consulted in divination were the spirits of the deceased kings, the *Ti*; but from requests made about the propriety of making sacrifices and performing rites, we know that, in addition to the spirits of the dead, the spirits of the hills, the streams, and other nature gods were worshipped. So, too, were the ancestors. From traces that still remain in the forms of certain graphs in the Shang writing system, and from the iconography of its ritual vessels, we know that a phallic element was present in such worship. Guidance was sought from the ancestors not only for conduct, but also for ensuring the fertility of man, his crops, and his beasts. Religion in the Shang dynasty is discussed by H. G. Creel in *The Birth of China* (London, Jonathan Cape, 1936). See also B. Karlgren, "Some Ritual Objects of Prehistoric China" in *Museum of Far Eastern Antiquities,* 14 (1942), 65–69.

B. The Ancient religion

Animism (the worship of the nature dieties), fertility rites and cults, and particularly ancestor worship not only are features of the earliest recorded Chinese religious practices, but are recurring elements in a variety of different forms of the "popular religion" of subsequent times.

C. The royal religion
(Western Chou, 11th–8th centuries B.C.)

The Shang dynasty was superseded by that of the Chou in 1027 B.C. From this period have survived some archival documents and inscriptions on bronze sacrificial vessels which tell us something of the religion of the Chinese Court and its kings. The royal religion was concerned with the cult of the royal ancestors, the "former kings." Over these deified kings, the supreme ancestor, *Shang-ti,* "God most high," presided. Kingship was thought to be invested by Heaven. Heaven gave its "charge"—the Mandate of Heaven—to one appointed to be its son. The Son of Heaven (*T'ien-tzŭ*) in turn enfeoffed his vassals with "charges," which were engraved on bronze ritual vessels and used in the worship of ancestors. The priest-king, Heaven's deputy upon earth, served his royal ancestors with sacrifice, engaged in ceremonial plowing and fishing to ensure the fertility of the earth, and sought to conserve his "virtue" (his *mana*), by means of which human society and the natural world were kept in accord. Since the whole of society, and of the state, was a projection of the extended family, the king was thus priest and paterfamilias of all mankind. His title to kingship lay in the ritual acceptability of the king to Heaven. If he lost "virtue," he surrendered his "mandate" to govern.

The *Book of Documents,* which includes "charges" of the kings of Western Chou, has been translated by J. Legge, *The Chinese Classics* (Oxford, 1893, rep. Hong Kong, Hong Kong Univ. Press. 1960), vol. 3, *The Classic of History,* but Legge includes a number of spurious chapters. B. Karlgren, *Glosses on the Book of Documents* (Stockholm, Östasiatiska Samlingarna, 1951), has translated those chapters thought to date from the pre-Han period. The "five charges" of the early Chou kings are translated in W. A. C. H. Dobson, *Early Archaic Chinese* (Toronto, Univ. of Toronto Press, 1962), where a selection of inscriptions, some of which describe religious ceremonials, are also translated.

In an appendix to *Early Archaic Chinese,* the palace and temple of the kings of Early Chou is described, together with an account of the religious rituals which took place there. The earliest section of the *Book of Songs* (the *Chou Sung*) contains the liturgy of these rituals. The *Book of Songs* has been translated by J. Legge, *The Chinese Classics* (Oxford, 1893; rep. Hong Kong, Hong Kong Univ. Press, 1960), see vol. 4, *The She King;* by A. Waley, *The Book of Songs* (London, George Allen and Unwin, 1937 and 1954; N.Y., Grove Press, 1960); and by B. Karlgren, *The Book of Odes* (Stockholm, Museum of Far Eastern Antiquities, 1950). In *Festivals and Songs of Ancient China,* (N.Y., E. P. Dutton, 1932), M. Granet connects the later poems in the *Book of Songs* with the fertility rites performed in spring and autumn when the country folk gathered, much as they do in certain parts of southeast Asia today.

D. Aristocratic religion
(Eastern Chou, 8th–3rd centuries B.C.)

The kings of Western Chou gradually declined in power and influence after the shift of the capital to the east in 771 B.C. With their decline came the rise of the city-states. Originally the feudatories of the royal house, the city-state rulers gradually asserted their independence and, with growing independence, increasingly arrogated to themselves "kingly privileges." Among these were the priestly functions of the ancient kings, such as presiding over the "altars of the soil and crops" and maintaining the ancestral cults in the family shrines, which became the symbols of sovereignty in the city-states. Most feudal lords attached their ancestry to the cult heroes of the past. Hou-chi, the Lord of Millet, was the putative ancestor of the Chi clan; Yü the Great, the hero of the primeval flood, was the putative ancestor of the Szu. Since these heroes were thought of as divinities, aristocratic tenure had religious sanction. The princes of the city-states, through their possession of the local altars and their right to serve the divinities of fertility, together with their access to the "mana" of the divine ancestors, asserted political domination over their subjects.

Studies which treat religion at this period in some detail are H. Maspero, "La Religion chinoise dans son développement historique" in *Les Religions chinoises* (Paris, Civilisations du Sud, S.A.E.P., 1950); *La Chine antique* (Paris, Imprimerie nationale, 1955), and M. Granet, *La Religion des chinois* (Paris, Gauthier-Villars, 1922).

E. Shamanism in the South (Eastern Chou)

The gods of the hills, the rivers, and the stars which figured little in kingly or aristocratic worship in West and North China, assumed an influential place in the South, particularly in the powerful city-state of Ch'u. The shamans *(wu)* who could draw down these spirits or recall the spirits of the sick and dead by dancing and incantation had a more important role there than in the North. It is likely that, through their exorcism, fortune telling, and services for the sick and dead, the shamans were the witch doctors of the popular religion everywhere, but we know more about the southern shamans, because the *Nine Songs,* a shaman's liturgy, is included in the *Songs of the South* which have survived.

See A. Waley, *The Nine Songs: A Study of Shamanism in Ancient China* (London, George Allen & Unwin, 1955), and D. Hawkes, *Ch'u Tz'u; The Songs of the South* (Oxford, UNESCO, 1959).

III. THE AGE OF PHILOSOPHY, 6TH–3RD CENTURIES B.C.

With the ritualists at the Courts of the city-states, and the shamans in the countryside, Chinese religion at the period when Chinese philosophies began to take shape had largely to do with the propitiation of ancestors, the worship of spirits, the ensuring of fertility, and the magic rites attendant upon birth, death, and marriage. It was almost totally concerned with the manipulation of powers, with engaging the sympathy of the powerful dead, with ensuring good luck. It had no ethical or moral content.

These elements of primitive religion were incorporated, changed, and elevated into ethical and moral systems by the philosophers. At some time prior to the rise of the philosophers, there arose a sense of moral conscience, a concern with right and wrong, with justice and with humanity. With the passing of the premoral stage, much of primitive religion was transferred into the elements of higher religions.

Philosophy, as distinct from customary lore, began with Confucius (551–479 B.C.). From the sixth century onward, other and rival teachers arose. They were characterized, together with their followers, as the "Hundred Schools." Beginning as teachers to the sons of the city–state aristocracy, these philosophers traveled from Court to Court, attempting to persuade the princes of the virtues of their systems, and seeking preferment in state government. Thus rival systems were evolved, aired, attracted adherents, and, in the process, elevated much in the religious sphere from the "primitive" to a higher order. Of these systems those of the Confucians and of the Taoists have historically been the most influential.

For a general introduction to Chinese philosophy, Fung Yu-lan, *History of Chinese Philosophy,* tr. by Derk Bodde (Princeton, Princeton Univ. Press, 1952), is standard. E. R. Hughes, *Chinese Philosophy in Classical Times* (London, J. M. Dent, 1942), is a handy companion to Fung. A very useful selection of readings will be found in W. T. De Bary, ed., *Sources of Chinese Tradition* (N.Y., Columbia Univ. Press, 1960), and in Wing-tsit Chan, *A Source Book in Chinese Philosophy* (Princeton, Princeton Univ.

Press, 1963). For further reading, consult Wing-tsit Chan, *An Outline and an Annotated Bibliography of Chinese Philosophy* (New Haven, Yale Univ. Press, 1969). Charles E. Moore, ed., *The Chinese Mind* (Honolulu, East-West Center Press, 1969) is a collection of general essays by contemporary authorities in the field, and F. W. Mote, *Intellectual Foundations of China* (N.Y., Knopf, 1971) is a stimulating essay.

A. Early Confucianism

Confucius was born in 551 B.C. in the city-state of Lu and died in 479 B.C. He was a tutor to the sons of the aristocracy. He taught the "wisdom of the ancients," taking as his texts the *Book of Documents* and the *Book of Songs,* which describe mainly, though not exclusively, life under Western Chou. This period, and in particular its founder-kings Wen and Wu and the regent, the Duke of Chou, provide for Confucius a golden age and model kings. He protested that he had "transmitted what was taught to me without making up anything of my own" (*Analects* 7.1). In reality, by using these documents as "scriptures," and by interpreting their already archaic language in a contemparary sense, he created from them the design for a model kingdom. *Te,* the magical force, the *mana* of antiquity, became "virtue" in an ethical and moral sense. *Yi,* a word for custom, became "justice." *Li,* originally simply a "rite," became a code for gentlemantly behavior. *Wang,* a king, became a king in more than name, and the prince (*chün-tzŭ*), the model gentleman of the Confucian ideal. Here kings governed by virtue, exemplified justice and humanity, and gathered their subjects into one large and harmonious family, whose conduct was regulated by *Li.* Confucius withdrew attention from the spirit world, directing it toward man in society. Thus the duty to serve ancestors through sacrifice became a duty to "serve them while they are still living." *Hsiao,* "filial piety," became, not so much the duty to a dead father, but the service to parents during their lifetime. And thus was born the system of familial obligations and duties, the "five relationships," that characterize Confucian teaching. Kingship, then, becomes model parenthood, and the sovereign acts as the "father and mother" of his people. Citizenship is conceived as an extension of familial duty. There is a sense in which the genius of Confucianism consisted in converting society from the domination of magic to the supremacy of morals. In the religious sphere the propitiation of ancestors became reverence for ancestors and was extended to reverence for parents, and to a rigid set of obligations among members of the family. Heaven became the God of all mankind, and not simply *Shang-ti*—the supreme ancestor of a kingly caste.

Mencius (*c.* 360–280 B.C.)—the most important of Confucius' successors—lived nearly a century and a half later. Important developments had occurred in the teaching of the School. For Mencius the world of myth, of founder-heroes and of sages, was secularized. These figures were constructed into a secular "history." Antiquity extended further back in time, and so did Mencius' golden age. It was the times of *"Yao"* and *"Shun."* In this more ample utopia, Confucianism became more secular still. "Any man might become a *Yao* or a *Shun.*" The Gods and demigods of shaman lore became exemplary human figures who personified the moral ideals of justice and humanity—the key tenets of Confucianism. Mencius was the first Confucian to speculate on man's nature. He said that man is born innately good and that it is only through external pressure, through evil environment, that he becomes bad.

Confucius' teaching is contained in the *Analects.* An excellent translation with an admirable introduction is that of A. Waley, *The Analects of Confucius* (London, Macmillan, 1938). A critical biography of Confucius will be found in H. G. Creel, *Confucius, The Man and the Myth* (N.Y., John Day, 1949), rep. as a Harper Torchbook under the title *Confucius and the Chinese Way* (N.Y., 1960); see also Shigeki Kaizuka, *Confucius* (London, George Allen & Unwin, 1956), tr. by G. Bownas. The works of Mencius are translated by W. A. C. H. Dobson in *Mencius* (Toronto, Univ. of Toronto Press, 1963). Both the *Analects* and *Mencius* have been translated, together with a Chinese text, by J. Legge in *The Chinese Classics* (*op. cit.*).

B. Hedonism and Utilitarianism (4th–3rd centuries B.C.)

Mencius stated that the prevailing philosophies of his time were the teachings of Yang Chu the Hedonist and of Mo Ti the Utilitarian. No Hedonist work has survived, and Yang Chu's philosophy must be recovered from the cautionary references his rivals made to it. *The Garden of Pleasure,* usually ascribed to him, is thought by most scholars to be a later work. Yang Chu's principal tenet, according to Mencius, was *wei ngo,* "I act in my own interests." While Confucianism was concerned with man as a social being, with his interrelationships and duties to society, Yang Chu was concerned with man as an individual. In fourth-century China great social upheavals were taking place. The city-state posed problems of an economic, political, and social kind for which the "old religion" was quite inadequate. In this turmoil was born the Hedonistic philosophy that sought, in an uncertain world, for the preservation of the integrity of the individual person.

Mo Ti or Micius (*c.* 486–390 B.C.) was born a century before Mencius. He argued that the sum total of human experience attests to the existence of a deity with a purpose and a will. That will and purpose are conceived in love and compassion, and order is the ultimate manifestation of the divine compassion. Since all men have the ear of Heaven, it follows that all are equal in the eyes of Heaven. Heaven rains upon the just and the unjust. Heaven manifests its love upon all regardless of person. Micius therefore argued that all men should love each other equally and without discrimination. Mencius sums up Micius' teaching in the phrase "Love all equally." To Mo Ti antiquity and its precedents were irrelevant. He sought to create an ideal society by beginning anew in the pure light of reason. He argued on the grounds of *li*, "utility." The criterion for what was right and wrong lay in the interests of the greatest number.

Neither Hedonism nor Utilitarianism survived the collapse of the city-states and the establishment of the Empire at the end of the third century B.C. But with the eclectic spirit that characterizes Chinese thought, something of their genius has contributed to the making of the Chinese ethos.

For Mo Ti (i.e., Motse, Mo Tzŭ, Micius), see Y. P. Mei, tr., *The Ethical and Political Works of Motse* (London, Arthur Probsthain, 1929) and *Motse, The Neglected Rival of Confucius* (London, Arthur Probsthain, 1934); B. Watson, *Mo Tzu: Basic Writings* (N.Y., Columbia Univ. Press, 1963); W. A. C. H. Dobson, "Micius," in Douglas Grant, ed., *The Far East: China and Japan* (Toronto, Univ. of Toronto Press, 1961), 299–310; and Hu Shih, *The Development of the Logical Method in Ancient China* (Shanghai, Oriental Book Co., 1922). For Yang Chu, see A. Forke, tr., *Yang Chu's Garden of Pleasure* (London, John Murray, 1912) and the comments thereon in A. C. Graham, *The Book of Lieh-tzŭ* (London, John Murray, 1960).

C. Mysticism (Philosophical Taoism, 4th–3rd centuries B.C.)

There is a close parallel between the images of the flight of the soul in trance used by the shamans of the south and the descriptions of the trance state in the Taoists' philosophical classic *Chuang Tzŭ*. The early mystics were concerned with the problem of knowledge. True knowledge, they insisted, is of the transcendental kind, the mystical knowledge known only to the adept in trance. In trance, one sees the universe as a unity, and indeed becomes identified with the One. Philosophical Taoism might be thought of as the elevation of the shamans' techniques and experiences to the level of metaphysics. To the adept in trance, all is so of itself. And this "so of itselfness" is *Tao*. Man finds his ultimate purpose in according with *Tao*, in refraining from "interfering" with the course of nature, and by rejecting such man-made artifices as moral systems and laws. The three main texts of philosophical Taoism are *Chuang Tzŭ*, the *Tao Te Ching*, and *Lieh Tzŭ*.

The best introduction to philosophical Taoism is contained in the introduction of A. Waley to *The Way and Its Power*, a study of the *Tao Te Ching* (London, George Allen & Unwin, 1934), and in *Three Ways of Thought in Ancient China* (London, George Allen & Unwin, 1939), in which Chuang Tzŭ, Mencius, and the Realists are contrasted. The *Tao Te Ching* has also been translated by J. J. L. Duyvendak, *Tao Te Ching, Lao Tzŭ* (London, John Murray, 1954), and by Wing-tsit Chan, *The Way of Lao-tzu* (Indianapolis, Bobbs-Merrill, 1963). The *Chuang Tzŭ* is translated in H. A. Giles, *Chuang Tzŭ, Mystic, Moralist and Social Reformer* (Shanghai, Kelly & Walsh, 1926); seven chapters only, but preferable to Giles', are translated by Yu-lan Fung in *Chuang Tzŭ, A New Selected Translation with an Exposition of the Philosophy of Kuo Hsiang* (Shanghai, Commercial Press, 1931). A modern translation is that of B. Watson, *The Complete Works of Chuang tzu* (N.Y., Columbia Univ. Press, 1968). *Lieh Tzŭ* has been translated by A. C. Graham, *The Book of Lieh-tzŭ* (London, John Murray, 1960).

D. Late classical Confucianism
(3rd–2nd centuries B.C.)

Hsün Tzŭ (*c.* 298–238 B.C.), who forms with Confucius and Mencius a trinity of classical Confucian philosophers, carries Confucian doctrine further towards naturalism. "Heaven" becomes, for Hsün Tzŭ, "nature." Hsün Tzŭ, in contrast to Mencius, argues that man's nature is evil.

For their influence in medieval Confucianism, the *Classic of Filial Piety* (*Hsiao-ching*), the *Doctrine of the Mean* (*Chung-yung*), and the *Great Learning (Ta Hsüeh)*—which postdate Hsün Tzŭ—are important Confucian treatises. H. H. Dubs, *Hsüntze . . . the Moulder of Ancient Confucianism* (London, Arthur Probsthain, 1927) is a study of Hsün Tzŭ's philosophy, and *The Works of Hsüntze,* by the same author (London, Arthur Probsthain, 1928), is a translation of Hsün Tzŭ's *Works.* A more recent work is B. Watson, *Hsün Tzu: Basic Writings* (N.Y., Columbia Univ. Press, 1963). *The Doctrine of the Mean* and the *Great Learning* have been translated by E. R. Hughes, *The Great Learning and the Mean-in-Action* (London, J. M. Dent, 1942).

Works on ritual and divination which were incorporated into the Confucian canon and which, because of the commentaries they accrued, are important in later philosophical development are the *Li Chi, Chou Li* and *Yi Li,* and the *Yi Ching.* See J. Legge, *The Lî Kî* (i.e., the *Li Chi;* The Book of Rites) in *Sacred Books of the East,* vols. XXVII and XXVIII (Oxford, 1885); E. Biot, *Le Tcheou-li ou rites des Tcheou* (i.e., the *Chou Li;* Rites of Chou) (Paris, Imprimerie nationale, 1851); J. Steele, *The I-Li or Book of Etiquette and Ceremonial,* 2 vols. (London, Arthur Probsthain, 1917); J. Legge, *The Yî King* (i.e., the *Yi Ching* or *Book of Changes*), *Sacred Books of the East,* vol. XVI (Oxford, 1889). See also H. Wilhelm, *Change: Eight Lectures on the I Ching* (N.Y., Harper and Row, 1960).

The *Analects, Mencius,* the *Doctrine of the Mean,* and the *Great Learning* form the "Four Books" of medieval Confucianism.

E. Other late classical philosophies

Confucianism, Taoism, and Mohism (from Mo Ti), the most important of the classical philosophies, emerge from a wide variety of schools, schisms, and intellectual movements that characterize the Philosophical Age. Collectively, these philosophies were known to later history as the "Hundred Schools." Certain of them are important in a study of Chinese religion.

Because of the contributions of the Logicians and Sophists to epistemology, of the Legalists to law, and of the Yin-Yang School to cosmological speculation, each has relevance to some aspects of religious thought. They are treated in the general histories of Chinese philosophy mentioned above. More detailed studies will be found in the bibliography of Wing-tsit Chan, *op. cit.* The Legalist classic has been translated by J. J. L. Duyvendak, *The Book of Lord Shang* (London, Arthur Probsthain, 1928). B. Watson has translated in part the works of the Legalist theorist, Han Fei Tzu in *Han Fei Tzu: Basic Writings* (N.Y., Columbia Univ. Press, 1964).

IV. RELIGION UNDER THE EMPIRE

With the unification of the city-states under the Ch'in dynasty (221–207 B.C.) and with the Han Empire (202 B.C.–A.D. 220), which succeeded Ch'in, the "Hundred Schools," which had flourished freely and with great individuality in the city-states, were replaced by an official state orthodoxy—Confucianism. After the introduction of Buddhism in the first century A.D., with its temples and religious orders, there also arose an indigenous movement with parallel institutions, claiming to find its inspiration in the writings of Taoist authors. This was religious Taoism.

A. Confucianism—the State Cult

Under the Han Empire, Confucianism came under the patronage of the Court, and in the hands of its devotees became the dominant philosophy in education. Through the selective civil service examination system, Confucianism became the philosophy of the bureaucracy. Confucian rituals were observed at Court. It became, as it were, the state cult and, as such, continued throughout much of Chinese imperial history. Confucian rituals provided the forms under which the emperors carried out their sacerdotal duties. This aspect of Confucianism is treated in J. K. Shryock, *The Origin and Development of the State Cult of Confucius* (N.Y., Century, 1932).

Apart from the cultic aspects of Confucianism as it affected Court ritual, the imperial sacrifices, and the like, Confucianism itself was subjected to progressive reinterpretations and reformulations. Under the Han—Confucianism in the hands of its apologists, and under attack from rival philosophies—a Confucianism that was characteristic of the period evolved. After the fall of Han, until the end of T'ang, Confucianism, though orthodox, was, in the hands of scholars, a sort of "classicism." Buddhism and Taoism played the major religious roles. With the Sung dynasty (A.D. 960–1279) came the Confucian revival; neo-Confucianism (a very different philosophy from the Classic and Han forms of Confucianism) became dominant and largely replaced Buddhism and Taoism.

B. Religious Taoism

With the breakdown of national unity and stability at the end of Han, a period of near chaos ensued (*c.* A.D. 220–589). Confucianism as imperial cult and as the orthodoxy of a highly organized bureaucracy lost much of its hold at this time. In this looser and freer soil, two religions were planted and flourished. The first, Buddhism, introduced from India in the first century A.D., is dealt with in Chapter 6 in this book. The second was religious Taoism.

Religious Taoism owes its beginnings to attempts in the first century B.C. to syncretize the classical philosophical Taoist teachings of the *Tao Te Ching* and *Chuang Tzŭ*, under the title *Huang-lao* (from Huang "yellow" in Huang-ti, "The Yellow Emperor" and *Lao*, in "Lao Tzŭ," the putative author of the *Tao Te Ching*—its cult heroes). The Huang-lao movement had a large popular following. In the second century A.D., the movement was exploited by one who set himself up as "Heavenly Teacher"—a religious title and office held hereditarily by his descendants. The Taoist "papacy" has continued into recent times. The Taoist "church" developed a canon of scriptures (the *Tao-tsang*), temples, and a priesthood—institutions paralleling those of the Buddhist church. Religious Taoism at brief periods enjoyed imperial patronage as the state religion, notably in the fifth and sixth centuries A.D., but after T'ang (A.D. 618–906) it survived largely as the religion of the masses. See H. Maspero, "Le Taoïsme" in his *Mélanges posthumes sur les religions et l'histoire de la Chine* (Paris, Civilisations du Sud, S.A.E.P., 1950); H. S. Levy, "Yellow Turban Religion and Rebellion at the end of Han," *Journal of the American Oriental Society*, LXXVI (1956), 214–27; H. Maspero, "Les procédés de 'nourrir le principe vital' dans la religion taoïste ancienne," *Journal Asiatique* (1937), 117–430; Chung-yüan Chang, *Creativity and Taoism* (N.Y., Julian Press, 1963); H. Welch, *The Parting of the Way; Lao Tzu and the Taoist Movement* (Boston, Beacon Press, 1957), and M. Kaltenmark, *Lao Tzu and Taoism* (Stanford, Stanford Univ. Press, 1969).

C. Myth and legend

The tendency in classical philosophical writing to reduce the rich and imaginative world of myth and legend to the sober proportions of secular and human history did not extinguish the hold of myth upon the popular imagination. Rather, myth began to proliferate after the classical period, and in Han and subsequent times appeared in literature and art in its unsecular mythological form. Or perhaps one should say "forms," for the "creation" myth, the myth of the separation of "heaven and earth," the "sun" myths, and the "flood" legend, in the complicated cosmogony of popular myth occur in a variety of forms, converge and diverge and become enriched and elaborated with elements from very disparate sources. One of the problems of scholarship is to sort this rich lore by cycle, period, and locale. The extent to which we should be justified in regarding myth as religious belief is a difficult question. As its elements occur in the iconography of temples and tombs, as its figures become objects of worship in popular cults and practices, we are presumably justified in regarding such myth as the "theology" of popular religion. But as these elements occur in the works of poets, much as the gods of Mount Olympus occur in the severely Christian Milton, or as myths are satirized in fiction (as in Wu Ch'êng-ên's *Monkey* translated by A. Waley [London, George Allen & Unwin, 1942]), they perhaps constitute a fantasy world in which the imagination has freer play and provide for the poet and writer a world of symbols divorced from the consequences of belief.

For ancient Chinese myths, W. Eberhard, *Lokalkulturen im alten China* (Leiden, E. J. Brill, 1942) should be compared with B. Karlgren, "Legends and Cults in Ancient China," *Bulletin of the Museum of Far Eastern Antiquities,* 18 (1946), 199–365, and with H. Maspero, "Légendes mythologiques dans le *Chou-king*," *Journal Asiatique* (1924), 1–100. General compendia of mythology are those of J. C. Ferguson, "Chinese Mythology," in J. A. MacCulloch, ed., *The Mythology of All Races* (Boston, Marshall Jones, 1930); E. T. C. Werner, *A Dictionary of Chinese Mythology* (Shanghai, Kelly & Walsh, 1932); and H. Maspero, "Mythology of Modern China," in P. L. Couchoud, ed., *Asiatic Mythology* (London, George C. Harrap, 1932), 252–384; and A. Christie, *Chinese Mythology* (London, Hamlyn, 1968). The above should, however, be read in conjunction with a recent study. D. Bodde, "Myths of Ancient China," in S. N. Kramer, ed., *Mythologies of the Ancient World* (N.Y., Doubleday, 1961). See also D. Hawkes, "The Supernatural in Chinese Poetry" in D. Grant, ed., *The Far East: China and Japan* (Toronto, Univ. of Toronto Press, 1961).

D. Neo-Taoism
(3rd–4th centuries A.D.)

The writings of classical philosophical Taoism, adopted, adapted, and augmented by the Taoist "church" provided scriptures and a canon for religious Taoism. But a revival of interest in the classical Taoist writings

themselves gave rise in the third and fourth centuries to a new philosophical movement known as neo-Taoism, which, among other things,
attempted a reinterpretation of Confucian texts in Taoist terms and in-
jected into philosophical Taoism itself certain social and political concepts
of Confucianism, alien to its earlier beliefs.

See D. Holzman, *La Vie et la pensée de Hi Kang* (Leiden, E. J. Brill,
1957); J. R. Ware, tr., *Alchemy, Medicine and Religion in the China of
A.D. 300* (Cambridge, M.I.T. Press, 1967), a translation of the esoteric
chapters of the *Pao-Pu Tzu;* with which compare E. Feifel, "Pao-p'u-tzu
Nei-p'ien" (Monumenta Serica, vol. 6, 1941; vol. 9, 1944; vol. 11, 1946).
See also the general histories of philosophy.

E. Neo-Confucianism
(11th–12th centuries A.D.)

From the end of Han (A.D. 200) to the beginning of Sung (A.D. 960),
Buddhism and Taoism dominated religious and much of intellectual life in
China. At times Buddhism and Taoism enjoyed imperial patronage,
threatening Confucianism as the state cult. With the rise of Sung, however,
Confucianism in a new formulation (neo-Confucianism), regained its intellectual supremacy. Part of the energies of the neo-Confucian movement
derived from its opposition to Buddhism and its determination to find, in
the Confucian classics, a philosophy and faith that would replace Buddhism.

The principal figure in the new movement was Chu Hsi (1130–1200),
who succeeded in synthesizing the new orthodoxy from the works of such
Confucians as Chou Tun-yi (1017–73); Ch'eng Yi (1033–1107); Ch'eng
Hao (1032–85), and Shao Yung (1011–67); Lu Hsiang-shan (1139–92),
a contemporary of Chu Hsi, apposed to Chu Hsi's rationalism an idealist
wing of Confucianism. This was developed later in Ming times by Wang
Yang-ming (1472–1529). For a synoptic view of neo-Confucianism, the
general histories of Fung Yu-lan, etc., should be consulted, together with
Carsun Chang, *The Development of Neo-Confucian Thought* (N.Y.,
Twayne Publishers, 1957) and by the same author, *Wang Yang-ming,
Idealist Philosopher of 16th Century China* (N.Y., St. John's Univ. Press,
1962). See also L. V. L. Cady, *The Philosophy of Lu Hsiang-shan,* 2 vols.
(N.Y., Union Theological Seminary, 1939), and for selected readings in
neo-Confucianism, chaps. 18–21 of De Bary, ed., *Sources of Chinese Tra-
dition* (N.Y., Columbia Univ. Press, 1960). Particular studies of neo-Con-
fucians are A. C. Graham, *Two Chinese Philosophers* (Toronto, Clarke,
Irwin, 1958) (i.e. Ch'eng Yi and Ch'eng Hûo); J. P. Bruce, *Chu Hsi and
His Masters* (London, Arthur Probsthain, 1923) and *The Philosophy of
Human Nature* (London, Arthur Probsthain, 1922); Wing-tsit Chan, trans.,
Reflections on Things at Hand; the Neo-Confucian Anthology (N.Y.,
Columbia Univ. Press, 1967) (a complete translation of the *Chin-ssu-lu of*

Chu Hsi, et al.); idem, *Instructions for Practical Living and other Neo-Confucian Writings by Wang Yang-ming* (N.Y., Columbia Univ. Press, 1963); and Siu-chi Huang, *Lu Hsiang-shan . . . a Twelfth Century Chinese Idealist Philosopher* (Philadelphia, American Oriental Series, vol. 27, 1944). See also W. Theodore de Bary, *Self and Society in Ming Thought* (N.Y., Columbia Univ. Press, 1970).

The extent to which Confucianism (whether in its classic form or in the progressive reinterpretations and reformulations of Confucianism which occurred in the history of the empire) influenced the religious attitudes and beliefs of the bureaucracy and the gentry is hard to define. Some studies, very miscellaneous in character (from the point of view of the reader interested in the religious aspects of Confucianism), which *en passant* may throw some light on this aspect are A. F. Wright, ed., *The Confucian Persuasion* (Stanford, Stanford Univ. Press, 1960); D. S. Nivison and A. F. Wright, eds., *Confucianism in Action* (Stanford, Stanford Univ. Press, 1959); A. F. Wright, ed., *Studies in Chinese Thought* (Chicago, Univ. of Chicago Press, 1953); J. K. Fairbank, ed., *Chinese Thought and Institutions* (Chicago, Univ. of Chicago Press, 1957); and A. F. Wright and D. Twitchett, eds., *Confucian Personalities* (Stanford, Stanford Univ. Press, 1962). A study of state Confucianism in its twilight is J. R. Levenson, *Confucian China and Modern Fate* (Berkeley, Univ. of California Press, 1958).

F. Religion in recent times

An emphasis on Confucianism and Taoism, in their more philosophical formulations and as they have influenced the educated official classes, has resulted in virtual neglect of studies of the influence of Confucianism and Taoism on popular religious movements and of the popular religions themselves. "Popular Religions and Secret Societies," chap. XXII of De Bary, ed., *Sources of Chinese Tradition* (N.Y., Columbia Univ. Press, 1960), treats this briefly. See also J. S. Burgess, *The Guilds of Peking* (N.Y., Columbia Univ. Press, 1928); W. Eberhard, *Chinese Festivals* (N.Y., Henry Schuman, 1952); C. K. Yang, *Religion in Chinese Society* (Berkeley, Univ. of California Press, 1961); Wing-tsit Chan, *Religious Trends in Modern China* (N.Y., Columbia Univ. Press, 1953). Popular religion in contemporary times is referred to in Hsiao-t'ung Fei, *Peasant Life in China* (London, George Routledge & Sons, 1939); S. D. Gamble, *Ting Hsien: A North China Rural Community* (N.Y., Institute of Pacific Relations, 1954); and F. L. K. Hsu, *Under the Ancestor's Shadow* (N.Y., Columbia Univ. Press, 1948). See too M. Freedman, "Ancestor Worship: Two Faces of the China Case," in *Social Organization: Essays presented to Raymond Firth* (Chicago, Aldine, 1967), and David C. Graham, *Folk Religion in Southwest China* (Washington, D.C., Smithsonian Institution,

1961). In Sung times, popular religious beliefs are described in J. Gernet, tr. by H. M. Wright, *Daily Life in China, on the Eve of the Mongol Invasion, 1250–1276* (London, George Allen & Unwin, 1962).

V. RELIGION IN CHINA SINCE 1949

Works which treat of the government's attitude to, and policy toward, religion in the People's Republic are: Donald E. MacInnis, *Religious Policy and Practice in Communist China* (N.Y., Macmillan, 1972); Richard C. Bush, *Religion in Communist China* (Nashville, Abingdon, 1970); and the *Source Book of Buddhism in Mainland China,* compiled and published by the Union Research Institute, Hong Kong, 1969. Holmes Welch, *Buddhism under Mao* (Cambridge, Harvard Univ. Press, 1972), is authoritative and also contains material on religion as a whole. The part played by tradition in present day China is dealt with by Albert Feuerwerker, ed., *History in Communist China* (Cambridge, Mass., M.I.T. Press, 1969), of which the following chapters are particularly noteworthy: Joseph R. Levenson, "The Place of Confucius in Communist China," 56–73; Hellmut Wilhelm, "The Reappraisal of Neo-Confucianism," 140–57; and Donald J. Munro, "Chinese Communist Treatment of the Thinkers of the Hundred Schools Period."

V

Hinduism

Norvin J. Hein

I. INTRODUCTIONS

T he early reading of books intended to be the first word rather than the last word is wise procedure for one who enters into the study of a tradition as ancient and as complex as Hinduism. If lasting confusion is not to kill his interest, he must develop, fairly quickly, a working understanding of the fundamental ideas, personalities, institutions, and chronological and sectarian developments that alone can enable him to organize Hinduism's boundless lore. For this reason the first titles to be named will help to establish these basic identifications in sizeable areas of the Hindu tradition.

Among the current religions of Asia Hinduism is unique, I believe, in often using English as a language of original expression, both in addressing the outer world and in its own internal communications. Therefore there is a fortunate array of English materials available on matters of major importance in Hinduism, and on the essentials of Hinduism as a whole. Satischandra Chatterjee, *The Fundamentals of Hinduism* (the author, 1950; Calcutta, Univ. of Calcutta, 1970) is a good introduction to the basic Hindu doctrinal teachings. It assumes the supremacy of Advaita Vedanta beliefs, but recognizes and respects the positions of other schools of Hinduism. The simple personal overview of another such neo-Vedantist is available in D.S. Sarma's *What Is Hinduism?* (Mylapore, Madras, Madras Law Journal Press, 3rd rev. ed., 1945). T.M.P. Mahadevan in his *Outlines of Hinduism* (Bombay, Chetana, 1956) provides a helpful catalogue of the principal scriptures, rituals, cults, and leaders of traditional Hinduism as well as of its central ideas. The Hindu presentation of Hinduism as a whole is carried out in greater detail in Kenneth Morgan, ed., *The Religion of the Hindus* (N.Y., Ronald Press, 1953), in which Hindu scholars of high standing explain in general terms the beliefs and practices related to their special fields. The last chapter, an anthology of Hindu scriptures, was produced by such radical selection and elision that it reflects poorly the historical peculiarities of the ages and documents on which it draws, but it does provide valuable insight into what is esteemed and actually used today. A unified view of a different sort is found in Jean Herbert's *Spiritualité hindoue* (Paris, Éditions Albin Michel, 1947), which scans Hinduism as an actuality of present observation, in fair detail and with much sympathy.

The writing of historical introductions is another kind of effort, in which western scholars have been involved more prominently. Thomas J. Hopkins, *The Hindu Religious Tradition* (Encino, Cal., Dickenson, 1971) is a thoughtful tracing of the chronological development of the religion, with creative interpretations that make the book much more than a primer of its subject. Robert C. Zaehner's *Hinduism* (Oxford Univ. Press, 1962, 1966) covers the same historical field, stressing the characteristics of selected major periods and historical traditions rather than the lines of development between them. Sir M. Monier Williams' old *Brahmanism and Hinduism* (London, J. Murray, 4th ed., 1891) is still a useful guide to the panorama of traditional Hinduism, and Frederick Harold Smith's *Outline of Hinduism* (London, Epworth Press, 1934) provides helpful identifications and general information about the major forms of Hinduism and their literatures. Still unavailable in English, but in a class by itself, is Jan Gonda's mature treatment of the whole of Hinduism in *Die Religionen Indiens,* vols. I and II (Stuttgart, W. Kohlhammer, 1960, 1963)—the most complete and dependable single work on the whole of Hinduism that is available today.

A. Collections of Hindu literature in translation

Even the best compilations of this kind use translations that are not the latest and finest. Of the anthologies of Hindu sacred writings that are readily available, Ainslee T. Embree's *The Hindu Tradition* (N.Y., Modern Library, 1966) will probably give most continuous satisfaction to readers whose interest is focused on religion. The editor interprets his selections more fully and effectively than does Louis Renou, ed., in his *Hinduism* (N.Y., George Braziller, 1961). Renou's lean and scanty introductions are of some importance, however, as the offhand pronouncements of a great authority on early India.

There are two good general anthologies of Indological material that deserve mention because they give some attention to Hindu religion. *Source Book in Indian Philosophy* (Princeton, Princeton Univ. Press, 1957), ed. by S. Radhakrishnan and Charles A. Moore, stresses the thought of the orthodox philosophical systems and is useful on philosophical aspects of Hindu thought. Here as everywhere, Radhakrishnan's historical interpretations are influenced by his sense of the responsibility to provide constructive guidance for modern Hindus. William Theodore de Bary et al., eds., *Sources of Indian Tradition* (N.Y., Columbia Univ. Press, 1958) includes striking selections from Hindu scriptures with excellent introductions, but it has been compiled for use in general survey courses in Indian civilization rather than in Indian religion specifically. Its selections from Hindu religious literature are too few, too fragmentary, and too rigidly structured to be the sole source of such materials in a major study of Hinduism.

There have been two great continuing efforts to make the most important Hindu scriptures available in English as unabridged documents: the *Sacred Books of the East,* ed. F. Max Müller, 50 vols. (Oxford, Clarendon Press, 1879–1910; Delhi, Motilal Banarsidass, 1959ff.), and *The Sacred Books of the Hindus,* 32 vols. (Allahabad, The Panini Office, 1909–37), of which a reprinting has also been begun. In *S.B.E.* and *S.B.H.* together, about thirty extensive religious writings have been translated and published as wholes. Many of these will be mentioned in the pages below.

B. General reference works

For general reference on all aspects of Hindu thought and practice, the *Encyclopedia of Religion and Ethics,* ed. James Hastings (N.Y., Charles Scribner's Sons, 1908–27, 1955), has not been replaced. George Benjamin Walker's *Hindu World* (N.Y., Frederick C. Praeger; London, George Allen & Unwin, 2 vols., 1968) is not a balanced work in its interests, judgments, or selection of sources, but as a reference work for mature people, it should not be ignored. John Nicol Farquhar's old *Outline of the Religious Literature of India* (London, Oxford Univ. Press; Delhi, Motilal Banarsidass, rep. 1967) has no successor as a guide to authors and documents and can still be used as a provisional encyclopedia of Hinduism. *Myths of the Hindus & Buddhists* by Ananda K. Coomaraswamy and the Sister Nivedita (London, George C. Harrap, 1913; N.Y., Dover Publications, 1967) is a pleasant primer of its particular subject. John Dowson's old *A Classical Dictionary of Hindu Mythology and Religion, Geography, History, and Literature* (London, Kegan Paul, Trench, Trübner, 1878; New Delhi, Oriental Books Reprint Corp., 1973) continues to be useful. *The Cultural Heritage of India,* 2nd rev. ed., Haridas Bhattacharya, ed.

(Calcutta, Ramakrishna Mission Institute of Culture, 1953–58), is a convenient summation of modern Hindu scholarship on the whole of Hinduism. K.A. Nilakanta Sastri gives us a valuable outline of a regional line of development in his *Development of Religion in South India* (Bombay, Orient Longmans, 1963).

To locate Hindu scriptures relating to a particular topic, one may use Moriz Winternitz, *A Concise Dictionary of Eastern Religion* (Oxford, Clarendon Press, 1925; Delhi, Motilal Banarsidass, 1966), which is an index to the many volumes of *S.B.E.* For locating translations as well as texts of rare works in American libraries, there continues to be some usefulness in Murray B. Emeneau's *A Union List of Printed Indic Texts* (New Haven, American Oriental Society, 1935).

II. PREHISTORIC RELIGION

The archeological work of the past fifty years points toward deep indigenous roots of the Hindu tradition that are still poorly known. Frank Raymond Allchin in his unusual *Neolithic Cattle-keepers of South India* (Cambridge, Univ. Press, 1963) and in *The Birth of Indian Civilization* (Harmondsworth, Penguin Books, 1968), written with his wife Bridget, finds evidence in the Deccan of very early religious practices, some of which survive in historic Hinduism. We are now sure that massive contributions to the Hindu tradition were made by the advanced civilization that occupied the Indus Valley in the second and third millennia B.C., even though those contributions cannot be demonstrated with certainty until the ideas and institutions of that early culture are much better known. Sir Mortimer Wheeler, *The Indus Civilization* (The Cambridge History of India, Supplementary Volume, 1953) and Ernest Mackay, *Early Indus Civilizations,* 2nd rev. ed. (London, Luzac, 1948), sketch this culture with some attention to evidences of its religion. These two surveys are convenient summarizations of the bulky original reports of the archeologists: Sir John Marshall, ed., *Mohenjo-Daro and the Indus Civilization,* 3 vols. (London, Arthur Probsthain, 1931), the official account of the excavations of 1922–27; Ernest J.H. Mackay, *Further Excavations at Mohenjo-daro,* 2 vols. (Delhi, Government of India, 1938), on the field work of 1927–31. Madho Sarup Vats, *Excavations at Harappā,* 2 vols. (Delhi, Government of India, 1940; Varanasi, 1974) on the work of the years 1920–21 and 1933–34; and Ernest J. H. Mackay, *Excavations at Chanhu-daro* (New Haven, American Oriental Society, 1943) also present details. Occasional later advances in knowledge have been reported in Stuart Piggott, *Prehistoric India to 1000 B.C.* (Harmondsworth, Penguin Books, 1952) and in Sir Mortimer Wheeler's chapter, "Ancient India" in Stuart Piggott, ed., *The Dawn of Civilization* (N.Y., McGraw-Hill, 1961). S.R. Rao,

Lothal and the Indus Civilization (Bombay and N.Y., Asia Publishing House, 1973) reports on the excavation of a major seaport of the culture in Gujarat and offers interpretations of its language and religion that will be of major importance if sustained.

Speculative work in the interpretation of Indus Valley religion has been continuous and intense since the appearance of Sir John Marshall's original report. These inconclusive efforts may be followed through the "Vedic" bibliographies of Renou and Dandekar mentioned in the following section. There is adequate reason for believing that the later Hindu cult of Śiva, the worship of female deities, and cultic concern with animals, trees and water derive from the Indus civilization. Important aspects of Hindu thought and practice must stem from this culture also, despite the inability of artifacts to reveal their presence there. Until the writing of the culture is deciphered and its seals are interpreted in the light of their inscriptions, it will not be possible to say anything with certainty that has not already been said by Sir John Marshall (*op. cit.,* I, 48–78) in his chapter, "Religion." Even regarding the firmest of our present suppositions, Herbert Sullivan makes a severe but necessary call for restraint in "A Re-examination of the Religion of the Indus Civilization," *History of Religions* 4 (1964), 115–25.

III. VEDIC RELIGION

Since the religion of the Indus Valley people remains largely unknown, substantial historical material on Hinduism begins with their successors, the Āryas, and their earliest literature, the Vedas and Brāhmaṇas.

Ignorance of French and German is a more serious handicap in approaching the Vedas than at any other point in the study of Hinduism. A century of intensive Vedic study in the West has been conducted in the form of a trilingual interchange, and the student who lacks even one of these languages must often use materials that are less than the best. Existing English translations of the Ṛigveda, for instance, fall seriously short of the best scholarly insight now available. For instructional purposes, A.A. Macdonell's annotated anthology, *Hymns from the Rigveda* (Calcutta, Association Press, 1922) is satisfactory. The selection translated in *S.B.E.* XXXII and XLVI is highly specialized and now antiquated. The only complete translation in English, Ralph T. H. Griffith, *The Hymns of the Rigveda,* 2 vols. (Varanasi, E.J. Lazarus, 1920–36; Chowkhamba Sanskrit Series Office, 1967), is unsatisfactory both because of its age and because is rests onesidedly on the interpretation of the medieval Hindu commentator Sāyaṇa. Hari Damodar Velankar has translated only the seventh book into English, *Ṛgveda Maṇḍala VII* (Bombay, Bharatiya Vidya Bhavan, 1963), and the ninth book is available in a translation by Shrikrishna Sakharam Bhawe, *The Soma-hymns of the Rgveda,* 3 vols. (Baroda, M.S. Univ. of Baroda Research Series, 1957–62). Those who work seriously in the Rigveda, however, must use the German translation of Karl Geldner, *Der Rigveda* (Harvard Oriental Series XXXIII–XXXVI, 1951–57), which sums up the insight of western Vedic scholarship until the year 1923, and the French translations in Louis Renou's *Études vediques et paninéens,* 17 vols. (Paris, E. de Boccard, 1955–67), which incorporate the improvements of an additional lifetime of scholarship. Renou's translation of any particular hymn can be found quickly with the aid of an index published by W. Rau in *Orientalistische Literaturzeitung* LXIV (1969), 72–83. The indices to Geldner's volumes are a minor Vedic research tool in themselves.

The shortcomings of Griffith's Rigveda translations characterize also his *The Hymns of the Samaveda* (Varanasi, E.J. Lazarus, 1893; Chowkhamba Sanskrit Series Office, 1963) and his *The Texts of the White Yajurveda* (Varanasi, E.J. Lazarus, 1899) and *The Hymns of the Atharvaveda,* 2 vols. (Varanasi, E.J. Lazarus, 1895–96; Chowkhamba Sanskrit Series Office, 1968). Arthur Berriedale Keith has translated *The Veda of the Black Yajus School Entitled the Taittiriya Sanhita* (Harvard Oriental Series XVIII, XIX, 1914). The Atharva-veda has been partially translated by Maurice Bloomfield, *Hymns of the Atharva-veda (S.B.E.* XLII, 1897; Delhi, Motilal Banarsidass, 1964), and more fully by William Dwight Whitney with extreme literalness and extensive critical notes, in *Atharva-veda Samhitā,* ed. C.R. Lanman (Harvard Oriental Series VII, VIII, 1905). Bloomfield followed his translations from the Atharvaveda with a secondary study, *The Atharva-veda and the Gopatha-Brahmana* (Strassburg, *Grundriss der indo-arischen Philologie und Altertumskunde,* II, 1, B, 1899).

The most acceptable books for beginning study of Vedic religion within the narrow options of English materials are Maurice Bloomfield, *The Religion of the Veda* (N.Y., G.P. Putnam's Sons, 1908; Ann Arbor, Univ. Microfilms, 1965; Varanasi, Indological Book House, 1972), and Arthur Berriedale Keith, *The Religion and Philosophy of the Veda and Upanishads* (Harvard Oriental Series XXXI, XXXII, 1925). Bloomfield's book is a clear personal exposition, judicious for its time. Keith's larger work is valuable for its comprehensive coverage and for its thorough survey and its conservative criticism of the views of earlier scholars. The most highly regarded book, however, is Hermann Oldenberg, *Die Religion des Veda,* 2nd ed. (Stuttgart–Berlin, Cotta, 1917).

All scholarship agrees that the best evidence on the nature of Vedic religion is provided by the internal materials of the Vedas themselves. But this internal evidence leaves many fundamental questions unsettled. In their searches for greater certainty, scholars have separated themselves into schools in two matters of approach, especially. They divide, first, on where to look for external material that will illuminate Vedic ideas and practices. Some have seen the Vedas as the religious literature of an Indo-European people only recently settled in India, and in interpreting the Vedas they have made extensive use of comparative philology and comparative mythology. Others have seen more significance in the fact that the Vedas are Indian scriptures, and have interpreted them with the help of Indian commentators and study of continuities with later Indian culture. Both groups are chastened now by fuller awareness of the great gaps of time that separate Vedic religion from all its parallels and successors.

The second dividing issue has been the reaction of scholars to an early and persistent interpretive hypothesis: that the Vedas can be understood as part of an attempt to conceptualize, and to establish relations with, the conspicuous forces of nature. Professor F. Max Müller of Oxford initiated this lasting debate by setting forth the theory of nature worship in an extreme form more than a century ago. It should be understood that Bloomfield, Keith, and Macdonell stand in this naturistic tradition, adhering to it in a more restrained and disciplined version. The reaction against overuse of the naturistic key has been carried on by Abel Bergaigne, Hermann Oldenberg, Alfred Hillebrandt, Georges Dumézil and others. The myths of the Vedas have been seen as originating in efforts to explain and reinforce established rituals; as records of the struggles of ethnic groups or of human heroes raised euhemeristically to the rank of gods; as representations of the interaction of personified abstractions of good and evil or light and darkness; as reflections of the functions and interests of the divisions of a tripartite Indo-European class structure; as symbolic expressions of monistic metaphysical teaching; and as part of a priestly white magic based upon the perception of esoteric correspondences among elements of the ritual and of the cosmos. Not much of this debate has been conducted in English. Accounts of the interchanges are available in Louis Renou, *Religion of Ancient India* (London, Athlone Press, 1953; N.Y., Schocken Books, 1968), and in R.N. Dandekar's initial chapter in *Progress of Indic Studies 1917–1942,* ed. by himself (Poona, Bhandarkar Oriental Research Institute, 1942). Renou's terse manual, *Vedic India,* tr. Philip Spratt (Calcutta, Susil Gupta, 1957) from Renou's *L'Inde classique* (Paris, Payot, 1947), I, 270–380, gives the succinct judgments of this wise scholar on these difficult questions.

The identity of the *soma* of the Vedic sacrifice has become a topic of active discussion again, through the publication by the mycologist Robert Gordon Wasson of *Soma, Divine Mushroom of Immortality* (N.Y., Harcourt Brace & World, 1968). Wasson's identification is being studied with great respect but not with universal acceptance. See John Brough, "Soma and Amanita Muscaria," *Bulletin of the School of Oriental and African Studies* XXXIV (1971), 331–62.

Renou's *The Destiny of the Veda in India* (Delhi, Motilal Banarsidass,

1965), tr. by Dev Raj Chanana from *Études vediques et paninéens,* vol. 6, surveys the manner and degree in which the Vedas were known and used in later Hinduism; and J. Gonda, *Change and Continuity in Indian Religion* (The Hague, Mouton,1965), traces the survival of particular Vedic elements in the transformations of later times. Franklin Edgerton, *Beginnings of Indian Philosophy* (Cambridge, Harvard Univ. Press, 1965) provides material in a well-selected anthology of his own annotated translations for the study of continuity in cosmological ideas in particular.

For general reference on Vedic myths and beliefs, one may use A.A. Macdonell, *Vedic Mythology* (Strassburg, *Grundriss der indo-arischen Philologie und Altertumskunde,* III, 1, A, 1897), supplemented if possible with Alfred Hillebrandt, *Vedische Mythologie,* 2nd rev. ed. (Breslau, M. & H. Marcus, 1927–29). Macdonell and Keith, *Vedic Index of Names and Subjects,* 2 vols. (London, J. Murray, 1912; Delhi, Motilal Banarsidass, 1967), excludes religious matter but is helpful in investigations on the social and literary boundaries of Vedic religion; non-Sanskritists can locate relevant material in it through the indices at the end of the second volume. The ultimate Vedic reference tool for readers of Sanskrit is the *Vaidika-Padānukrama-koṣa, A Vedic Word-Concordance,* ed. Viśva Bandhu Śāstrī, 5 vols. in 16 (Lahore and Hoshiarpur, the Vishveshvarananda Vedic Research Institute, 1942–65), which indexes every form of every word in the Vedas and dependent literature, including the Upanishads.

A mere handful of Brāhmaṇas have so far been translated into English: the Aitareya and Kaushītaki by A.B. Keith, *Rigveda Brahmanas* (Harvard Oriental Series XXV, 1920); The Panñcaviṃśa Brāhmaṇa of the Sāmaveda (called also the Tāṇḍya Mahā-Brāhmaṇa) by W. Caland, *Pancavimśa-brāhmaṇa.* (Calcutta, Bibliotheca Indica CCLV, 1931); and the Śatapatha-Brāhmaṇa of the White Yajurveda by Julius Eggeling, *The Śatapatha-Brāhmaṇa* (*S.B.E.* XII, XXVI, XLI, XLIII, XLIV, 1882–1900; Delhi, Motilal Banarsidass, 1966). Of the Jaiminīya, H.W. Bodewitz has just translated an important ritualistic section, *Jaiminīyabrāhmaṇa I, 1–65* (Leiden, E.J. Brill, 1973).

The speculative *Āraṇyaka* literature, transitional to the Upanishads, is represented in translation in A.B. Keith's edition and English rendering, *The Aitareya Āraṇyaka* (Oxford, Clarendon Press, 1909; Oxford Univ. Press, 1969).

On the interpretation of the religion of the Brāhmaṇas, Govind Vinayak Devasthali has published a series of clear introductory lectures entitled *Religion and Mythology of the Brahmanas* (Univ. of Poona, 1965). Jogiraj Basu brings together in his *India of the Age of the Brāhmaṇas* (Calcutta, Sanskrit Pustak Bhandar, 1969), 137–251, the Brāhmaṇa passages that are most illuminating regarding the sacrificial cult and its associated life and outlook. The standard work on brāhmanical theories regarding the ritual is Sylvain Lévi, *La Doctrine du sacrifice dans les brāhmaṇas* (Paris, Ernest Leroux, 1898).

With the end of the age of the Vedas and Brāhmaṇas we enter, in about the sixth century B.C., into the period of classical Hinduism. The essentials of this great religious culture have persisted down to the present century. During this immense sweep of time, hereditary caste occupation has given Hindu society a distinctive form. At the beginning of this period, the doctrines of karma and rebirth became key concepts in the Hindu view of life, and the old Vedic conceptions of the highest blessedness became subordinated to the hope of release from rebirth. In the first centuries of this age the goals and techniques of religious activity became so profuse and so varied that a unilinear chronological account will no longer describe the developments in Hinduism adequately. Hindu tradition itself divides orthodox Hindu religious life into three streams: the Way of Action (*karma-mārga*), the Way of Mystical Knowledge (*jñāna-mārga*), and the Way of Devotion (*bhakti-mārga*). These divisions are accepted here as a basis for classifying and describing the literature produced between the end of the Vedic period and the beginning of modern times.

IV. THE KARMA–MĀRGA

The literature of the Way of Action will receive first attention because it continues the central Vedic type of religious practice and governs the life of ritual and social duty, which has always had the position of chronological priority in the career of all Hindus. A Hindu may resort in mature years to the path of knowledge or of devotion, but he begins the religious life as a performer of acts required by Hindu tradition. Conformity to the *karma-mārga* is an essential preparation for entry into the finally-effective paths of liberation.

The Way of Action is a functional type only. The actions that it has required have differed from person to person and from age to age. They have always included elements of moral as well as of ritual action, but the degree of emphasis on moral action has varied greatly.

A. The Śrauta rites

In the immediately post-Vedic age, the form of religious observance that came to prominence first in literature was the Vedas' continuing cult of public sacrifice, the basic manuals of which are the Śrauta Sūtras. The few that have been translated into English include W. Caland, *Śāṅkhāyana-Śrautasūtra* (Nagpur, International Academy of Indian Culture, Sarasvati-Vihara Series XXXII, 1953), Chintaman Ganesh Kashikar, *The Śrauta, Paitṛmedha and Pariśeṣa Sūtras of Bharadvāja* (Poona, Vaidika Saṁśodhana Maṇḍala, 1964), and Asko Parpola, *The Śrautasūtras of Lātyāyana and Drāhyāyana and their Commentaries* (Helsinki, Societas Scientiarum Fennica, Commentationes Humanarum Litterarum, vol. 42:2, 1968, and 43:2, 1969). Kashikar describes the entire *sūtra* literature of the Vedic sacrifice in *A Survey of the Śrautasūtras,* published as *Journal of the University of Bombay,* n.s. vol. 35, Part 2 (Sept. 1966), 1–188. The Vaidika Saṃśodhana Maṇḍala's *Śrautakośa,* 2 vols. (Poona, 1958, 1962), translates and arranges the materials of the *Śrauta* texts according to the stages of the ceremonies that they govern.

An impression of the nature of these elaborate rituals can be had from the general descriptions in Pandurang Vaman Kane, *History of Dharmaśāstra* (Poona, Bhandarkar Oriental Research Institute, Government Oriental Series, Class B, No. 6, 1930–62), II:2, 976–1108; from Keith's *The Religion and Philosophy of the Veda and Upanishads* cited above, 252–358; and from Alfred Hillebrandt, *Ritual-Literatur* (Strassburg, *Grundriss der indo-arischen Philologie und Altertumskunde,* III:2, 1897), 97–166.

J. Gonda has written a full study of a rice offering comparable to the soma ritual, in *The Savayajñas* (Amsterdam, Verhandelingen der Koninklijke Nederlandse Akademie van Wetenschappen, n.s. vol. 71:2, 1965). J.A.B. van Buitenen, *The Pravargya* (Poona, Deccan College Postgraduate and Research Institute, 1968) describes in detail this preliminary ritual of the soma sacrifice, and gives in his preface a bibliography of the great monographs on the various *śrauta* rituals. We mention, for the importance of their topics, Johannes Cornelis Heesterman, *The Ancient Indian Royal Consecration* ('s-Gravenhage, Mouton, 1957) and Paul Émile Dumont's two works, *L'Aśvamedha* (Paris, E. Geuthner, 1923) and *L'Agnihotra* (Baltimore, Johns Hopkins Press, 1939).

The refining of rules and the propounding of theory regarding these ancient sacrifices were continued by specialists belonging to the tradition called Karma-mīmāmsā. A.B. Keith, *The Karma-Mīmāmsā* (Calcutta, Association Press, 1921) gives a general introduction to the history and outlook of this school. Reading in the treatises of the karma-mīmāṃsists themselves can begin profitably with Laugākshi Bhaskara, *Arthasaṃgraha* (Varanasi, Benares Sanskrit Series No. 4, 1882; Chowkhamba Amarabharati Prakashan, 1974), which has been translated by G. Thibaut with an excellent sketch of the essentials of the system. A similar work, Āpadeva's *Mīmāṃsānyāya-prakāśa,* has been translated under that title by Franklin Edgerton (New Haven, Yale Univ. Press, 1929). Both of these manuals are works of recent centuries and show a willingness to adjust the theory of sacrifice to the outlook of powerful theistic movements of their age. The fundamental ancient authority of the school, the Pūrva-mīmāṃsā-sūtra, has been translated by Mohan Lal Sandal, *The Mīmāmsā Sūtras of Jaimina* (Allahabad, *S.B.H.* XXVII–XXVIII, 1923–25). A commentary on that work is available in Gangānāth Jhā's translation, the *Śabarabhāṣya,* published in Gaek-wad's Oriental Series, vols. LXVI, LXX, LXXIII and CIII (Baroda, Oriental Institute, 1933–45). Jhā has translated also the *Ślokavārttika* and *Tantravārttika* of Kumārila Bhaṭṭa, an authoritative writer on the school's epistemology and exegetical principles (Calcutta, Bibliotheca Indica CXLVI, 1907, and CLXI, 1924).

B. The Gṛihya rites

The domestic rituals were the second type of religious actions to become the subject of authoritative books. The ceremonies of this class mark the round of life in the Hindu home and solemnize the great transitions in the careers of individual members of the family. The original manuals of such rites are the Gṛihya Sūtras, seven of the most important of which have been translated by Hermann Oldenberg, *The Grihya-sūtras (S.B.E.* XXIX–XXX, 1886, 1892; Delhi, Motilal Banarsidass, 1964). W. Caland has since translated the *Jaiminigṛhyasūtra* (Lahore, Punjab Sanskrit Book Depot, 1922) and the *Vaikhānasasmārtasūtram* (Calcutta, Bibliotheca Indica CCLI, 1929). Raj Bali Pandey in *Hindu Saṁskāras* (Varanasi, Vikrama Publications, 1949; 2nd rev. ed. Delhi, Motilal Banarsidass, 1969) collates the scriptural sources on each of the personal rituals and surveys the historical development of each. Many of these ancient family rites have fallen into disuse, and those that survive have often been modified in the course of rehandling in dharma-śāstras, purāṇas, and tantras. The best full treatment of the domestic ceremonies as now practiced is Mrs. Sinclair (Margaret) Stevenson's description of the sacraments and seasonal rites of the brahmans of Gujarāt in *The Rites of the Twice-Born* (London, Oxford Univ. Press, 1920; New Delhi, Oriental Books Reprint Corp., 1971). Joseph E. Padfield in his delightful *The Hindu at Home* (Madras, SPCK, 2nd rev. ed., 1908) gives a comparable account of the family rituals of Andhra. Representative liturgies for use in the individual's morning and noon *sandhyās* are given in detail in Srisa Chandra Vasu Vidyarnava, *The Daily Practice of the Hindus* (Allahabad, *S.B.H.* XX, 1918). The personal rituals of members of the sect of Rāmānuja are described in detail in K. Rangachari, *The Sri Vaishnava Brahmans* (Madras, Bulletin of the Madras Government Museum, n.s., general section, vol. II:2, 1931), 44–98.

C. Pūjā

By the beginning of the Christian era, the śrauta ceremonies had lost their dominant place in the Hindu approach to the gods. The newer practice was a simpler kind of ritual called *pūjā,* involving the worship of images erected in domestic shrines or public temples. For a general account of this development see Kane's aforementioned *History of Dharmaśāstra,*

II:2, 705–40, 889–916. The rules for making and worshipping images were slow to appear in Sanskrit literature; they have always found a significant part of their expression in obscure sectarian treatises and vernacular manuals. The most accessible sources are the iconographical and liturgical sections of the purāṇas, such as Agni Purāṇa, chaps. 21–104, *Agni Puranam* (tr. and published by M.N. Dutt, Calcutta, 1903, and Varanasi, Chowkhamba Sanskrit Series Office, 1967), vol. I, 91–423; and Matsya Purāṇa, 218–76, *Matsya-Puranam,* tr. S.C. Vasu (Allahabad, *S.B.H.* XVII:2, 1916; Delhi, Oriental Publishers, 1972). The *Paramasaṃhitā* ed. and tr. by S. Krishnaswami Aiyangar, Gaekwad's Oriental Series LXXXVI (Baroda, Oriental Institute, 1940), 20–45, 114–50, gives instructions particularly on the images and worship of Vishṇu. *The Vishṇudharmottara (Part III),* tr. Stella Kramrisch, 2nd rev. ed. (Univ. of Calcutta, 1938), is an inclusive manual on the images of the Hindu deities. The standard modern reference book for the identification of images is still T.A. Gopinatha Rau, *Elements of Hindu Iconography,* 2 vols. (Madras, Law Printing House, 1914–16; Varanasi, Indological Book House, 1971). The history of Hindu image worship is dealt with best by Jitendra Nath Banerjea, *The Development of Hindu Iconography* (Univ. of Calcutta, 2nd ed., 1956). Alice Boner, *Principles of Composition in Hindu Sculpture* (Leiden, E.J. Brill, 1962), makes advances in interpretation of the religious meaning of Vaishṇava and Śaiva images, as well as in the understanding of their design.

The Hindu temple, in which Hindu liturgy and religious sculpture find their grandest present-day expression, has been studied mainly by persons interested in architectural forms or general aesthetics. Frederic H. Gravely, *An Outline of Hindu Temple Architecture* (Madras, Bulletin of the Madras Government Museum, n.s., general section, vol. III:2, 1936) gives a simple analysis of the fundamental structural elements in temples and distinguishes their regional forms. Identification of the important temples of various regions and the collection of information on their customs and lore have been begun in a series of popular books published by the Bharatiya Vidya Bhavan in Bombay: M.S. Mate, *Temples and Legends of Maharashtra* (1962); N. Ramesan, *Temples and Legends of Andhra Pradesh* (1962); R.K. Das, *Temples of Tamilnad* (1964); and P.C. Roy Choudhury, *Temples and Legends of Bihar* (1965).

No one has yet written a full study of the temple as a house of worship. Stella Kramrisch, *The Hindu Temple,* 2 vols. (Univ. of Calcutta, 1946), begins her work by analyzing the symbolism of temples as understood in Hindu architectural literature of *advaita* outlook. A similar exploration of Tantric meanings has been carried out among the temples of eastern India by Alice Boner and Sadāśiva Rath Śarmā, trs., *Śilpaprakāśa: Medieval Orissan Sanskrit Text on Temple Architecture by Rāmacandra Kaulācāra* (Leiden, E.J. Brill, 1966). On the construction, history and ritual of a famous temple of Sūrya, Boner and Śarmā, again, have recovered and published information of rare authenticity in their *New Light on the Sun Temple of Konārka* (Varanasi, Chowkhamba Sanskrit Series Office, 1972). Various theories regarding the religious meaning of temple architecture are reviewed briefly by G.E. Monod-Herzen in "Evolution and Significance of the Hindu Temple," *Asia,* III (1953–54), 246–59. A.K. Coomaraswamy sets forth the view of one kind of worshipper in "The Indian Temple," *Śilpi,* II:3 (October, 1941), 83–90.

Detailed accounts of ceremonies performed in temples are scarce. T. Goudriaan, *Kāśyapa's Book of Wisdom (Kāśyapa-jñāna-kāndaḥ) A Ritual Handbook of the Vaikhānasas* (The Hague, Mouton, 1965) deals with Vaikhānasa temple rituals as well as with the building of temples. The acts and liturgies of the worship of Vishṇu in South Indian temples is Goudriaan's subject again in "Vaikhānasa Daily Worship according to the Handbooks of Atri, Bhṛgu, Kāśyapa, and Marīci," *Indo-Iranian Journal* XII (1970), 161–215. James Burgess, "The Ritual of Rameçvaram," *Indian Antiquary,* XII (1883), 315–26, describes the acts and words used in the six daily *pūjās* of a great Śaiva temple. Some information on such rites is found in Mrs. Stevenson's *Rites of the Twice-Born* and in Rangachari's *Sri Vaishnava Brahmans,* mentioned above. Carl Gustav Diehl, *Instrument and Purpose* (Lund, C.W.K. Gleerup, 1956) is an encyclopedic compendium and analysis of Tamil rituals, including the routine and special rites of South Indian temples.

The social and economic framework of the ritual activities of a famous temple is described by Nirmal Kumar Bose in the chapter, "Organization of the Services in the Temple of Liṅgarāj, Bhubaneswar," in his *Culture and Society in India* (Bombay, Asia Publishing House, 1967), 105–68.

D. Non-brahmanical rites

Yet another level of ritual is found in rural Indian life and is commonly described in works on "popular" or "village" Hinduism. The photographer of its shrines is Curt Maury in his *Folk Origins of Indian Art* (N.Y., Columbia Univ. Press, 1969). The ceremonies of its godlings are animistic in their theology, subliterary in their liturgies, and low-caste in their officiants. The purpose of the rites is neither liberation nor the creation of merit, but the practical goals of aversive magic, often in the interest of an entire village community. It can be denied that village practices are part of Hinduism, or even of religion, but since they are usually considered to be religious and because they are indigenous and peculiar to the country, we shall look at the literature. For South India, where these practices were particularly well established until recently, we have Henry Whitehead, *The Village Gods of South India,* 2nd rev. ed. (Calcutta, Association Press, 1921), and Wilber T. Elmore, *Dravidian Gods in Modern Hinduism* (Uni-

versity Studies of the Univ. of Nebraska, XV, No. 1, 1915). James Hor-
nell surveys the subject in "The Ancient Village Gods of South India,"
Antiquity, XVII (1944), 78–88. Notice of the existence of this type of
religion in North India also may be seen in L.S.S. O'Malley, *Popular
Hinduism* (Cambridge Univ. Press, 1935), and in Oscar Lewis, *Village
Life in North India* (Urbana, Univ. of Illinois Press, 1958), which describes the festivals and religious beliefs of a village near Delhi. The
nāgas, objects of cultic attention in the popular religion of every age, have
been studied in the materials of literature and folklore by Jean Philippe
Vogel, *Indian Serpent Lore* (London, Arthur Probsthain, 1926; Delhi,
Indological Book House, 1972). For a survey and criticism of current
anthropological literature in this area, see Louis Dumont and D. Pocock,
Contributions to Indian Sociology, No. III, *Religion* (Paris and the Hague,
Mouton, 1959).

The religions of India's primitive tribes, which relate to the mainstream
of Hinduism mainly at this level of Hindu culture, have been surveyed by
Christoph von Fürer-Haimendorf in *Die Religionen Indiens,* vol. III (Stuttgart, W. Kohlhammer, 1964). They are described in detail by Matthias
Hermanns, *Die Religiös-magische Weltanschauung der Primitivstämme Indiens,* 3 vols. (Wiesbaden, Franz Steiner, 1964, 1966, 1973). Hermanns'
historical theories are often questioned, but not the quality of his great
collection of data.

E. Social duties as religious actions

Behavior conforming to established ethical norms was recognized in
every period of the history of Hinduism as having some degree of significance in religion, but the ritualism of the Vedas and Brahmaṇas gave
social morality a position far from the center of religious life. With the
appearance of *sūtra* literature in the post-Vedic age, this ritualistic im-
balance was rectified by the appearance of the *Dharmasūtras*—treatises on
religious duties inclusive of ethical obligations. Sures Chandra Banerji,
Dharma-Sūtras: A Study of Their Origin and Development (Calcutta,
Punthi Pustak, 1962) provides a manual of this body of literature. Four
Dharmasūtras are translated by Georg Bühler, *The Sacred Laws of the
Āryas* (*S.B.E.* II, XIV, 1879–82; Delhi, Motilal Banarsidass, 1965). The
expansion and modification of the material of such *sūtras* produced the
Dharmaśāstras, which have remained the authoritative literature on Hindu
ethics. The most famous and influential of these is the Mānavadharmaśās-
tra, which has been translated by Bühler as *The Laws of Manu* (*S.B.E.*
XXV, 1886; Delhi, Motilal Banarsidass, 1964). The names and contents
of the many other works on *dharma* may be approached with the guidance
of Kane's monumental *History of Dharmaśāstra* cited above, an encyclopedic reference work on the vast *dharma* literature. The indices of Kane's

volumes can be used to uncover valuable material on almost any aspect of traditional Hindu practice. The most appreciated of all general introductions to these codes and their concepts is Robert Lingat, *The Classical Law of India* (Berkeley, Univ. of California Press, 1973), which was published in French in Paris in 1967 and translated by J. Duncan M. Derrett. Derrett's *Religion, Law and the State in India* (N.Y., Free Press, 1968) gives penetrating attention to the relation between religious norms and civil regulation from the first rise of the *dharma* literature until today.

The *Dharmaśāstras* distinguish between *sādhāraṇa-dharma*—norms applicable to all regardless of age and status—and *varṇāśrama-dharma*—prescriptions which are to be followed by persons of particular social rank (*varṇa*) and stage of life (*āśrama*). The duties of the first class, which are incumbent upon all Hindus, are described in passages which urge such ideal virtues as non-injury, truthfulness, non-stealing, purity, and forbearance. These general ideals receive only brief treatment in the ancient *dharma* literature. In the modern period, however, it is these abstract ideals which are being emphasized and developed, because their relevance is not limited, as in the case of most Hindu ethical literature, to a social structure that is now passing away. Some impression of the non-legalistic ethical material that can be culled from Hindu literature may be had in G.A. Chandavarkar, *A Manual of Hindu Ethics,* 3rd rev. ed. (Poona, Oriental Book Agency, 1925).

The duties of the *āśramas*—of student, householder, forest dweller, and hermit—are set forth in considerable detail in all the *Dharmasūtras* and *Dharmaśāstras.* The pattern of the four *āśramas* is highly theoretical; in practice, only a minority of Hindus has attempted to conform to them even roughly. The fourth or *sannyāsāśrama* lies beyond the limits of the Way of Action and will be discussed under *jñāna-marga,* below.

Regulations regarding the *varṇas* and their subdivisions, the *jātis,* are extremely elaborate both in the *dharma* literature and in the common law of typical rural Hindu communities. To understand the lasting ethical discipline that has shaped the lives of almost all Hindus for 2,500 years, one must study not only the prescriptions of Manu and the like, but also the modern sociological literature on caste and intergroup relations in villages today. G.S. Ghurye, *Caste and Class in India,* 2nd ed. (Bombay, Popular Book Depot, 1957), gives a history of the institution of caste and a clear general description of its lasting characteristics. For a sketch of the castes of a fairly representative modern village, with their duties and dignities, see Morris Opler and Rudra D. Singh, "The Division of Labor in an Indian Village," in Carleton S. Coon, ed., *A Reader in General Anthropology* (N.Y., Henry Holt, 1948), 464–96. William H. Wiser, *The Hindu Jajmani System* (Lucknow, Lucknow Publishing House, 1936, 1969) pioneered in showing the economic and social interactions of the village castes and in revealing the meaning of caste rank in terms of specific economic benefits. Subsequent studies of other village caste communities have shown that the great power of the brahmans in the village described by Wiser is not always found elsewhere, and have pointed out that kshatriyas or even lower castes, where they own much land or predominate in numbers, sometimes reduce the brahmans to a merely formal pre-eminence. But everywhere an hierarchical structure prevails, such as Wiser found. And Louis Dumont, *Homo Hierarchicus* (Paris, Gallimard, 1966; tr. Mark Sainsbury, Univ. of Chicago Press, 1970, 1974) denies the common western assumption that economic and political power determine caste rank, and sees position in the hierarchy as resting on discernments of levels of ritual purity or impurity. At any rate, social studies support the *dharma* literature in revealing the outlines of a strongly ranked society as the lasting background of traditional Hindu thought. The complementary relation between Hindu doctrine and the discriminations of this society cries out for fuller attention in the line of a suggestive study by William Stephens Taylor, "Basic Personality in Orthodox Hindu Culture Patterns," *Journal of Abnormal and Social Psychology* XLII (1948), 3–12, where some of the supportive relations between caste and dogma are identified.

Modern Hindu interpretation of caste ranges from total apologetic in Harendranath Maitra's *Hinduism: The World-Ideal* (N.Y., Dodd, Mead, 1916), 56–73, through S. Radhakrishnan's more moderate idealization in *The Hindu View of Life* (London, George Allen & Unwin, N.Y.; Macmillan, 1927), pp. 61–130, to vehement rejection in K.M. Panikkar, *Caste and Democracy* (London, Hogarth Press, 1933) and in B.R. Ambedkar, *Annihilation of Caste* (Bombay, B.R. Kadrekar, 1937). For an estimate of the continuing significance of caste among Hindus, see M.N. Srinivas, "Caste in Modern India," *Journal of Asian Studies* XVI (1956–57), 529–48.

V. THE WAY OF KNOWLEDGE

In the history of Hinduism the *jñāna-mārga* or Way of Mystical Knowledge, with its distinctive goals and methods, becomes explicit with the appearance of the Upanishads. The cause of the rise of this nonritualistic type of religion has been seen as a kshatriya revolt against brahman leadership, but this analysis has not stood the test of time. Other interpreters of the relation between Vedas and Upanishads have assumed a dynamic process in which decaying ritualistic religion gives way naturally to living religion of internal experience, or in which scattered cosmological speculation matures necessarily into systematic philosophical interpretations of the universe. Franklin Edgerton saw the Upanishads as the revolutionary completion of a search for power through insight into the oneness of things, sought with increasing intensity and self-consciousness as the tensions of a settled life bore down upon post-Vedic India. His writings include "The Philosophic Materials of the Atharva Veda" in *Studies in Honor of Maurice Bloomfield* (New Haven, Yale Univ. Press, 1920), 117–37; "The Upaniṣads: What Do They Seek, and Why?" in *Journal of the American Oriental Society* XLIX (1929), 97–121; and a volume of interpreted translations, *The Beginnings of Indian Philosophy* (Cambridge, Harvard Univ. Press, 1965).

Of the comprehensive English translations of the Upanishads, the most objective is Robert E. Hume, *The Thirteen Principal Upanishads* (Oxford Univ. Press, 2nd rev. ed., London, 1931; Madras, 1949; N.Y., 1971). S. Radhakrishnan, *The Principal Upanishads* (N.Y., Harper & Brothers, 1953), includes the Sanskrit texts, a scholarly translation, fragments of the commentaries of Śankara and others, references to approximately parallel modes of thought of occidental writers, and overall interpretation in terms of his own modern Vedanta doctrine. The center of his interest is not the discussion of puzzling passages but the exposition of clear passages that are important for modern Hindu belief. Swami Nikhilānanda has translated eleven major Upanishads into felicitous English in *The Upanishads,* 4 vols. (N.Y., Harper & Brothers, 1949–59). His translations are tendentious in the sense that they are purposely and openly conformed to the interpretations found in Śankara's commentaries and to the outlook of Advaita Vedanta. J.A.B. van Buitenen, *The Maitrāyaṇiya Upaniṣad* ('s-Gravenhage, Mouton, 1962) subjects a single late Upanishad to a textual analysis of rare thoroughness and translates its strands. Paul Deussen, *Sechzig Upanishad's des Veda* (Leipzig, F.A. Brockhaus, 1897) translates many sectarian and late Upanishads omitted by Hume, whose book includes only the universally-accepted Upanishads that are considered to be part of the Veda.

Paul Deussen, *The Philosophy of the Upanishads* (Edinburgh, T. & T. Clark, 1906; N.Y., Dover Publications, 1966) is a comprehensive well-documented secondary study. It has suffered telling criticism in certain of its historical and metaphysical interpretations, but it remains the most useful survey of the thought-world of these scriptures.

A. The Philosophies of the Jñāna-mārga

Works on Indian philosophy quite properly present the six orthodox *darśanas* in continuous treatment, in the traditional formal order, and with approximately equal attention to each system. But in this essay the various schools will be treated in an order determined by their place in the three *mārgas,* and the emphasis which each receives will be in accord with its importance in Hindu religion. The *Karma-mīmāṃsa,* first in the traditional list, has been discussed in connection with the Way of Action. The Yoga system of thought will be touched on in connection with the religious life of the yogis, below. The theistic varieties of Vedanta will be discussed in connection with various forms of bhakti religion. The others will be dealt with now.

The standard comprehensive works on Hindu philosophy are of prime importance in this realm of reading. The most detailed and authoritative is Surendranath Dasgupta's monumental *A History of Indian Philosophy,* 5 vols. (Cambridge Univ. Press, 1922–55). Out of scruple for preserving the unique character of Indian concepts, Dasgupta preserves the original Sanskrit terms, not converting them into their apparent European approximations. This policy gives his work a rare trustworthiness and, at the same time, makes it almost unassimilable for the beginner. On the other hand, S. Radhakrishnan, *Indian Philosophy,* 2 vols. (N.Y., Macmillan, 1923, 1927), achieves readability for the occidental by adopting western terminology, at the cost of a close relationship to its Indian sources. Radhakrishnan's work of historical interpretation is affected also by his responsibility as a religious leader: as he presents the traditions with which he identifies himself, he reconstructs them for modern use. On the conversion of Indian philosophical vocabulary, an advantageous middle position is taken by M. Hiriyanna, who in his succinct *Outlines of Indian Philosophy* (London, George Allen & Unwin, 1932) and other works combines accuracy with intelligibility as successfully as could be hoped. On an introductory level, S. C. Chatterjee and D. M. Datta, *An Introduction to Indian Philosophy* (Calcutta, Univ. of Calcutta, 1939) covers the systems dependably and with clarity. Radhakrishnan and Moore's *Source Book in Indian Philosophy,* cited above, is the best available philosophical anthology of its kind. Its extensive bibliography (pp. 643–69) offers remedy for our sketchy coverage of systems that are of lesser importance for religion.

Thus, with regard to the Nyāya and Vaiśeshika systems, we shall mention only Arthur Berriedale Keith's historical and doctrinal survey in his *Indian Logic and Atomism* (Oxford, Clarendon Press, 1921), a good first step for the reader who wishes to go beyond the treatment in the general works on Indian philosophy.

B. Sāṃkhya

The concepts of the Sāṃkhya philosophy are so pervasive of wide ranges of Indian thought that the system deserves the attention of all students of Hinduism. Hiriyanna explains this *darśana* with special lucidity in his already-cited *Outlines of Indian Philosophy,* in his *The Essentials of Indian Philosophy* (London, George Allen & Unwin, 1949), and in "The Samkhya System" in *The Cultural Heritage of India* mentioned above, vol. III,

41–52. The rise and development of the school are discussed by A.B. Keith, *The Sāṁkhya System* (Calcutta, Association Press, 1918). Gerald J. Larson, *Classical Samkhya* (Delhi, Motilal Banarsidass, 1969) is a useful guide to advanced study through its critical survey of Sāṃkhya scholarship and its detailed bibliography. For the fundamental text of the system see *The Sāṅkhyakārikā of Īśvara Kṛṣṇa,* tr. S.S. Suryanarayana Sastri, 2nd rev. ed. (Univ. of Madras, 1935).

C. Advaita Vedānta

The nontheistic branch of Vedanta as taught by Śaṅkarācārya and his followers demands full attention because of the dominant position it has achieved in intellectual Hinduism. Eliot Deutsch in his *Advaita Vedānta, A Philosophical Reconstruction* (Honolulu, Univ. Press of Hawaii, 1969) minimizes Indian vocabulary in a summary of Advaita philosophical teaching for untutored occidentals. M.K. Venkatarama Iyer, *Advaita Vedanta according to Samkara* (Bombay, Asia Publishing House, 1964), provides a brief, clear, unwesternized exposition of the system. Eliot Deutsch has compiled a useful teaching aid in his *A Source Book of Advaita Vedanta* (Honolulu, Univ. Press of Hawaii, 1971) which surveys the course of Advaita metaphysical thinking through its major representatives until the present day. However, he ignores the emotional and salvational aspects of the system. Because this disinterest is characteristic of the writings of modern academic philosophers, it is especially important to include in one's reading some original texts of the school, in order to recover the wholeness of the outlook, including its matrix of religious interests.

Śaṅkara's *magnum opus,* his commentary on the Vedānta Sūtras, is available in the translation of George Thibaut, *The Vedānta-Sūtras with the Commentary of Saṅkarākārya* (*S.B.E.* XXXIV, 1890, and XXXVIII, 1896; N.Y., Dover Publications, 1962). The introduction to the first volume provides a general view of Śaṅkara's thought. The continuous reading of the entire work can be a confusing and trying experience because Śaṅkara writes here as a commentator on a text and is not free to develop his own thought systematically. In this situation, Paul Deussen's closely documented *The System of the Vedanta* (Chicago, Open Court, 1912; Delhi, Oriental Publishers, 1972) performs a service in pulling these commentarial fragments together into a topical order. Deussen concludes (pp. 453–78) with a simple resumé that has been published separately, also, as *Outline of the Vedanta System of Philosophy according to Shankara* (N.Y., Grafton Press, 1906).

Agreeable systematic treatments of certain aspects of Advaita Vedānta can be found in several small doctrinal treatises that are attributed to Śaṅkara. A volume of minor works that could reasonably have been written by the master has been published by G.A. Natesan & Co. of Madras under the title, *Select Works of Sri Sankaracharya,* without date. The *Atmabodha* is available as *Self-Knowledge,* tr. Swami Nikhilananda (N.Y., Rama-krishna-Vivekananda Center, 1946). The *Vivekacudāmaṇi* has been rendered freely into English as *Crest-Jewel of Discrimination* by Swami Prabhavananda and Christopher Isherwood (Hollywood, Vedanta Press, 1947), and there is a literal translation of the same by Swami Madhavananda, *Vivekachudamani of Shri Shankaracharya* (Calcutta, Advaita Ashrama, 1921; 6th ed., 1957). The *Upadeśasāhasrī* is available as *A Thousand Teachings,* tr. Swami Jagadananda (Mylapore, Madras, Ramakrishna Math, 1941). Swami Muktananda's translation, *Aparokshanubhuti or Self-Realization* (Calcutta, Advaita Ashrama, 1938), is particularly revealing of the salvational longings and transcendental aspirations of old Advaita as a religious system.

Deeper understanding of Advaita involves life, as well as doctrine, and the study of living exemplars of the outlook. The twentieth-century representative of the faith who is most accessible in literature is Śrī Ramaṇa Mahārshi of Tiruvannamalai. We are able to meet both the mystic and his mystical experience in a natural manner through the experience, outer and inner, that Paul Brunton reports in his travel account, *A Search in Secret India* (N.Y., E.P. Dutton, 1935; Samuel Weiser, 1970). The life of the saint has been told hagiographically, in its own Indian terminology, by B.V. Narasimha Swami, *Self Realization, Life and Teachings of Sri Ramana Maharshi* (Tiruvannamalai, Sri Ramanasramam, 1931, 1968), and, in western terms, by Arthur Osborne, *Ramana Maharshi and the Path of Self-Knowledge* (London, Rider, 1954; N.Y., Samuel Weiser, 1969). Osborne has edited *The Collected Works of Ramana Maharshi* (London, Rider; and Tiruvannamalai, Sri Ramanasramam, 1959). Sri Ramanasramam publishes many books on the saint, his followers and his message, including S.S. Cohen's diary, *Guru Ramana* (1952) and the anonymous *Maha Yoga* (1967) on the Maharshi's meditational methods.

D. Yoga

Mircea Eliade's *Yoga: Immortality and Freedom* (N.Y., Pantheon Books, 1958) is recommended as the most comprehensive and penetrating interpretation of the standard techniques of yoga. Persons without any indological background might begin with advantage, however, with Claude Bragdon, *An Introduction to Yoga* (N.Y., Alfred A. Knopf, 1933), which is a simple, very general preliminary discussion of the objectives and methods of yoga. The eight-stage yoga of Patañjali is laid out by James Houghton Woods in his standard literal translation of that basic work, *Yoga-System of Patanjali* (Harvard Oriental Series, XVII, 1914; Delhi, Motilal Banarsidass, 1966) in which translations of the traditional commentaries are included. Surendranath Dasgupta, *Yoga as Philosophy and*

Religion (London, Kegan Paul, Trench, Trübner, 1924) is a lucid secondary description of the mystical discipline and of the metaphysical ideas with which they were originally associated. The most profound publication to date on the total system of Patañjali is Gaspar M. Koelman, *Pātañjala Yoga: From Related Ego to Absolute Self* (Poona, Papal Athenaeum, 1970).

VI. THE WAY OF DEVOTION

The article "Bhakti-mārga" by Sir George Grierson in *Encyclopedia of Religion and Ethics,* II, 539–51, is a convenient introduction to the special beliefs that are characteristic of devotional Hinduism in its many forms. The historical origins of the monotheistic religions of salvation have not yet been traced out conclusively. The findings that western scholarship regards as certainties are summarized by Sir Charles Eliot, *Hinduism and Buddhism,* 3 vols. (London, Edwin Arnold, 1921; N.Y., Barnes & Noble, 1953), II, 136–261. The proliferation of the cults of Vishnu and Śiva is covered in the secondary survey of Joseph Estlin Carpenter, *Theism in Medieval India* (London, Williams & Norgate, 1921), which goes over the ground of Eliot's work in greater detail. Nicol Macnicol, *Indian Theism from the Vedic to the Muhammadan Period* (London, Humphrey Milford, Oxford Univ. Press, 1915; New Delhi, Munshiram Manoharlal, 1968) deals primarily with the development of the various sorts of theistic doctrine during the vast period indicated. Of some value still is Sir R.G. Bhandarkar's pioneer historical work, *Vaiṣṇavism, Śaivism and Minor Religious Systems* (Strassburg, *Grundriss der indo-arischen Philologie und Altertumskunde,* III, 6, 1913; Varanasi, Indological Book House, 1965).

Much of the surviving literary evidence of early Indian theism has been preserved for us in the epics and *purāṇas*. The foremost of these depositories, and not the possession of any one particular theistic group, is the Mahābhārata. This great epic has now been edited critically, 19 vols. (Poona, Bhandarkar Oriental Research Institute, 1933–36), and a greatly superior translation has already begun to appear: J.A.B. van Buitenen, *The Book of the Beginning* (Univ. of Chicago Press, 1974), with valuable introductory treatment on the nature and history of the text. For some time, however, much use will have to be made of the best of the older translations, Kisari Mohan Ganguli, *The Mahabharata,* 10 vols. (Calcutta, Protap Chandra Roy, 1884–96; 2nd ed., 12 vols., Calcutta, Oriental Publishing Co., c. 1963). A useful sketch of the main plot of the Mahābhārata (and of the Rāmāyaṇa as well) is found in Sir M. Monier Williams, *Indian*

Epic Poetry (London and Edinburgh, Williams & Norgate, 1963). The most extensive critical study in English is E. Washburn Hopkins, *The Great Epic of India* (N.Y., Charles Scribner's Sons, 1901; New Haven, Yale Univ. Press, 1913, 1920; Calcutta, Punthi Pustak, 1969). We owe to Hopkins also an encyclopedic manual of the persons, gods and concepts of the Mahābhārata, *Epic Mythology* (Strassburg, *Grundriss der indoarischen Philologie und Altertumskunde,* III, 1, B, 1915; Varanasi, Indological Book House, 1968).

The editing and translating of the major *purāṇas* is being undertaken by the All India Kashiraj Trust, Fort Ramnagar, Varanasi, which has been publishing the specialized journal, *Purāṇa,* since July, 1959. The scholars of that center have now published *Vāmana Purāṇa* (1968) and *Kurma Purāṇa* (1972) in critical editions with English translations. For several major *purāṇas* we must still rely on uncertain versions of the turn of the century: *The Garūḍa Purāṇam,* tr. M.N. Dutt (Calcutta, Society for Resuscitation of Indian Literature, 1908; Varanasi, Chowkhamba Sanskrit Series Office, 1968); *The Markaṇḍeya Purāṇa,* tr. F. Eden Pargiter (Calcutta, Asiatic Society, Bibliotheca Indica CXXV, 1897, 1904; Delhi, Indological Book House, 1969); and the translations named under the heading "Pūjā" above and under "Krishna Worship" below.

The *bhakti-mārga* is a general type of religion only, without institutional unity. The social groups which produced its complex streams are often little known. In most cases we are able to follow the development of movements or cults only, rather than institutional histories. Outside these imperfectly defined bodies, blurring the historical outlines further, lie great numbers of polytheistic Hindus who worship the deities of these soteriological cults also, but as gods among others in their pantheon, and for ends short of salvation. The clearest lines of division within the bhakti-mārga are those that differentiate the cults of Śiva, on the one hand, and on the other those of the various *avatāras* of Vishṇu, among whom Rāma and Krishṇa are the most prominent. The worshippers of Rāma and of Krishṇa are united in connecting the deity of their worship with the Vedic god Vishṇu, usually through the conception that these gods are *avatāras* or descents of Vishṇu, the Creator and Lord of the universe. J. Gonda compares the two major branches of Hindu theism in *Viṣṇuism and Śivaism, a Comparison* (Univ. of London, Athlone Press, 1970); and in *Notes on the Name and the Names of God in Ancient India* (Amsterdam and London, North Holland Publishing Company, 1970) he describes devotional Hinduism's universal practice of reciting the divine names and traces its history and presuppositions. Again in *Aspects of Early Viṣṇuism* (Utrecht, N.V.A. Oosthoek, 1954) that prolific scholar collects and analyzes the elements in Vedic literature that were to become, in time, important materials for Vaishnava theology.

A. Rāma worship

The worship of Rāma has its earliest literary base in the *Rāmāyaṇa* attributed to Vālmīki. There is now a critical edition of this work, *The Valmiki-Ramayana,* gen. ed. G.H. Bhatt, 7 vols. (Baroda, Oriental Institute, 1961–75), but the principal English translation is old and out of date: Ralph T.H. Griffith, *The Rāmāyaṇa of Vālmīki* (Banaras, E.J. Lazarus, 1895). The medieval Rāma literature is surveyed by Charlotte Vaudeville in her *Étude sur les sources et la composition du Rāmāyaṇa de Tulsī-Dās* (Paris, Librairie d'Amerique et de Orient, 1955). Rāmaism in North India received a great impulse at the end of the sixteenth century A.D. from the appearance of Tulsī Dās' *Rāmcaritmānas,* of which we have two adequate English translations: Frederick S. Growse, *The Rāmāyana of Tulsī Dās* (Allahabad, North-Western Provinces Government Press, 1877; Ram Narain Lal, 7th ed., 1937), and William Douglas P. Hill, *The Holy Lake of the Acts of Rāma* (Indian Branch, Oxford Univ. Press, 1952, 1971). Growse provides pleasanter reading while Hill gives a closer translation based upon a better text. Frank Raymond Allchin has translated Tulsī Dās' *Vinaya Patrikā* as *The Petition to Rām* (London, George Allen and Unwin, 1964), and with the same publisher, his *Kavitāvalī* (1966). The Bengali Ramayana of Krittivāsa has been freely translated by Shudha Mazumdar, *Ramayana* (Calcutta, Orient Longmans, 1958). The cult of Rāma has not produced a systematic theologian, nor have Rāma worshippers usually distinguished themselves sharply from other Hindus by creating separate institutions.

B. Krishna worship

The earliest datable evidences of Krishna worship are laid out by Rama-prasad Chanda, *Archaeology and Vaishnava Tradition* (Calcutta, Memoirs of the Archaeological Survey of India, No. 5, 1920). *The Origin and Development of Vaiṣṇavism* by Suvira Jaiswal (Delhi, Munshiram Mano-harlal, 1967) provides entrance into study of the formative centuries of Vaishnavism and guidance to the scholarly secondary literature. Bimanbe-hari Majumdar, *Krṣṇa in History and Legend* (Univ. of Calcutta, 1969) offers a useful compendium of Krishna mythology with debatable historical analyses.

C. The *Bhagavadgītā*

This immortal poem, produced in about the second century B.C., is the earliest and greatest scripture of the Krishna cult. The irenic efforts of the author to relate his religion positively to older non-bhakti forms of Hinduism have made it possible for non-Vaishnavas to use the *Bhagavadgītā* also, and in their own way. An instance of this external use may be seen in the translation of Swami Prabhavananda and Christopher Isherwood, *The Song of God: Bhagavad-Gita* (N.Y., Mentor Books, 1954). This rendering has great literary charm, but it obscures the Vaishnava character of the book by tendentious interpretation and even interpolation, in the interest of subordinating it to *Advaita* doctrine. For those who must try to study the *Bhagavadgītā* seriously through a translation, we recommend Franklin Edgerton's *The Bhagavad Gītā* (Harvard Oriental Series XXXVIII and XXXIX, 1944)—not mellifluent, yet not excelled in dispassionate judgment and syllable-by-syllable accuracy. A romanized text is included, and the second volume contains a thorough study of the teaching of the *Bhagavadgītā*. One-volume paperback editions, omitting the Sanskrit text, are available in the Harper Torchbook series, and from the Harvard Univ. Press.

Sir Edwin Arnold's translation, *The Song Celestial,* has virtues opposite from those of Edgerton's. Arnold was a Sanskrit scholar, not unmindful of the consideration of accuracy, but his highest aim was to convey the general sentiments of the book in English verse of literary charm. His translation is appropriate for students of literature who are interested in general impressions only. Current editions include that of Routledge & Kegan Paul, London (1961). Several other translations combine good literary quality with good scholarship: Kāshināth Trimbak Telang, *The Bhagavadgītā with the Sanatsugātīya and the Anugītā* (S.B.E. VIII, 1882; Delhi, Motilal Banarsidass, 1965); William Douglas P. Hill, *The Bhagavadgītā* (London, Oxford Univ. Press, 1928, with text; 2nd abridged ed., without text, by Indian Branch, Oxford Univ. Press, 1953); and S. Radhakrishnan, *The Bhagavadgītā* (London, George Allen & Unwin, 1948)—a good translation, with a commentary that is generally useful, but which shifts often from exegesis to homily without notice. Robert C. Zaehner, *The Bhagavadgita* (London, Oxford Univ. Press, 1969) includes the text and good translations, but is to be valued above all for its comprehensive and judicious commentary that collects and considers the best opinions of modern scholarship.

KRISHNA MYTHS   The long-developing mythology of the Krishna cult has its primary ancient record in three great *purāṇas.* The Harivaṃśa, dominantly but not exclusively Vaishnava, is now available in a critical Sanskrit edition by P.L. Vaidya, *Harivaṃśa* (Poona, Bhandarkar Oriental Research Institute, 1969), but the old translation of Manmatha Nāth Dutt, *A Prose English Translation of the Harivamsha* (Calcutta, H.C. Dass, 1897), has not yet been superseded. The Vishnu Purāṇa, translated by Horace Hayman Wilson, is recommended in the edition of Fitzedward Hall, *The Vishnu Purāṇa,* 5 vols. (London, Kegan Paul, Trench, Trübner, 1864–77), but it is most easily available in a recent Calcutta reprint by

Punthi Pustak (1972). The third, the Bhāgavata Purāṇa, has not yet had an adequate complete translation. There is an English version by M.N. Dutt, *A Prose English Translation of Srimadbhagavatam* (Calcutta, 1896), but it is well to consult also the old French translation of Eugène Burnouf and his successors M. Hauvette-Besnault and Alfred Roussel, *Le Bhāgavata Purāna,* 5 vols. (Paris, Imprimerie Royal, 1840–98).

The mythological theme of the Rāsa dance of Kṛishṇa with the milkmaids may be studied with the help of several specialized booklets. Rādhākamal Mukerjee, *The Lord of the Autumn Moons* (Bombay, Asia Publishing House, 1957) collects the relevant texts in a free but fair translation. W.G. Archer brings Hindu artistic traditions to the appreciation of the Bālakṛishṇa tales in *The Loves of Krishna in Indian Painting and Poetry* (London, George Allen & Unwin, 1957). Hanumanprasad Poddar, *Gopi's Love for Sri Krishna* (Gorakhpur, Gita Press, 1941) sets forth the accepted modern theological interpretation of the erotic aspects of these stories. Adelbert Gail has published a penetrating and many-sided study of the devotional religion of the Bhāgavata Purāṇa in his *Bhakti im Bhāgavatapurāṇa* (Wiesbaden, Otto Harrassowitz, 1969).

The Bhāgavata Purāṇa itself, and the religious practices of those who belong to its tradition, come under attention in Milton Singer, ed., *Krishna: Myths, Rites and Attitudes* (Honolulu, East-West Center Press, 1966). The ritual practices of Krishnaites all over India are described in a general way from established literary sources by Rasik Vihari Joshi in *Le Rituel de la devotion kṛṣṇaite* (Pondichéry, Institut Français d'Indologie, Publication 17, 1959).

The literature and theology of several of the less prominent *avatāras* have received intensive study in several recent monographs. Paul Hacker, *Prahlāda, Werden und Wandlungen einer Idealgestalt* (Wiesbaden, F. Steiner, 1959) set the model, which was followed by Gaya Charan Tripath in *Der Ursprung und die Entwicklung der Vāmana-Legende in der indischen Literatur* (Wiesbaden, Otto Harrassowitz, 1968), and by Klaus Rüping in *Amṛtamanthana und Kūrma Avatāra* (Wiesbaden, Otto Harrassowitz, 1970).

THE PĀÑCARĀTRA TRADITION   An entrée into the thought and vast literature of the ancient Vaishnava group known as the Pāñcarātrins is given by F. Otto Schrader's book, *Introduction to the Pāñcarātra and the Ahirbudhnya Saṃhitā* (Madras, Adyar Library, 1916). Two of the basic treatises of the sect have so far been translated: *Parama Saṃhitā,* ed. & tr. S. Krishnaswami Aiyangar (Baroda, Gaekwad's Oriental Series No. 86, 1940); and *Lakṣmī Tantra,* tr. Sanjukta Gupta (Leiden, E.J. Brill, 1972). The latter is a rather atypical work, incorporating many Śākta practices and concepts. The Pāñcarātra tradition in image-making is the subject of H. Daniel Smith''s compilation of Sanskrit texts, *A Sourcebook of Vaiṣṇava*

Iconography (Madras, Pāñcarātra Pariśodhana Pariṣad, 1969), a work whose English introductions make its main points somewhat accessible to non-Sanskritists. A pass-key to all published Pāñcarātra texts has just become available in Smith's *A Descriptive Bibliography of the Printed Texts of the Pāñcarātrāgama* (Baroda, Gaekwad's Oriental Series No. 158, vol. I, 1975), which summarizes, chapter by chapter, the contents of thirty Pāñcarātra manuals.

THE KRISHNAISM OF MAHARĀSHTRA   The poetry of the Kṛishṇa devotees of Western India is introduced by Nicol Macnicol's translations from Marathi verse, *Psalms of the Marāthā Saints* (Calcutta, Association Press, 1920). The complete guide to the development of Kṛishṇa worship as seen in Marathi literature is Ramchandra Dattatreya Ranade, *Mysticism in Maharashtra* (Poona, Aryabhushan Press, 1933), a work that has been republished by the Bharatiya Vidya Bhavan as *Pathway to God in Marathi Literature* (Bombay, 1961). The chief work of Jñāneśvara, the thirteenth-century initiator of this tradition, is available in the translation of V.G. Pradhan, *Jñāneśvarī (Bhāvārthadīpikā): A Song-Sermon on the Bhagavadgītā,* ed. H.M. Lambert, 2 vols. (London, George Allen and Unwin, 1967, 1969). Another work of the founder has been studied and translated by Charlotte Vaudeville in her *Le Haripāth de Dñyāndev* (Paris, École Français d'Extrême Orient, 1969) in which a notable bibliography is included. G.A. Deleury, *The Cult of Vithobā* (Poona, Deccan College Postgraduate and Research Institute, 1960) is the most complete account of the history and practices of the Vārkarī Vaishṇavas whose great shrine is at Pandharpūr. Another major resource for entry into the world of this particular tradition of Kṛishṇa-worship is a series of translations by Justin E. Abbott (with occasional collaborators) called *Poet-Saints of Maharashtra,* published in Poona, mainly by the Scottish Mission Industries. Some of the individual titles are *Bhanudas* (1926); *Eknāth* (1927); *Bhikshugītā* (1929); *Stotramālā* (1929); *Tukārām* (1930); *Rāmdās* (1932); *Stories of Indian Saints,* 2 vols. (1933, 1934); and *Nectar from Indian Saints* (1935).

THE ŚRĪ VAISHṆAVAS   J.S.M. Hooper, *Hymns of the Ālvārs* (Calcutta, Association Press, 1929) translates specimens of a great body of ancient Tamil religious poetry that is claimed by the Śrī Vaishṇavas as a part of their early heritage. The institutional evolution of the various branches of this group is sketched by V. Rangacharya, "Historical Evolution of Śrī-Vaiṣṇavism in South India" in *Cultural Heritage of India,* 2nd ed., IV, 163–85.

Rāmānuja, the first great Vaishṇava theologian, rose among the Śrī Vaishṇavas of South India in the eleventh century. He remains the foundational thinker of this enduring group, and he has influenced the thinkers of most of the other theistic sects as well. His greatest work, the *Śrī Bhāshya,* has been translated by George Thibaut, *The Vedānta-Sūtras with the Commentary of Rāmānuja (S.B.E.* XLVIII, 1904; Delhi, Motilal Banarsidass, 1966). Rāmānuja's *Gītābhāshya* is available in a summarizing translation by J.A.B. van Buitenen, *Rāmānuja on the Bhagavadgītā* ('s-Gravenhage, the translator, 1953; Delhi, Motilal Banarsidass, 1969). Van Buitenen has translated also *Rāmānuja's Vedārthasaṃgraha* (Poona, Deccan College Monograph Series No. 16, 1956). There are other translations of this work by M.R. Rajagopala Ayyangar, *Vedartha Sangraha of Sri Ramanuja* (Kumbakonam, Cauveri Colour Press, 1956), and by S.S. Raghavachar, *Vedārthasaṁgraha of Śrī Rāmānujācārya* (Mysore, Sri Ramakrishna Ashrama, 1956). Rāmānuja's *Vedāntasāra,* tr. M.B. Narasimha Ayyangar, has been published by the Adyar Library (Madras, 1953).

Secondary studies of quality on Rāmānuja begin with Vasudev Anant Sukhtankar, *The Teachings of Vedānta according to Rāmānuja* (Vienna, the author, 1908), who explains the main doctrines of Rāmānuja clearly on the basis of the material of the *Śrī Bhāshya* and of the *Vedārthasaṃgraha.* Bharatan Kumārappa, *The Hindu Conception of Deity as Culminating in Rāmānuja* (London, Luzac, 1934) views Rāmānuja primarily in his role as polemicist against Śaṅkara, as had Thibaut and others. Dasgupta in his *History of Indian Philosophy* focuses on Rāmānuja's epistemology and metaphysics. Van Buitenen in the interpretive aspects of his works mentioned above shows a new interest in Rāmānuja as theologian and devotee. John Braisted Carman in his *The Theology of Ramanuja* (New Haven, Yale Univ. Press, 1974) brings this religious approach to culmination and provides the clearest and most sympathetic interpretation of Rāmānuja's mind that is now available.

After Rāmānuja, Vaishnava life becomes distinguishable into the activities of the various Vaishnava *sampradāyas* or sects and their sub-streams. Dasgupta's *History of Indian Philosophy,* vols. 3 and 4, surveys their systems of thought, and Bhandarkar describes the sects briefly in his *Vaiṣṇavism, Śaivism and Minor Religious Systems.* Their distinctive theological positions as expressed in their respective commentaries on the Vedānta Sūtras are described in two good studies: V.S. Ghate, *The Vedanta* (Poona, Bhandarkar Oriental Research Institute, 1926), and S. Radhakrishnan, *The Brahma Sūtra* (N.Y., Harper & Bros., 1960), 46–102. Rāmānuja's own Śrī Sampradaya soon bifurcated into the famous Tengalai and Vadagalai (cat-hold and monkey-hold) schools. Robert Lester deals with the differences between the thought of Rāmānuja and the positions of the later teachers of his school in "Rāmānuja and Śrī-Vaiṣṇavism: the Concept of Prapatti or Śaraṇāgati," *History of Religions* V (1966), 266–82.

The great themes of debate among the Śrī Vaishnavas are explained from a moderate Vadagalai point of view by P.N. Srinivasachari, *The Philosophy of Viśiṣṭādvaita,* 2nd ed. (Madras, Adyar Library, 1946), 352–540. On the points of difference see also A. Govindacharya, "The Aṣṭadaśa-bhedas," *Journal of the Royal Asiatic Society* (1910), 1103–12, and A. Govindacharya and George A. Grierson, "Tengalai and Vadagalai," *JRAS* (1912), 714–18. Vedānta Deśika, the crowning theologian of the Vadagalai school, has become much more accessible through M.R. Raja-gopala Ayyangar's translation from Tamil of that thinker's greatest work of positive theological construction, *Srimad Rahasyatrayasāra* (Kumba-konam, Agnihothram Ramanuja Thathachariar, 1956). Satyavrata Singh's *Vedānta Deśika: His Life, Works and Philosophy* (Varanasi, Chowkhamba Sanskrit Series Office, 1958) is a full-scale study; and S.M. Srinivasa Chari, *Advaita and Viśiṣṭādvaita* (N.Y., Asia Publishing House, 1961) gives a substantial account of Vedānta Deśika's major polemical work against *Advaita,* the *Śatadūṣhaṇī.*

A less satisfactory knowledge of the positions of the Tengalai or Cat-hold School is obtainable through translations of a few works of its earliest theologian, Pillai Lokācārya. Lokācārya's major metaphysical treatise, *The Vedanta Tattva-Traya,* tr. Manmatha Nath Paul (Allahabad, The Panini Office, Vedanta Series No. 5, 1904) is a difficult to obtain publica-tion. A. Govindacharya has translated his "Arthapanchaka," however, in *Journal of the Royal Asiatic Society* (1910), 565–98, and this work has just been translated and published again from a rather distinct Sanskrit version, *Artha-pañcakam,* tr. Dr. Surendranāth Śāstri (Indore, Indore Center, Bharati Research Institute, 1972). Dasgupta, *History of Indian Philosophy,* vol. III, 135–37, 374–81, offers brief summaries of Lokā-cārya's works, including his important *Śrīvacanabhushaṇa.* His *Nava-ratnamālā* and *Prapannaparitrāna,* two minor works, appeared in A. Go-vindacharya's translation in *Indian Antiquary* XXXIX (Nov. 1910), 316–19. An important religious work of Lokācārya is translated anony-mously in *The Visishtādvaitin* in a serial article "The *Mumukshuppadi* or *Rahasyatraya,* or the Way of the Seeker of Salvation," Aug. 1905, 1–6; Oct. 1905, 7–14; Jan. 1906, 15–18; and April–May 1906, 19–33.

THE MĀDHVAS   As introductions to the Mādhva Sampradāya we recommend Hiriyanna's sketch in his *Essentials of Indian Philosophy,* 187–99, and S. Subba Rau, "The Realism of Srī Madhvāchārya," in the first edition of *The Cultural Heritage of India* (Calcutta, Sri Ramakrishna Centenary Committee, 1937ff.), I, 582–96. The social and ritual life of this religious community in the 19th century is pictured in *Gazetteer of the Bombay Presidency,* XXII (Bombay, Government Central Press, 1884), 56–90. For examples of its hymnology, see Charles E. Gover, tr., *The Folk-Songs of Southern India* (Madras, Higginbotham, 1871; 2nd ed., Tirunelveli, South India Saiva Siddhanta Works Publishing Society, Publication No. 965, 1959), 3–63. The literary and general history of the movement to about A.D. 1400 is covered in B.N.K. Sharma, *A History of the Dvaita School of Vedanta and Its Literature* (Bombay, Booksellers' Publishing Co., 1960).

On the Mādhva theological system, reading can begin with K. Narain, *An Outline of Madhva Philosophy* (Allahabad, Udayana Publications, 1962). B.N.K. Sharma covers similar ground in two solid works: *Philosophy of Śrī Madhvācārya* (Bombay, Bharatiya Vidya Bhavan, 1962), and an anthology, *Śrī Madhva's Teachings in His Own Words* (same publisher, 1961). Helmuth von Glasenapp's *Madhva's Philosophie des Vishnu-Glaubens* (Bonn and Leipzig, Geistesströmungen des Ostens, Bd. 2, 1923) is thorough and lucidly arranged. P. Nagaraja Rao has written a specialized study, "The Epistemology of Dvaita Vedanta," *Adyar Library Bulletin,* XXII, Parts 3–4 (1958), 1–120. Of primary writings, several commentaries of Madhva have been translated or paraphrased by S. Subba Rau: *The Vedanta-Sutras with the Commentary by Sri Madhwacharya* (Madras, 1904) and *The Bhagavad-Gita, Translation and Commentaries in English according to Sri Madhwacharya's Bhashyas* (Madras, S. Subba Rau, 1906). R. Naga Raja Sarma, *Reign of Realism in Indian Philosophy* (Madras, National Press, 1937) summarizes ten works of Madhva as amplified and explained by the sectarian commentator Jayatīrtha; especially valuable are pp. 235–520 which condense one of Madhva's most comprehensive works. Suzanne Siauve's consummate study of Madhva's metaphysics, *La Doctrine de Madhva, Dvaita Vedanta* (Pondichéry, Institut Français d'Indologie, 1968) concludes with a select bibliography for further work.

THE NIMBĀRKAS   A good first reading in the thought of the Nimbārka Sampradāya is Roma Bose Chaudhuri, "The Nimbarka School of Vedanta," *The Cultural Heritage of India,* III, 333–46. For an ampler survey, see Umesha Mishra, *Nimbarka School of Vedanta* (Allahabad, Univ. of Allahabad Studies, Sanskrit Section, 1940; 2nd ed., Allahabad, Tirabhukti Publications, 1966). P.N. Srinivasachari, *The Philosophy of Bhedābheda,* 2nd rev. ed. (Madras, Adyar Library Series No. 74, 1950), 155–63, explains Nimbarkite positions in relation to those of other schools. The most substantial publication in the entire field is the three-volume work of Roma Bose (Chaudhuri), *Vedānta-Pārijāta-Saurabha of Nimbarka and Vedānta-Kaustubha of Srīnivāsa* (Calcutta, Asiatic Society of Bengal, Bibliotheca Indica CCLIX, 1940–43), the third volume of which is a detailed study of the principal theologians of the sect. William Crooke gives modest information on the life of the sect in *The Tribes and Castes of the North-Western Provinces and Oudh* (Calcutta, Government Press, 1896), vol. IV, 88ff.

THE VALLABHA SAMPRADĀYA   We recommend for the beginner two articles by Govindlal Hargovind Bhatt, "The School of Vallabha" in *The Cultural Heritage of India,* vol. III, 342–59, and "The Puṣṭimārga of Vallabhāchārya" in *Indian Historical Quarterly* IX (1933), 300–06.

There is a scarcity of writing for the outside world by members of the Vallabha Sampradāya. A sensational public scandal in the life of the sect in the middle of the last century caused its members to adopt seclusion as their defense. The situation can be understood by reading Yadunāthajī Vrajaratnajī, *Report of the Maharaj Libel Case* (Bombay, 1862) and the same writer's anonymous *History of the Sect of the Mahārājas, or Vallabhāchāryas, in Western India* (London, Kegan Paul, Trench, Trübner, 1865).

The most substantial works in English are Helmuth von Glasenapp, *Doctrines of Vallabhacharya,* translated from German by Ishverbai L. Amin (Kapadvanj, District Khaira, Gujarat, Shuddhadvaita Samsada, 1959); and Jethalal G. Shah, *A Primer of Anu-Bhāshya* (Nadiad, 1927; rev. ed., Kapadvanj, Shuddhadvaita Samsada, 1960). Vallabha's *Tattvārthadīpanibandha,* ed. H.O. Śāstrī (Bombay, Trustees of Sheth Narayandas and Jethananda Asanmal Charity Trust, 1943), includes an English translation of the basic text and an informative introduction by Jethalal G. Shah. In the three titles last mentioned, a constant quotation of materials in the *devanāgarī* alphabet will baffle many western readers. Mrudula I. Marfatia, *The Philosophy of Vallabhācārya* (Delhi, Munshiram Manoharlal, 1967) is valuable for the summaries of the major writings of Vallabha and his successors that fill two thirds of its pages.

Śriśa Chandra Vasu Vidyarnava, *Studies in the Vedanta Sutras* (Allahabad, *S.B.H.,* XXII, 1919), 66–98, analyzes Vallabha's interpretation of those authoritative *sūtras.* Sūr Dās, a disciple of Vallabha and a poet of the first rank in Hindī, is the subject of a study by Janardan Misra, *Religious Poetry of Surdas* (Patna, 1935; 2nd ed., Kumaitha, District Bhagalpur, Rajesh Misra, 1956). Pierre Johanns, S.J., *A Synopsis of "To Christ Through the Vedanta," Part III, Vallabha* (Ranchi, Catholic Press, Light of the East Series No. 9, 1944) provides a lucid summary of Vallabha's teaching in western terms, combining it with a critical examination from a Christian point of view.

THE FOLLOWERS OF CAITANYA   In contrast with the Vallabha sect, the Gauṙiyā Sampradāya, the school of Caitanya, has expressed itself fully and fluently in English; scarcity of literature is not a problem in understanding the group, but the peculiarities and scholastic complexities of Caitanyite thought are. In this situation, good primers are a desideratum. Edward C. Dimock, Jr., "Doctrine and Practice among the Vaiṣṇavas of Bengal," *History of Religions* III (1963), 106–27, is one such useful introduction. Rādhā Govind Nāth offers introductions in bare outlines in

"The Acintya–Bhedābheda School," *The Cultural Heritage of India,* 2nd ed., III, 366–83, and in "A Survey of the Caitanya Movement," *idem.,* IV, 186–200. The Gaudia Math, 16A Kali Prasad Chakravarti Street, Baghbazar, Calcutta 3, publishes many promotional booklets of which the following have an orientational value for beginners: Thakur Bhaktivinode, *Sri Chaitanya Mahaprabhu: His Life and Precepts* (1941); and *The Bhagavat: Its Philosophy, Its Ethics and Its Theology* (1936); Nisi Kanta Sanyal, *The Erotic Principle and Unalloyed Devotion,* 2nd ed. (1941). For mature and serious readers, however, the best introduction is Sushil Kumar De, *Bengal's Contribution to Sanskrit Literature and Studies in Bengal Vaisnavism* (Calcutta, Firma K.L. Mukhopadhyaya, 1960), 108–53. In the special function of introducing the missionary extension of the Caitanya school in America, J. Stillson Judah, *Hare Krishna and the Counterculture* (N.Y., John Wiley & Sons, 1974), gives a good account of its western development and literature, and the book's critical bibliography is a useful guide to the entire movement.

Melville T. Kennedy, *The Chaitanya Movement* (Calcutta, Association Press, 1925) is useful for its general factual outlines and for its information on the Caitanyites of recent times. Sushil Kumar De, *Early History of the Vaiṣṇava Faith and Movement in Bengal* (Calcutta, General Printers and Publishers, 1942) is indispensable for its critical account of the life of Caitanya and his immediate followers. Krishnadāsa Kavirājā's hagiographic verse biography of Caitanya exists in full translation now only in Nagendra Kumar Roy's *Sri Sri Chaitanya Charitamrita,* 6 vols. (Puri, Chaitanyacharitamrita Karyalaya, 1940–59), but Edward C. Dimock, Jr., is completing a new English version for the Harvard Univ. Press. Tapankumar Raychaudhuri has carried the history of the movement into the seventeenth century in his *Bengal under Akbar and Jehangir* (Calcutta, A. Mukherjee, 1953), 80–106.

The distinctive devotional hymnology of the Bengal Vaishnavas is described, with musical scores, by A.A. Bake in "Çri Chaitanya Mahāprabhu," *Mededelingen der Koninklijke Nederlandse Akademie van Wetenschappen,* Afd. Letterkunde, nieuwe reeks, Deel 11, No. 8 (1948), 279–305. On *kīrtan* see also Edward C. Dimock, Jr., "The Place of Gauracandrikā in Bengali Vaiṣṇava Lyrics," *Journal of the American Oriental Society,* LXXVIII (July–Sept., 1958), 153–69. Norvin Hein explains the religious experience cultivated in *kīrtan,* in the tradition's own theological terms, in "Caitanya's Ecstasies and the Theology of the Name," in Bardwell Smith, ed., *Hinduism: New Essays in the History of Religions,* forthcoming from E.J. Brill, Leiden.

On Bengal Vaishnava theology, the most profitable reading for those with some preparation is probably Sudhindra Chandra Chakravarti, *Philosophical Foundations of Bengal Vaisnavism* (Calcutta, Academic Publishers, 1969), which treats every aspect of doctrine lucidly and in detail, including comparisons with Christianity and other schools of Hindu thought. Girindra Narayan Mallik, *The Philosophy of Vaiṣṇava Religion* (Lahore, Punjab Sanskrit Book Depot, 1927) draws its material extensively from the Caitanya-caritāmṛita. Sukumara Chakravarit, *Caitanya et sa théorie de l'amour divin (prema)* (Paris, Presses universitaires de France, 1933) is a complete historical and theological survey. Nisi Kanta Sanyal's major work, *Sree Krishna Chaitanya* (1933), sold by the Gaudiya Math, devotes its first two hundred pages to a spirited and tenacious apologetic presentation of the theology of the sect. Swami Bhakti Hridaya Bon, tr., *Śrī Rūpa Gosvāmī's Bhakti-rasāmṛtaṣindhuḥ* (Vṛindāban, Institute of Oriental Philosophy, vol. I, 1965), gives us in translation, for the first time, one of the basic theological works of the sect.

The many doctrinal publications of the American Caitanyites can be obtained from the International Society for Krishna Consciousness, 3764 Watseka Avenue, Los Angeles, California 90034.

Certain hybrid offshoots or tantric perversions of Caitanya's tradition are described by Manindra Mohan Bose, *The Post-Caitanya Sahajiā Cult of Bengal* (Univ. of Calcutta, 1930); by Shashibhushan Dasgupta, *Obscure Religious Cults as Background of Bengal Literature* (Univ. of Calcutta, 1946; 2nd ed., Calcutta, Firma K.L. Mukhopadhyaya, 1962); and by Edward C. Dimock, Jr., *The Place of the Hidden Moon, Erotic Mysticism in the Vaiṣṇava-Sahajiā Cult of Bengal* (Univ. of Chicago Press, 1966). Dimock devotes a chapter to the Bāuls, who are the focus of a volume by Deben Bhattacharya, tr., *Songs of the Bards of Bengal* (N.Y., Grove Press, 1969).

The Krishnaism of Assam—distinct from that of Bengal though related to it—is introduced well by Maheswar Neog in his *Sankaradeva and His Times, Early History of the Vaiṣṇava Faith and Movement in Assam* (Gauhati, Univ. of Gauhati, 1965).

The Rādhavallabha Sampradāya is all but inaccessible in English. We have only Frederick S. Growse's *Mathurā*, 2nd ed. (North-Western Provinces and Oudh Government Press, 1880), 185–200, and Sir George Grierson's article "Rādhāvallabhīs" in *E.R.E.*, X, 559ff.

D. Śaivism

For elemental information on the varieties of Śaiva religion, please see the appropriate sections of several books already mentioned: Monier Williams' *Brahmanism and Hinduism,* Macnicol's *Indian Theism,* and Farquhar's *An Outline of the Religious Literature of India;* also, for the origin and special nature of this religion, Gonda's *Viṣṇuism and Śivaism.*

The mythology of Śaivism has recently become much more accessible through the translation by a board of scholars of *The Śiva-Purāṇa,* ed. J.L. Śastri, 4 vols. (Delhi, Motilal Banarsidass, 1970). Heinrich Zimmer,

Myths and Symbols in Indian Art and Civilization (N.Y., Pantheon Books, 1946; Harper Torchbooks, 1962) is helpful in the understanding of the central myths, and Wendy Doniger O'Flaherty, *Asceticism and Eroticism in the Mythology of Śiva* (London, Oxford Univ. Press, 1974), gives a luminous explanation of a striking paradox in the traditional characterization of Śiva.

Śaiva images get special treatment in Gabriel Jouveau-Dubreuil, tr. A.C. Martin, *Iconography of Southern India* (Paris, Paul Geuthner, 1937), 11–52. See also the plates by Auguste Rodin in "Sculptures Çivaites," *Ars Asiatica* III (1921), Pl. I–XII, and the interpretations of Zimmer, *op. cit.*, 123–89, and of A.K. Coomaraswamy, *The Dance of Siva* (N.Y., 1918; rev. ed., N.Y., Farrar Straus, 1957) in the chapter of that title.

Specimens of Śaiva hymnology are available particularly from South India, where the worship of Śiva emerges most clearly above the common polytheism. Aside from Gover's *The Folk-Songs of Southern India* (see "The Mādhvas" above), we have F. Kingsbury and G.E. Phillips, *Hymns of the Tamil Śaivite Saints* (Calcutta, Association Press, 1921), and Māṇikka-Vāchakar, *The Tiruvāçagam,* tr. by George Uglow Pope (Oxford, Clarendon Press, 1900), and Bishop Caldwell's translations of the more recent poems of the Śittar school in his *A Comparative Grammar of the Dravidian or South Indian Family of Languages,* 2nd rev. ed. only (London, Kegan Paul, Trench, Trübner, 1875), 146–49.

We have made some mention of materials on Śaiva rituals, particularly as practiced in Śiva-temples, in our reference to the writings of James Burgess, Margaret Stevenson, and Carl Gustav Diehl in the section on *Pūjā* above. The serious study of the regulatory literature of Śaiva ritual is now being pushed with vigor by scholars associated with the Institut Français d' Indologie in Pondichéry. Jean Filliozat gives a prospectus of the many and little-known *āgama* manuals in his introduction to the pioneering critical edition, *Rauravāgama,* ed. N.R. Bhatt (Publication No. 11 of that Institut, 1961). The opening up of the nature of required religious practices has progressed further in the publication of Hélène Brunner-Lacheux's translation, *Somaśambhupaddhati, Le rituel quotidien dans la tradition Śivaite de l'Inde du Sud* (Publication No. 25 of the Institut, 1963), and by her digest of the contents of a badly-preserved manual of the practices of the adherents of the Śaiva Siddhanta in "Analyse du Suprabhedāgama," *Journal Asiatique* CCLV (1967), 31–60. The same lady has given rare attention to the social attitudes of the Śaivas in her "Les Categories sociales védiques dans le Śaivism du Sud," *Journal Asiatique* CCLII (1964), 451–72.

The ideas and doctrinal literature of the many branches of Śaivism, including Kashmir Śaivism and the Vīra-Śaivism of the Lingāyat sect, are reviewed historically by S.N. Dasgupta in the fifth volume of his *History of Indian Philosophy.* The most prominent Śaiva system, the Śaiva Siddhanta of South India, is introduced by S.S. Suryanarayana Sāstri in "The Philosophy of Śaivism," *Cultural Heritage of India,* 2nd ed., III, 387–99. Mariasusai Dhavamony, *Love of God according to Śaiva Siddhanta* (Oxford, Clarendon Press, 1971), begins with a valuable sketch of the earlier history of Śiva-devotion and is unmatched for its analysis of fourteen little-known Tamil theological texts and for its sensitive final characterization of Śaiva theology as a whole. V.A. Devasenapathi, *Śaiva Siddhānta as Expounded in the Śivajñāna-siddhiyār and Its Six Commentaries* (Univ. of Madras, Madras Univ. Philosophical Series No. 7, 1960) is an advanced study of the metaphysics of this group. The comprehensiveness and clarity of H.W. Schomerus, *Der Çaiva Siddhanta* (Leipzig, J.C. Hinrichs'sche Buchhandlung, 1912) gives the publication some value still, despite its age. Violet Paranjoti, *Saiva Siddhānta,* 2nd rev. ed. (London, Luzac, 1954), sets forth the major doctrines as the school presents them in its apologetic literature. John H. Piet, *A Logical Presentation of the Saiva Siddhanta Philosophy* (Madras, Christian Literature Society for India, Indian Research Series No. 8, 1952) translates each verse of Meykaṇḍa's *Śiva-Jñāna-Bodha* and gives the traditional argumentation by which that article of faith has been defended. This fundamental work of Meykaṇḍa has been translated also by Gordon Matthews, *Siva-ñāna-bōdham* (Oxford, James G. Forlong Fund No. 24, 1948), and by J.N. Nallaswami Pillai, *Sivagnana Botham* (Dharmapuram, Gnanasambandam Press, 1945). Nallaswami Pillai has also translated a standard fourteenth-century theological work, *Thiruvarutpayan of Umapathi Sivacharya* (same publisher, 1945). A specialized epistemological study has been made by V. Ponniah, *The Saiva Siddhanta Theory of Knowledge* (Annamalainagar, Annamalai Univ., 1952). For further study of Śaiva thought, see the bibliography of D.I. Jesudoss, "The Literature of Saiva Siddhanta and Allied Schools," *Tamil Culture* I (Sept. 1952), 226–33.

For the study of Kashmir Śaivism, the practical beginning-point is still Jagdish Chandra Chatterji, *Kashmir Shaivism* (Śrīnagar, Research Department, Jammu and Kashmir State, 1914). The writings and ideas of the greatest thinker of this branch of Śaivism are described at length in Kanti Chandra Pandey, *Abhinavagupta: An Historical and Philosophical Study,* 2nd rev. and enl. ed. (Varanasi, Chowkhamba Sanskrit Series Office, 1963). Lilian Silburne has translated *Hymnes de Abhinavagupta traduits et commentés* (Paris, Publications of the Institut de Civilisation Indienne, University of Paris, No. 31, 1970) and Abhinavagupta's *Le Paramārthasāra* (same publisher, No. 5, 1957), and she has contributed in the same series a number of translations of works of other authors of the Kashmir Śaiva school: *Vātulanātha Sūtra* (No. 8, 1959); *Le Vijñāna-bhairava* (No. 18, 1961); *La Bhakti: Le Stavacintāmaṇi de Bhaṭṭanārā-yaṇa* (No. 19, 1964); and *La Mahārthamañjarī de Maheśvarānanda* (No.

29, 1968). Erich Frauwallner has translated into German Sadyojyoti's *Tattvasaṃgraha* and Utpaladeva's *Pratyabhijñākārikā* in his *Aus der Philosophie der Śivaitischen Systeme* (Berlin, Akademie Verlag, 1962). The mystical-metaphysical significance of the word in Kashmir Śaiva thought gets much attention in André Padoux, *Recherches sur la symbolique et l'énergie de la parole dans certains textes tantriques* (Paris, Éditions E. de Boccard, Publications of the Institut de Civilisation Indienne, No. 21, 1963).

VII. ŚĀKTISM AND TĀNTRISM

Śāktism on the popular level appears to be ordinary *bhakti* religion, different only in its dedication to feminine deities and in its predilection toward ties with Śaivism. But its historical roots are distinct, its ritual practices have pronounced peculiarities, and the more sophisticated reaches of its thought lead on into the unique philosophies and modes of adjustment known as tāntrism.

For preliminary classification and description of the adherents of this branch of Hinduism, see Horace Hayman Wilson, ed. Ernest R. Rost, *Religious Sects of the Hindus* (1861; 2nd ed., Calcutta, Susil Gupta, 1958), 135–48. No reading program is complete without exposure to Sir Charles Eliot's dry and discriminating historical and descriptive treatment in his *Hinduism and Buddhism,* already mentioned, vol. II, 188–91, 274–90.

Sudhendu Kumar Das, *Śakti or Divine Power* (Univ. of Calcutta, 1924) is a preliminary exploration of the central idea of *śāktism* in recognized scriptures, the orthodox philosophies, and in the thought of Kashmir Śaivism and in the doctrine of the Lingāyats. Ernest A. Payne, *The Śaktas* (Calcutta, Y.M.C.A. Publishing House, 1933) is a survey that stresses modern *śākta* practices. *Śākta* hymnology is illustrated from vernacular literature by Edward J. Thompson and Arthur Marshman Spencer, *Bengali Religious Lyrics, Śākta* (Calcutta, Association Press, 1923), and from Sanskrit sources by Arthur Avalon, *Hymns to the Goddess* (London, Luzac, 1913; Hollywood, Vedanta Society of Southern California, 1953). Vesudeva S. Agrawala provides a convenient text and translation of a basic *śākta* scripture, the *Devī-mahātmya,* in his *The Glorification of the Great Goddess* (Ramnagar, Varanasi, All-India Kashiraj Trust, 1963). *The Srimad Devi Bhagavatam,* tr. Swami Vijnanananda, 3 vols. (Allahabad, *S.B.H.* XXVI, 1921–22) is a large compendium of *śākta* mythology and ritual lore. An extensive *śākta* handbook of rituals addressed to Śiva's consort in many forms has been translated and published in part, in K.R. van Kooij, *Worship of the Goddess according to the Kālikāpurāṇa* (Leiden, E.J. Brill, 1972). Brill's forthcoming *Hinduism: New Essays in the His-*

tory of Religions, ed. by Bardwell Smith, will contain a pioneering chapter by David Kinsley on the historical origins and development of the mythology of Kālī. A booklet by Sister Nivedita, *Kali the Mother* (London, 1900; Almora, Advaita Ashrama, 1950) is helpful in understanding *śākta* theology and religious feeling, despite a burden of Victorian sentimentalism. A guide to a vast obscure medieval literature of goddess-worship is provided by R.C. Hazra in his digests and literary notes on the *śākta* upapurāṇas in his *Studies in the Upapurāṇas* (Calcutta, Sanskrit College, 1963).

The tantras are the special theological and liturgical literature of *śāktism,* and the repositories of its advanced and esoteric teachings (tāntrism). Poorly known, they are described generally by Moriz Winternitz in *A History of Indian Literature,* vol. I (Univ. of Calcutta, 1927), 591–606, where summaries of a number of the better-known tantras are given. The original popularizer of tāntrism was Sir John Woodroffe, who wrote under the pseudonym of Arthur Avalon. His most comprehensive and lucid book is *Shakti and Shākta, Essays and Addresses on the Shākta Tantrashāstra,* 3rd rev. and enl. ed. (Madras, Ganesh, 1929); his other works can be seen in the listings of standard catalogues. The special *kuṇḍalinī* yoga of advanced *śāktism* is described in detail in Woodroffe's *The Serpent Power* (London, 1919; 5th enl. ed., Madras, Ganesh, 1953), which is a translation and explanation of two Sanskrit manuals, the *Shat-cakra-nirūpana* and the *Pādūkapañcakā.* Mircea Eliade in *Yoga: Immortality and Freedom,* mentioned above, analyzes and interprets tantric yoga (pp. 200–73) with great ingenuity and insight. Agehananda Bharati, *The Tantric Tradition* (London, Rider, 1965; Garden City, Doubleday, 1970) includes a thirty-page bibliography and is probably the most up-to-date and comprehensive guide to tāntrism now available. The final chapter of Heinrich Zimmer, *Philosophies of India* (N.Y., Pantheon Books, 1951; Meridian Books, 1956) cuts its way through the murky field of tāntrism in bold lines of sympathetic interpretation. The grateful reader should remember that the ramifications of tāntrism are vast, complex, and little explored, and that no present scheme of explanation is likely to comprehend the whole neatly. Progress in understanding the tantras requires much lexicographical work like that of Ivo Fišer, *Indian Erotics of the Oldest Period* (Praha, Universita Karlova, Philologica Monographia XIV, 1966), which is a study of the sexual vocabulary of the Vedic age.

VIII. MODERN FORMS OF HINDUISM

During the past century and a half, under the impact of forces and influences from abroad, teachings and movements of such novelty have arisen that they burst the banks of the ancient streams of Hinduism and defy classification under the traditional categories. The new doctrines and developments are too numerous even to mention, and the amount of attention that should be given to any one of them in a survey of the whole of Hinduism is not clear. Gāndhī, Rāmakṛishṇa and Rādhākṛishnan, for example, are figures of great current influence, but only time will tell whether their names will endure with those of Śaṅkara and Rāmānuja. The Brāhmo Samāj and the Ārya Samāj have passed the crest of their activity and influence, but they plainly require attention for their vital place in the unfolding of modern thought. Unable to weigh our attention by the standards of eternity, we shall give space to men and movements according to their apparent present significance. We shall attempt to include what one needs to know in order to understand the panorama of Hindu activity in the present day.

For entering into the study of religious developments since 1800 it is still wise to read J.N. Farquhar, *Modern Religious Movements in India* (N.Y., Macmillan, 1915). Farquhar classifies the new movements according to their response to western influences, as characterized by radical reform (read, "westernization"), moderate defense of traditional Hinduism, full defense, and religious nationalism. Such an analysis is not the only reasonable possibility, but it does take note of the intercultural obsession of the modern period, and sets forth the phases of Hindu reaction in the order of their chronological unfolding. The developments of the sixty years since Farquhar will make necessary the addition of new categories. The defeat of the religious chauvinism of Farquhar's time has brought into prominence fully syncretic forms of religion that I shall call cosmopolitan Hinduism. A currently-emerging development is missionary Hinduism, as various types of Hinduism become rooted in the West.

The newer general books on the modern age begin with A.C. Underwood, *Contemporary Thought of India* (London, Williams & Norgate, 1930; N.Y., Alfred A. Knopf, 1931). D.S. Sarma, *The Renaissance of Hinduism* (Varanasi, Benares Hindu Univ. Press, 1944) parallels the coverage of Farquhar, omitting religious nationalism and adding chapters on the newly-emerged figures of Aurobindo, Tagore, Gandhi, and Radhakrishnan, and substituting an internal for an external point of view. Percival Spear, *India, Pakistan and the· West* (London and N.Y., Oxford Univ. Press, 1949) is a lively history of the commingling of Indian and western culture, useful to those in need of a primer of the subject. "Chanakya" (K.M. Pannikar), *Indian Revolution* (Bombay, National Information and Publications, 1951) adds to an overview of modern religion a general sketch of modern Indian social history from the perspective and interests of a Hindu intellectual of the mid-twentieth century. Milton Singer, *When a Great Tradition Modernizes* (N.Y., Praeger, 1972) reports current forms of religious life in South India and offers interesting generalizations on the principles and processes by which new forms of religion are being produced. Philip H. Ashby, *Modern Trends in Hinduism* (N.Y., Columbia Univ. Press, 1974) brings our information up to date on the main streams of modern institutional history and offers insightful estimates of current situations.

Several other books of wide coverage should be mentioned here for their value as resources on important persons and movements that are dealt with in their separate chapters. Hervey Dewitt Griswold, *Insights into Modern Hinduism* (N.Y., Henry Holt, 1934) includes chapters on less prominent figures not often discussed elsewhere. Benoy Gopal Ray, *Contemporary Indian Philosophers* (Allahabad, Kitabistan, 1947) gives sketches of the religious teaching of nine prominent leaders, beginning with Raja Rammohun Roy, without placing them in a frame of historical interpretation. The same author has made a loose collection of regional data, *Religious Movements in Modern Bengal* (Santiniketan, Visva-Bharati, 1965), useful on Bengal figures who are otherwise little known. Vishwanath S. Naravane, *Modern Indian Thought* (Bombay, Asia Publishing House, 1964) has the coverage of Ray's *Contemporary Indian Philosophers* with more attention to cultural history.

A. The Brahmo Samaj

The list of essential readings on the Brahmo Samaj, the first great modernist movement, begins with Sophia Dobson Collet's excellent biography of the founder, *Life and Letters of Raja Rammohun Roy,* ed. by Hem Chandra Sarkar (Calcutta, Baptist Mission Press, 1913). Information on Rammohun's life in the period up to 1823 has been brought up to date in Iqbal Singh's *Rammohun Roy,* vol. I (Bombay, Asia Publishing House, 1958). The anonymously edited *Raja Ram Mohun Roy, His Life, Writings and Speeches* (Madras, G.A. Natesan, 1925) includes fair representations of Rammohun Roy's religious, moral, and cultural views. Prosanto Kumar Sen, *Biography of a New Faith* (Calcutta, Thacker, Spink, 1950) is useful for the history of the movement from 1823 to 1866. Protap Chunder Mozoomdar, *The Life and Teachings of Keshub Chunder Sen* (Calcutta, Baptist Mission Press, 1887) gives a detailed account of the developments and schisms of the last half of the nineteenth century from the standpoint of a member of Sen's New Dispensation. The standard comprehensive history of the entire Brahmo movement, written by a moderate member of the Sādhāran Brāhmo Samāj, is Śivanāth Śāstrī's *History of the Brahmo Samaj,* 2 vols. (Calcutta, R. Chatterji, 1911–12).

B. The Arya Samaj

This society, founded by Swāmī Dayānanda Sarasvatī, occupies an inter-mediate position in the range of reactions to the West. It arose as a movement for radical social and doctrinal change, but its spirit is defensive. Full-scale books on the Arya Samaj in English have all been written by members of the sect. Lala Lajpat Rai's *The Arya Samaj, An Account of Its Origin, Doctrines, and Activities, with a Biographical Sketch of the Founder* (London and N.Y., Longmans, Green, 1915); 2nd rev. and enl. ed., *A History of the Arya Samaj* (Bombay, Orient Longmans, 1967) was written especially for occidentals and is still recommendable as a first book for the outsider. Ganga Prasad Upadhyaya, *The Origin, Scope and Mission of the Arya Samaj* (Allahabad, Arya Samaj, Chowk, 1940) is a concise booklet on the sect's history, practices and principles. For a clear outline of the life and social message of the founder, see Birendra Kumar Singh, *Swami Dayanand* (New Delhi, National Book Trust, National Biography Series No. 28, 1970). Har Bilas Sarda, *Life of Dayanand Saraswati* (Ajmer, Vedic Yantralaya, 1946) is a long anecdotal biography, eulogistic in intent but not entirely uncritical. It includes a valuable chapter on Dayānanda's principles of Veda interpretation and sections on aspects of his general teaching. Dayānanda's own major work, *Satyārtha-prakāśa,* has been translated from Hindi by Chīrañjīva Bhāradwāja, *Light of Truth* (Madras, Arya Samaj, 1932) and by Ganga Prasad Upadhyaya, *The Light of Truth* (Allahabad, Kala Press, 1946). This book is treated by the sect as an authoritative writing serving in many ways as scripture. It deserves reading in any serious study of Arya Samaj dogma. Satya Prakash, *A Critical Study of Philosophy of Dayananda* (Ajmir, Arya Pratinidhi Sabha of Rajasthan, 1938), attempts to systematize Dayānanda's metaphysics and theology as found in his *Satyārtha-prakāśa* and his *Ṛigvedādibhāshyabhumikā.* Ganga Prasad, *The Fountainhead of Religion* (Madras, Arya Samaj, 1941, and elsewhere), adds to Hindu solutions of the problem of the relation between religions the Arya Samaj's striking historical theory that the great world religions are decayed derivatives of the religion of the Vedas. We have a rare study of the life and condition of an Arya Samaj congregation today in P.D. Padale's *The Endowed Arya Samaj in Hindi-town* (Jabalpur, Leonard Theological College, Student Research Monographs No. II, 1953).

C. The Ramakrishna movement

Farquhar estimates this movement as more negative than the Arya Samaj with regard to acceptance of western influence. This rating is not based upon the cultural, social, and political attitudes of this group, but upon its religious complexion. It represents a return to a traditional form of Hindu mysticism. In its later phases, however, it moved in the direction of cultural nationalism under the influence of the extrapolitical patriotism of Swāmī Vivekānanda.

Romain Rolland's *Prophets of the New India* (N.Y., Albert & Charles Boni, 1930) is a good introduction to the entire Ramakrishna movement for Westerners. On the life and religion of Ramakrishna, three writings by his followers share the top position in quality and authority. *Life of Sri Ramakrishna compiled from Various Authentic Sources* (Almora, Advaita Ashrama, Mayavati, 1925; 2nd rev. ed., 1928), a collective work of the members of the Ramakrishna monastic order, is the most inclusive collection of data on Ramakrishna's life and the preferred source on questions of biographical fact. The most detailed biography is Swami Saradananda, *Sri Ramakrishna, the Great Master* (Mylapore, Madras, Sri Ramakrishna Math, 1952), tr. from Bengali by Swami Jagadananda. A voluminous work, it stops short of the final phase of Ramakrishna's life. It presents the thought of Ramakrishna in its relation to general Hindu positions in a way that is usually very instructive, but reserve is recommended with regard to Saradananda's stress—found in the anonymous biography also—that Ramakrishna understood the characteristic mystical experience of Advaita Vedanta to be the consummation of his spiritual life. On the relation between Ramakrishna's mystical experiences, await Walter Neevel's chapter, "The Transformation of Śrī Rāmakrishna" in Bardwell Smith, ed., *Hinduism: New Essays in the History of Religions,* forthcoming from E.J. Brill, Leiden. Because it shows balance on this matter, there is a place in early reading programs for Christopher Isherwood's easy biography, *Ramakrishna and His Disciples* (N.Y., Simon and Schuster, 1959). A great source-book on Ramakrishna's life is Mahendra Nath Gupta, *The Gospel of Sri Ramakrishna,* tr. Swami Nikhilananda (N.Y., Ramakrishna-Vivekananda Center, 1942). It is a remarkable transcript of conversations between Ramakrishna and his disciples and visitors between the years 1882 and 1886, recorded with almost stenographic completeness.

The story of the extension of the Ramakrishna movement overseas is inseparable from the life story of Vivekananda, which is told succinctly by Swami Nikhilananda in *Vivekananda, A Biography* (N.Y., Ramakrishna-Vivekananda Center, 1953). This and other biographies have been supplemented and at points corrected by Marie Louise Burke, *Swami Vivekananda in America, New Discoveries* (Calcutta, Advaita Ashrama, 1958), a large source book combed mainly from the American press, arranged chronologically, and interpreted. Vivekananda's own writings are available not only in *The Complete Works of Swami Vivekananda,* 7 vols. (Almora, Advaita Ashrama, Mayavati, 1919–22; 6th ed., 1940–46), but also in dozens of separate booklets published by Advaita Ashrama, 5 Dehi Entally Road, Calcutta 14. The approach of the Ramakrishna missionaries in

America is typified in Swami Akhilananda's *Hindu View of Christ* (N.Y., Philosophical Library, 1949).

D. Hindu religious nationalism

The union of religion with nationalism is already found in moderate degree in Dayānanda and Vivekananda. Dhanapati Pandey, *The Arya Samaj and Indian Nationalism* (New Delhi, S. Chand, 1972) demonstrates the initiatory role of the Arya Samaj in giving root in India to nationalism in an Indian form. The line of nationalistic religious movements and leaders is sketched with particular attention to political activities by Bimanbihari Majumdar, *Militant Nationalism in India and Its Socio-religious Background* (Calcutta, General Printers and Publishers, 1966).

The trend in the nineteenth century toward the combination of religious and national emotion culminated in the first decades of the twentieth century in open forms of violent religious nationalism. Valentine Chirol's *Indian Unrest* (London, Macmillan, 1910) surveys the early manifestations of such nationalism from a British point of view, using police records which were sometimes inaccurate. Lawrence J.L.D. Zetland, Earl of Ronaldshay, gives a general characterization of the movements in *The Heart of Āryāvarta; A Study of the Psychology of Indian Unrest* (London, Constable, 1925), 80–131. Lajpat Rai, *Young India* (N.Y., B.W. Huebsch, 1916), 187–220, provides a useful analysis of the types of religious nationalism, and an essential counterbalance in viewpoint. Bankim Chandra Chatterji's popular nationalist novel *Ānanda Math* has been translated from Bengali by Basanta Koomar Roy as *Dawn over India* (N.Y., Devin-Adair, 1941), with radical adaptations which make explicit a reference to the British which Chatterji had eliminated but which the Hindu nationalist has always read into it. Such theological depth as revolutionary nationalism possessed arose largely out of Bal Gangadhar Tilak's activistic interpretation of the Bhagavadgītā in his *Śrīmad Bhagavadgītā Rahasya,* a commentary which has been translated by Bhalchandra Sitaram Sukthankar, 2 vols. (Poona, Tilak Brothers, 1935). In "The Philosophy of Bal Gangadhar Tilak: Karma vs. Jnāna in the Gītā Rahasya," *Journal of Asian Studies,* XVII (Feb., 1958), 197–206, D. Mackenzie Brown gives a fine analysis of this work and points out its contribution to the social ethics of the nationalist movement. Religious ultra-nationalism continues to be represented at the present day, as a minority outlook, by religiopolitical organizations such as the Hindu Mahāsabhā and the Bhāratīya Jan Sangh. These groups are described in J.R. Chandran and M.M. Thomas, *Political Outlook in India Today* (Bangalore, Committee for Literature on Social Concerns, 1956), 91–139, and in J.A. Curran, *Militant Hinduism in Indian Politics* (N.Y., Institute of Pacific Relations, 1952). Religious chauvinism lost its pre-eminence, however, in the second decade of the present century, with the emergence into leadership in their various spheres of Aurobindo, Gandhi, Tagore, and Radhakrishnan, each representing a faith in universal human values.

E. Cosmopolitan Hinduism

AUROBINDO   Śrī Aurobindo Ghose illustrated in his own career the turning away from unlimited religious nationalism. His life story is sketched by A.B. Purani in the symposium, *The Integral Philosophy of Sri Aurobindo,* ed. by Haridas Chaudhuri and Frederic Spiegelberg (London, George Allen & Unwin, 1960), 332–40. Charles A. Moore in the same book (81–110, "Sri Aurobindo on East and West") shows how this man of international education and syncretistic attitudes is yet in the ultimate analysis a Hindu. The symposium terminates with "A Complete List of All the Books Published in English by Sri Aurobindo." A more inclusive bibliography is that of H.K. Kaul, *Sri Aurobindo, A Descriptive Bibliography* (New Delhi, Munshiram Manoharlal, 1972), listing English publications on Aurobindo and his ashram up to the year 1972. We assume that these bibliographies will take over the guidance of the advanced student. The reader who is hurried, or who finds Aurobindo's massive works confusing, can find help in Sushil Kumar Maitra's simple outline of Aurobindo's ideas in *An Introduction to the Philosophy of Sri Aurobindo* (Calcutta, Culture Publishers, 1941). Aurobindo's *The Life Divine* (Calcutta, 1939; N.Y., The Greystone Press, 1949), his *magnum opus,* is a detailed exposition of his system, stressing its metaphysics. In *Hymns to the Mystic Fire* (1952) and *On the Veda* (1956), both published by Sri Aurobindo Ashram, Pondicherry, Aurobindo uses the key of esoteric symbolism to find the seed of his mystical doctrine in the Rigveda. *The Human Cycle* (Pondicherry, Sri Aurobindo Ashram, 1949) and *The Ideal of Human Unity,* 2nd ed. (same publisher, 1950) are Aurobindo's interpretation of history and of the intellectual and spiritual evolution of man. His *Ideals and Progress* (Calcutta, Arya Publishing House, 4th ed., 1951) elaborates certain additional aspects of Aurobindo's philosophy of human social development. *Essays on the Gita* (1921–28; N.Y., E.P. Dutton, 1950), a major work of Aurobindo, interprets the Bhagavadgita in line with his metaphysical and ethical teaching. He lays down the requirements of the practical religious life in the light of his system in *Synthesis of Yoga* (1948; N.Y., Shri Aurobindo Library, 1953), in *The Mind of Light* (N.Y., E.P. Dutton 1953), and in *The Mother* (Pondicherry, Sri Aurobindo Ashram, 1928).

RABINDRANATH TAGORE   In approaching the religion of Rabindranath Tagore no reading has priority over an unhurried direct absorption of his

English masterpiece, *Gitanjali* (London, India Society, 1912; Macmillan, London, 1913; N.Y. 1952). A sensitive reader's direct understanding of this classic may leave little to be learned from all the rest of the vast literature by and about Tagore.

Rabindranath himself has generalized about his world view in various prose writings and speeches. *Sādhanā* (N.Y., Macmillan, 1913) was originally a series of sermons for the students at Śantiniketan. *The Religion of Man* (N.Y., 1931; Boston, Beacon Press, 1961), the Hibbert Lectures for 1930, is the fullest account of his religious experience and the most mature formulation of his beliefs. The first three chapters of both *Personality* (N.Y., Macmillan, 1917; London, 1921) and *Creative Unity* (N.Y., Macmillan, 1922) throw supplementary light upon his religion.

Secondary writings on Tagore's thought do not illumine his spirituality greatly. Sushil Chandra Mitter's *La Pensée de Rabindranath Tagore* (Paris, Adrien Maisonneuve, 1930) is a detailed and perceptive exposition. But S. Radhakrishnan, *The Philosophy of Rabindranath Tagore* (London, Macmillan, 1918; Baroda, Good Companions, 1961) interleaves the thought of Tagore very heavily with the thought of S. Radhakrishnan. Sigfrid Estborn, *The Religion of Tagore* (Madras, Christian Literature Society for India, 1949) gives little attention to Tagore in its preoccupation with arguments on the historical and theological relation of Tagore's religion to Christianity. Benoy Gopal Ray, *The Philosophy of Rabindranath Tagore* (Bombay, Hind Kitabs, 1941), is to be valued as an indirect access to Tagore's immense untranslated Bengali writings, and for its view of Rabindranath in relation to concurrent activity in Indian religious thought.

The other literary works of Tagore in English that reveal his religion significantly are contained for the most part in *Collected Poems and Plays of Rabindranath Tagore* (N.Y., Macmillan, 1937); the poems *Gitanjali* (with one regrettable abridgment) and *Fruit-Gathering,* and the plays *The Post Office, The Cycle of Spring, Sanyasi, Malini,* and *Sacrifice.* Three works are essential which are not included in that anthology. The first is *The King of the Dark Chamber* (N.Y., Macmillan, 1914), an allegorical drama. The other two are books of poetry translated from Bengali by Aurobindo Bose for the Wisdom of the East series: *A Flight of Swans— Poems from Balākā* (London, John Murray, 1955) and *Wings of Death, The Last Poems of Rabindranath Tagore* (London, John Murray, 1960), which carries as an appendix a striking letter in which Tagore expresses his fundamental religious convictions with rare compression.

A nearly complete bibliography of Tagore's writings in Bengali and English is included in *Rabindranath Tagore, 1861–1961, A Centenary Volume* (New Delhi, Sahitya Akademi, 1961), 504–19. For lists of translations into continental European languages and of books on Tagore published in the West in Occidental languages, including English, see A. Aronson, *Rabindranath through Western Eyes* (Allahabad, Kitabistan, 1943), 125–53.

MAHATMA GANDHI   Mahatma Gandhi was as original in his thought as Aurobindo, but he was by no means a metaphysician or systematizer. He was a practical moralist, working out his principles of action amid the crises of a many-sided life in which there was little time for elaboration and unification of his ideas. His thinking is best studied in conjunction with his life. Hence the special place of Gandhi's *An Autobiography; or The Story of My Experiments with Truth* (Ahmadabad, Navajivan Press, 1927; London, Phoenix Press, 1949; Boston, Beacon Press, 1959), tr. by Mahadev Desai.

The natural demand for succinct and orderly presentations of Gandhi's teachings has been met by editors who have assembled from his scattered speeches and writings the best expressions of his views on given topics. The compilations listed below are published by the Navajivan Publishing Co., Ahmadabad, and were edited—unless another name is mentioned—by Bharatan Kumarappa. *Hindu Dharma* (1950) and *In Search of the Supreme,* ed. V.B. Kher, 2 vols. (1961), are skillful efforts to assemble the materials of Gandhi's theological and ethical creed in his own words. *Truth Is God,* ed. R.K. Prabhu (1955), and *Ramanama,* 2nd enl. ed. (1949), give special attention to Gandhi's worship practices. *Communal Unity* (1949) and *What Jesus Means to Me,* ed. R.K. Prabhu (1959), express his views on other religions and their adherents. *Varnashramadharma,* ed. R.K. Prabhu (1962), and *The Removal of Untouchability* (1954) present Gandhi's attitudes toward caste. *Self-restraint v. Self-indulgence,* rev. ed. (1947), deals with birth control and sexual ethics. Various aspects of social morality are covered in *How to Serve the Cow* (1954), *Non-violence in Peace and War* (1942; 3rd ed., 1948), *For Pacifists* (1949), and *Satyagraha* (1951). These collections were combed primarily from the journals which Gandhi published in India during the last thirty years of his life. The original contexts of these excerpts can now be searched out in the many volumes of *The Collected Works of Mahatma Gandhi* (Delhi, Publications Division, Ministry of Information and Broadcasting, 1958ff.), which is near or at completion in about seventy volumes.

Three secondary works on Gandhi's religious outlook deserve special mention. Charles F. Andrews, *Mahatma Gandhi's Ideas* (London, George Allen & Unwin, 1929; N.Y., Macmillan, 1930) still has value. E. Stanley Jones's *Mahatma Gandhi: An Interpretation* (N.Y., Abingdon-Cokesbury Press, 1948) is a Christian appreciation of Gandhi's life and teachings. Dhirendra Mohan Datta's *The Philosophy of Mahatma Gandhi* (Madison, Univ. of Wisconsin Press, 1953) is a lucid summary of Gandhi's fundamental convictions by an eminent professor of philosophy.

Joan V. Bondurant, *Conquest of Violence* (Princeton Univ. Press,

1958; rev. ed., Berkeley, Univ. of California Press, 1965), is exceptional in observation and analysis of Gandhi's techniques of satyāgraha, but its theological perception is not deep.

Further study on Mahatma Gandhi can be carried on with the help of P.G. Deshpande's *Gandhiana* (Ahmadabad, Navajivan Publishing House, 1948) and Jagdish Saran Sharma's *Mahatma Gandhi, A Descriptive Bibliography* (Delhi, S. Chand, 1955).

VINOBĀ BHĀVE   The background and career of Vinoba Bhave, Gandhi's great disciple, is described briefly in Hallam Tennyson's general account, *India's Walking Saint* (Garden City, N.Y., Doubleday, 1955; English edition, *Saint on the March* [London, Victor Gollancz, 1955]). Suresh Ramabhai, *Vinoba and his Mission,* 3rd rev. ed. (Banaras, Sarva Seva Sangh, 1962), chronicles Bhave's land-redistribution campaigns and adds a section on his social and political attitudes. For significant material on Bhave's religious views it is necessary to turn back to his *Talks on the Gita* (Banaras, Sarva Seva Sangh, 1958) written originally in 1932. His economic and political ethics are most fully revealed in his booklet *Swaraj Sastra* (1945; 2nd ed., Wardha, Sarva Seva Sangh, 1955). Bhave's speeches and writings have been classified and compiled by his followers in useful booklets which include *Bhoodan Yajna* (Ahmadabad, Navajivan, 1953), *The Principles and Philosophy of the Bhoodan Yagna* (Tanjore, Sarvodaya Prachuralaya, 1955), and *Sarvodaya and Communism* (Tanjore, Sarvodaya Prachuralaya, 1957). Fifteen interpretive articles by intimates of Bhave have been brought together by P.D. Tandon, ed., *Vinoba Bhave; The Man and his Mission* (Bombay, Vora, 1952?). Study can be pushed further with the help of Jagdish Saran Sharma, *Vinoba and Bhoodan; a Selected Descriptive Bibliography of Bhoodan in Hindi, English and Other Indian Languages* (New Delhi, Indian National Congress, 1956).

SARVEPALLI RADHAKRISHNAN   Radhakrishnan has written his own life story and testament of faith in "My Search for Truth," *Religion in Transition,* ed. by Vergilius Ferm (London, George Allen & Unwin, 1937), 11–59. C.E.M. Joad summarizes the message of Radhakrishnan's earlier books in *Counter Attack from the East; The Philosophy of Radhakrishnan* (London, George Allen & Unwin, 1933). A.N. Marlow, ed., *Radhakrishnan: An Anthology* (London, George Allen & Unwin, 1952), illustrates Radhakrishnan's characteristic ideas from his writings. Radhakrishnan's lectures *Fellowship of the Spirit* (Cambridge, Mass., Center for the Study of World Religions, 1961) have the value of a review of the major emphases of his lecturing and writing over many years.

The immensity of Radhakrishnan's output is displayed dramatically in T.R.V. Murti's "Bibliography of the Writings of Sarvepalli Radhakrishnan" in Paul Arthur Schilpp, ed., *The Philosophy of Sarvepalli Radha-*

krishnan (N.Y., Tudor, 1952), 843–62. Our concern is with those writings which bear upon the study of Hinduism ancient and modern.

The first category which is relevant consists of primarily historical works. The more important of this class have already been mentioned: his *Indian Philosophy, The Brahma Sūtra,* and his translation of the major Upanishads and of the Bhagavadgita. We have mentioned that Radhakrishnan is always influenced by an acknowledged intent, even in his most serious historical writing, to find edification for Hindus of the present age.

Writings of a second category review the history of Hinduism also, but without serious effort to advance knowledge of descriptive history. The tone is homiletical, and the creation of authoritative norms for a progressive Hinduism is the real end in view. Such books include *The Hindu View of Life* (London, George Allen & Unwin; N.Y., Macmillan, 1927), *The Heart of Hindusthan* (Madras, Natesan, 1932), and *Religion and Society* (London, George Allen & Unwin, 1947). Their importance lies in their influence on the Hindu intellectuals of the present century, who often derive from them an inspiring conception of what their religion has been and should be.

A third type of writing ranges afar into the religious and cultural problems of the entire world. The universality of the themes considered and Radhakrishnan's wide reading in Occidental thought make him the first Hindu intellectual to become one of the fellowship of western intellectuals as well. These books involve Hinduism in exhorting the world to adopt, for the cure of its ills, a mystical idealism which has its strongest roots in a renovated Advaita Vedanta. The books of this class have a characteristic progression of ideas. They begin with a sketch of the degradation, confusion, and peril of a secularized world whose faiths are shattered beyond rebuilding. The argument moves on to the healing and unification of the world through a universalistic religion not identical with any now existing but to which monistic Hinduism will make contributions of central importance. Thus *An Idealist View of Life* (London, George Allen & Unwin, 1932; rev. ed., 1937; N.Y., Macmillan, 1932) describes the philosophic disorganizations of the scientific age and presents Radhakrishnan's most ambitious philosophical construction on behalf of a religion of intuitive experience. The negative counterpart of this work is his early book *The Reign of Religion in Contemporary Philosophy* (London, Macmillan, 1920), a polemic against representative pluralistic thinkers of the West on behalf of an absolute idealism close to the Vedanta. *Eastern Religions and Western Thought* (Oxford, Clarendon Press, 1939; N.Y., Oxford Univ. Press, 1940) follows the usual line of thought in urging upon a disunited and suffering world certain unifying insights of Eastern religions. In recommending them to the West, he devotes much of the book to a historical argument that the great creative periods in western thought were ages of openness to external influences. He suggests repeatedly that the flowering of Greek philosophy and the rise of the Christian gospel were responses to Indian impulses. Belonging to this class also are his shorter but equally eloquent books, *The Religion We Need* (London, Ernest Benn, 1928), *Kalki, or the Future of Civilization* (London, Kegan Paul, Trench, Trübner; N.Y., E.P. Dutton, 1929), and *Recovery of Faith* (N.Y., Harper & Bros., 1955).

Schilpp's *The Philosophy of Sarvepalli Radhakrishnan* includes some excellent analysis and criticism by academic philosophers of the U.S., Great Britain, and India. Criticism from the standpoint of various Protestant theologies is found in Hendrik Kraemer, *Religion and the Christian Faith* (London, Lutterworth Press, 1956; Philadelphia, Westminster Press, 1957) and David Gnanaprakasam Moses, *Religious Truth and the Relation between Religions* (Madras, Christian Literature Society for India, 1950), 97–122.

F. Missionary Hinduism

The foreign promotional activities of a few Hindu groups are of long standing. The Ramakrishna Mission's extension of its work throughout the world has been going on since the beginning of the century. See the materials under "The Ramakrishna Movement" above. The widespread present evangelism of the Caitanyites described in J. Stillson Judah's important book (see "The Followers of Caitanya" above) is the continuation of a tradition of zealous promotion that has been characteristic of the Caitanya movement from its beginnings. The new development of the last decade is the spread of missionary interest and activity to leaders and movements of many new kinds, as disillusion and alienation in the West have created a mass hearing for religious proposals from the East.

The study of this significant religious development is or should be a special field for scholarship. Currently a hesitant stream of publication on the phenomenon is emerging out of religious journalism. Marvin Henry Harper, *Gurus, Swamis and Avatars, Spiritual Masters and Their Western Disciples* (Philadelphia, Westminster Press, 1972) gives incidental attention to western followings as he describes new leaders and centers in India. Robert S. Ellwood, Jr., *Religious and Spiritual Groups in Modern America* (Englewood Cliffs, Prentice-Hall, 1973) includes in its casual overview some account of the followings of Paramahamsa Yogananda, Maharishi Mahesh Yogi, Swami Vishnudevananda, and Satya Sai Baba. In their westward expansion the Hindu movements have created new promotional literatures. We have mentioned the extensive Caitanyite literature of the highly disciplined International Society for Krishna Consciousness. For a panoramic view of the entire field of such exotic publication one can do no better than to look through a bookseller's catalogue, *Aquarian Pathfinder* (Washington, D.C., Yes! Inc., 1039 31st St. N.W., 1974). Its 140 pages list the titles that are the Vedas and Vedangas of American religious alienation and exploration. Robert A. McDermott has made the first effort to comprehend and classify these writings in "Indian Spirituality in the West: a Bibliographical Mapping," *Philosophy East and West,* XXV (April, 1975), 213–39. An analysis of Hinduism's intellectual rather than institutional proliferation, it sketches and criticizes American versions and views of Hinduism by standards that are philosophical and sometimes personal. It remains a uniquely useful guide.

G. The condition of Hinduism today

This guide to the study of Hinduism will end with notice of a few informed estimates of the vitality of Hinduism at the present time. All of our citations above on a broadening Hindu mission activity are of course testimonies to alertness and vigor. Hinduism has offerings that are interesting to the world, and there are Hindu leaders who are able and willing to make them.

The condition of Hinduism within India itself, however, is subject to mixed notices, and deserves discussion. Raymond Panikkar, "Contemporary Hindu Spirituality," *Philosophy Today* III (Summer, 1959), 112–27, offers a useful classification of modern Hindus with regard to religious belief and analyzes the current religious attitudes of the university-educated, the traditionally-educated, and the illiterate. The areas of doctrinal change and the reconstructions that are giving new shape to Hindu beliefs are the matters of concern in H. Heras, "Problèmes religieux de l'Inde moderne," *Le Bulletin des missions* XXV (1951), 196–203. Swami Abhishikteswarananda, "L'Hindouisme est-il toujours vivant?" in *Vitalité actuelle des religions non Chrétiennes* (Paris, Éditions du Cerf, 1957), describes the restoring and the eroding forces that are operating in and upon Hinduism.

The outstanding representative of secularism among the modern intelligentsia has been the late Jawaharlal Nehru, whose influential views on religion are clear in the chapter "What Is Religion?" in *Toward Freedom, The Autobiography of Jawaharlal Nehru* (London, John Lane, 1936; Boston, Beacon Press, 1958), 236–43, and also in *Discovery of India* (N.Y., John Day, 1946; Garden City, Doubleday, 1959), 9–20. The social attitudes of the traditionally religious, on which Nehru's hostility is based, are an actuality that has been outlined well in Harry H. Pressler's survey, *Social Thought in Benares* (Lucknow, Lucknow Publishing House, 1941). Since Nehru's feeling is often voiced by others, it is important to test its depth.

The studies of Edward Shils, *The Intellectual between Tradition and Modernity* (The Hague, Mouton, 1961), have not found this secularity to be typical of men in the educated professions, who continue for the most part not only to acquiesce in religious observance, but to engage in religious practices of personal choice and to testify to personal religious experience. The researches cited by Ashby in his *Modern Trends in Hinduism* confirm this continuing positive orientation toward Hinduism in recent generations of students. Singer's *When a Great Tradition Modernizes* describes a Hinduism that is retaining, through change, a dominant place in modern urban life, and J.D.M. Derrett, *Religion, Law and the State,* affirms the continuing role of religion in the support of contemporary culture. When one turns to reports from village India, the opinion is not different. M.G. Carstairs, "The Religious Temper of Two Indian Villages," *World Dominion* XXX (1952), 48–52, finds rural religion in various kinds of flux, but not dying out. The place of non-Śrauta rituals in the life of rural India is reported as prominent by Morris Opler in "The Place of Religion in a North Indian Village," *Southwestern Journal of Anthropology* XV (Autumn, 1959), 219–26. Taya Zinkin in "Hinduism and Communism: Are They Compatible?" *Eastern World* IX (Jan. 1955), 16ff., holds that only desperation could bring India to Communism. It appears that only the possibility of desperation raises any doubt about the future of Hinduism. That Hinduism is adapting to modern conditions, and can adapt, is clear.

BIBLIOGRAPHIES

Excellent bibliographical help is available on the earlier phases of Indian religion in Louis Renou's *Bibliographie védique* (Paris, Adrien-Maisonneuve, 1931) and its sequel by R.N. Dandekar, *Vedic Bibliography,* vol. I (Bombay, Karnatak Publishing House, 1949), and II (Univ. of Poona, 1961). The series is being continued. Both volumes include literature on the Indus civilization in their coverage, and Dandekar in particular includes much material on periods usually classified as post-Vedic. Their time coverage does not approach modern Hinduism, however. The *International Bibliography for the History of Religions* (Leiden, E.J. Brill, 1954ff. for 1952ff.) deals annually with the new publications of the Western world in particular on all aspects of Hinduism. The American Theological Library Association's *Index to Religious Periodical Literature,* published 1949ff. at McCormick Theological Seminary, Chicago, gives some attention to writing on Hinduism in non-specialists' publications.

A number of bibliographies by and about particular modern religious leaders have been mentioned above in the course of this essay.

Serious books on Hinduism in Western languages are reviewed critically in the *Journal of Asian Studies,* the *Journal of the American Oriental Society,* the *Journal of the Royal Asiatic Society,* the *Bulletin of the*

School of Oriental and African Studies (Univ. of London), the *Oriental-istische Literaturzeitung* (Berlin), and in the *Vishveshvaranand Indological Journal* (Hoshiarpur). *The Aryan Path* (Bombay) is useful for notices and reviews of general non-technical books on Hinduism, including many published in India.

Students of Hinduism can make much use of bibliographies that deal with their interests only incidentally or tangentially, such as the *Linguistic Bibliography* (Utrecht-Bruxelles, Spectrum, 1939ff.). The *Annual Bibliography of Indian Archaeology* of the Kern Institute (Leiden, E.J. Brill, 1928ff. for 1926ff.) covers interests that extend far beyond its title. Karl H. Potter, *Bibliography of Indian Philosophies* (Delhi, Motilal Banarsidass, 1970), is useful in aspects of Hindu thought that are strictly metaphysical. The *Review of Indological Research in the Last 75 Years* (M.M. Citrao Shastri Felicitation Volume), eds. P.J. Chinmulgund and V.V. Mirashi (Poona, Bharatiya Charitrakosha Mandal, 1967) is a critical survey of outstanding publications in many fields of Indology, including religion, and is a rare guide to works published in India, in particular. *The Indian National Bibliography* (Calcutta, Central Reference Library, 1958ff. for 1957ff.) and *Indian Books in Print* (Delhi, Indian Bureau of Bibliographies, 1955ff.) provide, in addition to the information one would expect, the mailing addresses of almost all of the Indian publishers mentioned in this essay. The journal *Prācī-Jyoti,* published by the Institute of Indic Studies of Kurukshetra University, 1963ff., digests articles on all realms of Indology, including Hinduism, from periodicals of many lands but particularly of India.

VI

Buddhism

Frank E. Reynolds

I. GENERAL WORKS

A. Gaining a perspective

Students interested in undertaking a study of Buddhism may choose from a variety of different approaches. One of the more mundane and traditional, but still perhaps the best, is to select a survey treatment which introduces the whole range of Buddhist traditions, to follow this survey with a set of essays which deal with the tradition in terms of topics of special interest, and then to proceed to a book which gives at least a sampling of primary texts. If it is necessary to restrict oneself to a single survey, good choices would be J.B. Pratt, *The Pilgrimage of Buddhism and a Buddhist Pilgrimage* (N.Y., Macmillan, 1928); Kenneth Chen, *The Light of Asia* (Woodbury, N.Y., Baron's Educational Series, 1968); or Richard Robinson, *Buddhism* (Belmont, Dickenson, 1970). A readily accessible set of essays which deal with topics of special interest and introduce the work of several prominent contemporary Buddhologists is included in vol. III of the new, 15th edition of the *Encyclopaedia Britannica* (Macropaedia); in the space of 71 pages the reader is treated to discussions on major Buddhological themes by Walpole Rahula, Giuseppe Tucci, Joseph Kitagawa, Hajime Nakamura, Herbert Guenther, and David Snellgrove. An excellent

I should like to express my thanks to John Holt, whose assistance in compiling and checking sources made it possible to complete this chapter in the time allotted.

anthology which draws from all of the major Buddhist traditions and includes not only philosophical but also cultic and popular materials in Stephan Beyer, *The Buddhist Experience* (Belmont, Dickenson, 1973).

Though the student will want to move quickly beyond broad introductory treatments such as these, it will nevertheless be worthwhile to mention other books covering the same or similar ground. During the past decade Edward Conze's *Buddhism: Its Essence and Development* (N.Y., Philosophical Library, 1951) has been one of the most widely used introductory texts; Alex Wayman's contribution on "Buddhism" included in C.J. Bleeker and G. Widengren, eds., *Historia Religionum,* vol. II (Leiden, E.J. Brill, 1969), 372–464, gives special emphasis to the Mahayana and Mantrayana traditions; and Richard Gard's *Buddhism* (N.Y., Braziller, 1961) includes a number of extensive quotations from original sources as well as classic descriptions of Buddhist life and practice. Though less ambitious than any of the above, Erik Zürcher's *Buddhism* (N.Y., St. Martin's, 1962) makes a unique contribution through the inclusion of 23 pages of excellent maps depicting the extension of Buddhism at various periods of its history.

Collections of essays comparable to that included in the new edition of the *Britannica* are difficult to find. However, there are at least three which can serve a useful function at the introductory level: Kenneth Morgan, ed., *The Path of the Buddha* (N.Y., Ronald, 1956) gathers together essays by various Asian Buddhist scholars; Charles Prebisch, ed., *Buddhism: A Modern Perspective* (University Park, Pa., Penn State Univ. Press, 1975) includes 45 short essays written by eight younger Buddhologists; and Edward Conze's *Thirty Years of Buddhist Studies* (Columbia, Univ. of South Carolina Press, 1968) is useful particularly because of an initial essay which raises important methodological issues that should be confronted by every student at an early stage of his studies.

Along with Stephan Beyer's anthology, the reader may also want to browse in Edward Conze, et al., *Buddhist Texts Through the Ages* (N.Y., Philosophical Library, 1954). Though this collection does not have quite the immediate appeal of Beyer's more recent work, its quality is excellent; and it covers a wide range of Buddhist sources. A third collection which also deserves to be singled out is *The Buddhist Tradition in India, China, and Japan,* ed. William T. de Bary (N.Y., Modern Library, 1969). Obviously certain major Buddhist traditions are not represented; however, the coverage is reasonably broad, and the selections are substantial. Among the many other published anthologies, three of the more adequate ones are E.A. Burtt, ed., *The Teachings of the Compassionate Buddha* (N.Y., Mentor, 1955); Clarence Hamilton, ed., *Buddhism: A Religion of Compassion* (N.Y., Liberal Arts, 1952); and Lucien Streik, ed., *World of Buddha: A Reader* (Garden City, N.Y., Doubleday, 1969).

In addition to these introductory studies and anthologies, the beginning student should also be aware of several dictionaries which may be useful in clarifying terminology; see, for example, Christmas Humphreys, a *Popular Dictionary of Buddhism* (N.Y., Citadel, 1963); Trevor Ling, *A Dictionary of Buddhism* (N.Y., Scribner's, 1970); and Mahathera Nyanaponika, *Buddhist Dictionary,* rev. ed. (Colombo, Frewin, 1956).

B. Surveys and other cross-cultural studies

At the time of the celebration of the 2500-year anniversary of Buddhism, a number of special volumes were published which contain important essays on a wide variety of Buddhological topics. Two major works of this kind are P.V. Bapat, ed., *2500 Years of Buddhism* (Delhi, Gov't. of India, 1956) and René de Berval, ed., *Présence du bouddhisme FA,* vol. XVI, 153–57 (Saigon, 1959). Two similar works which tend to emphasize Indian Buddhism are the special 1956 issues of the *IBRS* and the *IHQ.** In addition there are India-oriented collections not specifically related to the 2500-year celebration which contain interesting articles of very disparate character; see, for example, D.R. Bhandakar, et al., ed., *B.C. Law Volume* in two parts (Calcutta, 1945; Poona, 1956); B.C. Law, ed., *Buddhistic Studies* (Calcutta & Simla, Thacker, Spink, 1931); and A. Kunst, L. Cousins and K.R. Norman, eds., *Buddhist Studies in Honor of I.B. Horner* (Boston, Reidel, 1974). Similar collections pointed more toward East Asia are Kshitis Roy, ed., *Liebenthal Festschrift* (Santiniketan, Visvabharati, 1957) and *Studies of Esoteric Buddhism and Tantrism* (Koya San, Japan, Koya San Univ., 1965).

Another extremely valuable resource is provided by articles in various encyclopedias. Many of the articles on Buddhist subjects in the Hastings *Encyclopaedia of Religion and Ethics* (1908–27; rep. 1955) still retain their value, especially those contributed by the great French Buddhologist Louis LeVallée Poussin. Though the *Encyclopedia of Buddhism* (Colombo, Gov't. of Ceylon, 1961–   ) and the *Hôbôgirin* (Tokyo, Maison Française-Japonaise 1929–37 and 1967–   ) remain incomplete, they contain many definitive essays by outstanding scholars. Moreover, specific aspects of Buddhism can often be best pursued by utilizing the various entries in encyclopedias devoted to particular subject areas. For example, the history of Buddhist literature can be surveyed by examining the relevant articles on Buddhism and Buddhist countries in the *Encyclopedie de la Pléiade,* vol. I, *Histoire des littératures* (Paris, Gallimard, 1955). The easiest and most effective way to encounter the very best research on important topics in the history of Buddhist art is to consult the entries related

---

* For these and all the other abbreviations whose reference is not immediately apparent see the list at the end of this chapter.

to Buddhism and Buddhist countries in the *Encyclopaedia of World Art* (N.Y., McGraw Hill, 1959–68).

Turning to the works of individual scholars, one of the most basic cross-cultural treatments is Charles Eliot's three-volume study of *Hinduism and Buddhism* (N.Y., Barnes & Noble, 1954), which covers the major areas of Asian Buddhism with the exception of Japan. Though Eliot's style makes for rather dry reading, and though the work is at some points rather dated, the Buddhism sections provide the only reasonably comprehensive historical treatment presently available.

Another very different kind of cross-cultural approach, also historical in its own way, is pursued in René Grousset's *In the Footsteps of the Buddha* (N.Y., Grossman, 1971). Grousset utilizes the accounts of the Chinese pilgrims to describe the areas of the Buddhist world as they appeared in the seventh century A.D. when Buddhism was near the peak of its glory throughout Asia; and in so doing he produces a classic work which is as enjoyable as it is instructive. The reader may also consult the original accounts of the pilgrims themselves which are most accessible in Samuel Beal, tr., *Si-Yu-Ki: Buddhist Records of the Western World,* 2 vols. (N.Y., Paragon, 1968), which contains the works of Hsuan Tsang, Fa Hien and Sung-Yun; and in J. Takakusu, tr., *A Record of the Buddhist Religion as Practiced in India and the Malay Archipelago* (Oxford, Clarendon Press, 1896) which contains the account of I Ching.

Due both to the complex character of the Buddhist tradition and the vagaries of modern scholarship there is a real dearth of significant cross-cultural studies which deal with particular topics. In the area of Buddhist thought some relevant articles have been written; see, for example, Kenneth Inada, "Some Basic Misconceptions of Buddhism," *International Philosophical Quarterly,* IX, 1 (March, 1969), 101–19; Edward Conze, "Dharma: A Spiritual, Social and Cosmic Force" in Paul Kunz, ed., *The Concept of Order* (Seattle, Univ. of Washington Press, 1967); Shoshen Miyamoto, "Freedom, Independence and Peace in Buddhism," *PEW,* I, 4 (Jan., 1952); D.T. Suzuki, "Reason and Intuition in Buddhist Philosophy" in Charles Moore, ed., *Essays in East-West Philosophy* (Honolulu, Univ. of Hawaii Press, 1951); and J. Takakusu," Buddhism as a Philosophy of Thusness" in Charles Moore, ed., *Philosophy East and West* (Princeton, Princeton Univ. Press, 1944). A study of the Mahayana tradition has been provided by William McGovern in his *Introduction to Mahayana Buddhism* (N.Y., E.P. Dutton, 1922), and a more recent survey treatment is available in Douglas Fox, *The Vagrant Lotus* (Philadelphia, Westminister, 1973). For those who are seriously interested, however, the crucial work is still J. Takakusu, *Essentials of Buddhist Philosophy,* 3rd ed. (Bombay, Asia Publishing House, 1956), in which the positions of a wide variety of schools are presented. In this connection see also Hajime Nakamura, "A Critical

Survey of Mahayana and Esoteric Buddhism Based upon Japanese Studies," *Acta Asiatica,* 6 (1964), 57–88, and 7 (1964), 36–94; and "A Brief Survey of Japanese Studies on the Philosophical Schools of the Mahayana," *Acta Asiatica* 1 (1960), 56–88.

In the case of general works on Buddhist mythology, symbolism and art, the same problems exist, though again some helpful materials are available. In *Die Legende vom Leben des Buddha* (Berlin, Wegweiser-Verlag, 1929), Ernst Waldschmidt has translated a sampling of Buddha biographies from different parts of Asia. Waldschmidt's work can be complemented by Benjamin Rowland, *The Evolution of the Buddha Image* (N.Y., Asia House, 1963). The stupa, which is perhaps the most interesting and important Buddha-symbol, has been studied in summary fashion by Anagarika Govinda in *Some Aspects of Stupa Symbolism* (London, Kitabistan, 1940), and from a more historical perspective by G. Combaz in "L'Évolution du stupa en Asie," *MCB,* 2, 3, 4 (1933, 1934, 1935), 165–305, 93–114, 1–125; and by Paul Mus in his massive and highly technical *Barabaḍur* (Paris and Hanoi, Paul Geuthner, 1935), which ranges from the Brahmanic background though the development of the Pure Land traditions. Alice Getty has published a classic study of *The Gods of Northern Buddhism,* 2nd ed. (Oxford, Clarendon Press, 1928); and Paul Mus has treated an important figure in "The Thousand Armed Kannon," *JIBS,* XII, 1 (Jan., 1964), 1–33. "The Mirror as a Pan-Buddhist Metaphor-Simile" is discussed by Alex Wayman in *HR,* XIII, 4 (May, 1974), 251–69; and E. Dale Saunders opens up an important topic in his article on "Symbolic Gestures in Buddhism," *ArA,* 21 (1958), 47–68. Finally, the artistic expressions all across the Buddhist world are admirably surveyed by Dietrich Seckel in *The Art of Buddhism* (N.Y., Crown, 1964) and *Grundzüge der buddhistischen Malerei* (Tokyo, Deutsche Gesellschaft für Natur-und Völkerkunde Ostasiens, 1945).

In the area of meditational practice the reader will find "A Comparison of Theravada and Zen Meditational Methods and Goals" by Winston King in *HR,* IX, 4 (May, 1970), 304–15. For students interested in ritual practice useful sources include Helmut Von Glassenap, *Buddhistische Mysterien* (Stuttgart, Spemann, 1940), which deals with the esoteric traditions; and Paul Levy, *Buddhism: A Mystery Religion?* (London, Athlone, 1957), which draws together a great deal of material concerning Buddhist initiation.

A very important cross-cultural examination of Buddhist monasticism has been provided by Robert Bleichsteiner in his *Die gelbe Kirche* (Wien, Belf, 1937); it has been translated into French and published as *L'Église jaune* (Paris, Payot, 1937). Unfortunately most of the other studies which treat the communal and social dimensions of the tradition in a comprehensive manner are designed primarily as introductions; see for example overviews provided by Edmund Perry and Shanta Ratnayaka in *The Sangha of the Tri-ratana* (Evanston, Religion & Ethics Inst., 1974); and Peter Pardue, *Buddhism* (N.Y., Macmillan, 1968); as well as the much more substantial treatments in Joseph Kitagawa's chapter on "Buddhism and the Samgha" in his *Religions of the East* (Philadelphia, Westminster, 1960); and Richard Gard, "Buddhism and Political Power" in H.D. Laswell and H. Cleveland, eds., *The Ethics of Power* (N.Y., Harper, 1962).

It is also important to note that there are a number of cross-cultural studies which interpret or describe Buddhism in relation to the modern world. Among these a few, such as K.N. Jayatilleka's "Buddhist Relativity and the One World Concept" in Edward Jurji, ed., *Religious Pluralism and World Community* (Leiden, E.J. Brill, 1969), G.P. Malalasekera and K.N. Jayatilleke, *Buddhism and the Race Question* (Paris, UNESCO, 1958), and G.P. Malalasekera, "The Buddhist Point of View" in *Humanism and Education in East and West* (Paris, UNESCO, 1953) deal primarily with normative issues; whereas others, such as Ernst Benz, *Buddhism or Communism: Which holds the future of Asia?* tr. by Richard and Clara Winston (Garden City, N.Y., Doubleday, 1965), Jerold Schechter, *The New Face of Buddha* (N.Y., Coward-McCann, 1967), Donald Swearer, *The Samgha in Transition* (Philadelphia, Westminster, 1970), and Joseph Kitagawa's article on "Buddhism and Asian Politics," *Asian Survey,* II, 5 (July, 1962), 1–11, are primarily descriptive in character. An excellent overview of recent developments throughout the entire Buddhist world can be gained by consulting Heinrich Dumoulin, ed., *Buddhismus der Gegenwart* (Freiburg, Herder, 1970); moreover a new and updated English edition has been published by Macmillan in May, 1976.

II. BUDDHISM IN INDIA AND CENTRAL ASIA

A. Comprehensive discussions

In order to place the development of Buddhism within the context of Indian history and culture the reader may wish to consult one or two major works such as R.C. Majumdar's *The History and Culture of the Indian People,* vols. II–IV (Bombay, 1953–57); and Jean Filliozat and Louis Renou, *L'Inde classique* (Paris, Payot, 1947–1953), which give due attention to Buddhist traditions. Also there are collections of essays on India which contain significant contributions to the study of Buddhism; see, for example, *The Cultural Heritage of India,* rev. ed. (Calcutta, Ramakrishna Mission, 1953), and to a lesser extent B.C. Law, *Indological Studies,* I and II (Calcutta, India Research Institute 1950 & 1952) and III (Allahabad, Ganganath Research Institute, 1954).

Among the individually authored works Étienne Lamotte's *Towards the Meeting with Buddhism* (Rome, Ancora, 1970) and Trevor Ling's *Buddha: Buddhist Civilization in India and Ceylon* (N.Y., Scribner's 1973) provide introductory overviews. The standard surveys are Anthony Warder's *Indian Buddhism* (Delhi, Motilal Banarsidass, 1970) and Sukumar Dutt's excellent study of *Buddhist Monks and Monasteries of India* (London, Allen & Unwin, 1962). Another important dimension is considered by Lowell Bloss in "The Buddha and the Naga: A Study in Buddhist Folk Religiosity," *HR*, XIII, 1 (Aug., 1973), 36–53. In addition Taranatha's fascinating traditional chronicle of the *History of Buddhism in India* has been translated by Lama Chimpa and Alaka Chattopadhyaya and published by the Indian Institute of Advanced Study in Simla, 1970.

The Buddhist literature of India has been surveyed by Moriz Winternitz in the second volume of *A History of Indian Literature* (Calcutta, Univ. of Calcutta Press, 1933); a major segment of it has been covered by J.K. Nariman in his *Literary History of Sanskrit Buddhism* (Delhi, Motilal Banarsidass, 1972). Among the more comprehensive treatments of Buddhist philosophy, Edward Conze's *Buddhist Thought in India* (London, Allen & Unwin, 1962) is especially useful because of its conciseness and clarity; another important study which can be very helpful for beginners as well as for more advanced students is Guy Welbon, *The Buddhist Nirvana and Its Western Interpreters* (Chicago, Univ. of Chicago Press, 1968). Beyond these now-standard works, some older studies are still essential for those who wish to carry their studies further; see for example, E.J. Thomas, *History of Buddhist Thought,* (N.Y., Barnes & Noble, 1951); Th. Stcherbatsky, *The Buddhist Conception of Nirvana* (Leningrad, Academy of Science of USSR, 1927); Louis La Vallée Poussin, *Opinions sur l'histoire de la dogmatique* (Paris, Beauchesne, 1909); Maryla Falk, *Nama-rupa and Dharma-rupa* (Calcutta, Univ. of Calcutta, 1943); and André Bareau's important but technical study of *L'Absolu en philosophie bouddhique* (Paris, Centre de documentation universitaires, 1951). Finally it should be noted that some of the relationships between Buddhism and other intellectual traditions in India are neatly sketched out by David Ruegg in a lecture on *The Study of Indian and Tibetan Thought* (Leiden, E.J. Brill, 1967).

The broad range of Buddhist art is placed within its Indian context by Benjamin Rowland in *The Art and Architecture of India* (Baltimore, Penguin, 1953), especially Parts 2–4. A chronologically more limited treatment is given by V.S. Agrawala in *Indian Art: A History of Indian Art from the Earliest Times up to the 3rd century A.D.* (Varanasi, Prakashan, 1965). The very important Gandharan school is discussed by Madeleine Hallade in *Gandharan Art of North India* (N.Y., Abrams, 1968), by Hallade again in *The Gandharan Style* (London, Thames & Hudson, 1968), and by Sir John Marshall in *The Buddhist Art of Gandhara* (Cambridge, Cambridge Univ. Press, 1960). The closely related topic of Buddhist symbolism in India is surveyed by Willibald Kirfel, *Symbolik des Buddhismus* (Stuttgart, Hiersemann, 1959); while particular symbols are studied in greater detail in Ananda Coomaraswamy, *Elements of Buddhist Iconography* (Cambridge, Harvard Univ. Press, 1935), in Odette Viennot, *Le Culte de l'arbre dans l'Inde ancienne* (Paris, Presses universitaires de France, 1954), in Vasudeva S. Agrawala, *The Wheel Flag of India; Chakradhvaya* (Vanarasi, Prakashan, 1964), and in T.B. Karunaratne, *The Buddhist Wheel Symbolism* (Kandy, Buddhist Publication Society, 1969).

A survey of important architectural and artistic sites in India itself is provided by Debala Mitra in a work entitled *Buddhist Monuments* (Calcutta, Samsad, 1971). For studies of specific sites see Prudence Myer, "The Temple at Bodh—Gaya" *Art Bulletin* XL, 4 (1958), 277–98; *The Ajanta Caves: Early Buddhist Paintings from India* (Mentor UNESCO Art Book, 1965); Walter Spink, *Ajanta to Ellora* (Ann Arbor, Marg Publications, 1967); and André Bareau, "Le Stupa de Dhyanakataka selon la tradition tibetaine," *Ars Asiatica,* 16 (1967), 81–88. For Central Asia see Fred H. Andrews, *Wall Paintings from Ancient Shrines in Central Asia Recovered by Sir Aurel Stein,* 2 vols. (London, Oxford Univ. Press, 1948), and Basil Gray, *Buddhist Cave Paintings at Tun-Huang* (Chicago, Univ. of Chicago Press, 1959).

The practical and sociological aspects of the Indian Buddhist tradition have received less scholarly attention. In regard to Buddhist practice see Mircea Eliade, *Yoga: Immortality and Freedom* (N.Y., Pantheon, 1958), chaps. 5 and 6, and Edward Conze, *Buddhist Meditation* (London, Allen & Unwin, 1956); and for an interesting but deviant form of practice the reader may consult the articles by Étienne Lamotte and Jean Filliozat on "Le suicide religieux dans le bouddhisme ancien," *BCLS,* LI (1965), 156–58, and "Le Mort voluntaire par le feu et la tradition bouddhique indienne," *JA,* 251 (1963), 21–51. Studies which deal with the social aspects of Buddhism in a pan-Indian context include the important chapter on "Buddhist Education" in Radha K. Mookerji, *Ancient Indian Education* (London, Macmillan, 1947), and Hajime Nakamura's article on "The Indian and Buddhist Concepts of Law" in Edward J. Jurji, *Religious Pluralism and World Community* (Leiden, E.J. Brill, 1969).

B. Early Buddhism and the Hinayana schools

CONTEXT, ORIGINS, AND OVERVIEW   The first five to six centuries of Buddhist history constitute a crucial period during which the basic structural elements of the tradition became established. Those interested in a general introduction to the development during this early period may consult my essay on "The Two Wheels of Dhamma" in the book of the same name, Bardwell Smith, ed., published as No. 3 in the monograph series of the American Academy of Religion (Chambersburg, Penn., AAR, 1972). A more extended treatment is given by Sukumar Dutt in *Buddha and the*

Five After-Centuries (London, Luzac, 1957). Much more detailed discussions are provided by Nalinaksha Dutt's somewhat dated and uncritical *Early History of the Spread of Buddhism and the Buddhist Schools* (London, Luzac, 1925); G.C. Pande's *Studies in the Origins of Buddhism* (Allahabad, Univ. of Allahabad, 1957); and V.P. Varma's *Early Buddhism and Its Origins* (New Delhi, Munshiram Manoharlal, 1973). In addition, an interesting Japanese perspective is expressed by Kogen Mizuno in *Primitive Buddhism,* tr. by Kosho Yamamoto (Ube, Japan, Karinbunko, 1969).

Along with these more general treatments the reader may consult works which focus on two especially crucial moments: the period of the first beginnings, and the period during the reign of King Asoka when Buddhism underwent a significant reorientation. The context and emergence of early Buddhism are considered in Padmanabh Jaini's essay on the "Sramanas: Their Conflict with Brahmanical Society" in Joseph Elder, ed., *Chapters in Indian Civilization,* I (Dubuque, Kendall/Hunt, 1970), 39–81; in A.L. Basham, "The Rise of Buddhism in Its Historical Context," *Asian Studies* (Quezon), IV, 3 (Dec., 1966), 395–411; and in a very important article by André Bareau entitled "Le Parinirvana du Bouddha et la naissance de la religion bouddhique," *BEFEO,* LXI (1974), 275–300. For King Asoka and the influence of his reign see B.G. Gokhale, *Buddhism and Asoka* (Baroda, Padmaja, 1948); the *Edicts of King Asoka,* tr. by N.A. Nikom and Richard McKeon (Chicago, Univ. of Chicago Press, 1958); and Jean Przyluski, *The Legend of Emperor Asoka,* tr. D.K. Biswas (Calcutta, K.L. Mukhopadhyaya, 1967).

Moreover, in addition to some of the items mentioned above, every student who wishes to study more specialized aspects of early Buddhism should give careful attention to the appropriate segment of Étienne Lamotte's *Histoire du bouddhisme des origines à l'ère Saka* (Louvain, Publications universitaires, 1958). Lamotte's work is a masterpiece of over 800 pages which covers practically every aspect of early Buddhist development, and does so with the greatest of erudition and authority.

THE EARLY BUDDHIST COMMUNITY   Most scholars are now convinced that the Gautama Buddha was an historical figure who did, in fact, found the Buddhist community. Though the dates of the Buddha's birth and death are still a matter of some controversy, André Bareau has authoritatively examined the basic issues in "La Date du Nirvana," *JA* (1953), 27–62. Erich Frauwallner has presented "The Historical Data We Possess on the Person and Doctrine of the Buddha" in *East and West,* VII, 4 (Jan., 1957), 9–12. Beyond this there are three articles on the subject by B.C. Law entitled "The Buddha's Activities at Anga Magadha," *JBRS* (Buddha Jayanti Special Issue, 1956), vol. I, 7–32; "The Buddha's Activities at Kasi-Kosala," *JIH,* XXXIV (1956), 139–71; and "The Buddha's

Activities at Vesali," *JIH,* XXXV (1957), 7–36. There is also an important, though not easily accessible, study by Hajime Nakamura entitled "Sakyamuni's Activities at Rajagraha," *Annual of Oriental and Religious Studies* (Tokyo), IV (1968), 23–34.

The mendicants, or monastic component, of the early Buddhist community have been studied from several different perspectives. The relationship of the Buddhist monastic polity to that of the contemporary Indian republican states is discussed by Kachi P. Jayaswal in the chapter on "Republican Origins of the Buddhist Sangha and Republics in Buddhist Literature" in *Hindu Polity,* 3rd ed. (Bangalore, Bangalore Publishing, 1955). The polity of the monastic community is more directly examined in Gokulas De, *Democracy in the Early Buddhist Sangha* (Calcutta, Univ. of Calcutta Press, 1955); while the basic rules and regulations are presented by Durga M. Bhagvat, *Early Buddhist Jurisprudence—Theravada Vinaya Laws* (Poona, Oriental Book Agency, 1939), and discussed by Y. Krishnan in "Was It Permissible for a Sannyasi (Monk) to Revert to the Lay Life?," *ABORI,* 50 (1969), 75–89. A more sociological approach is taken by B.G. Gokhale, "The Early Buddhist Elite" *JIH,* XLIII, 2 (August, 1965), 131–37, and by Akira Hirakawa, "The Two-Fold Structure of the Buddhist Sangha," *Journal of the Oriental Research Institute (Baroda),* 16 (Dec., 1966), 131–37. In addition an interesting though mis-titled account is provided by Madan M. Singh in "Life in the Buddhist Monastery during the 6th century BC," *JBRS,* 40 (1954), 131–54.

During the early Buddhist centuries the monks convened a series of Councils which played a significant role in formulating the tradition and guiding the life of the community. The major studies on the subject have been concisely summarized by Charles Prebisch in his "Review of Scholarship on the Buddhist Councils," *JAS,* XXXIII, 2 (Feb. 1974), 239–54. Those who wish to pursue the matter further should consult the works which Prebisch cites, especially Jean Przyluski, *Le Concile de Rajagraha,* 3 vols. (Paris, Paul Guethner, 1926–29): Marcel Hofinger. *Étude sur la concile de Vaisali* (Louvain, Bureaux du Muséon, 1946); Paul Demiéville, "À propos du concile de Vaisali," *TP,* XL, 4–5 (1951), 239–96; and André Bareau, *Les Premiers conciles bouddhiques* (Paris, Presses universitaires de France, 1955).

In a development which was closely bound up with the deliberations and decisions of the Councils, the early community gradually came to be divided among various schools (the traditional number is 18) which the later Mahayana Buddhists called the schools of the Hinayana or Lesser Vehicle. There are two useful English language sources which deal with the emergence and orientation of these schools: Nalinaksha Dutt, *Buddhist Sects in India* (Calcutta, K.L. Mukhopadhyaya, 1970); and Ajay M. Sastri, *An Outline of Early Buddhism* (Vanarasi, Indological Book House, 1965). There are also two relevant texts available in English translation: see Shwe

Zan Aung and Caroline Rhys Davids, trs., *Points of Controversy* (PTS, London, Luzac, 1915); and Jiryo Masuda, tr., *Origins and Doctrines of Early Buddhist Schools: A Translation of Hsuan Chwang's Version of Vasumitra's Treatise* (Leipzig, Verlag der Asia Major, 1925). Those who read French will want to turn directly to the definitive study on the subject which is André Bareau's *Les Sectes bouddhiques du petit véhicule* (Saigon, EFEO, 1955), and to consult his "Trois Traités sur les sectes bouddhiques attribuées à Vasumitra, Bhavya et Vinitadeva," *JA*, 242 (1954), 229–66, and 244 (1956), 167–200.

In addition to these works which focus on the male order of monks there are a few studies which call attention to the fact that women (both "nuns" and lay women) and the laity constituted crucial elements in the structure of the early community. The basic studies of women and their activities are still Isaline B. Horner, *Women Under Primitive Buddhism* (London, Routledge and Kegan Paul, 1930), and B.C. Law, *Women in Buddhist Literature* (Colombo, W.E. Bastian, 1930), which can be supplemented on the mendicant side by the canonical collection of the *Psalms of the Sisters,* newly translated by K.R. Norman as the *Elder's Verses* II (PTS, London, Luzac, 1971). Three articles which deal specifically with the laity and its role are Nalinaksha Dutt, "The Place of the Laity in Early Buddhism," *IHQ*, 21 (1945), 163–83; Louis LaVallée Poussin, "Les Fidèles laïcs du Upasaka," *BCLS*, 1925, 15–34; and Étienne Lamotte, "Le Bouddhisme des laïcs" in Gadjin M. Nagao and Josho Nozawa, eds., *Studies in Indology and Buddhology* (Kyoto, 1955). It should also be noted that an important ritual involving both laymen and monks is treated by Kun Chang in *A Comparative Study of the Kathinavastu* ('s Gravenhage, Mouton, 1957) and by Heinz Bechert in "Some Remarks on the Kathina Rite'" in *JBRS,* 54 (1968), 319–39. Another such ritual is discussed by Jean Przyluski in his article on "Uposatha," *IHQ,* XII, 3 (Sept., 1936), 383–90.

LANGUAGES AND THE TRIPITAKA   Perhaps the greatest achievement of the early Buddhist community, and especially of the monastic community, was the establishment, maintenance, and codification of a body of teachings attributed to the Buddha and which came to be known as the Tripitaka or Three Baskets of scripture. A somewhat dated introduction to the language problems involved in the early stages is given by P.C. Bagchi in his article "On the Original Buddhism: Its Canon and Language" in *Sino-Indian Studies,* II, 3–4 (Oct., 1953; Jan., 1954), 107–35. Heinrich Lüders and E. Waldschmidt present some challenging hypotheses in their work, *Beobachtungen über die Sprache des buddhistischen Urkanons* (Berlin, Akademie der Wissenschaft zu Berlin, Klasse für Sprachen, Literatur und Kunst, 1952, 1954). The emergence and character of the Buddhist form of Sanskrit used by many later Hinayana Buddhists, as well as adherents of the Mahayana, is discussed by Franklin Edgerton in *Buddhist*

Hybrid Sanskrit Language and Literature (Benares, Benares Hindu Univ., 1954); by John Brough in "The Language of Buddhist Sanskrit Texts" in *BSOAS,* XVI, 2 (1954); and by Alex Wayman in "The Buddhism and the Sanskrit of Buddhist Hybrid Sanskrit," *JAOS,* LXXXIV, 4 (March, 1965), 111–15.

When we turn to the texts of Hinayana groups other than the Theravadins, we find some significant studies and translations; see, for example, Anukul C. Banerjee's general survey of *Sarvastivada Literature* (Calcutta, K.L. Mukhopadhyaya, 1957), J. Takakusu's commentary "On the Abhidharma Literature of the Sarvastivadins" in the *JPTS,* 1904–1905; Marcel Hofinger's translation of *Le Congrès du lac Anavatapata: Vies de saints bouddhiques* (Louvain, Bibliothèque du Muséon, 34, 1954) and Lavallée Poussin's translation of the very rich and difficult *Abihidharmakosa du Vasubandhu, MCB,* 16 (6 vols. in 3). There is a group of comparative studies reviewed by Charles Presbisch in his article on "The Pratimoksha Puzzle," *JAOS,* 94 (1974), 168–76; these include Erich Frauwallner's important exploration of *The Earliest Vinaya and the Beginnings of Buddhist Literature* (Rome, IMEO, 1956), and have now been supplemented by Presbisch's *Buddhist Monastic Discipline* (University Pk., Pa., Penn State Univ. Press, 1975). Thich Minh Chau has dealt with a different kind of text in *Chinese Agamas and the Pali Majjhima Nikaya* (Saigon, Institute of Higher Buddhist Studies, 1964) and in his *Milindapanha and Nagasenabhiksusutra: A Comparative Study through Pali and Chinese Sources* (Calcutta, K.L. Mukhopadhyaya, 1964). However the amount of work done in these areas cannot be compared with what has been done in the case of the Pali canon of the Theravadins.

Practically the entire Pali canon including the Vinaya texts (which form the first "basket of scripture" and serve as a kind of "constitution" for the monastic order), the Sutta texts (which form the second "basket" and are largely discourses attributed to the Buddha), and the Abhidhamma texts (which form the third "basket" and are later, more scholastic, summaries of the doctrine), as well as the semi-canonical *Questions of King Milinda,* have been translated into English in the Sacred Books of the Buddhists Series and the Translation Series of the PTS. An orientation to this vast collection of material can be gained by consulting E.J. Thomas, "The Theravada (Pali) Canon" which is an appendix to his *Life of the Buddha as Legend and History,* 3rd rev. ed. (N.Y., Barnes & Noble, 1952); B.C. Law, "Chronology of the Pali Canon" in *ABORI,* XII (1931), 171–201; Arthur C. March, "An Analysis of the Pali Canon," presented in revised form by I.B. Horner in Christmas Humphreys, ed., *A Buddhist Students' Manual* (London, Buddhist Society, 1956); and Thera Nyantiloka's invaluable *Guide Through the Abhidhamma Pitaka,* rev. ed. (Colombo, Buddhist Sahitya Sabha, 1957).

For those who find anthologies helpful the alternatives are legion. However, two compilations done in the nineteenth century have never been surpassed. The first is Henry Warren's *Buddhism in Translation* (Cambridge, Harvard Univ. Press, rep. 1953), and the second is T.W. Rhys Davids' *Buddhist Suttas* (N.Y., Dover, rep. 1969). Four other collections which may be used for particular purposes are J.G. Jennings, *The Vendantic Buddhism of Gotama the Buddha* (London, Oxford, 1947); George F. Allen, *The Buddha's Philosophy* (N.Y., Macmillan, 1959); I.B. Horner, *Early Buddhist Poetry* (Colombo, A. Semage, 1963); and Caroline Rhys Davids, *Poems of the Cloister and Jungle* (N.Y., Gordon, 1954).

STUDIES OF DOCTRINE   Given the knowledge which Buddhologists have generated concerning the gradual and relatively late development of the canon, it has long been recognized that it is not possible to reconstruct the specific content of the message which the Buddha himself taught. Although most scholars have not come to accept this fact, a number have nevertheless made serious attempts to identify a doctrinal orientation which preceded the orientation dominating the formation of the canonical tradition. Among the important studies which should be consulted in this regard are Stanislaw Schayer, "Precanonical Buddhism," *Archiv Orientali,* 7 (1935), 121–32; the response by Arthur S. Keith, in *IHQ* 12 (1936), 1–20; and the later evaluation by Constantin Regamey entitled "Le Schayer," *Rocznik Orientalistyczny,* 21 (1956), 37–58.

Most important studies of early Buddhist doctrines have, however, been efforts to elucidate various aspects or strands of the tradition found in the canonical texts. A few of the more interesting short contributions are the following: Maryla Falk's survey of La Vallée Poussin's work on "Nairatmya and Karman," *IHQ,* 16 (1940); Donald Swearer, "Two Types of Saving Knowledge in the Pali Suttas," *PEW,* 22 (1972), 355–71; Alex Wayman, "Buddhist Dependent Origination," *HR,* X, 3 (1971), 185–203; and B.G. Gokhale, "Dharma as a Political Concept in Early Buddhism," *JIH,* 44 (Aug., 1968), 249–61. Longer, book-length studies include La Vallée Poussin, *The Way to Nirvana* (Cambridge Univ. Press, 1917); I.B. Horner, *Early Buddhist Theory of Man Perfected* (London, Williams & Norgate, 1936); J. Evola, *The Doctrine of the Awakening* (London, Luzac, 1951); and Joseph Masson, *La Religion populaire dans le canon bouddhique pali* (Louvain: Bureaux du Muséon, 1942), which covers materials often ignored by modern scholars. Studies of the scholastic tradition are available in K.N. Jayatilleka, *Early Buddhist Theory of Knowledge* (London, Allen & Unwin, 1963); Anagarika Govinda, *The Psychological Attitude of Early Buddhist Philosophy and Its Systematic Representation according to the Abhidhamma Tradition* (London, Rider, 1969); and J. Kashyap, *The Abhi-Dhamma Philosophy, or the Social-Ethical Philosophy of Early Buddhism,* 2 vols. (Sarnath & Benares, Mahabodhi Society, 1942, 1943). In addition the reader may also consult Herbert V. Guenther, *Philosophy and*

Psychology in the Abhidhamma, rev. ed. (Berkeley, Shambhala, 1973), and Th. Stcherbatsky's classic study, *The Central Conception of Buddhism and the Meaning of the Word Dharma,* which was reprinted by Susil Gupta in Calcutta, 1956.

The other studies specifically on the distinctive doctrines of particular schools see Étienne Lamotte, "Buddhist Controversy over the Five Propositions,'" *IHQ,* 32 (1956), 148–62; Nalinaksha Dutt, "Doctrines of the Mahasanghika School of Buddhism," *IHQ,* 13 (1937), 549–80, and 14 (1938), 110–13; Nalinaksha Dutt, "Doctrines of the Sammitya School of Buddhism" *IHQ,* 15 (1939), 90–100; and Isaline B. Horner, "Buddhism: The Theravada" in R.C. Zaehner, ed., *The Concise Encyclopedia of Living Faiths* (London, Hutchison, 1959), 267–94.

DEVELOPMENTS IN BUDDHOLOGY   Though we have very little precise historical information concerning the life of the Buddha, we do know that the community—and especially its lay component—remembered aspects of his career, generated legends concerning his life and activities, and venerated the symbols associated with his person. The best overall introductions to the subject are Alfred Foucher, *The Life of the Buddha* (Middletown, Conn., Wesleyan Univ. Press, 1963) tr. and abr. by Simone Boas; E.J. Thomas, *The Life of the Buddha in Legend and History* (*op. cit.*) and Étienne Lamotte's article on "La Légende du Bouddha," *Revue de l'histoire des religions,* 134 (1947), 37–71, in which the stages in the development of the sacred biography are carefully delineated.

In more recent years much progress has been made in isolating and interpreting the various legendary cycles, particularly those which deal with the Buddha's final life as Gautama. However all of the really substantial studies have been in European languages, and none of them has thus far been translated. Paul Hirsch has published a fascinating article on "Buddhas erste Meditation," *ASES* (1964), parts 3/4, 100–154; but the major portions of the important work have been done by André Bareau and have been reported in a series of studies which include "Le jeunesse du Bouddha dans les Sutrapitaka et les Vinayapitaka anciens," *BEFEO,* 61 (1974), 199–274, and the three volumes of his *Recherches sur la biographie du Bouddha dans les Sutrapitaka et les Vinayapitaka anciens* (Paris, EFEO, 1963, 1970, 1971).

The earliest autonomous though still "incomplete" biographies which appeared in the first century A.D., the first "complete" biography which appeared in the second century A.D., and the classical Pali biography which appeared in the fifth century A.D., are all available in translation. For the "incomplete" biographies see Philippe E. Foucaux, tr., *Le Lalita Vistara,* 2 vols. (Paris, Leroux, 1884, 1892), and J.J. Jones, tr., *The Mahavastu,* 3 vols. (PTS, London, Luzac, 1949, 1952, 1956). For Asvagosha's more "complete" and readable text see E.H. Johnstone, tr., *The Buddhacarita or*

Acts of the Buddha, Part II (Lahore, Univ. of Punjab, 1936), which contains the first fourteen cantos, and "The Buddha's Mission and Last Journey: Buddhacarita XV–XVIII" in *AO,* XV, 1 (1936), 26–62. For the much later Pali treatment, which serves as an introduction to the Jataka Commentary, see C.A. Rhys Davids, ed., *Buddhist Birth Stories* (N.Y., E.P. Dutton, 1925). As for the Jatakas themselves a Sanskrit collection has been translated by Jacob Speyer, *The Gatakamala or Garland of Birth Stories* (London, Frowde, 1895), while the Pali collection has been translated by E.W. Cowell, et al., 6 vols. in 3 (PTS, London, Luzac, 1969).

Aspects of the development of Buddhology which paralleled the emergence of the literary biographies are traced by Adris Banerji in *Origins of Early Buddhist Church Art* (Calcutta, Sanskrit College, 1967); by Walter Spink in an article "On the Development of Early Buddhist Art in India," *Art Bulletin,* XL, 2 (1958), 95–104; by Alfred Foucher in *L'Orgine grecque de l'image du Bouddha* (Challon-sur Saone, Annals du Musée Guimet, 1912); and by Ananda Coomaraswamy in a well-known response to Foucher entitled "The Origin of the Buddha Image," originally published in the *Art Bulletin,* IX, 4 (June, 1927), 287–328, and recently reprinted in New Delhi by Munshiram Manoharlal, 1972. A rather different dimension is introduced by André Bareau and Mireille Bénisti in two technical but very important articles entitled "La construction et le culte du stupa d'après les Vinayapitaka," which appeared in *BEFEO,* L, 2 (1960), 229–74, and "Étude sur la stupa dans l'Inde ancienne" in *BEFEO,* L, 1 (1960), 37–116.

The developments expressed in these mythic, artistic and architectural images of the Buddha were closely related to the changing conceptions of his status and powers. An interesting study which touches upon these changing conceptions is carried through by André Bareau in his article. "The Superhuman Personality of the Buddha" in J.M. Kitagawa and C. Long, eds., *Myths and Symbols* (Chicago, Univ. of Chicago Press, 1969). For more technical studies which deal with conceptions of the Buddha's powers see Padmanabh S. Jaini's article on "The Buddha's Prolongation of Life" in *BSOAS,* 21 (1958), 546–52, and his article "On the Sarvajnatva (Omniscience) of Mahavira and the Buddha" in *Buddhist Studies in Honour of I.B. Horner* (*op. cit.*)

Though in the Hinayana tradition the Gautama Buddha and his career were in the foreground, other foci of Buddhological interest also developed. The very important figure of the Maitreya Buddha is treated by Sylvain Levi in his "Maitreya le consolateur," *Études d'orientalisme,* tome II (Paris, Leroux, 1932). Another dimension is explored by Theresa Rowell in her article on the "Background and Early Use of the Buddha-Ksetra Concept" in *EB,* 6 (1932–35), 199–246. Moreover, it is also worth noting that the early community supplemented its interest in Buddhology as such with an hagiographic and biographic interest in other key figures. For a prime example see André Migot, "Un grand disciple du Bouddha: Sariputra. Son rôle dans l'histoire du bouddhisme et dans le développement de l'Abhidharma," *BEFEO,* XLVI, 2 (1954), 405–554. For a fascinating study of the tradition which developed around the figure of the Buddha's cousin and archetypal opponent see Biswader Mukherjee, *Die Überlieferung von Devadatta, dem Widersacher des Buddha in den Kanonische Schriften* (München, Kitzinger, 1966) and the review by David Ruegg in *TP,* 54 (1968), 164–68.

EARLY BUDDHISM AND CONTIGUOUS TRADITIONS   In addition to the works which deal primarily with early Buddhism as such, there are a number of interesting studies focussing on its relationship to various Indian traditions that preceded or coexisted with it. In the first edition of this volume pp. 88–89, Richard Gard cited a number of older sources; but since that time several significant new studies have been published. For example, a comprehensive survey and analysis have been provided in chap. II of K.N. Upadhyaya, *Early Buddhism and the Bhagavadgita* (Delhi, Motilal Banarsidass, 1971). The Vedic and Upanishadic background has been considered in V.P. Varma, "The Vedic Tradition and the Origins of Buddhism," *JBRS,* 46 (1960), 276–308; in Pratap Chandra, "Was Early Buddhism Influenced by the Upanishads?" *PEW,* XXI, 3 (July, 1971), 317–25; and in a most provocative way by Orlan Lee in "From Acts to Non-Action to Acts," *HR,* VI, 4 (May, 1967), 273–302. Other aspects have been highlighted by N.N. Bhattacharyya in his article on "Brahmanical, Buddhist and Jain Cosmology," *JIH,* LXVII, 1 (April, 1969), and by B.C. Law in "The Concept of Morality in Buddhism and Jainism," *JRAS* (Bombay), ns. 34/35 (1959/1960), 1–21. And finally aspects of the complex relationships between early Buddhism and the Samkhya tradition have been considered by K.B. Ramakrishna Rao in "The Buddhacarita and the Samkhya of Arada Kalama," *Adyar Library Bulletin,* 28 (Dec., 1964), 231–44, and in a much more technical way in Esho Yamagushi's analysis of "The Problem of Dharma in Buddhism and the Dharma-Adharma in Samkhya," *JIBS,* XIII, 2 (March, 1965), 28–34.

Later developments and the Mahayana–Vajrayana traditions

HISTORICAL STUDIES: INDIA PROPER   Many of the best discussions of the later Buddhist tradition in India are contained in works previously cited; see, for example, the more comprehensive studies listed in Section II A, the relevant segments of the accounts and observations of the Chinese pilgrims, and many of the essays in the India-oriented collections of essays. However, there are also some studies which focus directly on various aspects of later Buddhist life and on the Mahayana and Vajrayana traditions.

In addition to Grousset's *In the Footsteps of the Buddha* (*op. cit.*) there are several other studies which use the accounts of the Chinese pilgrims to describe Buddhism and its condition in various periods and places in medieval India. Two book-length works of this type are Surendranath Sen, *India through Chinese Eyes* (Madras, Univ. of Madras, 1956), and Catherine Meuwese, *L'Inde du Bouddha vue par des pèlerins chinois sous la dynastie Tang* (Paris, Calman-Levy, 1968). Two articles which follow a similar procedure are Thich Minh Chau, "Monastic Life in India in the 5th century A.D. as Seen by Fa Hsien," *JBRS,* XLVII (1961), 65–71, and Jan Yun Hua, "South India in the VIIIth Century—Hui-chao's Description Re-examined," *OE,* 15 (1968), 169–77. Stephan Darian has contributed a description of "Buddhism in Bihar from the 8th to the 12th Century with Special Reference to Nalanda," *ASES,* 25 (1971), 335–52, which may be profitably supplemented by H.D. Sankalia, *The University of Nalanda* (Madras, B.G. Paul, 1934). The most substantial and detailed work which uses the widest range of sources is Lal Mani Joshi, *Studies in the Buddhistic Culture of India during the 7th and 8th Centuries A.D.* (Delhi, Motilal Banarsidass, 1967).

The decline of Buddhism in India has also been the subject of several articles. Among them three of the most helpful are: P.C. Bagchi, "Decline of Buddhism in India and Its Causes," *MSJV,* III, 3 (1925), 405–21; R.C. Mitra, "The Decline of Buddhism in India" in *Visva-Bharati Annals,* 6 (1954), 1–164, and *Visva-Bharati Studies,* 20 (1954), and Lal Mani Joshi, "Reviews of Some Alleged Causes of the Decline of Buddhism in India," *Journal of the Ganganath Jha Research Institute,* XX, 1/2 (Nov., 1965/ Feb., 1966), 23–38.

HISTORICAL STUDIES: NORTHWESTERN INDIA AND CENTRAL ASIA
From the time of King Asoka (third century B.C.) Buddhism was established in northwestern India; by the beginning of the Christian era it had spread into Central Asia; and during the following centuries Buddhist communities were prominent in both areas. Buddhism in northwestern India is discussed in Étienne Lamotte, "Alexandre et le bouddhisme," *BEFEO,* 44 (1947–51), 147–62, and "Du quelques influences grecques et scythes sur le bouddhisme," *Académie des Inscriptions et Belles Lettres, Comptes-rendus des séances* (1956), 485–504. In recent years the Kushana dynasty and subsequent developments have been explored by Alexander Belenitski in *Central Asia,* tr. by James Hogarth (London, Cresset, 1969); by B.A. Livitsky in "Outline History of Buddhism in Central Asia" in *Kushan Studies in the USSR* (Calcutta, India Past and Present, 1970), 53–132; and by Kshanika Saha in *Buddhism and Buddhist Literature in Central Asia* (Calcutta, K.L. Mukhopadhyaya, 1970). The relevant portions of Grousset's presentation of the observations of the Chinese pilgrims may also be consulted. These may be supplemented by Marc Aurel Stein, "La

traversée du désert par Hiuan-tsang en 630 ap. J.C.," *TP,* 20 (1921), 332–54.

Particular centers and developments in the northwest India–Central Asian area have been treated in G. Koshelenko, "The Beginnings of Buddhism in Margiana," *Acta Antiqua: Academie Scientarum Hungarica,* 14 (1966), 175–83; in John Brough, "Comments on the Third Century Shanshan and the History of Buddhism," *BSOAS,* 28 (1965), 582–612; in Jean-Paul Roux, "Les Religions des turcs de l'Orkhon des VIIe et VIIIe siècles," *Revue de l'histoire des religions,* 161 (Jan./March, 1962), 1–24; in Fredrick W. Thomas, "Buddhism in Khotan: Its Decline According to Two Tibetan Accounts," *MSJV,* III, 3 (1927), 30–52; and in Zenryu Tsukamoto, "Historical Outlines of Buddhism in Tunhuang," *MS,* 1, 1–10. Those interested in Buddhist texts will also want to consult Fredric R. Hoernle, *Manscript Remains of Buddhist Literature Found in Eastern Turkestan,* vol. I (London, Oxford, 1916); Pavel Pouchá, "Indian Literature in Central Asia," *AO,* 2 (1930), 27–38; and Lionel Giles, *Six Centuries at Tun-huang* (London, China Society, 1944).

Buddhism was established from a very early date in the valley of Kashmir in the Himalayan region of northwestern India where it had a rather separate and distinctive history. This history has been surveyed in booklength treatments by Sarla Khosla, *History of Buddhism in Kashmir* (New Delhi, Sagar, 1972) and Jean Nandou, *Les Bouddhistes kashmiriens au moyen-Age* (Paris, Presses universitaires de France, 1968); a shorter discussion can be found in Nalinaksha Dutt's essay on "Buddhism in Kashmir," included in his edited *Gilgit Manuscripts,* vol. I (Srinagar, Gov't. of Jammu and Kashmir, 1939), 1–40; and a special aspect is taken up in Jan Yun Hua's article on "Kashmir's Contribution to the Expansion of Buddhism in the Far East" in *IHQ,* 37 (June/Sept. 1961), 93–104.

THE MAHAYANA TRADITION   Any reader concerned with the later phases of Indian Buddhist history and the history of Buddhism in Central Asia must keep in mind that Hinayana Buddhism never lost its position as an important force in the thought and life of the Buddhist community. Nevertheless, it is also true that the most creative and interesting developments were those associated with the emergence and development of the Mahayana and Vajrayana traditions.

Good survey treatments of the Mahayana tradition as a whole are surprisingly rare. Edward Conze's essay on "Buddhism: The Mahayana" in R.C. Zaehner, ed., *The Concise Encyclopedia of Living Faiths (op. cit.)* provides one excellent starting point and may be supplemented by a booklength treatment such as Beatrice L. Suzuki's *Mahayana Buddhism* (N.Y., Macmillan, 1965); Nalinaksha Dutt's *Mahayana Buddhism* (Calcutta, K.L. Mukhopadhyaya, 1973); or Edward Conze, ed. of D.T. Suzuki on *Indian Mahayana Buddhism* (N.Y., Harper & Row, 1968). Useful anthologies of texts include E.J. Thomas, *The Quest for Enlightenment* (London, John Murray, 1952), and especially E.B. Cowell et al., eds., *Buddhist Mahayana Texts* (rep. N.Y., Dover, 1969).

The origins of Mahayana are explored by Ryukan Kimura in *A Historical Study of the Terms Hinayana and Mahayana and the Origins of Mahayana Buddhism* (Calcutta, Univ. of Calcutta Press, 1927); and in articles by B.M. Barua on "Mahayana in the Making," *MSJV,* III (1927), 163–80; by Étienne Lamotte "Sur la formation du Mahayana," *Asiatica,* 377–96; and by Rahula Sankrityayana on "Les Origines du Mahayana," *JA* (Oct./Dec., 1934). More recently Japanese scholars have made important new contributions; see, for example, Hajime Nakamura, "Historical Studies of the Coming into Being of Mahayana Sutras," *Proceedings of the Okurayama Oriental Research Institute,* II (Oct., 1956) 1–22, and especially Akira Hirakawa's article on "The Rise of Mahayana Buddhism and Its Relation to the Worship of Stupas," *MRDBT,* 22 (1963), 57–106. For the translation of a text which, though technically Hinayana, stands on the boundary line of Mahayana, see Hideo and Alex Wayman, trs., *The Lion's Roar of Queen Sri Mala* (N.Y., Columbia Univ. Press, 1974).

A body of literature which played a key role in the emergence and development of the Mahayana tradition has been surveyed by Edward Conze in *The Prajñaparamita Literature* ('s Gravenhage, Mouton, 1960) and by Ryusho Hikata in "An Introductory Essay on the Prajñaparamita" in his *Suvikrantavikramipariprccha Prajñaparamitra-sutra* (Fukuoka, Kyushu Univ., 1958). "A Summary of Various Research on the Prajñaparamitra Literature by Japanese Scholars" has been made available by Shoyu Hanayama in *Acta Asiatica,* 10 (1966), 16–93. In addition Edward Conze has written relevant articles including "The Ontology of the Prajñaparamita," *PEW,* III, 2 (July, 1953), 117–29, and "The Iconography of the Prajñaparamita," *Oriental Art,* II, 2 (Autumn, 1949), 47–52, and III, 3 (1951), 104–09. What is more important, he has provided an abundance of translations including earlier anthologies under the titles, *Selected Sayings from the Perfection of Wisdom* (London, Buddhist Society, 1955), and *Buddhist Wisdom Books* (London, Allen & Unwin, 1958), as well as an important collection of *The Short Prajñaparamita Texts* (London, Luzac, 1974), and *The Perfection of Wisdom in 8,000 Lines and Its Verse Summary* (Bolinas, Four Seasons, 1973).

The changing conceptions of the Buddha and particularly the emerging Mahayana conception of the three bodies of the Buddha have been the subject of a number of important investigations. Discussions which emphasize the conceptual aspects include a good introductory treatment by Gadjin Nagao, "On the Theory of the Buddha-body" in *EB,* 6 (1973), 25–53, and more technical essays by LaVallée Poussin entitled "Buddhist Dogma: The Three Bodies of the Buddha" in *JRAS* (1906), 943–77, and M.P. Masson-Oursel on "Les Trois corps du Bouddha," *JA* (1913), 581–

618. These works should, however, be supplemented by Herbert Guenther, "The Psychology of the Three Kayas," *Uttara Bharati*, 2 (1955), 37–50, and by Akanuma Chinzen's article on "The Triple Body of the Buddha" in *EB*, 2 (1922), 1–29, in which the important roles of religious faith and popular traditions are delineated.

Finally, those interested in a basic overview of the Indian Mahayana tradition must take into account the emergence of the Bodhisatva ideal and the role of the great Bodhisatvas in the religious life of the community. An excellent study has been done by Har Dayal on *The Bodhisatva Doctrine in Sanskrit Literature,* recently reprinted in Delhi by Motilal Banarsidass, 1970. An insight into the character of the great Indian Bodhisatvas and their role in later Indian Buddhism can be gained by consulting Alfred Foucher's *Étude sur l'iconographie bouddhique de l'Inde,* 2 vols. (Paris, E. Leroux, 1900 and 1905), esp. vol. I, 99–127, and vol. II, 22–49. Moreover, two excellent book-length studies of particular Bodhisatvas have been published by Theresa Mallman; see *Introduction à l'étude d'Avalokitesvara* (Paris, Civilization du Sud, 1948), and *Étude iconographique sur Manjusri* (Paris, EFEO, 1964). The reader who would like to consult an early Mahayana text in which Bodhisatvas play a prominent role has at his disposal Fredrick Kern's translation of *The Lotus of the True Law,* reprinted in N.Y. by Dover, 1963.

THE MAHAYANA SCHOOLS   The more philosophical side of Indian Mahayana Buddhism was developed in the context of two major schools: the Madhyamika and the Yogacara. The Madhyamika was the first of these schools to emerge, and it has been a prime focus of modern scholarly interest. A useful introduction to the Madhyamika position is presented in Richard Robinson, "Madhyamika" in Joseph Elder, ed., *Chapters in Indian Civilization,* vol. I (*op. cit.*), 202–10; while other short discussions have been provided in R.C. Pandeya, "The Madhyamika Philosophy," *PEW*, XIV, 1 (April, 1964) and in Alex Wayman's article, "Contributions to the Madhyamika School of Buddhism,'" *JAOS* (Jan./March, 1969), 141–52. An older but still useful book on the topic is T.R.V. Murti, *The Central Philosophy of Buddhism* (N.Y., Macmillan, 1955). For more recent book-length interpretations see Kenneth Inada's *Nagarjuna: A Translation of His Mulamadhyamikakarika with an Introductory Essay* (Tokyo, Hokuseido, 1970); Fredrick Streng's more comparatively oriented work on *Emptiness: A Study of Religious Meaning* (N.Y., Abingdon, 1967); and V. Vankata Ramanan's analysis of *Nagarjuna's Philosophy as Presented in the Mahaprajnaparamita-sastra* (Harvard Yenching Institute; Rutland, Vt., Tuttle, 1966). In this latter connection readers should at least be aware that portions of the voluminous and extremely rich text on which Ramanan's study is based have been translated by Étienne Lamotte under the title, *Le Traité de la grande vertu de sagesse de Nagarjuna,* 3 vols. (Louvain, Bibliothèque Muséon No. 19, 1944 and 1949; and Institut Orientalist 2, 1970). However, more important for most readers is Marion Matics' translation of Santideva's *Entering the Path of Enlightenment* (N.Y., Macmillan, 1970), in which the Madhyamika point of view is expressed in a relatively short poetic work of the highest literary quality.

An introduction to the Yogacara perspective can be gleaned from Richard Robinson's contribution on "Vijnanavada" in the Elder volume cited above, from Alex Wayman's article on "The Yogacara Idealism," *PEW,* XV, 1 (Jan., 1965), 65–73, and from Yoshifumu Ueda, "Two Streams of Thought in Yogacara Philosophy," *PEW,* XVII, 1–4 (Jan.–Oct., 1967), 155–65. More extensive treatments are provided by Surendranath Dasgupta in chaps. 4 and 5 of his *Indian Idealism* (Cambridge, Cambridge Univ. Press, 1969); by Sylvain Levi, et al. in *Matériaux pour l'étude de le système Vijnaptimatra* (Paris, Librairie Honoré Champion, 1932); by Jacques May in his article on "La philosophie bouddhique idéaliste," *ASES,* 25 (1971), 265–323; and by Ashok K. Chatterjee in a longer but less adequate study entitled *The Yogacara Idealism* (Benares, Benares Hindu Univ., 1962). The technical but important topic of Buddhist logic is treated in a definitive fashion by Giuseppe Tucci, *On Some Aspects of the Doctrines of Maitreya* (natha) and *Asanga* (Calcutta, Univ. of Calcutta, 1930), and more comprehensively by Th. Stcherbatsky in his two-volume *Buddhist Logic* (N.Y., Dover, 1962). In regard to translated texts it is unfortunate that there are none which can be easily utilized by beginning students; however, those who are seriously interested may consult Alex Wayman's translation of portions of the Yogacarabhumi sastra in his *Analysis of the Sravakabhumi Manuscript* (Univ. of California Pub. in Classical Philology No. 17; Berkeley, Univ. of California Press, 1961), 58–134 and 163–85, and especially Étienne Lamotte's *La Somme du grand véhicule d'Asanga* (Louvain, Bureaux du Muséon, 1938), vol. 2.

In addition to works which deal with the philosophical orientations of the two schools, a number of studies have been published which focus on key figures. Studies on figures important in the Madhyamika context include Max Walleser, "The Life of Nagarjuna from Tibetan and Chinese Sources" in Bruno Schindler, ed., *Hirth Anniversary Volume* (London, Arthur Probsthain, 1923), 421–55; Jan Yun Hua, "Nagarjuna, One or More?" *HR,* X, 2 (Nov., 1970), 139–55; P.S. Sastri "Nagarjuna and Aryadeva," *IHQ,* XXXI, 3 (Sept., 1955), 193–202; David F. Casey, "Nagarjuna and Chandrakirti: A Study of Significant Differences," *TICO,* 9 (1964), 34–45; and Amalia Pezzali, *Santideva: Mystique bouddhiste des VIIᵉ et VIIIᵉ siècle* (Firenze, Vallechi, 1968). Among those which give attention to figures in the Yogacara school are Hakuju Ui, "Maitreya as an Historical Personage" in *Indian Studies in Honor of Charles Rockwell Lanman* (Cambridge, Harvard Univ. Press, 1929); Erich Frauwallner, *On the Date of the Buddhist Master of the Law, Vasubandhu* (Rome, Serie

Orientale, 1951); Padmanabh Jaini, "On the Theory of the Two Vasu-bandhus," *BSOAS,* 21 (1958), 45–53; and Yuichi Kajiyama, "Bhavavi-veka, Sthiramati and Dharmapala," *Wiener Zeitschrift für die Kunde Süd und Ost-asiens und Archiv für Indische Philosophie,* XII–XIII (1968/ 1969), 193–203.

Alongside these works which focus primarily on the Mahayana schools and the important personages who represent them, there are also a few studies devoted primarily to the exploration of relationships between the philosophical thought of one or more of these schools and various aspects of Hindu philosophy. Short essays of this kind include Edward T. Jones, "Hinduism and the Development of Mahayana Buddhism," *Journal of the Society for Asian Studies* (Provo, Utah), II (April, 1969), 57–68; two essays entitled "Buddhism and Vedanta," one by P.T. Raju in *Indo-Asian Culture,* VI, 1 (July, 1957), 24–48, and the other by Chandradhar Sharma in his *Critical Survey of Indian Philosophy* (N.Y., Barnes and Noble, 1962), 318–34; Ajit R. Bhattacharya's article on "Sankara and the Bud-dhistic Speculations," *Journal of the Assam Research Society,* XIV (1960), 43–53, Karuna Bhattacharya's discussion of "Sankara's Criticism of Bud-dhism," *Journal of the Indian Academy of Philosophy* (Calcutta), I (July, 1961/Feb. 1962), 53–64; and T.R.V. Murti's essay on "Samvrti and Paramatha in Madhyamika and Advaita Vedanta" in *The Problem of Two Truths in Buddhism and Vedanta* (Boston, Reidel, 1973). Two books which develop the comparisons in a more extended and technical way are Chandradhar Sharma's *Dialectics in Buddhism and Vedanta* (Benares, Nand Kishore, 1962) and Dharmendra Nath Sastri's *Critique of Indian Realism* (Agra, Agra Univ., 1964).

THE VAJRAYANA TRADITION   In the earlier phases of modern Bud-dhist studies the last form of Indian Buddhism, which was known variously as Vajrayana, Mantrayana, Tantric Buddhism, or Esoteric Buddhism, et al., was considered to be a degeneration from the purer forms of Buddhist doctrine and practice, and therefore received relatively little serious study. In recent years, as this attitude has changed, attention has come to focus primarily on the Vajrayana tradition as it has been preserved and developed in Tibet. Thus adequate treatments specifically on the origins and develop-ment of the Vajrayana in India are difficult to find.

A substantial starting point is provided by Shashibushan Dasgupta's *Introduction to Tantric Buddhism,* recently reprinted with a helpful "fore-word" by Herbert Guenther (Berkeley, Shambhala, 1974). An interesting complement to Dasgupta's approach is provided by Benoytosh Bhatta-charyya in four closely related works: the "Introduction" to vol. II of his edition of the *Sadhanamala* (Baroda, Gaekwad's Oriental Series, No. 41, 1928), *An Introduction to Buddhist Esoterism* (London, Oxford, 1932), *Indian Buddhist Iconography,* rev. ed. (Calcutta, K.L. Mukhopadhyaya,

1958), and "The Buddhist Pantheon and Its Classification" in *Commemorative Essays Presented to Professor Kashinath Bapuji Pathak* (Poona, Bhandakar Oriental Research Institute, 1934). Relevant shorter discussions by other scholars include Rahula Sankrityayana, "L'Origine du Vajrayana," *JA* (Oct./Dec., 1934), 209–30; Mircea Eliade's chapter on "Yoga and Tantrism" in *Yoga: Immortality and Freedom* (*op. cit.*); Nalinaksha Dutt, "Tantric Buddhism," *Bulletin of Tibetology*, I, 2 (1964), 5–16; Bisheshwar P. Singh, "Naropa: His Life and Activities," *JBRS*, 53 (1967), 117–29; and David Snellgrove, "The Notion of Divine Kingship in Tantric Buddhism" in *The Sacral Kingship* (Leiden, E.J. Brill, 1959). Several of Alex Wayman's essays in *The Buddhist Tantras: Light on Indo-Tibetan Esoterism* (N.Y., Weiser, 1973) focus on Indian Buddhism; and Helmut Hoffman has examined "Das Kalacakra, die letze Phase des Buddhismus in Indien," in *Saeculum,* 15 (1964) 125–31. In addition Shashibushan Dasgupta has discussed some late offshoots of the Vajrayana tradition in *Obscure Religious Cults as Background of Bengal Literature,* 2nd rev. ed. (Calcutta, K.L. Mukhopadhyaya, 1962).

A good indication of the contents of a very early and important Vajrayana text can be gained from reading the rather detailed synopsis which Benoytosh Bhattacharyya provides as an introduction to his edition of the *Guhyasamaja Tantra or Tathagataguhyaka* (Gaekwad Oriental Series No. 53; Baroda, Oriental Institute, 1931), ix–xxxviii, and Giuseppe Tucci's commentary on Bhattacharrya's edition in "Some Glosses on the Guyhasamaja," *MCB,* 3, 339–53. For a full translation of a somewhat later but influential text accompanied by a helpful introduction, see David Snellgrove, tr., *The Hevajra Tantra,* vol. I (London, Oxford, 1959). For other Indian Vajrayana texts, presented along with later Tibetan interpretations, see below, Section V, A.

BUDDHISM IN MODERN INDIA   In India during the period from the thirteenth century to the end of the nineteenth century Buddhism existed only in a few very isolated areas. However, beginning at the very end of the nineteenth century there was a resurgence of interest in Buddhism, first among certain groups of intellectuals, and more recently among the so-called scheduled classes of "untouchables" led by the late B.H. Ambedkar. The revival of interest among Indian intellectuals in the late nineteenth and early twentieth centuries is discussed in several of the surveys and collections which deal with Buddhism in the modern world, perhaps most clearly in Ernst Benz's *Buddhism or Communism* (*op. cit.*); and this movement has produced the journal *Mahabodhi* which contains numerous short articles on all aspects of Buddhism. Though he was not a part of the Buddhist movement as such, Sarvapali Radhakrishnan reflects its spirit in his work, *Gautama the Buddha* (London, Milford, 1933), and in his

Buddha's Life by Modern Indian Painters (Madras, Associated Printers, 1957).

In contrast to the revival of interest in Buddhism in intellectual circles the so-called Neo-Buddhist movement touched off by B.H. Ambedkar's conversion in 1956 has brought several million converts at least nominally into the Buddhist fold. Short articles on the subject include Robert J. Miller, " 'They will not die Hindus': the Buddhist Conversion of Mahar Ex-Untouchables," *Asian Survey* (Sept., 1967), 637–44; Adele Fisk, "Religion and Buddhism among India's New Buddhists," *Social Research,* XXVI, 1 (Spring, 1969); and Eleanor Zelliott, "Background of the Mahar Buddhist Conversion" in Robert Sakai, ed., *Studies in Asia: 1966* (Lincoln, Univ. of Nebraska Press, 1966), 49–63; "Buddhism and Politics in Maharashtra" in Donald E. Smith, ed., *South Asian Religion and Politics* (Princeton, Princeton Univ. Press, 1966), and "The Revival of Buddhism in India," *Asia,* 10 (Winter, 1968), 33–45. Another important secondary source is Owen Lynch, *The Politics of Untouchability* (N.Y., Columbia Univ. Press, 1969), esp. 129–65; while the most interesting primary document is Ambedkar's fascinating re-telling of the Buddha's life, published under the title *The Buddha and His Dhamma* (Bombay, People's Education Society, 1957).

III. BUDDHISM IN SRI LANKA (CEYLON) AND SOUTHEAST ASIA

During the reign of King Asoka in the 3rd century B.C. Buddhist missionaries were sent out to establish Buddhism, not only in many areas of the Indian subcontinent, but also in Sri Lanka, and quite probably in certain areas of Southeast Asia as well. During a period of well over a millennium Sinhalese and Southeast Asian Buddhism developed in close relationship to Buddhism in India; and what is more, when Indian Buddhism went into decline and virtually passed out of existence, a reformed Theravada tradition established itself in Ceylon, Burma, Thailand, Laos, and Cambodia. Though it needs to be remembered that the whole range of Indian Buddhist schools have played a significant role in these areas, the Theravada tradition has held a position of particular historical importance and has, therefore, received the greatest amount of scholarly attention.

A. The Theravada tradition

BASIC ORIENTATION   Since there is no modern study which attempts anything like a full-blown structural and historical description of the Theravada tradition, the reader who seeks to gain a perspective on the whole is forced to resort to a variety of different materials. So far as I am aware, the only source providing a reasonably adequate account of Theravada Buddhology and its development is my own article on "The Many Lives of Buddha: A Study of Sacred Biography and Theravada Tradition," forthcoming in Frank E. Reynolds and Donald Capps, eds., *The Biographical Process: Essays in the History and Psychology of Religion* (The Hague, Mouton, 1976). Insights into the doctrinal orientation of the tradition, however, can be gained by reading any one of a number of books by modern Theravada scholars such as Walpole Rahula's *What the Buddha Taught* (N.Y., Grove, 1962); Widurupola Piyadassi's *The Buddha's Ancient Path* (London, Rider, 1964); H. Saddhatissa's *The Buddha's Way* (N.Y., Braziller, 1972); or K.N. Jayatilleke's *The Message of the Buddha* (London, Allen & Unwin, 1975). These may be supplemented by an account of the more traditional beliefs such as that by R. Spence Hardy in *A Manual of Buddhism,* 2nd ed. (London, Williams and Norgate, 1880). In addition, one may profitably consult the books of two Western scholars which take special account of the views of Burmese informants, viz.: Robert Slater's *Paradox and Nibbana* (Chicago, Univ. of Chicago Press, 1951), and Winston King's *A Thousand Lives Away* (Cambridge, Harvard Univ. Press, 1964).

The ethical aspect of Theravada teaching, including both its personal and more social emphases, is presented in two books entitled *Buddhist Ethics,* one by S. Tachibana (N.Y., Barnes & Noble, 1975) and one by H. Saddhatissa (N.Y., Braziller, 1971). The same topic is treated in a challenging and interesting way in Winston King, *In Hope of Nibbana* (LaSalle, Ill., Open Court, 1964). The Theravada perspectives on history and political ethics are the subject of a series of articles by B.G. Gokhale which include "The Theravada View of History," *JAOS,* LXXXV, 3 (July/Sept., 1965); "Dhamma as a Political Concept in Early Buddhism," *JIH,* XLIV, 1 (Nov., 1966); "The Early Buddhist View of the State," *JAOS,* LXXXIX, 4 (Oct./Dec., 1969), 731–38; and "Early Buddhist Kingship," *JAS,* XXVI, 1 (Nov. 1966). Related problems concerning secular involvement are discussed by Stanley J. Tambiah in an article on "Buddhism and This-Worldly Activity" which appeared in *Modern Asian Studies* VIII, 1 (1973), 1–20.

The important topic of Theravada meditation is taken up by Pe Maung Tin in his work on *Buddhist Devotion and Meditation* (London, S.P.C.K., 1964), and is explored in greater depth by Peravahera Vajiranana in *Buddhist Meditation in Theory and Practice* (Colombo, Gunasena, 1962). However, the best sources are perhaps Thera Nyanaponika, *The Heart of Buddhist Meditation* (London, Rider, 1962); Donald Swearer, "Control and Freedom: The Structure of Buddhist Meditation in the Pali Suttas," *PEW,* XXIII, 4 (Oct., 1973); and Daniel Coleman's important article on "The Buddha on Meditation and States of Consciousness" in the *Journal of Transpersonal Psychology,* 4 (1972), 2 parts. In the area of ritual, the very widespread practice of chanting particular Pali texts for the purpose of exorcism and protection has been studied by Otakar Perold, "A Protective Ritual of the Southern Buddhist," *JRAS* (Bengal), XII, 6 (1922–23), 744–89; by Marguerite La Fuente, tr., *Paritta* (Paris, Adrien Maisonneuve, 1941); and by Ernst Waldschmidt in *Von Ceylon bis Turfan* (Göttingen, Vandenhoeck and Ruprecht, 1967), 456–78. On the topic of communal life, Heinz Bechert has contributed a short but basic article entitled "The Theravada Buddhist Sangha," *JAS*, XXIX, 4 (1970), 761–78; and in addition his major work on *Buddhismus, Staat und Gesellschaft in den Ländern Theravada Buddhismus* (Hamburg, Frankfurt, and Berlin, Alfred Metzner, 1966, 67, 73) includes two volumes which deal with historical developments in the modern period and a third which contains a comprehensive bibliography.

Those who wish to develop an acquaintance with the original Theravada texts have at their disposal several translations of the *Dhammapada* including those of Irving Babbitt (N.Y., New Directions, 1965) and P.K. Lal, (N.Y., Farrar, Strauss & Giroux, 1967), as well as a less adequate one by S. Radhakrishanan (N.Y., Oxford, 1950). The very important *Dhammapada Commentary* has been translated by Eugene Burlingame under the title *Buddhist Legends,* 3 vols. (Cambridge, Harvard Univ. Press, 1969); a collection of *Buddhist Parables* has been translated by Burlingame (New Haven, Yale Univ. Press, 1922); and *Ten Jataka Stories* have been translated by I.B. Horner (London, Luzac, 1957). Two classic Theravada manuals, Buddhagosha's *Path of Purification* and Anuruddha's *Compendium of Philosophy,* are also available in English. The best rendering of the former is that of Bhikkhu Nanamoli (Colombo, R. Semage, 1959), but the reader may also consult Pe Maung Tin, *The Path of Purity,* 3 vols. (PTS, London, Luzac, 1922, 1928, 1931); for the *Compendium* see the version done cooperatively by Shwe Zan Aung and Caroline Rhys Davids (PTS, London, H. Milford, 1916). In order to supplement these and other translated sources the reader may turn to several surveys of the textual tradition including Wilhelm Geiger, *Pali Literature and Language* (Calcutta, Univ. of Calcutta, 1947); B.C. Law's book on the *History of Pali Literature,* 2 vols. (London, Kegan Paul, 1933); and the same author's article on "Non-canonical Pali Literature," *ABORI,* 12 (1931), 97–143.

GEOGRAPHICAL OVERVIEWS, COLLECTIONS, AND COMPARISONS
Though the majority of studies of Theravada Buddhism have focused on one particular national tradition, there are works of a broader scope. For example, the Southeast Asian scene has been surveyed by Robert Lester in *Theravada Buddhism in Southeast Asia* (Ann Arbor, Univ. of Michigan Press, 1973); while recent developments in all the various countries are described by Robert Slater, "Modern Trends in Theravada Buddhism,"

in Joseph Kitagawa, ed., *Modern Trends in World Religions* (LaSalle, Ill., Open Court, 1959); in Minoru Kiyota's "Buddhism and Social Change in Southeast Asia," *TICO,* 14 (1969), 66–83; and more recently in an article by Frank E. Reynolds and Joseph Kitagawa on "Theravada Buddhismus im 20 Jahrhundert" in Heinrich Dumoulin, ed., *Buddhismus der Gegenwart* (*op. cit.*); moreover a crucial contemporary event and the mythology associated with it are described by George Coedès, on "The Twenty-five Hundredth Anniversary of the Buddha," *Diogenes,* 15 (July, 1956), 95–111.

There also exist collections of essays useful in various contexts. G.P. Malalasekara's two-volume *Dictionary of Pali Names* (London, Murray, 1960) is an invaluable resource for anyone working with the canonical or commentarial tradition; and Thera Nyanaponika, ed., *Pathways of Buddhist Thought* (London, Allen & Unwin, 1971) contains a number of short popular essays. The general reader will likely be most interested in four recent collections which focus on the contemporary period see Manning Nash, ed., *Anthropological Studies of Theravada Buddhism* (New Haven, Yale Univ. Press, 1968); the winter, 1973, issue of *Daedalus* which includes essays on modern developments in Thailand, Burma and Ceylon; and vols. 4 and 8 of *Contributions to Asian Studies,* ed. by Bardwell Smith and Stephen Piker, entitled *Tradition and Change in Theravada Buddhism* and *The Psychological Study of Theravada Buddhism* (Leiden, E.J. Brill, 1973 and 1975).

In addition to these cross-cultural collections, there are also single articles in which the relations between different Theravada traditions are treated either historically or comparatively. The historical aspect is to the fore in the discussions of the life of Buddhagosha, the great 5th-century scholar who is claimed as a native son by several different local areas; see, for example, Pe Maung Tin, *Buddhagosha,* rev. ed. (Bombay, Royal Asiatic Society 1946) and R. Subrahmanian and S.P. Nainan, "Buddhagosha: His Place of Birth" in the *Journal of Oriental Research,* XIX (June, 1950), 278–84. Historical relations among various portions of the Theravada world in later periods are portrayed in Senerat Paranivatana, "Religious Intercourse between Ceylon and Siam in the 13th–15th Centuries," *JRAS* (Ceylon), (1932), 190–213; in D.B. Jayatilleka, "Sinhalese Embassies to Arakan," *JRAS* (Ceylon), 35 (1935), 1–6; and in P.E.E. Fernando, "An Account of the Kandyan Mission Sent to Siam in 1750," *CJHSS,* 2 (1959), 37–83.

Among the more serious intercultural studies of Theravada traditions the majority focus on Southeast Asia. The most substantial works of this kind are Robert Lingat's two articles, "Vinaya et droit laïque. Études sur les conflits de la loi religeuse et de la loi laïque dans l'Indochine hinayaniste," *BEFEO,* 37 (1937), 416–77, and "Evolution of the Conception of Law in Burma and Siam," *JSS,* XXXVIII, 1 (Jan., 1950), 9–31. See also the article by Francois Martini on a fascinating ritual called "Valukacetiya," *BEFEO,* LVII (1970), 155–68; and David Pfanner and Robert Ingersoll's very different kind of study of "Theravada Buddhism and Village Economic Behavior: A Burmese and Thai Comparison," *JAS,* XXI, 3 (May, 1962), 341–61. Among studies which compare Sinhalese traditions with those of other areas in Southeast Asia, the most interesting are Heinz Bechert's two articles, "Einige Fragen der Religionssoziologie und Struktur des südasiatischen Buddhismus," *International Yearbook for the Sociology of Religions,* 4 (1968), 251–95, and "Buddhism and Mass Politics in Burma and Ceylon" in Donald Smith, ed., *Religion and Political Modernization* (New Haven, Yale Univ. Press, 1974); an article by Hans Dieter Evers on "The Buddhist Sangha in Ceylon and Thailand," *Sociologus* (Berlin), 18 (1968), 20–35; and an essay by Donald Smith on "The Political Monks of Burma and Ceylon" in *Asia,* 10 (Winter, 1968), 3–10.

B. Buddhism in Sri Lanka (Ceylon)

THE PRE-MODERN PERIOD   With the notable exception of *Two Wheels of Dhamma,* ed. by Bardwell Smith (*op. cit.*) which covers both the pre-modern and modern periods (and contains my own bibliographical essay entitled "From Philology to Anthropology" which can be used to supplement the references given below), the available sources for Sinhalese history focus on a particular chronological period. For the whole range of pre-modern developments up to 1500 A.D. excellent sources are H.C. Ray, ed., *University of Ceylon, History of Ceylon,* 2 parts (Colombo, Univ. of Ceylon, 1959, 1960), which has many definitive articles on Buddhism and the abridged edition by C.W. Nicholas and Senerat Paranivatana, entitled *A Concise History of Ceylon* (Colombo, Univ. of Ceylon, 1961). Other secondary works which cover lengthy periods include my own article on "Dhammadipa: A Study of Buddhism and Indianization in Sri Lanka," *Ohio Journal of Religion,* II, 1 (April, 1974), 63–78, which deals with developments in the Anuradhapura and Polonnaruva kingdoms (3rd C. B.C.–13th C. A.D.); Evelyn Ludowyk's *The Footprint of the Buddha* (London, Allen & Unwin, 1958), which covers basically the same time-span; and Walpole Rahula's classic work on *The History of Buddhism in Ceylon. The Anuradhapura Period: 3rd C. B.C.–10th C. A.D.,* 2nd ed. (Colombo, Gunasena, 1966). Among the chronologically more limited studies, three covering developments that were particularly important for Buddhism are E W. Adikaram's *Early History of Buddhism in Ceylon* (Migoda, Ceylon, Puswella, 1946); Vincent Panditha's "Buddhism during the Polonnaruva Period," *CHJ,* 4 (1955), 113–29; and S. Dewaraja's *The Kandyan Kingdom of Ceylon: 1707–1760* (Colombo, Lake House Investments, 1972), esp. 119–49.

The fascinating chronicles which have provided the basis for much of the reconstruction of the pre-modern history of Sinhalese Buddhism are also available; see Hermann Oldenberg's translation of the *Dipavamsa* (London, Williams & Norgate, 1879); or B.C. Law's translation of the same work in *CHJ*, 7 (rep. as a separate volume in 1959); Wilhelm Geiger's translation of the *Mahavamsa* (London, Luzac, 1964); and the same scholar's translation of the *Cullavamsa*, PTS Tr. Ser., nos. 18 & 20 (rep. Colombo, Ceylon Government Information Dept., 1953). Moreover, a number of interesting discussions concerning these texts have been published including B.C. Law, *On the Chronicles of Ceylon* (Calcutta, Royal Asiatic Society [Bengal], 1947); Garrett C. Mendis, "The Pali Chronicles of Ceylon: An Examination of Opinions Expressed about Them since 1879," *Univ. of Calcutta Review*, V (Jan. 1947), 39–54; and the essays by L.S. Perera on "The Pali Chronicles of Ceylon" and A.K. Warder on "The Pali Canon and Its Commentaries as an Historical Record" in C.H. Phillips, ed., *Historians of India, Pakistan and Ceylon* (London, Oxford, 1961).

The variety of Hinayana schools which coexisted in Ceylon up to the time of the full establishment of the Theravada tradition in the 12th century are discussed in Heinz Bechert, "Zur Geschichte der buddhistischen Sekten in Indien und Ceylon," *Nouvelle Clio*, 7–9 (1955–57), 311–60; and more specifically in R.A.H.L. Gunawardene, "The Buddhist Nikayas in Medieval Ceylon," *CJHSS*, IX (1966), 55–66; and in D.J. Kalupahana, "Schools of Buddhism in Early Ceylon," *Ceylon Journal of the Humanities*, I, 2 (July, 1970), 159–90. The Mahayana presence is highlighted by Senart Paranivatane in "Mahayanism in Ceylon" which first appeared in the *Ceylon Journal of Science*, Section G, II, 1 (Dec., 1928), 37–51, and in L. Prematilleke and R. Silva, "A Buddhist Monastery Type of Ancient Ceylon Showing Mahayana Influences," *ArA*, XXX, 1 (1968), 61–84; while Vajrayana elements are noted by W. Pachow in "Ancient Cultural Relations between Ceylon and China" in *UCR*, XXXI, 3 (July, 1954), 113–29, and by Martin Wickramasinge in "Tantrism in Ceylon and Tisa Vera Lithic Diagram," *CHJ*, I, 4 (April, 1952), 55–66.

The literary traditions are surveyed by G. P. Malalasekera, *The Pali Literature of Ceylon* (London, Royal Asiatic Society, 1928), and by C.E. Godakumbura in his study of *Sinhalese Literature* (Colombo, Colombo Apothecaries, 1955). The Buddhological interest is represented by William H.D. Rouse's translation of a medieval Sinhalese life of the Buddha known as the *Jinacarita*, *JTPS* (1905–1906), 1–65. Various doctrinal developments are discussed by Richard Gombrich in several articles including "Merit Transference in Sinhalese Buddhism," *HR*, XI, 2 (Nov., 1971), 203–19; "Food for Seven Grandmothers," *Man*, VI, 1 (March, 1971), 5–17.

Various aspects of traditional Buddhist symbolism and art are presented in *Buddhist Paintings from Shrines and Temples in Ceylon* (UNESCO,

New American Library, 1964); in D.T. Devendra, *Classical Sculpture: 200 B.C.–1000 A.D.* (London, Tiranti, 1958); in Nandadeva Wijesekera's much more technical study of *Early Sinhalese Sculpture* (Colombo, Gunasena, 1962); and in Nandasena Mudiyanse, *Mahayana Monuments in Ceylon* (Colombo, Gunasena, n.d.). Sinhalese Buddha images are discussed in D.T. Devendra's *The Buddha Image and Ceylon* (Colombo, K.V.G. de Silva, 1957) and in an article by Siri Sunasinghe entitled "A Contribution to the Development of the Buddha Image," *CJHSS,* III (Jan./June, 1960), 59–71. An associated ritual is described by Richard Gombrich, "The Consecration of a Buddha Image," *JAS,* XXVI, 1 (Nov., 1966), 23–36. Senart Paranivatana has contributed an important monograph on *The Stupa in Ceylon* (Colombo, Ceylon Gov't. Press, 1946) which may be read in conjunction with N.A. Jayawickrama, tr., *Thupavamsa or Chronicle of the Stupa* (PTS, London, Luzac, 1971), which includes a traditional account of the construction of Ceylon's most famous stupa by the great national hero King Dutthagamani. For two fascinating studies which deal with a specific tradition that continues into the modern period see Arthur M. Hocart, *The Temple of the Tooth in Kandy* (London, Luzac for the Gov't. of Ceylon, 1931), and Victor Goloubew, "Le Temple de la dent à Kandy," *BEFEO,* XXXII (1932), 441–74. Finally, Jacques Maquet has recently published an interesting article on "Expressive Space and Theravada Values," *Ethos,* III, 1 (Spring, 1975), 1–21, in which he correlates the physical structuring of monasteries in Ceylon with the religious orientation of the Theravada tradition.

THE COLONIAL EXPERIENCE AND CONTEMPORARY BUDDHISM The changes which occurred in Sinhalese Buddhism during the difficult colonial period have been studied by Tennakoon Vimalananda in his book on *Buddhism in Ceylon under the Christian Powers* (Colombo, Gunasena, 1963), and *The State and Religion in Ceylon since 1815* (Colombo, Gunasena, 1970); by Hans Dieter Evers in "Buddhism and British Colonial Policy in Ceylon: 1815–1875," *Asian Studies (Quezon),* II, 3 (Dec., 1964); by Kitsiri Malagoda in a discussion of "Millennianism in Relation to Buddhism," *CSSH,* XII, 4 (1970), 424–41; by K.N. de Silva, "Buddhism and the British Government in Ceylon," *CHJ,* X, 1–4 (July/April, 1961); and by L.A. Wickremeratne, "Religion, Nationalism and Social Change in Ceylon: 1865–1885," *JRAS,* II (1969), 123–50. Gananath Obeyesekere has provided a fine study of the modern reformer, Anagarika Dharmapala, in Frank E. Reynolds and Donald Capps, eds., *The Biographical Process (op. cit.)*; and this article may be supplemented by some of Dharmapala's own writings published under the title *Return to Righteousness* (Colombo, Ceylon Gov't. Press, 1965). The role of Buddhism in the struggle for independence and its aftermath is discussed in Part IV of Donald E. Smith, ed., *South Asian Politics and Religion (op. cit.)*; and the militant spirit of the period following independence can be judged by reading D.C. Vijayavard-hana, *Revolt in the Temple* (Colombo, Sinha, 1953); the famous Buddhist Committee of Inquiry Report on the *Betrayal of Buddhism* (Balangoda, Dharmavijaya, 1956); and Walpole Rahula, *The Heritage of the Bhikkhu* (N.Y., Grove, 1974). Bardwell Smith, Donald Swearer and Nur Yalman respectively have discussed recent developments in articles titled "Toward a Buddhist Anthropology: The Problem of the Secular," *JAAR*, XXXVI, 3 (Sept., 1968), 203–16, "Lay Buddhism and the Buddhist Revival in Ceylon," *JAAR*, XXXVIII, 3 (Sept., 1970), 255–75; and "The Ascetic Buddhist Monks of Ceylon" which appeared in Peter Hammond, ed., *Cultural and Social Anthropology* (N.Y., Macmillan, 1964). The reader may also consult Edirweera Sarachandra, "Traditional Values and Modernization in a Buddhist Society," in Robert Bellah, ed., *Religion and Progress in Modern Asia* (N.Y., Free Press, 1966), and two articles by Michael Ames on "Ideological and Social Change in Ceylon," *Human Organization*, XXII, 1 (Spring, 1963), 43–53, and "Religion, Politics and Economic Development in Ceylon" in Melford Spiro, ed., *Symposium on New Approaches to the Study of Religion* (Proceedings of the American Ethnological Society, Seattle, Univ. of Washington, 1964).

In addition to these studies which focus on "modern" developments and the various Buddhist responses, there are a number of other works which deal with contemporary Sinhalese Buddhism from different perspectives. Philological, historical, and anthropological insights are neatly synthesized in Richard Gombrich's excellent and very rich analysis of *Precept and Practice: Traditional Buddhism in the Rural Highlands of Ceylon* (Oxford, Clarendon, 1971); and by Gananath Obeyesekere in his two articles on "Theodicy, Sin and Salvation in a Sociology of Buddhism" in Edmund Leach, ed., *Dialectics in Practical Religion* (Cambridge, Cambridge Univ. Press, 1968), and "The Great Tradition and the Little Tradition in the Perspective of Sinhalese Buddhism," *JAS*, XII, 2 (Feb., 1963), 139–53. For a less historical grappling with similar issues, see Michael Ames, "Magical Animism and Buddhism: A Structural Analysis of the Sinhalese Religious System" in Edward Harper, ed., *Religion in South Asia* (Seattle, Univ. of Washington Press, 1964).

Other efforts to deal with contemporary beliefs and practices include articles by Michael Ames on "Buddha and Dancing Goblins: A Theory of Magic and Religion," *AA*, LXVI (Feb., 1964), 75–82; by Edmund Leach on "Pulleyer and the Lord Buddha: An Aspect of Religious Syncretism in Ceylon," *Psychoanalysis and the Psychoanalytic Review*, XLIX, 2 (1962), 80–102; by Marguerite Robinson, on " 'The House of the Mighty Hero' or 'The House of Enough Paddy': Some Implications of a Sinhalese Myth" in Edmund Leach, ed., *Dialectics in Practical Religion* (*op. cit.*); and by H.L. Seneviratane, "The Asala Perahara in Kandy," *CJHSS*, VI (1963), 169–80. For studies which attend to communal organization and economic aspects see André Bareau, *La vie et l'organization des communautés bouddhiques modernes de Ceylon* (Pondichéry, Institut Français d'Indologie, 1957); H.W. Tambiah, "Buddhist Eccelesiastical Law," *JRAS (Ceylon)*, n.s. VII, 1 (1962), 71–107; and a series of studies by Hans Dieter Evers which include "Kinship and Property Rights in a Buddhist Monastery in Central Ceylon," *AA,* LXIX, 6 (Dec., 1967), 703–10; "Monastic Landlordism in Ceylon," *JAS,* XXVIII, 4 (Aug., 1969), 685–92; and his more comprehensive collection of essays entitled *Monks, Priests and Peasants: A Study of Buddhism and Social Structure in Ceylon* (Leiden, Brill, 1972).

C. Buddhism in Southeast Asia

THE INDIANIZED KINGDOMS IN JAVA, CAMBODIA, CHAMPA, AND MALAYA
The role of Buddhism in the "Indianization" of Southeast Asia is nowhere treated as an independent subject, and, therefore, piecing together a coherent picture is difficult. Anyone interested in the development and role of Buddhism in the early kingdoms of Indonesia, Malaya, Champa and Cambodia should begin by reading the appropriate sections of vol. III of Eliot's *Hinduism and Buddhism* (*op. cit.*), and he can then turn to some of the more specialized discussions of particular areas.

In the case of Java, a substantial treatment is provided by Pieter H. Pott in "Le Bouddhisme de Java et l'ancienne civilization javanaise," *Serie Orientale Roma,* V (1952), 109–56; which can be supplemented by R.M. Sutjipto Wirjosupara, "The Role of the Buddhism of South India in the Development of Buddhist Thought in Indonesia," *Proceedings of the International Conference of Historians of Asia, Manila 1960* (Manila, 1962), 211–23; and Himansu B. Sarkar, "The Evolution of the Siva-Buddha Cult in Java," *JIH,* XLV (Dec., 1967), 637–46. The great Buddhist stupa at Barabadur is treated not only in Paul Mus' massive work which we have previously cited, but also by C. Sivamurti in *Le Stupa du Barabadur* (Paris, Presses universitaires de France, 1961); by N.J. Krom, ed., *The Life of the Buddha on the Stupa of Barabadur According to the Lalitavistara-text* (The Hague, Martinus Nijhoff, 1926); and by Ryusho Hikata, "Gandavyuha and the Reliefs of Barabadur Galleries," *Studies in Indology and Buddhology (Tokyo)* (1959), 1–50. The final phase of the classical tradition in Indonesia is discussed in A.H. Johns, "From Buddhism to Islam: An Interpretation of the Javanese Literature of Transition," *CSSH,* IX (1966–67), 40–50.

The position of Buddhism in the early mainland kingdoms of Burma, Funan, and Champa is considered by Louis Finot in his "Outlines of the History of Buddhism in Indochina," *IHQ,* 2 (1926), 673–89. More specific areas are treated by Alastair Lamb in a rather dry fashion in his "Miscellaneous Papers on Early Hindu and Buddhist Settlement in Northern

Malaya and Southern Thailand," *Federation Museums Journal* (Kuala Lumpur), VI (1961), 1–90; and by Kalyan Sarkar in an article on "Mahayana Buddhism in Funan" in *Sino-Indian Studies,* VI, 1 (1955), 69–75. The fascinating and distinctive Hindu-Buddhist cults and monuments associated with the later Cambodian kingdom of Angkor are described and analyzed by George Coedès in *Angkor: An Introduction* (N.Y., Oxford, 1963); by Lawrence Briggs in his article on "The Syncretism of Religions in Southeast Asia, particularly in the Khmer Empire," *JAOS,* LXXI, 4 (Oct.–Dec., 1951), 230–49; by Paul Mus in his essay on "Angkor in the time of Jayavarman VII," in *Indian Arts and Letters,* ns, II (1937), 65–75; and by Mus again in a later and more original article entitled "Angkor vu du Japon," *FA,* 175–76 (1962), 521–38.

BURMA   Several different books, when taken together, can provide a fairly comprehensive historical overview of Burmese Buddhism. Nihar Ranjan Ray's *Theravada Buddhism in Burma* (Calcutta, Univ. of Calcutta, 1946), and his *Sanskrit Buddhism in Burma* (Amsterdam, H.J. Paris, 1936) cover the major developments in the classical tradition and can be usefully supplemented by B.C. Law's translation of the Burmese *History of the Buddha's Religion* (PTS, London, Luzac, 1952), and Mabel Bode's English introduction to the Pali edition of the same work, *Sasanavamsa* (PTS, London, H. Frowde, 1897). In addition there are two newer books which, though they focus on the modern period, cover aspects of the earlier history as well. The more inclusive of the two is Michael Mendelson's highly provocative study of *Samgha and State* (Ithaca, Cornell Univ. Press, 1975); the other, Emanuel Sarkisyanz' *Buddhist Backgrounds of the Burmese Revolution* (The Hague, Martinus Nijhoff, 1965), attends primarily to traditions associated with kingship and Buddhist conceptions of the "welfare state."

More narrowly focused historical problems are considered by Nihar Ranjan Ray in his article on "Early Traces of Buddhism in Burma" in the *Journal of the Greater India Society,* VI (1939), 1–52 and 99–123, which may be read in conjunction with the early chapters of Htin Aung's *History of Burma* (N.Y. & London, Columbia Univ. Press, 1967) in which an argument is made for a very ancient Buddhist presence in Burma.

Aspects of the ancient Mon tradition in Burma are discussed by Harry Shorto in two fascinating articles on "The Thirty-Two Myos in the Medieval Mon Kingdom," *BSOAS,* XXVI, 3 (1963), and "The Dewata Sotapan: A Mon Prototype of the Thirty-Seven Nats," *BSOAS,* XXX, 1 (1967). The important Burmese kingdom of Pagan is the subject of studies by Pe Maung Tin on "Buddhism in the Inscriptions of Burma," *JBuRS,* XVI, 1 (April, 1936), 52–70; by Than Thun on "Religion in Burma, 1000–1300" and "Religious Buildings of Burma, A.D. 1000–1300," *JBuRS,* XLII, 2 (Dec., 1959); and by Gordon Luce in his major two-volume work on *Old Burma–Early Pagan* (Locust Valley, N.Y., Augustin, 1969). Special esoteric elements in the tradition are traced by Charles Duroiselle in his article "The Ari Priests of Burma and Tantric Buddhism" in *Archaeological Survey of India, 1915–1916,* and by Htin Aung in *Folk Elements in Burmese Buddhism* (London, Oxford, 1962). Interesting religio-political patterns in the later Burmese kingdoms are depicted by John Badgley in "The Theravada Polity of Burma," *Tonan Asia Kenkyu* (*Kyoto*) (March, 1965) and by U Thang in "Burmese Kingship in Theory and Practice in the Reign of Mindon," *JBuRS,* XLII, 2 (Dec., 1959), 171–85.

A very helpful description of Burmese Buddhist life in the early years of British colonial rule is provided by James G. Scott in *The Burman: His Life and Notions* (London, Macmillan, 1910), and the responses of politically concerned Buddhists of the period are vividly portrayed in Htin Aung, tr., *Burmese Monk's Tales* (N.Y., Columbia Univ. Press, 1966). The whole range of modern religio-political development is surveyed in Donald E. Smith, *Religion and Politics in Modern Burma* (Princeton, Princeton Univ. Press, 1965). The situation during and after World War II is considered by Dorothy Guyot in "The Uses of Buddhism in Wartime Burma," *Asian Studies,* VII, 1 (April, 1969), 50–80; by Richard Butwell in his biographical study of U Nu of Burma (Stanford, Stanford Univ. Press, 1965), esp. 63–141; by Fred Van der Mehden in "The Changing Pattern of Religion and Politics in Burma," in Robert K. Sakai, ed., *Studies in Asia, 1961* (Lincoln, Univ. of Nebraska Press, 1961), 63–73; by Michael Mendelson in "The Uses of Religious Scepticism in Modern Burma," *Diogenes,* XLI (Spring, 1963), 94–116; and by Mendelson again in "Buddhism and the Burmese Establishment," *Archives de sociologie des religions,* XVII (Jan./June, 1964), 85–95. Manning Nash has provided a reasonably up-to-date account in his article on "Buddhist Revitalization in the Nation State: The Burmese Experience," which is available in Robert Spencer, ed., *Religion and Change in Contemporary Asia* (Minneapolis, Univ. of Minnesota, 1971).

The literature and the artistic traditions of Burmese Buddhism have received special attention from several modern scholars. A survey of the classical literature is provided by Mabel Bode in *The Pali Literature of Burma* (London, Royal Asiatic Society, 1909); one class of texts is surveyed by Shwe Zang Aung in his article on "Abhidhamma Literature in Burma," *JPTS* (1910–12), 112–32; and W.B. Boller identifies "Some Less Known Burmese Pali Texts" in J.C. Heesterman, et al., eds., *Pratidanam* (The Hague, Mouton, 1968), 493–99. The traditional cosmological literature is discussed in Paul Mus' important but extremely difficult *La Lumière sur les six voies* (Paris, Institut d'ethnologie, 1939), while another type is analyzed by Robert Spencer in a short article on "Ethical Expression in a Burmese Jataka," *American Folklore,* LXXIX (1966), 278–301. Burmese lives of the Buddha have been translated by Paul Bigandet,

The Life or Legend of Gaudama the Buddha of the Burmese, 2 vols. 4th ed. (London, Kegan Paul, 1911–12), and by Michael Edwards, *A Life of the Buddha* (London, Folk Society, 1959).

An overview of Burmese Buddhist art can be gained from an article by Reginald LeMay on "The Development of Buddhist Art in Burma" in the *Journal of the Royal Society of Arts,* 97 (June, 1949), 535–55. The works of the most important period are discussed by Gordon Luce in *Old Burma-Early Pagan* (*op. cit.*) and more briefly by Jane G. Mahler in "The Art of Medieval Burma in Pagan" in the *Archives of the Chinese Art Society of America,* 12 (1958), 30–47; and a famous depiction of the life of the Buddha is presented by Karl B. Seidenstucker in *Südbuddhistische Studien I: Die Buddha-Legende in den Skulpturen des Ananda-Temples zu Pagan* (Hamburg, Otto Meissners, 1916).

Various aspects of Burmese Buddhist belief, practice, and communal organization have been studied from the perspective of modern anthropology. The most ambitious and comprehensive work is certainly Melford Spiro's *Buddhism and Society* (N.Y., Harper & Row, 1970) which incorporates many of the insights presented in his book on *Burmese Supernaturalism* (Englewood Cliffs, N.J., Prentice-Hall, 1967) and his article on "Buddhism and Economic Saving in Burma," *AA,* 68 (1966), 1163–73. Manning Nash has included a lengthy discussion of Buddhism in *The Golden Road to Modernity* (N.Y., Wiley, 1965) and has published a later article on "Burmese Buddhism in Everyday Life" in *AA,* 65 (April, 1963), 285–95. Two other articles on Buddhism in the village context are John Brohm's study of "Buddhism and Animism in a Burmese Village," *JAS,* XII, 2 (Feb., 1963), 155–67 and A.W. Sadler, "Pagoda and Monastery: Reflections of the Social Morphology of Burmese Buddhism," *Journal of Asian and African Studies* (*Leiden*), V, 1 (Oct., 1970), 282–92. For fascinating anthropological accounts of more esoteric traditions see the series of articles by Michael Mendelson which includes "A Messianic Association in Upper Burma" in *BSOAS,* XXIV, 3 (1961), 560–80; "The King of the Weaving Mountain," *Royal Central Asian Journal,* XLVIII, 3 and 4 (1961); and "Observations on a Tour in the Region of Mt. Popa, Central Burma," *FA,* XIX, 179 (May/June, 1963).

THAILAND   Unfortunately the only historical surveys of Thai Buddhism in Western languages have been published in Bangkok and therefore may be difficult to locate. The best of these works is still Damrong Rajanubhab's *History of Buddhist Monuments in Siam* (Bangkok, Siam Society, 1962), which was translated by Sulak Sivaraksa from a Thai original written in 1926. However two slightly more up-to-date accounts are included in Luang Boriband Buribhand's chapter on "Buddhism in Thailand" in the volume *In Commemoration of the Year 2500 Buddhist Era in*

Thailand (Bangkok, Siva Phorn, 1957), and Dhani Niwat's short pamphlet entitled *History of Buddhism in Siam* (Bangkok, Siam Society, 1965). The reader may also consult the many issues of the Thailand Culture Series (Bangkok, Fine Arts Dept., 1956–   ) which deal with Buddhist topics, the annual Visakha Puja publications of the Buddhist Society of Thailand, and Phya Anuman's description of "Popular Buddhism" in his *Life and Ritual in Old Siam,* tr. and ed. by William Gedney (New Haven, Human Relations Area Files, 1961). For two articles which focus on particular aspects of the tradition but nevertheless may be helpful in providing a basic orientation, see Frank E. Reynolds "The Holy Emerald Jewel; Some Aspects of Buddhism and Political Legitimation in Thailand and Laos" in Bardwell Smith, ed., *Religion and Political Legitimation in Southeast Asia* (forthcoming, 1976) and "Buddhism as a Universal Religion and as a Civic Religion," *JSS,* LXIII, 1 (Jan., 1975), 28–43. For a book-length treatment which provides another kind of overview, see Stanley J. Tambiah, *World Conqueror and World Renouncer* (forthcoming from Cambridge Univ. Press, 1976.)

Buddhist developments in the important early Thai kingdom of Sukothai and the traditions of the northern Thai kingdom of Lannathai (Chiengmai) have been the subject of a number of special studies. In the case of Sukothai the main work is Alexander Griswold's *History of Sukothai Art* (Bangkok, Fine Arts Dept., 1967); however a shorter discussion is provided by Barbara Andaya in her article on "Statecraft in the Region of Lu Thai of Sukhodaya," *Cornell Journal of Social Relations,* VI, 1 (Spring, 1971). An overview of the development of the northern Thai tradition can be gained by reading Donald Swearer's recent monograph on *Wat Haripunjaya: The Royal Temple of the Buddha's Relic, Lamphun Thailand* published in Missoula, Montana, by the American Academy of Religion, 1975. The early period is covered in the local chronicle known as the *Sheaf of Garlands of the Epochs of the Conqueror,* tr. by N.A. Jayawickrama (PTS, London, Luzac, 1968); by Donald Swearer in his article on "Myth, Legend and History in the Northern Thai Chronicles," *JSS,* LXII, 1 (Jan., 1974); and by Swearer again in a follow-up article on "Tilokaraja and the Reform of Northern Thai Buddhism" in Smith, ed., *Religion and Political Legitimation (op. cit.).* In addition Charles Keyes has contributed a fascinating study of "Buddhist Pilgrimage Centers and the Twelve Year Cycle: Northern Thai Moral Orders in Space and Time," *HR,* XV, 1 (Aug., 1975), 71–89, and has dealt with more recent events in his study of "Buddhism and National Integration in Thailand," *JAS,* XXX, 3 (May, 1971).

The Buddhist traditions which developed in the central Thai kingdom have quite naturally received the most attention. A classic, firsthand account of Buddhism in the older Ayuddhya kingdom is provided by Simon de La Loubère in *The Kingdom of Siam,* recently repub. by Oxford Press (Kuala Lumpur, 1969); and the important subject of royal ritual, including its Buddhist elements, has been dealt with by H.G.Q. Wales in *Siamese State Ceremonies* (London, Quaritch, 1931). Buddhist developments in the Thonburi and early Bangkok periods are treated by Robert Lingat in "La Double crise de l'église bouddhique au Siam (1767–1851)," *Cahiers d'histoire mondiale,* IV, 2 (1958), 402–25, and by Klaus Wenk in *The Restoration of Thailand under Rama I, 1782–1809,* tr. by Greely Stahl (Tuscon, Univ. of Arizona Press, 1968). Studies of the life and work of King Mongut who was the major figure in the first phase of Buddhism's encounter with modernity have been carried out by Abbott L. Moffatt in *Mongkut, the King of Siam* (Ithaca, Cornell Univ. Press, 1961) and by Alexander Griswold in *King Mongkut of Siam* (N.Y., Asia Society, 1961). Different aspects of Buddhism in the late nineteenth and early twentieth centuries are presented by Henry Alabaster, *The Wheel of the Law* (London, Kegan Paul, 1871) in which the author translates a traditional Thai version of the life of the Buddha as well as a "modernist" defense of Buddhism, and by Ernest Young, *Kingdom of the Yellow Robe,* 3rd ed. (London, Constable, 1907). A survey of the situation as it has developed in recent decades is provided by Kenneth Wells, *Thai Buddhism: Its Rites and Activities* (Bangkok, Christian Book Store, 1960); and the important relationship between "Church and State in Thailand" is brought reasonably up-to-date by Yoneo Ishi in an article in *Asia Survey,* 8 (Oct. 1968).

The Buddhist Pali literature of Thailand is surveyed by H. Saddhatissa in his essay on "Pali Literature in Thailand" in *Buddhist Studies in Honor of I.B. Horner* (*op. cit.*). The most important and interesting Thai Buddhist text is translated by George Coedès and Charles Archaimbault under the title *Les Trois mondes* (Paris, EFEO, 1973); and Mani B. Reynolds and Frank E. Reynolds have also completed an English translation entitled *The Three Worlds According to King Ruang,* now awaiting publication by the Siam Society and Stanford University Press. Other translations of Thai works include *The Buddhist Attitude Toward National Defence* (Bangkok, 1916 and rep.), a sermon delivered by the Prince Patriarch to King Rama VI; *Red Bamboo* (Bangkok, Progress Publishing, 1968), a novel written by Kukrit Pramoj who is the present Prime Minister of the country; and Donald Swearer, tr., *Toward the Truth* (Philadelphia, Westminster, 1971), a collection of essays by Bhikkhu Buddadasa, a reform-minded monk who is an influential figure in contemporary Thai religion.

The traditions of Buddhist art are surveyed in Reginald LeMay's *Concise History of Buddhist Art in Siam* (Cambridge, Cambridge Univ. Press, 1939), in M.C. Subhadradis Diskul, *Art in Thailand* (Bangkok, Fine Arts Univ., 1970), and in Theodore Bowie, ed., *The Arts of Thailand* (Bloomington, Indiana Univ. Press, 1960); and these works may be supplemented by Alexander Griswold's *History of Sukothai Art* (*op. cit.*) which focuses on the most creative period. Some further acquaintance with Thai Buddhist painting can be gained from *The Life of the Buddha According to Thai Temple Paintings* (Bangkok, USIS, 1957); from Elizabeth Wray, et al., *Ten Lives of the Buddha: Siamese Paintings and Jataka Tales* (N.Y., Weatherhill, 1972); and from the magnificent illustrations of the "three worlds" cosmology (see above) reproduced by Klaus Wenk in *Thailändische Miniaturmalereien* (Wiesbaden, F. Steiner, 1965). Another important form of artistic expression is treated in general terms in Theodore Bowie, ed., *The Sculpture of Thailand* (N.Y,. Asia Society, 1972), and in C. Feroci, "The Aesthetics of Buddhist Sculpture," *JSS*, XXXVII, 1 (Oct., 1948), 39–46; and specialized discussions may be found in a number of articles by Alexander Griswold including his extremely important work on *Dated Buddha Images of Northern Siam* (Ascona, *ArA*, 1957). Those who are interested in the architecture and symbolism of Thai temples have at their disposal Karl Döhring's three-volume work on *Buddhistische Tempelanlagen in Siam* (Berlin, Asia Publishing House, 1920) and E.W. Hutchinson's article on "The Seven Spires: A Sanctuary of the Sacred Fig Tree at Chiengmai," *JSS*, XXXIX, 1 (June, 1951), 1–68.

In recent years the studies of Thai Buddhism by philologists, historians, and art critics have been supplemented by the descriptions and interpretations of a number of highly competent anthropologists. Lucien Hanks has made an important contribution in an article on "Merit and Power in the Thai Social Order," *AA*, 64 (1962), 1247–62; and in 1970 Stanley J. Tambiah published a truly superb analysis of *Buddhism and Spirit Cults in Northeastern Thailand* (Cambridge, Cambridge Univ. Press; paperback ed., 1975). Other extensive studies of this kind include a book by Jane Bunnag on *Buddhist Monks, Buddhist Laymen* (Cambridge, Cambridge Univ. Press, 1973) and a monograph by J.A. Niels Mulder on *Merit Monks and Motivation* (DeKalb, Ill., Northern Illinois Univ., 1968). Among the more interesting anthropological articles are Charles Keyes' "Tug of War for Merit: Cremation of a Senior Monk," *JSS*, LXI, 1 (Jan., 1975), 44–62; Stephen Piker's "The Relationship of Belief Systems to Behavior in Rural Thailand," *AS*, 8 (Oct., 1968); Tsuneo Ayabe's "*Dek Wat* and Thai Education: The Case of Tambon Ban Khem," tr. by Edward Tiffany and Toshikazu Arai, *JSS*, LXI, 2 (July, 1973), 39–52; Jasper Ingersoll's "Merit and Identity in Village Thailand" in G. William Skinner and A. Thomas Kirsch, eds., *Changes and Persistence in Thai Society* (Ithaca, Cornell Univ. Press, 1975), 219–51; and A. Thomas Kirsch's "Economy, Polity and Religion in Thailand," *ibid.*, 172–96. For additional studies on situations which have developed on the periphery of Thai Buddhism see Angela Burr, "Religious Institutional Diversity—Social, Structural and Conceptual Unity: Islam and Buddhism in a Southern Thai Coastal Fishing Village," *JSS,* LX, 2 (1972), 87–106; and T. Stern, "Ariya and the Golden Book: A Millennary Buddhist Sect Among the Karen," *JAS,* XXVII (1968), 297–328.

THERAVADA TRADITIONS IN LAOS AND CAMBODIA   Any reader who is limited to English language materials will have great difficulty in approaching a study of Buddhism in Laos and Cambodia (after the fall of Angkor). For Laos the three major English sources are the several articles on Buddhism in René de Berval, ed., *Kingdom of Laos* (Saigon, FA, 1959) which was originally published in a much more accessible French version as *Présence du royaume Laos, FA,* XII, 118–20 (Saigon, *FA,* 1956); Frank E. Reynolds, "Ritual and Social Hierarchy: Some Aspects of Traditional Religion in Buddhist Laos," *HR,* IX, 1 (Aug., 1969), 78–89; and Georges Condominas, "Phiban Cults in Rural Laos," Skinner and Kirsch, eds., *Change and Persistence in Thai Society* (*op. cit.*), 252–77. In the case of Cambodia the English materials are limited to a travel account by Alan Brodrick entitled *Little Vehicle* (N.Y., Hutchison, 1947) and an article by May Ebihara on "Interrelationships between Buddhism and Social Systems in Cambodian Peasant Culture" in Nash, ed., *Anthropological Studies of Theravada Buddhism* (*op. cit.*).

However, for those who read French the situation is considerably brighter. In addition to de Berval's volume mentioned above, Henri Deydier has included a chapter on religion in his *Introduction à la connaissance du Laos* (Saigon, Impr. française d'outremer, 1952). The literary aspects of the tradition in Laos and also in northern Thailand are covered in considerable detail in Louis Finot's "Recherches sur la littérature laotienne," *BEFEO,* XVII (1917), 1–221; and more recently Pierre Lafont has described "Les écritures du pali au Laos," *BEFEO,* L, 2 (1962), 395–405. The artistic and symbolic dimensions are surveyed by Henri Parmentier, *L'Art du Laos* (Paris, Imprimerie Nationale, 1954); and by Pierre Lafont, "Images Laotiennes," *Revue de psychologie des peuples* (Le Havre), XXI (1966), 472–88, and XXII (1967), 216–26.

Though the historical background is crucial for gaining a balanced perspective, most readers will probably find the most interesting treatments of Laotian Buddhism to be based on ethnological and anthropological observation. The most comprehensive works of this kind are Georges Condominas, "Notes sur le bouddhisme populaire en milieu rural lao," *Archives de sociologie des religions,* 25 (Jan.–June, 1968), 81–110, and 26 (July–Dec., 1968), 111–50; and especially Marcel Zago, *Rites et cérémonies en milieu bouddhist Laos* (Rome, Univ. Gregorian, 1973). In addition, fascinating accounts of particular rituals have been provided by Pierre Lafont and Pierre Bitard, "Ordination de deux dignitaires bouddhiques 'Tay lu'," *BSEI,* ns, 32 (1957), 199–221; and by Charles Archaimbault in a series of articles which include "La Fête du T'at à Luong Prabang" in *Essays Offered to G.H. Luce,* ed. by Ba Shin, et al., vol. I (Ascona, ArA, 1966), and "La Fête du T'at à S'ieng Khwang," *ArA,* XXIV, 3/4 (1961), 187–99. For two accounts which make some attempt to deal with the relationship between Buddhism and postindependence experiences in politics and national development see Joel Halpern, *Government, Politics and Social Structure in Laos* (New Haven, Yale Univ., 1964); and Boutsavath Vongsavanh and Georges Chapelier "Laos Popular Buddhism and Community Development," *JSS,* LXI, 2 (1973), 1–38.

In the case of Cambodia an historical introduction is provided by Pierre Dupont in his article on "La Propagation du bouddhisme indien en Indochine occidental," *BSEI,* XVIII, 1–2 (1943), 93–105; while a basic overview can be gained by reading Adhemar Leclere's *Le Bouddhisme au Cambodge* (Paris, Leroux, 1899). Leclere has translated a number of important texts including a Cambodian version of the life of the Buddha and published them under the title *Les Livres sacrés du Cambodge* (Paris, Bibliothèque d'études, 1906). Beyond this, Solange Thierry has analyzed a group of folk stories in his article on "La Personne sacrée du roi dans la littérature populaire cambodgienne" in *The Sacral Kingship* (*op. cit.*), 219–30; and André Bareau has examined "Les Idées sous-jacentes aux pratiques culturelles bouddhiques dans le Cambodge actuel," *Wiener Zeitschrift für die Kunde Süd- und Ost-asiens und Archiv für indische Philosophie,* 12/13 (1968–69), 23–32.

The ritual and communal aspects of Buddhism in Cambodia are dealt with in several different contexts. François Martini has published articles on "Le Bonze cambodgien" and "Organization du clergé bouddhique" in René de Berval, ed., *Présence du Cambodge, FA,* XII, 114–15 (Saigon, *FA,* 1955). A particular kind of ritual performance has been described by Paul Monie in his "Notes relatives à la crémation d'un personnage religieux au Cambodge," *Arts Asiatiques,* XI, 1 (1965), 139–55; and a different but equally important type of performance has been carefully analyzed by Madeleine Giteau, *Le Bornage rituel des temples bouddhique au Cambodge* (Paris, EFEO, 1969). Finally, André Bareau and a group of students from the Royal Faculty of Archaeology at Phnom Penh have published studies of specific monastic establishments as they were observed in the late 1960s; see "Quelques ermitages et centres de méditation bouddhique au Cambodge" and "Le Monastère bouddhique de Tep Pranam a Oudong," both of which were published in *BEFEO,* 56 (1969).

CONTEMPORARY BUDDHISM IN NON-BUDDHIST AREAS   Though they are sometimes forgotten, contemporary Buddhist communities do exist in other areas of Southeast Asia, notably in Bangladesh, Singapore, and Indonesia. The reformed Theravada community in Bangladesh has been studied by Heinz Bechert in an article on "Contemporary Buddhism in Bengal and Tripura," which appeared in *Educational Miscellany* (Tripura,

India), IV, 3–4 (Dec., 1967–March, 1968), 1–25. The Mahayana Buddhist presence in Singapore is discussed by Margaret Topley in the first portion of her article on "Chinese Religion and Religious Institutions in Singapore," *JRAS, (Malaya),* XXIX, 1 (May, 1956), 70–118; and a specific kind of institution is described in her study of "Chinese Women's Vegetarian Houses in Singapore," in the same journal, XXVII, 1 (May, 1954), 51–67. In the case of Indonesia a very special aspect of the medieval "syncretistic" tradition which has survived the rise of Islam is examined by Tyra de Kleen in her study of *Mudras: The Ritual Hand Poses of the Buddha Priests and Shiva Priests of Bali* (London, Kegan Paul, 1924).

IV. BUDDHISM IN EAST ASIA (EXCLUDING JAPAN)

A. China

INTRODUCTIONS AND HISTORICAL SURVEYS   The prospective student of Chinese Buddhism has at his disposal a wide variety of materials. Among the best of the short introductory essays are the China section of Richard Robinson's "Buddhism in China and Japan" in R. C. Zaehner, ed., *The Concise Encyclopedia of Living Faiths* (*op. cit.*); and Erik Zürcher, "Buddhism in China" in Raymond Dawson, ed., *The Legacy of China* (Oxford, Clarendon, 1964). Other short survey treatments include William T. de Bary, "Buddhism and the Chinese Tradition," *Diogenes,* 47 (Fall, 1964), 102–24; Hu Shih's two articles on "Buddhist Influence on Chinese Religious Life," *Chinese Social and Political Science Review,* 9 (1925), 142–50, and "The Indianization of China" in *Independence, Convergence and Borrowing in Institutions, Thought and Art* (Cambridge, Harvard Univ. Press, 1937); Kenneth Chen, "Mahayana Buddhism and Chinese Culture," *Asia,* 10 (Winter, 1968), 11–32; and Leon Hurvitz, "Toward a Comprehensive History of Chinese Buddhism," *JAOS,* LXXXIX, 4 (Oct.– Dec., 1969), 763–73. More limited aspects of the tradition are examined by Joseph Needham in his chapter on "Buddhist Thought" in vol. II of his *Science and Civilization in China* (N.Y., Cambridge Univ. Press, 1956), 396–431; by Kenneth Chen, "Filial Piety in Chinese Buddhism," *HJAS,* 28 (1968), 81–97; by J.J.M. de Groot, "Militant Spirit of the Buddhist Clergy," *TP,* II, 2 (1891), 127–39; and by Yang Lien-Shin, "Buddhist Monasteries and Four Money-raising Institutions in Chinese History," *HJAS,* XIII, 1–2 (June, 1950), 174–91. In addition a variety of more technical essays is included in Paul Demiéville, *Choix d'études bouddhiques* (Leiden, E. J. Brill, 1973).

A number of book-length works survey the Chinese Buddhist tradition in greater detail. Arthur Wright's *Buddhism in Chinese History* (Stanford, Stanford Univ. Press, 1959) provides a remarkably concise treatment; Kenneth Chen's *The Chinese Transformation of Buddhism* (Princeton, Princeton Univ. Press, 1973) emphasizes the process of acculturation; Karl Reichelt's *Truth and Tradition in Chinese Buddhism,* tr. by K.V.W. Bugge (Shanghai, Commercial Press, 1927), contains fascinating chapters on special topics such as the great epic novel, *Journey to the West* (see Arthur Waley's radically abridged and edited translation of this fascinating work which was published under the title, *Monkey,* by Grove Press, 1958), and Buddhist masses for the dead; and Reginald Johnston's *Buddhist China* (London, John Murray, 1913) describes many other popular aspects. Though it is more limited both in terms of chronological intention and subject matter, Jacques Gernet's *Les Aspects économiques du bouddhisme dans la société chinoise du Vᵉ au Xᵉ siècle* (Saigon, EFEO, 1956) deserves to be singled out, and should be read in conjunction with the article-length reviews by Arthur Wright and Dennis Twitchett; see "The Economic Role of Buddhism in China," *JAS,* XVI, 3 (May, 1957), 408–14, and "The Monasteries and China's Economy in Medieval Times," *BSOAS,* 19 (1957), 526–49. Finally, for serious students of Chinese Buddhism, a detailed and comprehensive account which can serve as an introduction and later as a reference work is Kenneth Chen's excellent volume entitled *Buddhism in China* (Princeton, Princeton Univ. Press, 1964).

MORE SPECIALIZED HISTORICAL STUDIES   Much scholarly effort has gone into the task of reconstructing the process through which Buddhism was introduced into China (about the beginning of the Christian era) and developed into a distinctively Chinese form of religious expression (by about the late sixth century A.D.). The major study of this development through the fourth century is Erik Zürcher's solid though somewhat mistitled *Buddhist Conquest of China,* 2 vols. (Leiden, E. J. Brill, 1959), to which may be added another book whose title fails to do it justice, namely, Alexander Soper's *Literary Evidence for Early Buddhist Art in China* (Ascona, ArA, 1959). Aspects of this very early period are discussed by Homer Dubs and James R. Ware in articles on "The 'Golden Man' of Former Han Times" and "Once More on the 'Golden Man'" in *TP,* 33 (1937), 1–14, and 34 (1938), 174–78; by Henri Maspero in a series of articles including "Le Songe et l'ambassade de l'empereur Ming," *BEFEO,* X (1910), 95–130, "Communautés et moines bouddhistes chinois au IIᵉ et IIIᵉ siècles," *BEFEO,* X (1910), 222–32, and "Les Origines de la communauté bouddhiste de Lo-Yang," *JA,* 225 (1934), 87–107; and by Maspero again in a short section of his *Mélanges posthumes sur les religions et l'histoire de la Chine,* vol. I, (Paris, Joseph Trias, 1950), 195–211. Interesting accounts of subsequent centuries are provided by Walter

Liebenthal, "Chinese Buddhism during the 4th and 5th centuries," *MN*, II (1955), 44–83, and by James Ware, tr., "Wei Shou on Buddhism" *TP*, 30 (1933), 100–81. Finally, various aspects of anti-Buddhist sentiment and Buddhist resistance to traditional Chinese modes of behavior receive special attention in Kenneth Chen's two articles on "Anti-Buddhist Propaganda during the Nan-Chao," *HJAS*, 15 (1932), 166–92, and "Some Factors Responsible for the Anti-Buddhist Propaganda," in Erik Zürcher, "Zum Verhältnis von Kirche und Staat in China während der Frühzeit der Buddhismus," *Saeculum*, 11 (1959), 73–81; and in Leon Hurvitz, " 'Render Unto Caesar' in Early Chinese Buddhism" in Kshitis Roy, ed., *Liebenthal Festschrift* (*op. cit.*), 80–114.

In addition to the more typically historical works concerning the early Buddhist development in China, there exist important studies focusing on the lives or views of particular Buddhist figures. See for example the account of the first Indian missionaries in P.C. Bagchi, *India and China,* rev. ed. (N.Y., Philosophical Library, 1951), 58–91; and P.N. Bose, *The Indian Teachers in China* (Madras, Ganesan, 1923). The biographies of the first translators are covered in vol. I of Robert Shih, tr., *Biographies des moines éminents de Houei-Kiao* (Louvain, Institut orientalist, 1968), and an excellent study of the full text has been published by Arthur Wright in his important article on "Biography and Hagiography of Hui-Chao's Lives of Emminent Monks," *Silver Jubilee Volume of Zinbun-Kagaku-Kyoto University* (Kyoto, 1954), I, 383–432. A major fourth century figure is given separate attention by Arthur Link in his "Biography of Shih Tao An," *TP*, 46 (1958), 1–48, and several studies have been devoted to Tao An's immediate successors. The most interesting examples are Walter Liebenthal, "Shih Hui-Yuan's Buddhism as Set Forth in His Writings," *JAOS*, 70 (1950), 243–59; Tairyo Makita, "Hui-Yuan—His Life and Times" tr. by Philip Yampolsky and published in *Zinbun*, VI (1962); Rudolf Wagner, "The Original Structure of the Correspondence between Shih Hui Yuan and Kumarajiva," *HJAS*, 31 (1971), 28–48; and Walter Liebenthal's two articles which present "A Biography of Chu Tao-sheng," *MN*, XI, 3 (Oct., 1955), 64–96, and "The World Conception of Chu Tao-sheng," *MN*, XII, (1956 and 1957), 65–104 and 241–68. Other figures of the period are discussed by Arthur Wright in two articles on the "Biography of the Nun An-ling-shou," *HJAS*, 15 (1952), 193–96, and "Fo-tu-teng: A Biography," *HJAS*, 11, 3–4 (Dec., 1948), 321–71; by Zenryu Tsukamoto in "The Sramana Superintendent Tan-yao and His Time," tr. by G.B. Sargent, *MS* 16 (1957), 363–96; and by Leon Hurvitz in a classic work on "Chih-i (538–97)," *MCB*, 12 (1962), which includes many other short biographies as well.

For the development of Buddhism from the late sixth century onward, two basic sources have been provided by Jan Yun-hua, his translation of *A Chronicle of Buddhism in China: 581–960* (Santiniketan, Visvabharati,

1966), and his related article on "The Fo-tsu-tung-chi: A Biographical and Bibliographical Study," *OE,* 10 (1963), 61–82. Two important articles on the early years of the period have been written by Arthur Wright, "The Formation of Sui Ideology: 581–604" in J.K. Fairbank, ed., *Chinese Thought and Institutions* (Chicago, Univ. of Chicago Press, 1957), 71–94, and "Fu I and the Rejection of Buddhism," *Journal of the History of Ideas,* XII, 1 (Jan., 1951), 33–47. For the Tang period the reader may consult Dennis Twitchett, "Monastic Estates in Tang China," *Asia Major,* 5 (1956), 132–46; Thich Minh Chau, *Hsuan Tang: The Pilgrim and Scholar* (Saigon, Vietnam Buddhist Institute, 1963); and Stanley Weinstein, "A Biographical Study of Tzu-en," *MN,* XV, 1–2 (April–July, 1959), 119–49. Buddhism in the mid-ninth century and the great persecution which it suffered at that time are depicted in Edwin Reischauer's translation of *Ennin's Diary* (N.Y., Ronald, 1966) and in his companion volume, *Ennin's Travels in Tang China* (N.Y., Ronald, 1955); while a specific aspect of the situation is analyzed by Kenneth Chen in his article on "The Economic Background of the Hui Chang Suppression of Buddhism." *HJAS,* XIX, 1–2 (June, 1956), 67–105.

Though it is often said—with some justification—that Buddhism never really recovered from the ninth-century persecutions, the point may easily be exaggerated. Developments during the next several centuries are considered by Jan Yun-Hua in his article on "Buddhist Relations Between India and Sung China," *HR,* VI, 1 and 2 (Aug. and Nov., 1966), 24–42 and 135–68; by Kenneth Chen in "The Sale of Monk Certificates during the Sung Dynasty," *Harvard Theological Review,* 49 (1956), 307–27; and by Karl Wittfogel and Feng Chia-Sheng, "Religion under the Liao Dynasty," *Review of Religion,* XII, 4 (May, 1948), 355–74. An important attack on Buddhism is presented by G.E. Sargent in "Tchou Hi contre le bouddhisme," *Mélanges publiés par l'Institut des hautes études chinoises* (Paris, 1957), 1–157. Daniel Overmeyer, however, has recently demonstrated the continued vitality and development of Chinese Buddhism right through to the seventeenth century; see his article on "Folk-Buddhist Religion" in *HR,* XII, 1 (Aug., 1972), and his book on the subject which will be forthcoming from Harvard, 1976.

Those readers interested in the condition of Buddhism in China during the twentieth century are extremely fortunate to have available Holmes Welch's magnificent three-volume work on the subject. The first volume deals with *The Practice of Chinese Buddhism: 1900–1950* (Cambridge, Harvard Univ. Press, 1967) and may be supplemented by Lewis Hodous, *Buddhism and Buddhists in China* (N.Y., Macmillan, 1924), and John Blofeld, *The Jewel in the Lotus* (London, Sidgwick and Jackson, 1948). Welch's second volume focuses on *The Buddhist Revival in China* (1968) and may be read along with Wing-tsit Chan, *Religious Trends in Modern China* (N.Y., Columbia Univ. Press, 1953) and the book by the Chinese reformer, Tai Hsu, entitled *Lectures on Buddhism* (Paris, Imprimerie Union, 1928). Volume three treats the very difficult topic of *Buddhism Under Mao* (1972) covering the topic up to the outbreak of the cultural revolution. Other discussions which may also be consulted include Kenneth Chen, "Chinese Communist Attitudes Toward Buddhism in Chinese History," *China Quarterly,* XXII (April–June, 1965), 14–30; Richard Bush, *Religion in Communist China* (N.Y., Abingdon, 1970) and David Yu, "Buddhism in Communist China," *JAAR,* 39, 1 (March, 1971), 48–61; however for more up-to-date accounts see Holmes Welch, "The Buddhists Return," *Far Eastern Economic Review* (July 16, 1973), and Sarah and John Strong, "A Post-Cultural Revolution Look at Buddhism," *China Quarterly,* 44 (April/June, 1973). For descriptions of Buddhism in Hong Kong and Taiwan see Holmes Welch, "Buddhist Organizations in Hong Kong," *JRAS* (*Hong Kong*) (1961), 1–17, and Joseph Kitagawa, "Buddhism in Taiwan Today," *FA,* ns, XVIII (July–Aug., 1962), 439–44. Further references on this subject may be found in the concluding section of chapter IV.

TEXTS AND SCHOOLS   Anyone interested in the literature of Chinese Buddhism should begin by acquainting himself with the texts which were generated within the Indian Buddhist tradition. The procedures and results of the process of translating the Indian texts into Chinese are carefully described in P.C. Bagchi, *Le Canon bouddhique en Chine,* 2 vols. (Paris, Paul Guethner, 1927, 1938). Other relevant items include R.H. Van Gulick *Siddham: An Essay on the History of Sanskrit Studies in China and Japan* (Nagpur, International Academy of Indian Culture, 1956); Probhat Mukherji, *Indian Literature in China and the Far East* (Calcutta, Greater India Society, 1931); and a more specialized article by V. Hrdlickova on "The First Translations of Buddhist Sutras in Chinese Literature and Their Place in the Development of Storytelling," *AO,* 26 (1958), 114–44. For those interested in an anthology of Chinese texts the two best are clearly Samuel Beal's *A Catena of Buddhist Scriptures* (London, Trübner, 1871) and the appropriate section of William T. de Bary, ed., *Sources of Chinese Tradition* (N.Y., Columbia Univ. Press, 1960).

In China as in India different texts and interpretations were emphasized by different Buddhist schools. In Chen's *Buddhism in China* (*op. cit.*) the history of these schools is carefully traced, but in order to clarify their different doctrinal orientations other works should be consulted. An excellent overview of the various positions can be gained from the appropriate sections of the second volume of Fung Yu-lan's *History of Chinese Philosophy,* tr. by Derk Bodde (Princeton, Princeton Univ. Press, 1953), and the relevant chapters of Wing-tsit Chan's *Source Book of Chinese Philosophy* (Princeton, Princeton Univ. Press, 1963). However the reader may carry his study further by consulting works devoted to particular schools and to the particular texts around which they rallied.

Though we know that the Hinayaya schools played an important role in the missionizing of China, the Mahayana traditions quickly became predominant, and at the philosophical level the Madhyamika (Three Treatises) and Yogacara (Consciousness Only) schools came to the fore. Studies which deal specifically with these schools include Richard Robinson, *Early Madhyamika in India and China* (Madison, Univ. of Wisconsin Press, 1967) and Clarence Hamilton's article on "Hsuan Chang and the Wei Shih Philosophy," *JAOS,* 51 (1931), 291–308. For two early texts that played an important role see Yoshita Hakeda, tr., *The Awakening of Faith* (N.Y., Columbia Univ. Press, 1967), which may actually have been written in China, and Charles Luk, tr., *The Vimalakirti Nirdesa Sutra* (Berkeley, Shambhala, 1972), which is discussed in Richard Mather, "Vimalakirti and Gentry Buddhism," *HR,* VIII, 1 (Aug., 1968), 60–73. For a text which emerged within the Madhyamika/Three Treatises School see Walter Liebenthal, tr., *The Book of Chao,* (Peking, Catholic Univ., 1948), and for one which was particularly significant for the Yogacara/Consciousness Only tradition see Clarence Hamilton, tr., *Vimsatika Wei Shih Er Lun or the Treatise in Twenty Stanzas on Representation Only* (New Haven, American Oriental Society, 1938).

In the course of time other more distinctively Chinese schools appeared on the scene. The very influential position of the Avatamsaka or Hwa Yen school has been presented and a few key texts translated by Garma C.C. Chang in *The Buddhist Teaching of Totality* (University Park, Pa., Penn State Univ. Press, 1971). In addition the reader may consult the excellent entries on the "Avatamsaka School" and the "Avatamsaka Sutra" in the *Encyclopedia of Buddhism* (*op. cit.*); D.T. Suzuki's very partial and "epitomized" translation of part of the Sutra in *EB,* 1 (1921), 1–13, 147–55, 237–42 and 282–90; and also Suzuki's long commentary in his *Essays in Zen Buddhism—Third Series* (London, Luzac, 1934), 1–185. The position of the other major philosophically oriented Buddhist tradition which developed in China is presented in R.C. Armstrong, "The Doctrine of the Tendai School," *EB,* 3 (1924), 32–54; in somewhat more detail in Bruno Petzold in "The Chinese Tendai Teachings," *EB,* 4 (1927–28), 299–347; and most fully in Leon Hurvitz's biographical study of its founder, *Chih-i (538–597)* (*op. cit.*). The basic text utilized by the Tendai teachers is the *Lotus Sutra* which is available in a translation from the Chinese version originally done by Bruno Kato and William Soothill, rev. by Wilhelm Schiffer and published as *The Sutra of the Lotus Flower of the Wonderful Law* (Tokyo, Rissho Kosei-kai, 1971).

At the same time that the Chinese Buddhist community was producing these more philosophical schools of interpretation, the equally important and historically more durable Chan (known in Japan as Zen) and Pure Land traditions were also coming to the fore. In the case of Chan the bibliographical resources are legion, and the problem is one of selectivity. An interesting way to begin is to read Hu Shih's article on "Chan (Zen) Buddhism in China: Its History and Method," *PEW,* III, 1 (April, 1953), and then D.T. Suzuki, "Zen. A Reply to Hu Shih," *PEW,* IV, 1 (April, 1954), 25–45. More substantive treatments are provided by Suzuki in his section on the "History of Zen Buddhism in China" in *Essays in Buddhism —First Series* (London, Luzac, 1927); and by Heinrich Dumoulin in a series of studies which includes an article on "Bodhidharma und die Angänge des Chan Buddhismus," *MN,* 7 (1951), 67–83, chaps. v–viii of his *History of Zen Buddhism,* tr. by Paul Peachey (N.Y., Pantheon, 1963) and *The Development of Chinese Zen,* tr. by Ruth Sasaki (N.Y., First Zen Institute in America, 1953), in which he provides the best available account of the development of the tradition from the eighth century onward. In addition a very different kind of introduction is provided by Chen-chi Chang in *The Practice of Zen* (N.Y., Rider, 1960).

One of the classical Indian texts which provides background for the development of Chan can be explored by reading D.T. Suzuki's translation of the *Lankavatara Sutra* (London, Routledge, 1932) along with the Chan-style interpretation which he develops in his *Studies in the Lankavatara Sutra* (London, Routledge, 1930). Very important stories concerning the early Chan masters have been helpfully introduced and translated by Chung-yuan Chang in *Original Teachings of Chan Buddhism* (N.Y., Pantheon, 1969); and the short "Sermon of Shen-hui" has been made available by Walter Liebenthal, *Asia Major,* III, 2 (1952), 132–55. Wing-tsit Chan has published an excellent translation of *The Platform Sutra* (N.Y., St. John's Univ. Press, 1963); however Philip Yampolsky's version entitled *The Platform Sutra of the Sixth Patriarch* (N.Y., Columbia Univ. Press, 1967) has the added advantage of an extended and very helpful introduction. Jacques Gernet has made available a "Biographie du maître Che-Houie du Ho Tso," *JA,* 239 (1951), 29–69. John Blofeld has translated two important works *The Zen Teachings of Huang Po* (N.Y., Grove, 1959) and the *Zen Teachings of Hui Hai on Sudden Illumination* (London, Rider, 1962); and Helen Chapin has translated an interesting text dealing with "The Chan Master Pu-tai," *JAOS,* 53 (1933), 47–52. A quite different kind of translation which also deserves to be singled out is Zenkei Shibayama, *Zen Comments on the Mumonkan* (N.Y., Mentor Books, 1975). For other Chinese (as well as Japanese) items see "A Bibliography of Translations of Zen (Chan) Works," *PEW,* 3/4 (1960–61), 149–66.

Though in China the Pure Land traditions have been at least as widespread and as durable as Chan, far less has been written about them. A good starting point is the article on "Amita" in the *Encyclopedia of Buddhism (op. cit.)*; and this may be supplemented by D.T. Suzuki, "The Development of Pure Land Doctrine in Buddhism," *EB,* 3 (1924–25), 285–326; by Gemmyo Ono, "On the Pure Land Doctrine of Tzu-min," *EB,* 5 (1929–31), 200–10; and by Allan Andrews, "Nembutsu in the Chinese Pure Land Tradition" *EB,* ns, 3 (1970), 20–45. The most important texts include the *Amitayus Dhyana-Sutra* and the *Sukhavati-Vyuha-Sutra* which are translated in Cowell et al., *Mahayana Buddhist Texts (op. cit.)* and Shan Tao's commentary on the former which is analyzed by Julian Pas in his article on "Shan Tao's Interpretation of the Meditative Vision of Buddha Amitayus," *HR,* 14 (1974), 96–116. In addition an early Pure Land catechism has been translated by Leo Pruden; see "Ten Doubts concerning the Pure Land" *EB,* ns, 6 (1973), 126–57. Richard Robinson has compiled a relevant anthology of *Chinese Buddhist Verse* (London, Murray, 1954).

Finally, for the only major treatment of the neglected tradition of esoteric Buddhism see the article by Yi-liang Chou on "Tantrism in China," *HJAS,* 8 (1945), 241–322.

MYTH, SYMBOL, AND ART   A fascinating Chinese version of the life of the Buddha is accessible in a translation by Leon Wieger in the second volume of his *Bouddhisme* (China, Hien-hien, 1913) in which extensive illustrations are also included. The "fully perfected saints" and their changing role in China are treated in an article by M.W. de Visser on "The Arhats in China and Japan" in *Ostasiatische Zeitschrift* (April/Sept., 1918), 78–102, and (April/Sept., 1920–21), 116–44; and in a more recent publication on *The Sixteen Arhats and the Eighteen Lohans,* compiled by the Shah Shin Buddhist Institute and published by the Buddhist Association of China (Peking, 1961). A number of studies have also been done focusing on particular Bodhisatvas; see, for example, Étienne Lamotte's article on "Manjusri," *TP,* 48 (1960), 1–96; and John H. Chamberlayne, "The Development of Kuan Yin, Chinese Goddess of Mercy," *Numen,* 9 (Jan., 1962), 45–52.

Among the many studies of Buddhist art in China a number focus specifically on representations of these figures. Hugo Munsterberg has written a very general introduction to *Chinese Buddhist Bronzes* (Tokyo, Charles Tuttle, 1967); Helen Chapin has contributed a monograph entitled *A Long Roll of Buddha Images* which was revised by Alexander Soper and published in Ascona by ArA (1972); Wen Fong has provided an important examination of *The Lohans and a Bridge to Heaven* (Washington, Freer Gallery of Art, 1958); and Helen Chapin has discussed the "Yunanese Images of Avalokitesvara," *HJAS,* 8 (1944–45), 131–86. For a similar study with a specifically textual focus see the excellent work by J. Leroy Davidson entitled *The Lotus Sutra in Chinese Art: A Study of Buddhist Art to the Year 1000* (New Haven, Yale Univ. Press, 1954).

Buddhist temples and pagodas of various types have been examined both for their historical and artistic interest. The remains from the Sui and Tang times have been intensively studied and represented by Tadashi Sekino and Daijo Tokiwa in their 5 volume *Buddhist Monuments in China* (Tokyo, Bukkyo-Shiseki Kenkyu Kwai, 1926); and a short article on "Buddhist Temples in the Tang Period" was written by A. Bulling and published in *Oriental Art,* 1 (1955), 115–22. Chinese forms of stupas have been analyzed by J.J.M. de Groot in his monograph on *Der Thupa: Das heiligste Heiligtum des Buddhismus in China* (Berlin, Akademie der Wissenschaft, 1919), and by G. Ecke and Paul Demiéville in *The Twin Pagodas of Zayton* (Cambridge, Harvard Univ. Press, 1935). Cave temples have been the subject of an excellent book by Zerukazu Akiyama and Saburo Matsubara entitled *Arts of China: Buddhist Cave Temples* (Tokyo, Kobansha, 1969), and of another major work by Michael Sullivan, *The Cave Temples of Maichisan* (Berkeley, Univ. of California Press, 1969). An important pilgrimage site has been described in general terms by Archibald Little, *Mt. Omi and Beyond* (London, W. Heinemann, 1901), and more recently an article on "Les temples bouddhiques du Mont O-Mei" was published by André Migot in *Arts Asiatiques* (1957), 20–34 and 131–42. Ferdinand Lessing's very rich study of *Yung-Ho-Kung—An Iconography of a Lamaist Cathedral in Peking* (Stockholm, Sino-Swedish Expedition, 18, 1964) must also be mentioned.

On the topic of Chinese Buddhist painting several interesting scholarly works are available. For example, Basil Gray has written on the *Buddhist Cave Paintings at Tun Huang* (*op. cit.*); Langdon Warner has published *Buddhist Wall Paintings: A Study of a Ninth-Century Grotto at Wan Fo Hsia* (Cambridge, Harvard Univ. Press, 1936); and William White has made available a study of *Chinese Temple Frescoes: A Study of Three Wall Paintings of the Thirteenth Century* (Toronto, Univ. of Toronto Press, 1940). In addition the important subject of Chan paintings has been discussed in a very helpful chapter in vol. II of Oswald Siren, *Chinese Painting: Leading Masters and Principles* (London, Lund Humphries, 1956).

RELIGIOUS LIFE AND PRACTICES   J. Prip Møller's classic work on *Chinese Buddhist Monasteries* (Hong Kong, Hong Kong Univ., 1967) provides an excellent idea of the setting and content of traditional monastic life in China; and Holmes Welch's *Practices of Chinese Buddhism 1900–1950* (*op. cit.*) as well as the same author's fascinating article on "Dharma Scrolls and the Succession of Abbots," *TP,* 50 (1963), 93–149, focus on the monastic community but include references to lay traditions as well. Some very important forms of Chinese Buddhist practice are discussed by Charles Luk in *The Secrets of Chinese Meditation* (London, Rider, 1964), which may be supplemented by W. Pachow, "A Buddhist Discourse on Meditation from Tun-Huang," *UCR,* XXI, 1 (April, 1963). A much more

unusual but nonetheless interesting form of Buddhist expression is traced
by Jacques Gernet in "Les Suicides par le feu chez les bouddhistes chinois
du Ve au Xe siècles," *Mélanges publiés par l'Institut des hautes études
chinoises,* tome II (Paris, 1962), 527–58, and by Jan Yun-Hua, "Buddhist
Self- Immolation in Medieval China," *HR,* IV, 2 (Winter, 1965), 243–68.
D.T. Suzuki has examined certain aspects of the popular "Cult of Kwan-
non," *EB,* 6 (1932–35), 339–53, and several scholars have described some
of the important Buddhist practices associated with death: see, for example'
W.P. Yetts, "Notes on the Disposal of the Dead in China," *JRAS,* 1911,
699–725; J.J.M. de Groot's account of the "Buddhist Masses for the Dead
in Amoy," *Actes du sixième congrès international des orientalistes,* IV, 4
(Leiden, 1885); and J.J.L. Duyvendak's examination of "The Buddhist
Festival of All-Souls in China and Japan," *AO,* V (1926), 39–48, which
should be read in conjunction with Jan Jaworski's translation of the story
of Mogallana's visit to hell, "L'Avalambanasutra de la Terre Pure," *MS,*
1 (1935), 82–107.

BUDDHISM AND OTHER TRADITIONS IN CHINA   A very sketchy overview of the interaction of "Buddhism and Native Chinese Ideologies" is
given by Richard Mather, *Review of Religion,* 20 (1955–56), 25–37.
Hajime Nakamura has carried out a more focused study on "The Influence
of Confucian Ethics on the Chinese Translations of Buddhist Sutras,"
Sino-Indian Studies, 5 (1957), 156–70; while Carsun Chang has centered
attention on the role of "Buddhism as a Stimulus to Confucianism," *OE,*
2 (1955), 157–66. In addition, Wing-tsit Chan has considered the question "How Buddhistic Is Wang Yang Ming?" in *PEW,* XII, 3 (Oct., 1962),
203–15, and has dealt with "Wang Yang Ming's Criticism of Buddhism"
in Ram Lee Singh, ed., *World Perspectives in Philosophy, Religion and
Culture* (Patna, India, Bharati Bhawan, 1968), 31–37.

The fascinating and enigmatic relationship between Buddhism and
Taoism has intrigued a number of scholars. Important articles have been
written by Kenneth Chen on "Neo-Taoism and the Prajna School during
the Wei and Chin Dynasties," *Chinese Culture,* I, 2 (Oct., 1957), 33–46,
and by Arthur Link on "The Taoist Antecedents of Tao-an's Prajna Ontology," *HR,* IX 2/3 (Nov., 1969/Feb., 1970), 181–215. Two Japanese
scholars, Mori Mikisubori and Mitsuji Fukunaga, have done studies on
"Chuang Tzu and Buddhism," *EB,* ns, V, 2 (Oct., 1972), 44–69, and
" 'No-mind' in Chuang-tzu and in Chan Buddhism," *Zinbun,* XII (1969),
9–45. Studies of the relationships and encounters in particular periods
have been published by W. Eichorn and Noritada Kubo; see *Beitrag zur
rechtlichen Stellung des Buddhismus und Taoismus im Sung-Staat* (Leiden,
E.J. Brill, 1968) and "Prolegomena to the Study of Controversies between
Buddhists and Taoists in the Yuan Period," *MROTB,* 26 (1968), 39–61.

The encounters between Buddhism and Christianity have been discussed for the "Nestorian" period by Svere Hoth in an article in *Ching Feng* (Hong Kong), XI, 3 (1968), 30–38; for the period from the fourteenth to the seventeenth century by Frederick Brandauer, *ibid.*, 30–38; and by Douglas Lancashire, *Journal of the Oriental Society of Australia* (Sydney), VI, 1/2 (1968/69), 82–103; and for the modern period by Winfried Gluer in an article in the same issue of *Ching Feng,* 39–57.

B. Korea

Korean Buddhism is introduced in short articles by Kwan Sang-no on the "History of Korean Buddhism," by Park Chang-hong on "Buddhist Influence on Korean Thought," and by Cho Myung-ki on "Prominent Buddhist Leaders and Their Doctrines," all of which appeared in the *Korean Journal,* IV, 5 (May, 1964), 8–21; as well as by Han Sang-ryun, in "The Influence of Buddhism in Korea," *Korea Observer,* III, 2 (1971), 17–25. Western observers in the early decades of the twentieth century have also provided introductory discussions which, though they are often superficial and dated, contain a great deal of interesting material; see, for example, Charles A. Clark, *Religions of Old Korea* (N.Y., F.H. Revell, 1932), 11–90; Frederick Starr, *Korean Buddhism* (Boston, Marshall Jones, 1918); and Mark Trollope, "Introduction to the Study of Buddhism in Korea" *TRASK,* 8 (1917), 1–41. However, the best available source for introducing Korean Buddhism to the serious student is Gari Ledyard's article on "Cultural and Political Aspects of Traditional Korean Buddhism," *Asia,* 10 (Winter, 1968), 46–61.

For those who wish to study particular aspects of the tradition a few resources are available. Peter H. Lee has translated the *Lives of Eminent Korean Monks* (Cambridge, Harvard Univ. Press, 1969) and has also contributed an article on "Fa-tsang and Uisang," *JAOS,* LXXXII, 1 (Jan./March, 1962). A number of studies of the development of art and iconography have been published, including Chewon Kim and Lena Kim Lee, *Arts of Korea* (Tokyo, Kodansha International, 1974); Hai Jin Kim, *Buddhism and Korean Culture* (New Delhi, Academy of Indian Culture, 1958); and Kye-Hyou Ahn, "Buddha Images in the Korean Tradition," *Korean Journal,* X, 3 (1970), 7–14. The reader may also consult two older studies by G.H. Jones and E.A. Gordon entitled "Colossal Buddha at Eun-Jin," *TRASK,* 1 (1901), 51–76, and "Some Recent Discoveries in Korean Temples and Their Relationship to Early Eastern Christianity," *TRASK,* 5 (1914), 1–39. An interesting reconstruction of the Chan tradition in Korea has been published by Do-Ryun Suk in a series of articles on "Son Buddhism in Korea" and "Modern Son Buddhism in Korea," *Korean Journal* IV and V (1964 and 1965). For other aspects of the contemporary situation see the special 1967 issue of *TRASK* which is devoted to The New Religions of Korea and contains a number of articles on Buddhist related groups including Lee Kang-o's discussion of "Jingsan-gyo: Its History, Doctrine and Ritual," and Benjamin Weems, "Ch'ondoyo Enters Its Second Century."

C. Vietnam

One of the very few short introductions to Vietnamese Buddhism is provided in the articles by Maurice Durand and Mai-tho-Truyen in *Présence du bouddhisme,* 797–812, the second and more extensive of which has been translated into English in *Le Bouddhisme au Vietnam* (Saigon, Pagoda XA-Loi, 1962). In addition the reader may consult the two chapters on Champa and Annam in vol. III of Eliot's *Hinduism and Buddhism* (*op. cit.*); the sections on Vietnam in André Migot's article on "Le Bouddhisme en Indochine" in *BSEI,* ns, XXI (2e semestre, 1946), 23–38; Tran-van-Giap's essay on "Les Deux sources du bouddhisme annamite: Ses rapports avec l'Inde et la Chine," *Cahiers EFEO,* 33 (1942), 17–20; Gustave Dumoutier, "Notes sur le bouddhisme tonkinois," *Revue d'ethnologie,* 7 (1888), 235–301; and L. Bezacier, "Le Panthéon des pagodes bouddhiques du Tonkin," *Cahiers EFEO,* 33 (1942). The one study which goes more deeply into the subject is Tran-van-Giap's classic article on "Le Bouddhisme en Annam: Des origines au XIIIe siècle" in *BEFEO,* XXXII, 1 (1932), 191–268.

In recent years there have, of course, been a number of studies and commentaries on the relationship between Buddhism and political developments, and particularly the controversy between many Buddhists and the regime of Ngo Dinh Diem. This conflict is discussed by Robert Scigliano, "Vietnam: Politics and Religion," *Asian Survey,* IV, 1 (Jan., 1964), 666–73; by Charles Joiner, "South Vietnam's Buddhist Crises," *Asian Survey,* IV, 7 (July, 1964), 915–29; and by David Halberstam in an essay on "The Buddhist Crisis in Vietnam" in Marvin Gettleman, ed., *Vietnam: History, Document and Opinion on a Major World Crisis* (Greenwich, Conn., Fawcett, 1965); and the issues are probed more deeply by Paul Mus in an article which has the somewhat misleading title, "Buddhism in Vietnamese History and Society," *Yearbook of the South Asia Institute, Heidelberg Univ.* (Wiesbaden, Otto Harrassowitz, 1967–68), 95–115; and in Joseph Buttinger, *Vietnam: A Political History* (N.Y., Praeger, 1968). In addition the reader may consult Thich Nhat Hanh's attempt to put his own contemporary situation into historical perspective in his book *Vietnam: Lotus in a Sea of Fire* (N.Y., Hill and Wang, 1967), and André Migot's discussion of "Le Suicide par le feu des religieux bouddhistes vietnamiens," *Guerres et paix,* I (1967), 18–27.

V. TIBET AND NEIGHBORING REGIONS

A. Tibet

INTRODUCTIONS AND SURVEYS.   In recent years a plethora of articles and books have appeared which deal with Tibetan Buddhism. Their quality, however, has been uneven, and the serious reader must exercise caution. Useful short introductions are provided by Li-Anche's essay on "Tibetan Religion" in Vergilius Ferm. ed., *Forgotten Religions* (N.Y., Philosophical Library, 1950), 251–69; and by Loban Jiavaka, "Le Bouddhisme tibetain," *FA,* XXI, 2 (Winter, 1966–67), 197–205; to which may be added William Weedon, "Tibetan Buddhism: A Perspective," *PEW,* XVII, 1/4 (Jan./Oct., 1967). For more extended treatments which set Buddhism within the context of Tibetan life and history the reader may depend upon Rolf Stein, *Tibetan Civilization,* tr. by J.E.S. Driver (Stanford, Stanford Univ. Press, 1972) and Hugh Richardson and David Snellgrove, *A Cultural History of Tibet* (London, Weidenfeld & Nicolson, 1968); or, for a rather different kind of orientation he may rely upon David Snellgrove's two works entitled *Buddhist Himalaya* and *Himalayan Pilgrimage* (Oxford, Cassirer, 1957, 1961). Among the basic surveys the most authoritative are Helmut Hoffman's *The Religions of Tibet,* tr. by Edward Fitzgerald (London, Allen & Unwin, 1961); and Marcelle Lalou's very neat and concise *Religions du Tibet* (Paris; Presses universitaires de France, 1959), which may be supplemented by the useful but more dated discussions in Charles Bell, *Religions of Tibet* (Oxford, Clarendon, 1931), and by the rich descriptions included in L. Austine Waddell, *Tibetan Buddhism* (rep. in N.Y. by Dover, 1972). Moreover, every serious student should become acquainted with the work of the great master of Tibetan studies, Giuseppe Tucci; for an introductory account see his *Tibet: Land of Snows,* tr. by J.E.S. Driver, (N.Y., Stein & Day, 1967), esp. 64–93; and for definitive chapters on a variety of major topics see his *magnum opus, Tibetan Painted Scrolls* (Roma, La Libreria dello Stato, 1949).

HISTORICAL DISCUSSIONS AND BIOGRAPHIES   A number of modern scholars have focused their attention on the unique religio-political traditions which developed and were maintained in Tibet until the Chinese took over the country in the late 1950s. Overviews of the central role of Buddhism in the traditional political and economic life of the country are provided in Pedro Carassco, *Land and Polity in Tibet* (Seattle, Univ. of Washington Press, 1959), and Rahul Ram, *The Government and Politics of Tibet* (Delhi, Vikas Publications, 1960). A very useful though consciously nationalistic treatment is provided in Tsepon Shakabpa, *Tibet: A Political History* (New Haven, Yale Univ. Press, 1967); while interesting discussions of the central religio-political institutions and figures are included in Guenther Schulemann, *Die Geschichte der Dalai Lamas* (Heidelberg, Carl Winter, 1911); in Rahul Ram's more comparative study of "The Role of Lamas in Central Asian Politics," *Central Asian Journal,* XII, 4 (1969), 209–27; and in Tieh-Tseng Li's *Tibet: Today and Yesterday* (N.Y., Bookman Associates, 1960). More specialized studies of particular periods include Giuseppe Tucci, *The Tombs of the Tibetan Kings* (Roma, IMEO, 1950), which deals with the very early period (seventh century A.D.); Ahmad Zahruddin, *Sino-Tibetan Relations in the 17th Century* (Roma, IMEO, 1970); and William Rockhill, "The Dalai Lamas of Lhasa and Their Relations with the Manchu Emperors of China, 1644–1908," *TP,* ser. II, XI (1910), 1–104.

On the other hand a few scholars have been concerned with the sectarian controversies and lineage traditions which have played a role in Tibetan Buddhist history. The very early and crucial encounter between representatives of the Indian and the Chinese expressions of Buddhism is presented in an authoritative manner by Paul Demiéville, *Le Concile de Lhasa* (Paris, Imprimerie nationale, 1952); and a basic document is provided by Giuseppe Tucci in *Minor Buddhist Texts, Part II: First Bhavanakarma of Kamasila* (Roma, IMEO, 1958). Particular sects and lineages have been studied by Li-Anche in a series of articles which includes "Rnin-ma-pa: The Early Form of Lamaism," *JRAS* (1948), 142–63; "The Bkah-Brgyud Sect of Lamaism," *JAOS,* LXIX, 2 (April/June, 1949), 51–59; "The Sakya Sect of Lamaism," *Journal of the West China Border Society,* XVI, ser. A (1945); by Giuseppe Tucci, "Diffusion of the Yellow Church in Western Tibet and the Kings of Guge," *HJAS,* 12 (1949), 477–96; and by Hugh Richardson, "The Karma-pa Sect" in *JRAS* (1958), 3/4, 139–64 and (1959), 1/2, 1–18. The doctrinal dimension of different groups is emphasized in David Ruegg, "The Jo nan pas: A School of Buddhist Ontologists according to the Grub mtha' sel gyi me lon," *JAOS,* LXXXIII, 1 (Jan./March, 1963), 73–91, and in Herbert Guenther "Some Aspects of Tibetan Religious Thought," *HR,* VI, 1 (Aug., 1966), 70–87.

The traditional chronicles on which most of the modern historical reconstructions are based are reviewed by A.I. Vostrikov in his work on *Tibetan Historical Literature,* tr. by Harish Gupta (Calcutta, IPP, 1970), and by Giuseppe Tucci in an article on "The Validity of Tibetan Historical Traditions" in F.D.K. Bosch, et al., *India Antiqua* (Leiden, E.J. Brill, 1947), 309–22. Two of the classic works are available in E. Obermiller, tr., *Bu-ston's History of Buddhism, Part II* (Heidelberg, Harrassowitz, 1932) and George Roerich, tr., *The Blue Annals,* 2 vols. (Calcutta, Asiatic Society, 1949, 1953). Also there are more recent histories written in the traditional mode: see, for example, the fourteenth Dalai Lama's *The Opening of the Wisdom Eye and the History of the Advancement of Buddhadharma in Tibet,* tr. by Thubten Katzang, et al. (Bangkok,

Social Science Press, 1968), 1–12; and Thubten Jigme Norbu and Colin Turnbull, *Tibet* (N.Y., Simon & Schuster, 1970).

For those interested in hagiographical and biographical material a variety of primary and secondary resources are available. A wide range of data is covered by Sarat S. Das in his still useful discussion of *Indian Pandits in the Land of the Snow* (Calcutta, Lahiri, 1893); and important early figures are dealt with separately by W.Y. Evans-Wentz in the section on Padmasambhava in his *Tibetan Book of the Great Liberation* (London, Oxford, 1954); in Herbert Guenther, tr., *The Life and Teachings of Naropa* (N.Y., Oxford, 1963); in Giuseppe Tucci's article "À Propos the Legend of Naropa," *JRAS,* (Oct., 1935), 677–85; in Alaka Chattopadhyaya, *Atisha and Tibet* (Calcutta, Indian Studies Past & Present, 1967); and in Jacques Bacot, *La Vie de Marpa le "traducteur"* (Paris, Geuthner, 1937).

A fascinating and very popular figure of the late eleventh and early twelfth century is presented in W.Y. Evans-Wentz, *Tibet's Great Yogi Milarepa,* 2nd ed. (London. H. Milford); which may be supplemented by Garma C.C. Chang, *The Hundred Thousand Songs of Milarepa* 2 vols. (New Hyde Park, N.Y., University Books, 1962); and Toni Schmid's *The Cotton-clad Mila: The Tibetan Poet-Saint's Life in Pictures* (Stockholm, Statens ethnografiska Museum, 1952); or, if shorter presentations are desired, by Humphrey Clarke, tr., *The Message of Milarepa* (London, Murray, 1958) and Toni Schmid, "The Life of Milarepa in a Picture Series," *Ethnos,* 1950, 1/2, 74–94. Accounts of the careers of significant figures who lived between the twelfth and sixteenth centuries have been published by George Roerich, *Biography of Dharmasvin: A Tibetan Monk and Pilgrim* (Patna, K.P. Jayaswal Research Institute, 1959; by E. Obermiller, "Tson-kha-pa le Pandit," *MCB,* III (1934–35), 319–38; and by David Snellgrove, *Four Lamas of Dalpo* (Oxford, Cassirer, 1967). For biographical studies of a more recent leader, see Charles Bell, *Portrait of the Dalai Lama* (London, Collins, 1946) and Tokan Tada, *The Thirteenth Dalai Lama* (Tokyo, Center for East Asian Cultural Studies, 1965).

VAJRAYANA PHILOSOPHY AND TECHNIQUES   Though Giuseppe Tucci's *Tibetan Painted Scrolls.* (*op. cit.*) was first published in 1949, the chapters on Vajrayana ideas and Tibetan religious literature still provide the best available overviews of these topics. Other works which are helpful in gaining an orientation to Vajrayana conceptions are the first chapters in John Blofeld's *Tantric Mysticism of Tibet* (N.Y., Dutton, 1970); and Herbert Guenther's two articles on "The Philosophical Background of Buddhist Tantrism," in the *Journal of Oriental Studies,* V, 1/2 (1959–60), 45–64, and on "Tantra and Revelation," in *HR,* VII, 4 (May, 1968), 279–301. In regard to texts, Charles Bell's *Religions of Tibet* (*op. cit.*) contains a very helpful section on "Sources," which may be supplemented by the more detailed studies of versions of the Tibetan canon and other texts noted on pp. 118 and 121 of Richard Gard's article in the previous edition of the present volume.

Among the more popular works which deal with Tibetan thought, techniques, and related primary sources, a number focus on the yogic aspects of the tradition. Though W.Y. Evans-Wentz's *Tibetan Yoga and Secret Doctrines* (London, Oxford, 1954) suffers from some of the same scholarly shortcomings which mar his other works, it can nevertheless be useful for those who read it with care; and Garma C.C. Chang, tr., *The Teachings of Tibetan Yoga* (New Hyde Park, N.Y., University Books, 1962) is also available. Bernard Bromage has provided a survey of *Tibetan Yoga* (N.Y., Samuel Weiser, 1971); and John Blofeld has published a study entitled *The Way of Power* (London, Allen & Unwin, 1970). Three related though rather different works involving translations of texts should be noted, namely, Geshe Wangyal, comp., *The Door of Liberation* (N.Y., Maurice Girodias, 1973); W.Y. Evans-Wentz, *The Tibetan Book of the Great Liberation* (*op. cit.*); and Francesca Fremantle and Chögyam Trungpa, trs., *The Tibetan Book of the Dead* (Berkeley, Shambhala, 1975), which should now replace the older translation by W.Y. Evans-Wentz (London, Oxford, 1927).

For those willing to grapple with the complexities of the tradition a number of additional resources are available. Anagarika Govinda has carried through a study entitled *Foundations of Tibetan Mysticism* (N.Y., Weiser, 1969) in which he interprets the Vajrayana mantra "Om Mani Padme Hum" on the basis of doctrines received from his own Tibetan teacher; and Rolf Stein has contributed a study "Du récit au ritual dans les manuscrits tibetaines de Touen-houang," *Études tibetains dédiées à Marcelle Lalou* (Paris, Adrien Maisonneuve, 1971), 497–574. Alex Wayman has published an important collection of essays entitled *The Buddhist Tantras: Light on Indo-Tibetan Esoterism* (*op. cit.*), which has been the subject of an important review by Reginald Ray, *JAS,* XXXIV, 1 (Nov. 1974), 169–76; and he has also cooperated with Ferdinand Lessing in the translation of a pivotal text, *The Fundamentals of Buddhist Tantra* (The Hague, Mouton, 1968). In addition Jeffrey Hopkins has recently published translations under the titles of *The Buddhism of Tibet and the Key of the Middle Way* and *Precious Garland; and the Song of the Four Mindfulnesses* (both published in N.Y. by Harper & Row, 1975).

Among the contemporary interpreters of Vajrayana thought Herbert Guenther is certainly the most prolific. In order to gain an orientation to Guenther's perspective and his very personal vocabulary the reader will be well advised to begin by consulting his study of *The Tantric View of Life* (Berkeley, Shambhala, 1969) and may then turn to his other interpretive works which include *Buddhist Philosophy in Theory and Practice* (Baltimore, Penguin, 1972); *Treasures of the Tibetan Middle Way* (Berkeley, Shambhala, 1972); and *Yuganaddha: The Tantric View of Life* (Varanasi,

Chowkhamba Sanskrit Studies III, 1969). In addition to these works every serious student of the Vajrayana tradition will also want to consult his translations of *The Royal Songs of Saraha* (Seattle, Univ. of Washington Press, 1969) and the *Jewel Ornament of Liberation* (Berkeley, Shambhala, 1959).

ART AND SYMBOLS   One of the most intriguing facets of Tibetan Buddhism is the richness of its symbolic and artistic expressions. Good introductions with illustrations are available in Pratapaditya Pal's two relatively short books on *The Art of Tibet* (N.Y., Asia Society, 1969) and *Lamaist Art* (Boston, Museum of Fine Arts, 1963). Other useful introductions are provided by Antoinette Gordon, *Tibetan Religious Art* (N.Y., Columbia Univ. Press, 1952) and *The Iconography of Tibetan Lamaism,* 2nd ed. (Rutland, Vt., Tuttle, 1959); and by Lumur Jisl, et al. in a simple but profusely illustrated book entitled *Tibetan Art* (London, Spring Books, 1957). More substantive discussions and analyses are provided in John Brzostoski's excellent *Collection of Tibetan Art with Commentary and Historical Essay* (N.Y., Riverside Museum, 1963); in several German works including Siegbert Hummel, *Geschichte der tibetischen Kunst* (Leipzig, Harrassowitz, 1953); and Helmut Hoffmann, *Symbolik der tibetischen Religionen und des Schamanismus* (Stuttgart, Hiersemann, 1967); and in Giuseppe Tucci's Tibetan Classification of Tibetan Images According to Their Style," *ArA,* XXII (1959), 179–87; as well as his magnificent study and reproduction of *Tibetan Painted Scrolls* (*op. cit.*). For an important study of the influences of Tibetan art in other areas of the Buddhist world, see Siegbert Hummel, *Die lamaistische Kunst in der Umwelt von Tibet* (Leipzig, Harrassowitz, 1955).

In Tibet, as elsewhere in the Buddhist world, the Buddha is a key figure in the religious and iconographic tradition. William Rockhill has translated the *Life of the Buddha and the Early History of the Buddhist Order* (London, K. Paul, 1884) from a basic Tibetan version; and aspects of the artistic tradition are presented in Tokan Tada, ed., *Tibetan Pictorial Life of the Buddha* (Tokyo, Tibet Bunka Senoykai, 1958); in Joseph Hackin, *Les Scènes figurées de la vie du Buddha d'après des peintures tibetaines* (Paris, Leroux, 1916); in Edna Bryner, *Thirteen Tibetan Tankas* (Indian Hills, Colo., Falcon Wings, 1956), and in the passage in Marco Pallis' *Peaks and Lamas* (London, Cassell, 1946) in which he describes the traditional lessons through which students learn to paint the figure of the Buddha. For an analysis of a very different but equally important form of Buddha-symbol see Anagarika Govinda, "The Historical and Symbolic Origins of Chortens" in the *Bulletin of Tibetology,* VII, 1 (Feb., 1970), 5–15.

Studies of bodhistvas, deities and saints and the ways in which they have been represented have been made by a number of different scholars. In the case of bodhisatvas and deities a broad range of subjects has been considered by Giuseppe Tucci in "Buddhist Notes I: À Propos Avalokitesvara," *MCB,* 9 (1948–51), 173–219; by Toni Schmid in *Saviours of Mankind; Dalai Lamas and Former Incarnations of Avalokitesvara* (Stockholm, Statens ethnografiska Museum, 1961); by Walter Clarke in two volumes of reproductions entitled *Two Buddhist Pantheons* (Cambridge, Harvard Yenching Institute, 1937); and by René Nebesky-Wojkowitz in *Oracles and Demons of Tibet* (The Hague, Mouton, 1956). In regard to the saints, Toni Schmid has published an important study of the *Eighty Five Siddhas* (Stockholm, Statens ethnografiska Museum, 1958) as well as the book on the *Cotton-clad Mila* previously cited; and in addition the procedure for the painting of representations of a variety of Buddhist saints used for magical purposes has been minutely described in Marcelle Lalou, *Iconographie des étoffes peintes (Pata) dans le Manjusrimulakalpa* (Paris, Guethner, 1931).

Other types of symbols have also been the subject of interpretive studies. José and Miriam Arguelles have published a book entitled *Mandala* (Berkeley, Shambhala, 1972) which deals with both the artistic and symbolic aspects of sacred circles; Giuseppe Tucci has provided another interpretation in his *Theory and Practice of the Mandala* (London, Rider, 1961); and Gladys Cairns has written an article on "The Philosophy and Psychology of the Oriental Mandala," *PEW,* XI, 4 (Jan., 1962), 219–29. Erik Haarch has published "Contributions to the Study of Mandala and Mudra," *AO,* XXIII, 1/2 (1958), 57–91; and Giuseppe Tucci has discussed a related pattern of orientation in his article on "The Symbolism of the Temple of bSam yas" in *East and West,* VI (1956), 279–81.

COMMUNAL PATTERNS AND RITUAL ACTIVITIES   Many insights into the communal and ritual life of Tibetan Buddhism can be gleaned from the more informed travel accounts. Giuseppe Tucci's *Shrines of a Thousand Buddhas,* tr. by J.E. Stapleton (N.Y., McBride, 1936), and the appropriate segments of John Blofeld's *Wheel of Life* (*op. cit.*) are especially helpful; while Mkcyen Brtse's *Guide to the Holy Places of Central Tibet,* ed. by Alfonso Ferari (Rome, IMEO, 1958) and L. Austine Waddell's *Lhasa and Its Mysteries,* 4th ed. (Freeport, N.Y., Books for Libraries, 1972), are both of considerable historical interest. The careful and discriminating reader can also profit from the numerous works of Alexandria David-Neal (see, for example, *Initiations and Initiates of Tibet* published in London by Rider, 1958) which contain fascinating but often undependable information, and from Anagarika Govinda's highly popularized *Way of the White Clouds* (Berkeley, Shambhala, 1972). Those who desire a more thorough description of a particular group should consult Louis Schram's extremely valuable description of *The Monguors of the Kansu-Tibetan Frontier, Part II, Their Religious Life* (Philadelphia, American Philosophical Society, 1957).

Scholarly presentations devoted specifically to describing the context and content of Tibetan monastic life are available in articles by Beatrice Miller and Li-Anche entitled "The Web of Tibetan Monasticism," *JAS,* XX, 2 (Feb., 1961), 197–203; and "A Lamasery in Outline," *Journal of the West China Border Society,* XIV, ser. A (1942), 35–68; and more extended treatments are provided in two older books by Wilhelm Filchner on *Das Kloster Kumbun in Tibet: Ein Beitrag zu seiner Geschichte* (Berlin; Mittler 1906) and *Kumbun Schamba Ling: Das Kloster der hunderttausend Bilder Maitrayas* (Leipzig, Brockhaus, 1933). Particular aspects of the monastic situation are highlighted in articles by Robert Ekvall on "Three Categories of Inmates in Tibetan Monasteries: Status and Function," *Central Asiatic Journal,* V (1960), 206–20; by R.J. Miller on "Buddhist Monastic Economy: the Jisa Mechanism," *CSSH,* III, 4 (July, 1961); by Li-Anche on "The Lamasery as an Educational Institution," *Asiatic Review,* XLVI (Jan., 1950), 915–22; and by Margaret Miller in a truly exemplary article which depicts "Educational Practices of Tibetan Lama Training," *Folklore Studies,* XVI (1957), 187–267.

The two outstanding works which focus on ritual expressions are Robert Ekvall's study of *Religious Observances in Tibet* (Chicago, Univ. of Chicago Press, 1964), which may be supplemented by Turell Wylie's review in *JAOS,* LXXXVI, 1 (Jan./March, 1966), and Stephen Beyer's comprehensive description and careful analysis of the *Cult of Tara* (Berkeley, Univ. of California Press, 1973). L. Austine Waddell has provided a dated though still useful account of an important aspect in his article on "The Dharani Cult in Buddhism," *Ostasiatische Zeitschrift,* I (1912), 155–95, Ferdinand Lessing has studied three specific rites in separate articles; see "Calling the Soul in a Lamaist Ritual" in Walter J. Fischel, ed., *Semitic and Oriental Studies* (Berkeley, Univ. of California Press, 1951), 253–84; "Structure and Meaning of the Rite Called the Bath of the Buddha," *Studia Serica Bernhard Kahlgren Dedicata* (Copenhagen, Munksgard, 1959); and "Wu-liang shou—A Comparative Study of Tibetan and Chinese Longevity Rites," *Bulletin of the Institute of History and Philology, Academia Sinica,* XXVIII, 2 (1957), 794–824. Finally, two very different types of ritual activities can be explored through Jacques Bacot's translation of *Three Tibetan Mysteries as Performed in Tibetan Monasteries* (N.Y., Dutton, 1923), and in Marion Duncan's two books on *Harvest Dramas of Tibet* (Hong Kong, Orient, 1955) and *More Festival Dramas of Tibet* (London, Mitre, 1967).

Recent Developments. The recent history of Tibetan Buddhism including the events leading up to the Chinese occupation, the occupation itself, and its aftermath are discussed in several different accounts written by Tibetan leaders; see, for example, the Dalai Lama, *My Land and My*

People, ed. by David Howarth (N.Y., Weidenfeld & Nicolson, 1962); Thubten Jigme Norbu, *Tibet Is My Country,* written with Heinrich Harrer (London, Rupert Hart-Davis, 1960); and Chögyam Trungpa as told to Esme Roberts, *Born in Tibet* (London, Allen & Unwin, 1966). The period which culminated in the flight of the Dalai Lama in 1959 is depicted from a Tibetan point of view by Rinchen Dola Taring in *Daughter of Tibet* (London, Murray, 1970), and from a pro-Chinese perspective by Stuart and Roma Gelder, *The Timely Rain* (London, Hutchinson, 1964). Different aspects of the situation which followed the occupation are described by Roger Brown, "The Policies of Communism and the Goal of Annihilation," *Journal of the Society for Asian Studies* (Provo, Utah), I (April, 1968), 1–19, and in the chapter on "Religion and Culture" in *Tibetans in Exile,* published by the Office of the Dalai Lama (Dharmsala, India, 1969).

B. The Himalayan kingdoms

Though the Buddhist traditions which have developed in the small kingdoms located along the border between India and Tibet have been heavily influenced by Buddhism in Tibet, they have a distinctive character of their own. A general overview of the forms of Buddhism practiced there may be gleaned from René Nebesky-Wojkowitz's colorful travel account entitled *Where the Gods Are Mountains* (London, Weidenfield & Nicolson, 1956); however, there are a number of more specialized discussions which focus on particular areas and examine the various forms of expression in greater detail.

Those who are interested in Nepal will find an excellent discussion in the appropriate segments of the introductory books by David Snellgrove cited in Section A, and especially in the chapter on Buddhism in Nepal in *Buddhist Himalaya* (*op. cit*); while those interested in historical questions may consult the English translation of *Buddhist History of Nepal,* ed. by Daniel Wright (Cambridge, Cambridge Univ. Press, 1877). Snellgrove has also published a helpful article on "Shrines and Temples of Nepal" in *Arts Asiatique* (1961), 3–10 and 93–120, to which may be added an article by Marietta Joseph on "Vibharas of the Kathmandu Valley," *Oriental Art,* VII, 2 (Summer, 1971), 121–44. The more specifically artistic traditions are considered by Stella Kramrisch in her essay on "The Art of Nepal and Tibet," *Philadelphia Museum of Art Bulletin,* LV (Spring, 1960), 23–38, and by Jean Eracle, "Un 'than-ka' nepalais: La terre heureuse du Buddha Amitabha," *ASES,* XX (1966), 41–71; and certain practical elements are highlighted by John Brough in an article on "Nepalese Buddhist Rituals," *BSOAS,* XII, 3/4 (1948), 668–76. For studies of one particularly fascinating ethnic group living in the northern part of the country see C. Fürer Haimendorf, *The Sherpas of Nepal* (London, Murray, 1964), 126 ff.; Friedrich Funks, *Religiöses Leben der*

Sherpa (Innsbruck, Universitäts Verlag Wagner, 1969); and Luther Jerstad's study of *Mani-Rimdu: Sherpa Dance Drama* (Seattle, Univ. of Washington Press, 1969).

Other Buddhist traditions of the border region are discussed by Rahul Ram in his work on *Modern Bhutan* (Delhi, Vikas, 1970); by C. Swaramamurti, "Buddhism in Sikkhim, Ladakh and Bhutan" *Light of the Buddha,* 5 (1960), 34–38; by Beatrice and Robert Miller in their article "On Two Bhutanese New Year's Celebrations," *AA,* LVIII (Feb., 1956), 179–83; and by the Second Marquis of Zetland in a book entitled *Lands of the Thunderbolt* (London, Constable, 1923) in which he describes Buddhist practices in Bhutan, Sikkhim, and Chumbi. For studies of a Buddhist ethnic group living in Sikkhim see John Morris, *Living with Lepchas* (London, Heinemann, 1938); René Nebesky-Wojkowitz and Geoffrey Gorer, "The Use of Thread-crosses in Lepcha Lamist Ceremonies," *Eastern Anthropologist,* 4 (1950), 65–87; and Nebesky-Wojkowitz, "Ancient Funeral Ceremonies of the Lepcha" in the same journal, 5 (1951), 27–40.

C. Mongolia

Those students who read German should begin any study of Mongolian Buddhism by turning to the survey by Walter Heissig in G. Tucci and W. Heissig, *Religionen Tibets und der Mongolei* (Stuttgart, Kohlhammer, 1970). However for those who are limited to English a good starting point is much more difficult to identify. Perhaps the best procedure is to consult the marvelously concise indigenous history, tr. by Sarat C. Das, under the title "Rise and Progress of Buddhism in Mongolia" which has been reprinted in his *Contributions to the Religion and History of Tibet* (New Delhi, Manjusri, 1970) and then to turn to Robert J. Miller, *Monasteries and Culture Change in Inner Mongolia* (Wiesbaden, Harrassowitz, 1959).

A number of other more specialized historical studies are now available. Henry Serruys discusses "Early Lamaism in Mongolia" *OE,* X (1963), 181–216, and has added an additional "Note on the Origin of Lamaism in Mongolia," *Ibid.,* XII (1966), 165–73. The same topic is covered by Sh. Natsagdorji in an article on "The Introduction of Buddhism into Mongolia" in *The Mongolia Society Bulletin,* VII, 1 (Jan./June, 1968), 1–12; while an interesting individual who lived during the early period is described in Igor de Rachewiltz's essay on "Yeh-Lu Chu-Tsai (1189–1243): Buddhist Idealist and Confucian Statesman," in Arthur Wright, ed., *Confucian Personalities* (Stanford, Stanford Univ. Press, 1962). Subsequent developments are treated by Sechin Jagchid in an article on "Buddhism in Mongolia after the Collapse of the Yuan Dynasty" in *The Mongolia Society Bulletin,* X, 1 (April, 1971), 48–61, and in Walter

Heissig, "A Mongolian Source Concerning the Lamaist Suppression of Shamanism in the 17th Century," *Anthropos,* XLVIII (1953), 1–29 and 493–536. Accounts of the disestablishment of Buddhism in the 1920s are included in Owen Lattimore, "Religion and Revolution in Mongolia" in *Modern Asian Studies,* I, 1 (Jan., 1967), 81–94, and in Charles R. Bawden, *The Modern History of Mongolia* (London, Weidenfeld & Nicolson, 1968). For an interpretation of the early interaction between Buddhism and Communism see the chapter on Lamaism in Emanuel Sarkisyanz, *Russland und der Messianismus des Orients* (Tübingen, J.C.B. Mohr, 1955), 369–78, and Nicholas Poppe, "The Destruction of Buddhism in the U.S.S.R.," *Mitteilungen, Institut zur Erforschung der UdS.S.R.* (July, 1956), 14–20; and for a firsthand description of the situation as it existed in 1957 see Lokish Chandra, "Buddhism in Mongolia," *Indo-Asian Culture,* 8 (1960).

In addition to the work of Das cited above, other indigenous histories have also been translated. The development of Buddhism and the role of the great lamas provide the primary foci of attention in George Huth, tr., *Geschichte des Buddhismus in der Mongolei,* vol. II (Strassburg, Trübner, 1896), and Charles Bawden, tr., *The Jebtsundamba Khutukhtus of Urga* (Wiesbaden, Harrassowitz, 1961); Charles Bawden's translation of *The Mongol Chronicle of Altan Tobci* (Wiesbaden, Harrassowitz, 1955) makes available a more general historical account written from an explicitly Buddhist perspective. Those who are interested in these translations will also profit by consulting Walter Heissig, "Zur lamaistische Beeinflussung des mongolischen Geschichtsbildes," *Serta Cantabrigiensia* (1954), 37–44.

Readers who prefer to adopt a topical rather than an historical approach also have a number of studies to which they can turn. The subject of "Buddhist Literature in Mongolia" is discussed by Prabat Mukerjee in the *Sino-Indian Journal,* July 1947, pp. 58–76; and particular items can be directly consulted. See, for example, Nicholas Poppe's translation of *The Twelve Deeds of the Buddha* (Wiesbaden, Harrassowitz, 1967), and the same scholar's rendering of a local version of *The Diamond Sutra* (Wiesbaden, Harrassowitz, 1971). Various symbolic and practical aspects of the traditions are presented by Maurice Percherons in *Dieux et démons, lamas et sorciers de Mongolia* (Paris, Denoel, 1953); basic elements of the meditation tradition have been studied by A.M. Pozdnejev in his *Dhyana und Samadhi im mongolischen Lamaismus* (Hannover, Lafaire, 1927); and Henry Serruys has published a major article entitled "A Mongol Lamaist Prayer: Incense Offering of Origin," *MS,* XXVIII (1969), 312–418. Those who are interested in the monasteries and communal aspects of the tradition may consult Robert Miller's comprehensive study mentioned above; Joseph can Hecken, "Les Lamaseries d'Oto (Ordos)," *MS,*

XXII, 1 (1963), 121–68; and the interesting though rather personal observations of John Blofeld in the appropriate segments of his *Wheel of Life* (*op. cit.*).

VI. BUDDHISM AND THE WEST

A. Buddhism and Western history

Any study of the impact of Buddhism in the Western world must first of all take account of the long and continuing history of cultural influence including the emergence and development of modern Buddhist studies. The most important books for those interested in exploring this history are Henri de Lubac's *La Rencontre du bouddhisme et de l'occident* (Paris, Aubier, 1952) and Guy Welbon, *The Buddhist Nirvana and Its Western Interpreters* (*op. cit.*). Particular aspects of the cultural influence of Buddhism in the pre-modern period are highlighted by Daniel Gimaret, "Bouddha et les bouddhists dans la tradition musulmane," *JA*, CCLVII, 3/4 (1969), 273–316; by David Lang, *The Wisdom of Balahvar: A Christian Legend of the Buddha* (N.Y., Macmillan, 1957); and by Jurgis Baltrusaitis in his *Le Moyen fantastique* (Paris, Armand Colin, 1955), 229–62, in which he discusses the Buddhist motifs brought back to Europe by the early Franciscan missionaries. Studies of more recent influences may be found in a number of sources including Dorothy Dauer, *Schopenhauer as a Transmitter of Buddhist Ideas* (Berne, Lang, 1969) and in the appropriate chapters of Raymond Schwab, *La Renaissance orientale* (Paris, Payot, 1950); and in addition the reader may also want to consult Edwin Arnold's poetic rendering of the life of the Buddha entitled *The Light of Asia* (Philadelphia, Altemus, 1879), which enjoyed a tremendous popularity in the late nineteenth and early twentieth centuries, particularly in America; Erich Fromm, et al., *Zen Buddhism and Psychoanalysis* (N.Y., Grove, 1963) which both expressed and fostered the American vogue for Zen in the 1950s and 1960s; and the many books of Alan Watts which have had a great impact on recent developments in American youth culture. Among the sources which deal with the nineteenth- and twentieth-century developments in Buddhology Edward Conze's essay on "Modern Buddhist Studies" in his *Thirty Years of Buddhist Studies* (*op. cit.*), and J.W. de Jong, "A Brief History of Buddhist Studies in Europe and America," *EB*, ns, VII (May, 1964), 56–106, provide readily accessible and authoritative accounts.

During the past century the more subtle modes of Buddhist impact have been supplemented by the appearance of Buddhist communities. The Buddhist groups which have developed in various Western countries are surveyed in a set of English and French articles in René de Berval, ed.,

Présence du bouddhisme (*op. cit.*); in an essay by Ernst Benz in Heinrich Dumoulin, ed., *Buddhismus der Gegenwart* (*op. cit.*); in Christmas Humphreys, *Sixty Years of Buddhism in England* (London, Buddhist Society, 1968); and in Joseph Kitagawa's article on "Buddhism in America with Special Reference to Zen," *Japanese Religions,* V, 1 (July, 1967), 32–57. A large and well entrenched Buddhist community which was established through immigration has been carefully studied by Louise Hunter in her book on *Buddhism in Hawaii* (Honolulu, Univ. of Hawaii Press, 1971), while an exile community is described by Peter Linfegger-Stauffer in his article on "Das klosterliche Tibet-Institut in Rikon/Zürich," *ASES,* XV (1971), 377–88. The very different kinds of Buddhist communities recently sprung up in the United States are briefly surveyed in Robert Ellwood, *Religious and Spiritual Groups in America* (Englewood Cliffs, N.J., Prentice-Hall, 1973), 74–79, 98–103, 125–30, and 225–75; and by Jacob Needleman, *The New Religions* (Garden City, N.Y., Doubleday, 1970), chaps. 2 and 7. In order to appreciate the number and diversity of Buddhist groups now operative on the American scene the reader may also consult the list of more than fifty organizations and their publications which Charles Presbisch and Roger Corless have included as a "Appendix" in Presbisch and Corless, eds., *Buddhism: A Modern Perspective* (*op. cit*), 255–58.

B. Comparative and dialogical studies

In each generation of modern scholars there have been a few who have undertaken the very sensitive and difficult task of comparing Buddhism with Christianity. In the early decades of the twentieth century a rash of studies appeared including Albert Edmunds (in cooperation with Masaharu Anesaki), *Buddhist and Christian Gospels* (Tokyo, Yuhokwan, 1905); Kenneth Saunders, *Buddhist Ideals: A Study of Comparative Religion* (London, Christian Literature Society, 1912); and B.H. Streeter, *The Buddha and the Christ* (London, Macmillan, 1932). In the 1950s Henri de Lubac, Fumio Masutani, and D.T. Suzuki published three still-useful works entitled *Aspects of Buddhism* (N.Y., Sheed & Ward, 1953), *A Comparative Study of Buddhism and Christianity* (Tokyo, Cultural Exchange Institute, rep. 1965), and *Mysticism: Christian and Buddhist* (N.Y., Harper & Row, 1957) respectively. During the 1960s I.A. Sparks contributed an article on "Buddha and Christ: A Functional Analysis," *Numen,* XIII, 3 (Oct., 1966), 190–204; Paul Tillich wrote a relevant chapter in his book on *Christianity and the Encounter of World Religions* (N.Y., Columbia Univ. Press, 1963) which was reviewed by Masao Abe in *EB,* ns, I, 1 (Sept., 1965). Abe and a variety of western Christian respondents carried on a stimulating dialogue in *Japanese Religions,* III–V

(1963–65); and Ninian Smart wrote *Buddhism and the Death of God* (Southampton, Univ. of Southampton, 1970). More recently still Heinrich Dumoulin has provided a relevant discussion in *Christianity Meets Buddhism,* tr. by John Maraldo (Chicago, Open Court, 1973); Michael Pye and Robert Morgan have edited *The Cardinal Meaning. Essays in Comparative Hermeneutics: Buddhism and Christianity* (The Hague, Mouton, 1973), in which a more specifically religio-scientific approach is delineated; and James Boyd has carried out an interesting analysis of *Satan and Mara: Christian and Buddhist Symbols of Evil* (Leiden, E.J. Brill, 1975).

Other scholars have limited the scope of their efforts by concentrating on one particular form of Buddhism. The Theravada perspective provides the focus in Winston King's interesting and helpful work on *Buddhism and Christianity* (Philadelphia, Westminster, 1962); in two sets of Thompson lectures by Bhikkhu Buddhadasa and Donald Swearer entitled *Christianity and Buddhism,* 2nd ed. (Bangkok, Sublime Mission, 1968), and *A Theology of Dialogue* (Bangkok, Church of Christ in Thailand, 1973); and in Roger Corless, "The Function of Recollection in Theravadian and Ignacian Ascesis," *Monastic Studies,* VIII, 159–69. Chan or Zen is the center of attention in Thomas Merton's very personal but interesting *Mystics and Zen Masters* (N.Y., Delta, 1961), and in Winston King's article on "Zen and the Death of God" in *Japanese Religions,* V, 2 (Dec., 1967), 1–21. In addition, comparisons between Buddhist Pure Land traditions and Christianity are presented in articles by Douglas Fox, "Soteriology in Jodo Shin and Christianity," *Contemporary Religions in Japan,* IX, 1/2, 30–51, and by Paul Ingram, "Shinran Shonin and Martin Luther: A Soteriological Comparison," *JAAR,* XXXIX, 4 (Dec., 1971), 430–47.

Still other scholars have sought to compare Buddhism, or aspects of it, with some explicitly philosophical orientations in the Western world. An excellent overview and evaluation of these kinds of comparisons is provided by Edward Conze in his two articles on "Buddhist Philosophy and Its European Parallels," *PEW,* XIII, 1 (April, 1963), 9–23, and "Spurious Parallels to Buddhist Philosophy," *PEW,* XIII, 2 (July, 1963), 105–15. In order to supplement Conze's discussion the reader should also consult some of the more recent studies in which attention is focused on particular Western thinkers; see, for example, L. Stafford Betty, "The Buddhist-Humean Parallel: Post-Mortem," *PEW,* XXI, 3 (July, 1971); Mitsuyoshi Saigusa, "Henri Bergson and Buddhist Thought," *Philosophical Studies of Japan* (Tokyo), IX (1969), 79–101; chaps. iv and vi of Anil K. Sarkar, *Changing Phases of Buddhist Thought* (Patna, Bharati Bhawani, 1968) in which aspects of Indian Buddhist thought are compared with the views of Whitehead and the Existentialists; Kenneth Inada's comparison of "Whitehead's 'Actual Entity' and the Buddhist Anatman," *PEW,* XXI, 3

(July, 1971); and Takeshi Umehara's essay on "Heidegger and Buddhism," *PEW,* XX, 3 (July, 1970), 271–82.

VII. FOR FURTHER STUDY

Readers who would like further bibliographical assistance will soon have at their disposal a full book-length *Guide to Buddhist Religion* which I am preparing with the assistance of John Strong and John Holt (Arts section by Bardwell Smith with the assistance of Holly Waldo) and a *Guide to Buddhist Philosophy* being prepared under the direction of Kenneth Inada (both forthcoming from G.K. Hall, Boston, 1976). The *Guide to Buddhist Religion* is organized in terms of fundamental religio-historical categories, such as History, Religious Thought, Mythology, and so forth; while the *Guide to Buddhist Philosophy* is organized in terms of nineteen basic philosophical categories which include History of Philosophy, Theories of Human Nature, Ethics, and so forth. In both cases all entries are fully annotated, and extensive indexes are provided.

Those who would like to keep up-to-date on the secondary literature may utilize the relevant sections of the *Bibliography for Asian Studies,* published annually by the *Journal of Asian Studies;* and those who are interested in new translations may consult Richard Gard, ed., *Buddhist Text Information,* published periodically by the Institute for Advanced Studies of World Religion (N.Y., Nov., 1974–   ).

ABBREVIATIONS

AA	*American Anthropologist*
ABORI	*Annals of the Bhandarkar Oriental Research Institute*
AO	*Acta Orientalia*
ArA	*Artibus Asiae*
ASES	*Asiatische Studien/Études asiatiques*
BCLS	*Bulletin de la classe des lettres et des sciences moraux et politiques Academie royal de Belgique*
BEFEO	*Bulletin de l'École française d'extrême-orient*
BSEI	*Bulletin de la Société des études indochinoises*
BSOAS	*Bulletin of the School of Oriental and African Studies*
CHJ	*Ceylon Historical Journal*
CSSH	*Comparative Studies of Society and History*
CJHSS	*Ceylon Journal of Historical and Social Sciences*
EB	*Eastern Buddhist*
EFEO	L'École française d'extrême-orient
FA	*France Asie*
HJAS	*Harvard Journal of Asiatic Studies*
HR	*History of Religions Journal*

IHQ	*Indian Historical Quarterly*
I(I)MEO	Istituto (Italiano) per il Medio ed Estremo Oriente
IPP	*India Past and Present*
JA	*Journal asiatique*
JAAR	*Journal of the American Academy of Religion*
JAOS	*Journal of the American Oriental Society*
JAS	*Journal of Asian Studies*
JBRS	*Journal of the Bihar Research Society*
JBuRS	*Journal of the Burma Research Society*
JIBS	*Journal of Indian and Buddhist Studies*
JIH	*Journal of Indian History*
JPTS	*Journal of the Pali Text Society*
JRAS	*Journal of the Royal Asiatic Society* (London, unless otherwise specified)
JSS	*Journal of the Siam Society*
MCB	*Mélanges chinoises et bouddhiques*
MN	*Monumenta Nipponica*
MRDTB	*Memoirs of the Research Department of Toyo Bunka*
MS	*Monumenta Serica*
MSJV	*Austosh Mookerjee Silver Jubilee Volumes*
OE	*Oriens Extremis*
PEW	*Philosophy East and West*
PTS	Pali Text Society
TICO	*Transactions of the International Congress of Orientalists in Japan*
TP	*Toung Pao*
TRASK	*Transactions of the Royal Asiatic Society of Korea*
UCR	*University of Ceylon Review*

VII

The Sikhs

Khushwant Singh

Max Arthur Macauliffe, in the preface to his monumental six-volume study, *The Sikh Religion,* published by Oxford Univ. at the Clarendon Press in 1909, wrote: "I bring from the East what is practically an unknown religion. The Sikhs are distinguished throughout the world as a great military people, but there is little known even to professional scholars regarding their religion in the English language." This statement was not strictly accurate. Many books on the Sikhs and their religion had been published in English in England and India before 1909.

The first and for many years regarded as the definitive work on the Sikhs was Joseph Davey Cunningham's *A History of the Sikhs from the Origin of the Nation to the Battles of the Sutlej,* published in London by John Murray in 1849. Only a few pages in the beginning and the appendices of this book dealt with the teachings of the Sikhs' ten Gurus and the contents of their scripture, the *Adi Granth.* The rest was devoted to a narration of events leading to the Sikhs' rise to power, the Sikh kingdom established by Maharajah Ranjit Singh, its rapid decline to chaos after the death of the Maharajah in 1839 and the first Anglo–Sikh War (1845). Since Cunningham did not fully subscribe to the official British version of the causes of the conflict between the Sikhs and the English, he was censored and his book proscribed. A revised second edition met the same fate, and the author died of a broken heart. It took many years before an acceptable edition of Cunningham's work could be made available to readers. Meanwhile a number of handbooks on the Sikhs were written by officers of the British army, chiefly for the guidance of recruiting officers. They make amusing reading because the information on the Gurus and their teachings was taken from the common soldiers serving under the authors, and for the most part the emphasis was on the fighting qualities of the different Sikh agricultural tribes.

As far as Sikhism as a religion is concerned, the chief importance of Cunningham's work lies in the theme he propounded. He was struck by the fact that the founder, Nanak (1469–1539), though born a Hindu, denounced the notion of multiplicity of gods and preached with an almost Islamic fervor, the One-ness of a supreme, undefinable but Omnipresent and Omniscient God. And though himself a Bedi (one who knows the Vedas) of the Kshatrya caste, Nanak castigated the Hindu caste system and like the Muslims emphasised the brotherhood of mankind. Since Nanak, acording to the *Janam Sakhis* (life stories), was reported to have started on his mission with the statement "there is no Hindu, there is no Musulman" and had gone on pilgrimage to Hindu holy places as well as to Mecca and Medina, Cunningham concluded that Nanak intended to build a bridge between the Hindus and the Muslims. He was impressed by the similarities of sentiment in the compositions of Shaykh Farīd al-Dīn of Pak Pattan, Kabir of Benares, and the hymns of Guru Nanak. He did not give adequate consideration to the fact that much of Nanak's teachings, including his monotheism, rejection of idolatry, and the ideal of a casteless society, could have been derived from the teachings of Hindu Vaishnavite saints known as the Bhaktas. Cunningham set the pattern for many succeeding writers who sought further evidence to confirm Nanak's image as the great bridge-builder summed up in the lines frequently quoted:

Guru Nanak, Shah Fakeer
Hindu Ka Guru, Musulman Ka Peer.
Guru Nanak, the King of Fakeers
The Guru of the Hindus, the Saint of the Muslims.

In 1870 "Her Majesty's Government of India . . . in due consideration of the importance of the work," commissioned a German missionary and professor regius of Oriental languages at the University of Munich, Dr. Ernst Trumpp, to undertake the study and translation of the scripture of the Sikhs. Dr. Trumpp described his commission as, "the first attempt on such a vast field which has hitherto hardly been touched" at a time when, according to him, "Sikhism is a waning religion, that will soon belong to history." Dr. Trumpp, a Sanskritist, found himself in difficulties with the language of the Granth which is largely the *Sant bhasha* (language of saints) used by religious poets of Northern India, in the 15th, 16th and 17th centuries. He arrived in Amritsar, the holy city of the Sikhs, and solicited the assistance of Sikh *Granthis* (scripture-readers). Not being familiar with Sikh tradition which forbids the use of tobacco, the German lit his cigar as he opened the holy book. Without a word of explanation the Sikh theologians dispersed.

Dr. Trumpp's translation of the first few pages of the holy book entitled *The Adi Granth or the Holy Scriptures of the Sikhs,* published in London in 1877 (W. H. Allen & Co.,) was prefaced by uncomplimentary remarks on the literary quality of the writings of the Gurus. He wrote:

> The greatest part of Grunth contains a sort of devotional hymn, rather poor in conception, clumsy in style, and wearisome to read. . . . The writings of the old Hindu Bhagats (or devotees) are on the whole far superior to those of the Sikh Gurus themselves as regards contents and style, especially those of Kabir from whom Nanak and his successors have borrowed all they know and preach. In fact so much is clearly seen from the Grunth itself that the Sikh Gurus taught nothing new whatever, and if a separate religion and a partially new nationality was in the course of time sprung from it, this was not owing in any way to the doctrine taught by them, but to their financial and political organizations which they gave their disciples.

The Sikhs were offended by Dr. Trumpp and viewed his commission as having been mischievously motivated.

To assuage the hurt feelings of the Sikh community, which provided a sizable proportion of soldiers to the British army, the Government of India in 1898 permitted Max Arthur Macauliffe to resign from the judicial service and undertake the task they had earlier entrusted to Dr. Trumpp. Macauliffe spent many years studying Panjabi and the Gurmukhi script and had a team of Sikh theologians headed by the scholarly Kahan Singh of Nabha to assist him. He criticized Trumpp as not a "trustworthy translator" and his work as "highly inaccurate," which not unnaturally "gave mortal offence to the Sikhs." Macauliffe patted the Sikhs on the back for their loyalties to the British and their rejection of "backward" Hindu practices. He wrote: "To sum up some of the moral and political merits of the Sikh religion: It prohibits idolatry, hypocrisy, caste exclusiveness, the concremation of widows, the immurement of women, the use of wine and other intoxicants, tobacco-smoking, infanticide, slander, pilgrimages to the sacred rivers and tanks of the Hindus; and it inculcates loyalty, gratitude for all favors received, philanthropy, justice, impartiality, truth, honesty, and all the moral and domestic virtues known to the holiest citizens of any country."

Whereas Dr. Trumpp had erred in making hasty and uncharitable judgments on the learning of the Sikh Gurus, Macauliffe went to the other extreme, being cautious that nothing he wrote would in any way offend the Sikh community. Without any discrimination he reproduced legends and miracles attributed by rustic scribes to the Gurus and saint-poets whose works were included in the holy book. He justified this as "an exact representation of the teachings of the Sikh Gurus and orthodox writers as contained in their sacred book." He judiciously excluded what he considered "a portrayal of the debased superstitions or heterodox social customs of the Sikhs who have been led astray from their faith by external influences." Macauliffe also made extensive translations of the hymns. But in so doing he stuck to the literal meaning of words and thus deprived them of their musical resonance. This was a pity because some of the hymns are poetry of the highest excellence specifically designed to be sung. Nevertheless Macauliffe's six volumes remain the standard books of reference on popular Sikhism. His translations should, however, be read with the knowledge that they are prosaic renderings of very beautiful poetry.

Among the first Sikhs to try their hand at explaining Sikhism in English was Khazan Singh of the Punjab Provincial Civil Service. His *History and Philosophy of Sikh Religion,* 2 vols., was published in 1914 (Lahore, printed at the Newal Kishore Press). This work is a faithful reproduction of the popularly accepted versions of the lives of the Sikh Gurus without scrutiny of the source-material or an attempt to interpret their teachings in the context of the development of Hinduism and Indian Islam. Khazan Singh's language is somewhat archaic. Mercifully he did not make many attempts at translating the hymns. The same could be said of the works of Bhagat Lakshman Singh who published the biographies of Guru Nanak, Guru Gobind Singh, and the Sikh martyrs in the 1920s. See, for example, his: *A Short Sketch of the Life and Work of Guru Gobind Singh, the 10th and Last Guru of the Sikhs* (Lahore, Tribune Press, 1909), and his: *Sikh Martyrs* (Madras, Ganesh, 1928).

Professor Teja Singh wrote over two dozen books on Sikhism and Sikh history. Among these are a number of translations. He translated Guru Nanak's morning prayer in *Japji, or Guru Nanak's Meditations* (2nd ed., Amritsar, Sikh Tract Society, 1924) and the morning hymns (Āsā dī vār) in *Āsā dī vār, Sikh Hymns from the Adi Granth* (Amritsar, Shiromani Gurdwara Prabandhal Committee, 1957). He also rendered into English Guru Arjun's Psalm of Peace: *Sukhmani, Sikh Hymns from the Adi Granth* (Bombay, Oxford Univ. Press, 1937). He wrote explanatory tracts such as *Thoughts on Forms and Symbols in Sikhism* (Lahore, 1927), *Guru Nanak and His Mission* (Lahore, Sikh Tract Society, 1918), *Are There Sects in Sikhism?* (published by the author, n.d.), and a comprehensive *Sikh Religion; An Outline of Its Doctrines* (Amritsar, Shiromani Gurdwara Prabandhal Committee, 1963). In collaboration with the historian Dr. Ganda Singh he began on an ambitious project to write a complete history of the community. Only one volume of *A Short History of the Sikhs,* vol. I, 1469–1765 (Bombay, Orient Longmans, 1950) was published. This covers the lives and teachings of the Sikh Gurus and has a few translations of their hymns as well. Though Teja Singh was a professor of English, his style of writing is somewhat naive and full of Indianisms. Besides this shortcoming, Teja Singh, though an academic, wrote more as a missionary of Sikhism than as an objective scholar.

Professor Sher Singh's *Philosophy of Sikhism* (Lahore, Sikh Univ. Press, 1944; 2nd edition, Delhi, Sterling Publishers, 1966), a thesis for which he earned a doctorate from London University, is a work of considerable merit. Although Dr. Sher Singh ignores Islamic influences that might have shaped some of Guru Nanak's thinking, he is very painstaking in tracing the development of Hindu philosophic thought and Vedantic concepts as they were reshaped by Nanak and his successors. Students of comparative religions will find Sher Singh's thesis illuminating. Two other writers following the same line of interpretation are Sohan Singh, *The Seeker's Path* (Bombay, Orient Longmans, 1959) and Dr. Surinder Singh Kohli, *A Critical Study of the Adi Granth* (New Delhi, Panjabi Writer's Cooperative Industrial Society, 1961). Sohan Singh's interpretations of Guru Nanak's morning prayer *Japji* which is often regarded as the quintessence of the Guru's teaching, though subjective, is thought-provoking. Dr. Kohli has gone farther and drawn attention to texts in the Upanishads from which Nanak derived many of his religious concepts.

An attempt to study Sikhism in the setting of contemporary religious movements in the Punjab is John Clark Archer's *The Sikhs in Relation to Hindus, Moslems, Christians and Ahmadiyyas: A Study in Comparative Religion* (Princeton, Princeton Univ. Press, 1946). The first section of this book describes the Sikh Pilgrimage to Amritsar. Since neither Christianity nor the Ahmadiyya schismatics had any bearing on Sikhism, the reader is left somewhat confused about what the author had in mind. Works of two American missionaries which have been well-received by the Sikhs deserve to be noticed. These are *The Sikhs and their Scriptures* (Lucknow, Lucknow Publishing House, 1958) by Clinton Herbert Locklin and *The Gospel of the Guru Granth Sahib* (2nd ed., Madras, Theosophical Publishing House, 1960) by Duncan Greenlees.

Students should bear in mind the two facets of Sikhism; the earlier quietist Sikhism of Guru Nanak and his four successors ending with the martyrdom of the fifth Guru, Arjun in 1606, is set out in the *Adi Granth*. The second militant aspect of Sikhism began with the sixth Guru, Hargovind, who girded himself with his swords symbolic of spiritual and temporal sovereignty (*miri piri da malik*) and was finally shaped with the establishment of the *Khalsa Panth* (community of the pure) by Guru Govind Singh in 1699; literature on this aspect is contained in the writings of Guru Gobind Singh and his contemporary bards compiled in the *Dasam Granth* and the ordinances (*Rahatnamas*) ascribed to Guru

Govind. Sir Gokal Chand Narang's *Transformation of Sikhism or How the Sikhs Became a Political Power* (Lahore, Tribune Press, 1912; 5th rev. ed., New Delhi, New Book Society, 1963) is regarded as the definitive work on this development in the community. Narang's thesis has been reprinted many times and though extensively quoted is regarded by contemporary Sikh scholars as biased because it assumes Sikhism to be an offshoot of Hinduism.

No proper study of Guru Gobind Singh's writings was made in English till the publication in 1959 of Dr. Dharam Pal Ashta's *Poetry of the Dasam Granth* (Delhi, Arun Prakashan, 1959). Dr. Ashta takes great pains to prove that the entire corpus of the *Dasam Granth* is the work of Guru Gobind Singh. This is most unlikely since the *Dasam Granth* is only a little smaller than the *Adi Granth*. (The latter consists of over 5,000 hymns which took a relay of readers reading non-stop at the *Akhand Path* ceremonies two days and nights to finish.) The short stormy life led by Guru Gobind hardly gave him time to compile a work of the size of the *Dasam Granth*. Besides, the varieties of language used and the styles of composition amply prove that these are works of different authors. The *Dasam Granth* also contains innumerable passages which have no religious significance. Sikh scholars reject most of the compilation as spurious.

In recent years there has been a spate of works on Sikhism. Of the present author's two volumes, *A History of the Sikhs* (Princeton, Princeton Univ. Press; and Oxford, Oxford Univ. Press, 1963–66), undertaken by a grant from the Rockefeller Foundation, a substantial portion of the first volume is devoted to the development of Sikhism; the appendices carry translations of a selection of the hymns from the *Adi Granth* and the *Dasam Granth*. The author has accepted Cunningham's thesis that Sikhism is a mélange of Hindu (Bhakti) thought and Islamic Sufism as developed in India. He goes further to maintain that the Gurus consciously propagated a third religion incorporating what they considered best in Hinduism and Islam in the hope of creating a religious system which would be acceptable to the people of northern India. He equates the rise of Sikhism with the resurgence of Panjabi nationalism, spearheaded by the Sikhs, but embracing both the Hindus and the Muslims. His point of view is not generally accepted by Sikh theologians or historians but finds favor with the younger generation of Sikhs.

A most important work on Sikhism is W.H. McLeod's *Guru Nanak and the Sikh Religion* (Oxford, Oxford Univ. Press, 1968). It is a detailed and thorough scrutiny of the sources, chiefly the *Janam Sakhis* (life stories) of Guru Nanak and the relics associated with the travels of the Guru. McLeod sets out to prove that the *Janam Sakhis* are utterly unreliable and that the relics, found as far apart as Baghdad in the West and Assam in the East, do not substantiate the theory that Nanak did in fact visit these places.

According to McLeod, the only authentic material on "the historic Nanak" as distinct from Nanak of tradition and legend are Nanak's own writings—which unfortunately have very few references to historical events. The book raised a storm of protest from the orthodox and a very lively controversy among scholars who maintain that McLeod did not give full weight to tradition which has been accepted without question from the days of Guru Nanak himself.

In 1960, on a commission by UNESCO, a panel of Sikh scholars combined to published an anthology *The Sacred Writings of the Sikhs* (London, Allen and Unwin). The translations were polished by the Irish poet John Fraser and are often quoted. The anthology has an excellent introduction on the Sikh religion by Dr. S. Radhakrishnan.

During the tricentenary celebrations of Guru Gobind Singh and the quincentenary celebrations of Guru Nanak respectively, the Guru Gobind Singh Foundation and the Guru Nanak Foundation sponsored translations of hymns and biographies of the Gurus. Of the many books published at the time, the following are noteworthy: J.S. Grewal, *Guru Nanak in History* (Chandigarh, Panjab Univ., 1969); J.S. Grewal and Dr. S.S. Bal, *Guru Gobind Singh: A Biographical Study* (Chandigarh, Panjab Univ., 1967); and Khushwant Singh, *Hymns of Guru Nanak* (UNESCO Collection of Representative Works, New Delhi, Orient Longmans, 1969).

Two attempts to translate the entire corpus of the *Adi Granth* also deserve mention. Dr. Gopal Singh Dardi's *Sri Guru Granth Sahib* in four volumes (Delhi, Attar Chand Kapur & Sons, 1960) and Manmohan Singh's translation, *Adi Granth,* published in six volumes by the S.G.P.C. (Amritsar) in 1969. There is little to recommend about Dr. Dardi's translations save the labor involved; the work could well do with a second rendering into correct English. Manmohan Singh, who had no pretensions to the English language, has more than made up for the deficiency by reproducing the original, a lexicon of difficult words with their interpretation and then his English translation. Nothing more thorough or as painstaking has been done on the *Adi Granth*.

So far no real work has been done on the *Rahatnamas* which would explain the significance of the symbols carried by Khalsa Sikhs (unshorn hair, comb, steel bracelet, sword, and the knee-length shorts) and the rules against the consumption of tobacco, narcotics, etc. For these one has to go to the Panjabi texts.

Currently Harbans Singh is engaged on an ambitious project of compiling an *Encyclopaedia of Sikhism* which he expects to complete in another two years. Students of Sikhism are further recommended to subscribe to magazines which frequently publish articles on the Sikh religion. Of these, four are indispensable: *Spokesman* published in Delhi, *The Sikh Review* published in Calcutta, *The Sikh Courier* published in London, and

The Journal of Sikh Studies published in Patiala. Most valuable for libraries and bibliographers are *A Bibliography of the Panjab* compiled by Dr. Ganda Singh, ed. (Patiala, Panjabi University, 1966) and *The Sikhs and Their Literature, A Guide to Tracts, Books, and Periodicals, 1849–1919* compiled by N. Gerald Barrier, ed., published by Manohar Book Service (Delhi, 1970).

VIII

The Jainas

Kendall W. Folkert

The Jainas,[1] though nowadays relatively few in number (less than three million), present a formidable challenge to one who sets out to learn something of them. Today's Jaina community is part of a very long, very firmly maintained tradition, reaching back at least to the time of the Buddha, whose contemporary Mahāvīra, the twenty-fourth Jaina Tīrthaṅkara,[2] is reckoned to have been. Throughout this 2,500 year history, moreover, the Jainas have been prodigious authors, producing a vast and complex literature in various Prākrits and Sanskrit, and showing an extraordinary respect —even love, perhaps—for the written word.

Thus not only did they produce a vast literature; they also preserved it. The libraries (*bhāṇḍāra*-s) attached to Jaina temples, large and small, contain countless carefully kept books and manuscripts, including a great

1. The name is derived from *jina,* conqueror, the honorific applied to the great ascetic teachers of the Jaina tradition.
2. The term "Tīrthaṅkara" is variously translated as "ford-maker," "crossing-maker," etc. Perhaps more apt than any translation is Louis Renou's comparison of the image to the Latin *pontifex,* literally "bridge-maker," in his *Religions of Ancient India,* p. 112 (London, Athlone Press; N.Y., Oxford Univ. Press, 1953; paperback, N.Y., Schocken Books, 1968).

many writings by non-Jainas—texts copied by scribes often commissioned by lay-Jainas, such an act being deemed meritorious or even simply auspicious. To see one of the catalogues of such a library, wherein are recorded the occasions upon which such copies were made, is to glimpse a remarkable attitude toward literary products of every kind, and perhaps to gain something of an insight into the firmness of purpose that has maintained the Jaina community for so long.

This ancient tradition and its vast literature have been studied far more than is often realized by students of religion, and the bibliographic selections that follow are admittedly very selective. This is so partly for reasons of space limitations, and partly because the Jainas as an object of study occupy an ambiguous position between being treated as a separate arena of study—as is Indian Buddhism—and being treated as a portion of the larger Hindu tradition. This ambiguity has been a part of Jaina studies from the beginning, and it makes the sources of information on the Jainas a very diffuse lot, since there exist not only studies that treat the Jainas alone, but also countless portions of larger studies of Hinduism that attempt to treat the Jainas in some way. The suggestions that follow attempt to point out the best material of both sorts, where space permits, and they can only serve as an introduction to the very broad and diverse field that comprises Jaina studies.

The Jaina teachings prescribe a rigorous course of ascetic practices, centering on *ahimsā,* non-injury, as the sole means of dissipating the *karma* that materially accumulates on the individual *jīva*-s, or souls, and binds them to earthly existence. When finally freed, each *jīva* attains its innate nature, which is pure knowledge and bliss, and abides in that state. This is *mokṣa,* and it is finally attainable only by practices that require the life of a homeless ascetic. The Jaina layman is not expected to attain release in this life; this will come only in a future birth, after lifetimes of increasing ascetic practice. There is no deity; Jainas do, however, venerate the Tīrthaṅkaras and some saints, and a temple cultus exists around these figures, who are not seen as intervening in any way in the lives of the devotee.

Given this set of teachings, the Jainas are often characterized as austere or sombre—in Louis Renou's words, "Buddhism's darker reflection," [3] and their position is often portrayed as somehow less vital or less compelling than that of Buddhism or other segments of the Indian tradition. It is not possible to argue these points here; but the person who seeks information concerning the Jainas is likely to confront such characterizations with almost monotonous regularity, and this brief introduction has been presented in the hope that students of the Jainas will thereby be prepared to reserve judgment on such points until they have made some wider acquaintance with the tradition.

3. *Religions of Ancient India,* p. 111.

I. MORE GENERAL STUDIES

Given the ancient and complex nature of the tradition, it seems wisest to begin with works of a general and introductory nature. Once these have been surveyed, a number of studies of particular aspects of the Jaina community and its history will be mentioned, and after that, the areas of art, literature, and philosophy will be touched upon.

Of the comprehensive studies, the best is still Helmuth von Glasenapp, *Der Jainismus, eine indische Erlösungsreligion* (Berlin, Alf Häger, 1925; repr., Hildesheim, Georg Olms, 1964). Excellently illustrated, its greatest claim to respect lies in its thoroughgoing attempt to provide a fully-rounded picture of Jaina thought, practice, and literature. To be sure, there are points where scholarship has now advanced beyond the level achieved in 1925; and if there is any significant weakness in the work, it lies in its handling of the Jaina scriptures. On the whole, however, it has not been replaced as a comprehensive introduction. For those who prefer reading French, one can still recommend Armand Guérinot, *La Religion djaïna, histoire, doctrine, culte, coutumes, institutions* (Paris, Paul Geuthner, 1926). Its title indicates its scope, and though it suffers in comparison with the detail in von Glasenapp, it remains an adequate basic guide.

Walther Schubring, *Die Lehre der Jainas, nach den alten Quellen dargestellt, Grundriss der Indo-Arischen Philologie und Altertumskunde*, III. Band, 7. Heft (Berlin und Leipzig, Walter De Gruyter, 1935), is also a comprehensive study of sorts; and by referring to it one might overcome the weakness in von Glasenapp's treatment of the scriptures. Schubring's work, however, limits itself to the Śvetāmbara [4] canon and its presentation of Jaina doctrine and practice. It is clearly authoritative in this area and indispensable for serious study of those scriptures. However, it is written in the formidable German Handbuch-style, and is not the best place for one to begin studying the Jainas. It has been translated into English (by Wolfgang Beurlen) as *The Doctrine of the Jainas* (Delhi, Motilal Banarsidass, 1962). Since the translation incorporates some revisions, it is useful to consult it; but the format of the original renders translation nearly impossible, the quality of the translation itself leaves much to be desired, and it lacks indices and bibliography.

Schubring's contributions to Jaina studies have been of major importance, and more of them will be detailed in the section on literature. At this point, one additional general work should be mentioned, namely, his contribution to *Die Religionen Indiens III, Religionen der Menschheit* 13.

---

4. The Jainas are divided into two major followings, the Śvetāmbaras, or "white-clad ones," and the Digambaras, "sky-clad ones," i.e., naked ones. The names refer to an ancient division in ascetic praxis, between those who felt the wearing of simple white garments to be proper, and those who maintain that only total nakedness is full asceticism. The two groups also disagree concerning the canon; see below.

Band (Stuttgart, W. Kohlhammer, 1964), entitled "Der Jinismus." This is a well-ordered, brief account, more general than his *magnum opus*. It, too, has been translated, by Amulyachandra Sen and T.C. Burke, and separately published as *The Religion of the Jainas* (Calcutta, Calcutta Sanskrit College Research Series lii, 1966). This translation, unlike the other, is excellent.

Should it have struck the reader that no survey originally written in English has yet been introduced, this will be a good time to note that at least in terms of general works on the Jainas, the literature in European languages is far superior to that in English. Still, there are some useful works that should be pointed out. [Alice] Margaret [Mrs. Sinclair] Stevenson, *The Heart of Jainism* (London, Humphrey Milford, Oxford Univ. Press, 1915), and J.L. Jaini, *Outlines of Jainism,* ed., with preliminary note, by F.W. Thomas (London, Jain Literature Society, Cambridge Univ. Press, 1916; repr., with corrections, 1940), are perhaps the two best-known general studies in English.

Mrs. Stevenson's work, largely based on her own tireless observations of Jainas among whom she lived in India, is useful in its emphasis on daily life and the state of the community early in this century, but weak on history and literature. Despite its colonialisms and theological framework (namely, that the heart of Jainism is empty, lacking the love and trust that can only obtain where there is faith in a compassionate God), and its occasionally dense recitals of utterly unexplained detail, it is an adequate introduction. Yet it has serious flaws, and is generally repudiated by Jainas. J.L. Jaini's slim volume has the virtue of being an exposition of Jaina thought by a Jaina. However, it is more a compact presentation of Jaina philosophy (including a selection of texts in translation) than a general introduction.

In addition to these better-known works, one should also consult Mohan Lal Mehta, *Jaina Culture* (Varanasi [Banaras], P.V. Research Institute, n.d. [1969?]), a compact and wide-ranging account. This work also presents matters from a Jaina viewpoint, and may be very useful as an introduction or more comprehensive supplement to other studies. The reader will also find a host of brief works in English, some by Europeans and some by Indians, listed in catalogues and other bibliographies, most of them published around the turn of the century. To list them all here is impossible; most are now outdated, or are very much simplified apologetic works. It cannot hurt to consult them, but they are certainly not to be ranked as comprehensive sources. The plain fact is that a new introduction to the Jainas in English is a major desideratum.[5]

5. This situation should improve with the forthcoming publication of Padmanabh S. Jaini's introductory text on the Jainas, *The Path of Purification,* to appear in 1976 in the series The Religious Life of Man, Frederick J. Streng, series ed. (Belmont, Calif., Dickenson).

As mentioned earlier, almost every general survey of Indian religion includes something of a brief section on the Jainas. These are so numerous that to survey them thoroughly is impossible. Yet their quality varies so widely that some sort of recommendation is in order. Out of all such brief notices, perhaps the best balanced and most engaging is that by A.L. Basham in William Theodore de Bary, *et al., Sources of Indian Tradition* (N.Y., Columbia Univ. Press, 1958), which has the virtue of including brief readings from texts. One might supplement this with Basham's contribution, "Jainism," to R.C. Zaehner, ed., *The Concise Encyclopedia of Living Faiths* (N.Y., Hawthorn Books, 1959; paperbound: Boston, Beacon Press, 1967), or the section on the Jainas in his own *The Wonder That Was India* (3rd rev. ed., N.Y., Taplinger, 1968; paperbound: N.Y., Grove Press, 1959).

Among other such portions of texts on religion in India, one may consult the brief but adequate chapter on Jainism in Louis Renou, *Religions of Ancient India* (London, Athlone Press; N.Y., Oxford Univ. Press, 1953; paperbound: N.Y., Schocken Books, 1968). There are also various chapters in the volumes of *The Cultural Heritage of India,* 2nd rev. ed. (Calcutta, Ramakrishna Mission Institute of Culture, 1953ff.), some of which are excellent, others less satisfactory. Also, because of its general availability, Heinrich Zimmer's treatment of the Jainas in his *Philosophies of India,* ed. Joseph Campbell (Princeton, Princeton Univ. Press, 1951; paperbound: 1969) should be mentioned. This is, in the style of the remainder of the book, a highly interpretive presentation, and Joseph Campbell's notes carry certain interpretive points even further. Yet it has considerable virtues, for it is lively and engaging; and the reader, armed with the knowledge that Zimmer's portrait of the Jainas is something of a *tour de force,* may find it better reading than many· other accounts.

It may also be useful to point out certain encyclopedia articles. Walther Schubring's article, "Jinismus" (and others to which it refers), in *Die Religion in Geschichte und Gegenwart,* Dritter, völlig neu bearbeitete Auflage (Tübingen, J.C.B. Mohr [Paul Siebeck], 1957–65) is a possible starting point. It is also a pleasure to note the very readable articles, "Jainism" and "Mahāvīra," by U.P. Shah, in the 15th Edition of the *Encyclopaedia Britannica (Macropaedia).* Shah's articles have perhaps at last replaced Hermann Jacobi's "Jainism" in James Hastings, ed., *Encyclopedia of Religion and Ethics* (N.Y., Charles Scribner's Sons, 1908–27; repr., 1955), though the latter is still an excellent brief account despite its now outdated sources.

Although it is the oldest of the three, mention of Jacobi's article has been made last because it raises one further way of getting an introduction to the Jainas. Jacobi's efforts to introduce the Jainas to the Western world were truly gigantic in scope, although they never resulted in a major expository volume. Now that his many articles (not including the one in

Hastings) have been collected and published, it is possible to read almost all of his briefer statements on the Jainas without searching through numerous periodicals and smaller publications. They may be found in: Hermann Jacobi, *Kleine Schriften,* 2 vols., herausgegeben von Bernhard Kölver (Wiesbaden, Franz Steiner, 1970). Also, since Jacobi often chose to write in English, so as to ensure that his work would be accessible to Indians, these shorter studies of his do not impose the language barrier that other European scholarship often raises.

In addition to works intended as general introductions, there are also numerous studies of the historical development of the Jaina tradition in India, many of them focusing on specific regions or periods. These generally contain a basic introduction to Jaina thought. Jyoti Prasad Jain, *The Jaina Sources of the History of Ancient India, 100 B.C.–A.D. 900* (Delhi, Munshi Ram Manohar Lal, 1964), is an interesting, occasionally somewhat speculative study, whose prime value lies in its focus on the Digambara Jainas. Jagdish Chandra Jain, *Life in Ancient India, As Depicted in the Jain Canons* (Bombay, New Book Co., 1947), is largely an unrelieved catalogue of technical terms culled from Śvetāmbara texts, perhaps useful as a research tool. Epigraphical evidence available early in this century has been collected in Armand Guérinot, *Répertoire d'épigraphie jaina, précédé d'une esquisse de l'histoire du Jainisme d'après les inscriptions* (Paris, E. Leroux, 1908). Chimanlal J. Shah, *Jainism in North India, 800 B.C.–A.D. 526* (London, Longmans, Green, 1932), contains a lengthy general introduction, as well as accounts of the growth of Jainism in the regions of India where it, like Buddhism, originated and enjoyed its early successes. This should now be supplemented by accounts such as Upendra Thakur, *Studies in Jainism and Buddhism in Mithilā* (Varanasi [Banaras], Chowkhamba Sanskrit Series Office, 1964); and P.C. Roy Choudhury, *Jainism in Bihar* (Patna, I. Roy Choudhury, 1956).

Although the present concentration of Jaina communities in western and northern India would not seem to indicate it, the Jainas enjoyed some of their most creative and productive eras in central and south India. No picture of the Jaina tradition is complete without some study of this part of its history, and a number of excellent accounts of those areas and periods are available. An early study is M.S. Ramaswami Aiyangar and B.S. Rao, *Studies in South Indian Jainism* (Madras, Hoe & Co., 1922). One should also consult Bhasker Anand Saletore, *Mediaeval Jainism, with Special Reference to the Vijayanagara Empire* (Bombay, Karnatak Publishing House, n.d. [1938?]); S.R. Sharma, *Jainism and Karnāṭaka Culture* (original title: *Jainism in South India;* Dharwar, N.S. Kamalapur, 1940); and most recently, P.B. Desai, *Jainism in South India and Some Jaina Epigraphs* (Sholapur, G.H. Doshi, 1957). The background of the present situation in western India can be explored through Kailash Chand Jain, *Jainism in Rajasthan* (Sholapur, G.H. Doshi, 1963); and Chimanlal

Bhailal Sheth, *Jainism in Gujurat, A.D. 1100 to 1600* (Bombay, Shree Vijayadevsur Sangh Gnan Samity, n.d. [1953?]). The quality of the latter, unfortunately, is far below that of all the other regional studies.

There are also some excellent non-historical studies of the Jaina community, both monastic and lay. The former is covered in general by Shantaram Bhalchandra Deo, *History of Jaina Monachism, From Inscriptions and Literature* (Poona, Deccan College Postgraduate and Research Institute, 1956). This work, however, is more a catalogue of items than an analysis. A briefer general account of Jaina monastic praxis can be found in sections of Dayanand Bhargava, *Jaina Ethics* (Delhi, Motilal Banarsidass, 1968), though it, too, is short on analysis. Specific practices and the theoretical bases for those practices are better covered in K.C. Sogani, *Ethical Doctrines in Jainism* (Sholapur, Jaina Saṁskṛti Saṁrakshaka Sangha, 1967). This is a well-informed, methodical study. The scriptural basis of monastic practice is minutely covered in Schubring's *Die Lehre der Jainas,* and von Glasenapp's *Jainismus* is also a useful source. One should also consult Colette Caillat, *Les Expiations dans le rituel ancien des religieux jaina* (Paris, Éditions, E. de Boccard, 1965). This excellent study covers the monastic community in general in addition to the specific practices that are its focal point.

Sogani, Bhargava, Schubring, von Glasenapp, and Mrs. Stevenson can introduce one to the life of a lay-Jaina. The non-canonical sources and their presentation of the rules of conduct for laymen are best covered by R[obert Hamilton Blair] Williams, *Jaina Yoga, A Survey of the Mediaeval Śrāvakācāras* (London, Oxford Univ. Press, 1963). This is a superb study, whose introductory section and accounts of major Jaina authors are also highly valuable. The specific topics of Williams' study, however, require a good deal of general familiarity with the Jaina tradition, and are not to be approached lightly. Specific texts dealing with the life of the layman will be mentioned below. On the contemporary Jaina community there is Vilas Adinath Sangave, *Jaina Community, A Social Survey* (Bombay, Popular Book Depot, 1959). Its sources of information for the early tradition are spotty, but the whole is a valuable piece of work.

Virtually every volume mentioned thus far—and those yet to be covered —contains a bibliographic section of its own. Thus, while this list of general, historical, and specific studies is far from complete, it should enable the reader to find such sources of more specific data as may be desired.

II. SPECIALIZED STUDIES

A. Art

Some of the studies detailed next are for more serious scholars; others, however, provide another valuable and pleasurable way of acquainting oneself with the Jainas. It is in some ways true that the scholarly predilection for doctrine and sacred literature overlooks the lively and charming side of any religious tradition, and this is particularly true of the Jainas, given the attitudes noted above toward their literature and teachings. Thus it seems worthwhile to draw the reader's attention to several works through which one can gain a vision of the Jainas that is very different from that presented by the standard introductions. These works are W. Norman Brown's three studies of Jaina miniature-paintings, particularly those done as manuscript illustrations: *The Story of Kālaka* (Washington, D.C., Lord Baltimore Press, 1933); *Miniature Paintings of the Jaina Kalpasūtra* (Washington, D.C., Smithsonian Institution, 1934); and *Manuscript Illustrations of the Uttarādhyayana Sūtra* (New Haven, American Oriental Society, 1941).

These can be studied both alone and in conjunction with the texts that the manuscript paintings illuminate, in particular the Uttarādhyayana Sūtra (see below). The latter method is a very good way of approaching Jaina texts themselves. Should one's appetite be whetted by Brown, the following further studies can be consulted: Moti Chandra, *Jain Miniature Paintings from Western India* (Ahmedabad, Sarabhai Manilal Nawab, 1949); Sarabhai M. Nawab, *Masterpieces of the Kalpasutra Paintings* (Ahmedabad, the author, 1956), this work being particularly useful because of its lavish use of color plates, though portions of the text are utterly dependent on Brown; and perhaps also *idem, The Oldest Rajasthani Paintings from Jain Bhandars* (Ahmedabad, the author, 1959).

The reader who has an interest in the general artistic activity of the Jainas—which was considerable and very important—would perhaps do well to consult one of the major general works on Indian art and architecture, or the specific reading lists in Benjamin Rowland, *The Harvard Outline and Reading Lists for Oriental Art,* 3rd ed. (Cambridge, Harvard Univ. Press, 1967). Jaina art is one of the areas that is almost inseparable from study of the Indian tradition as a whole. However, one might turn to B.C. Bhattacharya, *The Jaina Iconography* (Lahore, Motilal Banarsidass, 1939), of which a revised edition is said to be forthcoming from the same publisher; or more important tò U.P. Shah, *Studies in Jaina Art* (Banaras, Jaina Cultural Research Society, 1955), the latter being perhaps the most generally reliable guide to Jaina art as a specific arena within the Indian tradition.

B. Literature

Jaina literature, as noted earlier, is vast in extent and is preserved both in Sanskrit and several Prākrits. Maurice [Moriz] Winternitz, *A History of Indian Literature,* vol. 2, *Buddhist Literature and Jaina Literature,* tr.

S. Ketkar, and rev. by the author (Calcutta, Univ. of Calcutta, 1927; New Delhi, Oriental Books Reprint Corp., 1972), remains a valuable guide to the literature as a whole. It is important to note that the English translation cited here contains a far more complete account of Jaina literature than do the earlier German editions. Thus the translation should be viewed as a significantly revised edition of the original, at least where Jaina materials are concerned. Unfortunately, not since the time of that translation has a truly comprehensive account of Jaina literature been produced.

The discovery of Jaina literature actually served as the major impetus to early Jaina studies in the West. It was the Śvetāmbara (see above) sacred texts that first drew scholars' attention, and they have remained the focus of scholarly activity. Schubring's *Die Lehre der Jainas* reviews the early scholarship; more recent developments are explored in Ludwig Alsdorf, *Les Études jaina, État présent et tâches futures* (Paris, Collège de France, 1975). This brief and engaging account is essential reading for one who desires a full picture of the study of the Śvetāmbara canon. Matters are less fortunate for those interested in Digambara writings. The non-specialist will be hard-put to find much in the way of Digambara writings available in good translations. It is commonly held that the Digambaras reject *in toto* the scriptures to which the Śvetāmbaras give canonical status. Yet the history of that canon and of the Digambara attitude toward it is in need of a thorough reëxamination. The reader is bound to be struck by the brevity of the remarks on the Digambaras that are to be found in intro-ductory—and even specialized—studies of Jaina literature, and should be warned against underestimating the Digambara share in the whole.

As far as confronting the Digambara texts themselves is concerned, it should be noted that J.L. Jaini was a Digambara layman; thus his *Outlines of Jainism* approaches the matter of scripture from a Digambara point of view, though it does not take up the issues involved. Jyoti Prasad Jain, *The Jaina Sources of the History of Ancient India,* should also be men-tioned again here as presenting the Digambara position. The writings of two of the major Digambara philosophers will be mentioned shortly. Other Digambara texts, of various sorts, were published in the 1920s and '30s as *The Sacred Books of the Jainas,* 13 vols. (Arrah and Lucknow, Central Jaina Publishing House, 191ff; repr. N.Y., AMS Press, 1973).[6] These volumes generally include the text plus an English translation and modern commentary in English; unfortunately, the quality of the transla-tions is not high, and the modern commentaries are not very useful. Out of all these, perhaps the best text for the general reader to approach is Nemi-

6. Some of the volumes in the series appeared under the series heading Bibliotheca Jainica; still others as part of the J.L. Jaini Memorial Series. The reader should be aware of this when consulting catalogues and bibliographies.

candra Siddhāntacakravartin, *Davvasaṁgaha* [*Dravyasaṁgraha*],[7] ed. and trans. by Sarat Chandra Ghoshal, *Sacred Books of the Jainas,* vol. 1 (Arrah, Central Jaina Publishing House, 1917; repr. N.Y., AMS Press, 1973), which can give one some notion of the complexity and intensity of Jaina scholasticism ca. A.D. 1000. (J.L. Jaini's translation for this series of the *Tattvārthādhigamasūtra* will be mentioned below.) On the whole, however, there is no good set of translations of very early Digambara writings or of those which they treat as authoritative.[8]

The Śvetāmbara canon, on the other hand, is fairly accessible to those seeking to read texts in translation. Walther Schubring's *Die Lehre der Jainas* is, as mentioned, based on those scriptures and can serve as a guide to this mass of material which, in its current form, consists of some 45 texts of varying lengths. The 45 texts are divided into several groups, the most basic and important of which is that of the eleven extant *aṅga*-s (these are held to have been twelve in number, the twelfth now being lost); attached (though not originally) to these are twelve *uvaṅga*-s [*upāṅga*-s]. By common reckoning, the remaining 22 texts comprise ten *painna*-s [*prakīrṇa*-s], miscellaneous writings; six *cheyasutta*-s [*chedasūtra*-s] and four *mūlasutta*-s [*mūlasūtra*-s], these two groups dealing with disciplinary matters and basic teachings, respectively; and two works of a more comprehensive, systematic nature, the Nandīsutta [Nandīsūtra] and Anuogadāra [Anuyogadvāra]. The language of these texts is the Prākrit known as Ardha-Māghadī, though the process of redaction and compilation has added numerous features of later Prākrits to many of the texts.

The classic detailed study of all these texts is Albrecht Weber, "Über die heiligen Schriften der Jaina," *Indische Studien* XVI–XVII (1883–85), 211–479, 1–90 (repr. Hildesheim and N.Y., Georg Olms, 1974). This was translated by H. Weir Smyth as "Weber's Sacred Literature of the Jains," *The Indian Antiquary* XVII–XXI (1888–92); Smyth's translation was then reprinted, with consecutive pagination, in 1893 (Bombay, at the Education Society's Steam Press). Weber was truly performing a pioneering work, and on many points there is now much better information. Hiralal Rasikdas Kapadia, *A History of the Canonical Literature of the Jainas* (Bombay, printed at the Gujurati Printing Press, 1941), incorporates many of the later discoveries, is conversant with major European scholarship on the texts, and has the virtue of presenting an Indian approach to the texts as scripture; though the reader may find the style of the whole to be a bit trying at times.

---

7. Since Jaina texts were composed in both Prakrit and Sanskrit, their titles often present a problem. If the text is Prakrit, the Prakrit title is given here, with Sanskritized title in brackets.

8. Two important chapters of the *Mūlācāra,* one of the definitive early Digambara texts, are treated in two soon-to-be-printed doctoral theses by Kiyoaki Okuda and R.P. Jain, Universität Hamburg, Germany.

As for available translations, most of them are of *anga*-s, *cheyasutta*-s and *mūlasutta*-s. However, since these are generally the oldest and most important of the texts, the person who reads English and/or European languages can gain entrée to the basic scriptures of the Śvetāmbaras without too much difficulty. Unfortunately, translations have not been made of the commentaries to these texts, and thus the reader is cut off—save for the information in an occasional footnote—from the Jaina tradition's own understanding and continuous interpretation of these ancient texts.

The pioneer in editing and translating these texts was Hermann Jacobi, whose *Gaina Sûtras,* 2 vols., *Sacred Books of the East,* vols. 22 and 45 (Oxford, Clarendon Press, 1884, 1895; repr. Delhi, Motilal Banarsidass, 1968, and N.Y., Dover Publications, 1968), contains translations of the first and second *anga*-s, the Āyāraṅga and Sūyagaḍaṅga [Ācārāṅga and Sūtrakṛtāṅga]; of the Uttarajjhāyāsutta [Uttarādhyayana Sūtra], and of the Kappasutta [Kalpa Sūtra], the latter two being a *mūlasutta* and a *cheyasutta,* respectively. Jacobi's introductions to these two volumes provide an interesting glimpse of the problems besetting early scholars of the Jainas, prominent among which was the debate over the relationship between the Jainas and Buddhists. Jacobi relied on later Sanskrit commentaries for help in translating and interpreting these texts, the oldest parts of which probably date to ca. 300 B.C.

Important portions of the Āyāra and Sūyagaḍa have been admirably translated into German by Walther Schubring in *Worte Mahāvīras, kritische Übersetzungen aus dem Kanon der Jaina* (Göttingen, Vandenhoeck & Ruprecht, 1926). These translations should be consulted, if possible, in conjunction with Jacobi's translations of the same passages. There are useful English translations of three other *anga*-s. The Uvasagadasāo [Upāsakadaśāh], which is an important account of the prescriptions for the lay-Jaina (see above) set in illustrative tales, has been edited and translated by A.F. Rudolf Hoernle (Calcutta, Published for the Bibliotheca Indica, vol. 1 [Text], 1885, vol. 2 [Translation], 1888). Hoernle's translation style is very smooth, and handles well the repetitive portions of the text. (A characteristic of Jaina texts is the use of lengthy, stereotyped descriptions of typical settings for Mahāvīra's sermons and dialogues, and their general use of repetition elsewhere is also striking. This often gives the original texts a very plodding atmosphere, and makes smooth translation very difficult.) The second volume of Hoernle's work also contains an abbreviated translation of the fifteenth book of the Viyāhapaṇṇatti [Vyākhyāprajñaptī, or more commonly, Bhagavatī], the fifth *anga,* which contains the major Jaina account of the career of Maṅkhaliputta Gosāla, the leader of the Ajīvikas. The text itself has been masterfully handled by Jozef Deleu, *Viyāhapannatti (Bhagavaī). The fifth Anga of the Jaina Canon. Introduction, Critical Analysis, Commentary and Indexes* (Bruges, Rijksuniversiteit te Gent, Fac. Lett. 151, 1970). L.D. Barnett has translated the *Antagadadasāo* [Antakṛtadaśāḥ] and *Aṇuttarovavāiyadasāo* [Anuttaraupapātikadaśāḥ], Oriental Translation Fund, n.s. XVII (London, Royal Asiatic Society, 1907). Each of these consists of ten tales of pious ascetics and their progress toward *mokṣa*.

There are few translations into western languages of the six *cheyasutta*-s. Jozef Deleu and Walther Schubring, *Studien zum Mahānisīha* [Mahāniśītha], *Kapitel*, 1–5 (Hamburg, Cram, De Gruyter, 1963) contains an English translation of chapters 1–3 (by Deleu) and a German translation of chapters 4–5 (by Schubring). The Vavahārasutta [Vyavahāra Sūtra] has been translated into French by Colette Caillat, in *Drei Chedasūtras des Jaine-Kanons, Āyāradasāo, Vavahāra, Nisīha,* bearbeitet von Walther Schubring, mit einem Beitrag von Colette Caillat (Hamburg, Cram, De Gruyter, 1966). The Kappasutta translated by Jacobi (see above) is actually part of the Āyāradasāo, and is not the Kappasutta that the reader will commonly find listed as a separate *cheyasutta*. These texts deal primarily with monastic order and discipline.

The four *mūlasutta*-s, which are so named apparently because they contain material that is considered to be basic and thus to be studied at the outset of one's monastic career, have been translated in part. Jacobi's translation of the Uttarajjhāyā has been mentioned. The Dasaveyāliyasutta [Daśavaikālika Sūtra] has been edited by Ernst Leumann and translated into English by Walther Schubring (Ahmedabad, Managers of Sheth Anandji Kalianji, 1932). This is an important compendium of rules for ascetics. The Āvassayasutta [Āvaśyaka Sūtra], a text of great import, based on discussions of the six "essential" *(āvaśyaka, āvassaya)* daily practices of a Jaina, is actually extant only insofar as the original is preserved in several layers of commentary. The classic study of this complex text-mass is Ernst Leumann, *Übersicht über die Āvaśyaka-Literatur,* aus dem Nachlass herausgegeben von Walther Schubring (Hamburg, Friederichsen, De Gruyter, 1934). Bits and portions of major commentaries on the Āvassayasutta have been translated, many of these partial translations being very unsatisfactory. The whole remains largely inaccessible to the non-specialist.

One of the more important *paiṇṇa*-s has been translated by Colette Caillat, *Candāvejjhaya* [Candravedhyaka], *Introduction, édition critique, traduction, commentaire* (Paris, Éditions E. de Boccard, 1971). Its title might be translated as "Taking Aim," and it covers several subjects including teacher-pupil relationships, problems of proper conduct, and behavior at the time of death.

Finally, two further translations by Walther Schubring should be mentioned. *Isibhāsiyāiṃ, Aussprüche der Weisen,* aus dem Prākrit der Jainas übersetzt von Walther Schubring, nebst dem revidierten Text (Hamburg, Cram, De Gruyter, 1969), is a set of "sayings of the seers" whose age is apparently as great as the texts nowadays held to be canonical. Schubring has also produced an anthology-style set of translations from various texts, under the title "Die Jainas," in Alfred Bertholet, herausgeber, *Religionsgeschichtliches Lesebuch 7* (Tübingen, J.C.B. Mohr [Paul Siebeck], 1927). This work is composed of brief passages from a number of texts, arranged topically, and has the effect of being a systematic presentation of Jaina teachings in the words of the Śvetāmbara scriptures.

In addition to the Digambara and Śvetāmbara dogmatic texts, there remains a vast amount of narrative and poetic literature that cannot, perhaps, be construed as "religious" or "philosophical" in the narrower, western senses of the terms. However, it is a vital part of the Jaina tradition, particularly because a great deal of this literature is based on legends and tales incorporated in older scriptures, or in commentaries thereon. A glance at Winternitz, or at von Glasenapp's account of such literature, will show how large is its extent. Little of it is easily available to the general reader, but there are certain works that can be consulted, and even this brief account would be incomplete without mentioning them.

Perhaps the capstone of Jaina epic narrative writing is Hemacandra's monumental Triṣaṣṭisalākāpuruṣacaritra, "The Lives of the 63 Great Persons," with its "appendix," the Pariśiṣṭaparvan, which comprises a history of the early Jaina church. The former is a history of world-events and great personages up to Mahāvīra; the appendix restricts itself to accounting for Mahāvīra's major followers. The composition of the whole is dated to the twelfth century A.D.

This great *opus,* the work of the grammarian/theologian/poet who was called "The Omniscient One of the Kali-Age," is a veritable encyclopedia of Jaina beliefs and practices. Thanks to the efforts of Helen M. Johnson, "The Lives of the 63 Great Persons" is fully available in an eminently readable and carefully researched English translation: Hemacandra, *Triṣaṣṭisalākāpuruṣacaritra,* 6 vols., The Gaekwad Oriental Series, vols. 51, 77, 108, 125, 139, 140 (Baroda, The Oriental Institute, 1931–62). These volumes present the reader with a very engaging and interesting entrée to the Jaina tradition, and cannot be recommended too highly. The 63 Great Persons are the 24 Tīrthaṅkaras, 12 Cakravartins (Universal Monarchs), and 27 other patriarchs and heroes. By "lives" is meant the stories of the various incarnations of all these figures prior to each one's final birth and attainment of release. Thus these are equivalent, particularly in the case of the Tīrthaṅkaras, to the *jātaka*-s more commonly associated with the Buddhist tradition.

Parts of the "appendix" are available in Johannes Hertel, tr., *Ausgewählte Erzählungen aus Hemacandras Pariśistaparvan* (Leipzig, W. Heims, 1908). Concerning Hemacandra himself, one can consult [Johann] Georg Bühler, *Über das Leben des Jaina Mönches Hemachandra* (Wien, Oesterreichische Akademie der Wissenschaften, 1889); English translation: *Life of Hemacandrācārya,* tr. M. Patel (Śāntiniketan, 1936).

One can also sample the Jaina epic/narrative material in two more brief collections: Maurice Bloomfield, *Life and Stories of the Jaina Savior Pārçvanātha* (Baltimore, Johns Hopkins Press, 1919); and John Jacob Meyer, *Hindu Tales* (London, Luzac, 1909). The latter is an English translation of the tales in Hermann Jacobi, *Ausgewählte Erzählungen in Mâhârâshṭrī, Grammatik, Text, Wörterbuch* (Leipzig, 1886), which contains no translations, having been designed as a textbook for the study of Jaina Prākrit. The materials are drawn from commentaries on the Uttarajjhāyā; thus, while the tales in Bloomfield are more engaging that those in Meyer/Jacobi, the latter gain dimension by being read in conjunction with Brown's book on Uttarajjhāyā illustrations.

Because of the amount of material that is here omitted, it seems almost worse to mention only these few examples than it would be to pass over the material altogether. However, these samples of Jaina narrative material should serve as something of an introduction to the greater mass of literature; again, the bibliographies of the various volumes should certainly be consulted for further information.

C. Philosophy

Partly because of the intended scope of this volume, and partly because Jaina philosophy would require a full bibliographic statement by itself, only a few observations on Jaina philosophical texts and secondary studies will be made here. Like much of the introductory material on the Jainas, their philosophy is covered at least briefly in almost every general study of Indian thought. Also as before, the quality of such brief treatments varies widely, and it seems in order to recommend that the reader examine several such accounts in order to insure getting a balanced picture.

Beyond this, there are specific treatments of Jaina philosophy that can better be used, if they are available. Mohan Lal Mehta, *Jaina Philosophy* (Varanasi [Banaras], P.V. Research Institute, 1971), is a balanced, if occasionally somewhat simplified and confessional presentation. Another good general account is Subramania Gopalan, *Outlines of Jainism* (N.Y., Halsted Press, 1973); the title should not mislead one into thinking that it is a general introduction to the tradition.

From these, one might move on to Satkari Mookerjee, *The Jaina Philosophy of Non-Absolutism* (Calcutta, Bhāratī Mahāvidyālaya, 1944; a reprint is said to be forthcoming from Tara Publications, Banaras). This is an excellent study, particularly of the Jaina notion of universals in relation to the position of other Indian schools. Nathmal Tatia, *Studies in Jaina Philosophy* (Banaras, Jain Cultural Research Society, 1951), is a very readable apologetic study, focusing on the notion of *avidyā,* nescience, in Jaina thought and other Indian schools. Also, any clear understanding of Jaina analytical thought requires some familiarity with the Jaina notion of *karma* and its effects. Still unsurpassed as a concise introduction to this problem is Helmuth von Glasenapp, *Die Lehre vom Karman in der Philosophie der Jainas* (Leipzig, O. Harrassowitz, 1915); English translation: *The Doctrine of Karman in Jain Philosophy,* tr. G. Barry Gifford and rev. by the author, ed. H.R. Kapadia (Bombay, Bai Vijibai Jivanlal Panalal Charity Fund, 1942).

The basic text of Jaina philosophy is the Tattvārthādhigamasūtra of Umāsvāti (whom the Digambaras refer to as Umāsvāmin). The author is claimed by both major sects, and the text is accepted by both, though they preserve it in slightly different versions. Hermann Jacobi first translated the *sūtra*-s themselves into German, in his *Eine Jaina-Dogmatik, Umās-vāti's Tattvārthādhigama Sūtra* (Leipzig, in Kommission bei F.A. Brockhaus, 1906; this being a separate reprint from the *Zeitschrift der deutschen morgenländischen Gesellschaft* LX [1906]). Jacobi added brief comments of his own, based on the commentary that the Śvetāmbaras hold to be Umāsvāti's own commentary to the *sūtra*-s (the Digambaras reject the commentary and the claim concerning its authorship). The Digambara version of the text is adequately translated by J.L. Jaini as volume 2 of the *Sacred Books of the Jainas* (Arrah, Central Jaina Publishing House, 1920; repr. N.Y., AMS Press, 1973); Jaini also provides a good deal of information concerning the different versions of the text, and lists the commentaries by various authors from both sects. The commentary of the Digambara philosopher Pūjyapāda, the Sarvārthasiddhi, has been very nicely translated by S.A. Jain, and published under the title *Reality* (Calcutta, Vira Sasana Sangha, 1960).

All of Jaina philosophy is certainly not a series of footnotes to Umāsvāti. The work of creative and skillful logicians and metaphysicians such as Kundakunda, Siddhasena Divākara, Akalaṅka, Samantabhadra, Haribhadra, et al., comprises a philosophical tradition that is as intriguing and exciting as any other in India. It is simply impossible to give even an outline of that tradition here. A thorough history of Jaina thought in English is another major desideratum in the field of Jaina studies; in the meantime, students will have to exercise a bit of extra resourcefulness in order to get at the full Jaina tradition of analytical thought.

III. CONCLUSION

Finally, the reader should be aware of some bibliographic works that can be of great aid. Armand Guérinot, *Essai de bibliographie jaina* (Paris, Annales du Musée Guimet, 1906) is a very thorough account of early Jaina studies, including a very useful survey of periodicals. Chhote Lal Jain, *Jaina Bibliography (to 1925)* (Calcutta, Bhāratī Jaina Pariṣat,

1945), seeks to supplement and update Guérinot, and is again useful in its attention to periodical literature. Colette Caillat, "Notes de bibliographie jaina et moyen-indienne," *Journal Asiatique* (1972), 409–32, is a very important source of information on recent textual and general works, in particular the later scholarly output of Walther Schubring. Also, the American reader and scholar should be aware of the fact that various Japanese scholars have done a great deal of work on the Jainas. This work, along with a mass of detailed bibliographic information on Jaina studies outside Japan, is admirably covered by Hajime Nakamura in "Bibliographical Survey of Jainism," *The Journal of Intercultural Studies* (Hirakata City, Osaka; Intercultural Research Institute, Kansai Univ. of Foreign Studies), Inaugural Number (1974), 51–75. (One must, unfortunately, beware of misprints.)

For those who read *nāgarī* script, Hari Damodar Velankar, *Jinaratnakośa, An Alphabetical Register of Jain Works and Authors,* vol. 1, Works (Poona, Bhandarkar Oriental Research Institute, 1944), is a list of all known (at that date) Jaina texts, with references to manuscript catalogues and generally accurate listings of published editions and translations. The projected second volume has not materialized.) Unfortunately for the general reader, the works are listed according to the Indian alphabet, and all titles printed only in *nāgarī* script (and in their Sanskritized form). Also, mention should be made of the bibliographic section in Schubring's *Die Lehre der Jainas.* This is an extremely useful tool (not found in the English translation, alas), even though Schubring firmly disclaims any pretense of exhaustiveness.

In conclusion, what this brief account should reveal is that there is available a reasonable amount of material for introductory and general study of the Jainas. Though gaps and *desiderata* have been pointed out, the primary problem in studying the Jainas has not been lack of material, but lack of interest. Whether this is due to the nature of the Jaina tradition itself, or to the nature of the Western perception of it, or a combination of these, is a question worthy of study.

IX

The Religions of Japan

J. M. Kitagawa

Anyone who attempts to study the religions of Japan will soon discover the ambiguities involved. Some people interpret the designation "religions of Japan" in a narrow sense, as referring to the religions that developed on Japanese soil without including Buddhism and other religions introduced from abroad. In this article we have permitted ourselves to be more inclusive and have dealt with religions of non-Japanese origin that exerted significant influences within Japan, though we have made no attempt to deal with their origins, doctrines, and development prior to their introduction to the Japanese homeland.

We have also faced another ambiguity in regard to the term "religion" itself. We have found, for example, that some people do not classify Confucianism as a religion and that even Shinto is often regarded as a "national cult"—that is, as something other than a religion, properly speaking. We have, however, included Shinto, Japanese Confucianism, and various other systems and movements in our discussion because we feel them to constitute important elements in the religious life and history of the Japanese people. On the other hand, we have excluded militarism, nationalism, and communism from this discussion even though they have semireligious or pseudoreligious features.

Some readers may ask why the Ainu religion is included in our discussion. Although the Ainus are not "Japanese" in their ethnic affiliation, the largest concentration of them has lived in the northern section of Japan for over two millennia; hence, if for no other reason, some knowledge of Ainu religion is pertinent to one's understanding of the religious situation in prehistoric Japan.

Another problem we must clarify is that of perspective, since the religions of Japan may be, and have been, studied from a number of different viewpoints. For example, Japanologists, Buddhologists and Sinologists approach Japanese religious history from their own respective perspectives, while students of world history, archeology, prehistory, folklore, and anthropology study Japanese religions in the light of their own perfectly valid disciplines. In this article we will use the perspective of *Religionswissenschaft,* commonly known as the "history of religions" or the "comparative study of religions." Thus our concern will be to reach an understanding of these religious phenomena *qua* religious rather than to arrive at any philosophical, theological, anthropological, or socioeconomic conclusions about them.

A few words may now be said about Japanese study in the West as it affects our materials. During the period of roughly thirty years between the 1880s and World War I, a number of Western teachers, missionaries and diplomats in Japan were engaged in serious scholarly investigations of Japanese language, history, culture, and religions. Among them were Sir Ernest M. Satow, Basil Hall Chamberlain, William George Aston, Ernest F. Fenollosa, Hans Haas, Michel Revon, Sir Charles Eliot, Karl Florenz, August Karl Reischauer, and John Batchelor, to name only the best known. Their books and articles contributed much toward the West's understanding of Japan and the Japanese people.

The initiative taken by Western scholars in Japanology also stimulated the study of able Japanese scholars, notably Bunyiu Nanjio (Buddhology), Masaharu Anesaki (Science of Religions), Genchi Kato (Shinto Study), D.T. Suzuki (Zen Buddhist Study), Nobuhiro Matsumoto (Mythology), and Kunio Yanagida (Folklore). The period between the two world wars was marked by an impressive growth in Japanese scholarship and also by a concomitant general decline of Western scholarship in the field. Unfortunately, most Japanese scholars published their works only in Japanese, and thus the Japanese contribution to the study of Japanese religions, for example, was virtually inaccessible to Western scholars during this period. To be sure, there were some able Westerners, such as Sir George B. Sansom, Wilhelm Gundert, and Daniel C. Holtom, who continued their research, but for the most part Western understanding of Japanese religions and culture depended upon the works by earlier Western scholars or upon works by a very limited number of Japanese scholars who wrote in Western languages.

This observation does not imply that there is a scarcity of Western books on matters Japanese. However, many of those in use, if not dated, are either too technical or too popular. Moreover, while some aspects of religion in Japan, such as Zen, have attracted the attention of many people, other important dimensions of Japanese religion have not as yet even begun to be touched.

Happily, in recent years a number of younger Western scholars have become interested in Japanese religions, and an increasing number of younger Japanese scholars in the field have begun to write in Western languages. It is to be hoped that cooperation between Japanese and Western scholars will provide for greater "understanding" of the complex but fascinating religious phenomena that Japan offers for serious consideration.

I. GENERAL SURVEY

A. Information on Japan

Religions in Japan, as in any other part of the world, are more than systems of beliefs and practices. Japanese religions do not exist in isolation from the social and cultural life, as well as the historic experience, of the Japanese people. Therefore, those who study the religions of Japan are advised to acquaint themselves with the general characteristics of Japanese culture and the historical development of Japan.

Probably the most comprehensive (1,077 pages in all) and up-to-date single volume on Japan in general is *Japan: Its Land, People and Culture,* compiled by the Japanese National Commission for UNESCO (Tokyo, Bureau of Ministry of Finance, 1958); the religious development of Japan is briefly sketched in chapter XIX, "The Formation of the Thoughts of the Japanese and Their Spiritual Characteristics," 491–528. *The Encyclopaedia Britannica* (1971 ed.) has a comprehensive article on "Japan." For geographical information concerning Japan, one might consult G.T. Trewartha, *Japan: A Physical, Cultural and Regional Geography* (Madison, Univ. of Wisconsin Press, 1945) or George B. Cressey, *Asia's Lands and Peoples,* 3rd ed. (N.Y., McGraw-Hill, 1963).

Some of the older books, though naturally dated, still provide helpful insights regarding various aspects of the Japanese tradition. For example, the popularity of B.H. Chamberlain, *Things Japanese* (London, John Murray, 1902; Rutland, Vt., C.E. Tuttle, 1970) was such that it is still used by some people. Likewise, Edmond Papinot, *Dictionnaire d'histoire et de géographie du Japon* (Tokyo, 1906) and its English translation, *Historical and Geographical Dictionary of Japan* (Yokohama, 1909; Rutland, Vt., C.E. Tuttle, 1971) have been widely circulated. Some of the books written by Japanese authors soon after the turn of the century, such as Kakuzo Okakura, *The Awakening of Japan* (N.Y., Century, 1904) and Inazo Nitobe, *The Japanese Nation* (N.Y., G.P. Putnam's Sons, 1912), both of which are still read in some quarters, reflect the attitude of Japanese intellectuals of that period. Also in this connection, mention should be made of Lafcadio Hearn, an eccentric, romantic, and very gifted interpreter of Japan. Born in the Ionian islands of an Anglo-Irish father and Maltese mother, he was educated in Ireland, England, and France and became a newspaper reporter in America. He went to Japan in 1890, married a Japanese woman, and eventually renounced his British citizenship in order to become a naturalized Japanese with the name Yakumo Koizumi. Hearn died in 1904, leaving behind him numerous articles, short stories, and sixteen books, the most important being *Japan: An Attempt at Interpretation* (N.Y., Macmillan, 1904; Rutland, Vt., C.E. Tuttle, 1955). His critics are no doubt right in characterizing him as a conservative romanticist who loved those aspects of Japanese life that were passing away even during his time. Nevertheless, his poignant description of his adopted land should be read by those who try to understand Japanese religions and culture. See two recent anthologies of his works: Henry Goodman, ed., *The Selected Writings of Lafcadio Hearn* (N.Y., Citadel Press, 1949) and Edwin McClellan, ed., *Tales and Essays from Old Japan* (Chicago, Regnery Gateway Editions, 1956).

Some of the publications of the Society for International Cultural Relations (*Kokusai Bunka Shinkokai*), Tokyo, have been useful in introducing Japan to Westerners. For example, their production, "The Japanese Arts through Lantern Slides" with companion handbooks, has been profitably used in some circles. Among the handbooks, *Japanese Architecture* (Tokyo, 1938) contains fairly good factual materials concerning Shinto shrines and Buddhist temples. Some travel books, such as Atsushi Sakai, *Japan in a Nutshell—Religion, Culture, Popular Practices* (Yokohama, 1949) and Japan Travel Bureau, *Japan: the Official Guide*, rev. ed. (Tokyo, 1952), are goldmines of factual information. The Japan Travel Bureau also publishes handy topical booklets in a series called the *Tourist Library;* among them, *What Is Shinto?* by Genchi Kato (No. 8), *Japanese Buddhism* by D.T. Suzuki (No. 21), and *Ainu Life and Legend* by Kyosuke Kindaichi or Kindaiti (No. 36) are important for students of religions.

During World War II a number of books and articles on Japan appeared in the West. The wartime slant of many of these works is well illustrated in *Fortune,* XXIX, 4 (April, 1944), the issue dedicated to "Japan and the Japanese." While many wartime publications on Japan are no longer taken seriously, some have continued to be read as good introductory materials. For example, John F. Embree, an anthropologist well known for his study of a peasant village, *Suye Mura* (Chicago, Univ.

of Chicago Press, 1939), published *The Japanese Nation, A Social Survey* (N.Y., Farrar & Rinehart, 1945) which is a well-balanced account of Japanese culture and society. Ruth Benedict, *The Chrysanthemum and the Sword—Patterns of Japanese Culture* (Boston, Houghton Mifflin, 1946; N.Y., World Publishing, 1967) has some good insights into certain cultural features of Japan, although her work is more controversial than Embree's. One wishes that Embree and Benedict had lived longer, so that they could have revised certain sections of their books by incorporating the criticisms and suggestions of others.

Space does not permit us to list the numerous works on Japanese culture that have appeared since the end of the second World War, but a number of helpful collections of essays may be cited: *Japanese Culture: Its History and Development,* ed. by Robert J. Smith and Richard K. Beardsley (Chicago, Aldine, 1962); *Japanese Character and Culture,* ed. by Bernard S. Silberman (Tucson, Univ. of Arizona Press, 1962); *Studies in Japanese Culture,* ed. by Joseph Roggendorf (Tokyo, Sophia Univ., 2nd ed., 1965); *Twelve Doors to Japan,* ed. by John Whitney Hall and R.K. Beardsley (N.Y., McGraw-Hill, 1965); and *Personality in Japanese History* (Berkeley, Univ. of California Press, 1970), ed. by Albert M. Craig and Donald H. Shively in honor of E.O. Reischauer's sixtieth birthday. Focusing on modern cultural changes are Donald H. Shively, ed., *Tradition and Modernization in Japanese Culture* (Princeton, Princeton Univ. Press, 1971); R.P. Dore, ed., *Aspects of Social Change in Modern Japan* (Princeton, Princeton Univ. Press, 1967); and Marius B. Jansen, ed., *Changing Japanese Attitudes toward Modernization* (Princeton, Princeton Univ. Press, 1965).

Turning to the materials dealing with the general historical orientation of Japan, no one will go wrong by starting with *Japan: The Story of a Nation* (N.Y., Alfred A. Knopf, 1946; new ed., 1970) by Edwin O. Reischauer, the United States Ambassador to Japan, the son of August Karl Reischauer and brother of Robert Karl Reischauer. This small book, unlike his other more technical works, presents Japanese history in general and broadly interpretive terms with a significant degree of success and clarity. Another merit of the revised edition is its inclusion of a sober analysis of the postwar period of Japanese history. John Whitney Hall, *Japan: From Prehistory to Modern Times* (N.Y., Delacorte Press, 1970), presents a valuable supplement to Reischauer's book in that he is especially strong on the medieval and early modern periods in Japan. An older but very readable one-volume survey of Japanese history up to 1963 is Sir George B. Sansom, *Japan: A Short Cultural History* (N.Y., Appleton-Century-Crofts, 1931; rev. ed., 1943; N.Y., Appleton, 1962). It is a mature production, reflecting the many years of Sansom's research and thought on his subject. His own perspective is succinctly discussed in his *Japan in World History* (N.Y., American Institute of Pacific Relations, 1951). Having the two foci of world history and Japanese history, and using the comparative method in the broad sense of the term, Sansom tries to differentiate what is general and what is characteristically Japanese in historical phenomena. Sansom's work culminated in his three-volume history of Japan, reflecting the thoroughness and lucidity that are characteristic of his writing: *A History of Japan to 1334; A History of Japan, 1334–1615;* and *A History of Japan, 1615–1867* (Stanford, Stanford Univ. Press, 1958–63). Some people have also found Arthur L. Sadler, *Short History of Japan* (Sydney, Angus & Robertson, 1946) useful. For classroom purposes, *A History of East Asian Civilization,* by E.O. Reischauer and John K. Fairbank, 2 vols. (Boston, Houghton Mifflin, 1960–65) and *Sources of Japanese Tradition,* comp. by Ryusaku Tsunoda, William Theodore de Bary, and Donald Keene (N.Y., Columbia Univ. Press, 1958) are to be highly recommended. Of a more limited nature, Peter Duus, *Feudalism in Japan* (N.Y., Alfred A. Knopf, 1969), and John Whitney Hall, *Government and Local Power in Japan 500 to 1700: A Study Based on Bizen Province* (Princeton, Princeton Univ. Press, 1966), survey important political developments up to the early Tokugawa period.

We do not imply, however, that the earlier works dealing with Japanese history should be discarded altogether. For example, Captain F. Brinkley, *Japan: Its History, Arts and Literature,* 8 vols. (Boston, J.B. Millet, 1901–02) uncritical though they are, have some good descriptions of certain periods, and *History of Japan,* 3 vols., by James Murdoch and Isoh Yamagata (London, Kegan Paul, Trench, Trübner, 1910), which are just as dated as Brinkley's *magnum opus,* are still to be consulted regarding some political events. Similarly, E. Honjo, *The Social and Economic History of Japan* (Kyoto, Institute for Research in Economic History of Japan, 1935; repr. 1965) and Yosaburo Takekoshi, *The Economic Aspects of the History of the Civilization of Japan,* 3 vols. (N.Y., Macmillan, 1930) are invaluable in the study of the socioeconomic factors involved in the religious development of Japan. For the most part, historical works written in Japanese during the same period share the virtues and failings of the books mentioned here. All these authors lived in a period when the task of the historian was regarded as the amassing of data without much effort in interpretation.

The modern period of Japanese history has attracted the attention of many able scholars, both Western and Japanese, such as Chitoshi Yanaga, *Japan Since Perry* (N.Y., McGraw-Hill, 1949); G.B. Sansom, *The Western World and Japan* (N.Y., Alfred A. Knopf, 1950); Jintaro Fujii, ed., *Outline of Japanese History in the Meiji Era,* tr. by H.K. Colton and Kenneth Colton (Tokyo, Obunsha, 1958); Hugh Borton, *Japan's Modern Century* (N.Y., Ronald Press, 2nd ed., 1970); and Richard Storry, *A History of Modern Japan* (Baltimore, Penguin, 1960). Works that lean heavily on the political and economic aspects of modern Japan include

Walter W. McLaren, *A Political History of Japan during the Meiji Era, 1867–1912* (London, George Allen & Unwin, 1916); G.C. Allen's two books, *A Short Economic History of Modern Japan, 1867–1937* (London, George Allen & Unwin, 1946) and *Japan's Economic Recovery* (London, Oxford Univ. Press, 1958); W.W. Lockwood, *The Economic Development of Japan: Growth and Structural Change, 1868–1938* (Princeton, Princeton Univ. Press, 1954); E.H. Norman, *Japan's Emergence as a Modern State* (N.Y., American Institute of Pacific Relations, 1940); H. Feis, *The Road to Pearl Harbor* (Princeton, Princeton Univ. Press, 1950); F.C. Jones, *Japan's New Order in East Asia: Its Rise and Fall, 1937–1945* (London, Oxford Univ. Press, 1954); E.J. Lewe, Baron van Aduard, *Japan from Surrender to Peace* (Hague, M. Nijhoff, 1953); Edwin M. Martin, *Allied Occupation of Japan* (Stanford, Stanford Univ. Press, 1948); R.A. Feary, *The Occupation of Japan—Second Phase, 1948–1950* (N.Y., Macmillan, 1950); T.A. Bisson, *Prospects of Democracy in Japan* (N.Y., Macmillan, 1949); C. Yanaga, *Japanese People and Politics* (N.Y., John Wiley & Sons, 1956); A.T. von Mehren, ed., *Law in Japan: The Legal Order in a Changing Society* (Cambridge, Harvard Univ. Press, 1963); and Theodore McNelly, *Contemporary Government of Japan* (Boston, Houghton Mifflin, 1963).

While many of these publications do not make direct reference to religions as such, they provide the general framework of Japanese culture and history that is essential for understanding the religious development of Japan.

B. Works on Japanese religions

It is almost impossible to evaluate all the books that deal directly or indirectly with the religions of the Japanese nation. Some indication must be given, however, of the different approaches used by writers on the subject.

First, let us look briefly at books that may be classified as reading materials for the general history of religions or the comparative study of religions. In North America, be it noted, the interest in this field developed gradually from the end of the last century. The popularity of comparative religion reached its peak in the 1920s, and then steadily declined in the 1930s and early 1940s. Since the end of World War II, study of world religions has again become a favorite subject. Publications in this field reflect the rise, decline, and the renewed popularity of the discipline. For the most part, scholars in the history of religions or comparative religion are more concerned with "major world religions," such as Buddhism, Hinduism, Islām, Judaism, Christianity, and Chinese religions, at the expense of the so-called "minor religions," including Shinto. However, even books that have no section on Shinto or Japanese religions usually discuss some aspects of Japanese religions *per se* in connection with the development of Buddhism.

Among the earlier American works, both George Foote Moore, *History of Religions,* vol. I (N.Y., Charles Scribner's Sons, 1913) and George A. Barton, *The Religions of the World* (Chicago, Univ. of Chicago Press, 1929) have special chapters on Japanese religions. Others that include sections on Japanese religions are John Clark Archer, *Faiths Men Live By* (N.Y., Thomas Nelson & Sons, 1934; 2nd ed., N.Y., Ronald Press, 1958); Selwyn G. Champion, *The Eleven Religions and Their Proverbial Lore* (N.Y., E.P. Dutton, 1945); Horace L. Friess and Herbert W. Schneider, *Religion in Various Cultures* (N.Y., Henry Holt, 1932); A. Eustace Haydon, *Biography of the Gods* (N.Y., Macmillan, 1941; N.Y., Frederick Unger, 1967); E. Washburn Hopkins, *The History of Religions* (N.Y., Macmillan, 1918); Robert E. Hume, *The World's Living Religions* (N.Y., Charles Scribner's Sons, 1924; rev. ed., 1959); and Edmund D. Soper, *The Religions of Mankind* (N.Y., Abingdon Press, 1921; 3rd ed., 1951). The chief merit of these discussions of Japanese religions is their brevity; but so far as their quality is concerned, none of them approaches A. Bertholet and E. Lehmann, *Lehrbuch der Religionsgeschichte,* 4th ed., ed. by P.D. Chantepie de la Saussaye (Tübingen, J.C.B. Mohr, 1925), vol. I, section on "Die Japaner" by Karl Florenz, 262–422.

Many recent publications also include brief descriptions of Japanese religions; see, for example, Charles S. Braden, *The Scriptures of Mankind: An Introduction* (N.Y., Macmillan, 1952); Vergilius Ferm, ed., *Religion in the Twentieth Century* (N.Y., Philosophical Library, 1948); Jack Finegan, *The Archeology of World Religions* (Princeton, Princeton Univ. Press, 1952); Edward J. Jurji, ed., *The Great Religions of the Modern World* (Princeton, Princeton Univ. Press, 1946); Quinter M. Lyon, *The Great Religions* (N.Y., Odyssey Press, 1957); John B. Noss, *Man's Religions* (N.Y., Macmillan, 1949; 4th ed., 1969); R.C. Zaehner, ed., *The Concise Encyclopedia of Living Faiths* (N.Y., Hawthorn Books, 1959); W. Richard Comstock, ed., *Religion and Man: An Introduction* (N.Y., Harper & Row, 1971); and C.J. Bleeker and Geo. Widengren, *Historia Religionum: Handbook for the History of Religions,* vol. II, *Religions of the Present* (Leiden, E.J. Brill, 1971). In the main, the quality of the postwar publications is superior to the older works in regard to Japanese religions. Those who have access to *Proceedings of the IXth International Congress for the History of Religions, Tokyo and Kyoto, 1958* (Tokyo, Shinto Committee Report, 1960) will find many excellent papers by Western and Japanese scholars on various aspects of Japanese religions.

Secondly, there are many works that are concerned primarily with one of the religions of Japan. While some of them are fairly adequate treatises on the respective religions, they do not always help readers in relating the specific religion under discussion to the total historical development of Japanese religions.

On Shinto, one of the oldest works, and yet still helpful in some ways, is W.G. Aston, *Shinto, The Way of the Gods* (London, Longmans, Green, 1905), even though his classification of Shinto deities and his naturalistic interpretation of religion have been rightly questioned. K. Florenz, *Die historischen Quellen der Shinto-religion* (Leipzig, J.C. Hinrichs, 1919) and H. Haas, "Shintoismus," *Die Religion in Geschichte und Gegenwart,* V, 466–70, though naturally dated, are still read with profit. On the other hand, more recent works are not always reliable or well balanced. Even D.C. Holtom's careful study, *Modern Japan and Shinto Nationalism* (Chicago, Univ. of Chicago Press, 1943; 2nd ed., 1963), to say nothing of R.O. Ballou, *Shinto: The Unconquered Enemy* (N.Y., Viking Press, 1945), betray the wartime psychology, and Chikao Fujisawa's *Zen and Shinto* (N.Y., Philosophical Library, 1959) and *Concrete Universality of the Japanese Way of Thinking* (Tokyo, Hokuseido, 1958) are but part of the sad legacy of a chauvinistic ethnocentricism. The two most frequently cited works on Shinto are Genchi Kato, *A Study of Shinto: The Religion of the Japanese Nation* (Tokyo, Meiji Japan Society, 1926, repr. 1971) and Daniel C. Holtom, *The National Faith of Japan* (N.Y., Kegan Paul, Trench, Trübner, 1938, repr. 1965). Readers must be aware, however, that Kato, using a now dated evolutionary theory, tries too hard to show the development of Shinto from its earliest stage of nature religion to that of an ethical and intellectual religion, while at the same time trying to maintain a lofty place for the divine emperor. Holtom's *The National Faith of Japan,* together with his "The Political Philosophy of Modern Shinto: A Study of the State Religion of Japan," *Transactions of the Asiatic Society of Japan,* XLIX (1922), Part 2, 1–325, his *The Japanese Enthronement Ceremonies* (Tokyo, Sophia Univ., 1928, repr. 1972), and other articles are still good sources concerning the general characteristics and history of Shinto, even though readers may not agree with Holtom's own ethical liberalism and evolutionary conception of religion. A.C. Underwood, *Shintoism* (London, Epworth Press, 1934), depends heavily on the works of Anesaki, Aston, W.E. Griffis, Kato, and Michel Revon. Although it has no particular originality, this small book is a handy introduction to the study of Shinto. It is interesting to note that Shinto intrigued Raffaele Pettazzoni, the well-known Italian historian of religion, as evidenced by his *La mitologia giapponese* (Bologna, N. Zanichelli, 1929) and *Religione e politica religiosa del Giappone moderno* (Rome, Istituto Italiano per il Medio ed Estremo Oriente, 1934).

In recent years a number of non-definitive but helpful works (that is, without the older evolutionary perspective or the World War II psychology) have been published. Among these might be mentioned Jean Herbert, *Shinto: At the Fountain-Head of Japan* (London, Allen & Unwin, 1967); Motonori Ono, *Shinto: The Kami Way* (written by Sokyo Ono in collaboration with William P. Woodard; Tokyo, and Rutland, Vt., Bridge-way Press, 1961); Muraoka Tsenetsugu, *Studies in Shinto Thought,* tr. by Delmer M. Brown and James T. Araki (Tokyo, Ministry of Education, 1964); Floyd H. Ross, *Shinto: The Way of Japan* (Boston, Beacon Press, 1965); and Hirai Naofusa, *Understanding Japan: Japanese Shinto* (Tokyo, International Society for Educational Information, 1966). Finally, the reader is referred to the *Proceedings, The Second International Conference for Shinto Studies: Continuity and Change* (Kyoto, Kokugakuin-daigaku, 1968), and to the volume *Basic Terms of Shinto,* ed. by Jinja-honchō and Kokugakuin-daigaku (Kyoto, Kokugakuin-daigaku, 1958), for specific studies and definitions of Shinto terms and concepts.

Books on Japanese Buddhism are many and varied. Bunyiu Nanjio (also spelled Bunyu Nanjo), *A Short History of the Twelve Japanese Buddhist Sects* (Tokyo, Meiji, 1886) and Arthur Lloyd, "Development of Japanese Buddhism," *Transactions of the Asiatic Society of Japan,* XXII (1894), Part 3, 361–405, are important pioneering works. Lloyd's later work, *Creed of Half Japan* (N.Y., E.P. Dutton, 1912) suffers from his too lively imagination. Robert C. Armstrong's *Buddhism and Buddhists in Japan* (N.Y., Macmillan, 1927) and *Introduction to Japanese Buddhist Sects* (a posthumous publication, privately printed somewhere in Canada, 1950) are good as introductory materials. E. Steinilber-Oberlin and K. Matsuo, *The Buddhist Sects of Japan,* tr. by Marc Loge (London, George Allen & Unwin, 1938) may be characterized as a sensitive religious travelogue. Two important scholarly works on the subject are A.K. Reischauer, *Studies in Japanese Buddhism* (N.Y., Macmillan, 1917) and Sir Charles Eliot's posthumous publication, *Japanese Buddhism* (London, 1935; repr., N.Y., Edward Arnold, 1959). Both are dull reading, and both undoubtedly need revision in the light of current research; yet they are substantial works to be reckoned with by serious students of Japanese religions. A more popular introduction to Buddhism in Japan, emphasizing the significance of esoteric Buddhism, is Ernest Dale Saunders, *Buddhism in Japan, with an Outline of Its Origins in India* (Philadelphia, Univ. of Pennsylvania Press, 1964). An additional resource on Japanese Buddhism is the *Japanese-English Buddhist Dictionary* (Tokyo, Tokyo Daito Shuppansha, 1965).

In addition to works on Japanese Buddhism, most books on Buddhism in general, especially those on Mahayana Buddhism, make reference to Japanese Buddhism. Among them, James B. Pratt, *The Pilgrimage of Buddhism and a Buddhist Pilgrimage* (N.Y., Macmillan, 1928) devotes chapters XXI–XXXI to Buddhism in Japan, and Kenneth W. Morgan, ed., *The Path of the Buddha* (N.Y., Ronald Press, 1956) includes an important section on Buddhism in Japan, 307–63. Junjiro Takakusu, *The Essentials of*

Buddhist Philosophy, ed. by C.A. Moore and W.T. Chan (Honolulu, Univ. of Hawaii, 1974) is in fact a book on the doctrines of eleven Japanese Buddhist schools. One should also refer the reader to the very helpful articles on Japanese Buddhism that are published in almost every issue of *The Eastern Buddhist* (new series since 1965; Kyoto, Eastern Buddhist Society, Otani Univ.).

Some of the Japanese Buddhist schools have been studied by specialists; these will be mentioned later in their proper context. The abundance of books on Zen, however, calls for some comment at this time. Briefly, Zen Buddhism in Japan should not be linked solely with the name of D.T. Suzuki. To be sure, some of his writings, especially *The Training of the Zen Buddhist Monk* (Kyoto, Eastern Buddhist Society, 1934) and *Zen and Japanese Culture* (N.Y., Pantheon Books, 1959; Princeton, Princeton Univ. Press, 1970) deal directly with Zen Buddhism in Japan, but most of his books are interpretations of Zen Buddhism in general. It must also be noted that there are many other books on Zen Buddhism in Japan, such as, for example, Kaiten Nukariya, *Religion of the Samurai, A Study of Zen* (London, Luzac, 1913); Reiho Masunaga, *The Soto Approach to Zen* (Tokyo, Layman Buddhist Society Press, 1958); Heinrich Dumoulin, *A History of Zen Buddhism,* tr. by Paul Peachey (N.Y., Pantheon Books, 1963); Isshu Miura and Ruth Fuller Sasaki, *Zen Dust: The History of the Koan and Koan Study in Rinzai (Linchi) Zen* (N.Y., Harcourt, Brace and World, 1966); *The Tiger's Cave* (London, Rider, 1964), a translation of Japanese Zen texts by Trevor Leggett; Philip Kapleau, ed., *The Three Pillars of Zen* (Tokyo, John Weatherhill, 1965); Eugen Herrigel, *Zen,* tr. by R.F.C. Hull (N.Y., McGraw-Hill, 1964); and Ernest Wood, *Zen Dictionary* (N.Y., Philosophical Library, 1962). In our discussion, only those works that deal directly with Zen in Japan—or with other Japanese Buddhist schools, for that matter—will be treated.

In sharp contrast to the abundance of works on Japanese Buddhism, those on Japanese Confucianism are very meager, to say the least. This is all the more surprising and distressing because of the significant role that the Confucian tradition has played in Japanese history. Those who wish to study Japanese Confucianism must either learn to read Japanese or go through such works as A. Lloyd, "Historical Development of the Shushi (Chu Hsi) Philosophy in Japan," *Transactions of the Asiatic Society in Japan,* XXXIV (1906), Part 4, 80, or R.C. Armstrong, *Light from the East: Studies in Japanese Confucianism* (Toronto, Univ. of Toronto Press, 1914), both of which are quite dated. Its modern development is studied in Warren Smith, *Confucianism in Modern Japan* (Tokyo, Hokuseido Press, 1959). There is a brief historical study of Japanese Confucianism in Joseph J. Spae, *Ito Jinsai, A Philosopher, Educator and Sinologist of the Tokugawa Period* (Peking, Catholic Univ. of Peking, 1948; *Monumenta Serica,* no. 12; N.Y., Paragon, 1967). Some of the studies of Japanese Confucianist leaders include Olaf Graf, *Kaibara Ekken* (Leiden, E.J. Brill, 1942); Galen M. Fisher's "Kumazawa Banzan, His Life and Ideas," *Transactions of the Asiatic Society of Japan,* 2nd Series, XVI (1938), 221–58; Ken Hoshino, *The Way of Contentment,* translations of selections from Kaibara Ekken (London, Orient Press, 1904); T. Yoshimote, *A Peasant Sage of Japan* (London, Longmans, Green, 1912); J.R. McEwan, *The Political Writings of Ogyū Sorai* (Cambridge, Cambridge Univ. Press, 1962); and *Ogyu Sorai's Distinguishing the Way: An Annotated English Translation of the Bendo,* tr. by Olog G. Lidin (Tokyo, Sophia Univ., 1970). Also D.S. Nivison and A.F. Wright, eds., *Confucianism in Action* (Stanford, Stanford Univ. Press, 1959, repr. 1969) makes reference to Japanese Confucianism.

The complex field of Japanese folk religion has recently been studied in a number of important works. Ichiro Hori, *Folk Religion in Japan,* ed. Joseph M. Kitagawa and Alan Miller (Chicago, Univ. of Chicago Press, 1968), looks at a number of important aspects of Japanese folk traditions. More specialized studies include Cornelis Ouwehand, *Namazu-e and Their Themes* (Leiden, Brill, 1964); U.A. Casal, *The Five Sacred Festivals of Ancient Japan: Their Symbolism and Historical Development* (Tokyo, Sophia Univ., 1967); Geoffrey Bownas, *Japanese Rainmaking* (London, George Allen & Unwin, 1963); and Byron Earhart, *A Religious Study of the Mount Haguro Sect of Shugendo* (Tokyo, Sophia Univ., 1970). One should also refer to important work done on Japanese folklore; see especially Richard Dorson, ed., *Studies in Japanese Folklore* (Bloomington, Indiana Univ. Press, 1963). For the religious traditions of Okinawa, see William P. Lebra, *Okinawan Religion* (Honolulu, Univ. of Hawaii Press, 1966).

Many of the Christian publications dealing with Japanese religions are apologetic or evangelical in character. There are some historical studies of Christianity in Japan, however. The two earliest works that are still consulted are Hans Haas, *Geschichte des Christentums in Japan* (Tokyo, Der Rikkyo Gakuin Press, 1902–04) and Otis Cary, *A History of Christianity in Japan,* 2 vols. (N.Y., F.H. Revell, 1909, repr., Scholarly Press, 1971). A more recent historical study is Richard Drummond, *A History of Christianity in Japan* (Grand Rapids, Eerdman's, 1971). On the Catholic development, one might read Johannes Laures, *The Catholic Church in Japan* (Westport, Conn., Greenwood Press, 1970) and Joseph Jennes, *History of the Catholic Church in Japan—From Its Beginnings to the Early Meiji Period: 1549–1873* (rev. ed., Tokyo, Oriens Institute, 1972). On the Protestant development, Winburn T. Thomas, *Protestant Beginnings in Japan—The First Three Decades: 1859–89* (Rutland, Vt., Charles E. Tuttle, 1959) and Charles W. Iglehart, *A Century of Protestant Christianity in Japan* (Rutland, Charles E. Tuttle, 1959) will provide basic information.

Thirdly, some scholars have undertaken the very difficult task of studying, not the individual religions and their schools, but the ethos and development of the multidimensional religious history of Japan. The older works, such as William E. Griffis, *The Religions of Japan: From the Dawn of History to the Era of Meiji* (N.Y., Charles Scribner's Sons, 1895 and 1901) and George W. Knox, *The Development of Religion in Japan* (N.Y., G.P. Putnam's Sons, 1907), remind us of a quickly moving kaleidoscope without any central theme. The standard works in this area are Masaharu Anesaki, *History of Japanese Religion, with Special Reference to the Social and Moral Life of the Nation* (London, Kegan Paul, Trench, Trübner, 1930; repr. Rutland, Vt., Tuttle, 1963); Wilhelm Gundert, *Japanische Religionsgeschichte* (Stuttgart, D. Gundert, 1943); and Joseph M. Kitagawa, *Religion in Japanese History* (N.Y., Columbia Univ. Press, 1966). An historical survey of a more popular nature is H. Byron Earhart, *Japanese Religion: Unity and Diversity* (Belmont, Calif., Dickenson, 1969). In our historical survey, we will assume that readers will follow Anesaki, Kitagawa, and Tsunoda et al. (*Sources of Japanese Tradition,* cited before) as basic readings and source material.

In addition, mention should be made of *Religious Studies in Japan,* ed. by the Japanese Association for Religious Studies (Tokyo, Maruzen, 1959), which is a collection of papers by leading Japanese scholars on Shinto, Japanese Buddhism, and so on. Some Buddhist materials are also to be found in philosophical works. For example, *Philosophical Studies of Japan,* comp. by the Japanese National Commission for UNESCO (Tokyo, 1959), has an excellent article on Japanese Buddhism by H. Ui; and H. Nakamura, *The Ways of Thinking of Eastern Peoples* (rev. ed., Honolulu, East-West Center, 1964), Part IV, "The Ways of Thinking of the Japanese," is important for the study of Japanese religions. See also Nakamura's short study, *A History of the Development of Japanese Thought from A.D. 592 to 1868,* 2 vols. (2nd ed., Tokyo, Kokusai Bunka Shinkokai, 1969). For the religious basis of traditional Japanese philosophy, the reader may consult Joseph M. Kitagawa, "Japanese Philosophy (History)," *Encyclopaedia Britannica* (1971 ed.), and *The Japanese Mind: Essentials of Japanese Philosophy and Culture,* ed. Charles A. Moore (Honolulu, East-West Center Press, 1967). T. Harada, *The Faith of Japan* (N.Y., Macmillan, 1914) is still useful as an introductory study, and T. Kishinami, *The Development of Philosophy in Japan* (Princeton, Princeton Univ. Press, 1915); K. Tsuchida, *Contemporary Thought of Japan and China* (N.Y., Alfred A. Knopf, 1927); and Gino K. Piovesana, *Recent Japanese Philosophical Thought, 1862–1962: A Survey* (rev. ed., Tokyo, Sophia Univ. 1968), deal with modern philosophical trends in Japan. The reader will be able to appreciate the Buddhist structure of thought that undergirds even modern Japanese philosophy by reading the English translations of some of the important works that are now available, for example, Kitaro

Nishida's *A Study of Good,* tr. by V.H. Viglielmo (Tokyo, Ministry of Education, 1960), and Nishida's *Fundamental Problems of Philosophy,* tr. by David Dilworth (Tokyo, Sophia Univ., 1970).

It has been the experience of many who have tried to "understand" Japanese religions that some knowledge of Japanese art is extremely helpful. In fact, some go so far as to say that "religion is art" and "art is religion" in Japan. One of the pioneers in this field was Ernest F. Fenollosa, whose *Epochs of Chinese and Japanese Art,* 2 vols. (London, William Heinemann, 1912) were important contributions of his time. More up to date and comprehensive are *Pageant of Japanese Art,* 6 vols., published by the Tokyo National Museum (Tokyo, 1952); Yukio Yashiro and P.C. Swann, *Two Thousand Years of Japanese Art* (N.Y., H.N. Abrams, 1958); Hugo Munsterberg, *The Arts of Japan: An Illustrated History* (Rutland, Charles E. Tuttle, 1957); Seiroku Noma, *The Arts of Japan, Ancient and Medieval,* tr. and adapted by John Rosenfield, 2 vols. (Tokyo, 1965–66); and Peter Swann, *The Art of Japan: From Jōmon to the Tokugawa Period* (N.Y., Crown, 1966). There are also several excellent interpretations of Japanese art, such as Laurence Binyon, *The Spirit of Man in Asian Art* (Cambridge, Harvard Univ. Press, 1935); René Grousset, *The Civilization of the East,* tr. by C.A. Philipps (N.Y., Alfred A. Knopf, 1941, repr., Cooper Square, 1967); Robert T. Paine, Jr., and Alexander Soper, *The Art and Architecture of Japan* (Middlesex, Penguin Books, 1955); P.C. Swann, *An Introduction to the Arts of Japan* (Oxford, Bruno Cassirer, 1958); Langdon Warner, *The Enduring Art of Japan* (Cambridge, Harvard Univ. Press, 1952); and Shuichi Kato, *Form—Style—Tradition: Reflections on Japanese Art and Society,* tr. by J. Bester (Berkeley, Univ. of California Press, 1971). Dealing with aesthetic theories are Makoto Ueda, *Literary and Art Theories in Japan* (Cleveland, Western Reserve Univ. Press, 1967), and Seni'ichi Hisamatsu, *The Vocabulary of Japanese Literary Aesthetics,* tr. by H. McCullough (Tokyo, Center for East Asian Cultural Studies, 1963). Since much of Japanese art is closely connected with Zen Buddhism, it is very helpful to consult the books that deal with Zen aesthetics, such as Toshimitsu Hasumi, *Zen in Japanese Art: A Way of Spiritual Experience,* tr. by John Petrie (N.Y., Philosophical Library, 1962); Seni'ichi Hisamatsu, *Zen and the Fine Arts* (Tokyo, Kodansha International, 1971); Hugo Munsterberg, *Zen and Oriental Art* (Tokyo and Rutland, Vt., Charles E. Tuttle, 1965); and Kōichi Awakawa, *Zen Painting,* tr. by John Bester (Tokyo, Kodansha International, 1970).

Among books on the arts of Japan, those that deal with music, especially religious music, are extremely rare. Sir Francis Piggott, *Music and Musical Instruments of Japan* (London, Kelly & Walsh, 1909, repr., N.Y., Plenum Publications, 1971); Katsumi Sunaga, *Japanese Music* (Tokyo, Maruzen, 1936); H. Tanabe, *Japanese Music* (Tokyo, 1959); and William P. Malm, *Japanese Music and Musical Instruments* (Rutland, Vt.,

Charles E. Tuttle, 1959), provide some information concerning this difficult subject. Students of religions are also strongly advised to listen to recordings, such as the seven volumes of Gagaku classical court music, transcribed by Sukehiro Shiba into Western notation (Tokyo, 1956?) and the record accompanying Douglas G. Haring, *Japanese Buddhist Ritual* (N.Y., 1954; record No. P449, Ethnic Folkways Library). On traditional dance, one should consult *Introduction to the Classic Dances of Japan,* by R. Umemoto and Y. Ishikawa (Tokyo, Sanseido Co., 1935), and on classical theater, Donald Keene, *Nō: the Classical Theater of Japan* (Tokyo, Kodansha, 1966).

II. HISTORICAL SURVEY

A. Japanese religion in the prehistoric and early periods

Despite many years of research and speculation by devoted scholars, we are not at all certain about the religious development in the Japanese islands during the early period. The expression "primitive Shinto" is often used in referring to early Japanese religion, but the term "Shinto" arose only in the sixth century to distinguish Buddhism from traditional Japanese religious beliefs and practices that were not in themselves united within a single religious entity. The earliest chronicles of Japan are the *Kojiki* and the *Nihongi* (or *Nihon-shoki*), both of which are considered to be semisacred scriptures of Shinto. See B.H. Chamberlain's translation of Jo-ji-ki: "Records of Ancient Matters," Supplement to *Transactions of the Asiatic Society of Japan,* X (Tokyo, 1906), now superseded, finally, by Donald L. Philippi's translation of the *Kojiki* (Tokyo, Tokyo Univ. Press, 1968), and W.G. Aston's translation of *Nihongi; Chronicles of Japan from the Earliest Times to A.D. 697* (London, George Allen & Unwin, 1956; repr., N.Y., Paragon, 1969; originally published by the Japan Society of London, 1896). We must bear in mind, however, that both the *Kojiki,* which appeared in 712, and the *Nihongi,* which appeared in 720, were colored by Chinese influence, although they were both supposed to be faithful collections and compilations of ancient oral traditions. Thus, we cannot reconstruct the early history of Japan by basing it solely on these chronicles. There are references to Japan in the Chinese sources which are conveniently collected in Tyusaku Tsunoda and L.C. Goodrich, eds., *Japan in the Chinese Dynastic Histories* (South Pasadena, P.D. & I. Perkins, 1951). But, again, we cannot depend on the Chinese records alone to reconstruct the prehistory of Japan.

Fortunately, thanks to the untiring efforts of many scholars, we know considerably more today than fifty years ago, about Japanese origins. Three excellent recent publications on the subject are G.J. Groot, *The Pre-*

history of Japan, ed. by B.S. Kraus (N.Y., Columbia Univ. Press, 1951), Charles Haguenauer, *Origines de la civilisation Japonaise,* Part I (Paris, Imprimerie nationale, 1956), and Jonathan E. Kidder, *Japan before Buddhism* (N.Y., F.A. Praeger, 1959, rev. ed., 1966). In the main, scholars agree that the Japanese islands were inhabited as early as two or three millennia B.C. and that the earliest dwellers there were in part of northern Asiatic origin and in part from southern Asia. There seems, however, to be a variety of opinions as to which group migrated to which section of Japan at which age and by which route. Also, while most scholars accept the fact that there were two stages in prehistoric Japanese cultural development—namely, the Jōmon ("The rope-pattern") and the Yayoi (so named because of certain characteristic pottery found in a Neolithic site at a place called Yayoi in present-day Tokyo)—their opinions differ widely on how to trace specific cultural influences to Ural-Altaic or South Sea origins.

To complicate the matter further, scholars are also confronted with the question of the Ainu, one of the Paleo-Asiatic groups that originated in the arctic or subarctic zones of Asia. That the Ainus dwelt in the northern part of Honshu (the main island of Japan) in the prehistoric period is clear. But how and when they migrated from Asia to Sakhalin, Kurile, and Hokkaido, and their relation to non-Ainu peoples on Honshu, cannot be ascertained accurately. Understandably, many pioneers in Japanology, such as W.G. Aston, B.H. Chamberlain, E.O.E. von Baelz, Hans Haas, and Frederick Starr, were intrigued by the Ainus. The best-known Ainu scholar was John Batchelor, an Anglican missionary who worked among the Hokkaido Ainus for fifty years; he wrote numerous articles and books, such as *The Ainu of Japan* (London, Religious Tract Society, 1892), *The Ainu and Their Folk-lore* (London, Religious Tract Society, 1901), *Ainu Life and Lore* (Tokyo, Kyobun Kwan, 1927; repr. N.Y., Johnson Reprint, 1971), and "The Ainu Bear Festival," *Transactions of the Asiatic Society of Japan,* 2nd Series, IX (1932), 37–44.

The Ainus pose a number of interesting questions. Having no written language of their own, they have preserved an impressive quantity of their oral tradition. And, although they lived in close geographical proximity to the Japanese for centuries, they maintained intact their own social and cultural patterns until quite recently. One of the main questions arising in this situation is the relation of the Ainus to other peoples of arctic or subarctic origins who also practice the bear festival and similar rites. This problem is dealt with in A. Irving Hallowell, *Bear Ceremonialism in the Northern Hemisphere* (Philadelphia, 1926; published Ph.D. thesis). It must be mentioned, however, that R. Torii and other scholars hold that the bear festival was not a fundamental feature of the Ainu tradition but that it was probably borrowed from neighboring peoples. Some of these issues are discussed in J.M. Kitagawa, "Ainu Bear Festival (Iyomante)," *History of Religions,* I, 1 (Chicago, 1961), 95–151.

Another question presented by the Ainus is their relation to the Japanese people, especially in regard to their religious beliefs. The Batchelor-Chamberlain controversy—Batchelor, "On the Ainu Term 'Kamui'," *Transactions of the Asiatic Society of Japan,* XVI (1888), 17–32, vs. Chamberlain, "Reply to Mr. Batchelor on the Words 'Kamui' and 'Aino'," *ibid.,* 33–38—aroused great interest among scholars concerned with possible connections between the Ainu religion and primitive Shinto, but this problem is far from being solved. Meanwhile, a number of Japanese scholars have taken up Ainu study. The most prominent and productive is Kyōsuke Kindaichi (also spelled Kindaiti); unfortunately, his only work available in English is *Ainu Life and Legends* (Tokyo, Board of Tourist Industry, 1941). Also lamentable is the fact that none of the writings of Mashio Chiri, himself an Ainu and an eminent professor of linguistics at Hokkaido University, is available in Western languages. John A. Harrison deserves our gratitude for translating and annotating S. Takakura's difficult work "The Ainu of Northern Japan: A Study in Conquest and Acculturation," *Transactions of the American Philosophical Society,* n.s., L, Part 4 (1960), although it does not have much to say about the prehistoric aspects of the Ainu. A reading of current work on the Ainu problem by Japanese scholars can be obtained from Martin Gusinde and Chiye Sano, eds., *An Annotated Bibliography of Ainu Studies by Japanese Scholars* (Nagoya, Nanzan Univ., 1962). A recent helpful English account of the religious traditions of the Ainu is Niel Munro's *Ainu Creed and Cult,* ed. by B.Z. Seligman (N.Y., Columbia Univ. Press, 1963). Suggestions about the interpretation of the Ainu mythic traditions are made by Joseph M. Kitagawa in "Ainu Myth," *Myths and Symbols: Studies in Honor of Mircea Eliade,* ed. by Joseph M. Kitagawa and Charles H. Long (Chicago, Univ. of Chicago Press, 1969), 309–23, and in "The Ainu Bear Festival" (previously cited). There have been some articles on the Ainus appearing from time to time in such places as the *Journal of the Royal Anthropological Institute,* LXXIX (1949); *Contemporary Japan,* XVIII (1949); the *Journal of American Folklore,* LXIV (1951) and LXV (1952); and the *Southwest Journal of Anthropology,* X (1954). All the writers on the Ainu question realize that it is a risky undertaking to reconstruct the prehistoric religion and culture of the Ainus and their relation to the Japanese solely on the basis of a study of their descendants in our own period.

In recent years scholars have not been as optimistic as Chamberlain once was in depending on Ainu studies for a clarification of the prehistoric culture of Japan. Cf. B.H. Chamberlain, "The Language, Mythology, and Geographical Nomenclature of Japan Viewed in the Light of Ainu Studies," *Memoirs of the Literature College,* no. 1 (Tokyo, Imperial Univ., 1887). Rather, they are turning toward archeology, folklore, and mythology for possible clues. The most detailed historical study of Japan is Robert K. Reischauer, *Early Japanese History,* 2 vols. (Princeton, Princeton Univ.

Press, 1937). For a very good brief discussion of Japanese mythology, see E. Dale Saunders, "Japanese Mythology," *Mythologies of the Ancient World,* ed. by S.N. Kramer (N.Y., Doubleday Anchor Books, 1961), 409–40. On this subject, Post Wheeler's attempt to reconstruct a coherent story of the origin of the cosmos to the seventh century A.D. out of various Shinto myths in *The Sacred Scriptures of the Japanese* (N.Y., Henry Schuman, 1952) is neither successful nor reliable. The difficulty lies in learning how to correlate the analysis of the myths with archeological, historical, and other types of evidence, even though the main lines of development of the prehistoric peoples in Japan are fairly well established.

It is more or less taken for granted among scholars that various tribes from both northern and southern Asia infiltrated the Japanese islands during the Neolithic and Ecolithic ages, and that they intermarried among the people there. Another question is not settled so easily, however, in respect to how and when the so-called Tennō clan (the dominant group among the Japanese) arrived. This tribe is believed to have brought with it the horseback-riding culture and the "uji" or clan social organization. Many scholars hold that the Tennō clan, originally one of the Altaic peoples, moved southward to the Korean peninsula about the beginning of the Christian era and migrated from there to Kyūshū island around the third century A.D. Eventually, this group established the so-called Yamato kingdom in the present Nara prefecture around the fourth century A.D. On the other hand, many scholars argue that the myths of the Tennō clan, especially those of the Sun-Goddess (Amaterasu-Ōmikami), share similarities with South Asian myths. The standard work on Japanese mythology is Nobuhiro Matsumoto, *Essai sur la mythologie japonaise: Austro-Asiatics,* vol. II (Paris, P. Geuthner, 1928), and the best-known ethnological work, though not published, is Masao Oka's dissertation, *Kulturschichten in Alt-Japan* (Wien, 1934?). Oka's influence is clearly evident in Alexander Slawik, "Kultische Geheimbünde der Japaner und Germanen," *Wiener Beiträge zur Kulturgeschichte und Linguistik,* IV (Salzburg-Leipzig, 1936), 675–764, and his "Zur Etymologie des japanischen Terminus marebito 'sakraler Besucher'," *Wiener volkundliche Mitteilungen,* II, 1 (1954), 44–58. For a summary of Oka's hypothesis, with an interpretation of how it relates to prehistoric religious traditions, see Joseph M. Kitagawa, "Prehistoric Background of Japanese Religion," *History of Religions,* II (Winter, 1963), 292–328.

What, then, were the main features of primitive Shinto? This is a difficult question, indeed; for the term Shinto probably referred to a loosely organized religious cult that developed with the growth of the Yamato kingdom, which was *de facto* a confederation of semiautonomous clans with the imperial clan as the center. All we are certain of is that the early Japanese accepted the whole of life and the cosmos as sacred because the *kami* nature pervaded everything, and that the Shinto religion developed as a manifestation of the tribal and communal cult with simple ceremonies. On the term *kami,* see D.C. Holtom, "The Meaning of Kami," *Monumenta Nipponica,* III, 1 (1940), 1–27. Judging from the Chinese records concerning early Japanese myths, female shamanic-diviners played significant roles both in the religious and the sociopolitical domains, but their relation to the tradition of Korean shamanism, for example, is not clear at all. For material on Japanese shamanism see William P. Fairchild, "Shamanism in Japan," *Folklore Studies,* XXI (1962), 1–122. While Satow, Chamberlain, and Griffis held that ancestor worship was an original feature of Shinto, Aston and Florenz believed that primitive Shinto presented no conception of ancestor worship. Michel Revon, in his *Le Shinntoisme* (Paris, E. Leroux, 1907) and "Ancestor-worship and the Cult of the Dead (Japan)," *Encyclopaedia of Religion and Ethics,* I, 455–57, characterized primitive Shinto primarily as nature worship, containing the seed for veneration of the ancestors, the full growth of which occurred only after Chinese influence penetrated Japan. Edmund Buckley, on the other hand, sought the meaning of Shinto in terms of a combination of ancestor worship, nature worship, and phallicism; cf. his *Phallicism in Japan* (Chicago, Univ. of Chicago Press, 1895; published doctoral thesis). A more recent and balanced study of phallicism in Japan is that of U.A. Casal, "Der Phalluskult in alten Japan," *Deutsche Gesellschaft für Natur-und Völkerkunde Mitteilungen,* 44, pt. 1 (1963), 72–94. Franz Kiichi Numazawa, an ethnologist and a leading Japanese Roman Catholic, contributed an article on the subject, "Die Religionen Japans," to F. König, ed., *Christus und die Religionen der Erde,* III (Freiburg, 1951), 393–436. Controversy on this subject will undoubtedly continue for many years to come. Meanwhile, for a Japanese Shinto scholar's evaluation of the views of Western scholars, see Motokiko Anzu, *Shinto as Seen by Foreign Scholars* (Los Angeles, Perkins Oriental Books, 1938).

B. Penetration of Chinese civilization and Buddhism

During the fifth and sixth centuries, Sino-Korean civilization began to penetrate Japan, introducing the ethical teachings of Confucianism, the magico-mystical system of Taoism, and the gospel of Buddhism. The administration of Prince Shōtoku (d. 621), the regent under the Empress Suiko (reigned 592–628), was an important landmark in Japanese history, for it was he who envisaged the establishment of a unified empire, patterned after the Chinese political structure. The underlying principles of Shōtoku's "Seventeen-article Constitution," assigning national and communal cults to Shinto, public and private morality to Confucianism, and the spiritual and metaphysical domains to Buddhism, exerted significant influence on the subsequent religious and social development. After the overthrow of the Soga clan, which resisted Shōtoku's policies, the court depended heavily on Sinified aristocrats and scholars who enhanced the introduction of Chinese thought and institutions into Japan. For the religious development of this period, see Clarence H. Hamilton, *Buddhism in India, Ceylon, China and Japan: A Reading Guide* (Chicago, Univ. of Chicago Press, 1931), Part IV; M. Anesaki, *Prince Shotoku, the Sage Statesman* (Rutland, Charles E. Tuttle, 1949); and K. Asakawa, *The Early Institutional Life of Japan, A Study in the Reform of 645 A.D.* (Tokyo, Shueisha, 1903, repr., N.Y., Paragon, 1963).

The eighth century was an important period for the religious, cultural, and artistic development of Japan. In the metaphor of L. Warner, "the T'ang dynasty of China was hanging like a brilliant brocaded background, against which we must look at Japan and its capital city of Nara to watch the eighth century, while the Japanese were at work weaving their own brocade on patterns similar but not the same" (Warner, *op. cit.*). One finds brief expositions of the doctrines of the so-called Nara Buddhist schools—The Kusha ("Abhidharmakosa"), Jōjitsu ("Satyasiddhi"), Hossō ("Yogacara"), Sanron ("Madhyamika"), Kegon ("Avatamsaka"), and Ritsu ("Vinaya")—in most of the general works on Japanese Buddhism. The Buddhist scriptures and rites used in the seventh and eighth centuries in Japan are discussed in M.W. de Visser, *Ancient Buddhism in Japan,* 2 vols. (Leiden, E.J. Brill, 1935), while the religious arts of this period are discussed in International Buddhist Society, ed., *History of Buddhist Art in Japan* (Tokyo, International Buddhist Society, 1940).

The Nara period produced not only the *Kojiki* ("Records of Ancient Matters") and the *Nihongi* ("Chronicles of Japan"), which have been mentioned earlier, but also a number of provincial historical records known as "Fūdoki," which preserve valuable local traditions; see the most complete of these, the *Izumo Fudoki,* tr. by M.Y. Aoki (Tokyo, Sophia Univ., 1971). The *Kogoshūi,* which is an historical account of early Japan according to the Imbe clan, an hereditary Shinto priestly family and the traditional rival of another priestly family called the Nakatomi, was translated by G. Kato and Hikoshiro Hoshino under the title *Kogoshūi: Gleanings from Ancient Stories,* 3rd rev. ed. (N.Y., Barnes & Noble, new impression, 1972). J.S. Snellen translated another historical work, "Shoku-Nihongi: Chronicles of Japan, Continued, from 697–791 A.D." *Transactions of the Asiatic Society of Japan,* 2nd Series, XI (1934), 151–239; XIV (1937), 209–79. Unfortunately, the *Shinsen Shojiroku* ("The New Compilation of the Register of Families"), a very important document, dating from 815, has not been translated into Western languages. The importance of the *Manyōshu,* which is a collection of ancient poems, for the understanding of Japanese religions cannot be exaggerated. Among several translations, we recommend the Japanese Classics Translation Committee's edition, *The Manyōshu: One Thousand Poems* (N.Y., Columbia Univ. Press, 1965). Ichiro Hori discusses religious beliefs that can be traced to the pre-Nara and Nara periods in "Japanese Folk-beliefs," *American Anthropologist,* LXI (June, 1959), 405–24. The precarious relationship between Shinto and Buddhism during the eighth century is briefly discussed in J.M. Kitagawa, "Kaiser und Schamane in Japan," *Antaios,* II, 6 (1961), 552–66, and J.H. Kamstra takes up this problem in his *Encounter or Syncretism: The Initial Growth of Japanese Buddhism* (Leiden, E.J. Brill, 1967).

In the transition from the Nara period (710–94) to the Heian period (794–1192), as a result of the transfer of the capital from Nara to Kyoto, there was a general decline in the Nara Buddhist schools together with the growth of two new Buddhist movements—the Tendai and the Shingon schools—that were introduced from China by Saichō (Dengyō-daishi) and Kūkai (Kōbō-daishi), respectively. Both schools gave doctrinal justification to the pattern of coexistence between Shinto and Buddhism; see Alicia Matsunaga, *The Buddhist Philosophy of Assimilation* (Tokyo, Sophia Univ., 1969). The Tendai scheme, known as "Sannō-ichijitsu Shinto," is discussed in T. Ishibashi and H. Dumoulin, "Yuitsu-Shinto-Myōbō-Yōshū: Lehrabriss der Yuitsu-Shinto," *Monumenta Nipponica,* III, 1 (1940), 187–239. The scheme of Buddhist-Shinto coexistence that lasted until the nineteenth century came to be known under the Shingon title "Ryōbu ('Two Aspects') Shinto." The Shingon school, being of the "esoteric" variety, stressed elaborate rituals and the use of art objects. These aspects of Shingon are discussed in M. Anesaki, *Buddhist Art in Its Relation to Buddhist Ideals, with Special Reference to Buddhism in Japan* (Boston, Houghton Mifflin, 1915), and E. Dale Saunders, *Mūdra: A Study of Symbolic Gestures in Japanese Buddhist Sculpture* (N.Y., Pantheon Books, 1960). The most concise description of Shingon Buddhism is R. Tajima, *Les Deux grands mandalas et la doctrine de l'ésotérisme Shingon* (Paris, Presses universitaires de France, 1959), and the best summary of Tendai doctrine is H. Ui, "A Study of Japanese Tendai Buddhism," *Philosophical Studies of Japan, op. cit.,* 33–74. The most important figure of Kūkai (or Kōbō Saishi), founder of Shingon Buddhism, is discussed, and his major works translated, in Yoshito S. Hakeda, *Kūkai and His Major Works* (N.Y., Columbia Univ. Press, 1972). Hakeda's somewhat one-sided view of Kūkai should be supplemented with Joseph M. Kitagawa, "Master and Savior," in *Studies of Esoteric Buddhism and Tantrism* (Koyasan, Japan, Koyasan Univ., 1965), 1–26. During the Heian period, the worship of Amida Buddha became important in the Tendai school especially. A classic theoretical statement of faith in Amida's Pure Land is Genshin's *Ōjō-yōshū* (Essentials of salvation); see Allan A. Andrews, *The Teachings Essential for Rebirth: A Study of Genshin's Ōjōyōshū* (Tokyo, Sophia Univ., 1973). E.O. Reischauer, *Ennin's Travels in T'ang China*

(N.Y., Ronald Press, 1955), and his translation of *Ennin's Diary* (N.Y., Ronald Press, 1955) are important documents concerning the contacts between Japanese and Chinese Buddhism in the ninth century.

In spite of the prosperity of the Tendai and the Shingon schools, during the Heian period Buddhism did not exterminate the cults of Onmyō-dō (Taoist-Shinto exorcism) or of Shugen-dō (the Shinto-Buddhist order of mountain priests). Percival Lowell studied some of these practices in his "Esoteric Shinto," *Transactions of the Asiatic Society of Japan,* XXI (1893), 106–35; XXI, 152–97; XXI, 241–70; XXII (1894), 1–26. See, more recently, I. Hori, "On the Concept of Hijiri (Holy-Man)," *Numen,* V (1958), fasc. 2, 128–60; fasc. 3, 199–232. Other studies dealing with Shugendō include Georges Renondeau, *Le Shugendo: Histoire, doctrine et rites des anchorites dits yamabushi* (Paris, Imprimerie nationale, 1965); and H. Byron Earhart, *A Religious Study of the Mount Haguro Sect of Shugendo* (previously cited). The Heian period also produced the *Engi-Shiki,* a compilation of laws and ritual regulations from A.D. 927, which includes many ancient Shinto prayers (*Norito*) and other material important for Shinto studies. See Sir Ernest M. Satow, "Ancient Japanese Rituals (Norito)," *Transactions of the Asiatic Society of Japan,* VII (1879), Part 2, 97–132; VII, Part 3, 409–55; IX (1881), Part 2, 183–211; Karl Florenz, "Ancient Japanese Rituals," *Transactions of the Asiatic Society of Japan,* XXVII (1900), 1–112; *Norito: A New Translation of the Ancient Japanese Ritual Prayer* by Donald L. Philippi (Tokyo, Institute for Japanese Culture and Classics, 1959); and Felicia Bock's recent translation, *Engi-Shiki: Proceedings of the Engi Era* (Tokyo, Sophia Univ., Bks. I–V, 1970; Bks. VI–X, 1972).

The peaceful atmosphere of Kyoto helped to create an elegant culture centering around the court during the Heian period; see Ivan I. Morris, *The World of the Shining Prince: Court Life in Ancient Japan* (N.Y., Alfred Knopf, 1964). Among literary works available in English are "Kagero Nikki (Journal of a 10th Century Nobleman)," tr. by Edward Seidensticker, *Transactions of the Asiatic Society of Japan,* 3rd Series, IV (1955), 1–243; *Konjaku Monogatari* (Ages Ago: Thirty-seven Tales from the Konjaku Monogatari Collection), tr. by S.W. Jones (Cambridge, Harvard Univ. Press, 1959); the *Tosa Diary,* tr. by W.N. Porter (London, 1912); *Japanese Poetic Diaries,* tr. by Earl Miner (including Tosa Nikki of Tsurayuki, Izumi Shikibu Nikki, Oku no Hosomichi, Botan Kuroku of Shiki; Berkeley, Univ. of California Press, 1969); and *The Izumi Shikibu Diary, A Romance of the Heian Court,* tr. by Edwin A. Cranston (Cambridge, Harvard Univ. Press, 1969). By far the most famous available work from this period is Arthur Waley's translation of *The Tale of Genji,* 2 vols. (London, George Allen & Unwin, 1935). One may also consult *Translations from Early Japanese Literature* by E.O. Reischauer and J. Yanagiwa (Cambridge, Harvard Univ. Press, 1951), the Kokusai Bunka Shinkokai,

Introduction to Classical Japanese Literature (Tokyo, 1948), and Samuel P. Brower and Earl R. Miner, *Japanese Court Poetry* (Stanford, Stanford Univ. Press, 1961). These poetical and literary works are invaluable resources for our understanding of the religious and cultural atmosphere of the Heian period.

C. Indigenous religious movements

The refined, aristocratic, and somewhat artificial culture of the Heian period gave way to the austere atmosphere of the Kamakura period (1192–1336) under the military rule of the Minamoto and the Hōjō families, followed by the eventful and chaotic "Warring States" period (1338–1568) under the nominal rule of the Ashikaga Shogunate. With the establishment of the military regime (*Bakufu*) in 1192, the imperial court became a powerless institution, and, with the exception of a short-lived restoration of direct imperial rule (1333–36), remained in obscurity until the latter half of the nineteenth century. For the general historical background of this period, one might consult Minoru Shinoda, *The Founding of the Kamakura Shogunate, 1180–1185, with Selected Translations from the Azuma Kagami* (N.Y., Columbia Univ. Press, 1960); Helen C. McCullough, tr., *The Taiheiki: A Chronicle of Medieval Japan* (N.Y., Columbia Univ. Press, 1959); H. Paul Varley, *Imperial Restoration in Medieval Japan* (N.Y., Columbia Univ. Press, 1971); and Peter Duus, *Feudalism in Japan* (cited previously).

The Kamakura period is noted for the vigorous spiritual awakening of Japan. The return from China of Eisai (d. 1215), founder of the Rinzai sect of Zen Buddhism, in 1191 ushered in an all but new religious age. Another branch of Zen, called the Sōtō, was established in Japan by Dōgen (d. 1253), and a third, the order of homeless mendicancy, known as the Fuke, was founded by Kakushin in 1255. Among the numerous works on Zen, the most concise historical account of its development in Japan is given in Heinrich Dumoulin, *A History of Zen Buddhism* (previously cited). One might also consult Nukariya's *Religion of the Samurai,* which was mentioned earlier. Undoubtedly, Bushido ("The Code of the Samurai or Warrior") was greatly influenced by Zen Buddhism. On this subject, see Inazo Nitobe, *Bushido: The Soul of Japan* (N.Y., G.P. Putnam's Sons, 1905; repr., Rutland, Charles E. Tuttle, 1969); D.T. Suzuki's *Zen and Japanese Culture* (*op. cit.*); and H. Paul Varley with Ivan and Nobuko Morris, *Samurai* (N.Y., Delacorte Press, 1971).

The most colorful religious leader during the Kamakura period was Nichiren (d. 1282), a patriotic prophet who became the founder of the Nichiren sect. His warning of a foreign invasion and his bitter denunciation of other Buddhist schools brought a death sentence upon him, which he skillfully avoided. His prestige soared when his prophecy was fulfilled in the Mongol invasions (of 1274 and 1281). Nichiren's life and his teaching, based on the Lotus Sutra, are succinctly portrayed in M. Anesaki, *Nichiren, the Buddhist Prophet* (Cambridge, Harvard Univ. Press, 1916) and G.B. Sansom's article, "Nichiren," in Eliot's *Japanese Buddhism* (*op. cit.*). The most dogmatic view of the Nichiren school is found in K. Satomi, *Japanese Civilization: Its Significance and Realization, Nichirenism, and the Japanese National Principles* (London, Kegan Paul, Trench, Trübner, 1923). One should also consult N.R.M. Ehara, tr., *The Awakening to the Truth or Kaimokushō, by Nichiren* (Kyoto, Perkins Oriental Books, 1941).

The Kamakura period also witnessed the growth of the Amida Pietist sects. Amida Pietism, it should be noted, had its roots in the popular "Nenbutsu" movement ("Recitation of prayers offered to the Buddha Amitabha who reigns over the 'Jōdo' or the Western Pure Land") that was widely spread among the masses in the tenth and eleventh centuries. In the thirteenth century Hōnen (d. 1212), inspired by the writings of a Chinese Pure Land Buddhist, reformed the "Nenbutsu" movement and established the Jōdo sect. His disciple, Shinran (d. 1262), founded the Jōdo Shin ("The True Pure Land") sect, which, incidentally, is the largest Buddhist group in Japan today. The third branch of Amida Pietism, known as the Ji ("the Perpetual Invocation") sect, was founded by Ippen (d. 1289). The more detailed study of Hōnen is H.H. Coates and R. Ishizuka, *Hōnen the Buddhist Saint, His Life and Teaching* (Kyoto, Kyon, 1925). For Shinran, see A. Lloyd, *Shinran and His Work* (Tokyo, Kyōbun Kwan, 1910); G. Nakai, *Shinran and His Religion of Pure Faith* (Kyoto, 1946); Ryosetsu Fujiwara, tr., *Tamnishō; Notes Lamenting Differences* (Kyoto, Ryukoku Translation Centre, Ryukoku Univ., 1962; 3rd. ed., 1966); G. Sasaki, *A Study of Shin Buddhism* (Kyoto, Eastern Buddhist Society, 1925); Alfred Bloom, *Shinran's Gospel of Pure Grace* (Tucson, Univ. of Arizona Press, 1965); Alfred Bloom, *The Life of Shinran Shonin: The Journey to Self Acceptance* (Leiden, E.J. Brill, 1968); D.T. Suzuki, *Shin Buddhism* (N.Y. Harper & Row, 1970); Hisao Inagaki et al., tr., *The Kyō gyō shinshō: The Teaching, Practice, Faith and Enlightenment* (Kyoto, Ryukoku Univ., 1966); Ryukyo Fujimoto et al., tr., *The Jōdo wasan: Hymns on the Pure Land* (Kyoto, Ryukoku Univ., 1965); and, on the fifteenth-century leader Rennyo, *The Works of St. Rennyo: Complete Translations of the Rennyoshonin-Goichidaiki-Kikigaki and the Anjinketsujosho,* tr., Kōshō Yamamoto (Ube, Karinbunko, 1968).

The spiritual revival of the Kamakura period encompassed Shintoists as well. Under the leadership of the hereditary priests of the Watarai family of the Ise shrine, Shintoists, adding a new element to the interreligious exchange, asserted that the Buddhas and Bodhisattvas of India were manifestations of the great *kami* of Shinto. The decline of the Kamakura feudal regime in 1333 and the restoration of imperial rule, even though it lasted as it did for only three years, nevertheless helped to encourage Shinto resurgence. A famous loyalist, Kitabatake Chikufusa (d. 1354), wrote the Jinnō Shōtōki ("Records of the Valid Succession of the Divine Emperor"); excerpts from this important document are included in Tsunoda et al., *Sources of Japanese Tradition* (*op. cit.*), 273–82. We may add that G.B. Sansom, tr., "The *Tsurezure Gusa* of Yoshida no Kaneyoshi, Being the meditations of a recluse in the fourteenth century," *Transactions of the Asiatic Society of Japan,* XXXIX (1911), 1–141, enables us to appreciate the original author's sharp criticisms of the social conditions of his time and to share in his inner spiritual struggle.

The "Warring States" period (1338–1568) is also known as the Ashikaga period because of the nominal rule of the nation at that time by the Ashikaga Shogunate. It is also called the Muromachi period, from the city of Muromachi not far from the imperial court in Kyoto. This troublesome time was marked by social and political chaos on the one hand and by the growth of various arts on the other. Cultural contacts with China were resumed, which accounts for some of the new artistic inspiration. During this period Zen Buddhist priests were the social and cultural elite whose influence was felt in education, foreign trade, the establishment of the tea cult, and various other cultural activities. In this period also a unique synthesis of the spirit of Zen and the ethos of Shinto was achieved, as exemplified in the so-called Nō play. Besides Zen and Shinto, the Tendai, Shingon, Nichiren and the Jōdo Shin Buddhist sects were active; and they were often involved in bloody battles resulting from jurisdictional disputes. All in all, the religious mood of this period can be appreciated through studies of general history and of the arts, particularly K. Okakura, *The Book of Tea* (N.Y., Fox, Duffield, 1906; repr., Rutland, Charles E. Tuttle, 1972); Horst Hammitzsch, *Cha-do: Der Tee-Weg* (München-Planegg, Otto Wilhelm Barth-Verlag, 1958); John Kirby, *From Castle to Teahouse: Japanese Architecture of the Momoyama Period* (Rutland, Charles E. Tuttle, 1962); Shin'ichi Hisamatsu, *Zen and the Fine Arts* (cited previously); B.L. Suzuki, *Nogaku: Japanese Nō-plays* (London, John Murray, 1932); A. Waley, *The Nō Play of Japan,* new ed. (London, George Allen & Unwin, 1950); and Wilhelm Gundert's excellent study, "Der Shintoismus im japanischen No-Drama," *Nachrichten der (Deutschen) Gesellschaft für Natur- und Völkerkunde Ostasiens,* XIX (Tokyo, 1925).

D. "Kirishitan" and national seclusion

One of the by-products of foreign trade in the sixteenth century was the arrival of merchants and Roman Catholic missionaries from Europe. The famous Jesuit, Francis Xavier, reached Japan in 1549 and initiated the missionary activities of Catholicism, then known as "Kirishitan" in Japan.

Oda Nobunaga (d. 1582), the "strong man" of that time, favored Catholicism, partly to counteract the power of uncooperative Buddhist groups. The guiding principle of the later Tokugawa feudal regime (1603–1867), which did not favor Catholicism, was the Neo-Confucianism of the Chu Hsi tradition. The Kirishitan movement was virtually wiped out after the revolt of Japanese Catholics (1637–38), and every Japanese family was required to belong to some Buddhist temple. Furthermore, the Tokugawa regime took the drastic step of declaring national seclusion, cutting off all contacts with foreign nations with the exception of China and the Netherlands. For the historical background of this period, see Walter Dening, *The Life of Toyotomi Hideyoshi, 1536–1598* (Tokyo, Hokuseido Press, 1955); A.L. Sadler, *The Maker of Modern Japan: The Life of Tokugawa Ieyasu* (London, George Allen & Unwin, 1937); M. Takizawa, *The Penetration of Money Economy in Japan and Its Effect upon Social and Political Institutions* (N.Y., Columbia Univ. Press, 1927); T.C. Smith, *Agrarian Origins of Modern Japan* (Stanford, Stanford Univ. Press, 1959); Charles D. Sheldon, *The Rise of the Merchant Class in Tokugawa Japan* (Locust Valley, N.Y., J.J. Augustin, 1958); John W. Hall, *Tanuma Okitsugu, 1719–1788: Forerunner of Modern Japan* (Cambridge, Harvard Univ. Press, 1955); Donald Keene, *The Japanese Discovery of Europe: Honda Toshiaki and Other Discoverers, 1720–1798* (London, Routledge & Kegan Paul, 1952; repr., 1969); *Studies in the Institutional History of Early Modern Japan,* ed. John Hall and Marius Jansen (Princeton, Princeton Univ. Press, 1968); David Earl, *Emperor and Nation in Japan: Political Thinkers of the Tokugawa Period* (Seattle, Univ. of Washington Press, 1964); Conrad Totman, *Politics in the Tokugawa Bakufu, 1600–1843* (Cambridge, Harvard Univ. Press, 1967); Toshio Tsukahira, *Feudal Control in Tokugawa Japan: the Sankin Kōtai System* (Cambridge, Harvard Univ. Press, 1966); and Ronald P. Dore, *Education in Tokugawa Japan* (Berkeley, Univ. of California Press, 1965).

During the Tokugawa period the populace was sharply divided into the four distinct social classes of the warrior farmer, artisan, and merchant in that descending order. The warriors were expected to live by Bushido (the "Code of the Samurai"), as exemplified by the famous 47 retainers who sacrificed their lives in order to maintain the honor of their master. For this incident, see F.V. Dickins, tr., *Chūshingura, or the Loyal League* (London, 1880). The lot of women then was anything but enviable, judging from S. Takaishi, *Women and Wisdom of Japan* (London, John Murray, 1905). Yet strange as it may seem, under "permanent martial law" the Tokugawa period produced all kinds of poetry (*waka* and *haiku*) and other literature. The theatrical arts (*kabuki* and *bunraku*) flourished, and schools of painters from the great Koyetsu tradition to that of popular *ukiyo-e* were prominent. For the cultural development of this period, for example, see R.H. Blyth, *Haiku,* 4 vols. (Tokyo, Kamakura Bunka, 1949–52), and his translation of *Senryū: Japanese Satirical Verses* (Tokyo, Hokuseido Press, 1949); H.H. Honda, tr., *A Hundred Poems from a Hundred Poets: Ogura-Hyakunin-Isshu* (Tokyo, Hokuseido Press, 1948); A. Miyamori, *An Anthology of Haiku, Ancient and Modern* (Tokyo, Maruzen, 1932); H.G. Henderson, *An Introduction to Haiku* (N.Y., Doubleday, 1958); Basho's *Oku no Hosomichi,* tr. by Y. Isobe (Tokyo, 1933); Makoto Ueda, *Matsuo Bashō* (N.Y., Twayne Publishers, 1970); Max Bickerton, "Issa's Life and Poetry," *Transactions of the Asiatic Society of Japan,* 2nd Series, IX (1932), 111–54; A.L. Sadler, *Japanese Plays: No, Kyogen, Kabuki* (Sydney, Angus & Robertson, 1934); Earle Ernst, *The Kabuki Theatre* (London, Oxford Univ. Press, 1956); Earle Ernst, ed., *Three Japanese Plays from the Traditional Theatre* (London, Oxford Univ. Press, 1959); F. Bowers, *Japanese Theatre* (N.Y., Hermitage House, 1952); A.C. Scott, *The Kabuki Theatre of Japan* (London, George Allen & Unwin, 1955); A. Miyamori, *Masterpieces of Chikamatsu, the Japanese Shakespeare* (N.Y., E.P. Dutton, 1926); Donald Keene, *The Battle of Coxinga: Chikamatsu's Puppet Play* (London, Taylor's Foreign Press, 1951); Howard Hibbett, *The Floating World in Japanese Fiction* (London, Oxford Univ. Press, 1959); Jippensha Ikku, *Hizakurigé,* tr. by T. Satchell (Japan, Kobe Chronicle, 1929); L. Binyon, *Japanese Colour Prints* (N.Y., Charles Scribner's Sons, 1923); J. Hillier, *Japanese Masters of the Cloud Print* (London, Phaidon Press, 1954); and J.A. Michener, *The Floating World* (N.Y., Random House, 1954).

The standard work on the Kirishitan movement is C.R. Boxer, *The Christian Century in Japan, 1549–1650* (Berkeley, Univ. of California Press, 1951; rev. ed., 1967), while *Monumenta Nipponica* published by Sophia University, Tokyo, also has good materials such as *Kirishito-ki und Sayo-yoroku* by G. Voss and H. Cieslik (1940), *Nobunaga und das Christentum* by J. Laures (1950), and *Kirishitan Bunko* by J. Laures (1957). Also useful is F.V. Williams, *The Martyrs of Nagasaki* (Fresno, Academy Library Guild, 1956). The general features and the role of Japanese Confucianism during the Tokugawa period are discussed in R.C. Armstrong, *Light from the East,* which was mentioned earlier; Joseph J. Spae, *Ito Jinsai, a Philosopher, Educator and Sinologist of the Tokugawa Period* (*op. cit.*); John W. Hall, "The Confucian Teacher in Tokugawa Japan," *Confucianism in Action,* ed. by D.S. Nivison and A.F. Wright (Stanford, Stanford Univ. Press, 1959); and Ogyu Sorai's *Distinguishing the Way* (cited previously).

In the main, Buddhism lost its spiritual vitality during the Tokugawa period, and was content to uphold the *status quo.* Zen Buddhism did produce one of its greatest masters in the person of Hakuin Zenji of the Rinzai school; see *The Zen Master Hakuin,* by Philip B. Yampolsky (N.Y., Columbia Univ. Press, 1971), and *The Embossed Tea Kettle,* tr. by R.D.M. Shaw (London, Allen & Unwin, 1963). Shinto, on the other hand, received the cooperation and support of Neo-Confucian scholars. Toward the latter part of the Tokugawa period, able Shinto leaders, such as Kamo Mabuchi (d. 1769), Moto-ori Norinaga (d. 1801), and Hirata Atsutane (d. 1843) greatly expedited the Shinto revival. For Shinto development during the Tokugawa period, see Horst Hammitzsch, *Die Mito Schule* (Tokyo, Tokugawa-Zeit, 1940); H. Dumoulin, *Kamo Mabuchi* (Tokyo, Sophia Univ. Press, 1943: *Monumenta Nipponica* Monograph); Shigeru Matsumoto, *Motoori Norinaga, 1730–1801* (Cambridge, Harvard Univ. Press, 1970); Tsunoda et al., *Sources of Japanese Tradition* (*op. cit.*), 506–51; and Naofusa Hirai, *The Concept of Man in Shinto* (unpublished M.A. thesis, Univ. of Chicago, 1954). In the meantime, the folk elements in Shinto began to break through the traditional framework, especially among the oppressed peasantry; and several messianic movements sprang up under charismatic leaders; among them were Tenri-kyo and Kurozumi-kyo, who were destined to play important roles in the modern period. There were also semireligious movements, such as that of Ninomiya Sontoku, "Hōtoku" ("Repay the Indebtedness"), and Ishida Baigan's "Shingaku" ("Mind Learning") movement. For information on these movements, see R.C. Armstrong, *Just before the Dawn, The Life and Work of Ninomiya Sontoku* (N.Y., Macmillan, 1912); Ingrid Schuster, *Kamada Ryūkō und seine Stellung in der Shingaku* (Wiesbaden, Otto Harrassowitz, 1967); and Ishida Baigan's *Seirimondo: Dialogue on Human Nature and Natural Order,* tr. by Paolo Beonio Brocchieri (Rome, Istituto Italiana per il Medio ed Estremo Oriente, 1967). Robert N. Bellah's excellent sociological analysis, *Tokugawa Religion: The Values of Pre-Industrial Japan* (Glencoe, Free Press, 1957), makes special reference to Ishida Baigan and the "Shingaku" movement.

E. Modern period

The decline of the Tokugawa regime was accelerated by the Perry expedition (1853–54), and the last Tokugawa *shogun* resigned in 1867. Thus began the Meiji era (1868–1912), followed by the Taisho era (1912–26) and the Shōwa era (1926 to the present). The architects of the Meiji regime attempted to establish a modern nation state without losing Japan's traditional religious and cultural foundation. The best single volume on the religious development of this period is H. Kishimoto, ed., *Japanese Religion in the Meiji Era,* tr. and adapted by J.F. Howes (Tokyo, Obunsha, 1956), which has separate chapters on Shinto, Buddhism, and Christianity. Among numerous other works, especially useful for our purposes are M. Kōsaka, *Japanese Thought in the Meiji Era,* tr.

by D. Abosch (Tokyo, Pan-Pacific Press, 1958); Inazo Nitobe et al., *Western Influence in Modern Japan* (Chicago, Univ. of Chicago Press, 1931); Shigenobu Ōkuma, ed., *Fifty Years of New Japan,* 2 vols. (London, Smith, Elder, 1909–10); K. Shibusawa, ed., *Japanese Life and Culture in the Meiji Era,* tr. by A.H. Culbertson and M. Kimura (Tokyo, Obunsha, 1958); and some of the biographical and autobiographical studies, such as M.E. Cosenza, ed., *The Complete Journal of Townsend Harris* (N.Y., 1930; rev. ed., Rutland, Charles E. Tuttle, 1959); Y. Fukuzawa, *The Autobiography of Fukuzawa Yukichi, 1834–1901,* tr. by E. Kiyooka (Tokyo, Hokuseido Press, 1934); Carmen Blacker, *The Japanese Enlightenment: A Study of the Writings of Fukuzawa Yukichi* (N.Y., Cambridge, Univ. Press, 1964); H. van Straelen, *Yoshida Shōin: Forerunner of the Meiji Restoration* (Leiden, E.J. Brill, 1952); K. Obata, *An Interpretation of the Life of Viscount Shibusawa* (Tokyo, Bijutsu insatsucho, 1937); K. Hamada, *Prince Ito* (Tokyo, Sanseido Press, 1936); and J. Ijichi, *The Life of Marquis Shigenōbu Ōkuma* (Tokyo, Hokuseido Press, 1940).

The Meiji regime lifted the edict banning Christianity, and religious freedom was guaranteed, at least officially, in the 1889 constitution. Encouraged by this action of the government, Protestant, Eastern Orthodox, and Roman Catholic missionaries engaged in evangelistic activities. The Meiji regime also issued a separation edict in an attempt to abolish the age-old pattern of Shinto-Buddhist cooperation. Some of the messianic movements were separated from Shinto proper and were classified as Sect (*Kyōha*) Shinto; thirteen of them were recognized by the government as "churches" (kyōha or kyōkai) between 1882 and 1908. These measures were taken by the regime in order to restore the ancient Japanese pattern of Saisei-itchi ("unity of religion and state"). Thus Shinto was proclaimed the national cult for all subjects of the emperor, who was revered as the living manifestation of the *kami.* In addition, the imperial edict on education was promulgated as the guiding principle for universal education. For Christian development in modern Japan, see, in addition to the above-mentioned books, J. Natori, *Historical Stories of Christianity in Japan* (Tokyo, Hokuseido Press, 1957), Part III, "Modern Times"; Kanzo Uchimura, *How I Became a Christian* (Tokyo, Keiseisha, 1913); and R.P. Jennings, *Jesus, Japan, and Kanzo Uchimura* (Tokyo, Kyo Bun Kwan, 1958). For Sect Shinto, a description is found in Holtom's previously mentioned *National Faith of Japan.* One of the Sect Shinto denominations, the Kurozumi-kyo, is portrayed in C.W. Hepner, *The Kurozumi Sect of Shinto* (Tokyo, Meiji Japan Society, 1935), while another school, called Tenri-kyo, is the subject of Henry van Straelen's *The Religion of Divine Wisdom* (Kyoto, Veritas Shion, 1957); Delwin B. Schneider studies yet a third Shinto sect in his *Konko-kyo, A Japanese Re-*

ligion (Tokyo, International Institute for the Study of Religion, 1962). For the Confucian influence in the Meiji era, see Warren W. Smith, *Confucianism in Modern Japan* (Tokyo, Hokuseido Press, 1959) and D.H. Shively, "Motoda Eifu: Confucian Lecturer to the Meiji Emperor," *Confucianism in Action* (*op. cit.*), pp. 302–33. For the guiding principles of the Meiji regime, see R.K. Hall, *Kokutai no Hongi* (Cambridge, Harvard Univ. Press, 1949) and his *Shūshin: The Ethics of a Defeated Nation* (N.Y., Columbia Univ. Press, 1949).

No one has yet attempted a systematic study of religious developments during the period between 1912 (the beginning of the Taisho era) and World War II. In this era two of Japan's neighbors, China and Russia, underwent political revolutions, while Japan itself took part in World War I, the Siberian expedition, and engaged in an undeclared war with China. Internally, she suffered from the tensions existing between liberal democratic tendencies and chauvinistic militarism. There is a brief description of the relation between government and various religions during this eventful period in William K. Bunce, *Religions in Japan—Buddhism, Shinto, Christianity* (Rutland, Vt., Charles E. Tuttle, 1955; repr., 1959). Christian activities were minutely reported in various denominational publications, as well as in *Monumenta Nipponica,* the *Japan Christian Quarterly,* and the *Japan Christian Year Book.* There are a number of books and articles about Toyohiko Kagawa, but probably the best way to understand him and his life is to read his own writing, *Christ and Japan* (N.Y., Friendship Press, 1934). Michi Kawai, a leading Christian woman educator, also wrote an interesting book, *My Lantern,* 3rd ed. (Tokyo, Kyo Bun Kwan, 1949). Buddhist activities were reported in the *Young East,* the *Eastern Buddhist,* and other journals. There were a number of articles written in English by eminent Japanese Buddhists, such as M. Anesaki, Junjiro Takakusu, and D.T. Suzuki. One book that reflects a popular Buddhist view of this period is Haya Akegarasu, ed., *Selections from the Nippon Seishin Library* (Kōsōsha, Kitayasuda, Ishikawaken, Nippon, 1936). The Shinto activities of this period are succinctly presented in D.C. Holtom, *The National Faith of Japan* and in his *Modern Japan and Shinto Nationalism,* both cited earlier.

Memoirs and biographical accounts are also helpful for an understanding of this period. See, for example, B. Omura, *The Last Genro: Prince Saionji* (Philadelphia, J.B. Lippincott, 1938); Joseph Grew, *Ten Years in Japan* (N.Y., Simon & Schuster, 1944); C. Hull, *The Memoirs of Cordell Hull,* 2 vols. (N.Y., Macmillan, 1948); Shigenori Togo, *The Cause of Japan,* tr. by F. Togo and B.B. Blakeney (N.Y., Simon & Schuster, 1956); Mamoru Shigemitsu, *Japan and Her Destiny,* tr. by Oswald White (N.Y., E.P. Dutton, 1958); and Toshikazu Kase, *Journey to the Missouri* (New Haven, Yale Univ. Press, 1950, repr., 1969). The life of women in this transitional period is portrayed in Etsu I. Sugimoto, *A Daughter of the Samurai* (Garden City, Doubleday, 1925; Rutland, Vt., Charles E. Tuttle, 1966), as well as in her *A Daughter of the Narikin* (Garden City, Doubleday, 1932) and *A Daughter of the Nohfu* (Garden City, Doubleday, 1935); see also Shidzue Ishimoto, *Facing Two Ways* (N.Y., Farrar Rinehart, 1935); Katherine Sansom, *Living in Tokyo* (N.Y., Harcourt, Brace, 1937); and S. Akimoto, *Family Life in Japan* (Tokyo, Japanese Government Railways, 1937).

One of the interesting features of the postwar (1945 to the present) period is the quantity of feverish activity on the part of various religious groups. Two good introductory works on the postwar religious situation are Bunce's *Religions in Japan,* which was mentioned previously, and Niels C. Nielsen, Jr., *Religion and Philosophy in Contemporary Japan* (Houston, 1957; Rice Institute, Pamphlet XLIII, No. 4, Monograph in Philosophy). On the two thorny issues of the emperor system and the religious juridical persons in law, see G. Okubo, "Problems of the Emperor System in Postwar Japan" (Tokyo, 1948; Institute for Pacific Relations, Pacific Studies Series) and William P. Woodard, "The Religious Juridical Persons Law," *Contemporary Japan* (Tokyo, Foreign Affairs Association of Japan, 1960), 1–84. This period is thoroughly documented in William P. Woodard, *The Allied Occupation of Japan 1945–1952 and Japanese Religions* (Leiden, E.J. Brill, 1971). As a result of the initiative of the occupation authorities, technically referred to as General Headquarters (GHQ) of the Supreme Commander for the Allied Powers (SCAP), State Shinto was disestablished; but Shinto as a religion (Shrine Shinto) continues to attract adherents. Of about 110,000 shrines governed before the war by the Home Ministry, over two-thirds now belong to the Association of Shinto Shrines (*Jinja Honcho*). Sect (*Kyōha*) Shinto denominations enjoy freedom and independence; and two of them, Tenri-kyo and Konko-kyo, are not only expanding rapidly in Japan but are also attempting missionary work abroad. Buddhist denominations, while suffering from internal ecclesiastical divisions, are holding their strength both among the intelligentsia and the rural populations. Among Christian groups, Roman Catholics and the so-called fundamentalist wings of Protestantism have made rapid advances, while older Protestant denominations are also making some progress. By far the most significant development in the postwar religious scene in Japan is the emergence of new religions (*Shinkō Shūkyō*). Some of these are more properly splinter sects that were identified either with Shinto or Buddhism before the war. About one hundred of them belong to the Union of New Religions (*Shin-shū-ren*).

Regarding the contemporary religious situation, a useful volume is *Japanese Religion: A Survey by the Agency for Cultural Affairs* (Tokyo, Kodansha, 1972). Good up-to-date information can be secured from the publications of the International Institute for the Study of Religions (*Kokusai Shukyo Kenkyu Sho*), Tokyo. This Institute not only publishes an English quarterly, *Contemporary Religions in Japan,* but also produces a number of informative bulletins on such topical subjects as *Religion and Modern Life* (1958), *Religion and State in Japan* (1959)*, The Kami Way: An Introduction to Shrine Shinto* by S. Ono (1960), and *Living Buddhism in Japan,* by Y. Tamura and W.P. Woodard (1959). The Christian Center for the Study of Japanese Religions, Kyoto, publishes a bilingual quarterly, *Japanese Religions,* which has good articles on new religions. Another group called the Institute for Research in Religious Problems (*Shukyo Mondai Kenkyu Sho*), Tokyo, occasionally publishes reports in English called *Religions in Japan—At Present.*

Recently Edward Norbeck has provided insights into the contemporary religious situation from the viewpoint of cultural anthropology in his *Religion and Society in Modern Japan: Continuity and Change* (Houston, William Marsh Rice Univ., 1970). A number of sociological studies of Japanese religion have also added to the material available for understanding current developments: Kiyomi Morioka and William Newell, *The Sociology of Japanese Religion* (Leiden, E.J. Brill, 1968); F.M. Basabe, *Japanese Youth Confronts Religion* (N.Y., Prentice-Hall, 1967); F.M. Basabe, *Religious Attitudes of Japanese Men* (Tokyo, Sophia Univ., 1968); and Robert N. Bellah, ed., *Religion and Progress in Modern Asia* (N.Y., Free Press; and London, Collier-Macmillan, 1965).

On Shinto and related subjects, the Institute for Japanese Culture and Classics (*Nihonbunka Kenkyusho*) at Kokugakuin University, Tokyo, has been actively engaged in scholarly research. While most of its publications are in Japanese, in conjunction with the Association of Shinto Shrines it has published various informative booklets, such as *An Outline of Shinto Teachings* (1958) and *Basic Terms of Shinto* (1958). Wilhelmus Creemers has made a study of post-war Shinto, *Shrine Shinto after World War II* (Leiden, E.J. Brill, 1968). The postwar publications on Japanese Buddhism provide a true panoply, ranging from scholarly works to popular apologetics, and including as well quarterlies and bulletins such as *Young East* and *Zen Culture. The Journal of Indian and Buddhist Studies* and books published in honor of prominent scholars (D.T. Suzuki and S. Yamaguchi, for example) include articles in Western languages. In 1959 the Association of the Buddha Jayanti printed *Japan and Buddhism* and many short pieces in English. Saburo Ienaga's study, "Japan's Modernization and Buddhism," *Contemporary Religions in Japan,* VI (March, 1965), 1–41, might be mentioned, as well as Shōkō Watanabe, *Japanese Buddhism: A Critical Appraisal* (Tokyo, Kokusai Bunka Shinkokai, 1968). Articles by Japanese Buddhist scholars have appeared in international academic journals, also. Somewhat unique is the account of Shinsho Hanayama, a Buddhist chaplain who spent three years with the condemned Japanese war criminals in the Sugamo prison, *The Way of Deliverance* (London, Victor Gollancz, 1955). On the Christian side, both Roman Catholic and Protestant books and articles in Western languages have appeared in large quantity, including such works as Everett F. Briggs, *New Dawn in Japan* (Toronto and N.Y., Longmans, Green, 1948); R.T. Baker, *Darkness of the Sun* (Nashville, Abingdon-Cokesbury Press, 1947); W.C. Kerr, *Japan Begins Again* (N.Y., Friendship Press, 1949); C.W. Iglehart, *Cross and Crisis in Japan* (N.Y., Friedberg Press, 1957); N. Ebizawa, *Japanese Witness for Christ* (London, Association Press, 1957); Masao Takenaka, *Reconciliation and Renewal in Japan* (N.Y., Friendship Press and Student Volunteer Movement for Christian Missions, 1957); T. Ariga, "Christian Mission in Japan as a Theological Problem," *Religion in Life,* XXVII, 3 (Summer, 1958), 372–80; Carl Michalson, *Japanese Contributions to Christian Theology* (Philadelphia, Westminster Press, 1960); Charles Germany, *Protestant Theologies in Modern Japan: A History of Dominant Theological Currents from 1920–1960* (Tokyo, International Institute for the Study of Religion, 1965); Kitamori Kazoh, *Theology of the Pain of God* (translator not identified; Richmond, John Knox Press, 1965); and a number of books by Joseph Spae, including *Japanese Religiosity* (Tokyo, Oriens Institute for Religious Research, 1971).

Some of the Sect (*Kyōha*) Shinto denominations have been actively engaged in presenting their histories and doctrines in Western languages. This is especially true of Tenri-kyo, Konko-kyo, as well as of the semi-religious movement called Itto-en. On the so-called new religions (*Shinkō Shūkyō*), a variety of books and studies have been published recently, including much material published by the headquarters of the various new religions. Among the better comprehensive works are M.A. Bairy, *Japans neue Religionen in der Nachkriegzeit* (Bonn, Ludwig Röhrscheid, 1959); Harry Thomsen, *The New Religions of Japan* (Rutland, Charles E. Tuttle, 1963); Clark B. Offner and Henry van Straelen, *Modern Japanese Religions with Special Emphasis upon Their Doctrines of Healing* (Leiden, E.J. Brill, 1963); and H. Neill McFarland, *The Rush Hour of the Gods: A Study of New Religious Movements in Japan* (N.Y., Macmillan, 1967). The movement called Sōka Gakkai has recently received especially much attention; see, for example, Noah S. Brannen, *Sōka Gakkai: Japan's Militant Buddhists* (Richmond, John Knox Press, 1968); Kiyoaki Murata, *Japan's New Buddhism: An Objective Account of Soka Gakkai* (N.Y., Walker/Weather-Hill, 1969); James Allen Dator, *Soka Gakkai, Builders of the Third Civilization* (Seattle, Univ. of Washington Press, 1969); and James W. White, *The Sokagakkai and Mass Society* (Stanford, Stanford Univ. Press, 1970). For further bibliographical references on the various new religions, including materials published by each new religion, see H. Byron Earhart, *The New Religions of Japan: A Bibliography of Western-Language Materials* (Tokyo, Sophia Univ., 1970).

APPENDIX

I. Reference works relevant to religions of Japan

Bibliotheca Japonica, by Henri Cordier (Paris, Imprimerie nationale, 1912).

A Catalogue of the Chinese Translation of the Buddhist Tripitaka, by Bunyiu Nanjio (Oxford, Clarendon Press, 1883); reprint with additions, Daijo Tokiwa, et al., eds. (Tokyo, 1929).

Encyclopaedia Britannica, 1971 edition.

Encyclopedia of Buddhism, Japan Compilation Office, ed. (Tokyo, 1957).

An Encyclopedia of Religion, Vergilius Ferm, ed. (N.Y., Philosophical Library, 1943).

Encyclopedia of Religion and Ethics, James Hastings, ed. (N.Y., Charles Scribner's Sons, 1908–26).

Hôbôgirin: Dictionnaire encyclopédique du bouddhisme d'après les sources chinoises et japonaises, Paul Demiéville, ed. (Tokyo, 1929–37).

Japan Christian Year Book (Tokyo: Kyo Bun Kwan).

Japan—Its Land, People and Culture, by the Japanese National Commission for UNESCO (Tokyo, Printing Bureau, Ministry of Finance, 1958).

Proceedings of the IXth International Congress for the History of Religions, Tokyo and Kyoto, 1958 (Tokyo, Maruzen, 1960).

Die Religion in Geschichte und Gegenwart, H. Gunkel, and L. Zscharnack, eds. (Tübingen, J.C.B. Mohr, 1927–31).

Religionswissenschaftliches Wörterbuch, Franz König, ed. (Freiburg, Herder, 1956).

Religious Studies in Japan, Japanese Association for Religious Studies, ed. (Tokyo, Maruzen, 1959).

Sources of Japanese Tradition, comp. by Ryusaku Tsunoda, William Theodore de Bary, and Donald Keene (N.Y., Columbia Univ. Press, 1958).

II. Published bibliographies

A. General bibliographies on Japan

Hugh Borton, Serge Elisseef, William W. Lockwood, and John C. Pelzel, *A Selected List of Books and Articles on Japan,* rev. ed. (Cambridge, Harvard Univ. Press, 1954).

John W. Hall, *Japanese History: A Guide to Japanese Reference and Research Materials* (Ann Arbor, Univ. of Michigan Press, 1954).

D.G. Haring, *Books and Articles on Japan: A Reference List* (mimeo) (Syracuse, Syracuse Univ. Book Store, 1960).

Japan—Economic Development and Foreign Policy: A Selected List of References (Washington, Library of Congress, 1940).

Hyman Kublin, *What Shall I Read on Japan? An Introductory Guide* (N.Y., Japan Society, 1956).

Oskar Nachod, *Bibliography of the Japanese Empire,* vols. 1 and 2 (London, E. Goldston, 1928), vols. 3 and 4 (Leipzig, K.W. Hiersemann, 1931–35).

Kokusai Bunka Shinkokai, *A Short Bibliography on Japan* (English Books) (Tokyo, 1936).

————, *Kurze Bibliographie der Bücher über Japan, in Deutsch, Hollandisch, Danisch, Schwedisch und Norwegisch* (Tokyo, 1938).

Friedrich von Wenckstern, *A Bibliography of the Japanese Empire,* vol. I (Leiden, E.J. Brill, 1895), vol. 2 (Tokyo, Z.P. Maruya, 1907).

Robert E. Ward, *A Guide to Japanese Reference and Research Materials in the Field of Political Science* (Ann Arbor, Univ. of Michigan Press, 1950).

[*See also* in the annual bibliography of the *Journal of Asian Studies* (formerly the *Far Eastern Quarterly*), the section on Japan.]

B. Shinto

Jean Herbert, *Bibliographie du Shintō et des sectes shintōistes* (Leiden, E.J. Brill, 1968).

Genchi Kato, et al., *A Bibliography of Shinto in Western Languages from the Oldest till 1952* (Tokyo, 1953).

C. Japanese Buddhism

Shōjun Bando, et al., *A Bibliography on Japanese Buddhism* (Tokyo, C.I.I.B. Press, 1958). (This bibliography, pp. 1–7, lists other bibliographies that contain references to Japanese Buddhism.)

D. New Religions

Christian Center for the Study of Japanese Religions, *Bibliography on the New Religions* (Kyoto, 1960).

H. Byron Earhart, *The New Religions of Japan: A Bibliography of Western-Language Materials* (Tokyo, Sophia Univ., 1970).

E. Religions in general

International Association for the History of Religions, *International Bibliography of the History of Religions* (Leiden, E.J. Brill, 1954 ff.)

III. Periodicals relevant to religions of Japan

Bulletin de l'École française d'extrême-orient   (BEFEO)
Bulletin de la Maison Franco-Japonaise   (BMFJ)
Contemporary Religions in Japan   (CRJ)
Eastern Buddhist   (EB) (New series, 1965–   )
East and West   (EW)
Folklore Studies   (FS)
France-Asie   (FA)
Harvard Journal of Asiatic Studies   (HJAS)
History of Religions, An International Journal for Comparative Historical Studies   (HR)
Japan Quarterly   (JQ)
Japanese Religions   (JR)

Journal asiatique   (JA)
Journal of the American Oriental Society   (JAOS)
Journal of Asian Studies   (JAS) formerly *Far Eastern Quarterly* (FEQ)
Journal of the Royal Asiatic Society of Great Britain and Ireland   (JRAS)
Monumenta Nipponica   (MN)
Nachrichten der Deutschen Gesellschaft für Natur- und Völkerkunde Ostasiens
    (NDGNVO)
Numen, International Review for the History of Religions   (NMN)
Ostasiatische Zeitschrift   (OAZ)
Philosophy East and West   (PEW)
Proceedings of the Imperial Academy of Japan   (PIAJ)
The Middle Way   (TMW)
The Young East   (TYE)
Transactions of the Asiatic Society of Japan   (TASJ)
Weiner völkerkundliche Mitteilungen   (WVM)
Zeitschrift für Missionskunde und Religionswissenschaft   (ZMKR)

X

Early and Classical Judaism

Judah Goldin

I. INTRODUCTION

Drawing up a select bibliography on the Jewish religion * presents a serious problem, particularly if the works to be included are limited essentially to the English language. To take but one example, no study of Judaism may ignore the investigation of the use and interpretation of Scripture in the Synagogue, for this was central to Jewish worship as well as intellectual development; but there is nothing in English to replace, or even correspond to, L. Zunz's classic *Die gottesdienstlichen Vorträge der Juden,* which appeared in 1832—and, incidentally, inaugurated the modern critical-historical study of Judaism—and was amplified in its second edition in 1892. Since the modern critical study of Judaism, its history and literature, began in Germany, German was the language in which many pioneering and important works were written, and the earnest student must refer to them again and again.

Zunz's volume is today available in Hebrew translation, *Ha-Derashot be-Yisrael* (Jerusalem, Mosad Bialik, 5707–1946), and by adding his notes to this edition, Ch. Albeck has enriched the work and brought it up to date. But even more serious is the problem created by the fact that quite

---

* I want to thank Doctor Leon Nemoy for a number of valuable suggestions which I have incorporated in the following pages.

a number of works such as this, which are fundamental requirements for the understanding of major aspects of Judaism, are written in Hebrew. Without a knowledge of Hebrew it is almost hopeless to gain insight into this complex religion and its traditions: despite its limitations and its being out of date, there is no counterpart either in English or in any European language to I.H. Weiss's *Dor Dor ve-Doreshav* (several times reprinted; I have before me the Wilna, Buchhandlung L. Goldenberg in Elisawetgrad, 1911 ed.), which attempted to trace the development of the tradition that became normative for Judaism through the authoritative role of the oral Torah and the Talmud. (On this work, see at least S. Schechter's essay, "The History of Jewish Tradition," in *Studies of Judaism,* first series [N.Y., Macmillan, 1896; Philadelphia, Jewish Publication Society, 1938], pp. 182–212.) Or, again, for critical study of the development and character of the Mishnah, that "code" which is the cornerstone of the whole talmudic structure, one must still turn and return to the literature from Z. Frankel's *Darke ha-Mishnah* (Warsaw, M.L. Cailingold, 1923) to J.N. Epstein's *Mabo le-Nusah ha-Mishnah* (Jerusalem, the author, 5708–1947)—there is no substitute for such works.

It is tempting to give illustration after illustration to make adequately vivid how dependent one is on Hebrew, not only for the study of the religion's primary sources (which goes without saying), but also for access to responsible and illuminating secondary ones. The language problem is serious enough, but there are two further problems which cannot be solved by a simple formula (that is, to learn the languages) and to which attention must be directed even in a bibliographical essay, although they are of more than bibliographical consequence. The first is that when a work describes the religion as it is reflected in the primary literary source—the Bible, let us say—to what extent is the description a description of the actual religious mentality and practice of the moment and to what extent is it a description of the idealized formulation? Are the collections of laws incorporated in the Pentateuch, for example, a record of generally accepted norms of conduct (when? right after the conquest of the Holy Land? during the period of the kings? in post-exilic times?) or merely idealized constructions of priestly or prophetic demands while the current religious practice, sincerely followed and faithfully obeyed and conventionally approved, was something different? When in postbiblical times a particular ceremony is described in the Mishnah—say, the ordeal for the suspected wife (Numbers 5:11–31)—how much, if any, of the description is an actual account of the proceedings, and how much is merely the result of academic imagining and exegetical exercise?

This is a serious problem for the historian; but it is no less a problem for the bibliographer who wishes to select a partial but properly representative list of works which describe the Jewish religion *as it was.* This kind of problem, however, faces the student of other religions too. Special complications arise for Judaism because there is an indivisible connection between the people called Jews and the religion called Judaism. Often the very character of the religion can be understood only in terms of the history of the Jews. Had it not been for the destruction of the Jerusalem Temple in the first century, presumably Jewish worship would still include institutions now of archeological interest only—or of eschatological yearning. The specific texture or flavor of Jewish cultural life was often determined by conditions governing the particular country where one of the diaspora communities was located (for example, the intellectual idiom of eleventh-century Spanish Jewry was quite different from that of Franco-German Jewries of the same century), and proper appreciation of the religious life of the Jews involves frequently not only the study of purely religious expression but also attention to the history of the people. Furthermore, since so much *cultural* activity was related to the religious sources and the religious life—poetry being the poetry of the synagogue, philosophy being a rational defense of the faith, grammar being an attempt to explain holy scriptures, and so on—the study of Judaism always becomes more profound and more revealing as more and more attention is paid to the study of Jewish literature as a whole—at least so long as we deal with Judaism and Jewish life up to the beginnings of modern times (let us say, up to the latter part of the eighteenth century). And even in modern times, by way of one final word, much of so-called secular Jewish literature can be properly understood only against the background of—as in response to or reaction against—the religious life and ideal.

II. JUDAISM AND THE JEWS

The relationship between Judaism and the Jews, the extraordinary vitality of the religion and the people under various and frequently disastrous circumstances, the continuity of a recognizable tradition despite varieties of adaptation, the role of the religion not only in the history of the Jews but in the history and context of the world, the future direction of Judaism as well as the future of the Jews—in short, the meaning of the total Jewish experience—have been subjects for reflection on the part of practically every serious Jewish thinker and historian. It would be most naive to imagine that such reflection began with modern times; in one form or another, the meaning of Jewish existence and experience is already contemplated by the prophets, is reflected upon by Philo and by the talmudic rabbis in many Midrashim, is a compelling theme for post-talmudic homilists and compilers of chronicles, and so on down through the centuries. On the other hand, it is very probably true that the modern formulation of questions about the meaning of Jewish experience is characterized by its nontheological idiom; even if the answer given in the end is not entirely dependent on exclusively rational categories, the modern man attempts to ask his question and to make answer in the vocabulary and framework which are independent of dogmatic considerations and credal imperatives. A great many essays have been written on the meaning of Judaism and the Jews, some in English. (Since below we shall be speaking of H. Graetz, let me mention his fine essay *Die Konstruktion der jüdischen Geschichte* [Berlin, Schocken, 1936], with an epilogue and useful bibliography.) We shall refer to four (but see by the way the essay by M.R. Cohen, "Philosophies of Jewish History," in the first volume of *Jewish Social Studies* [1939], 39–72).

In S.M. Dubnow's *Jewish History* (Philadelphia, Jewish Publication Society of America, 1903) (a short book which appeared originally in 1893 as an essay in Russian) the distinguished historian and author of the *Weltgeschichte* does not yet make the sociological emphasis which characterized so much of his subsequent thinking and writing—that is, the emphasis on Jews and Judaism as a national minority culture and their autonomy within a larger majority political framework. But he does attempt to answer the question, "What is the essential meaning, what the spirit, of Jewish history?" After a compact review of Jewish history from its beginnings through the nineteenth century, Dubnow presents briefly what are to him the lessons of that long experience (his language is characteristically nineteenth-century spiritual-idealistic): Jewry is a spiritual nation at all times permeated by a creative principle which is itself the product of religious, moral, and philosophical ideals; of historic memories; and of a consciousness that it has yet great deeds to accomplish in the future, as it accomplished them in the past. In the light of the events of the past four decades, there is even a kind of pathos to the last sentence of Dubnow's essay: "Jewish history in its entirety is the pledge of the spiritual union between the Jews and the rest of the nations."

Views much more characteristic of Dubnow's reflections on Jews and Jewish history are available in *Nationalism and History. Essays on Old and New Judaism by Simon Dubnow,* ed. by K.S. Pinson (Philadelphia, Jewish Publication Society of America, 1958) (in which, by the way, his essay *Jewish History* is reprinted). In his introductory essay Pinson also discusses Dubnow's theories of nationalism.

More philosophical, and possibly more profound, is the essay *Galut,* by Y.F. Baer (N.Y., Schocken Books, 1947), originally written in German. This work by the leading authority on the Jews in Christian Spain (vol. I of his history has now been translated into English by L. Schoffman and issued by the Jewish Publication Society of America, Philadelphia, 1961, under the title *The History of the Jews in Christian Spain*) begins with the proposition that because "of the Jews' exalted consciousness of religious superiority and of their mission among the nations, a consciousness all the more infuriating because it exists in a nation totally without power," the Jew is inseparably bound up with Galut—that is, not only exile but all the outrages of being an exile, an alien. For Baer the principles historians employ when they attempt to understand and explain all other nations are inadequate for the understanding of Jewish history and experiences. That is not to say that economic and social and political and international forces do not operate within Jewish history, but that these "natural" laws fail to explain the Jewish character, the persistence of this tiny people that has been without the basic material equipment the successful nations have enjoyed. ". . . The history of the Jewish people remains distinct from the astrologically determined history of the nations (i.e., a history determined by causes operating within the finished framework of nature), for the Jewish people in its special relationship to God is removed from the context of natural law." Jewish history, therefore, follows its own laws. One may put it this way perhaps: whereas in his essay Dubnow's categories were spiritual and hopeful, Baer's are more forthrightly religious, growing particularly out of the cataclysm in German-Jewish life. This will explain why so much of the essay concentrates on aspects of redemption and messianism.

One Jewish thinker and writer very well known among intellectuals of the Western world (his impact on some contemporary Protestant expression has been profound) is M. Buber. Much of his writing has been devoted to an exploration of the meaning of the Jewish spirit and the Jewish word and Jewish living, but for our immediate purpose the volume of essays called *Israel and the World. Essays in a Time of Crisis* (N.Y., Schocken Books, 1948) is probably most relevant. The essays were not all written at one time or for one particular audience; nevertheless, taken together, they "combine into a theory," as Buber says, "representing the teachings of Israel." For Buber the most essential fact of the Jewish faith is that history, of all nations and of every individual, is a dialogue with God; not dogma but encounter is of primary importance in Judaism. Under the headings "Jewish Religiosity," "Biblical Life," "Learning and Education" (in connection with the essays in this section it would be profitable to see Franz Rosenzweig, *On Jewish Learning,* ed. by N.N. Glatzer [N.Y., Schocken Books, 1955]), "Israel and the World," "Nationalism and Zion," Buber undertakes not only to "clarify the relation of certain aspects of Jewish thinking and Jewish living to contemporary intellectual movements," but also to "analyze and refute" whatever current ideologies within Jewish life lead to the weakening and defeat of the internal authentic Jewish teaching. Since the whole world of humanity is intended to achieve a genuine unity, that one nation (Israel) which once heard the charge and assented to it must so live, not merely as masses of individuals but entirely as a nation, as to bring true humanity into fulfillment. It is in terms like these that Buber finds the meaning of Judaism and the Jews; but in nothing less than terms like these does he see the meaning of Zionism too (see further below).

On the relationship of Jews and Judaism, it will be wise to consult also the opening chapter of S.W. Baron's multivolume history, *A Social and Religious History of the Jews* (N.Y., Columbia Univ. Press, 1952–58; on this work, see further below). The essay in a sense serves to make prominent what are, to the author, the distinctive features of Jewish society and religion: the interdependence of Jews and Judaism, the historical-ethical direction given by the religion to what may have been in remote origins nature festivals, the ethical dimension of the chosen-people concept, the independence, ultimately, of the religion from the fate of any particular state or territory, simultaneous affirmation by Judaism of nationalism and universalism. It is the presence of these features within Judaism that gives both the people and the religion their particular insights into reality, their historical preoccupations, and the impulse toward achievement in certain directions.

Reflections more or less along the lines of the four works we have referred to occur in many other writings to which reference will be made under other rubrics. One work, written in Hebrew, Yehezkel Kaufmann's *Gola Ve-Nekar (In Exile and among Aliens;* 1929–32, Tel Aviv, Debir; 2nd ed., 1954), would especially have to be consulted by the serious student concerned with the philosophy of history, for Kaufmann's two-volume work is one of the most serious and thoroughgoing historical-sociological investigations of Jewish history and fate in any language, and by any thinker. To attempt to summarize this work in a sentence or two would be almost caricaturing it, for it is a detailed review of basic issues and movements from biblical days to the present time. Only against Kaufmann's full discussion can justice be done to his emphasis on the ideals of national redemption, of which not even independent statehood is the realization, let alone fulfillment. To Kaufmann what national redemption involves is a completely radical reorientation on the part of the people as it recognizes in itself the *need* for redemption from the political and cultural servitude of generations of dependence on others and the yearning to lose its individuality.

At all events, whatever the direction taken by any particular thinker on the theme of Jews and Judaism, one point is clear (and perhaps this is the most significant fact about such works): none of them is able to assume that this relationship, and the destiny that may be in store for it, is only accidental, and that, therefore, no special meanings are to be sought. On the contrary, even when the reflection is carried on in purely secular discourse, all of these thinkers try to clarify the organic nature of that relationship and to evaluate its significance in terms not only of the past but also of the future. The relation of Jews and Judaism, in short, is for them not only a datum of past history or current events but also a condition for the future vitality of the religion and achievement of the people, whatever that may be. Thus this very relationship between Jews and Judaism brings the student of Judaism to a study of the history of the Jews.

III. HISTORIES AND STANDARD WORKS

As for full-scale histories, one inevitably begins with H. Graetz's six-volume *History of the Jews* (Philadelphia, Jewish Publication Society of America, 1891, but frequently reprinted), and again I must apologize for not being able to refer to the original German work (*Geschichte der Juden,* 11 vols. in 13, 1897–1911) with its copious notes, or to the Hebrew translation, which is also rich in notes of its own (although because of the Russian censor, some of the German notes had to be omitted). The English version is a condensation of the original German volumes but has no notes at all; however, while in the original the account went from the beginnings to 1848, in the English version the history is continued (not too fully) to 1870. A companion volume on Jewish life from the middle of the nineteenth century to Hitler's war against the Jews was published in 1944 by the Jewish Publication Society of America (Philadelphia): I. Elbogen, *A Century of Jewish Life.*

Of course, in many ways Graetz's work is outdated; major sources of Jewish history which were discovered at the end of the last and beginning of the present century were unknown to him, let alone momentous discoveries of recent decades and the results of archeological work. Moreover, on some subjects Graetz disqualified himself: he was totally impatient with mysticism in any of its manifestations, and he was insensitive to the color of life in the eastern European centers. Even more serious is the charge by the critical historians that Graetz saw Jewish history principally as response to persecution, as suffering on the one hand and spiritual and literary creation on the other.

The fact remains that Graetz's performance is still overwhelming. His single-handed attempt at a *complete* critical accounting of Jewish history from the beginnings to the mid-nineteenth century, not only using the results of research by other men but himself furnishing the material he would require in synthesis, is one of the principal achievements of nineteenth-century Jewish scholarship. Especially because he wrote with fervor, his work is still eminently readable, and for a coherent account (even if sometimes we would prefer a different scheme or organization), his work is still where one begins. Even when one disagrees, he does not pass Graetz by.

More sociological, and much more understanding of the eastern European milieu and its movements and personalities, is S. Dubnow's ten-volume work, to which we have already referred, *Die Weltgeschichte des jüdischen Volkes* (1925–29). A Hebrew translation of this work exists, but unfortunately no English one (his three-volume *History of the Jews in Russia and Poland,* tr. by I. Friedlaender [Philadelphia, Jewish Publication Society of America, 1916–20] is an excellent counterbalance to Graetz). Dubnow's history takes much more into account social and economic influences than does Graetz, his attention to purely secular manifestations is much more lively than is Graetz's, and the organization of his subject matter along the lines of development within different geographical centers makes his chapters more immediately comprehensible than does a purely chronological scheme.

An ambitious and impressive undertaking, still in the course of appearing, is S.W. Baron's *A Social and Religious History of the Jews.* An earlier and shorter version in three volumes first appeared in 1937 (N.Y., Columbia Univ. Press), but in 1952 the longer version began to appear. To date eight volumes plus an index volume have been published (N.Y. and Philadelphia), covering the history from the beginning to 1200. Baron's work is particularly noteworthy on three scores. First, it provides one of the most comprehensive bibliographies on Jews and Judaism one is likely to find anywhere; the references in the notes especially are a rich source of assistance not only to a beginner but often to specialists as well. Second, the organization of themes and problems offers a fresh approach for students of Jewish history. Baron is concerned with principal motifs of the history rather than aspects of chronicling, either by way of centuries or geographical centers: one may say that Baron is eager to describe not events, even major ones, but major patterns of development. Thus the *History* is not a narrative but a commentary on the narrative one has learned in other and earlier works. Third—and this obviously is related to the second point—Baron has approached Jewish history with the skills and perspective of the modern general social scientist. His approach is familiar to the modern student of general history. By exploring, for example, demographic factors, by paying especially close attention to economic and sociological influences in the milieu at large, Baron has often provided explanations for the dynamics of Jewish life which were not anticipated, inevitably, by earlier historians. The *Social and Religious History* is thus a characteristic *modern* work; that is to say, it is the product of the advances made by the social science disciplines in modern times and an awareness of modern historiographical tendencies.

As a companion to Baron's *History,* it is often instructive to examine his three-volume study of *The Jewish Community* (Philadelphia, Jewish Publication Society of America, 1942) from the biblical Palestinian municipality down to the period of the American revolution. The principal focus of the work is on the structure of the European community of the Middle Ages and early modern times. Here too we see Baron preoccupied with the social institution, the features of and the forces operative in a complex societal reality. And while he is expressly aware of the ambiguities of the term "community" in relation to diverse Jewish settlements in the Diaspora, his analysis helps create coherence in what might otherwise be a confused picture with a host of disjointed facts—and this in a universe of discourse especially congenial to the modern social scientist and historian.

There is today no longer any dearth of shorter, one-volume histories of the Jews, though unfortunately not many are either reliable or particularly illuminating. The three works we shall refer to have at least the merit of trustworthiness and competence in understanding the original sources, despite their other limitations. *A History of the Jewish People* by M.L. Margolis and A. Marx (Philadelphia, Jewish Publication Society of America, 1927 and frequently reprinted), is, strictly speaking, a chronicle of events, persons, and achievements, with hardly any attempt at interpretation or explanation. As a handbook of "facts," it is still perhaps the most convenient and accurate single-volume collection.

A History of the Jews by S. Grayzel (Philadelphia, Jewish Publication Society of America, 1947) begins its account, not with the biblical period, but with the Babylonian exile and goes down to the end of World War II. Grayzel's volume is essentially a textbook, the kind of work one would use for classroom instruction, and while it suffers from a homiletical tone of voice and point of view, it is by and large a dependable account of Jewish experience and achievement. Furthermore, the author's attitude can at least suggest which aspects of Jewish history have taken on special value for Jews devoted to their tradition and settled in Western countries.

The third one-volume work is a collaborative enterprise by a number of scholars, *Great Ages and Ideas of the Jewish People,* ed. by L.W. Schwarz (Toronto, Random House of Canada, 1956). As the title itself reveals, the various chapters are essentially essays attempting to present principal intellectual and cultural developments during key periods of Jewish history, from biblical days to modern times. Perhaps the aim of the work may best be suggested by the following sentence from the editor's introduction: "We do not hesitate to say that four thousand years of experience have evolved a cluster of ideas and values that are uniquely Jewish and that remain significant for modern men and women." In other words, the individual chapters seek, each for its own period, to find the principal ideas growing out of the Jewish experience and governing Jewish expression and expectation.

There are, even in English, a number of historical studies of particular Jewries in particular countries, and of particular periods, to which the student with special interests will turn (and to some of which reference will be made below in relevant sections). But if it is true that a knowledge of what was happening to the Jews will often make the emphases of their religion intelligible, it is even more true that a knowledge of Jewish culture, especially literature, will introduce one to the intellectual and articulate form—to the very vocabulary, one might say—of the religious substance.

Here, too, we are not dealing with an altogether simple phenomenon. Despite the strong attachment of Jewish intellectual activity to religious living and conduct, one is often hard put to classify certain Jewish writings even before modern times—even before, that is, Jewish society, like Western society in general, was secularized. First of all, one might say that the abundance of secular medieval Hebrew poetry, for example, is *not* relevant to the religion. But, secondly and more importantly, a historian of literature might well and justly classify certain works as studies (let us say) in lexicography and grammar—categories which to a modern Westerner hardly suggest religious exercise. (And possibly for the original grammarian too *as he worked,* the purely technical and substantive problems of his work proved so entirely engaging that for the time being he too thought more in terms of his immediate problems than in terms of the religious background to which his work belonged.) Nevertheless, these works may constitute an active expression of religious concern—an undertaking, for instance, to explain the language or the teaching of a sacred text. Especially since for Judaism the study and interpretation of sacred texts became a paramount activity in *piety,* and the range of study and interpretation was as extensive as the resources and the age provided, a considerable amount of Jewish literature has direct bearing on Jewish religious thought and the very life of the religion. That is why some study of Jewish literature is germane to the study of Judaism as a religion. And a convenient survey of this literature from the close of the Bible down to almost the present is available in the five volumes by M. Waxman, *A History of Jewish Literature* (N.Y., Thomas Yoseloff, latest ed., 1960): the discussions do attempt to be comprehensive and incorporate the results of much modern research.

Finally, among such general accounts might be mentioned several useful standard works of reference, most prominent of which (though in many ways outdated) is *The Jewish Encyclopedia* in twelve volumes (N.Y., Funk & Wagnalls, 1901–06). Leading scholars and authorities were among the contributors of articles, and, especially in the first few volumes, there are a number of studies that are still of prime significance. The discussions of classical literature and subjects uppermost in the minds of nineteenth-century western European Jewish scholars are especially valuable. In German and not completed because of the Hitler disaster (only ten volumes appeared through "Lyra," Berlin, 1928–34) is the *Encyclopedia Judaica;** like the *Jewish Encyclopedia* in English, this is a very serious work on the highest possible standards, with many articles by very distinguished scholars who incorporated the results of their own (and others') major

* There is now an English version of *Encyclopedia Judaica.* It is not a translation of the German version but contains many articles from it.

research. *The Universal Jewish Encyclopedia,* 10 vols. (N.Y., Universal Jewish Encyclopedia, 1939–43), is largely a popular work, particularly for the historical subjects covered more fully in the older *Jewish Encyclopedia;* but on certain subjects related to modern times—above all, events and developments in the twentieth century—it is not only more up to date but at times truly extensive in treatment.

In addition to the encyclopedias, there are available two excellent works which present not only surveys of Jewish history but also studies of the wide range of Jewish thought and expression and experiences in both the past and the present. They are both popular in that they deliberately avoid the speech of the technical monograph and the specialist's tone of voice, but the serious and responsible presentations are admirable as introductions to the study of numerous aspects of Judaism. One is *The Jewish People: Past and Present* (N.Y., Central Yiddish Culture Organization, 1946–52) in four volumes (based principally on an earlier version in Yiddish); the other is *The Jews: Their History, Culture and Religion,* ed. by L. Finkelstein, 3rd ed. (N.Y., Harper & Brothers, 1960), which is more extensive than the two earlier editions. Both works are handsomely published. Especially valuable are the bibliographies they provide in connection with each subject discussed. Above all, they convey a genuine sense of the dynamic character of Jewish life—its manifoldness, its tensions and resolutions, its response to external and internal pressures in the different periods of its existence. And in both a concern for continued Jewish existence and achievement is evident. (For an earlier collection of essays on what might be called aspects of the Hebrew and Jewish genius, still both readable and instructive, see E.R. Bevan and C. Singer, *The Legacy of Israel* [Oxford, Clarendon Press, 1927]).

It is probably true to say that such works are themselves illustrative of a ferment or restlessness or vitality within Jewish society, especially since the third decade of the present century. As a result of critical and historical research of the previous hundred years, the beginnings of summary formulation and synthesis could finally be contemplated. Moreover, as a result of the shift of center of gravity, particularly from eastern Europe to America, and the rise of a generation whose language was English, whose sense of relationship to a Jewish past was fading, and whose identity as Jews might to them be meaningless except on terms of ethnic liability, it was inevitable that Jewish scholars should once again (as in previous ages) undertake to explore the origins and direction of Jewish existence in an idiom which would be comprehensible to contemporaries. Furthermore, the extent of the disasters which overtook Jews in Europe and various parts of Asia and Africa unavoidably stirred up a renewed self-consciousness among Jews, one of whose phases was bound to be a re-examination of what they were and what they could expect of and for themselves. It is a safe guess that just as in recent general fiction Jewish themes and characters have begun to appear with a frequency unanticipated early in the century, so in the next two to three decades there will be increasing attention to Judaism by Jewish and non-Jewish students of religion and culture and social science (compare, for example, the essay by Edmund Wilson, "The Need for Judaic Studies" in his *A Piece of My Mind* [N.Y., Farrar, Straus & Cudahy, 1956] pp. 151–58). And the existence of the independent State of Israel will add to the liveliness of curiosity and speculation and argument.

IV. A FEW REMARKS ON PRIMARY SOURCES IN TRANSLATION

The very circumstances which have led to the creation of a growing body of literature in English *on* Judaism have, at the same time, led to the translation into English of primary literary sources, hitherto either not translated at all or translated into one of the other European languages (most often in the past century into German). Although it may not seem to be immediately germane to our discussion of books in English, something of the vigorous efforts being made in the present to revive preoccupation with the roots of the classical intellectual and religious tradition may be conveyed by the fact that in the State of Israel basic works of research composed in the past century in German (the work of Zunz and Geiger and Goldziher, for example) are now being translated into Hebrew and brought up to date through the addition of notes. These include not only secondary sources, but primary ones as well: a Hebrew translation of the Babylonian Talmud (from the original Aramaic) is being prepared, and substantial portions of the Kabbalistic classic, the *Zohar,* have been translated into Hebrew (and also rearranged in organization to help study particular motifs).

Of course, there is more than one reason for such developments. Evidently, even with a knowledge of Hebrew one may be far removed from the basic texts and sentiments of the classical religious tradition. The point is that in order properly to appreciate why increased activity of translation into English is taking place, it is necessary to look upon that activity not as some accidental and local phenomenon, but against the larger background of contemporary Jewish life as a whole. That the primary sources require translation everywhere is a sign not only of the results of alienation, but also of the resolution to recover for a new generation a sense of immediate kinship with the past. And the translations into Hebrew as well as English must be understood as an expression of that same resolution. But obviously the problem is much more serious where there is no knowledge of Hebrew at all.

Rather than list each and every work now available in English translation, we will refer only to some general series of publications; and only in the appropriate sections will specific reference be made to the relevant individual items. At this point it will be sufficient therefore if we call attention to the following: the Schiff Classics of the Jewish Publication Society of America; the translations by the scholars associated with the Soncino Press in England: *The Babylonian Talmud,* under the editorship of I. Epstein (London, Soncino Press, 1936), *Midrash Rabbah,* under the editorship of H. Friedman and M. Simon (1939), and *The Zohar,* by H. Sperling and M. Simon; the various Jewish texts published in translation by scholars for the Society for Promoting Christian Knowledge; the translations published by the East and West Library in England (Phaidon Press); and the Yale University Judaica Series. For apocrypha and pseudepigrapha there is not only the well-known collection in two volumes under the editorship of R.H. Charles, *The Apocrypha and Pseudepigrapha of the Old Testament in English* (Oxford, Clarendon Press, 1913), but a series of text and translation, in the Dropsie College Jewish Apocryphal Literature Series, of which six volumes have thus far appeared.

V. ON THE RELIGION OF ISRAEL AND THE HEBREW SCRIPTURES

Even if one limits himself to works in the English language, there is such a fantastic volume of studies on the history, literature, and religion of Israel and the Hebrew Scriptures (what Christians call the Old Testament), that if we were to do no more than list a long bibliography, even incomplete, the titles themselves would run on, seemingly endlessly. But this would achieve only a hypnotic effect. We shall deliberately choose only a few works—naturally such choice does reflect a personal value judgment—and content ourselves with the following additional observation: in several of the works referred to there are excellent bibliographical lists, which will lead the student to further discussion of the particular subject he decides to explore.

So closely related to the problems of the *literature* of the Hebrew Scriptures are the problems of the *religion,* that some orientation toward the literature is required before one can properly appreciate the discussions and presentations of the religion. For an approach characteristic of what is called the "higher critical school," associated especially with the epochal work of J. Wellhausen (for the English reader there is available, now in paperback, his *Prolegomena to the History of Ancient Israel* [Toronto, Longmans, Green, 1957])—the different documentary sources it distinguishes, the dates it attaches to these respective sources, its view of the line of development of Israelite thought and faith—and for detailed discussion in defense of that approach, plus a very full bibliography and documentation, R.H. Pfeiffer's *Introduction to the Old Testament* (N.Y., Harper & Brothers, 1941) is about as thorough and painstaking a one-volume work on the subject as is available. On the basis of conclusions arrived at by such literary analysis, there are many histories of Israelite religion, and we shall mention three: H.P. Smith, *The Religion of Israel* (N.Y., Charles Scribner's Sons, 1914), W.O.E. Oesterley and T.H. Robinson, *Hebrew Religion, Its Origin and Development* (N.Y., Macmillan, 1930), and, most recently, R.H. Pfeiffer's own posthumous *Religion in the Old Testament* (N.Y., Harper & Brothers, 1961), edited by C.C. Forman. It would be preposterous to say that these three works, and others that are close to them in outlook and spirit, agree in every detail or present the same outline of the religion from beginning to end. Nor are they necessarily the best of their kind. But they are representative and essentially united by the following: a robust dismissal of the possibility that a number of traditions ascribed to the Age of Moses is credible; a conviction that most of the narratives about the periods before the Conquest of the Promised Land are later legends pure and simple; an evolutionary hypothesis that explains the development of the religion of Israel from primitive conceptions and institutions, in the beginnings regarded as legitimate and proper, to an exalted monotheism of profound spiritual and ethical content arrived at gradually and only in the course of the prophetic period; and a strong feeling that notions and practices and expressions recorded by Scripture, if they can be compared with parallels in other cultures, almost certainly have the same meaning in Scripture as they have in the other contexts. (For a strong protest against this last presumption see N.H. Snaith, *The Distinctive Ideas of the Old Testament* [Philadelphia, Westminster Press, 1946].)

Altogether opposed to these conclusions, and indeed to all the more or less current accounts of Israelite religion, is Y. Kaufmann, whose great work *The Religion of Israel* has finally been superbly abridged and translated from the original eight volumes in Hebrew by M. Greenberg (Chicago, Univ. of Chicago Press, 1960: strictly speaking, the translation and abridgment are of the first seven volumes). Kaufmann accepts the idea that different documentary sources were combined to form the present Pentateuch no less than do the critics generally, but, by attentive study of these very sources, and especially by close analysis of the critical argumentation in defense of the chronological scheme imposed on those sources, he is led to fundamental revisions of dating and a presentation of the religion of Israel radically and most profoundly different from that at which the critics arrive. In the first place, Kaufmann derives from the biblical sources themselves the concept that Israel's monotheism was not an idea gradually attained (after many centuries) and then only by an intellectual, prophetic, or priestly elite, but, on the contrary, was an original, primary intuitive conception held by the folk at large, governing all Israelite thinking from the Mosaic period on (to such a degree that no longer can one find in the biblical record an adequate or just understanding of the pagan religions of Israel's neighbors; these religions to Israel are mere fetishism). Second, the added knowledge today of the high civilizations in the ancient Near East makes unwarranted many of the critics' assumptions about the necessary late dates for some forms of biblical speculation. In the third place, although Israelite life and thought were rooted in the high civilizations of the ancient Near East, a comparative study of religious forms (cult, mythology, magic, morality, notions of sin) underscores the *essential* differences that separate pagan religions from the religion of Israel. The distinguishing mark of pagan thought is "the idea that there exists a realm of being prior to the gods and above them, upon which the gods depend, and whose decrees they must obey," while "the biblical religious idea, visible in the earliest strata, permeating even the 'magical' legends, is of a supernal God, above every cosmic law, fate, and compulsion; unborn, unbegetting. . . . An unfettered divine will transcends all being—this is the mark of biblical religion and that which sets it apart from all the religions of the earth." Biblical religion is thus *absolutely* different from the religion of the pagan world. (In this connection see also the important essay by M. Greenberg, "Some Postulates of Biblical Criminal Law" in *Yehezkel Kaufmann Jubilee Volume* [Jerusalem, 1960], 5–28.)

Whatever else Kaufmann's biblical studies may accomplish (and their influence was felt among those scholars who were reading his volumes as they appeared in Hebrew from 1937 on), it is clear that they have made much more tentative a number of propositions which had been regarded as basic and almost beyond dispute by European and American biblical criticism. This is particularly true as regards the relationship between Pentateuch and former prophets' literature and the writings of the literary prophets.

Kaufmann's history of the religion of Israel does represent a milestone in biblical studies (see in this connection N.M. Sarna, "From Wellhausen to Kaufmann," *Midstream* [N.Y., Summer, 1961], 64–74 and, even earlier [Sept., 1950], H.L. Ginsberg's essay, "New Trends in Biblical Criticism," in *Commentary,* 276–84); but it would be inaccurate to leave the impression that, except for his challenge, studies of Israelite religion have otherwise been uniformly written along the lines suggested by the classical *literary* criticism. Archeology and the advances made in the knowledge of ancient Near Eastern languages have also had a strong effect on biblical studies (and yet in this connection see the remarks by J.J. Finkelstein, "The Bible, Archaeology and History," in *Commentary* [April, 1959], 341–49); inevitably this has led to reconsideration of the character of the religion. Especially noteworthy of the new trends in biblical research has been the distinguished work of A. Alt, whose investigations of what he calls "territorial history" have related the problems of Palestinian events and records to the larger Near Eastern framework as a whole and thus made intelligible the information provided in biblical data by the data available in extra-biblical sources or resulting from fastidious topographical and inscriptional studies. Alt writes in German (see his 3 vols., *Kleine Schriften zur Geschichte des Volkes Israel* [Münich, C.H. Beck, 1953–59]), but the English reader may get some notion of the point of view of Alt and his school from M. Noth, *The History of Israel*, tr. by S. Godman (London, Adam & Charles Black, 1958).

The many writings of W.F. Albright have also been influential in this respect, and in particular his two volumes *From the Stone Age to Christianity* (first published in 1940 but it is important to consult the latest edition, [Baltimore, Johns Hopkins Press, 1957] because of the considerable revisions) and *Archaeology and the Religion of Israel* (Baltimore, Johns Hopkins Press, 1942; latest edition, 1959), which is both a complement and amplification of the former volume. Albright has insisted that biblical history can become a scientific discipline only through archeological research, and that research, he declares, "has confirmed the substantial historicity of Old Testament tradition"; though divergences from historical fact are present in the biblical record, he feels these are explicable as due to oral tradition, but they do not seriously affect the historical picture. And his emphasis is perhaps best conveyed in his own words, for they reveal at the same time the direction of concern and interpretation adopted by a number of Albright's students (such as G.E. Wright and F.M. Cross, Jr.) in their writings (see, for example, G.E. Wright, *God Who Acts* [Chicago, Henry Regnery, 1952]; or, even earlier, *The Challenge of Israel's Faith* [Chicago, Univ. of Chicago Press, 1944]) as they contemplate the nature of biblical religion: "The tradition of Israel represents Moses as a monotheist; the evidence of ancient Oriental religious history, combined with the most rigorous critical treatment of Israelite literary sources, points in exactly the same direction. The tradition of Israel represents the Prophets as preachers and reformers, not as religious innovators; rigid historical and philological exegesis of our sources agrees with tradition." For the student of biblical literature and religion, the very tenor of such statements has constituted a challenge to re-examine the religion of Israel in the light of newly acquired data and the alternative perspective and development they suggest.

Special mention must be made of R. de Vaux's *Ancient Israel: Its Life and Institutions*, tr. by J. McHugh (N.Y., McGraw-Hill, 1961), for it incorporates the latest results of literary and archeological research. Its detailed descriptions of the family and the civil and political, military, and religious institutions are a model of compactness and careful statement; it is no less valuable for its critical appraisal of current theories about the origins, and meaning, of some of Israel's institutions.

For histories of Israel, T.H. Robinson and W.O.E. Oesterley, *History of Israel* (Oxford, Oxford Univ. Press, 1st ed., 1932, and reprinted several times), while in some respects outdated, is still an excellent historical summary; but now the student should also consult J. Bright, *A History of Israel* (Philadelphia, Westminster Press, 1959). For introductions to the Old Testament, in addition to Pfeiffer's *Introduction* referred to earlier, the little book by M.L. Margolis, *The Hebrew Scriptures in the Making* (Philadelphia, Jewish Publication Society of America, 1922) might be used with profit. G.E. Wright and F.V. Filson, *The Westminster Historical Atlas to the Bible,* rev. ed. (Philadelphia, Westminster Press, 1956) is an excellent volume. In the field of comparative studies of texts and rituals in the ancient Near East, the texts and pictures assembled by J.B. Pritchard in *Ancient Near Eastern Texts Relating to the Old Testament,* 2nd ed. (Princeton Univ. Press, 1955) and *The Ancient Near East in Pictures Relating to the Old Testament* (Princeton, Princeton Univ. Press, 1954) are indispensable; a stimulating discussion of ritual and myth in the ancient Near East is presented by T.H. Gaster, *Thespis* (N.Y., Henry Schuman, 1950). On "Authority and Law in the Ancient Orient," consult the symposium prepared as a *Supplement to the Journal of the American Oriental Society,* Supp. 10–17, No. 17 (July-Sept., 1954).

New translations of the Bible, commentaries on individual books of the Bible, and biblical encyclopedias all help in various ways to arrive at a better understanding of the religion. In recent years a number of textbooks for school use have attempted a synthesis of technical discussion of the individual books of the Hebrew Bible, history of the people of Israel, and theological discussion of principal religious teachings of the Hebrew Scriptures, particularly as compared with the ideas to be found in important ancient Near Eastern literary sources; such works may serve the general reader, as well as the student in the classroom. See for example B.W. Anderson, *Understanding the Old Testament* (Englewood Cliffs, N.J., Prentice-Hall, 1957; 2nd ed., 1966) and N.K. Gottwald, *A Light to the Nations* (N.Y., Harper & Brothers, 1959); in the latter, there are thumbnail characterizations of many works in English recommended for further reading.

A final word about one more work, J. Pedersen's *Israel, Its Life and Culture* (Oxford, Oxford Univ. Press, vols. 1–2, 1926, vols. 3–4, 1946), which explores patiently and in detail social institutions and, above all, the psychology behind and within key biblical concepts. By penetrating into the thinking process that inheres in the terms for these key concepts, this instructive study of biblical anthropology is able to suggest the ideas that governed Israelite mentality, the thoughts associated with various forms of conduct and acts and expressions, and the auxiliary notions that cluster about a word as it is employed in a specific statement. As the richness of these terms is uncovered and their movement is traced, something of the depth of biblical religion is apprehended. At the same time, it is likely that through such analysis and interpretation one can discern those elements, or categories, which lie at the base of all the biblical literary sources, the late ones no less than the earliest ones, and thus examine the literature as a unit and not merely as an assembly, fortuitous or tendentious, of independent documents. Nevertheless, see the strong protest by J. Barr, *The Semantics of Biblical Language* (Oxford, Oxford Univ. Press, 1961).

VI. IN CONTACT WITH THE GREEKS

Products of Greek, and especially Athenian, industry apparently made their way to Palestine, as to other western parts of the Persian empire, even prior to the time of Alexander the Great; and while in the middle of the fourth century B.C. a decline in trade with Athens set in, both archeological and literary sources reveal that Jewish life in Palestine not only could not escape Hellenistic influence but in a sense received such influence without hostility, particularly from the late fourth century and mid-third century B.C. on. The encounter of Judaism with Hellenism was to have major consequences, not only in political and materialistic, but also in intellectual and religious, spheres; and, fortunately, there are available in English several good studies to make this encounter and its consequences vivid. M.I. Rostovtzeff's monumental *Social and Economic History of the Hellenistic World* (Oxford, Clarendon Press, 1941)—and for the later period see his *Social and Economic History of the Roman Empire* (Oxford, Clarendon Press, 1957)—is obviously devoted to the Hellenistic world at large, not merely to Palestine. But precisely this extensive treatment helps put events and developments within Palestine into proper perspective by making it possible for the student of Judaism to appreciate why some aspects of Hellenism could almost imperceptibly penetrate Jewish thought and conduct, with hardly a murmur of protest; why other aspects would produce a spirit of outright rejection; and, above all, why still others—though at times passively accepted—would become subjects of strong feelings and debate in the course of strained relations between Jews and Gentiles. Even this is hardly a just summary of the effects of the encounter of Hellenism and Judaism: a not unknown phenomenon of the millennium from about the fourth century B.C. to the fifth century A.D. is this at times severe general criticism of the ways of the Gentiles, on the one hand, and the innocent (and deliberate too!) adoption of particular notions and customs and even turns of speech which are not part of the earlier biblical tradition, on the other. This should hardly surprise us, for the truism that realities are subtler than rules had best be recalled to mind again and again in the study of Judaism from the time Greek ideas and artifacts came to the attention of Jews until the classical forms of the Jewish religion were crystallized.

A brief and still useful account of Jewish history from the Babylonian captivity in the sixth century B.C. to the fourth century A.D. is available in M. Radin's *The Jews among the Greeks and Romans* (Philadelphia, Jewish Publication Society of America, 1915). Unlike writers such as Hugh Willrich, for example, Radin does attempt to understand the sentiments of the Jews in their response to and reaction against the political and intellectual milieu in which they found themselves. The volume is by now too elementary, however. Much more instructive is *Hellenistic Civilization and the Jews* by V. Tcherikover, tr. from the Hebrew by S. Applebaum (Philadelphia, Jewish Publication Society of America, 1959), which investigates "the material foundation of Jewish life in the Hellenistic period and the political, economic and public bases of Jewish life in the Greek world" and discusses religious and literary questions only insofar as these bear on the material aspects. Tcherikover does not limit himself to a study of Hellenism in Palestine but studies also the effects of this civilization in the Diaspora. In effect, this means principally (but definitely not exclusively) Alexandria; and in this connection, the student will find it profitable to read that introductory essay, "Prolegomena," in V.A. Tcherikover and A. Fuks, *Corpus Papyrorum Judaicorum,* vol. I (Cambridge, Mass., Harvard Univ. Press, 1957), 1–111, which gives an account of Egyptian Jewry down to the seventh century in the Byzantine period.

Since we are dealing with the over-all theme of Hellenism and Judaism, it is important to call attention to the many-volumed and major work by E.R. Goodenough, *Jewish Symbols in the Greco-Roman Period* (the first three volumes appeared in 1953 in the Bollingen Series, N.Y., Pantheon Books; to date thirteen volumes have been published). This extremely impressive, pioneering, and challenging collection, description, and discussion of artistic representations in Jewish tombs, homes, and synagogues, on household and ornamental objects, buildings, and sarcophagi furnishes us with the very realia one needs to supplement the picture that emerges otherwise from purely literary sources. The data assembled are not only material for the filling in of historical outlines but raise the fundamental question of the conception of Judaism held by the Jews themselves in Hellenistic-Roman times (note, for example, C.H. Kraeling's discussion in *The Synagogue of Dura* [New Haven, Yale Univ. Press, 1956], 340ff.). Granted that even within a particular tradition there are dissenting groups and points of view (and on sectarians see further below); what in the last analysis was the *normative* conception? Or are we still in a time of flux, and, strictly speaking, has no one particular view triumphed as normative? This need not necessarily suggest that the Judaism reflected by midrashic-talmudic sources is unrepresentative of Judaism of the time, nor that the artifacts demonstrate the existence of a different kind of Judaism; but perhaps current interpretations of rabbinic sources are still too narrowly, too partially formed. Even the literary texts may reveal hitherto only partially understood details when the realities this art reflects are taken into account.

The meaning of Judaism's contact with Hellenism is nowhere so beautifully and fastidiously analyzed as in the writings of E.J. Bickerman. His studies are primary not only for a proper chart of the historical course of events but also for the appreciation of religious consequences. It would be wise, indeed, for the student to begin with Bickerman's essay on "The Historical Foundations of Postbiblical Judaism" in L. Finkelstein's first volume of *The Jews* (N.Y., Harper & Brothers, 1949), 70–114, for here the orientation provided toward the whole period of the Second Commonwealth applies to subsequent periods of Judaism no less. Because he never loses sight of "the polarity of Jerusalem and the Dispersion," Bickerman escapes many superficialities which unfortunately are still current (for example, the idea that what distinguishes Diaspora Judaism from Palestinian Judaism is that the former adapted itself happily to Hellenistic civilization while the latter utterly rejected it). But, more positive and important is that Bickerman is sensitive to the richness and complexity of Jewish civilization in Hellenistic times, and, once again, reference must be made to a work not in English: his brilliant German volume, *Der Gott der Makkabäer* (Berlin, Schocken, 1937). It is the best discussion of the events which led to the Maccabean revolt and the *religious* crisis of the age, of the conflict *within Jewry* as a result of the resistance to attempts on the part of Hellenized Jews in Palestine to "modernize" an ancestral faith. Since preservation and change are like two opposing forces pressing simultaneously on a living tradition, Bickerman's study makes understandable not only the specific chapter of Jewish history to which his study is devoted but suggests as well an approach to the understanding of developments in subsequent periods. For example, Bickerman demonstrates beautifully in his little book *The Maccabees* (N.Y., Schocken Books, 1947) how the triumphant Maccabees themselves assimilated Hellenistic notions: "With the Maccabees . . . the internal Jewish reconcilement with Hellenism begins." By strengthening their people, and by appropriating from Hellenism what they could use to enrich Torah teachings, the Maccabees saved Judaism "from the mummification that overtook the religion of the Egyptians, for example, which shut itself off from Hellenism completely." *The Maccabees* and "The Historical Foundations of Postbiblical Judaism" are both reprinted in *From Ezra to the Last of the Maccabees* (N.Y., Schocken Books, 1962, paperback).

Along entirely independent lines, a kind of "chapter and verse" confirmation of this thesis is superbly furnished for the English reader in two volumes by S. Lieberman: *Greek in Jewish Palestine* (N.Y., Jewish Theological Seminary of America, 1942) and *Hellenism in Jewish Palestine* (N.Y., Jewish Theological Seminary of America, 1950). Although his individual essays are devoted to somewhat technical and textual problems, the lucidity of Lieberman's expositions makes the material accessible even to the non-specialist. And, again, we have here the kind of discussion absolutely essential for the proper understanding of the vocabulary, the institutions, and the attitudes of the religious tradition. What Palestinian talmudic Judaism was trying to teach, what some of its preoccupations were, and what the character of its discourse was—insofar as these are the products of a particular time and place—become intelligible to the historian and student of Judaism through studies like these. Lieberman makes us see that not merely Jews in general but the talmudic Rabbis themselves were influenced by the Hellenistic world. It should be added that our understanding of Judaism during Hellenistic-Roman times has been immensely deepened by Lieberman's many publications, particularly his commentaries, and at present especially his commentary to the Tosefta which is appearing: to date, on the first part of the Tosefta, three volumes have appeared (N.Y., Jewish Theological Seminary of America, 1955), on the second part four more volumes (N.Y., Jewish Theological Seminary of America, 1961)—but these are in Hebrew.

Even at the risk of some repetition, let us consider the significance of these recent studies to which we have referred. Judaism's meeting with Hellenism we now know did not inevitably mean clash and antagonism. And obviously it did not mean submerging Judaism in the waves of a conquering civilization. A truly complex interrelationship began, aspects of the biblical religion being modified, forms and substance of speculation making their appearance now for which no background is provided in the biblical *literature* at least. For example, a religion rooted in this-worldly conceptions, so firmly expressed by Scripture (except for the late sections in Daniel), is gradually superseded by a religion whose yearning and goal become other-worldly; specific cultic features have such close counterparts in Hellenistic religious practice that the impression is inescapable that more or less direct influence is here at work; echoes of exegetical methods familiar in Alexandrian schools reverberate in the rabbinic academy.

Additional details the student will accumulate from his careful attention to the works to which we have already referred, and it will reward him greatly if he will follow the bibliographical leads suggested by the footnotes in these volumes. I am thinking specifically of such studies as E.J. Bickerman, "The Maxim of Antigonus of Socho" in the *Harvard Theological Review*, XLIV (1951), 153–65, which in the course of analyzing social institutions illuminates at the same time religious conceptions. (See also M. Smith, "The Image of God," in the *Bulletin of the John Rylands*

Library [March, 1958], 473–512.) In short, what is to be kept in mind is that contact with the "Greeks" did not produce a Judaism insulated from Hellenism, but in fact the very reverse: a complex of revised and enriched traditions which added vitality to the religion, affecting by the way the character of Christianity and later Islām too.

The immediately recognizable Hellenistic influence is, of course, to be located in those Jewish writers who wrote in Greek. As for Josephus, the most sober and instructive study is still that by H. St. John Thackeray, *Josephus, the Man and the Historian* (N.Y., Hebrew Union College Press, 1929). Together with Ralph Marcus, Thackeray has translated *The Jewish Wars* (N.Y., Washington Square, 1965; London, New English Library, 1966) which was abridged and edited by I. Finley. Very useful too is a little volume done by Thackeray in 1919 for the Society for Promoting Christian Knowledge, *Selections from Josephus* (London). In addition to introductory comments, the passages translated are accompanied by fine brief notes, but, to return to Thackeray's biography of Josephus, its real value lies in the author's disciplined assessment of that writer against the actualities and literary fashions of Josephus' own time. More recently N.N. Glatzer's selection of Josephus' writings, *Rome and Jerusalem: The Writings of Josephus* (N.Y., Meridian Books, 1960), has a neat introduction.

Fragments from the works of Hellenistic Jewish writers are conveniently assembled in W.N. Stearns, *Fragments from Graeco-Jewish Writers* (Chicago, Univ. of Chicago Press, 1908). We have already referred to the collections of apocrypha and pseudepigrapha by Charles and the editors of the Dropsie College Series; and the bibliographies listed in those works will serve well for deeper study of specific texts and the religious thought expressed therein. Of some interest in this connection is the volume by R.H. Charles, *Religious Developments between the Two Testaments* (N.Y., Henry Holt, 1914); see also R.T. Herford, *Talmud and Apocrypha* (London, Soncino Press, 1933). For consideration of some specific aspects of religion related to apocryphal literature, one may want to consult R. Marcus, *Law in the Apocrypha* (N.Y., Columbia Univ. Press, 1927); H.J. Wicks, *The Doctrine of God* (London, Hunter & Longhurst, 1915); N.B. Johnson, *Prayer in the Apocrypha and Pseudepigrapha* (Philadelphia, Society of Biblical Literature & Exegesis, 1948). For additional literature on this subject and related matters discussed in this and the following section, R.H. Pfeiffer's discussion and bibliography in his *History of New Testament Times* (N.Y., Harper & Brothers, 1949) are very useful.

We come finally to Philo, in whose work interest has grown considerably during the last four to five decades. Fortunately for the English reader, there is an excellent translation of Philo's works in the Loeb Classics (thus far ten volumes plus two supplementary volumes, begun by F.H.

Colson and G.H. Whitaker, then continued by the former alone) and the two volumes of *Philo Supplement* by R. Marcus (N.Y., G.P. Putnam's Sons, 1929–53). For Philo's *Legatio ad Gaium,* not yet translated in the Loeb Series, see now the learned edition with commentary by E.M. Smallwood (Leiden, E.J. Brill, 1961). A little book of *Philo* selections with a learned and sensitive introduction and some comments was prepared by H. Lewy for the East and West Library Series (Oxford, 1946). (This fine scholar's studies deserve careful reading and should be translated into English and presented like the superior studies in Jewish Hellenism brought together in his posthumous Hebrew volume *Olamot Nifgashim* [Jerusalem, Mosad Bialik, 1960].) Still another anthology worth reading is that drawn up by C.G. Montefiore, "Florilegium Philonis," in the old series of the *Jewish Quarterly Review,* VII (London, 1894–95), 481–545.

What Philo represents, and the significance of his writings for an understanding of Judaism, is a subject still stirring discussion. To get two distinct points of view on this subject, one should examine E.R. Goodenough's *By Light, Light* (New Haven, Yale Univ. Press, 1935) and H.A. Wolfson's two-volume *Philo* (Cambridge, Harvard Univ. Press, 1947). (Goodenough's short *Introduction to Philo Judaeus* [New Haven, Yale Univ. Press, 1940] is also relevant in this connection.) The former sees in Philo the great articulation of a mystic conception of Judaism distinctive of Alexandrian intellectual-religious Jewry: "The fact is, it seems to me," says Goodenough, "that by Philo's time, and long before, Judaism in the Greek-speaking world, especially in Egypt, had been transformed into a Mystery."

For Wolfson, on the other hand—for whom the work on Philo, incidentally, is a kind of "prolegomenon to the major problems of religious philosophy for the seventeen centuries following Philo"—the Alexandrian Jewish philosopher no doubt represents a Judaism being brought into intimate contact with the thought patterns of Hellenistic culture, but his distinctive Jewish heritage and idiom are in no way radically different from what one could find in Palestine and even in rabbinic teaching. Not only is this true of Philo himself but of Hellenistic Judaism in general. If, says Wolfson, the Alexandrian Jewish writers "happen to use the terminology of the mysteries in their presentation of Jewish rites, it is either for the purpose of emphasizing the contrast between the religion of the Jews and the mysteries of the heathen, or because the terms derived from the mysteries have become part of the common speech and are used in a sense completely divorced from their original meaning." And Philo himself, Wolfson reaffirms (in the prefatory statement of his *Religious Philosophy* [Cambridge, Belknap Press of Harvard Univ. Press, 1961])

. . . is the interpreter of Greek philosophy in terms of certain fundamental teachings of his Hebrew Scripture, whereby he revolutionized philosophy and remade it into what became the common philosophy of the three religions with cognate Scriptures, Judaism, Christianity, and

Islam. This triple religious philosophy, which was built up by Philo, reigned supreme as a homogeneous, if not a thoroughly unified, system of thought until the seventeenth century, when it was pulled down by Spinoza.

The data at our disposal demonstrate that the effect of Hellenism on the Jewish mind and thought was a profound and highly complicated phenomenon. Any attempt to simplify it is almost sure to become *over*simplification, and to that extent misleading.

VII. THE FORMATION OF CLASSICAL JUDAISM

There is bound to be a certain overlapping in our discussion, for several works referred to in the previous section (such as those by Lieberman and Bickerman) are relevant to this section, and, contrariwise, a number of volumes referred to here are no less relevant to the preceding section. And perhaps it would be helpful to come to an understanding of what is meant by the expression "classical Judaism" before we proceed to the bibliographical statement. What, then, is classical Judaism?

"Classical" Judaism, with the biblical books and emphases as its heritage, appropriated what it found in the world congenial to the passion of the law and prophetic ideal and by intellectual exercise found sanction for its adaptations and innovations in those books that had become authoritative; while anticipating an otherworldly destination for man (to which "this world is an antechamber"), it was rooted firmly in the historical affiliation with the Holy Land and the indestructibility of the folk Israel, and so convinced of God's ultimate triumph that it demanded an immediate practice and acting out of His commands and regulations, the behavior patterns of the Messianic age. Some of the clauses in this long sentence might not have been subscribed to by the Sadducees, for example (who are reported to have rejected the belief in Resurrection, for instance, and the authority of the oral Torah); but it is likely that not only Pharisees but philosophical Jews like Philo, the different sectarians of whom Josephus speaks, the groups represented by material from the Dead Sea region, and the early Jewish Christians too (until they removed to Pella)— indeed, all the varieties of Jews until almost a millennium after Alexander the Great—were engaged in a life which was sometimes more and sometimes less an expression of this Judaism I have called "classical." The tensions and controversies and animosities among these groups—and even within Pharisaism, which ultimately triumphed through talmudism—were the result of conflicts over whether this or that particular interpretation or institution contributed to or detracted from the strengthening of this Judaism. If our description of classical Judaism does not do justice to the

Sadducees and those in sympathy with them, it may indeed be because even before they disappeared, the Sadducees had already lost that interior confidence in the capacity of Judaism to appropriate and transform without losing contact with its past—in other words, had already then confused the archaic with the classical. But a word of caution is in order: what little we know of the Sadducees we know only from their critics and antagonists. If groups like the Essenes did not in the end survive, it may be that they cut themselves off so radically from what the larger surrounding civilization could offer them that they starved to death on a limited diet.

In the actual mêlée of Hellenistic-Roman times, then, classical Judaism was in the process of being formed. As it developed, the talmudic approach eventually succeeded, for reasons that can to some extent be suggested by a number of works to which we must now turn. (A very helpful bibliographical tool for what follows is H.L. Strack, *Introduction to the Talmud and Midrash* [Philadelphia, Jewish Publication Society of America, 1931] also in paperback.)

For primary sources, there is the English translation of the Talmud and the Midrash Rabbah to which reference has already been made. The English translation of the *Mishnah* by H. Danby (Oxford, Clarendon Press, 1933) is fine but is to be used with care, for a number of passages are not properly translated (or understood). In recent years a translation with useful commentary and notes (and a printed Hebrew text) has been prepared by P. Blackman (London, Mishna Press, 1951–56). For a first-rate pointed Hebrew text of the Mishnah, there is nothing even to compare with the edition by Ch. Albeck and Ch. Yalon, *Shishah Sidre Mishnah* (The Six Orders of the Mishnah) (Tel Aviv, Mosad Bialik, 1952–59). An excellent translation of the Mishnah treatise on relations with idol-worshippers, *Abodah Zarah,* with important philological and historical notes, was done by W.A.L. Elmslie (Cambridge, Cambridge Univ. Press, 1911); in 1945 the first three treatises of the *Mishnah* were issued by the H. Fischel Institute scholars (Jerusalem) in Danby's translation (with corrections) and a good. commentary. This may be a bit too technical for the general reader, but one can learn a lot from it. There is also an edition by P.R. Weis with translation by E. Robertson of the treatise *Horayoth* (Manchester, Manchester Univ. Press, 1952) and of *Mishnah Megillah* by J. Rabbinowitz (London, Oxford Univ. Press, 1931). Several other treatises, with corresponding sections of the Tosefta, were prepared by different scholars under the auspices of the Society for Promoting Christian Knowledge (see above), and these are of a more popular character.

A particularly important treatise of the Mishnah for the understanding of classical Judaism is *Pirke Aboth.* The most valuable edition (with translation and commentary in English) is that by C. Taylor, *Sayings of the Jewish Fathers,* 2nd ed. (Cambridge, Cambridge Univ. Press, vol. I, 1897; vol. II, 1900); although out of print, it will richly reward the specialist, and the general reader can acquire solid instruction by concentrating on volume I. Every traditional Jewish prayerbook which is accompanied by a translation will provide also a translation of *Pirke Aboth*, for it was incorporated into the prayerbook as "liturgical" reading and study at an early time. The translation with commentary by R.T. Herford, *Pirke Aboth, the Tractate "Fathers,"* 3rd rev. ed. (N.Y., Jewish Institute of Religion, 1945, recently reissued in paperback), although not always correct, is marked by a sympathetic approach to Pharisaism in reaction against the antipharisaic prejudice current generally among Christian scholars. J. Goldin's *The Living Talmud: The Wisdom of the Fathers* (N.Y., 1957, Chicago, Univ. of Chicago Press, 1958, and Mentor paperback) is an attempt to transmit the literary quality of the text with strict attention to philological detail, and to provide for the first time in English selections from the great early-medieval commentators on this treatise. And in connection with *Pirke Aboth*, there is available the talmudic companion volume, *The Fathers According to Rabbi Nathan*, also by J. Goldin (New Haven, Yale Univ. Press, 1955).

A reliable translation of the *Mekilta de Rabbi Ishmael* accompanies the splendid edition by J.Z. Lauterbach (Philadelphia, Jewish Publication Society of America, 1933). Parts of the *Sifre* on Numbers were translated by P.P. Levertoff, *Midrash Sifre on Numbers* (London and N.Y., Macmillan, 1926). Of later Midrashim there is in English the careful two-volume work by W.G. Braude, *The Midrash on Psalms* (New Haven, Yale Univ. Press, 1959); G. Friedlander's learned *Pirkê de Rabbi Eliezer* (London, Kegan Paul, Trench, Trübner, 1916); and a beautiful little book of selections by N.N. Glatzer, *Hammer on the Rock: A Short Midrash Reader,* tr. by J. Sloan (N.Y., Schocken Books, 1948).

Probably one of the most useful anthologies of talmudic passages is still that by C.G. Montefiore and H. Loewe, *A Rabbinic Anthology* (reprinted in Philadelphia, Jewish Publication Society of America, 1960), for it has some fine notes on a number of passages. But the apologetics and tone of the introductory essays are acutely irritating.

Finally (though doubtless some texts have been omitted inadvertently), there has recently been reprinted the French translation of the Palestinian Talmud, M. Schwab, *Le Talmude de Jérusalem* (Paris, Maisonneuve, 1871–89). This should be used with much caution; I mention it since there is no English translation of this important source.

Relevant chapters and sections on the history of this period, which for our present purpose might be delimited as 200 B.C.–A.D. 500, the reader will find in the histories referred to earlier. Here we shall refer to only one work, despite its very serious limitation, E. Schürer's *History of the Jewish People in the Time of Jesus Christ,* which appeared in Edinburgh, 1886–90, and apparently eleven issues of this English translation of the original German, in its second edition, came out until 1924 (N.Y., Charles

Scribner's Sons). Since this work is a deservedly standard presentation and discussion of what is generally called Judaism in New Testament Times, a few comments on its nature are in order. The time scope it sets for itself is from about 175 B.C. to about A.D. 200, although the political history it outlines goes only to the end of the Bar Kochba revolt in A.D. 135.

The English translation is excellent, although in a few places (in Division II) the translators misunderstood the original German, and their version is misleading. This is not the most serious limitation of the translation—which to repeat, lest a wrong impression be left, is an excellent one. Schürer was a very exacting scholar, and his *Geschichte* appeared in four constantly revised editions. If a student is eager to learn Schürer's final conclusions, it is essential that he check with the German volume in either its third or fourth edition (ed. 1901, 1907, 1909, 1911).

As a summary of political history, a compilation of data on some institutions or literary sources, or a synthesis of what the primary sources preserve regarding specific problems of the period (for example, the three principal groups, Sadducees, Pharisees, Essenes, or what the daily service in the Jerusalem temple was like, according to the Mishnah), Schürer's is still the best work to consult. About some matters we are of course better informed today than Schürer could be: discoveries relating to the Dead Sea sectarians have furnished us with data Schürer did not have, and we can listen, for instance, to Essene or Essene-like groups as they expressed themselves rather than as they were paraphrased. Our knowledge of the state of post-biblical Hebrew is better grounded than Schürer's could be because of these finds. Thanks especially to the researches of Bickerman and Lieberman, our understanding of the penetration of Hellenism into Jewish Palestine is more profound and richer than Schürer's

But it is noteworthy that so painstaking was Schürer in his work that the basic outline he drew up of events (in large part following Josephus) is still the basic outline of our picture of the period. And Schürer's disciplined gathering of literary sources, epigraphic material, coinage, and results of archeological expeditions is a model for every historian. Schürer's work is therefore strongly recommended to the student; and in the recent paperback abridgment (the volume is confined to political history) prepared by N.N. Glatzer, *A History of the Jewish People in the Time of Jesus* by Emil Schürer (N.Y., Schocken Books, 1961), one will find not only a very useful selected bibliography to cover results of scholarship in the years 1900–60, but a sensitive evaluation of Schürer's work and outlook.

The serious limitation of this work, alluded to above, is that it is absolutely tone-deaf to the spirit of talmudism and the mood of rabbinic preoccupation with the law (see his discussion "Life under the Law" in Division II, Volume II). Moreover, Schürer persists in presenting Judaism as no more than a preparation for Christianity, and hence as something that had to be outgrown. Schürer reads like an accurate reporter of all the finger exercises a concert pianist has prepared for himself who then says: "From this catalogue, judge the concert performance." Inevitably such an outlook was bound to stir up opposing reactions, from Jews and non-Jews (and, alas, the reactions have sometimes involved all sorts of unnecessary special pleadings).

One specific aspect of the problems of this period has to do with the Pharisees. A sympathetic presentation of what the Pharisees were and stood for is available in R.T. Herford's *Pharisaism* (N.Y., G.P. Putnam's Sons, 1912)—see also his *The Pharisees* (London, George Allen & Unwin, 1924)—which argues against the group being judged by Christian standards and attempts to see Pharisaism's merits even in the conflict between the Pharisees and Jesus (as well as Paul): "The conflict," Herford feels, "was one between two fundamentally different conceptions of religion, viz. that in which the supreme authority was Torah, and that in which the supreme authority was the immediate intuition of God in the individual soul and conscience. The Pharisees stood for the one; Jesus stood for the other."

Somewhat of the same tenor, though disagreeing in details, and certainly more learned, and exploring Pharisaic teaching more fully, is J.Z. Lauterbach's essay "The Pharisees and Their Teachings," reprinted in his posthumous volume *Rabbinic Essays* (Cincinnati, Hebrew Union College Press, 1951). This volume incidentally has several studies of importance for the understanding of talmudic Judaism.

An ambitious undertaking, attempting to explain Pharisaic and rabbinic law and thought and institutions by reference to economic and sociological forces in Palestine, is the two-volume work by L. Finkelstein, *The Pharisees* (Philadelphia, Jewish Publication Society of America, 1938; but one should consult the 1962 edition, since Finkelstein has been trying to refine his original presentation in the light of severe criticism). The approach has the merit of being a fresh one, of attempting to see the "sect" against the larger social background rather than against the purely doctrinal one— even if serious reservations are retained against specific interpretations. The cue for his approach Finkelstein found in L. Ginzberg's essay— originally in Hebrew (Jerusalem, 5691–1931) and now reprinted in English translation, by A. Hertzberg, as "The Significance of the Halachah for Jewish History," in the volume of essays *On Jewish Law and Lore* (Philadelphia, Jewish Publication Society of America, 1955)—which was, if I am not mistaken, the first attempt to view aspects of rabbinic law (specifically as reflected by the controversies of the famous schools of Shammaites and Hillelites) against economic conditions.

Recent attempts at presenting the Pharisees must undertake to establish some correlation between the teachings of the group and the milieu to which the group belongs. In this connection, but with different results from Finkelstein's, see M. Smith's essay "Palestinian Judaism in the First Century" in *Israel: Its Role in Civilization,* ed. by M. Davis (N.Y., Jewish Theological Seminary of America, 1956), 67–81. The student especially interested in the Pharisees will find a useful essay by R. Marcus in vol. XXXII of the *Journal of Religion* (Chicago, 1952), 153–64, "The Pharisees in the Light of Modern Scholarship"; and since Marcus not only discusses a number of important works on this subject, but also lists a selected bibliography at the end of his paper, we shall leave the Pharisees as such, and move on to more comprehensive themes.

There is, first, S. Schechter's *Some Aspects of Rabbinic Theology,* chapters of which began to appear toward the end of the nineteenth century in the *Jewish Quarterly Review* (old series), and later (1909) appeared as a volume (the edition before me is N.Y., 1936; the original volume has been out of print for some time, and now a paperback edition [N.Y., Shocken Books, 1961] has appeared, with an Introduction by L. Finkelstein). The presentation is still instructive, vigorous and relevant, because Schechter wrote with a keen sense of the fervor of original sources and was not averse to engaging in polemic, where he felt that less than justice had been done to the life reflected by midrashic-talmudic texts. Without passion, but excellently written (with a refreshing cleanliness in the prose) is the more extensive and systematic three-volume work of G.F. Moore, *Judaism in the First Centuries of the Christian Era, the Age of the Tannaim* (Cambridge, Harvard Univ. Press, 1927; vol. III appeared in 1940). It has become fashionable recently to take issue with this work, and some of the criticism is certainly justified. But Moore's remains one of the best introductions to and presentations of basic features of classical Judiasm, for he tried most earnestly to listen to the rabbinic texts he studied and was attentive to critical problems raised by this literature. "The aim of these volumes," wrote Moore at the beginning of his Preface, "is to represent Judaism in the centuries in which it assumed definitive forms as it presents itself in the tradition which it has always regarded as authentic." This aim the writer realized to a remarkable degree.

But one can no longer assume that the teachings of the tradition—which Moore said characterized Judaism in the age of the Tannaim—but in actuality treated as though they characterized the later Amoraic age too—were quite as uniform, as stable, as unaffected by reinterpretation and change as Moore assumed them to be. And even within the first two centuries, the age of the Tannaim—more especially, within the period from Sirach to the compilation of the Mishnah, from roughly 200 B.C. to A.D. 200—there is good reason to see gradual developments, so that emphases of one period give way to other emphases entirely, even if the vocabulary seems to be the same for both periods.

What is more, a basic assumption made by Moore is just the matter which today calls for re-examination and demonstration. In reaction against those scholars who had largely adopted the idea that the sentiments and thoughts derived from the apocrypha, the pseudepigrapha, and even the New Testament were essentially normative for Judaism, and that talmudism was an unfortunate deviation which, however, finally conquered the main expressions and institutions of the religion, Moore assumed that the very reverse was true (see also Schechter's volume already referred to)—namely, that what was normative *in those early centuries* was the Judaism reflected by the midrashic-talmudic sources. But this is the very issue which confronts the historian, particularly today, because of many realia to which archeology especially has alerted us, and because of forms of speculation and expression, gnostic and otherwise, which research has underscored in recent years and talmudists were prone to underestimate.

It is not that Moore has been proven wrong, but the question, simply, of what *was* normative in the Judaism of Greco-Roman times remains. No answer to this question can be given yet, for very much painstaking research is required along new lines, and this will very likely be one of the primary items on the agenda of Judaica scholars in the coming decades.

But a brief comment is in order, for it is pertinent to the way we read not only the primary sources but also the major secondary ones which attempt to represent Judaism. When we seek to discover what is normative for these centuries, we must recognize that *all* sources are a record of particular teachings striving to become normative, all represent the ambition of particular groups to have the whole of Israel adopt their particular emphases. And so long as they were still vigorously arguing *with each other,* Judaism was *in process toward final formulation,* one might say it was feeling its way toward definitiveness (and in some respects finality was never attained). What made the teachings of some one or other group *not* normative was the withdrawal of the particular group from the common argument, from this resolution to press its point of view on the folk as a whole, where the folk as a whole was located. Issuing polemical statements from a reservation to which one has retired, and where one has adopted a particular routine for privileged initiates, is already an expression of giving up and disengagement, and a sign of having become tangential. Whatever else talmudism was, it was the determination of its exponents, the Rabbis, to engage themselves with what was daily happening in society as a whole and to engage that society with the terms of their, the Rabbis', debates and values. This does not mean that therefore their word was "everywhere" law; but it does mean that there was a widespread consciousness of their law, considerable contact with its demands and the value structure these exhibited. By being aggressively present within Palestinian Jewish society at all times, talmudic Judaism asserted itself on that society as a kind of norm, to which gradually more and more of the religious life related (and later still, accommodated) itself. I am tempted to say that early talmudism was the one form of the inchoate classical Judaism which won a dominant position even in these early Tannaite and Amoraic centuries because, on the one hand, it was relatively open to many influences and points of view crisscrossing that society and, on the other hand, its leading representatives stayed on the scene, never allowing their own pre-occupations to get too far removed from the concerns of the folk at large and not giving the folk at large the impression that *its* common practices and predilections were exempt from rabbinic judgment.

What happened later, when classical Judaism came to be defined vir-tually in terms of talmudism, we shall see below. But the marginal com-ment introduced above was essential if we are properly to appreciate what the studies we go on to list have to cope with.

A number of aspects of rabbinic Judaism, which are treated by Moore as chapters of his full presentation, receive more elaborate treatment in sev-eral special studies. Much information is offered and carefully analyzed in the works of A. Büchler; specifically, *Types of Jewish-Palestinian Piety from 70* B.C.E. *to 70* C.E. (London, Oxford Univ. Press, 1922) and *Studies in Sin and Atonement in the Rabbinic Literature of the First Cen-tury* (London, Oxford Univ. Press, 1928). Several essays in his posthu-mously published *Studies in Jewish History,* ed. J. Brodie and J. Rabbino-witz (London, Oxford Univ. Press, 1956) may also be mentioned. Büchler is learned and exact, though his wandering discussion and pedestrian style sometimes discourage the general reader—regrettably, for Büchler supplies a healthy corrective to a number of seemingly plausible generalizations.

Even more closely related to purely "theological" themes are J. Abelson, *The Immanence of God in Rabbinical Literature* (London, Macmillan, 1912) and A. Marmorstein, *The Doctrine of Merits in Old Rabbinical Literature* (London, Oxford Univ. Press, 1920). Marmorstein also has two volumes on *The Old Rabbinic Doctrine of God* (London, Oxford Univ. Press, 1927 and 1937; the second of these volumes, *Essays in Anthropo-morphism,* is relevant to the study of Philo); and finally there is his volume of essays, *Studies in Jewish Theology,* ed. J. Rabbinowitz and M.S. Lew (London, Oxford Univ. Press, 1950). For serious studies of what might be called the way of rabbinic thinking, and a thoroughly original approach to basic concepts indigenous to midrashic-talmudic discourse, there are three volumes by M. Kadushin: *The Theology of Seder Eliahu* (N.Y., Bloch, 1932), *Organic Thinking* (N.Y., Jewish Theological Seminary of America, 1938), and *The Rabbinic Mind* (N.Y., Jewish Theological Seminary of America, 1952).

Without commenting in detail on the following works, I shall call atten-tion to them as valuable and sometimes sensitive analyses of the problems they treat: N.N. Glatzer's essay "A Study of the Talmudic Interpretation of Prophecy," *Review of Religion* (N.Y., 1946), 115–37; B.J. Bamberger, *Proselytism in the Talmudic Period* (Cincinnati, Hebrew Union College Press, 1939)—a careful and fresh dissertation on a theme which had been discussed by a number of leading scholars and not always with as close study of the texts as Bamberger brought to them (conclusions fairly similar to the ones arrived at by Bamberger, that the dominant rabbinic attitude towards proselytism remained favorable, were reached also by W.G. Braude in his doctoral dissertation, *Jewish Proselytizing in the First Five Centuries of the Common Era* [Providence, Brown Univ. Press, 1940]); and, also by Bamberger, *Fallen Angels* (Philadelphia, Jewish Publication Society of America, 1952), which has two sections (Parts Two and Five) relevant to the period we are discussing and other sections treating the themes of the fallen or rebel angels in Christianity and in post-talmudic Judaism.

For studies of the Messianic theme as it is treated in the literature of Hellenistic-Roman times, see J. Klausner, *The Messianic Idea in Israel* (N.Y., Macmillan, 1955) and W.D. Davies, *Torah in the Messianic Age and/or the Age to Come* (Philadelphia, Society of Biblical Literature and Exegesis, 1952). In this connection it is also illuminating to consult R. Wischnitzer, *The Messianic Theme in the Paintings of the Dura Synagogue* (Chicago, Univ. of Chicago Press, 1948).

What Jewish imagination did with its biblical heritage—especially biblical narratives and personalities—is nowhere better presented than in L. Ginzberg's *Legends of the Jews* (Philadelphia, Jewish Publication Society of America, 1909–38; the first four volumes consisting of the text; vols. 5 and 6 of the notes, nothing short of a treasury of learning; vol. 7, the index volume, was drawn up by B. Cohen). For the folklorist and the student of religion this work is indispensable; the material assembled and the critical discussion in the notes reveal not only what interpretation and reinterpretation can do to an inherited corpus of writings when they are endowed with canonical authority, but also how speculative themes of universal range are naturalized and are given a specific Jewish character and idiom. For Judaism this is not only of literary and purely cultural importance; it is consequential for the religion. This is the haggadic substance and vocabulary which the pietists will invoke and with which the homilists especially will fill the minds of the folk. An abridged one-volume edition of this monumental work, omitting the notes, was published under the title *Legends of the Bible* (Philadelphia, Jewish Publication Society of America, 1956), with an introductory essay by S. Spiegel which is one of the most beautiful and illuminating statements of the nature of haggadah and Jewish legend in any language. (Students of folklore who do not read Hebrew are unfortunately deprived of Spiegel's outstanding study of the Binding of Isaac legends and theme, *Me-Agadot Ha-Akedah,* which appears in the *Alexander Marx Jubilee Volume,* Hebrew section, 471–547 [N.Y., Jewish Theological Seminary, 5710–1950]. It is a pity that this work has not yet been translated into English.) Ginzberg also has a suggestive essay on "Jewish Folklore: East and West," originally prepared as a lecture at the Harvard Tercentenary in 1936, included in the volume *On Jewish Law and Lore,* to which we have referred previously. All the essays in the volume are relevant to this period (even the one on the "Cabala," to which we shall refer later).

The way haggadic material was molded into sermonic form is painstakingly studied and presented by J. Mann in *The Bible as Read and Preached in the Old Synagogue,* vol. I (Cincinnati, the author, 1940)—a technical study to be sure, but a very important one.

On the nature of the mystical teachings, particularly of an esoteric kind, in these early centuries, there is now the important and exciting volume by G.G. Scholem, *Jewish Gnosticism, Merkabah Mysticism, and Talmudic Tradition* (N.Y., Jewish Theological Seminary of America, 1960), which has established the existence of a Jewish gnosis ("That is to say," to quote him, "knowledge of an esoteric and at the same time soteric . . . character") in rabbinic circles in the very period when the classic tradition as a whole was being shaped. Not only does this open up vistas for students of Judaism on the varieties of expression of the Jewish religion, but for students of Gnosticism too certain roots and origins are uncovered. For the charting of the inner religious development of Judaism, studies along such lines as Scholem's are a prime requirement.

On the subject of synagogue worship there is in English a passable volume by A.Z. Idelsohn, *Jewish Liturgy and its Development* (N.Y., Henry Holt, 1932); but the standard work is still that by I. Elbogen in German, *Der jüdische Gottesdienst in seiner geschichtlichen Entwicklung* (Leipzig, G. Fock, 1913)—although, perhaps needless to say, specific phases of the liturgy continue to be studied and discussed by scholars, and specific views of Elbogen are modified. Useful explanatory notes to the Jewish prayerbook are provided by I. Abrahams. *A Companion to the Authorized Daily Prayer Book* (London, Eyre & Spottiswoode, 1922); for a translation of the prayerbook, see *The Authorized Daily Prayer Book,* tr. by S. Singer (London, Eyre & Spottiswoode, 1944, but frequently reprinted before and after that date) or, more recently, *Daily Prayer Book, Ha-Siddur Ha-Shalem,* tr. by P. Birnbaum (N.Y., Hebrew Publishing Co., 1949).

There are several so-called biographies in English of rabbinic personalities, such as N.N. Glatzer, *Hillel the Elder: The Emergence of Classical Judaism* (N.Y., B'nai B'rith Hillel Foundations, 1956); B.Z. Bokser, *Pharisaic Judaism in Transition: R. Eliezer the Great and Jewish Reconstruction after the War with Rome* (N.Y., Bloch, 1935) and L. Finkelstein, *Akiba* (N.Y., Covici, Friede, 1936)—(the bibliographies and notes in these volumes will lead the reader further on). These are to some extent useful, but such works are hardly biographies in the serious sense of the word (though the studies are undertaken seriously), for not only do the primary sources disappoint us deeply in the amount of reliable *historical* detail they provide, but even as regards the opinions and teachings of the Sages, one is left to guess what is early and what is late. In short, there is practically no way to get at *development,* surely and desperately necessary for the historian and biographer. These books therefore are filed with speculation, sometimes plausible, sometimes not. As reflections of the author's own imagination and interpretation, however, and as *collections* of data about the specific sage, they are informative exercises.

Though the following are in Hebrew, mention must be made of them: G. Allon's two-volume history, *Toledot ha-Yehudim be-Erez Yisrael bi-Tekufat ha-Mishnah veha-Talmud*—the History of the Jews in Palestine in Mishnaic and Talmudic Times (Tel Aviv, Ha-Kibbuz Ha-Meuhad, 1952–55)—and two volumes of collected essays, *Mehkarim be-Toledot Yisrael*— Studies in Jewish History (Tel Aviv, Ha-Kibbuz Ha-Meuhad, 1957–58), particularly the latter and the first volume of the former, are very important for the serious student. Allon brings to the exegesis of the talmudic and Hellenistic sources the acute sensibilities and skills of the social historian: in his hands texts which seemed dry as dust and problems that for many general historians were too technical or recherché have been made to release fundamental information on religious thought and practice of this period. See at least his essay on "The Attitude of the Pharisees to the Roman Government and the House of Herod," in *Scripta Hierosolymitana,* vol. VII (Jerusalem, 1961), 53–78.

The Hellenistic-Roman age, as has been suggested, was the age when the biblical traditions were assembled and given both a refreshed and fresh consistency and a new momentum by the native wit and whatever techniques could be safely appropriated from the larger civilization surrounding the Jews. It took almost a millennium to achieve this. But once it was achieved, and particularly after the Palestinian and Babylonian Talmuds were redacted (*c.* 400 and 500 respectively), the *groundwork* of the classical tradition had been laid. Thereafter, the post-talmudic scholarly and religious authorities, the Geonim, did everything in their power to establish this Judaism as standard. This, in turn, required almost another half-millennium to accomplish fully. Of course, all variety did not henceforth disappear, and all the tensions of further development were not painlessly resolved; but from this time, whatever developments were recommended or elaborated or accepted (cheerfully or reluctantly) had to be in accommodation with talmudic law and the main lines of talmudic teaching. The climax of classical Judaism was reached with the establishment of the Babylonian Talmud as authoritative by the Geonim. On this theme, see L. Ginzberg's essay "An Introduction to the Palestinian Talmud," reprinted in his volume *On Jewish Law and Lore* (Philadelphia, Jewish Publication Society of America, 1955), and the first volume of his *Geonica* (N.Y., Jewish Theological Seminary of America, 1909).

VIII. THAT WHICH IS SECTARIAN

What is a sect? For the purpose of our discussion, it is sufficient, I believe, if we classify as a sect any group within the larger communion which insists on persisting as a distinct association even after its terms have been essentially adopted by society, or—more particularly our concern in this section—which in the course of time fails to impose its terms—its articulated principal doctrines and its "heroes" and its institutional forms—on that establishment it is battling against and wishes to replace. Some sects are longer-lived than others, and within sects further fission is possible. Often sects have a profound influence on the development and even revitalization of their strongest opposition (and, of course, never have been officially recognized for or credited with their influence); many an establishment, speaking historically, began originally as a sectarian push and demand. But the fact remains that that group within any large complex which fails to impose its terms, as we have said, and therefore fails to be acknowledged as *representative* of the society, is a sect.

Sects fail—in other words, remain sects—for different reasons under different circumstances for different sects; and from the bibliography listed below the student may try to form some idea of what prevented the various sects from successfully making Judaism in their image. I would like to suggest that, whatever else is responsible for the sects' failures, within Jewish history at least it has always been the sects' confusing prevalent forms of real discontent on the part of the folk with the folk's capacity totally to reject the past, or even the irritations of the present.

On the earliest Jewish sect that we have any knowledge of, the best work is still J.A. Montgomery, *The Samaritans* (Philadelphia, John C. Winston, 1907); M. Gaster's *The Samaritans* (London, Oxford Univ. Press, 1925) does not replace it. Some very pertinent remarks are made by Y. Kaufmann in the last volume (especially 185ff.) of his history of the religion of Israel (see above), not yet translated from the Hebrew, to suggest that the Samaritans were *not* of Israelite stock: "they adopted (their) new God not as the God of *Israel,* but as the God of the Land of Israel" (p. 190, author's italics). For an outline and summary of the kind of defense of the Samaritan position which would be drawn up in later times to bolster Samaritan morale, see A.S. Halkin's monograph, "Samaritan Polemics against the Jews," in vol. VII of *Proceedings of the American Academy for Jewish Research* (Philadelphia, 1936), 13–59.

That the Jewish colony at Elephantine ought to be included in our section here seems to me far from certain. Pockets of Jewish settlement in different places doubtless, and at all times, came under local influences and therefore reflect variations of expression and custom, but they were not necessarily attempting to impose their customs or emphases on Catholic Israel, to use S. Schechter's famous expression. But those interested in following up some discussion of this subject might consult the Introduction in A.E. Cowley, *Aramaic Papyri of the Fifth Century B.C.* (Oxford, Clarendon Press, 1923) and E.G. Kraeling's discussion, especially pp. 83–99, in his *The Brooklyn Museum Aramaic Papyri* (New Haven, Yale Univ. Press, 1953).

We know of the famous sects in the period of the Second Commonwealth chiefly through Josephus, talmudic sources, and Philo, and now through discoveries in the neighborhood of the Dead Sea. Literature on the Pharisees has already been cited above; Pharisaism ceased to be a sectarian phenomenon once it triumphed, and in this connection I would like to call attention to a lecture delivered in 1960 by H.L. Ginsberg, "New Light on Tannaite Jewry and on the State of Israel of the Years 132–135 C.E.," published in vol. XXV of the *Proceedings of the Rabbinical Assembly of America* (N.Y., 1961), 132–42. In the works listed the reader will again and again find discussion of the Sadducees. L. Finkelstein's *Pharisees* (Philadelphia, Jewish Publication Society of America, 1938) provides an extensive bibliography which is most useful and a number of specific items (though not in English) concentrate more specifically on the Sadducees. Many works devoted to a study of the Pharisees inevitably deal also with the Essenes; but of the older literature on this group, I should like to mention C.D. Ginsburg, *The Essenes* (London, Longmans, Green, 1861); in addition to his own discussion and a review of leading "modern" opinions, Ginsburg reproduces also the descriptions of this sect as these are furnished by the ancient sources, from Philo to Epiphanius.

The Essenes have once again become a subject of considerable interest because of the discoveries in the caves of the Dead Sea region. It would serve little purpose, even in a bibliographical essay, to try to list all the works which deal with the Dead Sea literature: one can hardly improve on the *Revue de Qumran* appearing in Paris since 1958, and the reader keenly concerned with this material ought to keep consulting that periodical. For the general student, I believe the following works are not only easily accessible but dependable and fair—that is, avoiding excessive speculation and polemic—in treatment: M. Burrows, *The Dead Sea Scrolls* (N.Y., Viking Press, 1955) and *More Light on the Dead Sea Scrolls* (N.Y., Viking Press, 1958); F.M. Cross, Jr., *The Ancient Library of Qumrân and Modern Biblical Studies* (N.Y., Doubleday, 1958). Writings of the Dead Sea sectarians are available in translation not only in M. Burrows' volumes (where, by the way, there are excellent bibliographies too), but also in T.H. Gaster's *The Dead Sea Scriptures in English Translation* (N.Y., Doubleday, 1956) which is accompanied by notes; there is a translation by S.S. Nardi of *A Genesis Apocryphon,* ed. N. Avigad and Y. Yadin (Jerusalem, Hebrew Univ. Magnes Press, 1956), and of the much talked about copper scroll by J.M. Allegro, *The Treasure of the Copper Scroll* (N.Y., Doubleday, 1960).

Regarding some phases of sectarian practice, particularly as it may be related to practices recorded in the Talmud, there is a most illuminating study by S. Lieberman, "Light on the Cave Scrolls from Rabbinic Sources" in vol. XV, 395–404, of *Proceedings of the American Academy for Jewish Research* (N.Y., 1951); see also his paper "The Discipline in the So-Called Dead Sea Manual of Discipline" in *Journal of Biblical Literature,* LXXI (1952), 199–206. Finally, H.L. Ginsberg's essay, "The Dead Sea Manuscript Finds" in *Israel: Its Role in Civilization* (N.Y., Harper & Brothers, 1956), 39–57, discusses problems significant not only for biblical *textual* study but also for the understanding of early biblical interpretation (and *its* relation to crisis in the religious life) and the idiom of liturgy.

The reader will find literature on the early Christians, when they were still a sect within the framework of Jewish society, in the essay on Christianity in this volume.

During Second Commonwealth times there were very likely still other sects than the ones we have referred to: the Mishnah, for example, refers to certain forms of liturgical recitation which must have characterized some Jews deviating from Rabbinic practice—and who exactly these people were, we still cannot say; their specific identity has not yet been established.

For the period after the redaction of the Talmud and its adoption by the academies as the authoritative source for Jewish orthodoxy, a good deal (but not all) of the difficulty in deciding what is sectarian is removed. The post-talmudic authorities regarded as a sectarian one who rejected talmudic authority. This of course did not mean that henceforth absolute uniformity of thought or practice or expression prevailed, but, whatever the varieties or vagaries endorsed or urged, precedent and sanction for them had to be found in the Talmud. There were those, alongside the Judaism governed by the Talmud, who refused to acknowledge the Talmud's authority. On this famous anti-talmudic sect, itself the culmination of several inchoate dissident movements, see J. Mann, "An Early Theologico-Polemical Work" in vols. XII–XIII of the *Hebrew Union College Annual* (1937–38), 411–59; and on the affinities of such sectarianisms with heterodoxies in the Islāmic world, see the important study by I. Friedlaender, "Jewish-Arabic Studies" in the *Jewish Quarterly Review,* I–III (1910–12). Ultimately—the early Rabbanite authorities still wondered at times how according to talmudic law these new dissenters were to be regarded—this sect became a branch *severed* from the main stock, the Karaites.

An excellent anthology of Karaite writings up to 1500 (including, however, extracts from the Karaite prayerbook after that date) is available in L. Nemoy, *Karaite Anthology* (New Haven, Yale Univ. Press, 1952). The histories and encyclopedias listed earlier obviously discuss the Karaite movement as part of Jewish history, but, as Nemoy writes in his Introduction, "Modern critical study of Karaite history and theology is as yet in its infancy." One of the best general presentations of the movement is still that by S. Poznanski in his article, "Karaites," written for vol. VII of Hastings' *Encyclopedia of Religion and Ethics,* 662–72; see, in addition, J. Mann, "New Studies in Karaism" in vol. XLIV of the *Yearbook of the Central Conference of American Rabbis* (1939), 220–41, and *Texts and Studies in Jewish History and Literature,* vol. II (Philadelphia, 1953) for essential source material.

An important contribution to this field of study is Z. Ankori's *Karaites in Byzantium* (N.Y., Columbia Univ. Press, 1959). In addition to its discussion of the specific region upon which it concentrates, the volume is a sophisticated assessment of the character of dissent from Babylonian talmudism and the relation of such nonconformity to messianic frustrations. There is a rich bibliography at the end of the book—most of it, alas, not in English.

The subject of the Karaites brings us at last into the period when, as we have said, the dominant cultural-religious reality is represented by the concentrated activity to establish Babylonian talmudic teaching as authoritative.

XI

Medieval and
Modern Judaism

Seymour Cain

I. INTRODUCTION

Judah Goldin's contribution has brought us to the Geonic age, which established the Babylonian Talmud as authoritative for Jews everywhere. This complement will take us from there to contemporary times and touch on a few topics not mentioned above. It is assumed that the reader has perused Goldin's piece attentively, and that we may refer to literature cited there by the author's surname and a key title term where necessary, without confusion. The histories and standard works cited in III, above, are most useful and illuminating for the intelligent, curious lay reader and should be referred to constantly; they contain comprehensive surveys and short treatises on many of the topics discussed below, and, hence, we shall cite them frequently. In addition, the following works will prove useful: Isidore Epstein, *Judaism: A Historical Presentation* (Harmondsworth, Penguin Books, 1959), a superbly organized and expressed work, especially valuable for its coverage of the Talmudic and Medieval periods (hereafter cited as Epstein); Jacob Neusner, *The Way of Torah: An Introduction to Judaism* (Belmont, Cal., Dickenson, 1970), with deftly chosen bibliographies; Nahum N. Glatzer, *A Jewish Reader: In Time and Eternity* (N.Y., Schocken Books, 1946, 2nd ed., 1961), a consummately selected and edited work; Arthur Hertzberg, *Judaism* (N.Y., George Braziller, 1961; also in a cheap paperback edition), another excellent reader, with citations and brief commentaries, arranged under Judaic religious categories (People, God, Torah, etc.); Israel Abrahams, *Chapters on Jewish Literature* (Philadelphia, Jewish Publication Society of America, 1899; called *Short History of Jewish Literature* in other editions), a clear, brief, yet comprehensive survey, from first-century Palestine to eighteenth-century Germany: Israel Zinberg, *A History of Jewish Literature*, 12 vols. (Cleveland and London, The Press of Case Western Reserve Univ., 1972–   ), a beautifully produced translation from the Yiddish, by Bernard Martin, of this monumental work (vols. I–V available, 1977); Abraham Millgram, *Jewish Worship* (Philadelphia, Jewish Publication Society, 1971), both a systematic and historical presentation of the liturgy enabling the reader to consult it for particular topics or periods of development, with footnotes and bibliographies indicating the basic literature on the subject, and a superbly helpful index; Judah Goldin, ed., *The Jewish Expression* (N.Y., Bantam Books, 1970), a collection of jewels of twentieth-century scholarship in Judaica; *The Study of Judaism: Bibliographical Essays* (N.Y., Ktav, 1972), put out by the Anti-Defamation League of B'nai B'rith with a superb section on Modern Jewish Thought by Fritz Rothschild and Seymour Siegel (*Bibliographical Essays in Medieval Jewish Studies: The Study of Judaism,* vol. II, is promised for 1975–76); Cecil Roth and Geoffrey Wigoder, eds., *The New Standard Jewish Encyclopaedia* (N.Y., Doubleday, 1970), the most useful and comprehensive one-volume work; R.J.Z. Werblowsky and Geoffrey Wigoder, eds., *The Encyclopaedia of the Jewish Religion* (N.Y., Holt, Rinehart and Winston, 1966), centered on religion and with somewhat longer articles than the preceding.

References to the *Encyclopaedia Judaica* (*EJ*) below are to the new English version (1972). *EB=The New Encyclopaedia Britannica* (15th ed., 1974), the 19 vol. Macropaedia segment (the 10 vol. Micropaedia is also useful for particular topics, terms, and persons). JPS=The Jewish Publication Society of America (Philadelphia). Baron, followed by a Roman numeral, refers to a volume in the 2nd ed. (1952–   ) of Salo Baron, *A Social and Religious History of the Jews;* other Baron works and editions will be specified. Waxman, followed by a Roman numeral, refers to a volume of his *A History of Jewish Literature*. Medieval Judaism, in this essay, covers the period from the 7th to the 18th century with some necessary blurring and inconsistency.

II. A DIASPORA RELIGION

In post-talmudic times, Judaism became almost entirely a Diaspora religion, with its main centers and predominant influences outside of Palestine. A distinctive period, the age of the Geonim (c. 640–1038), takes its name from the dominance of the Geonim (singular, Gaon), the heads of the talmudic academies at Sura and Pumbedita in Babylonia. They claimed and usually held supreme authority in Jewish religious law everywhere, and the Babylonian Talmud became the accepted norm of Jewish society and religion for all Jewish communities. (Note, however, Louis Ginzberg's statement, in the aforementioned essay on the Palestinian Talmud, about its continued authority in Palestine and its importance as a subject of study in Egypt, North Africa, and southern Italy.) Moreover, Judaism in the lands where most Jews lived, including Palestine, was subjected to the influence of an alien culture and religion, Arabic Islam, in an interplay which shaped its forms of expression and patterns of thought significantly and creatively, eventuating in one of the two main branches of European Judaism, the Sefardic. Under the usually tolerant Muslim rule, the Jews had self-governing communities, with freedom to practice their religion and to maintain and develop their tradition. It is the prevailing historical consensus, with some vehement dissent, that despite the oppressive taxation and irksome, even degrading humiliations they suffered, along with other "unbelievers," and occasional fanatical persecutions, their situation was good compared with that of Jews under Christian regimes, enabling the growth and expansion of the Jews and Judaism.

For overviews of the whole medieval period, see Gerson Cohen, "Rabbinic Judaism," in "Judaism, History of," *EB*, 10; A. Steinberg, "The History of the Jews in the Middle Ages and Modern Times," *The Jewish People* I; and Ben Zion Dinur, "Israel in Diaspora," *Israel and the Diaspora* (Philadelphia, JPS, 1969), written by a great Israeli historian who sees Palestine as central in Jewish faith and life during the Diaspora experience and provides a critical consideration of the main lines of Jewish historical thought on this question. For the specific Geonic development, see Grayzel, Book II; Marx and Margolis, Book II; Graetz, III; Judah Goldin, "The Age of the Talmud," sec. 10–12, in Finkelstein, *The Jews;* and Abrahams, *Jewish Literature,* ch. V. For a clear, concise yet comprehensive and balanced presentation of the Judeo-Islamic period as a whole (7th to 13th centuries) see Abraham S. Halkin, "The Judeo-Islamic Age," in Schwartz, *Great Ages and Ideas of the Jewish People.* For the situation of the Jews in medieval Islam, see Baron, III; Nissim Rejwan, "Arab-Jewish Relations Through the Ages: A Problem for the

Historian," *Dispersion and Unity,* 19/20 (1973), 87; and S.D. Goitein, *Jews and Arabs* (N.Y., Schocken Books, 1964). On the question of the influence of Judaism on Islam, see Abraham Geiger, *Judaism and Islam* (N.Y., Ktav, 1970); Charles C. Torrey, *The Jewish Foundation of Islam* (N.Y., Jewish Institute of Religion Press, 1933); Abraham I. Katsh, *Judaism in Islam* (N.Y., Bloch, 1954); and S.D. Goitein, "Muhammad's Inspiration by Judaism," *The Journal of Jewish Studies,* vol. IX (1958), 149.

After the period of Babylonian dominance other centers, some of long standing and some newly created, flourished independently, and major talmudic academies were to be found in North Africa, Spain, Italy, Provence, Germany, and Poland/Lithuania. The European Jew and his rendering(s) of Judaism became predominant for almost a millennium. It was in Christian Europe that Jews and Judaism suffered the cruelest and most relentless persecution in their history, and yet achieved such a remarkable creativity in scholarship, life-ways, and religious experience that Judaism came to be identified with the European (and even the Ashkenazic!) version in the common, unhistorical mind. (Important centers also arose in Palestine, Egypt, and Turkey during this period.)

A good introduction to the history, achievements, and ways of European Jewry is provided by Cecil Roth, "The European Age," in Schwartz, including a chapter on "a day in the life of an ordinary Jewish household." See also his earlier, "The Jews in the Middle Ages," *Cambridge Medieval History,* VII (N.Y. and Cambridge, Macmillan and Cambridge Univ. Press, 1932), with a very extensive bibliography. With these should go a most enjoyable work on the Jewish Middle Ages, Israel Abrahams, *Jewish Life in the Middle Ages* (N.Y., Meridian Books; Philadelphia, JPS, 1958; paperback, Atheneum, 1969). For the Spanish-Jewish development, see Zinberg, I (on Muslim Spain); Yitzhak Baer, *A History of the Jews in Christian Spain,* 2 vols. (Philadelphia, JPS, 1961), one of the monumental works of contemporary Jewish scholarship; Abraham A. Neuman, *The Jews in Spain,* 2 vols. (Philadelphia, JPS, 1942); and Cecil Roth, *A History of the Marranos* (N.Y., Harper & Row, 1966)—elucidatory and elaborative footnotes, including bibliographical sources, for the chapter entitled "The Religion of the Marranos," are appended to the original version in *The Jewish Quarterly Review,* n.s., XXII (1931–32). On Italy, see again Cecil Roth, *The History of the Jews of Italy* (Philadelphia, JPS, 1946) and *The Jews in the Renaissance* (Philadelphia, JPS, 1959); and Moses A. Shulvass, *The Jews in the World of the Renaissance* (Leiden, E.J. Brill and Spertus College of Judaica Press, 1973). On England see Cecil Roth, *A History of the Jews in England* (Oxford, Oxford Univ. Press, 1949). For France see Robert Anchel, *Les Juifs de France* (Paris, J.B. Janin Éditeur, 1946). For Germany see Guido Kisch, *The Jews in Medieval Germany* (N.Y., Ktav, 1970); Marvin Lowenthal,

The Jews of Germany (Toronto, Longmans, Green, 1936); and Ismar Elbogen, *Geschichte der Juden in Deutschland* (Berlin, Jüdische Buch-Vereinigung, 1935). On the Eastern European developments, see the aforementioned work of Dubnow on the Jews of Russia and Poland, with a systematic index of some 200 pages, which not only lists but identifies and informs; Bernard Weinryb, *The Jews of Poland* (Philadelphia, JPS, 1972) covering the period 1100–1800; and these two essays in Finkelstein, *The Jews:* Israel Halpern, "The Jews in Eastern Europe (From Ancient Times until the Partitions of Poland, 1772–1795)," and Abraham Menes, "Patterns of Jewish Scholarship in Eastern Europe." A special jewel in the literature on Eastern European Jewry is Abraham Joshua Heschel, "The Earth Is the Lord's" in *The Earth Is the Lord's and the Sabbath* (Philadelphia, JPS, 1963).

For Christian anti-Semitism, see Cecil Roth, "The Medieval Conception of the Jew," in Israel Davidson, ed., *Essays and Studies in Memory of Linda R. Miller* (N.Y., Jewish Theological Seminary, 1938); Joshua Trachtenberg, *The Devil and the Jews* (New Haven, Yale Univ. Press, 1943); Leopold Zunz, *The Sufferings of the Jews during the Middle Ages* (N.Y., Bloch, 1907); Edward H. Flannery, *The Anguish of the Jews* (N.Y., Macmillan, 1965); James Parkes, *The Conflict of the Church and the Synagogue* (Philadelphia, JPS, 1961), *The Jew in the Medieval Community* (London, Soncino Press, 1938), *Judaism and Christianity* (Chicago, Univ. of Chicago Press, 1948); Leon Poliakov, *The History of Anti-Semitism,* I & II (N.Y., Vanguard Press, 1965 and 1973), the first of four promised volumes; Graetz, III–V, *passim.* For the special case of Spain, see Baer and Neuman and Roth's books on the Marranos. For the Italian Ghetto see Roth's *Jews of Italy.* For polemic and debate, see O.S. Rankin, *Jewish Religious Polemic* (Edinburgh, Edinburgh Univ. Press, 1956); Hans Joachim Schoeps, *The Jewish-Christian Argument* (N.Y., Holt, Rinehart and Winston, 1963); and Baron, IX.

III. LITURGY, LIFE–DISCIPLINE, AND CUSTOMS

The basic structure of Jewish liturgy had been established in the first century by Gamaliel II at Yavneh, but a great many additions were made during the talmudic and Geonic ages, including the development of a new prayer-form, the *piyut* (plural, *piyutim*) or prayer-poem, which came to take over an ever-larger part of the service. The greatest liturgical contribution of the Geonim was the production of the first *Siddur* (Order, or Prayerbook), an innovative break with the traditional ban on writing down the prayers. This was first done in the 9th century by Amram bar Sheshna, Gaon at Sura, and for a wider readership, with commentaries in Arabic, in the 10th century by Saadia ben Joseph. For the first prayerbook, see

David Hedgard, *Seder R. Amram Gaon: Part I* (Lund, A.-B. Linstdets Universitets-Bokhandel, 1951), including Hebrew text, English translation, and notes. During the later, post-Geonic Middle Ages, further additions took place, including the emphasis on Yahrzeit and Yizkor memorial observances, dirges and martyrologies, and penitential prayers, in response to the grim situation of Jewry in Christendom. The mystical movement (see VI below), with its intense concentration on prayer, produced its own prayerbooks (e.g. the *Siddur Ha-Ari*) and table-hymns, and left its imprint on the standard prayerbooks. It was in this time that the *hazan,* or cantor, became the central participant in the synagogue service, so that often the congregation of worshippers became an audience of listeners. But at the same time devotional prayers in the vernacular were being created, usually for women and often by women, and in the Hasidic conventicles later on the emphasis was on the most active participation and intense piety, including group singing, by the lay members. The old-time emphasis on the homily or sermon, going back to the Pharisees, declined—there was hardly time for it with all the *piyutim* and the virtuoso performances of the cantors. Besides, the official rabbi was a legal scholar and judge rather than a preacher. It was the itinerant lay preacher, or *maggid,* feeling called upon to preach to the common people, who often performed that necessary function.

The best available work for the English-speaking reader to follow these developments is Millgram, *Jewish Worship,* esp. Part III. See also Idelsohn, *Jewish Liturgy,* chs. IV–VII, and the Introduction to Jacob J. Petuchowski, ed., *Contributions to the Scientific Study of Jewish Liturgy* (N.Y., Ktav, 1970). For German readers the historical section, "Geschichte des jüdisches Gottesdienstes," in Elbogen, *Der jüdische Gottesdienst,* cited above, including a long discussion of the era of the *piyut* and Leopold Zunz, *Die synagogale Poesie des Mittelälters* (Berlin, J. Springer, 1855), are recommended. The essays on homilies and worship in Baron, VI and VII, are very helpful. See also the presentation of sacred poetry in Waxman, I, with many examples, and the translations of religious poems, prayers, hymns and dirges in Abraham Millgram, *An Anthology of Medieval Hebrew Literature* (N.Y., Abelard-Schuman, 1961); and read Shalom Spiegel, "On Medieval Hebrew Poetry," in Finkelstein, *The Jews,* also in Goldin, *Jewish Expression.* A beautifully printed and translated selection of prayers, including occasional and vernacular women's prayers, is presented in Nahum N. Glatzer, *Language of Faith* (N.Y., Schocken Books, 1967). On the *maggid* and his preaching, see "Introduction: Maggidim and Hasidim: Their Preaching Method and Art," in Louis I. Newman, ed., *Maggidim and Hasidim* (N.Y., Bloch, 1962). On the special liturgy for the High Holy Days, see Max Arzt, *Justice and Mercy* (N.Y., Holt, Rinehart and Winston, 1963), with an excellent Introduction on

Jewish liturgy. For liturgical music, see Abraham Z. Idelsohn, *Jewish Music in Its Historical Development* (New York, Schocken Books, 1967), probably the best introduction in English; and his monumental *Thesaurus of Hebrew Oriental Melodies,* 10 vols. in 4 (N.Y., Ktav, 1973); Eric Werner, *From Generation to Generation* (N.Y., American Conference of Cantors, 1968) and *The Sacred Bridge* (N.Y., Columbia Univ. Press, 1959); Reuben R. Rinder, ed., *Music and Prayer* (N.Y., Sacred Music Press of the Hebrew Union College-Jewish Institute of Religion, 1959); "Music," *Encyclopaedia Judaica,* with extensive bibliography; "Cantillation," *Jewish Encyclopaedia,* on the intonation of prayers and Scripture readings; and, more fully, Solomon Rosowsky, *The Cantillation of the Bible* (N.Y., Reconstructionist Press, 1957).

Medieval Judaism, as also its lineal successors, was as much a home religion as a public liturgical cult, indeed, even more so. Moreover, the Jew was regulated in all the aspects of daily existence, including prescribed individual prayers, by a sacral life-discipline from the moment he got up in the morning until the moment he went to bed at night; and his life rhythm was regulated by a sacral calendar, punctuated each week by the holy Sabbath and culminating annually in the Days of Awe from the New Year to the Day of Atonement. In addition, local patterns of observances, customs, and folkways arose in the various lands of dispersion. For this all-embracing pattern see "Basic Practices and Institutions," in Lou Silberman, "Judaism," *EB;* Sid Leiman, "Jewish Religious Year," *ibid.;* Epstein, *Judaism,* ch. 16; Abrahams, *Jewish Life,* ch. VII–X; Meyer Waxman, *A Handbook of Judaism* (Chicago, L.M. Stein, 1953); Abraham Z. Idelsohn, *The Ceremonies of Judaism* (Cincinnati, The National Federation of Temple Brotherhoods, 1930); Samuel H. Dresner, *The Jewish Dietary Laws* (N.Y., Burning Book Press, 1959); Jacob Z. Lauterbach, *Studies in Jewish Law, Custom and Folklore* (N.Y., Ktav, 1970), also "Tashlik," in *Rabbinic Essays;* Simon M. Lehrman, *Jewish Customs and Folklore* (London, Shapiro, Vallentine, 1949), from a traditionalist viewpoint; Theodor H. Gaster, *Customs and Folkways of Jewish Life* (N.Y., William Sloane Assoc., 1955), from a comparative folklorist viewpoint; Harry M. Rabinowicz, *A Guide to Life: Jewish Laws and Customs of Mourning* (London, Jewish Chronicle Publications, 1964); Hayyim Schauss, *Guide to Jewish Holy Days* (N.Y., Schocken Books, 1962); Theodor H. Gaster, *Festivals of the Jewish Year* (N.Y., William Sloane Assoc., 1953); Shmuel Yosef Agnon, *Days of Awe* (N.Y., Schocken Books, 1948), truly "a treasure of traditions, legends, and learned commentaries"; A.J. Heschel, "The Sabbath," in *The Earth Is the Lord's and the Sabbath;* Joshua Trachtenberg, *Jewish Magic and Superstition* (Philadelphia, JPS, 1961); Louis M. Epstein, *Sex Laws and Customs in Judaism* (N.Y., Ktav, 1948).

IV. INTERPRETATION, COMMENTARY, AND CODIFICATION

It is a truism that post-Biblical Judaism was essentially interpretive and commentative. The Talmud is a commentary on the Mishnah, which itself has been presented as a commentary on the Torah, and in medieval times there were commentaries on the Talmud too, not to speak of commentaries on the commentaries. During this period significant linguistic and exegetical studies on the Hebrew Bible preceded or accompanied talmudic commentary. Stimulated by the Arab example of linguistic studies and the challenge of the Karaite back-to-the-Bible movement, a phenomenal development of Hebrew textual, grammatical, and exegetical studies took place. First came the Masoretic standardization of the biblical text (6th–10th centuries), then systematic work on Hebrew grammar and lexicography, accompanied and indeed motivated by biblical exegesis. "Normative" rabbanite exegesis was the response of "heretical" Karaite exegesis. The first great biblical exegete was Saadia, with his Arabic translation and commentary. Later, in France, it was the commentary of Rashi of Troyes (Rab Solomon Yitzhaki), especially on the Pentateuch, that became the standard for Jews, down to our own times. And in Iberia and Provence, luminaries such as Nachmanides, Jacob ben Asher, Gersonides, and Don Isaac Abrabanel made significant contributions to biblical exegesis. For these philological and exegetical developments see Waxman, I and II; Baron, VI and VII; W. Bacher, "Bible Exegesis—Jewish," *The Jewish Encyclopaedia;* Avraham Grossman, "Medieval Rabbinic Commentaries," *Encyclopaedia Judaica;* Louis Ginzberg, "Allegorical Interpretation of Scripture," in *On Jewish Law and Lore;* Bernard M. Casper, *An Introduction to Jewish Bible Commentary* (N.Y., Thomas Yoseloff, 1960). For Rashi, see *Pentateuch with Targum Onkelos, Haphtaroth and Prayers for Sabbath and Rashi's Commentary* (London, Shapiro, Vallentine, 1932), or *Rashi: Commentaries on the Pentateuch,* selected and tr. by Chaim Perl (N.Y., W.W. Norton, 1970). For the Masoretes see "Text. Old Testament," Sec. A.4, and "Masoretic Accents," *The Interpreters Dictionary of the Bible* (N.Y., Abingdon Press, 1962); Christian D. Ginzburg, *The Masorah,* 4 vols. (London, 1880–1905).

The Talmud ruled liturgy and life, communal and personal existence, during the Middle Ages. In order to do this effectively in post-talmudic times and circumstances, in widely varying regions and milieus, the text required interpretation and codification. Commentaries were written in the Geonic period, notably by Saadia and Hai, of which only parts are extant. The great work of talmudic commentary was done in the post-Geonic era in the new centers, i.e., Kairwan in North Africa (notably

Al-Fasi), Spain (notably Maimonides), France-Germany (notably Ger-shom ben Yehuda, Rashi, and the Tosafists), Italy, and Provence. Codi-fication began quite early, even before the commentaries, because of the practical need for a systematization and application of the mass of mate-rials in the Talmud. The most notable commentaries in the Geonic era were the *Sheiltoth, Halakoth Pesuqoth,* and the *Halakoth Godoloth,* with Saadia and Hai again making contributions. The great work of codification took place later in the new centers, especially North Africa and Spain, where the great names again are Al-Fasi and Maimonides, and France-Germany. Maimonides' Code, the *Mishne Torah,* was in effect Maimonides' own Talmud, for he claimed a man would need no other book to under-stand the Oral Law (Mishnah) and, by implication, the Written Law too. The next great code was the widely accepted *Sefer-ha-Turim* (Book of Rows), by the Provencal rabbi Jacob ben Asher, a modestly presented work, limited to laws applicable after the Fall of the Temple. And finally came the *Shulhan Arukh* (Prepared Table) by Joseph Karo, a Spanish-Bulgarian legal scholar and mystic who settled in Palestine. This work, a digest of a much larger work of Karo's based on the *Turim,* while essen-tially Sefardic in tradition and authorities cited, also became the standard code for Ashkenazic Jews, when combined with the annotations, entitled *Mapah* (Tablecloth), of the great Polish scholar Moses Isserles. In modern time a condensation for lay readers, *Kitzur* (Abbreviated) *Shulhan Arukh,* by Solomon Ganzfried, gained wide acceptance. Naturally, in a commentative religious culture, the codes also drew commentaries, espe-cially the *Mishneh Torah,* the *Turim,* and the *Shulhan Arukh.*

A special type of literature, directly related to the commentaries and codes, was the *Responsa,* replies to questions on points of law, originally initiated by the Babylonian Geonim in response to queries from outlying communities. About a dozen collections (*She'elot-u-Teshuvot*) of Geonic *Responsa* are available, besides numerous fragmentary *Responsa;* they constituted prime authorities for later legal decisions. Later on, the North African and Spanish scholars wrote *Responsa,* e.g. Ibn Megash, Al-Fasi, and Maimonides (including his famous "Letter to Yemen"), so also the Franco-German, Provençal, and other regional scholars. Indeed the largest part of Rabbinic literature in the period of the great commentaries and codes was in the *Responsa* genre. Because of the specific character of the queries, the *Responsa* provide a firsthand source for the everyday life of Jews in the Middle Ages. For an excellent and fascinating example of studies based on such Rabbinic literature, see Louis I. Rabinowicz, *The Social Life of the Jews of Northern France in the XII–XIV Centuries,* 2nd ed. (N.Y., Hermon Press, 1972).

For a comprehensive survey of Talmudic commentaries, codes, and re-sponsa, see Waxman, I and II; Baron, VI; Epstein, ch. 17, 20; Louis Ginz-berg, "The Codification of Law," in *Jewish Law and Lore;* Menachem

Elon, "Codification of Law," *Encyclopaedia Judaica.* On the *Mishneh Torah,* generally regarded as the greatest work in Rabbinic literature, see Isidore Twersky, ed., *A Maimonides Reader* (N.Y., Behrman House, 1972), which includes the Introduction and selections from all 14 books of the work; or Maimonides, *The Mishneh Torah,* 3 vols., ed. and tr. Moses Hyamson (N.Y., Bloch, 1949), a translation of the first two books ("Knowledge" and "Love") in full; or *The Code of Maimonides,* 14 vols. (New Haven, Yale Univ. Press, 1949, 1963), a publication of the whole of the *Mishneh Torah* in English. For Karo's code, see *Code of Hebrew Law: Shulhan 'Aruk,* 5 vols., tr. and ed. Chaim N. Denburg (Montreal, Jurisprudence Press, 1955–   ), a publication of the whole work with extensive commentaries (Vols. I–IV available, 1974); or Solomon Granzfried, *Code of Jewish Law: Kitzur Shulhan Aruk,* tr. Hyman E. Goldin, annotated rev. ed. (N.Y., Hebrew Publ. Co., 1961), the 19th-century digest for everyman. See also Isidore Twersky, "The *Shulhan 'Aruk:* Enduring Code of Jewish Law," *Judaism,* XVI, 2, Spring, 1969, 141; also in Goldin, *Jewish Expression.* On the *Responsa,* see Solomon B. Freehof, *The Responsa Literature and a Treasury of Responsa* (N.Y., Ktav, 1973); Abrahams, *Jewish Literature,* ch. 5; and Maimonides, "Epistle to Yemen," and "Letter on Astrology," in Twersky, *Maimonides Reader.* For the application of the rabbinical rules (*Takkanot*) by communal and intercommunal organizations, see Louis Finkelstein, *Jewish Self-Government in the Middle Ages* (N.Y., Philipp Feldheim, 1964); Neuman, *Jews in Spain,* I; Jacob Katz, *Tradition and Crisis* (Glencoe, Free Press, 1961); Baron, *The Jewish Community;* and Louis Rabinowicz.

V. MEDIEVAL PHILOSOPHY AND ETHICS

Medieval Jewish philosophy is one of the main evidences of the shaping influence of Arab Muslim culture on the Jewish spirit (Sefardic). Not only was the Aristotelianism and Neo-Platonism received through Arabic sources of a special kind, but many early medieval Jewish philosophers belonged to a school generated by Islam, the Kalam. It is also noteworthy, as S.D. Goitein points out, that it was in an alien culture far removed in space and time from the Hellenistic culture in which Jews had once lived that Greek ideas and science first made a deep and decisive inroad into the very heart of Judaism (as, notably, in the works of Maimonides). Moreover, in the later Middle Ages the Jews were the transmitters of Arabic-Greek thought and science to Western Christendom, and influenced and were influenced by Christian philosophy and theology. The medieval Jewish philosophers, however, should not be labelled as rationalists in the modern sense of being opposed to biblical faith, talmudic tradition, and mystical experience and speculation. Some, in fact, were anti-rationalist or anti-philosophic (against Greek philosophy); many were centered in biblical and talmudic inspiration and studies, and some of them were definitely mystical. Biblicism, talmudism, philosophy, and mysticism could be present at the same time in a Jewish philosopher.

Since Isaac Husik lamented the dearth of books on Jewish philosophy in English a half-century ago, there have been many additions to the literature. Husik's own work, *A History of Medieval Jewish Philosophy* (N.Y., Atheneum, 1969, first pub. in 1916) still remains a sound and useful manual, containing an instructive introduction and excellent index. Section II, "Jewish Religious Philosophy in the Middle Ages," in Julius Guttmann, *Philosophies of Judaism* (N.Y., Holt, Reinhart, and Winston, 1964) is also an indispensable aid for its presentation of the broad sweep and main schools of medieval Jewish philosophy. For another excellent introduction see Georges Vajda, *Introduction à la pensée juive du moyen âge* (Paris, Librairie Philosophique J. Vrin, 1947), with a superb annotated bibliography by an eminent contemporary scholar of medieval Jewish philosophy and mysticism. See also Jacob B. Agus, *The Evolution of Jewish Thought* (N.Y., Abelard-Schuman, 1959), chaps. 6–8; Joseph L. Blau, *The Story of Jewish Philosophy* (N.Y., Random House, 1962), chaps. 5–8; Goitein, *Jews and Arabs,* 140–48; Epstein, ch. 18, esp. 198–222; Baron, VIII; Graetz, III; Waxman, I and II; and Zinberg, I. For an excellent brief treatment by an outstanding scholar, see Shlomo Pines, "Jewish Philosophy," *EB,* 10, especially 208–14.

On Saadia, the great, many-sided Gaon, see Henry Malter, *Saadia Gaon: His Life and Works* (Philadelphia, JPS, 1921); David Neumark, "Saadya's Philosophy: Sources, Characteristics and Principles," in *Essays in Jewish Philosophy* (Cincinnati, Central Conference of American Rabbis, 1929); Saadia Gaon, *The Book of Beliefs and Opinions,* tr. Samuel Rosenblatt (New Haven, Yale Univ. Press, 1949); and the excellent, short bibliography in Moses Zucker, "Sa'adia ben Joseph," *EB.* Abridged editions of Saadia's *Beliefs and Opinions* and of Judah Halevi, *Kuzari,* are available in Hans Lewy et al., *Three Jewish Philosophers* (Philadelphia, J.P.S., 1960); a paperback edition of the unabridged Kuzari is available in Judah Halevi, *The Kuzari* (N.Y., Schocken Books, 1964). On Halevi, see Jefim H. Schirmann, "Judah ha-Levi," *EB;* "Jehuda Hallevi's Philosophy," in Neumark; Graetz, III, chap. xi. For Maimonides, the greatest medieval Jewish philosopher, see Moses Maimonides, *The Guide of the Perplexed,* tr., introduced, and annotated by Shlomo Pines, with an illuminating introductory essay by Leo Strauss, a master of the Guide; also available in a handy paperback edition is the older Michael Friedlander translation, called *The Guide for the Perplexed* (N.Y., Dover Press, 1956). An abbreviated version, with introduction and commentary by Julius Guttman, appears in Moses Maimonides, *The Guide of the Perplexed,* tr. Chaim Rabin (London, East and West Library, 1952), and there is a generous selection from Pines' translation in Twersky's *Maimonides Reader,* which also contains an excellent introduction on Maimonides' life and works. For a stimulating discussion of the perplexities of the *Guide,* see "The Philosophy of Maimonides," in Isaac Husik, *Philosophical Essays,* eds. Milton C. Nahm and Leo Strauss (Oxford, Basil Blackwell, 1952). For the intrusion of philosophical rationalism into the very heart of law and its codification, see Isidore Twersky, "Some Non-Halakhic Aspects of the Mishnah Torah," in Alexander Altmann, ed., *Jewish Medieval and Renaissance Studies* (Cambridge, Harvard Univ. Press, 1967).

For ethics, see Bachya Ibn Pakuda, *Duties of the Heart,* tr. M. Hyamson, 5 vols. (N.Y., Bloch, 1925–45), one of the most popular and influential of medieval Jewish ethical writings; Judah Ben Samuel, *Book of the Pious (Sefer Hasidism),* listed as Sholom Alchanan Singer, tr., *Medieval Jewish Mysticism: Book of the Pious* (Wheeling, Ill., Whitehall, 1971), a favorite book of medieval Ashkenazic Jewry, a major ethical work, and also central in medieval German mystical pietism; and Israel Abrahams, ed., *Hebrew Ethical Wills,* 2 vols. (Philadelphia, JPS, 1958). The latter is a selection from "a distinctive Jewish genre" of ethical literature, written on various occasions by fathers for their families, which despite a good deal of tedious sententiousness provides a vivid portrait of the personal religion and socio-cultural milieu of Jews in medieval times. On this special genre, see Abrahams, "Jewish Ethical Wills," *The Jewish Quarterly Review,* o.s., vol. III (1891), 436; and "Jewish Ethical Wills: Texts and Additions," *ibid.,* vol. IV (1892), 333. See also the selections from medieval Jewish philosophical and ethical writings in Nahum N. Glatzer, ed., *Faith and Knowledge* (Boston, Beacon Press, 1963), an excellent collection by the prince of Jewish anthologists.

VI. MYSTICISM, MESSIANISM, AND HASIDISM

Also of primary importance in the medieval contribution to the Jewish spirit was the development of mysticism, or Kabbala, which with its major work the *Zohar,* once held a place in the Jewish community practically on a par with the biblical and talmudic expressions. The outstanding scholar on this subject is Gershom Scholem, who has made its study a methodical, respected academic discipline. See, above all, *Major Trends in Jewish Mysticism* (N.Y., Schocken Books, 1941), still the best introduction; "Jewish Mysticism and Kabbalah," *The Jewish People, I: On the Kabbalah and Its Symbolism* (N.Y., Schocken Books, 1965); and the article "Kabbalah" in *Encyclopaedia Judaica,* with a very extensive bibliography, also published separately as *Kabbalah* (N.Y., Quadrangle Books, 1974). For other introductions, see J. Abelson, *Jewish Mysticism* (London, G. Bell and Sons, 1913); Ernst Mueller, *A History of Jewish Mysticism* (Oxford, East and West Library, 1946); Georges Vajda, "Jewish Mysticism," *EB;* Louis Ginzberg, "The Cabbala," in *Jewish Law and Lore;* and Christian David Ginsburg, *The Kabbalah: Its Doctrines, Developments, and Literature* (London, G. Routledge and Sons, 1920), a pioneer work, originally published in 1865. For the background of Lurianic Kabbala, see Solomon Schechter, "Safed in the Sixteenth Century," in *Studies in Judaism* (Philadelphia, JPS, 1958), also valuable on Karo as a mystic; and Rivka Schatz-Uffenheimer, "Luria, Isaac ben Solomon," *EB*. For more on Karo's mysticism, see R.J. Zwi Werblowsky, *Joseph Karo: Lawyer and Mystic* (Oxford, Oxford Univ. Press, 1962). For the influence of Kabbala on folk beliefs and practices, see Joshua Trachtenberg, *Jewish Magic and Superstition* (Philadelphia, JPS, 1961). On Kabbalism, see also Graetz, III–IV–V; Baron, VIII; Zinberg, III; Waxman, II; and Baer, *History,* I. Remember in reading Graetz that he is filled with disgust for Kabbala, Hasidism, and all their works and worthies. He is cited here as a famous and eloquent example of a certain point of view (which is by no means dead). For an excellent survey of the work of contemporary scholars on salient problems in the study of Jewish mysticism, see Georges Vajda, "Recherches récents sur l'ésoterisme juif," *Revue de l'histoire des religions,* 147–48 (1955), 62; 163–64 (1963), 39, 191; and 165–66 (1964), 49. For original sources on Kabbala, see *The Zohar,* tr. J. Harry Sperling and Maurice Simon, with introduction by Dr. J. Abelson, 5 vols. (London, Soncino Press, 1933); Gershom G. Scholem, ed., *Zohar: The Book of Splendor* (N.Y., Schocken Books, 1963), a tiny selection with introduction by Scholem; Moses Cordovero, *The Palm Tree of Deborah,* tr. Louis Jacobs (London, Valentine, Mitchell, 1960); Glatzer, *Faith and Knowledge,* ch. IX; Millgram, *Anthology,* ch. V.

Messianism is of central importance during this era, not only as idea and belief, but increasingly as socio-religious movements, sometimes vast and cataclysmic in scope, as in the case of Sabbatianism. Diaspora meant not only the physical condition of dispersion, but even more the spiritual trauma of exile—from the Holy Land, from the center of Jewish existence, from Zion—a state from which Jewish souls constantly sought relief, living always in expectation of imminent liberation. Someday the Messiah would come and the Jews would return to their Land, and freely and fully observe God's Torah in the restored kingdom; but beyond that, all mankind and the whole universe would be regenerated and saved, made whole and new (even the Torah would be made new, or revealed anew in its fullness, in some views). The sufferings of the Jews were for the sake of all mankind, indeed, for all creation; and they would come to an end on a day that some claimed could be calculated by various methods, which others insisted could not be fathomed by the human mind, or by divine power alone, or also by human effort.

For the Jewish response to the Exile, Baer's little jewel of a book, *Galut,* should be read and reread again. The ancient background of Messianism is covered in Joseph Klausner's, *The Messianic Idea in Israel* (London, Allen and Unwin, 1956); the biblical and rabbinical views of Torah in the Messianic Age are discussed in W.D. Davies' *Torah in the Messianic Age;* Messianic ideas and movements in the earlier Middle Ages are treated in Baron, V; the whole scope of Messianic development from biblical times to Reform and Zionism, including Kabbalistic views, is presented in Julius H. Greenstone, *The Messiah Idea in Jewish History* (Philadelphia, JPS, 1906); views from Saadia to Abrabanel, but excluding Kabbalistic views as non-normative, are covered in Joseph Sarachek, *The Doctrine of the Messiah in Medieval Jewish Literature* (N.Y., Jewish Theological Seminary of America, 1968); the various methods of "calculating the end" and anti-calculationist views, from the 1st to the 17th centuries, are presented in Abba Hillel Silver, *History of Messianic Speculation in Israel* (N.Y., Macmillan, 1927). Brief introductory articles on Messianic movements are presented in *The Jewish People,* I: A. Steinberg, "Messianic Movements up to the End of the Middle Ages," and Gershom G. Scholem, "Messianic Movements after the Expulsion from Spain." Scholem has provided profound and rich analyses and interpretations of Messianism in *The Messianic Idea in Judaism* (N.Y., Schocken Books, 1971) and *Sabbatai Sevi* (Princeton, Princeton Univ. Press, 1973), a monumental work on the leading figure in the greatest and most disastrous Messianic movement in Jewish history. For Scholem's view of Messianism see Seymour Cain, "Gershom Scholem on Jewish Messianism," *Midstream,* XVII, 10 (1971), 35. On Sabbatianism and its aftermath, see also Weinryb, *Jews of Poland.*

Hasidism, the life-affirming pietistic movement that arose in mid-18th century Eastern Europe—not to be confused with the ethical-ascetic German Hasidism of the 13th-14th centuries—is discussed here for topical convenience as stemming in a direct line from Kabbalistic and Sabbatian developments, although in its contemporary historical context it belongs with the modern movements discussed in the next section. Hasidism is covered in Scholem's *Major Trends* and *Messianic Idea;* Mueller's *History;* Graetz V, with venom; the histories of Grayzel, Marx and Margolis; Waxman, III; Dubnow's *Jews in Russia and Poland,* with mixed feelings; Weinryb's *Jews of Poland,* with rare objectivity; Raphael Mahler, *A History of Modern Jewry,* 1780–1815 (N.Y., Schocken Books, 1971), including a lengthy consideration of Hasidism in its early creative phase, from a national and social viewpoint, by a great Israeli Marxist historian; "Hasidism," by various hands, including Louis Jacobs and Rivka Schatz-Uffenheimer, *Encyclopaedia Judaica;* and J.B. Agus, *The Evolution of*

Jewish Thought. Martin Buber, the preeminent presenter of Hasidism to the contemporary Western world, has written many Hasidic works, of which these few are recommended: *Hasidism* (N.Y., Philosophical Library, 1948), also in a new translation somewhat altered in form, entitled *The Origin and Meaning of Hasidism* (N.Y., Harper Torchbooks, 1958); *Hasidism and Modern Man* (N.Y., Harper Torchbooks, 1958); *Ten Rungs: Hasidic Sayings* (N.Y., Schocken Books, 1947), a little jewel; *The Way of Man* (London, Routledge & Kegan Paul, 1950), a significant opuscule; *The Tales of the Hasidim,* 2 vols. (N.Y., Farrar, Strauss & Young, 1947–48), Buber's monumental recreation of the original Hasidic oral literature, an event in modern Western cultural history; and his Hasidic "novel," *For the Sake of Heaven* (N.Y., Harper & Bros., 1953). For a critical scholarly attack on Buber's view of Hasidism, see Scholem, "Martin Buber's Interpretation of Hasidism," in *Messianic Idea,* and Rivka Schatz-Uffenheimer, "Man's Relation to God and World in Buber's Rendering of the Hasidic Teaching," in Paul Arthur Schilpp and Maurice Friedman, eds., *The Philosophy of Martin Buber* (La Salle, Ill., Open Court, 1967), and for Buber's riposte, see *ibid.,* pp. 731–44.

Many cardinal works on Hasidism are written in modern Hebrew and will be unavailable to most readers. However, Dubnow's history of Hasidism, *Toledot Ha-hasidut,* is available in German, *Geschichte des Chassidismus,* 2 vols. (Berlin, Jüdischer Verlag, 1951); and Samuel A. Horodetsky, noted for his four volume study of Hasidism, *Ha-Hasidut veha-Hasidism,* is represented in English by *Leaders of Hassidism* (London, Hasefer Agency for Literature, 1928), a direct, quite simple, partisan presentation of the Hasidic leaders and community; and there is also the Israeli author Eliezer Steinmann's *The Garden of Hassidism* (Jerusalem, World Zionist Organization, 1961), presenting the Habad version of Hasidism. Among introductory works for the general reader, one of the best is Harry M. Rabinowicz, *The World of Hasidism* (London, Valentine, Mitchell, 1970); Louis Jacobs, *Hasidic Prayer* (London, Routledge and Kegan Paul, 1972) treats a central Hasidic act and provides many citations on the doctrines of the masters; and Samuel H. Dresner, *The Zaddik* (N.Y., Abelard-Schuman, 1960) gives a careful, perceptive study of one of the masters. The late Joseph G. Weiss, a brilliant young English disciple of Scholem's, has left behind a number of valuable papers on Hasidism among which are "Contemplative Mysticism and 'Faith' in Hasidic Piety," *The Journal of Jewish Studies,* IV (1953), 19; "R. Abraham Kalisker's Concept of Communion with God and Men," *ibid.,* VI (1955), 87; and "The Kavvanoth of Prayer in Early Hasidism," *ibid.,* IX (1958), 163.

Among other collections of Hasidic tales and legends, besides Buber's, are Dan Ben-Amos and Jerome R. Mintz, tr. and ed., *In Praise of the Baal Shem Tov* (Bloomington, Univ. of Indiana Press, 1970), an English version of the first printed collection (1814); Jerome R. Mintz, *Legends of the Hasidim* (Chicago, Univ. of Chicago Press, 1968), including a collection of oral tales among Hasidim in America; and Louis I. Newman, tr. and ed., *The Hasidic Anthology* (N.Y., Schocken, 1963), with a topical arrangement of the tales and sayings, and an index of the Hasidic rabbis cited. Original sources of the important Habad (Lubavitcher) sect, now centered in New York, include the basic work of the founder, Schneur Zalman of Liadi, *Tanya*, 5 vols. (N.Y., Kehot Publication Society, 1962–68), and Dov Baer of Lubavitch, *Tract on Ecstasy,* tr. Louis Jacobs (London, Valentine, Mitchell, 1963).

Hasidism and its leaders have had a great appeal to Jewish fiction writers. Israel Zangwill has a fictionalized portrait of the Baal Shem Tov, in "The Master of the Name," in *Dreamers of the Ghetto* (Philadelphia, JPS, 1898); Maurice Samuel, *Prince of the Ghetto* (Philadelphia, JPS, 1959) covers the rendition of Hasidism in the stories of Isaac Loeb Peretz (1852–1915); Scholem Asch, *Salvation* (N.Y., G.P. Putnam's Sons, 1934) belongs to the genre of Hasidic fiction; "A Wonder Worker," in Shalom Spiegel, *Hebrew Reborn* (Philadelphia, JPS, 1962) shows the response of Jewish writers to the Hasidic movement; and one should add that a brilliant post-Auschwitz Jewish novelist, Elie Wiesel, has retold the tales and legends of the Hasidic masters in *Souls On Fire* (N.Y., Random House, 1972).

VII. MODERNITY: SOCIAL AND RELIGIOUS DEVELOPMENTS

In the past it has been customary to mark the entrance of the Jews into modernity by the specific legal guarantees or rights that followed the American and French Revolutions; and this so-called "Emancipation" was placed a century or more later in relatively backward Eastern Europe. Even where cultural development in Western modes was made the criterion, the transition was put only a generation earlier with the beginning of the German Haskalah (Enlightenment). Twentieth-century Jewish historiographers, however, have questioned the narrowly legal criterion of modernity, and have insisted that the actual entrance of Jews into modern Western modes of life and culture occurred much earlier in a movement that covered several centuries and was governed by various social, economic, and political factors. As for cultural participation, we are referred to the Renaissance Italian and Iberian-Dutch communities or even back to Spanish Jewry before them. Furthermore, there has been a reassessment of the meaning and value of the Emancipation for Judaism and Jewishness and a radical challenge to the standard view of the Jewish Middle Ages as a monochromatic (dark) period of wretchedness and persecution that was followed by a new (light) Messianic Age of freedom and fulfillment. (The publications cited above on Jewish medieval status and self-government and on Italian and Spanish developments are relevant to this discussion; for the significant Dutch development, see Baron, XV, ch. I, "Dutch Jerusalem.") In any case, whenever the process began, Emancipation and Enlightenment have had revolutionary effects on Jewish social and religious life for the past two centuries, and the consequences have elicited responses from leading Jewish thinkers.

Two excellent readers are available on this era: Raphael Mahler, *Jewish Emancipation* (N.Y., American Jewish Committee, 1941), a selection of historical documents from 1657 to 1917; and Nahum N. Glatzer, *The Dynamics of Emancipation* (Boston, Beacon Press, 1965), a selection of writings from leading Jewish thinkers and doers, from Mendelssohn's day to Auschwitz and after. For a concise survey of the modern period, see Arthur Hertzberg, "Modern Judaism," in "Judaism, History of," *EB;* for a longer, more detailed presentation, see Salo Baron, "The Modern Age," in Schwartz, or Grayzel, Bk. V; for a Zionist view, see Ben Zion Dinur, "The Modern Period," in *Israel and the Diaspora.* The standard view of modernity as the release from medieval darkness is found in Graetz, V; a narrative continued down to the Nazi era in Elbogen's *A Century of Jewish Life.* Salo Baron is responsible for the most radical and probably earliest of the revisionist views of Emancipation and the medieval experience. See especially his "Ghetto and Emancipation: Shall We Revise the Traditional View?", *The Menorah Journal,* XIV (1928), 6, 515; "Newer Approaches to Jewish Emancipation," *Diogenes,* No. 29 (Spring, 1960), 56; and the chapter "Emancipation" in vol. II of the first edition of his *History* (1937). See also Joseph Katz, "The Term 'Jewish Emancipation': Its Origins and Historical Impact," in Alexander Altmann, *Studies in Nineteenth-Century Jewish Intellectual History* (Cambridge, Harvard Univ. Press, 1964); the many excellent articles on Emancipation in the Leo Baeck Institute Yearbooks; and Joachim Prinz, *The Dilemma of the Modern Jew* (Boston, Little, Brown, 1962). For the discussion of particular periods and/or regions, see Mahler's *History;* Michael A. Meyer, *The Origins of the Modern Jew* (Detroit, Wayne State Univ. Press, 1967), on Germany, 1749–1824; H.G. Adler, *The Jews in Germany* (Notre Dame, Univ. of Notre Dame Press, 1969); Henry Lucien-Brun, *La Condition des juifs en France depuis 1789,* 2nd ed. (Paris and Lyon, Victor Retaux and Adrien Enfantin, n.d.); Lowenthal's *Jews of Germany*; Arthur Hertzberg, *The French Enlightenment and the Jews* (N.Y. and Philadelphia, Columbia Univ. Press and JPS, 1968); Arnold Ages, *French Enlightenment and Rabbinic Tradition* (Frankfurt am Main, Vittorio Klostermann, 1970); Cecil Roth, *Jews in England;* Salo Baron, "The Emancipation Movement and American Jewry," in *Steeled by Adversity* (Philadelphia, JPS, 1971); Dubnow, *Jews in Russia and*

Poland; Salo Baron, *The Russian Jew Under Tsars and Soviets* (N.Y., Macmillan, 1964); Bernard D. Weinryb, "East European Jewry (Since the Partitions of Poland, 1772–1795)," in Finkelstein, *The Jews.*

Most of the above cited publications have something to say about the Haskalah, the Jewish Enlightenment movement, which preceded the official legal Emancipation and for many interpreters is a far more important indicator of the Jewish entrance into modernity. It was an endeavor, originating in mid-18th-century Germany, to make Jews full participants in European culture, while at the same time preserving what were conceived to be the essential Jewish values and tradition. Hence it emphasized Hebrew language and literature, as well as that of the country of residence. It involved the secularization of Jewish learning and a reform of religious customs and observances, and hence was vigorously opposed by what came to be called Orthodox Jewry as being destructive to the Jewish religion and people. In central Europe the emphasis on Hebrew was soon abandoned, and radical forms of assimilation and reform were embraced. In Eastern Europe, however, the renaissance of Hebrew letters continued, and a strong sense of Jewish identity ("Jewishness") remained. In both cases, a distinctive Jewish community was preserved; not annihilated, as Jacob Katz points out, but transformed (that is, before the Holocaust). Both the Central and Eastern movements and literatures are covered comprehensively in Waxman, III; on the literary renaissance, see Spiegel, *Hebrew Reborn;* on the Central European development, Katz, *Out of the Ghetto;* on the Eastern Haskalah, Mahler's *History* and Jacob S. Raisin, *The Haskalah Movement in Russia* (Philadelphia, JPS, 1918); on Germany, Meyer. Zinberg, VIII–XII (to be published) covers the Central and Eastern movements. The greatest personality of the Haskalah, certainly the model man of German Enlightenment Jewry, was Moses Mendelssohn. Besides Graetz, V, and Meyer, see the monumental biographical study by Alexander Altmann, *Moses Mendelssohn* (Philadelphia, JPS, 1973), and Moses Mendelssohn, *Jerusalem and Other Jewish Writings,* tr. and ed., Alfred Jospe (N.Y., Schocken Books, 1969). A vivid personal account of the exodus from the Eastern Ghetto into modern Western culture is provided in *The Autobiography of Solomon Maimon* (London, East and West Library, 1954).

Religious renovation was an essential aim of the Haskalah movement and an ineluctable result of the external transformation of the Jewish social, cultural, and civic situation. The system of self-government by rabbinical authorities, recognized by the secular régimes in the various lands of residence, was now a thing of the past, and religious association in the modern state was in theory the free choice of individual citizens, not a matter of ethnic belonging. The anti-medievalism of the apostles of Emancipation and Enlightenment brought with it an anti-Talmudism and an emphasis on Judaism as a spiritual-ethical stance, for which the traditional life-disciplines and ceremonies were obsolete trappings. Rabbinic Judaism, far from being considered "normative" or "orthodox," was pilloried as a degenerate deviation from the true Judaism arising out of the Bible, particularly the Prophets. The main thing was to get to the essentials of the Judaic faith and to strip everything else away, particularly the prescribed "oriental" practices. The Reform movement historically began in France, but had its greatest impact and sway in Germany and the United States, beginning in the first quarter of the 19th century; indeed, in the U.S. it was practically the only form of Judaism until the Eastern European Jewish immigration began.

David Phillipson, *The Reform Movement in Judaism,* new rev. ed. (N.Y., Macmillan, 1931), first published in 1907 and written from a committed Reform viewpoint, is a good introduction to the movement's spirit, development, doctrines and practices before the Hitler era. Excellent sourcebooks, including theological statements as well as historical documents, are provided in W. Gunther Plaut, *The Rise of Reform Judaism* and *The Growth of Reform Judaism* (N.Y., World Union for Progressive Judaism, 1963 and 1965). See also Joseph L. Blau, ed., *Reform Judaism* (N.Y., Ktav, 1973), a collection of significant essays by leading American spokesmen of the movement, including theological and liturgical papers, selected from the Yearbook of the Central Conference of American Rabbis. For a critical study of American Reform, see Beryl Harold Levy, *Reform Judaism in America* (N.Y., Bloch, 1933). For developments in Reform liturgy and other practices, see Jacob J. Petuchowski, *Prayerbook Reform in Europe* (N.Y., World Union for Progressive Judaism, 1968); also his "Manuals and Catechisms of the Jewish Religion in the Early Period of Emancipation;" and Alexander Altmann, "The New Style of Preaching," in Altmann, *Studies;* Lou H. Silberman, "The Union Prayerbook; a Study in Liturgical Development," in Bertram W. Korn, ed., *Retrospect and Prospect* (N.Y., Central Conference of American Rabbis, 1965); Solomon B. Freehof, *Reform Jewish Practice and Its Rabbinic Background* (Cincinnati, Hebrew Union College, 1944) and the various volumes of Reform *Responsa* put out by him and published by Hebrew Union College and Ktav. A biography of the great German Reform leader, Abraham Geiger, and excerpts from his writings are provided in Max Wiener, *Abraham Geiger and Liberal Judaism* (Philadelphia, JPS, 1962); and two American Reform theologians have written systematic theologies: Kaufmann Kohler, *Jewish Theology* (N.Y., Macmillan, 1918), and Samuel S. Cohon, *Jewish Theology* (Assen, Holland, Royal Van Gurcum; Beaverton, Ore., 1971).

The *Wissenschaft des Judentums* (Science of Judaism) movement endeavored to reconstruct Judaism and to attain respectability and pride through secular, critical-historical studies. It was a central factor in the culture of Emancipation Jewry and significant for both Reform and Conservative developments. See Waxman, III; Luitpold Wallach, *Liberty and Letters: the Thoughts of Leopold Zunz* (London, East and West Library, 1959); Louis Ginzberg, "Zechariah Frankel," in *Students, Scholars and Saints* (Philadelphia, JPS, 1958); and Nahum N. Glatzer, "The Beginnings of Modern Jewish Studies," in Altmann, *Studies.*

Conservative Judaism, now largely an American phenomenon, traces its derivation from the moderate wing of German Reform, which sought to retain a basic core of religious customs and traditions, modified by a critical-historical view of their origins, and endeavored to combine time honored values with new ways of thought and life and to maintain the Jews as a religious people. Originally called the Historical School, it appealed to rabbis in both the Orthodox and Reform camps in 19th-century America and in the 20th century became the favored middle way for millions of American Jews. Besides Ginzberg's essay on Frankel, the mid-19th-century herald of the movement, see Moshe Davis, *The Emergence of Conservative Judaism: The Historical School in 19th Century America* (Philadelphia, JPS, 1963); Marshall Sklare, *Conservative Judaism* (N.Y., Schocken Books, 1972), a sociological study; Solomon Schechter, *Essays in Judaism* and *Selected Writings* (Oxford, East and West Library, 1956), the latter including a biography, by Norman Bentwich, of Schechter, the leading theologian of Conservative Judaism in the English-speaking world; Herbert Parzen, *Architects of Conservative Judaism* (N.Y., Jonathan David, 1964). See also the journal, *Conservative Judaism.*

Orthodoxy (so named pejoratively by its Reform opponents) also underwent changes and generally adapted to the new situation, trying to maintain the corpus of traditional religious practices and beliefs while acting productively in the modern secular world. It was rich, especially in Eastern Europe, in various types of new movements: Hasidism, already covered above; the Musar movement, a spiritual-pietistic-ethical school, originating in Lithuania and spreading to *yeshivot* in many lands; acute Talmudic scholasticism, also centered in Lithuania and embodied paradigmatically in the great Vilna Gaon, Elijah Ben Solomon Zalman, the arch-opponent of Hasidism; the neo-Orthodoxy proclaimed by Samson Raphael Hirsch, originating in Germany and spreading to Western Europe. The various Eastern movements are covered in the already cited essay by Abraham Menes in Finkelstein, *The Jews;* Musar in H.H. Ben-Sasson, "Musar Movement," *Encyclopaedia Judaica,* and in Louis Ginzburg, "Rabbi Israel Salanter," in *Students,* which may be read in Goldin's *Jewish Expression* along with Gedalyahu Alon, "The Lithuanian Yeshivas," and Menachem M. Glenn, *Israel Salanter* (N.Y., Bloch, 1953); the Vilna Gaon, in Solomon Schechter, *Studies in Judaism,* Ginzberg, *Students,* and H.H. Ben-Sasson, "Elijah Ben Solomon," *EB;* the German developments in Herman Schwab, *The History of Orthodox Jewry in Germany* (London, Mitre Press, 1950) and Samson Raphael Hirsch, *Judaism Eternal,* 2 vols.

(London, Soncino Press, 1956), a selection from Hirsch's writings. For a vivid portrait of life and religion in the Eastern European villages where the masses of Orthodox Jews lived, besides Heschel's *The Earth is the Lord's,* see Mark Zborowski and Elizabeth Herzog, *Life is with People* (N.Y., Schocken Books, 1962) and Maurice Samuel, *The World of Sholom Aleichem* (N.Y., Schocken Books, 1965). The Eastern European Jewish response to modernity is reflected concretely in Lucy S. Davidowicz, *The Golden Tradition* (N.Y., Holt, Rinehart and Winston, 1967) through personal documents, with an extensive introduction on "The World of East European Jewry." The mainline voice of present-day American Orthodoxy may be found in the Studies in Torah Judaism series, published by Yeshiva University in New York. A valuable collection of these papers is presented in Leon D. Stitskin, ed., *Studies in Torah Judaism* (N.Y., Yeshiva Univ. Press and Ktav, 1969). *Tradition* and *The Jewish Observer* are journals that express the viewpoints of two main segments of American Orthodoxy. For present-day Hasidism, besides Rabinowicz, see "Part One: The Hasidic People," in Mintz; Herbert Weiner, "The Lubavitcher Movement," in *9 1/2 Mystics* (N.Y., Holt, Rinehart and Winston, 1969); Philip Garvin and Arthur A. Cohen, *A People Apart* (N.Y., E.P. Dutton, 1970), photographed and written perceptively, *con amore;* and two social-science studies: Israel Rubin, *Satmar: An Island in the City* (Chicago, Quadrangle Books, 1921), and Solomon Poll, *The Hasidic Community of Williamsburg* (Glencoe, Free Press, 1962). The writings of Joseph I. Schneersohn, the late, venerated leader of the Lubavitcher community, and other Habad writings are published by Kehot Publication Society, 770 Eastern Parkway, Brooklyn, N.Y., 11213.

Reconstructionism, a twentieth-century American movement, operative in Reform and Conservative circles, seeks to combine a naturalist-humanist philosophy with historical Jewish tradition, viewing Judaism as a distinctive cultural entity or civilization, of which religion is a partial expression, and emphasizing Jewish peoplehood—the community of all Jews, of various shades of belief and non-belief. It is best approached through books by and about Mordecai M. Kaplan, its founder and leading spirit. See particularly Mordecai M. Kaplan, *Judaism as a Civilization* (N.Y., Schocken Books, 1967), and *The Greater Judaism in the Making* (N.Y., Reconstructionist Press, 1960); and Ira Eisenstein and Eugene Kohn, eds., *Mordecai M. Kaplan* (N.Y., Jewish Reconstructionist Foundation, 1952), with concluding piece by Kaplan, "The Way I Have Come."

Zionism may be viewed as a twentieth-century expression of the national aspect of Judaism, and for many present-day Jews it has taken on the character of a secular religion. For a deeply religious view of Zionism, see Martin Buber, *Israel and Palestine: The History of an Idea* (London, East and West Library, 1952); for a spiritual-humanist view, see Ahad Ha-Am, *Essays, Letters, Memoirs,* tr. and ed. Leon Simon (Oxford, East and West

Library, 1946); for an excellent historical introduction and magnificent anthology of Zionist writings, see Arthur Hertzberg, ed., *The Zionist Idea* (N.Y., Atheneum, 1970). And refer again to Dinur's *Israel and the Diaspora.* The chapter on "Nationalism" in the 1937 edition of Baron's *History* provides a broad and thoughtful presentation.

A lucid, very readable presentation of most of the above developments is provided in Joseph L. Blau, *Modern Varieties of Judaism* (N.Y., Columbia Univ. Press, 1966), and also in Part One of Jacob B. Agus, *Guideposts in Modern Judaism* (N.Y., Bloch, 1954). Nathan Glazer, *American Judaism,* 2nd ed. (Chicago, Univ. of Chicago Press, 1972) is an excellent, brief presentation of the various phases and forms of American Judaism. See also Marshall Sklare, *American Jews* (N.Y., Random House, 1971), a keen, brief, sociological study. A very important work on modern Jewish religious developments is the still untranslated book of Max Wiener, *Jüdische Religion im Zeitalter der Emanzipation* (Berlin, Philo Verlag und Buchhandlung, 1933).

VIII. MODERN JEWISH RELIGIOUS PHILOSOPHY

Because of their radical challenge to traditional Jewish beliefs and practices, it is justifiable to begin the study of modern Jewish philosophy with the seventeenth-century Iberian-Dutch thinkers, Uriel Acosta and Benedict (originally Baruch) Spinoza. For Spinoza's philosophy of, or rather against, Judaism, see the remarks in Guttmann, 265–85; Leo Strauss, *Spinoza's Critique of Religion* (N.Y., Schocken Books, 1965), preface also available in Goldin, *Jewish Expression;* J.B. Agus, *Evolution of Jewish Thought;* Harry A. Wolfson, *The Philosophy of Spinoza* (Cleveland, World, 1958); and Benedict de Spinoza, *A Theological-Political Treatise and a Political Treatise* (N.Y., Dover Books, 1951). For a concise survey of Jewish philosophy from Acosta to Buber, with a very long section on Spinoza, see Pines' *EB* article; for excellent coverage from Mendelssohn to Rosenzweig, see Guttmann, ch. III, and Nathan Rotestreich, *Jewish Philosophy in Modern Times* (N.Y., Holt, Rinehart & Winston, 1968). Also useful are the surveys in Waxman, III–V; Jacob Agus, *Modern Philosophies of Judaism* (N.Y., Behrman House, 1941); the excellent little guide by Samuel H. Bergman, *Faith and Reason;* and the incisive essay by Alexander Altmann, "Theology in Twentieth-Century German Jewry," in *Leo Baeck Institute Yearbook I* (London, East and West Library, 1956).

Since Mendelssohn (covered above), the major Jewish religious philosophers have been Hermann Cohen, Franz Rosenzweig, and Martin Buber. On Cohen, besides the general surveys listed above, see Trude Weiss Rosmarin, *Religion of Reason* (N.Y., Bloch, 1936); Jehuda Melber, *Hermann Cohen's Philosophy of Judaism* (N.Y., Jonathan David, 1968), from a traditional viewpoint; Mordecai M. Kaplan, *The Purpose and Meaning of Jewish Existence* (Philadelphia, JPS, 1964), from a Reconstructionist's viewpoint, with a 200-page epitome of Cohen's *Religion of Reason;* and Hermann Cohen, *Religion of Reason out of the Sources of Judaism,* with introductory essays by Leo Strauss and Simon Kaplan (N.Y., Frederick Ungar, 1972), and *Reason and Hope* (N.Y., W.W. Norton, 1971), a selection of Cohen's "Jewish writings," by the translator, Eva Jospe. On Rosenzweig, see Nahum N. Glatzer's *Franz Rosenzweig: His Life and Thought* (N.Y., Farrar, Strauss and Young, and Schocken Books, 1953), an illuminating introduction, deftly presented through Rosenzweig's letters, diaries, and published writings; Eugen Rosenstock-Huessy, ed. *Judaism Despite Christianity* (University, Univ. of Alabama Press, 1969), an exchange of letters on Christianity and Judaism between a Jewish friend who was a Christian convert and Rosenzweig. For Rosenzweig's philosophic and Jewish writings, besides Glatzer, see Franz Rosenzweig, *The Star of Redemption* (N.Y., Holt, Rinehart & Winston, 1971), his *magnum opus,* a profound and difficult work on the Judaic and Christian revelations; *Understanding the Sick and the Healthy* (N.Y., Noonday Press, 1954), a subtle sliver of a book on world, man, and God; and *On Jewish Learning,* ed. N.N. Glatzer (N.Y., Schocken Books, 1955), including an interchange of opposing views on Revelation and Law with Martin Buber.

On Martin Buber, the best available book on his religious philosophy is Malcom L. Diamond, *Martin Buber* (N.Y., Harper Torchbooks, 1968). Maurice Friedman, *Martin Buber* (N.Y., Harper Torchbooks, 1960) covers all aspects of Buber's thought; Schillp and Friedman contains critiques and interpretations by thirty scholars, together with Buber's "Autobiographical Fragments," and "Replies to My Critics," and a bibliography of his writings from 1897 to 1966. For Buber's philosophical and Judaic works, see especially Martin Buber, *I and Thou,* 2nd ed. (N.Y., Charles Scribner's Sons, 1958), his major work, a philosophic lyric which has played a seminal role in 20th-century thought; *On Judaism,* ed. Nahum N. Glatzer (N.Y., Schocken Books, 1967), challenging and sometimes abrasive addresses delivered on various occasions between 1909 and 1951; *Israel and the World* (N.Y., Schocken Books, 1965), another significant collection of addresses and essays on various occasions which expound Buber's basic view of Judaism, in the face of an uncomprehending, disturbing, and often hostile non-Judaic world, and *Eclipse of God* (N.Y., Harper Torchbooks, 1957), comprising mainly his American addresses in 1951. His considerable work in biblical interpretation may be approached through *On The Bible* (N.Y., Schocken Books, 1968), an excellent selection by Nahum N. Glatzer.

Space forbids dealing with the writings of other eminent twentieth-century philosophers and theologians. Pre-eminent among those who have passed on are Leo Baeck and Abraham Joshua Heschel; among the living, Emil Fackenheim has assumed a towering rank; and attention should also be paid to the theological writings of Eliezer Berkovits, Eugene B. Borowitz, Arthur A. Cohen, David Polish, Jacob J. Petuchowski, and Richard L. Rubenstein. For excellent bibliographical coverage on these and other contemporary religious philosophers and theologians, see Rothschild and Siegel's essay referred to above. Robert Gordis and Ruth B. Waxman, eds., *Faith and Reason: Essays in Judaism* (N.Y., Ktav, 1973), comprises selected theological essays by contemporary Jewish thinkers that have appeared in the journal *Judaism*. The cataclysmic, traumatic experience of the Holocaust—the extermination of 6,000,000 Jews by the Nazis during World War II—has had a pronounced and still growing effect on Jewish theological thought. Seymour Cain, "The Question and the Answers after Auschwitz," in Gordis and Waxman, deals with theologizing on this agonizing question by Ignaz Maybaum, Rubenstein, and Fackenheim. See also Eliezer Berkovits, *Faith and the Holocaust* (N.Y., Ktav, 1973), a moving presentation by an orthodox theologian. Arthur Cohen, *Arguments and Doctrines* (Philadelphia, JPS, 1970), subtitled "A Reader of Jewish Thinking in the Aftermath of the Holocaust," is a perceptive selection of various kinds of writings on Judaism and Jewish existence in this spiritual ambiance, ending significantly with Stephen S. Schwartzchild's "The Personal Messiah: Toward the Restoration of a Discarded Doctrine."

XII

Christianity

H. H. Walsh
revised by Jaroslav Pelikan

I. INTRODUCTION

Christianity, together with the other two "monotheisms of the Book," Judaism and Islam, claims to base its message not merely on the way things really are in the universe nor on the symbolic truth of myths that took place "once upon a time," but upon a particular series of events of history whose center and climax is the life, death, and resurrection of Jesus of Nazareth, confessed as "the Christ," the chosen of God and the Son of God. It follows, then, that an understanding of the Christian view of history is a necessary preliminary to a critical examination of the relevant material upon which the Christian faith is based—namely, the New Testament. The New Testament, however, is not comprehensible without some acquaintance with the Old Testament and with Jewish literature produced between the two Testaments (which is generally referred to as intertestamental literature). Some overlapping of this chapter with the two on Judaism is therefore unavoidable, but only to the extent of indicating how Christians interpret Jewish literature in the light of New Testament insights.

More germane to an understanding of Christianity is the literature concerned with Christian beliefs about the central figure of the New Testament, Jesus Christ; it is also important to know how Christians have responded to the demands that Christ has made upon them. The first of these concerns is usually classified under "Christian doctrine," which often shades off into a philosophy of Christianity; the second may be considered under the general heading of "Christian sociology." As is the case with all institutions with high moral goals, the ideal and reality are often in conflict. The failure of the Christian Church to achieve its chief goal, to be "perfected into one" (John 17:23), has produced a large body of literature which is usually classified under the term "irenics." Irenics, in turn, has given rise to an ecumenical movement which has produced a peculiar literature of its own.

All the material so far suggested would fail to give a true reflection of Christianity as a way of life if it did not include some reference to the struggles and temptations of Christians trying to do the work of Christ and to keep themselves "unspotted from the world" (James 1:8). No doubt such literature comes under the overall heading of Christian sociology, but in this case sociology must include such specifically Christian disciplines as liturgy, pastoral theology, moral theology, ethics, and social welfare. Nor are the inner recesses of the Christian life exhausted under these more activist disciplines: for fundamentally the Christian life is one of worship, in which personal devotion, meditation, and mysticism play most significant roles. From this inner life of devotion Christianity has found its mood and the creativity to develop its own specific culture.

It is in the cultural sphere that we will be introduced to the most lively writings on Christianity today, for this is an age of meeting and crossing of different cultures. Consequently this chapter will appropriately conclude on the theme of Christianity and other religions.

A. The Christian view of history

It goes without saying that the Christian view of history has been molded by the Christian faith. This fact creates the suspicion that those who composed the earliest Christian documents were under the restraint of maintaining a thesis that the prophecies of the Old Testament were fulfilled in Jesus, the Messiah. There was also an inclination on the part of early Christians to disparage past history because of the expectation of the immediate culmination of the historical process. Martin Werner's *The Formation of Christian Dogma,* tr. by S.G.F. Brandon (London, A. & C. Black, 1957), seeks to assess the importance of this expectation, and of its disappointment, for the development of early Christianity. But, as R.L.P. Milburn observes in *Early Christian Interpretations of History* (London, Adam & Charles Black, 1954), Christians inherited much of their conception of history from the Jews, and this gave them a vision of history with a definite plan; this plan is for both Jews and Christians in the hands of God, but for the Christians it has its center in Jesus and his redemptive work. Thus the Christian historian sets forth a series of historic events in which God himself acts, but the full meaning of these events is beyond history. Such a view of history has been called by German writers *Heilsgeschichte,* "salvation-history," or perhaps better, "sacred-history." The relation of sacred history to the complex phenomena of world history has been explained in some detail by E.C. Rust in *The Christian Understanding of History* (London, Lutterworth Press, 1947). A thorny problem for sacred history is the ambiguity of the primitive Christian conception of time and history. The first Christians believed that Christ had won in their day an eschatological victory, but there is also evident in their writings a future expectation of a coming kingdom. The relation between what has been called the "realized eschatology" of the New Testament and its future reality is a subject much debated among Christian writers today, particularly since the publication of C.H. Dodd's *History and Gospel* (N.Y., Charles Scribner's Sons, 1938). It has also been the subject of an interesting and highly controversial monograph by O. Cullman, *Christ and Time,* tr. by F.V. Filson (Philadelphia, Westminster Press, 1950), in which he attempts to set forth a consistent interpretation of the Christian view of salvation.

B. Christian historiography

The role played by sacred history in historiography is an interesting story in itself and has brought about many modifications and reinterpretations of the Christian view of history. The story begins with the Acts of the Apostles, the author of which, as pointed out by M. Dibelius in *Studies in the Acts of the Apostles,* tr. by Mary Ling (N.Y., Charles Scribner's Sons, 1956) and by Henry J. Cadbury in *The Making of Luke-Acts* (N.Y., Macmillan, 1927), not only produced a consecutive narrative but also endeavored to interpret events in the light of divine rather than human activity. After this first tentative approach in Acts, there is no formal attempt to write church history until we come to Eusebius (c. 260–c. 340), who wrote a monumental *Ecclesiastical History,* tr. by K. Lake (N.Y., G.P. Putnam's Sons, 1926–32) in seven books, covering the history of the church from apostolic times down to 303; the story is continued in his *Life of Constantine.* Eusebius is extremely important in that he was not only the first systematic historian of the origin and expansion of the Christian church, but also embodied in his history the earliest Christian theme, carried over from Jewish history, the vindication of God's justice, emphasizing God as the controller of history.

It remained for Augustine of Hippo (354–430) to set forth this theme in philosophical form. The great challenge that Augustine had to face in his day was the obvious disintegration of the Roman Empire during the opening phases of the Christian era. He met the challenge by pointing out that the calamities under which society was then reeling were not so great as those which had overtaken earlier empires and at the same time by emphasizing that there was still a reasonable sequence running through history in accordance with the divine plan. This was set forth in the *City of God,* an outline of a theology of history in which all human events are seen as carrying out a plan foreordained by God. The book is a first example of Christian philosophy of history in which oriental conceptions of eternally recurring phases of history are abandoned and time becomes linear, not cyclical. Its philosophy has been summarized by G.L. Keyes in *Christian Faith and the Interpretation of History* (Lincoln, Univ. of Nebraska Press, 1966) and by Charles Norris Cochrane in *Christianity and Classical Culture* (Oxford, N.Y., and Toronto, Oxford Univ. Press, 1939).

The work of Augustine is a landmark in Christian thought and has had a permanent influence on the Christian interpretation of history. It was carried on by Orosius (c. 380–c. 420), who was directed by Augustine to set out in greater detail the providential acts of God even in the midst of calamities. This he did in *The Seven Books of History against the Pagans,* ed. by G. Golsuinge (N.Y., Columbia Univ. Press, 1936), in which he deals with four world empires and comments on their rise and fall. He enlarges upon their calamities in order to minimize the calamities of his own day. Despite calamities besetting the tottering Roman Empire, even greater than those faced by Augustine and Orosius, Salvian (c. 400), a priest of Marseilles, in a treatise entitled *The Governance of God,* tr. by J.F. O'Sullivan (N.Y., Fathers of the Church, 1947), still held that these events indicate the providential purposes of God. He wrote in the manner of the Old Testament prophets, denouncing the Romans and the lukewarm Christians of his day, and concluded that the barbarian invaders were a scourge of sinners, a proof that God controls history. This theme was continued in the sixth and seventh centuries by Gregory, Bishop of Tours (538–594), and by the Venerable Bede (672–723), the former in *The History of the Franks,* tr. by O.M. Dalton (Oxford, Clarendon Press, 1927) and the latter in *The Ecclesiastical History of the English Nation,* tr. by J.E. King (N.Y., Loeb Classical Library, 1930). Their influence is evident throughout the medieval period, during which annals and chronicles rather than interpretive history were the vogue.

There are some exceptions to this generalization, of which Bishop Otto Freising (c. 1114–c. 1158) is an illustrious example. His *The Two Cities,* tr. by C.C. Mierow (N.Y., Columbia Univ. Press, 1928), may be regarded as a philosophy of history rather than a chronicle but borrows its ideas chiefly from Augustine. Also of special interest are contemporary histories of the Crusades: J.A. Brundage, *The Crusades: A Documentary Survey* (Milwaukee, Marquette Univ. Press, 1962) is a useful guide, together with A.S. Atiya, *Crusade: Historiography and Bibliography* (Bloomington, Indiana Univ. Press, 1962). Other exceptional medieval historians are Jean Froissart (1337–1410), whose *Chronicles of England, France, Spain and Adjoining Countries,* tr. J. Bourchier (Carbondale, Southern Illinois Univ. Press, 1963) is concerned with the manners and customs of these countries, and Philip de Comines (1445–1509), whose *Memoirs,* tr. A.R. Scoble (London, H.G. Bohn, 1855–56) are a commentary on contemporary events. This concern reflects the displacement of the providential view of history. Both these writers dwell strongly on the underlying motives behind the trend of events, and they mark a transition to the Renaissance mood, in which the emphasis upon divine providence in history begins to recede before the revived classical interest in human events.

The rise of humanism in western Europe brought about a gradual secularization of history, first discernible perhaps in Petrarch's (1304–74) *History of Rome,* but even more so in the writings of Machiavelli (1469–1527) and of Guicciardini (1483–1540), both of whom pioneered in modern political and national historical writing. Thus was brought about a close association of history with political science, as set forth by Jean Bodin (1530–96) in *Method for the Easy Comprehension of History,* tr. by B. Reynolds (N.Y., Columbia Univ. Press, 1945), in which he also laid great emphasis upon the geographical factors in history. Both these ideas were taken up in the age of Enlightenment and helped to bring about the secularization of historical writing in Europe.

The age of Enlightenment contributes little to the development of Christian historiography except for the problems it created for the Christian view of history. It was the remarkable development of science that most influenced historical writers, both secular and Christian, during this era and was evidenced in a more critical analysis of all historical documents, biblical as well as nonbiblical, thus abolishing the distinction between sacred and profane history. Perhaps the most influential historian of the Enlightenment was Giovanni Battista Vico (1668–1744) who in *The New Science,* tr. by T.G. Bergin and M.H. Fisch (Ithaca, Cornell Univ. Press, 1948), put forth a theory of cycles in history through which all nations pass: heroic, classical, and a new barbarism. In his analysis he found that each cycle is differentiated from the preceding one and that there is a spiral movement of progress. Thus arose the general idea of an inevitable progress based upon the idea of the perfectibility of human nature. Through all this development ran a constant emphasis upon the capability of human reason to discover the true causes of events and thus to improve human relations. Historians entered upon a campaign to free men from bigotry and superstition, and especially from the dominance of the church. All this led to the composition of nationalistic histories in which the providential purpose of God was abandoned as a principle of explanation and replaced by geographic, commercial, and fiscal interpretations of events. From the point of view of Christianity, the most significant history of the era was Edward Gibbon's *The History of the Decline and Fall of the Roman Empire* (1776–88) with its famous fifteenth and sixteenth chapters dealing with the rise of Christianity—or, as he termed it near the end of the book, "the triumph of barbarism and religion"—in what purported to be a completely objective manner, colored by "grave and temperate irony." The "clamor" following the publication of the first volume created "what might almost be called a library of controversy."

But even during the age of Enlightenment there was a reaction against a purely rationalist approach to historical phenomena, of which Rousseau was the outstanding voice. Rousseau's influence on historiography is to be found among the romantics of the nineteenth century rather than in the eighteenth, particularly in François René Chateaubriand, who in 1802 published *The Genius of Christianity,* tr. by Charles I. White (Philadelphia, J.B. Lippincott Co., 1868 and after), an elaborate defense of Christianity based upon history and aesthetic experience. The summary of his argument in proof of Christianity may be put in this way: the works of Christianity indicate its perfection; a perfect consequence cannot spring from an imperfect principle; the logical conclusion is, therefore, that Christianity is not the work of men, but of God.

Romantic church history, which became allied with nationalistic and liberalistic trends, proved to be a weak defense for the Christian faith. As was inevitable, a gradual reaction set in against highly colored church history. The reaction is evidenced in the works of Leopold von Ranke (1795–1886), who is generally regarded as the father of scientific history. During 1834–36, there appeared three volumes of his *History of the Popes,* tr. into English by W.K. Kelly in 1844 (Philadelphia, Lea & Febiger), and with new editions in 1845 and 1847; his *History of the Reformation in Germany,* tr. by Sarah Austin (N.Y., E.P. Dutton, 1905), despite its evident Protestant bias, helped to give the impetus to modern research on the Reformation. Ranke based his work on the most careful and detailed research and set a pattern for church historians to adhere vigorously to the rules of scientific method. One of the most brilliant of Ranke's school was Johann Döllinger, whose *Church History,* tr. by E. Cox (London, 1840), was a revolution in the interpretation of Christian documents, particularly in its stress upon evidence and the testing of facts. Döllinger's ideas were carried to England by his pupil, Lord Acton, who was to have a decisive influence upon the writing of church history in England, particularly upon Mandell Creighton, whose *History of the Papacy during the Period of the Reformation* (Boston, Houghton Mifflin, 1882–94) is a landmark in balanced historical writing on a very controversial subject.

Scientific history, however, did not solve the problem of history, for with its attempt to be purely objective it showed a bias toward contemporary liberal ideas and failed to answer the question of the ultimate force or forces which determine historical developments. Such doubts arose out of G.F.W. Hegel's *Lectures on the Philosophy of History,* which appeared in Germany in 1837 and was made available to English readers by J. Sibree's translation in 1852. In this first direct approach to a philosophy of history Hegel attempted to show that mankind has developed through a dialectical process, culminating in the ultimate self-realization of the idea of freedom. Hegel's philosophy of history was to have a stimulating effect upon Christian historians, but this enthusiasm was somewhat dampened by Karl Marx, who adopted Hegel's dialectical conception but, in place of Hegel's idealism, proclaimed that material conditions rather than spiritual forces underlie historical development, from thesis through antithesis to synthesis. These steps in the dialectic of development he held were open to scientific study. Not dissimilar to Marx's view was Auguste Comte's, who in his *Positive Philosophy* (1830–42), tr. by Harriet Martineau (2 vols.; London, J. Chapman, 1953), outlined a three-stage historical development— the theological, the metaphysical, and the scientific or positive eras—and foresaw in the final positivistic era a world ruled by a sociological priesthood. In this same general mood were the social evolutionists, such as Herbert Spencer in his *The Principles of Sociology,* 3rd ed. (N.Y., Appleton-Century-Crofts, 1895), who assumed that historical development is an evolutionary process governed by unrelenting forces that cannot be changed by human action and that this inevitable development is in the direction of perfection and ultimate happiness for the human race.

HISTORISM.   It is against this background of utopian ideas and a concern with simple or scientific explanations of history, often called "historism," that modern Christian historians have attempted to reassert a specifically Christian interpretation of history. An early approach to the problem raised by "historism" was made by W.E. Collins in *The Study of Ecclesiastical History* (N.Y., Longmans, Green, 1903). Collins undertook to distinguish church history from other historical disciplines by pointing out that it is not subject to the deductive method because the history of the church is not finished. More recently, Herbert Butterfield, in *Christianity and History* (London, G. Bell & Sons, 1949), issued a similar warning against the pitfalls into which the scientific approach to history may lead the church historian. and made a strong plea for a reassertion of the providential view of history. Writing from the perspectives of Protestant liberalism and of "the social history of Christianity," Shirley Jackson Case, in *The Christian Philosophy of History* (Chicago, Univ. of Chicago Press, 1943), attempted to meet the problem raised by secular historians as to the purpose and meaning of history by freeing the study of history from the perversions of metaphysical theories apart from historical data. He insisted that history can serve as a tonic against threatening evils.

Moving somewhat away from this defensive position was R.W. Mc-

Laughlin, who in *The Spiritual Element in History* (N.Y., Abingdon Press, 1926) found an agreement among Hegel, Marx, and Augustine on the "why" or meaning of history and arrived at the conclusion "that in Christianity is found the most convincing proof of the continuity of history." With even more confidence M.C. D'Arcy, S.J., in *The Sense of History: Secular and Sacred* (London, Faber & Faber, 1959), taking Christian truths for granted, attempted to see what light they throw on the human scene. In a similar vein Christopher Dawson in *The Dynamics of World History*, ed. by J. Mulloy (London, Sheed & Ward, 1957), contends that "Christianity laid the foundations for a new view of history, which is both universalist and progressive." He sees history moving toward an ultimate goal; so also does Nicholas Berdyaev, who in *The Meaning of History* (London, Geoffrey Bles, 1936) accepted much of the Marxian dialectic and used it for a dynamic interpretation of Christianity. He found an interior dialogue underlying European literature from Augustine to Dostoevski, Proust, Joyce, and even some of the Soviet writers which has helped to shape Christianity. A novel exposition of the dynamics of history is to be found in Karl Löwith's *Meaning in History* (Chicago, Univ. of Chicago Press, 1949), in which he puts forth the idea that the historical consciousness of Europe has been "determined by an eschatological motivation from Isaiah to Marx, from Augustine to Hegel and from Joachim to Schelling." His conclusion is that "cyclic motion and eschatological direction have exhausted the basic approaches." It follows that Christians must repudiate both these approaches and fall back on the radical Christian faith that "the Christian times are Christian only in so far as they are the last time," which makes a "Christian history" nonsense. Despite this pessimistic view of Christian history, there are a number of what may be called theological historians who still find an eschatological view of history to be the Christian answer to the historical relativism of secular historians. Among them is Paul Tillich, who in his *Interpretation of History* (London, Charles Scribner's Sons, 1936) accepts the existentialist approach to history and provides it with several categories, such as philosophical, political, and theological. Erich Frank suggests in chapter five of his *Philosophical Understanding and Religious Truth* (London, Oxford Univ. Press, 1945) that "the Christian is a contemporary of Christ, and time and the world's history are overcome." For Reinhold Niebuhr in *Faith and History* (London, James Nisbet, 1949), none of the problems of history can be solved in time, since the end of history lies outside time; the Christian can only overcome history within the community of grace. The Neo-Thomist Jacques Maritain accepts much of the existentialist insight, but he also relies on many axiomatic or functional laws for the study of history. His views have been set forth in a volume edited by J.W. Evans, entitled *Jacques Maritain on the Philosophy of History* (N.Y., Charles Scribner's Sons, 1957). Although it does not confine itself to theological interpretations, R.G. Collingwood's *The Idea of History* (Oxford, Clarendon Press, 1946), has succeeded, more perhaps than any other work of the past several decades, in raising the questions with which any theological interpretation of history is obliged to deal.

The most drastic attempt to deal with the problems that historism has posed for the modern students of Christianity, and particularly for New Testament scholars, has been made by K. Rudolph Bultmann in *Kerygma and Myth*, tr. by R.H. Fuller (London, Society for Promoting Christian Knowledge, 1953) and in *History and Eschatology* (Edinburgh, Edinburgh Univ. Press, 1957), both of which serve as good introductions to the literature on the problem of the interpretation of Scripture. Not all Christian scholars are in agreement with his radical ideas of interpretation of Christian documents, but many theologians welcome his approach to the Scriptures as a way through the maze of modern historical criticism of the Bible and as an escape from historical nihilism. The story of this controversy has been told by Friedrich Gogarten in *Demythologizing and History,* tr. by N.H. Smith (London, Student Christian Movement Press, 1955), and by Schubert M. Ogden in *Christ Without Myth* (N.Y., Harper & Row, 1961). The reason for the controversy, Gogarten explains, is that Bultmann insists upon a fundamentally different understanding of reality than that assumed in the classical form of Christian dogma. The change has come about because modern man does not, as medieval man did, try to adapt himself to a preestablished order. History for modern man can only be envisaged from the point of view of his own responsibility for it; thus history cannot be a subject–object pattern, in that man cannot take himself out of it. Consequently, he must approach history within the historical character of human existence. The essence of history, then, is that man tries to understand himself by participating in it; so Bultmann believes that one must try to understand the character of the New Testament revelation in accordance with the nature of history. To give an objective history of the so-called redemptive facts of the New Testament, he feels, would be a rationalization which would cause it to lose its own historical character. For Bultmann, Jesus is not perceptible from the standpoint of historical investigation, so we must take seriously that "reality which discloses itself in faith," faith in the kerygma as the proclamation of the work of God. This, however, according to Bultmann, does not exclude applying to the study of Scripture all the principles of historical and literary criticism, which are the common tools of both sacred and profane historians.

C. The holy Scriptures

Like several other of the world religions, Christianity has a sacred literature—the written record of God's communication to his people. The core of that communication for Christians is what the New Testament calls the kerygma, or the proclamation of good news that is the fulfillment of a promise made by God to his people. Thus, as C.H. Dodd has emphasized in *According to the Scriptures* (N.Y., Charles Scribner's Sons, 1953), the church was committed by the terms of its proclamation "to a formidable task of biblical research," both for its own understanding of the gospel and to make its message intelligible to the outside world. The earliest fathers of the church found the ultimate source and authority for the kerygma in the person and work of Jesus Christ, but they explained this in the context of the Old Testament, which was for them, as also for the writers of the New Testament, "the Scriptures." The significance of the Old Testament for the early Christians is briefly told by W.F. Lofthouse in chap. X of a volume edited by H.W. Robinson, *Record and Revelation* (Oxford, Clarendon Press, 1938), in which he undertakes to help his readers understand the profound meaning of Augustine's dictum "the Old Testament is patent, lies open in the New" and "the New Testament is latent, lies hidden in the Old." Nevertheless, for the first hundred years of the church's history, the term "Scriptures" meant the Old Testament alone. This entire area has been newly illuminated with the publication of Hans von Campenhausen's *The Formation of the Christian Bible,* tr. by J.A. Baker (Philadelphia, Fortress Press, 1972).

II. THE OLD TESTAMENT

Since the Old Testament was the doctrinal norm for the primitive church, it is evident that it cannot be overlooked in any study of Christianity. In order to bring the Old Testament into accord with the gospel message, Christians early began to make use of two methods of exegesis: typology and allegory. The first took as its premise that the events and personages of the Old Testament were types which anticipated the events and personages of the new dispensation. That this is still an acceptable form of exegesis is the contention of G.W.H. Lampe and K.J. Woolcombe in *Essays and Typology* (London, Student Christian Movement Press, 1957). This book provides an interesting analysis of the difference between allegorism and typology, with the balance in favor of typology. In allegorical exegesis the text was treated more as a symbol of deeper spiritual truths, but this often led to a disregard of the content and the original meaning of the text. Nevertheless, these two methods of interpretation became almost universal for Christian exegetes, particularly during the medieval period, in a development described by Beryl Smalley in her *The Study of the Bible in the Middle Ages,* 2nd ed. (Oxford, B. Blackwell, 1952). The persistence of these methods into the period of the Reformation is shown in such studies as Jaroslav Pelikan's *Luther the Expositor*

(St. Louis, Concordia Publishing House, 1959). Thus the continuity of the two Testaments was accepted; all the writers were regarded as inspired by the selfsame divine Spirit, and little interest was shown by the exegetes in dating the books of the Old Testament or analyzing the conditions under which they were written. From them could be drawn a continuing theme or a divine epic in which all the parts fitted together, as was brilliantly done by J.B. Bossuet in *An Universal History,* originally published in 1681, and translated into English by James Elphiston (Dublin, R. Marchbank, 1785, and reprinted). But with the rise of the scientific spirit during the century in which Bossuet was writing, all the comfortable acceptance of a divine epic began to fade away. The new spirit of the time, with its quest for sources and origins and with its greater knowledge of the evolution of the universe, could no longer accept the simple biblical explanation. This change of outlook is briefly told by G.W. Anderson in an introductory chapter to his *A Critical Introduction to the Old Testament* (London, Gerald Duckworth, 1959). Linguistic and literary methods of criticism were used with startling effect in an analysis of Old Testament writings by a German scholar, J.G. Eichhorn, in his *Einleitung in das Alte Testament,* 3 vols. (Leipzig, Weidmann, 1803).

It was not, however, until the latter part of the nineteenth century that J. Wellhausen and other German scholars began to apply in a systematic way all the critical apparatus that was being made known to English students by S.R. Driver in 1891, in his justly famous *An Introduction to the Literature of the Old Testament* (N.Y., Charles Scribner's Sons, 1891), of which a ninth edition appeared in 1913. Under the impact of literary criticism, the Old Testament was broken up into its constituent elements, and this development caused Christian scholars to revise their earlier conceptions of revelation in the Old Testament. Still a very readable book on this subject is A. Loisy's *The Religion of Israel,* tr. by A. Galton (London, George Allen & Unwin, 1910). Loisy, a leader of the Modernist movement in the Roman Catholic church, bluntly asserted that the old theory of an inspired book dictated by God from cover to cover must be abandoned and that the legendary character of many Old Testament stories must frankly be recognized. At the same time, he held that the study of the evolution of prophecy and messianism is still valuable for an understanding of Christianity. We must, as it were, see the Old Testament as pioneering in ideas that were finally taken over by the Christian church. This is a theme that occupies a great many Christian writers on the Old Testament today and has been dealt with in some detail by R.H. Pfeiffer in his *Introduction to the Old Testament* (N.Y., Harper & Brothers, 1941).

Today, however, a new school of Old Testament scholars, the tradition–historical school, is compelling a revision of much of the work of the literary–critical school. The new school was preceded by a development associated with the name of Herman Gunkel, who made a rather drastic criticism of the "Wellhausen fabric of learning." The tradition–historical school led by Professor Ivan Engnell accepts Gunkel's view that it is impossible to carry through an exact chronological treatment of Israelite literature by the old literary methods, that there must be a recognition of conventional forms of literature appropriate to particular occasions. It is the function of literary history to recognize and classify these forms, to relate each to its setting in life (*Sitz im Leben*) and thus to trace their development with an exactitude impossible to the older literary–critical school. H.H. Rowley, in *Worship in Ancient Israel* (London, Society for Promoting Christian Knowledge, 1967), has drawn the implications of some of these insights for contemporary scholarship. Carrying such suggestions even further, the tradition–historical school centered at Uppsala, Sweden, is applying this new approach vigorously to the books of the Old Testament. A good summary of the accomplishments of these Scandinavian scholars has been made by E. Nielsen, *Oral Tradition, A Modern Problem in Old Testament Introduction* (Naperville, Ill., A.R. Allenson, 1954).

For those desirous to keep up with the latest developments in the field of Old Testament interpretation there are available two excellent quarterlies: *Vetus Testamentum* (1951–   ), published by the International Organization for the Study of the Old Testament, at Leiden, Netherlands, and *Interpretation, A Journal of Bible and Theology* (1947–   ), published at Richmond, Virginia.

A. Biblical archeology

All these new approaches to an understanding of the Old Testament are inspired by the modern desire to have as authentic documents as possible in order to gain a clearer comprehension of the origin of fundamental Christian beliefs. Naturally the findings of biblical archeologists are of great importance in this quest, particularly in establishing the age and authenticity of many key documents. Although biblical archeology is concerned with stratigraphy and typology, its underlying motive is to understand and expound the Scriptures. A brief introduction to this fascinating study was provided by G.E. Wright, assisted by R. Tomes, in *An Introduction to Biblical Archeology* (N.Y., Doubleday, 1960). Professor Wright gave a more detailed account of the subject in his *Biblical Archeology* (Philadelphia, Westminster Press, 1957). The introductory chapter enlarges upon the connection between archeology and biblical theology.

Archeological investigation by both professionals and amateurs has enjoyed a vogue in the state of Israel. Yigael Yadin, *The Art of Warfare in Biblical Lands in the Light of Archeological Study*, tr. M. Pearlman (N.Y., McGraw-Hill, 1963), is an interesting illustration. A good summary of the work of biblical scholars in recent years and their contribution to an understanding of the Christian background, particularly through archeological research, is provided in a volume entitled *The Old Testament and Modern Study* (Oxford, Clarendon Press, 1951). This book, edited by H.H. Rowley, consists of essays by members of the Society for Old Testament Study.

B. Intertestamental literature

Almost equal in importance to the Old Testament for understanding the underlying doctrines of the New Testament is the literature produced by Jewish writers after the Old Testament period and before the New Testament had become a canonical book. As is now well known, Judaism was much more complex than one would suppose from a reading of the New Testament alone. It had been in great ferment during those years and had divided into many parties, particularly on the question of the messianic hope. It was from this dream of the ultimate triumph of the Jewish nation through a messianic deliverer that Christianity issued. The subsidiary doctrines that arose around it, such as an apocalyptic judgment, separatism, asceticism, the nature of the Messiah, the resurrection of the dead, are all of significant importance for the origins of Christian beliefs. They are preeminently the subject of intertestamental literature. An excellent introduction to these intertestamental speculations is S.B. Frost's *Old Testament Apocalyptic, Its Origin and Growth* (London, Epworth Press, 1952), a book which deals with the whole field of apocalyptic thought both in the Old Testament and in noncanonical Jewish literature. The latter literature as well as the Apocrypha, composed roughly between 200 B.C. and A.D. 100, has been collected by R.H. Charles in two large volumes under the title, *The Apocrypha and Pseudepigrapha of the Old Testament in English* (Oxford, Clarendon Press, 1913). In this work he had the aid of many scholars, and each of the books is provided with an introduction and critical explanatory notes. These are formidable volumes for the layman but are indispensable for the serious student of the background of Christian beliefs. Less formidable is C.C. Torrey's *The Apocryphal Literature, A Brief Introduction* (New Haven, Yale Univ. Press, 1945), which defines the term "apocrypha" as applying to all Jewish religious writings not found in the canon of sacred scripture. An even simpler approach than Professor Torrey's is R.C. Dentan's *The Apocrypha, Bridge of the Testaments* (Greenwich, Seabury Press, 1954), which attempts to explain in nontechnical language how to understand this literature as a key to much New Testament writing. Nor should one overlook a popular manual by the great scholar of this literature, R.H. Charles, whose *Religious Development between the Old and New Testament* (N.Y., Holt, Rinehart & Winston, 1914) is an interesting analysis of the development of both Jewish and Christian ideas on the ultimate destiny of mankind.

C. The Dead Sea Scrolls

The Dead Sea Scrolls have become an exciting addition to intertestamental literature as well as an aid to textual criticism of the Old Testament. Eleven caves in the area of Qumran, northwest Jordan, have yielded to the archeologists very important material for the critical study of both Old and New Testaments. Every book of the Old Testament is represented in fragments, but there are also fragmentary remains of the library of the Essenes, a Jewish sect that lived in the area, probably during the second century B.C. Other fragments are of a later date, but all are earlier than A.D. 68.

The most ambitious work in connection with the scrolls is still Millar Burrows, *The Dead Sea Scrolls* (N.Y., Viking Press, 1955), in which he discussed the problem of dates, identification, and significance and also included six translations. It has been supplemented with a second volume, *More Light on the Dead Sea Scrolls* (N.Y., Viking Press, 1958), in which Professor Burrows discussed new scrolls and new interpretations and also included new translations. A good part of the second book is devoted to the question whether the "Essene" teacher of righteousness anticipated Christian beliefs, a suggestion made by J.M. Allegro in a series of lectures delivered over the B.B.C. in the spring of 1956 and since enlarged upon in his work, *The Dead Sea Scrolls* (N.Y., Penguin Books, 1956). In this book Allegro gives many parallels between documents from Qumran and New Testament writings, particularly on messianic and eschatological concerns. This so-called challenge to Christian faith has been addressed by twelve New Testament scholars whose opinions have been collected in a book edited by Krister Stendahl, *The Scrolls and the New Testament* (N.Y., Harper & Brothers, 1957), and in a brief volume entitled *The Dead Sea Scrolls and Primitive Christianity,* by Jean Daniélou, S.J., tr. by Salvator Attanasio (Baltimore, Helicon Press, 1958). Since the discovery of the Scrolls is quite recent, there will undoubtedly be new evaluations of their significance; these may be followed in such learned journals as *Bulletin of American Schools of Oriental Research* (1919–   ), *Bulletin of John Rylands Library* (1903–   .), *Catholic Biblical Quarterly* (1939–   ), *Journal of Biblical Literature* (1881–   ), *Revue d'histoire des religions* (1880–   ), and *Zeitschrift für die alttestamentliche Wissenschaft* (1881–   ).

III. THE NEW TESTAMENT

A. Text and canon of the New Testament

The ordinary reader of the New Testament may give little thought to its original composition, or to the long history behind the collection of the books that make up either authorized or revised versions. Nevertheless, this is important information for any student of Christianity, since the collection of Christian books was part of the evolution of the church; and it is through textual criticism that we can get at the original reading of Christian documents preserved through the centuries.

TEXTUAL CRITICISM.   Textual criticism is necessary because the twenty-seven documents which constitute the New Testament have not been preserved in their original form. As new copies of the originals are discovered, they often show variant readings from the texts in use. The object of the textual critic is to recover as nearly as possible the original text. A splendid introduction to the whole field of textual criticism is Bruce M. Metzger, *The Text of the New Testament: Its Transmission, Corruption and Restoration,* 2nd ed. (Oxford, Oxford Univ. Press, 1968). This erudite volume describes the principal manuscripts, the Latin, Syriac, and other versions, and the alternative methods of determining the best text of the New Testament.

The history of the discovery of manuscripts and the significance of each discovery add to the interest of any book in textual criticism. G.F. Kenyon tells, in his *Handbook to the Textual Criticism of the New Testament,* 2nd ed. (London, Macmillan, 1912), the story of such important manuscripts as *Codex Sinaiticus,* ed. by C. Tischendorf (London, 1862), discovered by Constantine Tischendorf in the Monastery of St. Catherine at Mount Sinai in 1844 and now preserved in the British Museum. As a matter of fact, all the important manuscripts such as the *Codex Vaticanus,* ed. by H. Fabiani (London, 1859), preserved in the Vatican Library, and the *Codex Alexandrinus,* ed. by E.M. Thompson (London, 1881–83), now after many hazardous adventures safely housed in the British Museum, have romantic stories attached to them. It is beyond the compass of this chapter to detail the various manuscripts of the New Testament, but very few of them are omitted from Kenyon's and Metzger's books. Nor does the research rely wholly upon manuscripts and ancient versions. Quotations of New Testament writings found in the works of early ecclesiastical writers are also extremely valuable in the quest for the proper reading, since these quotations often come from manuscripts long since lost. A book highly recommended for the inquiring student in this field of research is *The Text and Canon of the New Testament* by A. Souter, first published in 1912 and recently revised by C.S.C. Williams, 2nd rev. ed. (London, Gerald Duckworth, 1954).

It was to A. Souter that the editors of the Oxford series of Greek and Latin classics entrusted the task of preparing a critical edition of the New Testament in Greek, with a selected critical apparatus of variant readings. His *Novum Testamentum Graecae* (Oxford, Oxford Univ. Press, 1910; 2nd ed., 1947) gives the text which by inference lies behind the English Revised Version (1881), to some extent behind the American Standard

Revised Version (1946) and the New Testament of the New English Bible (1961). Still useful is the edition of the Greek New Testament by B.F. Westcott and F.J.A. Hort, originally published in 1881 and after reprinted.

A much valued text based upon meticulous research is E. Nestles' convenient pocket edition of the *Greek Testament,* first published in 1898 and constantly being revised, now under the editorship of Kurt Aland.

CANON.   Closely allied with textual criticism is the problem of the canon of the New Testament. "Canon" used in this sense may be defined as the rule whereby some of the writings of early Christians were recognized as divinely inspired, while others were not. This history of the collection and official approval of New Testament Scriptures is very involved and begins with a consideration of the writings of the earliest fathers of the church, includes heretical writers as well, and continues into the fourth century and even beyond. Indeed, B.F. Westcott, who wrote *A General Survey of the History of the Canon of the New Testament* (London, Macmillan, 1881) carries his story through eight centuries. This book has long been a standard authority on the subject.

It is interesting to note that the first known person to draw up a list of New Testament books was the heretic Marcion. He had rejected the Old Testament and sought for an alternative set of scriptures for his heretical following. This occurred around A.D. 144, and there seems little doubt that he was revising a list of books currently in use in the church; and so it would appear that there was a fixed list or canon around the middle of the second century. This development is described in a fascinating little book by John Knox, *Marcion and the New Testament* (Chicago, Univ. of Chicago Press, 1942).

EXCLUDED BOOKS.   A study of the canon raises the question, Why were some Christian writings of the first two centuries admitted and others rejected? Obviously the canon was drawn up to prevent heretical books from masquerading as Christian, but there were Christian books in circulation to which no doctrinal objection could be made but which failed to be recognized as canonical. It would seem that the church in its contest with heretics laid down a criterion which prevented the acceptance as canonical of many books that could still be read with profit. One such criterion was apostolicity: a canonical book must have been written by an apostle or at least have apostolic authority behind it.

Besides those rejected because of lack of apostolic authority, other books in circulation in the primitive church were referred to as apocryphal. For the most part they are imaginative works, written either to edify or to commend a peculiar doctrinal view. This apocryphal literature has been gathered together and translated into English by M.R. James in a volume entitled *The Apocryphal New Testament* (Oxford, Clarendon Press,

1924). To it may be added a supplementary volume entitled *Excluded Books of the New Testament* (London, Nash & Grayson, 1927), tr. by J.B. Lightfoot, M.R. James, H.B. Sweet, and others, with an Introduction by J.A. Robinson. The latter includes not only apocryphal literature, but also books that may have some genuine historical value.

Interest in this literature has been greatly stimulated in recent years by the discovery of Gnostic documents unearthed in Egypt in 1945, near a village called Nag Hammadi, far up the Nile. These documents are now being published, the most interesting being the *Gospel according to Thomas,* a Coptic text, established and translated by A. Guillaumont and others (N.Y., Harper & Brothers, 1959), and *The Gospel of Truth,* ed. by Kendrik Grobel (Nashville, Abingdon Press, 1960). The significance of this discovery for New Testament students has been commented on by R.M. Grant in collaboration with D.N. Freedman in a book entitled *The Secret Sayings of Jesus* (N.Y., Doubleday, 1960).

Spurious or rejected Christian literature has a long and checkered history. Even today there are in circulation writings professing to be genuine documents of Christian antiquity. Since many people have been misled by them, it has become the task of Christian scholars to apply to them the same tests applied to early apocryphal literature. Some of these modern forgeries have been analyzed by E. Goodspeed in *Strange New Gospels* (Chicago, Univ. of Chicago Press, 1931), to which he has added a supplement, *Modern Apocrypha* (Boston, Beacon Press, 1956).

B. New Testament interpretation

The critical study of the New Testament is a fairly modern discipline. A century or two ago the Christian student would have relied upon typology and allegory for interpreting the Christian Scriptures. The new method of interpretation has created, as it were, a serious breach between the modern student and his Reformation and medieval predecessors. To Richard Simon (1688–1712), a French Oratorian priest, goes the distinction of pioneering in the application of literary criticism to New Testament writings. His essay on the New Testament was translated into German in 1750 and started a series of critical works on Christianity, which became forerunners of the Tübingen school of research. An outstanding member of this school was F.C. Baur (1792–1860), whose *The Church History of the First Three Centuries,* tr. by A. Menzies, 3rd ed. (London, Williams & Norgate, 1878–79), stimulated a revolutionary interpretation of early Christian documents. Peter C. Hodgson, *The Formation of Historical Theology* (N.Y., Harper & Row, 1966) is the only satisfactory account in English of Baur's work. The narrative of these changes has been briefly told by J. Moffat in the prolegomena to his *Introduction to the Literature of the New Testament* (N.Y., Charles Scribner's Sons, 1911), and the development from patristic times to the present has been admirably summarized by Robert M. Grant in *The Bible in the Church* (N.Y., Macmillan, 1948).

SYNOPTIC PROBLEM.   Any study of the nature and quality of Christianity must give pre-eminence to the first three Gospels. In recent years there has been great concentration on what has been called the synoptic problem—that is, how to relate the variations of the Gospels when they narrate similar events. Another problem is presented by the fact that similarity of the Gospels is so great that when a good deal of the material from all three is placed in three parallel columns striking resemblances in phrasing and wording can be perceived. In 1907 A. Huck made such a harmony, which was translated into English by R.L. Finney, with the title *Huck's Synopsis of the First Three Gospels* (N.Y., Methodist Book Concern, 1929). The similarities thus revealed strengthened an hypothesis put forward by G.E. Lessing as early as 1778, and developed by J.G. Eichhorn in 1794, that the authors of these Gospels drew much of their material from an older, primitive gospel, perhaps in Aramaic. This was still a respectable theory when B.F. Westcott wrote his *Introduction to the Study of the Gospels* in 1862 (Boston, Gould & Lincoln), but now seems no longer tenable. As A.H. McNeile has expressed it in his very useful *Introduction to the Study of the New Testament* (1927), 2nd ed., rev. by C.S.C. Williams (Oxford, Clarendon Press, 1953), there is considerable agreement that oral tradition played a role in the formation of the Gospels, but "the idea of a primary stereo-typed corpus of preaching has been abandoned." The balance of opinion is that written Gospels appeared only after the church had entered the Greek-speaking world.

Most scholars today regard Mark as the foundation document used by both Matthew and Luke. They used other sources as well, one of which they had in common, designated as "Q" (from *Quelle,* the German word for source). Pioneer works supporting this theory are Hund's *Kommentar zum Neuen Testament,* 4 vols. (Freiburg, Mohr, 1889–91), and B. Weiss's *Die Quellen der synoptischen Überlieferung* (Leipzig, J.C. Hinrichs, 1908). Two scholars who brought the problem of sources forcibly to the attention of English students were J.C. Hawkins, with his *Horae synopticae* (Oxford, Clarendon Press, 1909), and W. Sanday, with his *Studies in the Synoptic Problem* (Oxford, Clarendon Press, 1911). B.H. Streeter's *The Four Gospels, A Study of Origins* (London, Macmillan, 1924) was one of the most notable contributions of British scholarship to this area of New Testament criticism. He, along with V. Taylor in *Behind the Third Gospel* (Oxford, Clarendon Press, 1926), suggested a Proto-Luke theory—namely, that someone, perhaps Luke, gathered into one document, "L," previously unwritten stories and teachings. Then Luke combined L with Q to form Proto-Luke; later Luke inserted large sections of Mark into Proto-Luke to form the Third Gospel. Streeter also suggested that behind the First Gospel lies a Jewish-Christian document, "M," which makes Matthew's sources: Mark, Q, M, and L. This four-document theory has been vigorously challenged by M.S. Enslin in *Christian Beginnings* (N.Y., Harper & Brothers, 1938). On the other hand, F.C. Grant in *The Gospels: Their Origin and Their Growth* (London, Faber & Faber, 1959) advocates a "multiple source" theory somewhat similar to Streeter's four-document theory. Involved in all these speculations are questions relating to the origin, place of writing, and dating of the Gospels. Exact dating is impossible, and authorities vary in their conjectures from A.D. 40 to the opening of the second century. The suggestion of W.L. Knox in *The Sources of the Synoptic Gospels, II: St. Luke and St. Matthew* (Cambridge, Cambridge Univ. Press, 1957) that Luke was written somewhere in the middle of the second century is not generally accepted by New Testament scholars. A succinct exposition on the problem of dating Gospels is to be found in A.H. McNeile (*op. cit.,* pp. 25–31).

FORM CRITICISM.   Form criticism came into prominence in the early 1920s as a method in the interpretation of the New Testament. This method, as explained by M. Dibelius in *From Tradition to Gospel,* tr. by B. Woolf (London, Nicholson & Watson, 1934), is to put into their original purity the forms which the Gospel material assumed during the shaping of the tradition—that is, to explain the origin of these forms and their development before they were committed to writing. To some extent it is the application to the New Testament of the categories which H. Gunkel (*op. cit.*) applied to the Old Testament in looking for the formative influence of a people's life pattern (*Sitz im Leben*) upon literary composition. One of the pioneers of this school of research, R. Bultmann, in *The History of the Synoptic Tradition,* tr. by John Marsh (N.Y., Harper & Row, 1963), has used the method with great skill to show that the Gospels are primarily witnesses to the life and teaching of the early church. A smaller book by Bultmann, *Die Erforschung der synoptischen Evangelien* (1929; 4th ed., Berlin, 1961) on the same subject has been translated into English by F.C. Grant and is included in a book entitled *Form Criticism: A New Method of New Testament Research* (Chicago, Willet, Clark, 1934). In the same volume is also included a translation of Karl Kundsin's *Primitive Christianity in the Light of Gospel Research.*

In their attempt to classify the forms of Gospel material form critics are not always in agreement, but there appears to be a fairly unanimous opinion that the Passion Story took form first and that it is the one exception to the claim that each event as a teaching story was originally a separate unit. V. Taylor in *The Formation of the Gospel Tradition* (London, Macmillan, 1933) has laid special emphasis upon the typical forms he finds in the Gospels, particularly upon what he has designated the Pronouncement

Story, which is preceded by either a problem, a controversy, or a miracle and reaches its climax in a pronouncement of Jesus. It has also been observed by P. Carrington in *The Primitive Christian Catechism* (Cambridge, Cambridge Univ. Press, 1940) that stories about Jesus were preserved by those who were in constant touch with the worship and teaching of the church, and who would emphasize their points by saying, "Hear what our Lord Jesus Christ says!" A good summary of the achievements as well as the drawbacks of form criticism is to be found in E.B. Redlich's *Form Criticism: Its Values and Limitations* (London, Gerald Duckworth, 1939).

THE FOURTH GOSPEL.   Form criticism as a method of New Testament interpretation is useful only to a limited degree beyond the Synoptic Gospels. This is particularly true in the case of the Fourth Gospel, which is obviously the work of an outstanding personality rather than merely the product of popular tradition. Much has been written on the purpose of John's Gospel. Among the early church fathers there was general agreement that the author's purpose was to supplement the Synoptics; in the nineteenth century the idea was put forth that the author shaped his material with the purpose of giving depth to the picture of Jesus conveyed in the other Gospels, the so-called improvement theory. At the beginning of the twentieth century there emerged the displacement theory—namely, that the author wrote with the intention of displacing or replacing the other gospels. R. Bultmann, for example, in what is perhaps the outstanding commentary on this Gospel in the twentieth century, *The Gospel of John,* tr. G.R. Beasley-Murray (Philadelphia, Westminster Press, 1971), sees signs of Hellenistic and even Gnostic strains of thought influencing the doctrinal outlook of the Gospel. B.W. Bacon is in accord with this interpretation and entitled his work on John's Gospel, *The Gospel of the Hellenists* (N.Y., Henry Holt, 1933). Moving in the opposite direction, C.F. Burney, impressed with the Semitic mind of the author, entitled his work *The Aramaic Origin of the Fourth Gospel* (Oxford, Clarendon Press, 1922). An excellent summary of the critical debate that has raged around John's Gospel during the twentieth century is E. Malatesta, S.J., *St. John's Gospel 1920–1965* (Rome, Analecta Biblica, 1967). Critical debate is by no means over, but recent books on this gospel such as C.H. Dodd's *The Interpretation of the Fourth Gospel* (Cambridge, Cambridge Univ. Press, 1953) leave critical questions to one side and concentrate on the background and the dominant concepts within which the author wrote. Thus Aileen Guilding's *The Fourth Gospel and Jewish Worship* (Oxford, Clarendon Press, 1960) attempts to assess "the relation of the Fourth Gospel to the ancient Palestinian synagogue lectionary system."

PAULINE LITERATURE.   The Pauline epistles are very much an aspect of New Testament criticism, since the question of date and authorship (whether written by St. Paul or not) reflects upon other books of the New Testament. These are important questions to solve, in that they are vital for establishing the earliest forms of Christianity. A classic work on the whole Pauline problem is A. Deissmann's *St. Paul; A Study in Social and Religious History* (London, Hodder & Stoughton, 1912). A brief but very useful book is A.D. Nock's *St. Paul* (London, Butterworth, 1938), which provides the reader with an extensive bibliography.

Chronology is always an important factor in any study of St. Paul. Most scholars attempt to synchronize the Acts and Paul's epistles with Jewish and Roman history, so that archeological discoveries in either of these fields usually revive interest in Pauline studies. A recent archeological discovery has helped to fix the date of Gallio's proconsulship, leading to reconstructions of chronology, such as John Knox's *Chapters in a Life of Paul* (N.Y., Abingdon Press, 1950), in which the historical accuracies of Paul's letters are emphasized against the inaccuracies of Acts. Each of Paul's epistles has come in for exhaustive treatment; all of them are dealt with adequately in *The Interpreters Bible,* 12 vols. (N.Y., Abingdon-Cokesbury, 1951–57), an excellent guidebook to all the books of the Bible. There are, however, some monographs on many of Paul's epistles that the inquiring reader should not overlook. For example, E.J. Goodspeed in *The Meaning of Ephesians* (Chicago, Univ. of Chicago Press, 1933) emphasized the encyclical character of this epistle, and C.L. Mitton's *The Epistle to the Ephesians* (Oxford, Clarendon Press, 1951) has revived considerable interest in the very thorny problem of Paulinism, to which this letter is a vital key. Ernst Percy, *Die Probleme der Kolosser und Epheserbriefe* (Lund, C.W.K. Gleerup, 1946), is an attack on the conventional wisdom of current New Testament scholarship dealing with these two letters.

The so-called pastoral epistles, I and II Timothy and Titus, because of their vocabulary and style, are difficult to ascribe to Paul. P.N. Harrison in *The Problem of the Pastoral Epistles* (Oxford, Oxford Univ. Press, 1921) thinks he finds five genuine Pauline fragments embedded in the letters but does not indicate how these fragments might occasion a letter. C. Spicq in *Les Épitres pastorales* (Paris, J. Gabalda, 1947) maintains the traditional view of Pauline authorship, asserting that there is counseling in all Pauline epistles and that all vary in style. J.N.D. Kelly's commentary, *The Pastoral Epistles* (London, Black's New Testament Commentary, 1963), has also argued for this position, but most New Testament scholars remain unconvinced.

Many Pauline terms—justification by faith, being in Christ, grace, and so on—call for close definition. For a definition of such terms as well as for specialized words used throughout the New Testament, G. Kittel's *Theological Dictionary of the New Testament,* tr. by J.R. Coates (Grand Rapids, Eerdmans, 1964) is indispensable.

HOMILIES AND PASTORALS.   With the exception of Acts, the rest of the canonical literature may be classified under the caption "homilies" and "pastorals." In chapter III of his *Introduction,* Moffatt points out that none of these writings contains any narrative, as they are mainly intended for edification. The Revelation of John belongs to a different category from the others and must be studied in close association with Jewish eschatology. The suggestion of R.B.Y. Scott in *The Original Language of the Apocalypse* (Toronto, Univ. of Toronto Press, 1928) that our present book is a Greek translation of an Hebrew original has not been generally accepted by scholars, nor has C.C. Torrey's suggestion in *Documents of the Primitive Church* (N.Y., Harper & Brothers, 1941) that the author wrote in Aramaic. What the author was trying to achieve has been interestingly set forth by C.H. Allen in *The Message of the Book of Revelation* (Nashville, Cokesbury Press, 1939), and by Paul S. Minear, in *I Saw a New Earth: An Introduction to the Visions of the Apocalypse* (Washington, Corpus Books, 1968).

The Epistles of Peter and Jude, though they may be regarded as homilies or tracts, belong to some extent to the realm of eschatology. They are generally linked together in commentaries, particularly Jude and II Peter, as J.W. Wand does in *The General Epistles of St. Peter and St. Jude,* prepared for the Westminster Commentaries (London, Methuen, 1917). Recently there has arisen a considerable interest with widely fluctuating conclusions, over the date of I Peter. F.W. Beare in *The First Epistle of Peter* (Oxford, B.H. Blackwell, 1947; 2nd ed., 1958) dates it about A.D. 112, whereas F.G. Selwyn in *The First Epistle of St. Peter* (London, A.R. Mowbray, 1940) suggests that it was sent out about Easter A.D. 64.

Because of the fluency and grammatical niceties of the Greek in the Epistle of James, it is thought doubtful that it could have been written by James the Apostle. It is considered probable by A.T. Cadoux in *The Thought of St. James* (London, James Clarke, 1944) and by other commentators that James may have secured the services of an Hellenist to write the epistle for him. There are many theories about the authorship and date of Hebrews, fully dealt with by T.W. Manson in *The Epistle to the Hebrews, an Historical and Theological Reconstruction* (London, Hodder & Stoughton, 1951).

It is fairly well accepted that an eminent church leader in Asia Minor, who called himself the "Elder," wrote the First, Second, and Third Epistles ascribed to John. He may also have been the author of John's Gospel. But C.H. Dodd in an article, "The First Epistle of John and the Fourth Gospel" in the *Bulletin of John Ryland's Library,* XXI (1937), 129–56, cannot agree that they were written by the same person, because of the differences of style and thought between I John and the Fourth Gospel. W.F. Howard in an article in *The Journal of Theological Studies,* XLVIII

(1947), does not concur with Dodd and makes out a good case for his opinion.

The Acts of the Apostles, which belongs to the topic of church history, also plays an important role in New Testament interpretation, being, as H.J. Cadbury notes in his *The Making of Luke-Acts,* an independent history of the apostolic age; but it is also a sequel to Luke's Gospel and completes a chronological story that opens with the birth of John the Baptist and continues down to the anticipated departure of Paul from Rome to Spain.

It is evident even from this brief review of literature relating to New Testament interpretation that there remain many open questions in the field of biblical criticism. These are being constantly debated in theological journals; besides those mentioned above, the following are particularly devoted to New Testament criticism: *Novum Testamentum: An International Quarterly for New Testament and Related Studies, Based on International Cooperation* (Leiden, 1956–   ) and *New Testament Studies* (N.Y., 1954–   ), an international journal published quarterly under the auspices of Studiorum Novum Testamenti Societas.

IV. PATRISTICS AND PATROLOGY

From New Testament literature the student of Christianity normally proceeds to a study of patristic literature, the writings of those who have been designated "fathers of the church." The logic behind this is the recognition that Christianity cannot be fully understood apart from the contemporary literature reflecting the environment in which it arose, developed, and defined its faith. H.B. Swete in a brief outline of *Patristic Study,* 3rd ed. (London, Longmans, Green, 1904), felt so strongly the need of some acquaintance with the fathers of the church for an understanding of Christianity that he provided in his book a suggested minimum reading course. J. Quasten in the standard modern manual on the subject, *Patrology* (Westminster, Newman Press, 1950ff.), calls for an even broader course of reading after the New Testament and includes within patrology not only orthodox writers of Christian antiquity but heretical writers as well—as, indeed, did many collectors of the patristic writings. Quasten defines patrology "as the science of the fathers of the church" and "includes in the West all Christian writers up to Gregory the Great (d.604) . . . and in the East it usually extends to John Damascene (d.749)."

Special importance has always been attached to the apostolic fathers, so designated first by J.B. Coltelier in his *Apostolic Fathers* (Paris, 1672), in which he described Barnabas, Clement of Rome, Hermos, Ignatius, and Polycarp as "The Fathers who flourished in the times of the Apostles." Since then the list has been extended, and J.B. Lightfoot in his *The Apostolic Fathers,* edited and completed by J.R. Harmer (N.Y., Macmillan, 1907), includes also *The Epistle to Diognetus, The Teaching of the Apostles, The Fragments of Papius,* and *The Reliques of the Elders Preserved in Irenaeus.*

A. Origins of patrology

In an introductory chapter to the first volume of his *Patrology (op. cit.),* Quasten provides an interesting commentary on the development of the idea of a history of Christian literature in which the theological point of view predominated. Eusebius pioneered in this field, and his *Ecclesiastical History (op. cit.)* remains one of the most important sources for patrology. The first writer, however, to compose a history of theological literatures was Jerome in *De viris illustribus* (392), which covered the period from the apostles to his own time. Around 480 Gennadius, a priest of Marseilles, made an addition to Jerome's work; a further continuation was made by Isidore of Seville between 615 and 618. Another contributor was Isidore's disciple Ildephonsus (d.667).

After Ildephonsus there was a pause in the development of patrology until the end of the eleventh century, when Sigebert of Gembloux (d.1112) again took up the task of bringing the history of Christian literature up to date. In his *De viris illustribus* he closely followed Jerome and Gennadius and then added some biographical notes on the Latin theologians of the early medieval period. There were a few other compilations around this time, but nothing significant until the appearance of Johannes Trithemius, who composed *De scriptoribus ecclesiasticis* (c. 1494), which includes biographical and bibliographical details of about 693 writers. The term "patrology" itself, however, appears to have been coined by the Orthodox Lutheran theologian, Johann Gerhard (1582–1637).

B. Great collections

In the sixteenth and seventeenth centuries an era of great collections of patristic works was inaugurated. Cardinal Bellarmine's *De scriptoribus ecclesiasticis liber unus* appeared in 1613, followed by the L.S. Nain de Tellemont's *Mémoires pour servir à l'histoire ecclésiastique des six premiers siècles,* 16 vols. (Paris, G. Robustel, 1693–1712), and R. Ceillier, *Histoire générale des auteurs sacrés et ecclésiastiques,* 23 vols. (Paris, 1729–63). The existing collections, including especially the classic editions produced by the Maurists—described by M. David Knowles in *Great Historical Enterprises* (N.Y., Nelson, 1963), pp. 33–62—were compiled by

J.P. Migne into his *Patrologia Latina,* 221 vols. (Paris, 1844–64) and *Patrologia Graeca,* 162 vols. (Paris, 1857–66). Such collections were much enriched in the nineteenth century by new discoveries of patristic writings, and so the need arose for new critical editions. The Academies of Vienna and Berlin responded to the challenge and began to put forth critical editions of the Latin and Greek series of the fathers, while French scholars began critical editions of Oriental Christian literature: *Corpus scriptorum ecclesiaticorum latinorum,* ed. by the Academy of Vienna since 1866; *Die griechischen christlichen Schriftsteller der ersten drei Jahrhunderte,* ed. by the Academy of Berlin since 1897; *Corpus scriptorum christianorum orientialium,* ed. by J.B. Chabot and others, published in Paris, since 1903. Since 1948 the Benedictine monks of St. Peter's Abbeye, Steenbrugge, Belgium, have been publishing an enormous *Corpus Christianorum.* Along with patristic texts are included conciliar and legal documents and inscriptions, and also the intention is to include non-Christian writers in this huge collection.

C. Translations

Along with the collection of texts in their original languages has proceeded the work of translation into vernacular languages. A famous Oxford series in English is the *Library of the Fathers,* 45 vols. (1838–88), ed. by Pusey, Keble, and Newman. At Edinburgh was produced *The Ante-Nicene Christian Library,* 25 vols. (Edinburgh Univ. Library, 1867–97), ed. by A. Roberts and J. Donaldson. An American reprint of the Edinburgh edition was made under the title *The Ante-Nicene Fathers,* 8 vols. (1884–86), with a supplement by A. Menzies (Vol. 9); a tenth volume has been added containing a bibliographical synopsis and a general index (N.Y., Charles Scribner's Sons, 1925). Between 1886 and 1900 P. Schaff and H. Wace issued *A Select Library of Nicene and Post-Nicene Fathers of the Christian Church,* 28 vols., 2 series (N.Y., Christian Literature Co.), now reprinted. More recent ambitious works are *Ancient Christian Writers* (Westminster, Newman Press, 1946–   ) ed. by J. Quasten and J.C. Plumpe; the series *The Fathers of the Church,* ed. by Roy J. Deferrari and others (N.Y., 1961 ff.); and *The Library of Christian Classics* (Philadelphia, Westminster Press, 1953–   ) under the general editorship of J. Baillie, J.T. McNeill, and H.P. Van Dusen.

It has been recognized that the general reader of Christian literature is not going to be able to read extensively in the fathers, and so smaller collections of selected portions of this literature have been made for such readers. An older collection of selections was made by H.M. Gwatkins. His *Selections from Early Writers Illustrative of Church History to the Time of Constantine,* rev. ed. (London, Macmillan, 1897) has long been a popular textbook. Equally popular are B.J. Kidd's *Documents Illustrative of the*

History of the Church, 2 vols. (N.Y., Macmillan, 1920), and Henry S. Bettenson, *Documents of the Christian Church,* 2nd ed. (Oxford Univ. Press, 1963). F.L. Cross has made a useful set of extracts for the purpose of illustrating church doctrine, *The Early Christian Fathers* (London, Gerald Duckworth, 1956).

D. Background studies

Obviously, patristic literature was not produced in a vacuum; so it is part of the discipline of patrology to become acquainted with the contemporary literature with which early Christian writers would be familiar as well as with the conditions of the society in which they formulated their ideas. It is particularly important that the student in this field should know something of the rhetorical devices and the topics of the popular philosophies of the first few centuries of Christianity. Also, though in the analysis of Christian texts the basic method is philological, the style and literary methods of Christian writers must be investigated against the background of Greek and Roman rhetoric. An excellent little book for patristic background is M.L.W. Laistner's *Christianity and Pagan Culture in the Later Roman Empire* (Ithaca, Cornell Univ. Press, 1951). The author deals with the interesting phenomenon of the decline of ancient science at the time of the emergence of Christianity. G.B. Caird's *The Apostolic Age* (London, Gerald Duckworth, 1955), though primarily concerned with the Christian community, provides in an appendix a painstaking chronology of the apostolic age, a very important element in patristic studies.

V. CHRISTIAN DOCTRINES

The work of scholars in the field of patristics has for its object a clearer understanding of Christian doctrine. It is also intended as an aid to the systematic theologian who has the perilous task of discriminating between orthodoxy and heterodoxy. The task begins logically enough with an analysis of the kerygma; but as the kerygma was proclaimed against the background of Old Testament and intertestamental thought, it can only be understood in relation to Old Testament theology.

A. Old Testament theology

In recent years there has been much interest displayed in this subject. Prominent students in the field are M. Burrows, who in *An Outline of Biblical Theology* (Philadelphia, Westminster Press, 1946) stresses the Old Testament view of God as the Lord of history and nature, and H.W. Robinson, who in *Inspiration and Revelation in the Old Testament* (Oxford, Clarendon Press, 1946) gives special attention to the concept that man, as God's chief creation, has a special relation to God, expressed in the Old Testament term "covenant." Both these writers are in agreement that the dominant concepts in the Old Testament which are carried over into the New are the creative and redemptive acts of God in history. The redemptive aspect arises out of the covenant relationship, which was righteous for God's people to observe and sinful to disregard. In a provocative article on "Biblical Theology" in *The Interpreter's Dictionary of the Bible,* 4 vols. (Nashville, Abingdon Press, 1962), I, 418–32, Krister Stendahl has identified, with great clarity and force, the issues raised by this problematic field.

It is probably the concept of a compact between God and his people that accounts for what Christians sometimes see as the legalistic character of Jewish religion, but, as G.E. Wright takes pains to illustrate in an article "The Faith of Israel" in *The Interpreters Bible* (*op. cit.*), I, 348–89, the legal aspect was overcome by the introduction of the term "grace" which bound the people to God with an attachment stronger than legal bonds. Nevertheless, these writers agree that there are many frustrations and unresolved problems in Old Testament theology, particularly in the realm of prophetic eschatology with its messianic overtones; and it was the unfulfilled hopes of Israel that New Testament theology was challenged to explain.

B. New Testament theology

Although the New Testament writers make Jesus of Nazareth their central theme, he always appears as the climax to the unfinished work of the Old Testament. This aspect of New Testament theology has been clearly outlined by C.H. Dodd in *According to the Scriptures: The Substructure of New Testament Theology* (*op. cit.*). Dodd finds "according to the scriptures" to be the key phrase which gives a unity of outlook to the whole of the New Testament. All the writers, he says, are concerned to show how the evangelical facts took place "according to the scriptures"; thus arose "the fundamental and regulative ideas of Christian Theology"—namely, "that the Church according to the testimonia from the Old Testament is the true and ultimate people of God" and its "operative centre was the passion and death and resurrection of Jesus Christ." From this conviction emerged the problem of Christology, a problem not fully faced by the early fathers until after they had defined Jesus' relation to God by a Trinitarian formula.

C. Trinitarianism

The transition of New Testament Christianity to early Catholicism is the basic problem in the study of the doctrines of the early church. Long the best book in English on this problem was H.F. Bethune-Baker's *An Intro-*

duction to the Early History of Christian Doctrine (1903; 6th ed., London, Methuen, 1938); but it has been somewhat displaced by J.N.D. Kelly's *Early Christian Doctrines* (London, Adam & Charles Black, 1958), and by Jaroslav Pelikan's *The Emergence of the Catholic Tradition* (*to A.D. 600*), the first volume of his *The Christian Tradition: A History of the Development of Doctrine* (Chicago, Univ. of Chicago Press, 1971 ff.). The problem of the Trinity arose, as G.L. Prestige so succinctly phrased it in *God in Patristic Thought* (London, Society for Promoting Christian Knowledge, 1956), because "The overwhelming sense of divine redemption in Christ led Christians to ascribe absolute deity to their Redeemer." Consequently, logos theories were adopted by the apologists to try to frame an intellectually satisfying explanation of the relation of Christ to God. But, as Prestige says, "the doctrine of the Logos, great as was its importance for theology, harbored deadly perils in its bosom." Prestige is an excellent guide through the many perils Christian theism had to survive (adoptionism, Christ deified only after his ascension; subordinationism, the Son an impersonal function of the Father, etc.) until the church resolved at the Council of Nicea (325) that there was an identity of substance of Father and Son. A good analysis of the evolution of this doctrine is to be found in *Essays on the Trinity and the Incarnation,* ed. A.E.J. Rawlinson (N.Y., Longmans, Green, 1928). This book is particularly helpful for understanding later developments of the doctrine as formulated at the Council of Constantinople (381), where the Holy Spirit was also declared consubstantial with the Father and the Son.

D. Christology

The problem of Christology—how could full and perfect divinity and full and perfect humanity be united in one person, and what are the relations existing between them when united in one person?—was not resolved in the first two ecumenical councils of the church. Two further councils, Ephesus (431) and Chalcedon (451), battled with this problem. At both councils, two schools of thought were in conflict: the Alexandrine, emphasizing the reality of the Godhead, and the Antiochene, emphasizing the reality of the manhood of Jesus. An excellent study of these two points of view has been made by R.V. Sellers in *Two Ancient Christologies* (London, Society for Promoting Christian Knowledge, 1940), in which he points out that the extremes of both schools were condemned at the Council of Chalcedon (451). At the 1500th anniversary of this council, A. Grillmeier, S.J., and H. Bacht, S.J., edited a three-volume collection of studies in several languages, *Das Konzil von Chalkedon* (Würzburg, Echter-Verlag, 1951); Grillmeier expanded his own study into an entire book, *Christ in Christian Tradition,* tr. by J.S. Bowden (N.Y., Sheed and

Ward, 1965). In 1953 R.V. Sellers published his readable and informative *The Council of Chalcedon* (London, S.P.C.K., 1953).

But even after Chalcedon the problem of Christology was not solved, as John Meyendorff has shown in his *Christ in Eastern Christian Thought* (Washington, D.C., Corpus Books, 1969). Nor is it even yet a closed subject for Christian theologians. In the latter half of the nineteenth century it was eclipsed by the search for the Jesus of history, a search stimulated by Sir John Seeley's *Ecce Homo* (Toronto, J.M. Dent & Sons [Canada], 1865), in which the emphasis was upon the human personality of the historical Jesus of Nazareth. Thus arose kenotic (self-emptying of the divine) theories regarding the human knowledge of Jesus. This new approach was adopted by A. Harnack in *What Is Christianity?* (N.Y., Harper Torchbooks, 1957; first published in 1900 under the title *The Essence of Christianity*) in which he drew a distinction between the gospel about Jesus and the gospel of Jesus.

The assumption that it was possible to gain an historical portrait of Jesus apart from Christology was challenged by A. Schweitzer in *The Quest of the Historical Jesus,* tr. by W. Montgomery (London, Adam & Charles Black, 1910). James M. Robinson continued and corrected this account in *A New Quest for the Historical Jesus* (London, Student Christian Movement, 1961). Form critics also arrived at the conclusion, as D.M. Baillie points out in *God Was in Christ* (N.Y., Charles Scribner's Sons, 1948), that the New Testament story of Jesus is Christological from beginning to end.

Both Emil Brunner in *The Mediator,* 2nd impression (N.Y., Macmillan, 1934) and Karl Barth in *Dogmatics in Outline* (N.Y., Philosophical Library, 1949) affirm a "high" Christology, but Brunner has reservations on the Chalcedonian formula and hesitates to define the relations between the divinity and humanity of Christ in two-nature terms.

There have been attempts to abandon Greek philosophical terms to explain Christ's person and to replace them with either modern philosophical or psychological expressions. A pioneer attempt is L. Thornton's *The Incarnate Lord* (N.Y., Longmans, Green, 1928), based upon the organic philosophy of A.N. Whitehead; Thornton's lead was followed in Leonard Hodgson's *The Doctrine of the Trinity* (London, Nisbet, 1943). Even earlier W. Sanday in *Christologies, Ancient and Modern* (N.Y., Oxford Univ. Press, 1910), had sought a solution of Chalcedonian dualism by placing the divinity of Christ in the subliminal consciousness. More recently W.R. Matthews has suggested in *The Problem of Christ in the Twentieth Century* (N.Y., Oxford Univ. Press, 1950) that Jung's theory of the racial unconscious may help us to understand the corporate significance of Christ's redemptive work. An excellent criticism of these modern Christologies is to be found in W.N. Pittenger's *The Word Incarnate* (N.Y., Harper & Brothers, 1959). He also offers a restatement of his own.

E. Human destiny

Christological speculation, which is so often concerned with fallen human nature, inevitably raises the problem of human destiny. A classic on this subject is still F.R. Tennant's *The Sources of the Doctrines of the Fall and Original Sin* (Cambridge, Cambridge Univ. Press, 1903). This book deals with the Fall story in Genesis II, and follows its development through the intertestamental literature down to the fathers before Augustine. During this period there was a division between East and West, the former being more optimistic than the latter as to the nature of man. Though both agreed that man was a composite of body and soul, they did not always agree on where the soul came from. Many held a traducianist view—that each soul is somehow generated from the parent's soul—while others held a creationist view—that each soul was created by God at the moment of its infusion into the body.

H.W. Robinson in *The Christian Doctrine of Man* (Edinburgh, T. & T. Clark, 1911) supplements Tennant's book by continuing the story through the medieval and Reformation periods; the latter period introduces a new division in the West, since the Reformation theologians have been far less optimistic about the nature of man than the Counter-Reformation theologians. Robinson's book also deals with current views.

N.P. Williams in *The Ideas of the Fall and Original Sin* (London, Longmans, Green, 1927) justifies his rather large volume, covering the same ground as Tennant, by the fact that the "new psychology" and the revival of the theory of a cosmic fall call for a new constructive view of the whole subject of the nature of man.

A massive study of human nature and human destiny has been made by Reinhold Niebuhr in his Gifford Lectures, *The Nature and Destiny of Man,* 2 vols. (N.Y., Charles Scribner's Sons, 1941–43), based upon the belief that "there are resources in Christian faith for an understanding of human nature that have been lost in modern culture." Niebuhr's work owed a considerable debt to Emil Brunner's *Man in Revolt,* tr. by Olive Wyon (Philadelphia, Westminster Press, 1947). A less ambitious but more optimistic book on the subject is E.L. Mascall's *The Importance of Being Human* (N.Y., Columbia Univ. Press, 1958).

F. Soteriology

Implicit in all Christian discussion of human nature is the belief that man through self-determined rebellion has become enmeshed in evil and is in need of redemption or restoration of his original righteousness. The Christian solution to this aspect of evil is that the image of God in man is restored through the Incarnation and the Atonement; but the latter is a doctrine that has never received an official dogmatic formulation. Nor was attention particularly directed toward it until Anselm in his famous book

Why God Became Man (1098) proclaimed that Christ on behalf of men through his death made the satisfaction for sin which God's justice demands; Anselm's work had been translated before, but it was given a fresh English rendering and a learned introduction by Eugene R. Fairweather in *A Scholastic Miscellany: Anselm to Ockham* (Philadelphia, Westminster Press, 1956). It is often contended that this emphasis on the death of Christ as an isolated event stands in sharp contrast to the patristic view, in which the death of Christ is the climax of a long conflict and constitutes a victory. The patristic view, however, as H.E.W. Turner makes evident in *The Patristic Doctrine of Redemption* (London, A.R. Mowbray, 1952), was never consistent. It consists of a variety of theories; a mystical theory (human nature sanctified by Christ becoming man), a ransom theory (Christ's death regarded as a ransom paid to the devil), and a realist theory (Christ took upon himself the penalty which justice demanded). Associated with all these is a theory derived from Paul and developed by Irenaeus, which sees Christ as the representative of the whole human race, the recapitulation theory. All these theories were brought together by Augustine and passed on to the Middle Ages, where they provided Anselm with the material upon which he based his satisfaction theory. No sooner was it put forth than it was challenged by Peter Abelard (1079–1142), with his doctrine that Christ's example had a subjective effect upon mankind, the so-called subjective view of the Atonement, set forth in his *Expositio* of the Epistle to the Romans and referred to in his *Christian Theology*. The latter work has been translated into English by J.R. McCallum (Oxford, B.H. Blackwell, 1948).

It was the Anselmian view that prevailed in the Middle Ages and on into the Reformation period, but, as G. Aulén in *Christus Victor* (N.Y., Macmillan, 1951) has pointed out, with some very significant modifications. Aulén's book is a useful study of the changes that came about in the interpretation of the doctrine of the Atonement through the Later Middle Ages, the Reformation, and the Enlightenment.

In recent days a strong attack has been launched against the satisfaction theory. It began with Horace Bushnell's *God in Christ* of 1849 (N.Y., AMS Press, 1972) and *The Vicarious Sacrifice* (N.Y., Charles Scribner, 1866); and with McLeod Campbell's controversial book *The Nature of the Atonement* (London, Macmillan, 1886); and was continued by R.C. Moberley's *Atonement and Personality* (N.Y., Longmans, Green, 1901). These writers repudiated penal satisfaction and stressed Christ as representative man, not merely as substitute. P.T. Forsyth in *The Cruciality of the Cross,* 2nd ed. (London, Independent Press, 1948), sought to reinterpret the traditional theory of vicarious satisfaction.

There has also been considerable criticism of the use of individual categories in relation to the Atonement. The objection was raised by R. Niebuhr in *Moral Man and Immoral Society* (N.Y., Charles Scribner's Sons,

1932); also by J.G. Bennett in *Social Salvation; A Religious Approach to the Problems of Social Change* (N.Y., Charles Scribner's Sons, 1935); Nels F.S. Ferré in *The Christian Understanding of God* (N.Y., Harper & Brothers, 1951); and Karl Heim in *Jesus the World's Perfecter,* tr. by D.H. van Daalen (Edinburgh, Oliver & Boyd, 1937; 2nd ed., 1959). A fair summary of these modern views of redemption, including those who regard the "Fall" as a step upward, based upon the idea of evolution, is to found in T.H. Hughes' *The Atonement—Modern Theories of the Doctrine* (London, George Allen & Unwin, 1949).

G. Ecclesiology

An emphasis upon the corporate aspect of redemption through Christ leads, as K. Heim (*op. cit.*) stresses, to a recognition of the importance of the church as the body which "carries on His Life's work with supra-spatial and supra-temporal power." The doctrine of the church has always been closely associated with the doctrine of the Holy Spirit. Consequently, when Charles Gore came to write the third volume of his famous trilogy The Reconstruction of Belief, he entitled it *The Holy Spirit and the Church* (London, John Murray, 1924). The reason, he said, was that Jesus "gave few directions to His Church but left it to organize itself under the guidance of the Holy Spirit."

Unfortunately, the doctrine of the church has been subject to much controversy. Roman Catholics, Eastern Orthodox, Anglicans, and Protestants all hold varying views about its constitutional structure, its source of authority, and the relative prestige of its ancient sees. But the subject is even more complicated for in almost all the major churches there is a "high" and "low" view on the nature of the church. C. Gore, for example, represents a high church view within Anglicanism, while J.B. Lightfoot in a notable study, *The Christian Ministry* (London, Macmillan, 1903), presents a radical departure from Anglicanism on the historic status of the episcopate.

The primacy of the papacy has long been a controversial subject, for which Karl Adam makes a convincing case in *The Spirit of Catholicism* (London, Sheed & Ward, 1929). Eastern churches, on the other hand, have regarded Rome as first among equals. The point of view of the Orthodox churches has been carefully set forth by B.J. Kidd in *The Roman Primacy to A.D. 461* (N.Y., Macmillan, 1936), and by Francis Dvornik in *Byzantium and the Roman Primacy* (N.Y., Fordham Univ. Press, 1966). An excellent historical examination of the Reformed tradition is Geddes MacGregor's *Corpus Christi: The Nature of the Church according to the Reformed Tradition* (Philadelphia, Westminster Press, 1958). All the traditional concepts of the church have been gathered together in a volume prepared by the Theological Commission on the Church, set up by the

World Conference on Faith and Order, entitled *The Nature of the Church,* ed. by R.N. Flew (London, Student Christian Movement Press, 1952). Paul S. Minear has examined *Images of the Church in the New Testament* (Philadelphia, Westminster Press, 1960), and Avery R. Dulles, S.J., has proposed his own useful classification of various theories in *Models of the Church* (Garden City, Doubleday, 1974).

H. The sacraments

Vital to the doctrine of the church and its ministry is the place of the sacraments. All the books referred to in the previous section give a prominent position to the sacramental aspect of church life. In the earliest Christian literature there is the implicit assumption that the sacraments are the outward and visible signs of invisible but genuine grace, but it was a long time before their number and nature were fixed.

A learned treatise on the sacraments is B. Leeming's *Principles of Sacramental Theology* (Westminster, Md., Newman Press, 1956), covering the general principle upon which sacraments are based and their origins and development in the Christian church as well as the attitudes of the various branches of Christianity. Such matters as validity, objective efficacy, causality, and intention are minutely discussed. The book also contains a bibliography, in which all points of view are represented. A good cross section of denominational views is set forth in a volume prepared by the Theological Commission appointed by the Continuation Committee of Faith and Order, entitled *The Ministry and the Sacraments,* ed. R. Dunkerly (1937).

Pre-eminent among the sacraments are Baptism and the Eucharist, and much has been written on both. A recent book on Baptism which has received favorable comment from many quarters is G.W. Lampe's *The Seal of the Spirit* (London, Longmans, Green, 1951), which deals with the confusing question of the relation of Baptism to Confirmation. The controversial aspect of the Eucharist is the problem of the "real presence." An historical examination of this doctrine has been made by E. Masure in *The Christian Sacrifice* (N.Y., P.J. Kenedy & Sons, 1944).

During the Middle Ages the number of the sacraments was eventually fixed at seven, with Penance taking a far more prominent position than it ever held in the early church. This was due to medieval concentration on grace and merit as an aspect of personal religion. Thus arose an insistence on private confession to a priest. The origin of this practice has been the subject of careful research by R.C. Mortimer in *The Origins of Private Penance in the Western Church* (Oxford, Clarendon Press, 1939), and by Bernhard Poschmann in *Penance and the Anointing of the Sick,* tr. by Francis Courtney (N.Y., Herder & Herder, 1964). It was the Reformers' attack upon the system of merits and indulgences that constituted the first step toward creating the great difference between medieval and modern society in the West. The differences between Roman Catholic and Protestant sacramental views have been candidly discussed by O.C. Quick in *The Christian Sacraments* (N.Y., Harper & Brothers, 1928). The occasional sacraments such as Holy Orders, Matrimony, and Extreme Unction are all discussed in great detail by B. Leeming (*op. cit.*).

I. Eschatology

Systematic Christian theology always closes on the theme of eschatology —the doctrine of the last things. Although Christian history is supposed to have reached its climax in the coming, death, and resurrection of Jesus Christ, yet there is a final dénouement. Four chief moments are prominent in the dénouement: (1) the return of Christ, the Parousia; (2) the resurrection; (3) the judgment; (4) the catastrophic end of the present world order. There has sometimes been a tendency to regard these moments as symbols rather than literal facts, but how to interpret these symbols is a matter of controversy. A theory gaining much approval, set forth by C.H. Dodd in *The Apostolic Preaching* (N.Y., Willett, Clark, 1937), is that the final age is here ("realized eschatology")—that is, the final phase of God's dealing with men has already arrived—and yet "there remains a residue of eschatology" which is implied in the second coming of the Lord and the last judgment, which can only be expressed in mythological terms. J. Baillie in *The Belief in Progress* (N.Y., Charles Scribner's Sons, 1951) speaks of this final phase as "years of Grace" and regards the second coming, the last judgment, and the resurrection as "symbols of a reality unimaginable by us except in symbolic form"; but they are necessary defenses against "secular progressiveness." R. Niebuhr in the second volume of *The Nature and Destiny of Man* (*op. cit.*) sees the significance of eschatology as a symbol of the fact that the final consummation of history is beyond time; but O. Cullman in *Christ and Time* (*op. cit.*) returns to the Hebraic idea that eternity is a simple extension of time and suggests abandoning the Greek idea of a qualitative difference between time and eternity. He sees the Christian drama as a continuous redemptive line, "unlimited in one direction." W.C. Robinson in *Christ the Hope of Glory* (Grand Rapids, Mich., Wm. B. Eerdmans, 1945) reasserts the position of historic Protestantism that Christ will return, but objects to the Premillennialists' programming of the future. The latter base their views on the promise in Revelation (20:6) that "they, the saints, shall reign with him [Christ] a thousand years." Various interpretations of this hope have been set forth by E.T. Clark in *The Small Sects in America,* rev. ed. (N.Y., Abingdon Press, 1949). Eschatological timetables have occupied groups of Christians from earliest days down to the present time. These have been the subject of careful research by S.J. Case in *The Millennial Hope* (Chicago, Univ. of Chicago Press, 1918), who begins his book with an analysis of pre-Christian Millennarianism and concludes with a modern estimate of millennial hopes. Norman Cohn's *The Pursuit of the Millennium,* rev. ed. (N.Y., Oxford Univ. Press, 1970), documents the history of such hopes in an exciting way.

VI. CHRISTIAN PHILOSOPHY

In the background of all discussion of Christian doctrines lurks the question: How do Christians know that God revealed Himself in Jesus Christ, or how do they know that God exists? It is the task of Christian philosophy to answer these and allied questions. A good introduction to the subject is Geddes MacGregor's *Introduction to Religious Philosophy* (Boston, Houghton Mifflin, 1959), which opens with the preliminary question: What is religion? MacGregor also provides simple definitions of the many technical terms that occur in philosophical discussions of Christianity.

J.S. Whale in *Christian Doctrine* (N.Y., Macmillan, 1941; reissued, 1957) frankly regards Christian doctrine as a philosophical problem and reviews the traditional arguments for the existence of God as a preface to his presentation of the Christian faith.

A. Reason and revelation

There are, however, many theologians vigorously opposed to the term "Christian philosophy." Conflicting views on the subject have been collected by J. Baillie and H. Martin, eds., *Revelation* (London, Faber & Faber, 1937), in which representatives of various Christian traditions— Roman Catholic, Lutheran, Reformed, Orthodox, Anglican, and Baptist— discuss the antithesis of reason and revelation and also raise the question whether God has revealed himself in non-Christian religions. One contributor, K. Barth, considers that Christian philosophy is a contradiction in terms and asserts that the Christian faith is based solely on revelation; the theologian's task is to provide scientific conceptions of this revelation. M.C. D'Arcy, representing the Roman Catholic point of view, defends a long-standing distinction between natural and revealed religion, but partly agrees with Barth in asserting that there is only a limited revelation outside Jesus Christ. S. Bulgakoff, speaking for the Orthodox, finds a glimmer of revelation in all pagan religions. A difficulty associated with this book is that the representatives of the various traditions do not necessarily speak for a consensus within their respective traditions. E. Brunner, who was often aligned with the neo-orthodox school of K. Barth, conceded, in *The Philosophy of Religion from the Standpoint of Protestant Theology* (London, Nicholson & Watson, 1937) and in *Revelation and Reason,* tr. Olive

Wyon (Philadelphia, Westminster Press, 1946), that there was a legitimate relation between revelation and rational knowledge. An Anglican, L. Hodgson, is hardly in agreement with the Anglican representative in *Revelation* (*op. cit.*) when in *Towards a Christian Philosophy* (London, James Nisbet, 1942) he questions whether revelation and philosophical inquiry can still be united as they were in former eras, since philosophy is now bogged down in analyzing its own procedures. On the other hand, John Wilson in *Language and Christian Belief* (N.Y., St. Martin's Press, 1958) suggests that Christian theologians, by using the new methods of analytical philosophy, could greatly improve the language of religion. H. Richard Niebuhr's *The Meaning of Revelation* (N.Y., Macmillan, 1941) is one of the most profound discussions of this issue in recent decades.

B. Early Christian philosophy

The history of Christian philosophy began, as A. Harnack says in *What Is Christianity?* (*op. cit.*), when Christian apologists laid down the equation, "The Logos is Jesus Christ"—perhaps even earlier, when the writer of the Fourth Gospel said, "In the beginning was the Word . . ." (John 1:1) or when Paul spoke of Christ as the wisdom (sophia) of God.

With Justin Martyr's *Apologies* (c. 155), ed. by A.W.F. Blunt (Cambridge, Cambridge Univ. Press, 1911), the claim was made that all good philosophies are "the property of the church." A little later Athenagoras in his *Plea* (c. 176) attempted to show that Christianity is a respectable philosophy. Closely associated with this interest in a philosophical statement of Christianity is the problem that the Gnostics were creating for the church fathers in trying to use Christianity for their own purposes. Good studies of this problem are Hans Jonas, *The Gnostic Religion: The Message of the Alien God and the Beginnings of Christianity* (Boston, Beacon Press, 1958), a "systematic theology" of the teachings of the Gnostic masters, and R. McL. Wilson's *The Gnostic Problem* (London, A.R. Mowbray, 1958), which stresses the fact that Gnosticism was a problem for Hellenistic Judaism before it became a problem for the church. In combatting Gnosticism, both were compelled to use contemporary philosophical terms.

Some Jews, such as Philo (born about 25 B.C.), frankly sought to justify Judaism by the use of Hellenistic philosophical language and thus paved the way for a similar use by Christian theologians. Hans Lewy in *Philo: Philosophical Writings* (Oxford, East & West Library, 1956) has made brief selections from Philo's works which are good background introduction to the philosophy of the early church fathers, as is also H.A. Wolfson's *Philo* (Cambridge, Harvard Univ. Press, 1947). The latter is a monumental study of Philonic problems as they relate to patristic problems and is continued in Wolfson's *The Philosophy of the Church Fathers,* vol. I

(Cambridge, Harvard Univ. Press, 1956). An important book in this field is C. Bigg's *The Christian Platonists of Alexandria* (1886; rep., Oxford, Clarendon Press, 1913), particularly good for its comments on the writings of Clement of Alexandria and on Origen's *On First Principles,* which has been translated by G.W. Butterworth (N.Y., Harper Torchbooks, 1966). Both these writers imported a great deal of Platonism into Christian theology, a tradition carried on by the Cappadocian fathers, whose contribution to Christian philosophy is clearly outlined in G.L. Prestige's *Fathers and Heretics* (N.Y., Macmillan, 1940). Jean Daniélou, S.J., in *Platonisme et théologie mystique* (Aubier, Éditions Montaigne, 1944) has examined the place of Gregory of Nyssa (c.330–c.395) in this development.

C. Augustinian Platonism

It was, however, in the writings of Augustine of Hippo that philosophical speculation was to reach its highest peak in Christian theology. His monumental contribution to Christian thought and culture has been well documented by seventeen contributors to *A Companion to the Study of Saint Augustine,* ed. R.W. Battenhouse (N.Y., Oxford Univ. Press, 1955), and both his life and his thought have been illumined by Peter Brown in his *Augustine of Hippo* (Berkeley, Univ. of California Press, 1967), a model of what the biography of a man of letters or ideas should be.

It was early recognized by the church fathers that there were serious difficulties with a Platonic or a Neo-Platonic interpretation of Christian doctrine, but no alternative was considered possible until the scholastics of the Middle Ages discovered Aristotle. In the meantime the Platonic tradition was preserved in a mystical garb by the Pseudo-Dionysius in his *The Celestial Hierarchy* and *Concerning the Divine Names,* first appearing about 532, and by Joannes Scotus Erigena (c.800–c.877) in a great work entitled *The Division of Nature* or *Periarchon,* now appearing in a new critical edition of the Latin text with an English translation by I.P. Sheldon-Williams (Dublin, Scriptores Latini Hiberniae, 1968ff.). This work was condemned by the church, which was becoming alarmed with the "illumination" approach to understanding, but it survived underground and came to the surface in the speculative mysticism of later medieval thinkers.

D. Scholasticism

After Erigena the hierarchical church was opposed for some time to any speculation on the data of faith, but with the revival of learning in the eleventh century there was a distinct change of attitude. This is evidenced in the *Monologion* and *Prosologium* of Anselm (1033–1109). In the first

Anselm made his famous utterance *credo ut intelligam,* and in the second he developed his famous ontological proof of God's existence. This so-called "father of Scholasticism," whose work has been carefully summarized, with an extensive bibliography by Jasper Hopkins, *A Companion to the Study of St. Anselm* (Minneapolis, Univ. of Minnesota Press, 1972), raised a subject which was to be much debated throughout the Middle Ages, the nature of universals (whether they exist in reality or whether they are merely names). Those who asserted the former were known as realists, the latter as nominalists. Such speculation had been formulated by Porphyry (233–c.304) in an *Introduction to Aristotle,* tr. into Latin by Boethius (480–524) and used in the Middle Ages as a compendium of Aristotelian logic.

The questions raised by Porphyry were taken up by Roscellin (c.1050–1122), who accepted the nominalist point of view, and by William of Champeaux (1070–1121), who held a realist view; and so the great medieval debate began. Its opening phases are told by Abelard in his *History of Calamities,* in which he himself took a mediating view known as conceptualism. The story of medieval philosophy from the beginning to its dénouement in William of Ockham is told by G. Leff in a very readable book, *Medieval Thought: St. Augustine to Ockham* (Middlesex, Penguin Books, 1958), and in Fairweather's *Scholastic Miscellany* (*op. cit.*).

After Abelard the story of medieval Christian philosophy takes on a new dimension because of the acquisition of a greater knowledge of both Plato and Aristotle through the mediation of Islamic scholars. This phase is satisfactorily dealt with by Leff, but a more detailed account can be obtained in J.W. Sweetman's *Islam and Christian Theology,* 2 vols. (London, Lutterworth Press, 1945–47).

The new era was characterized by the making of "summaries," such as the *Summa Universae Theologiae* of Alexander of Hales (d.1245), ed. P. Bernardini Klumper (Florence, Claras Aquas [Quaracchi], 1924), that of Albert the Great (c.1206–80), and that of Bonaventure (1221–74), several of whose writings have been translated in J. deVinck (ed.), *The Works of Bonaventure* (Patterson, N.J., St. Anthony Guild Press, 1960–70). Bonaventure is also famous for his commentary on the *Sentences of Peter Lombard,* a much used theological textbook written between 1145 and 1150. From it the medieval masters raised many questions (*quaestio disputa*); hence the remarkable number of questions asked and answered in the medieval summaries of theology.

The greatest of the summaries was from the pen of Thomas Aquinas (c.1227–74), whose *Summa Theologica,* now appearing in a new Latin-English version, the so-called "Blackfriars Edition," (N.Y., 1964ff.) with introductions and notes, is still accepted as the basis of the theological position of the Roman Catholic Church. Thomas Gilby's *St. Thomas Aquinas' Philosophical Texts* (London, Oxford Univ. Press, 1952) is a selection of translations with notes from the many works of the great Catholic doctor and is useful for those who cannot hope to read all of his works. This may be supplemented by a very excellent collection by A.C. Pegis: *Basic Writings of St. Thomas Aquinas,* 2 vols. (N.Y., Random House, 1948). Shortly after Aquinas' death a doctrinal storm broke out in Europe, heralded by Duns Scotus (c. 1266–1308), who in *Commentaries on the Sentences of Peter Lombard* began a retreat of reason from faith. With the advent of William of Ockham (c. 1300–49) and his *Sentences* and *Quodlibeta,* the collaboration of faith and reason as it had prevailed in high scholasticism came to an end. For both the Reformation and the Counter-Reformation, philosophy no longer appeared to be a buttress of faith; the former relied upon justification by faith alone, the latter upon the authority of the church and mysticism. In Anglican circles, however, a rational approach to faith was not wholly abandoned, as evidenced in R. Hooker's (1553–1600) *Laws of Ecclesiastical Polity* (Oxford, Clarendon Press, 1905, and many other editions).

E. Cartesianism

In the seventeenth century Christian philosophy received a new lease on life when René Descartes (1596–1650) published his *Discourse on Method* with its famous *cogito ergo sum,* and thus laid the foundations of modern philosophical rationalism. Both Blaise Pascal in his *Pensées* (N.Y., Modern Library, 1941), and J.B. Bossuet in *De la connaissance de Dieu* (1732; rev. ed., 1741; also Paris, Garnier, 1937) attempted to use the Cartesian method in defense of faith; the former held, however, that actual faith is a gift of divine grace, while the latter added Thomism to Cartesianism.

The story of the attempt to re-establish faith on a rationalistic foundation can be followed in A. Caldecott and H.R. Mackintosh, eds., *Selections from the Literature of Theism,* 3rd ed. (Edinburgh, T. & T. Clark, 1931); it opens with the ontological argument of Anselm and includes some reference to scholastic philosophy, but it is particularly useful for its selections from the outstanding philosophers of modern rationalism, including Descartes, Spinoza, the Cambridge Platonists, Berkeley, Kant, Schleiermacher, Comte, Lotze, Sorley, and Ritschl. Two notable omissions are Joseph Butler's *Analogy* (1736), and William Paley's *View of the Evidences of Christianity* (Philadelphia, 1795).

F. Liberalism

The above writings to a large extent belong to the age of the Enlightenment, but even during this era it became evident to most serious Christians that the Cartesian philosophy and its subsequent development were leading nowhere. But there was a revived hope for an alliance of philosophy and religion with the publication of Immanuel Kant's *Critique of Practical*

Reason (1788), in which Kant attempted to base religious faith on the categorical imperative. G.W.F. Hegel sought to buttress this approach with an emphasis upon the universe as a constant development of the Absolute. An interesting collection of the theological writings of Hegel, who played an unusually significant role in the development of liberal Christianity, has been made by T.M. Knox and Richard Kroner in a volume entitled *Early Theological Writings* (Chicago, Univ. of Chicago Press, 1948). Prominent among the liberal theologians are: Friedrich Schleiermacher, whose *On Religion,* tr. by John Oman (N.Y., Harper Torchbooks, 1958), was an effort at a new apologetic, while *The Christian Faith,* tr. by H.R. Mackintosh and J.S. Stewart (Edinburgh, T. & T. Clark, 1928), sought to recast systematic theology; Albrecht Ritschl, whose principal work was *The Christian Doctrine of Justification and Reconciliation* (Edinburgh, T. & T. Clark, 1900); and Adolph Harnack, whose *What Is Christianity?* (*op. cit.*) is the classical statement of liberal theology.

G. Crisis, or dialectical, theology

Liberalism, however, was constantly challenged for its use of a relativist interpretation of Christian faith. As early as the middle of the nineteenth century Sören Kierkegaard (1813–55) denounced the spectator-like attitude of the Hegelian philosopher indulging in speculative theories apart from existential experience. Stimulated by Kierkegaard's works, particularly *Training in Christianity* and *Concept of Dread* (which have been made available to English-speaking readers by the translations of W. Lowrie, the former in 1941 [Oxford Univ. Press, N.Y.] and the latter in 1944 [Princeton Univ. Press, New Jersey]), there arose a theology of crisis in which theological analysis is based upon a dialectical method of thinking as one way of overcoming the contradictions of human existence—or, as it has otherwise been expressed, that actual relations between God and man can only be described in paradoxical terms (hence, the alternative title "dialectical theology").

Several books have been written on this modern approach to theological problems; among them W. Lowrie's *Our Concern with the Theology of Crisis* (Boston, Meador, 1932), J. McConnachie's *The Barthian Theology and the Man of Today* (N.Y., Harper & Brothers, 1933), and F.W. Camfield's *Reformation, Old and New* (London, Lutterworth Press, 1947).

H. Distinctive philosophies

It is perhaps necessary to add that liberal theology has not yet wholly abandoned the scene, or at least there are still many supporters of a modified liberalism, such as H.H. Farmer, who in *God and Men* (Nashville, Abingdon-Cokesbury, 1947) adheres to the Bible as the supreme authority of faith. There is a continuation of the naturalist tradition, represented by H.N. Wieman in *The Growth of Religion* (Chicago, Willett, Clark, 1938); Neo-Thomism has been attractively expounded by E.H. Gilson in *Elements of Christian Philosophy* (N.Y., Doubleday, 1960). Philosophical theology on the basis of believing in order to understand was stoutly maintained by W. Temple in *Nature, Man and God,* 2 vols. (London, Macmillan, 1932–35); Nels F.S. Ferré in *The Christian Understanding of God* (N.Y., Harper & Brothers, 1951) combines evangelical insight with the metaphysics of Whitehead. P. Tillich's *Systematic Theology* (Chicago, Univ. of Chicago Press, 1951–64) was a new and bold statement of the position that Christian theology can make philosophical sense. There is, therefore, little evidence that the philosophical debate on Christian doctrines is in decline; its future development may be followed in such magazines as *The Hibbert Journal* (London, 1902–   ), *Revue d'histoire et de philosophie religieuses* (Strasbourg, 1921–   ), *Journal for the Scientific Study of Religion* (1961–   ), and *The Modern Churchman* (1911–   ).

VII. CHRISTIAN SOCIOLOGY

Not all Christians are in agreement that there is a sociological approach to Christianity; those dissenting hold that what is primarily a proclamation of good news cannot be subject to a scientific analysis, such as the term "sociology" implies. Nevertheless, there does seem to be need for some designation of a study concerned not only with the collective behavior of Christians, but also with the functional relation of Christianity to society in general. Since Ernst Troeltsch wrote *The Social Teaching of the Christian Churches* (1912; English translation, N.Y., Macmillan, 1931), a brilliant analysis of the influence of the Christian spirit upon the ancient, medieval, and modern world and of the influence of the natural and political structure of these worlds upon the church, there has arisen a deep interest in the sociological approach to religion. J. Wach in *Sociology of Religion* (Chicago, Univ. of Chicago Press, 1944), a study of the sociology of all religions, concedes the influence of Troeltsch upon his own work. But he gives Max Weber the credit for conceiving a systematic sociology of religion. The latter in a very controversial essay, *The Protestant Ethic and the Spirit of Capitalism,* tr. by T. Parsons (London, George Allen & Unwin, 1930), identified business acumen with Calvinism. There have been many refinements upon this theme, the best known being R.H. Tawney's *Religion and the Rise of Capitalism* (London, John Murray, 1926). A more recent discussion of the same theme is V.A. Demant's *Religion and the Decline of Capitalism* (N.Y., Charles Scribner's Sons, 1952).

Weber's and Troeltsch's researches stimulated H.R. Niebuhr to make a similar analysis of American denominational religion; his *The Social Sources of Denominationalism* (N.Y., Holt, Rinehart & Winston, 1929) is an outstanding contribution to the sociology of religious sects.

A. The social gospel

A variant approach to the sociological problem, known as the social gospel, emphasizes what ought to be the collective behavior of Christians. V.A. Demant in *Theology of Society* (London, Faber & Faber, 1947) defends this approach on the basis that since "the Christian religion is a religion of redemption" and "redemption is always a restoration," the essential nature of the Christian approach to the social problem is therefore to restore things to their true nature.

At the opening of the nineteenth century it became the hope of many Christians that the application of Christian principles to the ordering of society would pave the way for the establishment of a better world order. In Europe this new interest was manifested by H.R. de Lamennais in France, G. Mazzini in Italy, H. Kutter in Switzerland, and A. Harnack in Germany. The theology of the movement, particularly among Roman Catholics, is set forth by A.R. Vidler in *Prophecy and Papacy: A Study of Lamennais, the Church and the Revolution* (N.Y., Charles Scribner's Sons, 1954). Although the movement initiated by Lamennais and other liberal Roman Catholics was condemned by the papacy, the concern for better social order was nevertheless clearly manifest in the papal encyclical *Rerum Novarum* (May 15, 1891), and in the many epochal documents issued by Pope Leo XIII, which have been arranged and annotated by J. Husslein in *Christian Social Manifesto* (N.Y., Bruce, 1939).

A pioneer historical study of the influence of the social gospel in the early days of the church is A. Harnack's *The Expansion of Christianity in the First Three Centuries,* tr. by James Moffatt, 2 vols. (N.Y., G.P. Putnam's Sons, 1904–05), in which he illustrates from early Christian literature the growing popularity of the church in the first three centuries because of its warmth and kindliness to those in distress. A similar study is S.J. Case's *The Social Origins of Christianity* (Chicago, Univ. of Chicago Press, 1923).

The study of the social gospel has been greatly intensified by the impact of the industrial revolution upon social life. It was seen by many churchmen that the individualistic social philosophy that had been accepted by Christians generally was inadequate in a world of large-scale production in which economic power was concentrated in few hands. This was particularly the stimulus behind the Christian socialist movement initiated in England by J.F.D. Maurice and Charles Kingsley, and kept alive in the writings of such prominent Anglicans as A.C. Headlam, B.F. Westcott, H. Scott Holland, C. Gore, and W. Temple; Temple, while Archbishop of

York, wrote his justly famous *Christianity and Social Order* (N.Y., Penguin Books, 1942). The origin and early history of the movement has been well told by C.E. Raven in *Christian Socialism 1848–1854* (London, Macmillan, 1920); its later development may be followed in M.B. Reckitt's *Maurice to Temple: A Century of Social Movement in the Church of England* (London, Faber & Faber, 1947).

The most startling evidences of the change that had been taking place in the social outlook of the churches in England were the reports issued by a Conference on Christian Politics, Economics and Citizenship (C.O.P.E.C.), held at Birmingham in 1924. From this conference emerged twelve volumes of reports dealing with every aspect of social life, with recommendations based upon the conference's interpretation of the social gospel. The series concludes with *Historical Illustrations of the Social Effects of Christianity* (Birmingham, 1924). In the United States the social gospel made little headway until the closing years of the nineteenth century, when Washington Gladden began to urge a more humane approach to social problems on the part of Christians, a theme which he set forth in *Social Salvation* (N.Y., Houghton Mifflin, 1902); he was followed by Walter Rauschenbusch, who made considerable advance towards a Christian socialism in *Christianity and the Social Crisis* (N.Y., Macmillan, 1920). The story of the movement initiated by these two men has been told by C.H. Hopkins in *The Rise of the Social Gospel in American Protestantism 1865–1915* (New Haven, Yale Univ. Press, 1940), which may be supplemented with H.M. May's *Protestant Churches and Industrial America* (N.Y., Harper & Brothers, 1949). R.T. Handy has collected important documents from the movement in *The Social Gospel in America 1870–1920* (N.Y., Oxford Univ. Press, 1966).

Orthodox churches until recent times seem to have remained somewhat remote from these social movements, but there were some stirrings within the Russian church which have been touched upon by N. Berdyaev in *The Origin of Russian Communism* (London, Geoffrey Bles, 1937).

B. Pastoral theology

The social gospel, as set forth by its more radical advocates, met with considerable opposition from many clergy concerned with the cure of souls. These clergy saw Christian vocation as a guidance of individuals in moral development; they held that the unique contribution of the Christian pastor to human welfare is his shepherding function. This point of view has been set forth by F. Greeves in *Theology and the Cure of Souls* (London, Epworth Press, 1960). It is generally recognized by most writers on pastoralia, however, that pastoral care is not a unique Christian activity but that all religions have provided guides to the good life here on earth. John T. McNeill in *A History of the Cure of Souls* (N.Y., Harper &

Brothers, 1951) has made a study of these guides in the antique world, in Israel, and in the Hellenic world, with a special emphasis upon the rise of the confessional in medieval Christianity; he also includes the specialized functions of the Protestant pastors in the contemporary scene. William A. Clebsch and Charles R. Jaekle, in *Pastoral Care in Historical Perspective* (Englewood Cliffs, N.J., Prentice-Hall, 1964), have redefined both pastoral and historical theology.

Pastoral theology is heavily weighted on the side of methodology, as is the case of A. Curran's *Counseling in Catholic Life and Education* (N.Y., Macmillan, 1953), a book designated for "sure guidance" in every conceivable eventuality in Christian counseling. C.A. Wise, however, in *Pastoral Counseling: Its Theory and Practice* (N.Y., Harper & Brothers, 1951), emphasizes the decisive factor that the pastor's religious interpretation of man must play in all counseling. This is also the emphasis of A.T. Boisen in *The Exploration of the Inner World* (Chicago, Willett, Clark, 1936), in which he urges the importance of relating pastoral training to the theology and philosophy of religion. Seward Hiltner's *Preface to Pastoral Theology* (N.Y., Abingdon Press, 1958), set forth a program for the discipline that is being worked out in his later works.

C. Moral theology and Christian ethics

An association of theology with counseling raises the problem of the foundations of moral consciousness. A good introduction to this problem is E. Westermarck's *Christianity and Morals* (London, Kegan Paul, Trench, Trübner, 1939), which views the subject from a very broad perspective.

Christian moral theology begins with the assumption that Christian conduct is guided by the revelation of God's own character as depicted in both the Old and New Testaments; thus Christian morals have been greatly affected by the prophetic insights of the Old Testament as has been pointed out in R.B.Y. Scott, *The Relevance of the Prophets* (N.Y., Macmillan, 1944). From the prophets Christianity inherited the basic idea that religion and morals are inextricably bound together, but the eschatological setting of Jesus' teaching obscured any long-term specifically Christian ethic and has complicated the task of Christian moral theology. The difficult struggle of early Christian thinkers to apply the ethical principles of Jesus to society in general has been well told by C.J. Cadoux in *The Early Christian Church and the World* (Edinburgh, T. & T. Clark, 1925). As has been pointed out by A. Nygren in *Agape and Eros,* tr. by Philip Watson, 2 vols. (London, 1932–39; republished in one volume, Philadelphia, Westminster Press, 1953), Christians such as Paul and Augustine fell back upon the freedom of love to decide moral issues. An outstanding exponent of Christian morals during the medieval period was Thomas Aquinas, who worked out a natural moral law as a basis for the church to provide moral guidance. A diligent student of Aquinas, E. Gilson in *Moral Values and Moral Life* (London, B. Herder, 1931) has used Thomist insights to answer some of the more pressing moral issues of contemporary life. Concern with natural law and the opposition raised against it by the passions of men led the fathers of the church to evolve a system of casuistry for solving doubtful cases of conscience. This system has a long history. A very readable book on the subject is K.E. Kirk's *Conscience and Its Problems* (N.Y., Longmans, Green, 1931). Its application to the economic area has been examined by B.N. Nelson, *The Idea of Usury* (Princeton, Princeton Univ. Press, 1949; rev. ed., 1969).

Casuistry to a large extent is confined to individual cases, as is also moral theology, and so is distinguished, as it were, from Christian ethics. The latter tries to answer the question: What does it mean to be a Christian, a Christian with civic responsibilities? An excellent study from his point of view is P. Ramsey's *Basic Christian Ethics* (N.Y., Charles Scribner's Sons, 1950). W. Beach and H.R. Niebuhr have collected into one volume, *Christian Ethics: Sources of the Living Tradition* (N.Y., Ronald Press, 1955), representative selections on ethics from the writings of leading Christian thinkers down through the ages. It is the opinion of the editors that these selections indicate that Christian ethics inevitably lead on to a Christian sociology. In *Can Ethics be Christian?* (Chicago, Univ. of Chicago Press, 1975), James M. Gustafson has opened up the central issues of Christian ethics in a stimulating and serious way.

D. Welfare work

Because of the New Testament imperative to go about doing good, Christians have always been engaged in some kind of welfare work. Very early in Christian history there emerged orders of both men and women dedicated in some specific way to the service of the Master. Although there were many motives behind the rise of monasticism, the most prominent, as H.B. Workman has pointed out in *The Evolution of the Monastic Ideal* (London, C.H. Kelly, 1913), was the opportunity to do good works unhampered by selfish distractions. With the repudiation of monasticism by the reformed churches, Protestants for a time lacked the techniques for relieving human distress. In more recent days this lack has been overcome by trained Christian social workers. A good account of this modern development is to be found in an article by B.M. Boyd, "Protestant Social Work," in the *Social Work Year Book* (N.Y., American Association of Social Workers, 1951). Social service activity, carried on not only by Protestants but also by Roman Catholics and Jews, has been outlined by L.A. Stidley in *Sectarian Welfare among Protestants: A Comparative Study of Protestant, Jewish, and Roman Catholic Welfare Federations* (N.Y., Association Press, 1944). Within the present century there has been a considerable revival of monasticism within both the Anglican and the reformed churches of Europe that has spread to the North American continent. This revival has been sympathetically discussed by J.D. Benoit in *Liturgical Renewal Studies in Catholic and Protestant Developments on the Continent* (London, Student Christian Movement Press, 1958). The prominent part played by women in Christian social service is obvious from the large number of female religious communities. Their role has been set forth by Kathleen Bliss in *The Service and Status of Women in the Churches* (London, Student Christian Movement Press, 1952).

There are several journals concerned with the pastoral work of the church, among them the *Journal of Religion and Health* (1961–   ), published by the Academy of Religion and Mental Health; *The Journal of Pastoral Care* (1947–49), published by the Council for Clinical Training, Kutztown, Penn.; *Religion in Life* (N.Y., Abingdon Press, 1932–   ). *The Student World* (N.Y., 1908–   ), a quarterly published by the World Student Christian Federation, devotes a great deal of space to the social aspects of Christianity.

VIII. CHRISTIAN WORSHIP

An appreciation of the inner life of Christianity can only be achieved by an intimate knowledge of its worship from which so much of its doctrinal affirmation and moral practice arise. As Charles Gore has pointed out in his *Body of Christ: An Inquiry into the Institution and Doctrine of the Holy Communion* (London, John Murray, 1907), if an observer were able to return to any period of the Christian era, he would find Christians at some time or other gathering together for a service of worship in which bread and wine would be a prominent feature. This service of Holy Communion has from apostolic days to the present time remained a permanent feature of Christian worship.

It is well known, however, that Christian public worship began in the Jewish temples and synagogues, and, therefore, no historical introduction to Christian worship is complete without some reference to Jewish piety. Although Christians and Jews early drifted apart, yet, as Eric Werner has phrased it, "a sacred bridge still spans the abyss and allows for an exchange of views and moral concepts." His *Sacred Bridge* (N.Y., Columbia Univ. Press, 1959) is an excellent study of the origins of Christian worship, as is W.O.E. Oesterley, *Jewish Background of the Christian Liturgy* (Oxford, Clarendon Press, 1925). The latter must be read with some caution as not all Oesterley's conclusions are acceptable to modern scholarship.

A. Liturgy

"Liturgy" is an over all term for fixed forms of service in public worship. It is agreed that in the early church, apart from Jewish models, there were no rigid forms but rather a fluid rite based upon accounts of the last supper of Christ with his disciples. Gradually there grew up collections of prescribed forms of public worship; interest in the origin and form of these early liturgies has recently been greatly stimulated by Gregory Dix's *Shape of the Liturgy* (London, Dacre Press, 1945); J.H. Srawley in *The Early History of Liturgy* (Cambridge, Cambridge Univ. Press, 1947) covers much the same ground as Dix but is more cautious in his conclusions.

Along with the development of the liturgy, there emerged the Christian year. The association of the Christian year with liturgical practices has been set forth by A.A. McArthur in *The Evolution of the Christian Year* (London, Student Christian Movement Press, 1953) and by J. van Goudoever, *Biblical Calendars* (Leiden, E.J. Brill, 1959).

Liturgical study divides into periods and areas. The books recommended above cover fairly adequately the early church both East and West; H. De Lubac's *Corpus Mysticum: L'Eucharistie et l'Église au moyen âge* (Paris, Aubier, 1944) provides an illuminating analysis of the medieval period; it is also an interesting commentary on the decline in frequency of communion and in congregational participation in worship from late antiquity through the Middle Ages.

E.E. Yelverton's *The Manual of Olavus Petri* (London, Society for Promoting Christian Knowledge, 1953) is a study of the first vernacular prayer book to appear in a modern language. Liturgical and sacramental questions are carefully analyzed in Yngve Brilioth, *Eucharistic Faith and Practice, Evangelical and Catholic,* tr. by A.G. Hebert (London, 1953). The first two prayer books of the Church of England (1549 and 1552) were also in the vernacular but were mainly translations and revisions of medieval service books. The liturgy as received by the Church of Scotland in 1564, commonly called *John Knox's Liturgy* (rep. 1886), is a good illustration of a reformed church liturgy. A full bibliography of Roman Catholic reformed liturgies may be found in H. Jedin's "Das Konzil von Trient und die Reform des Römisch Messbuches," *Ephemerides Liturgicae,* LIX (1945).

B. The liturgical revival

The modern period has been marked by a great revival of interest in the history and meaning of Christian worship. Books on the subject are many; only a few can be mentioned here. E.B. Koenker's *The Liturgical Renaissance in the Roman Catholic Church* (Chicago, Univ. of Chicago Press, 1954) provides a good outline of the modern liturgical movement within the Roman communion. That movement helped to bring about the most far-reaching reform in Roman Catholic liturgical history, the Constitution on the Sacred Liturgy promulgated by the Second Vatican Council in 1963; the text of the Constitution, as well as of other decrees, appears in Walter M. Abbott, S.J., ed., *The Documents of Vatican II* (N.Y., Guild Press, 1966). A.G. Hebert's *Liturgy and Society, The Function of the Church in the Modern World* (London, Faber & Faber, 1935), though an Anglican work, has been deeply influenced by modern Roman Catholic development.

It is inappropriate to speak of a liturgical revival within the Orthodox churches, since they have never experienced a decrease in liturgical practices; but there has been on the part of both Protestants and Catholics a desire to become better acquainted with Eastern liturgical worship, a desire that has been partially met by F.E. Brightman's *Liturgies Eastern and Western,* vol. I, "Eastern Liturgies" (Oxford, 1896). Alexander Schmemann, *Introduction to Liturgical Theology,* tr. by A.E. Moorhouse (London, Faith Press, 1966), is a contemporary summary of the Eastern Orthodox view of liturgy.

A study of liturgy is incomplete without some acquaintance with Christian music and hymnody. A detailed study of the subject is to be found in Winfred Douglas' *Church Music in History and Practice* (N.Y., Charles Scribner's Sons, 1937). John Julian's *A Dictionary of Hymnology* (London, J. Murray, 1908) is a standard reference work. A brief book covering the whole field of church music and its relation to theology and morals which can be highly recommended is E. Routley's *Church Music and Theology* (London, Student Christian Movement Press, 1959). The latter is particularly valuable for its comments on Christian hymnody and for a section dealing with Bach and pietism.

There are several periodicals that concentrate on liturgical subjects. One of the best of these, published in Paris, is *La Maison de Dieu* (1964–   ); frequently it has numbers devoted to one aspect of liturgical thought and practice. Another valuable periodical is *Worship* 1926–   ), published by the Liturgical Press, Collegeville, Minn. *Jahrbuch für Liturgik und Hymnologie* (1955–   ), is a Protestant publication from Kassel, Germany, with an international contributing staff.

C. Art and symbolism

The close association of art and religion has long been recognized, and the claim is well founded that religion has been the fountainhead of art. Art and symbolism are also closely associated with the subject of worship, since art and architecture provide the aesthetic framework in which public worship is conducted; but it is important to remember that this aesthetic framework is the outcome of the inner spirit of Christianity. Consequently, to gain an intimate understanding of Christian art it is necessary to have some knowledge of the inner meaning of the sacramental life of the church. A helpful book for this purpose is N. Clark's *An Approach to the Theology of the Sacraments* (London, Student Christian Movement Press, 1956); also useful is F.W. Dillistone's *Christianity and Symbolism* (Philadelphia, Westminster Press, 1955), in which the author discusses the signs, symbols, and sacraments of the church and relates them to the poetic image. *Signs and Symbols in Christian Art* (N.Y., Oxford Univ. Press, 1954) by G. Ferguson is a well-arranged book, beautifully illustrated with paintings from the Renaissance period. It also provides explanations of all the symbols connected with Christian art.

Christian architecture is a study in itself. E. Short, *A History of Religious Architecture,* 3rd rev. ed. (N.Y., W.W. Norton, 1951), provides a broad perspective of the subject; it begins with the first God's house of ancient Egypt and concludes with two modern cathedrals, a Roman Catholic and an Anglican, at Liverpool, England. A very practical book is P. Hammond, *Liturgy and Architecture* (London, Barrie & Rockliff, 1960), which relates past developments in church symbolism to the contemporary setting. Sir Basil Spence, *Phoenix at Coventry: The Building of a Cathedral* (N.Y., Harper & Row, 1962), is an interesting case-study.

D. Mysticism

Imperceptibly one moves from the aesthetic aspect of religion to mysticism, so much dependent upon symbolism. Mystic contemplation is sometimes spoken of as the highest form of Christian worship, a thought carried over from the classical world, where contemplation, following the lead of Aristotle, was regarded as the most significant activity of which human nature is capable. It was in the thought of Plato, however, that contemplation assumed the character of religious aspiration. Mediated to western Europe by the Pseudo-Dionysius in his *The Celestial Hierarchy* (*op. cit.*), in a Neo-Platonic form based upon the philosophy of Plotinus, contemplation gave to Christianity a goal of union with God through a state of ecstasy in which discursive reasoning has been transcended. The classic work on this subject in modern times is W.R. Inge, *The Philosophy of Plotinus* (N.Y., Longmans, Green, 1924), which is an outstanding apologetic for the retention of the mystical element of religion.

Not all Christian mysticism has followed Plotinus and Dionysius in what has been called the "way of negation." In contrast to this anti-intellectualism was the school of St. Victor, which emphasized intellectual travail as well as renunciation. Thomas Aquinas also insisted on a study of the works of God as well as a quest for an intuitive vision. Two books which discuss these contrasting methods are K.E. Kirk, *The Vision of God* (London, Longmans, Green, 1931) and E.C. Butler, *Western Mysticism* (London,

Constable, 1922). Rudolf Otto, *Mysticism East and West,* tr. B.L. Bracey and R.C. Payne (N.Y., Macmillan, 1960), is an effort to relate Christian mysticism to other traditions.

Many Protestants have turned to the devotional writings of Catholic mystics for consolation and inspiration. Among these was Evelyn Under-hill, who, in *Mysticism, A Study in the Nature and Development of Man's Spiritual Consciousness* (1911; 12th rev. ed., N.Y., E.P. Dutton, 1930), has in her own right made a remarkable contribution to the literature of mysticism. In an appendix she gives an historical sketch of European mysticism from the earliest times to the death of Blake; she also provides a bibliography that covers almost everything written on mysticism up to 1930. Friedrich von Hügel, in *The Mystical Element of Religion* (N.Y., Dutton, 1923), used Catherine of Genoa to delineate the various components in mysticism.

E. Priest and prophet

Integral to the liturgical life of the church is the ministry of word and sacrament, a subject already dealt with under the headings of pastoralia and ecclesiology; but, apart from a social ministry, there is the concern of the church over safeguards for the proper administration of the sacraments and an equal concern for the freedom of preaching as fundamental to the inspirational life of the body of believers. On this whole subject the church has been seriously divided, since in it is involved the question of the validity of the ministry. The question has been frankly discussed by Anglican contributors to *The Apostolic Ministry* (London, Hodder & Stoughton, 1946), ed. by K.E. Kirk. A reply to this volume has been written by T.W. Manson in *The Church's Ministry* (London, Hodder & Stoughton, 1948). A more recent statement is that of Daniel Jenkins, *The Gift of Ministry* (London, Faber & Faber, 1947).

Prophecy, which had been much valued by Christians in apostolic and subapostolic times, came under suspicion during the church's contest with the Montanists, who were extravagant in their reliance upon an "inner light." The story of this contest and its influence upon the church has been brilliantly told by John De Soyres in *Montanism and the Primitive Church* (London, G. Bell & Sons, 1878). One result of this episode in church history was that for a thousand years Christian faith was largely mediated by priest and ritual. Nevertheless, there were throughout this period sporadic outbursts of the Montanist spirit which became particularly pronounced during the Reformation era. These have been set forth by E.B. Box in *Rise and Fall of the Anabaptists* (London, Macmillan, 1903). R.M. Jones in *Spiritual Reformers of the Sixteenth Century* (London, Macmillan, 1914) deals with the radical concepts of the ministry that arose during the Reformation era, particularly the emphasis upon prophecy.

Recently there has arisen a new interest in prophecy from an historical point of view, as well as a revised concept of the function of a priest in the Old Testament era. Two important books that have created this interest are A.C. Welch's *Prophet and Priest in Old Israel* (London, Student Christian Movement Press, 1936) and J. Hoschander's *Priests and Prophets* (N.Y., Jewish Theological Seminary of America, 1938). Various signs now indicate that the pulpit is more and more guided by prophetic preaching, as has been advocated by K.M. Yates in *Preaching from the Prophets* (N.Y., Harper & Brothers, 1942). At the same time, there has been a decline in Protestant churches of a bias against liturgical forms of worship and priestly guidance of an individual's moral development.

F. Christian education

Part of the Christian ministry is the guiding of children, youths, and adults into a mature discipleship. As in so many instances in Christian origins, such educational activity is a Jewish inheritance from the synagogue schools. Very early, church schools rivaled the synagogue schools, particularly the Catechetical school at Alexandria founded about A.D. 185. The story of the development of Christian education from Hebrew foundations on to the medieval schools has been briefly told by L.J. Sherrill in *The Rise of Christian Education* (N.Y., Macmillan, 1950).

Before Constantine, when the church lived in a pagan world, Christian education consisted mainly in teaching converts the morals, creed, and discipline of the church; after Constantine all education gradually came under the control of the church with the attempt, as can be seen in A.C. Pegis' *The Wisdom of Catholicism* (N.Y., Random House, 1949), to make Christian faith the basis of knowledge.

Modern secular education was born during the Renaissance, and the churches were compelled to find new means to impart biblical knowledge. The Roman Catholic Church as well as many Protestant churches fell back upon catechisms as a method of inculcating fundamental doctrines and morals. The substance of the Roman teaching as set forth by the catechism of the Council of Trent can be found in *The Catholic Catechism* (N.Y., P.J. Kenedy & Sons, 1936), drawn up by Peter Cardinal Gasparri. The catechisms of the reformed churches are too numerous to be mentioned here; several of them have been compiled by Thomas F. Torrance in *The School of Faith* (London, J. Clarke, 1959).

In Protestant circles there has been much debate on the content and method of Christian education. Horace Bushnell in his epoch-making book, *Christian Nurture* (N.Y., Charles Scribner's Sons, 1847), opposed the individualistic revivalism of his day as a means of conversion and sought to establish a biblical basis for teaching within the home and the church. Most denominations have attempted to carry on Christian education with a complex set of agencies: the Sunday school, vacation school, and released time from day schools, but with somewhat frustrating results. For this reason there has arisen a large collection of literature devoted to ways and means of Christian education. G.A. Coe in *What Is Christian Education?* (N.Y., Charles Scribner's Sons, 1929) attempts to make Christian education relevant to contemporary life. Some penetrating questions on the subject have been posed by H. S. Elliott in *Can Religious Education Be Christian?* (N.Y., Macmillan, 1940) and by R.C. Miller in *The Clue to Christian Education* (N.Y., Charles Scribner's Sons, 1959).

IX. CHRISTIANITY AND CIVILIZATION

A tension between civilization, which is a human achievement, and an organization which belongs primarily to the eternal and the absolute would appear to be inevitable. Nevertheless, the church which arose within an advanced civilization could not fail to be affected by its surrounding environment and attempt to make some accommodation to it. As W.F. Albright has pointed out in *From the Stone Age to Christianity* (1940; 2nd ed. Baltimore, Johns Hopkins Press, 1946), even if Hellenism had little influence on Jesus' idea of God, it did have some effect "in the formation of Jesus' other religious ideas." Nor does Albright think it possible to deny that the religious emotions and impulses that had swayed the Near East for three millennia were "part of the divine preparation for Christianity." This is a subject to which a great deal of attention has been given in recent years by A.J. Toynbee, who in *Civilization on Trial* (N.Y., Columbia Univ. Press, 1948) takes issue with Sir James Frazer's theory set forth in *The Golden Bough,* 3rd ed. (London, Macmillan, 1915), that Christianity has been a destroyer of civilization; on the contrary, he holds that it has been the reproducer of civilizations. Toynbee has somewhat modified this view by seeing civilizations as the handmaids of religion.

Be that as it may, Christianity, as Christopher Dawson in *Understanding Europe* (London, Sheed & Ward, 1952) says, has from the beginning been a missionary and, hence, a world-transforming movement. Because of its proclamation of a coming new order, it has been essentially a dynamic force in society and, consequently, has never been at peace with the world around it. This has led to continuous conflict, usually dealt with by historians under the over all heading "church and state."

A. Church and state

The church's approach to the state has been historically one of cooperation when possible, but also of judgment. It is in the act of judgment that it has come into conflict with the state. This conflict has produced an immense library of literature, part of which has been critically analyzed by F. Gavin in *Seven Centuries of the Problem of Church and State* (Princeton, Princeton Univ. Press, 1938).

A good introduction to what has been called the struggle between "Christ and Caesar" is H.B. Workman, *Persecution in the Early Church,* 3rd ed. (London, C.H. Kelly, 1911). Hans Lietzmann's *From Constantine to Julian,* vol. III of *A History of the Early Church,* tr. by B. Lee Woolf (London, Lutterworth Press, 1950), gives a good insight into the relations of church and state immediately following upon the recognition of the church as a favored religion of the Roman Empire.

During the medieval period there was much discussion about the division of authority between secular and spiritual powers. This may be followed in G. Tellenbach's *Church, State and Christian Society at the Time of the Investiture Contest,* tr. R.F. Bennett (Oxford, B.H. Blackwell, 1940); also in J. Bryce's *The Holy Roman Empire,* 8th ed. (N.Y., Macmillan, 1889). A parallel contest in the Eastern church, centering around the veneration of icons, is described by G. Every in *The Byzantine Patriarchate 451-1204* (N.Y., Macmillan, 1947).

The relations of church and state during the Reformation era were much complicated by an internal quarrel within the Christian community. This struggle had considerable influence on the attitudes of both churchmen and statesmen toward political matters, as can be seen in J.W. Allen's *A History of Political Thought in the Sixteenth Century* (N.Y., Dial Press, 1928) and also in R.H. Bainton's *The Travail of Religious Liberty* (Philadelphia, Westminster Press, 1951).

With the rise of modern nationalism and new conflicting ideologies, the problem of the relations of church and state has taken on a new complexity. Two books dealing with this new phase in Europe are A. Keller, *Church and State on the European Continent* (London, Epworth Press, 1937), and L. Pfeffer, *Church, State and Freedom* (Boston, Beacon Press, 1953). A.L. Drummond, *German Protestiantism since Luther* (London, Epworth Press, 1951) is concerned with some peculiarly German problems, particularly in Part II, which deals primarily with the relations of church and state.

W.K. Jordan, *The Development of Religious Toleration in England,* 4 vols. (London, George Allen & Unwin, 1932–40) is a detailed study of many phases of church and state development in England. A work on the same scale, dealing with the intricacies of church-state relations in the United States is A.P. Stokes, *Church and State in the United States,* 3 vols. (N.Y., Harper & Brothers, 1950). A one-volume study, *Religious Liberty: An Inquiry* (N.Y., International Missionary Council, 1945) by M. Searle Bates, carried on under the auspices of a Joint Committee appointed by the Foreign Missions Conference of North America and the Federal Council of Churches of Christ in America, covers the whole field of the relations of church and state down to the present time. It is particularly good concerning Latin America and also the present situation of the churches in non-Christian lands. The entire issue was put into a new perspective with the publication of John Courtney Murray, S.J., *We Hold These Truths: Catholic Reflections on the American Proposition* (N.Y., Sheed and Ward, 1960), a book that helped to shape the Declaration on Religious Liberty promulgated in December 1965 by the Second Vatican Council.

B. Christian missions

The Christian imperative to go into all the world to preach the gospel has, down through the ages, created novel problems in the relations of church and state. The missionary imperative has compelled the church to assume civilizing activities—that is, to attempt to enlighten and refine newly converted people. Such activities have often aroused the suspicion of the state into which the church has expanded. The story of this expansion is practically a history of Christianity itself, and it is in this sense that K.S. Latourette wrote his monumental *A History of the Expansion of Christianity,* 7 vols. (N.Y., Harper & Brothers, 1937–45). A less formidable work is W.O. Carver's *The Course of Christian Missions,* rev. ed. (N.Y., Fleming H. Revell, 1939).

With the collapse of the Roman Empire, Europe became a great field for Christian expansion, posing a challenge for a systematic form of missionary work; the challenge was met by religious orders dedicated to the spread of the gospel. A good account of the work and method of these orders can be found in C.H. Robinson's *The Conversion of Europe* (N.Y., Longmans, Green, 1917); a brief but painstaking study which supplements Robinson's book is J.T. Addison's *The Medieval Missionary* (N.Y., International Missionary Council, 1936).

The age of exploration and the discovery of a new world in the fifteenth century provided a new challenge to the missionary imperative. It was the Roman Catholic Church that first accepted this challenge through the instrumentality of its older orders; also new orders emerged to meet the new conditions. The complexity of the work in non-Catholic lands led to the establishment in the seventeenth century of the Sacred Congregation *de Propaganda Fide* to coordinate the work of evangelization. Its history has been told by R.H. Song, *The Sacred Congregation for the Propagation of the Faith* (Washington, D.C., Catholic Univ. of America, 1961).

Although the Protestant churches were rather slow in taking up missionary work, they did finally help to make the nineteenth century, as Latourette has emphasized (*op. cit.*), one of the most expansive centuries in all Christian history. For the origins of Protestant missions both G. Warneck, *History of Protestant Missions* (N.Y., Fleming H. Revell, 1904) and R.H. Glover, *The Progress of World-wide Missions,* rev. and enl. by J.H. Kane (N.Y., Harper & Brothers, 1960), are useful books. To some extent the Orthodox church shared in this expansive mood, as is indicated in S. Bolshakoff, *The Foreign Missions of the Russian Orthodox Church* (London, Society for Promoting Christian Knowledge, 1943).

Because of the rapid expansion of the church during the nineteenth century, there has developed a science of missions such as has been set forth in J.H. Bavinck, *An Introduction to the Science of Missions,* tr. by D.H. Freeman (Philadelphia, Presbyterian & Reformed Pub. Co., 1960), which seeks to ascertain the scriptural basis of missions and their status in the life of the church. A Roman Catholic definition of this science has been propounded by J. Schmidlin in *Catholic Mission Theory,* tr. by M. Braun (Techny, Ill., Mission Press, 1923). This new interest has led to the establishment of chairs and missions in theological colleges and the founding of societies to engage in missionary research and publication; the fruits of such investigation are reported in such journals as *The International Review of Missions* (Edinburgh, 1912–   ) and the *Allgemeine-Missions Zeitschrift* (Berlin, 1874–   ).

X. THE ECUMENICAL MOVEMENT

While the nineteenth century was an era of expansion for the Christian church, it now appears that the twentieth may well be an era of integration. Such integration is best exemplified in the ecumenical movement, the history of which has been carefully compiled by R. Rouse and S.C. Neil in *A History of the Ecumenical Movement 1517–1948* (London, Society for Promoting Christian Knowledge, 1954). Roman Catholic interpretations of the movement include George Tavard, *Two Centuries of Ecumenism,* tr. by R.W. Hughes (N.Y., New American Library, 1960), and John M. Todd, *Catholicism and the Ecumenical Movement* (N.Y., Longmans, Green, 1956).

A. Faith and order

As R.S. Bilheimer has emphasized in his *The Quest for Christian Unity* (N.Y., Association Press, 1952), the origins of ecumenicity reach back to the sixteenth century and even beyond; yet he, along with other writers such as H.P. Van Dusen in *World Christianity: Yesterday–Today–Tomorrow* (Nashville, Abingdon-Cokesbury, 1947), gives credit to the gathering together of missionary societies in world conferences for stimulating efforts toward organic church unions, the most successful to date being the church of South India, whose exciting story has been told by B. Sundkler in *Church of South India: The Movement towards Union 1900–1947* (London, Lutterworth Press, 1954). Preceding this historic event had been many international gatherings of churchmen, the most notable being a meeting of a World Missionary Conference at Edinburgh (1910), which formed a continuation committee known as the International Missionary Council. A brief but adequate account of the purpose of this council as well as the significance of Edinburgh is given by N. Goodall in *The Ecumenical Movement* (London, Oxford Univ. Press, 1961). He points out that, although matters of faith and doctrine were excluded from the Edinburgh Conference, yet this conference was responsible for the origin of the Faith and Order Movement.

To find a satisfactory doctrinal and disciplinary basis for the reunion of Christendom has been the avowed task of the World Conference on Faith and Order. Descriptions and interpretations of these conferences are contained in E.S. Wood's *Lausanne* (1927), H. Martin's *Edinburgh* (1937), and E.H. Robertson's *Lund* (1952).

B. Life and work

Parallel with the search for doctrinal unity was an attempt to bring the mind of Christ to bear on the great social, industrial, and international questions so urgent in twentieth-century civilization. The leaders of this movement were Nathan Söderblom and the Ecumenical Patriarch of Constantinople, who simultaneously issued appeals for the church to cooperate in social and moral action. These appeals led to the formation of a Universal Christian Conference on Life and Work at Stockholm in 1925, to be followed by several similar conferences. Official reports of these conferences are *Report of the Stockholm Conference, 1925,* ed. by G.K. Bell (1926), and *The Churches Survey Their Task, The Report of the Conference at Oxford, July 1937, on Church, Community and State* (London, George Allen & Unwin, 1937).

C. World Council of Churches

It soon became evident that there was much overlapping in the aims and activities of the Faith and Order and Life and Work committees, and this led to their integration into the World Council of Churches. The First Assembly met at Amsterdam, Holland, in 1948 and adopted a constitution which proclaimed, "The World Council of Churches is a fellowship which accepts our Lord Jesus Christ as God and Saviour." Official reports of the *First and Second Assemblies of the World Council of Churches* were published in 1948 (London) and 1955 (N.Y.), ed. by W.A. Visser't Hooft. A most comprehensive collection of documents on all phases of the ecumenical movement leading up to and beyond the formation of the

World Council has been made by G.K. Bell in *Documents on Christian Unity,* 3 series (London, Oxford Univ. Press, 1920–48). More recent developments as well as reports on the progress of negotiations for unity may be followed in *The Ecumenical Review* (Geneva, 1948–   ), a quarterly published by the World Council of Churches.

D. Christian dialogue

Until recently the Roman Catholic Church has remained somewhat aloof from the ecumenical movement, but with the establishment by John XXIII of a secretariat for Christian unity, there has arisen a keen "dialogue" between Roman and non-Roman churches, with a preliminary attempt to understand one another's point of view. Such an attempt was foreshadowed in G.H. Tavard's *The Catholic Approach to Protestantism* (N.Y., Harper & Brothers, 1955), which outlines steps that have been taken by Roman Catholic authorities for the promotion of ecumenism. Another interesting book on the same theme is Y.M. Congar's *After Nine Hundred Years* (N.Y., Fordham Univ. Press, 1959).

XI. TRADITION AND TRADITIONS

Christianity has expressed itself in variant forms in different ages and in different places. These distinctive developments are loosely termed "traditions"; the acceptance of these traditions as part of the ongoing life of the church is based upon faith in the uninterrupted and abiding presence of the Lord in his church. Also implicit in this faith is the belief that behind divergent expressions of Christianity is a common tradition or history from which these separated traditions derive their true existence. The concept of "tradition," with its presuppositions and implications, has been carefully examined in Yves-Marie Congar, *Tradition and Traditions,* tr. by M. Naseby and T. Rainborough (London, Burns & Oates, 1966).

This frank recognition of a living tradition which expresses itself in different ecclesiastical forms associated with certain ways of thinking or molded by certain temporal circumstances has permitted church historians to divide church history into distinct fields of research—early, medieval, orthodox, reformed, modern—all of which represent different expressions of the original apostolic tradition. Modern church history is also subdivided into European, Eastern, Oriental, American, African, and so on. No one historian can hope to deal adequately with all these traditions but must, for the most part, confine himself to one or two fields of research, that is, either to a period (such as the medieval) or to an aspect of the history (such as the history of doctrine).

A. A common tradition

Nevertheless, there have been serious attempts to find one common tradition to which all the various traditions might be related or by which they may be tested. One such attempt is A.C. Outler's *The Christian Tradition and the Unity We Seek* (N.Y., Oxford Univ. Press, 1957). Also there have been many attempts to write an overall history of the church. Reference has already been made to K.S. Latourette's monumental work on the expansion of Christianity, but the same author has also written in one volume *A History of Christianity* (N.Y., Harper & Brothers, 1953), in which he essays "to place the story of Christianity in the setting of universal history." A similar and more concise account of the onward march of the Christian faith is *Twenty Centuries of Christianity* (N.Y., Harcourt, Brace, 1959) by P. Hutchinson and W.E. Garrison. Earlier A.H. Newman produced a notable compendium of Christianity entitled *A Manual of Church History,* 2 vols. (Philadelphia, American Baptist Publication Society, 1900).

A similar kind of manual, extremely condensed, is Williston Walker's *History of the Christian Church* (N.Y., Charles Scribner's Sons, 1918), which has been revised and brought up to date by Cyril C. Richardson, Wilhelm Pauck, and Robert Handy (1959). All these histories suffer seriously from compression, which necessitates arbitrary selection, and also from the fact that one author or even several cannot be proficient in all the various traditions. An obvious method of overcoming this deficiency is to ask experts in the various fields of historical research to write articles on those aspects of Christianity with which they are most familiar and to bring such articles together in Christian dictionaries or encyclopedias. *The Oxford Dictionary of the Christian Church* (London, Oxford Univ. Press, 1957), ed. by F.L. Cross, is one recent attempt to provide an authoritative account of Christianity; a second and revised edition was published in 1974. *The New Schaff-Herzog Encyclopedia of Religious Knowledge,* 13 vols. (N.Y., Funk & Wagnalls, 1908–14), is an earlier attempt to cover the same field; it has recently been extended by *Twentieth Century Encyclopedia of Religious Knowledge,* 2 vols. (Michigan, Baker Book House, 1955), ed. by L.A. Loetscher. *The Catholic Encyclopaedia,* 17 vols. (N.Y., Encyclopaedia Press, 1907–22), as its preface indicates, is intended to provide "full and authoritative information on the entire cycle of Catholic interests." *New Catholic Encyclopedia,* 15 vols. (N.Y., McGraw-Hill, 1967) was not a revision of the earlier work, but a brand-new reference book, with articles by scholars of many traditions; the bibliographies in the set are very helpful. *The Encyclopedia of Religion and Ethics,* 13 vols. (N.Y., Charles Scribner's Sons, 1908–27), ed. by J. Hastings, is probably the most comprehensive of all these encyclopedias, dealing as it does with other religions in addition to Christianity.

B. Early church history

Earlier portions of this chapter have already dealt at length with the major periods of church history, including collections of sources and secondary studies. What follows here is merely a listing of some of the most important books, which can, in turn, provide a guide to further reading.

Early church history has long been a most intensive field of research for church historians, so that it is extremely difficult to give any fair or adequate selection from the mass of literature on the subject. B.J. Kidd's *A History of the Church to 461,* 3 vols. (Oxford, Clarendon Press, 1922), is a carefully documented piece of work and a mine of information. A much-valued study of the early church is H. Lietzmann's four-volume series, tr. by B.L. Woolf, *The Beginnings of the Christian Church* (London, Nicholson and Watson, 1937), *The Founding of the Universal Church* (London, Nicholson & Watson, 1938), *From Constantine to Julian* (London, Lutterworth Press, 1950), and *The Era of the Church Fathers* (N.Y., Charles Scribner's Sons, 1952). L. Duchesne, *The Early History of the Christian Church,* tr. from the 4th French rev. ed. by Claude Jenkins, 3 vols. (London, John Murray Publishers, 1909–24), is a classic history of the ancient church. An extended bibliography on the period is furnished in *A Bibliographical Guide to the History of Christianity,* ed. by S.J. Case (Gloucester, Mass., Peter Smith, 1952).

C. The medieval period

It is impossible to extricate medieval church history from general medieval history; consequently, the justly famous *The Cambridge Medieval History,* 8 vols. (N.Y., Macmillan, 1911–36), currently being issued in a greatly revised edition, is indispensable for the student of Christianity. A good overall survey of the period is H. Pirenne's *A History of Europe from the Invasions to the XVI Century,* tr. by B. Miall (London, George Allen & Unwin, 1939).

D. Crusades

One of the most dramatic episodes of the medieval period was the long-drawn-out contest between Christendom and the Islamic world generally designated as the "crusades." The crusades have given rise to a voluminous literature, of which a recent contribution is S. Runciman's *A History of the Crusades,* 3 vols. (Cambridge, Cambridge Univ. Press, 1951–54). A series of interesting historical essays on the crusades is to be found in *The Crusades and other Historical Essays* presented to Dana C. Munro by his former students, ed. by L.J. Paetow (N.Y., F.S. Crofts, 1928). Other studies include those of Atiya (*op. cit.*).

E. Reformation

It is difficult to separate the period known as the Reformation from the Renaissance and the Counter-Reformation, as they are inextricably bound together but antipathetic to one another. All of them are part and parcel of the decline of the medieval synthesis. This is clearly brought out in J. Huizinga's *The Waning of the Middle Ages,* tr. by F. Hopman (1924; rev. ed. N.Y., Doubleday, 1954). There is again an embarrassment of literature on the period, but all the significant aspects are encompassed in E.M. Hulme's *The Renaissance, the Protestant Reformation, and the Catholic Reformation,* 2 vols. (N.Y., Century House, 1914).

Reformation literature, like the patristic, has long been subject to minute analysis by specialized scholars. For this reason, much interest has been manifested in great collections of the works of the leading reformers, such as the *Corpus Reformatorum,* ed. by K.G. Bretschneider and H.E. Bindseif (Halle, Hallis Saxonum, 1834–   ). There are also large collections of the works of leading individual figures, such as the famous Weimar edition of Martin Luther's *Werke (Kirtische Gesamtausgabe)* (Bohlau, 1883–   ). This edition, which is almost indispensable for the student of Luther, has been translated, though not in full and with some departures from its readings and findings, by a group of American scholars under the overall title *Luther's Works,* 55 vols., ed. by J. Pelikan and H.T. Lehman (St. Louis, Concordia Publishing House and Fortress Press, 1955–   ). Of almost equal interest to Luther's are the works of John Calvin, particularly his *Institutes of the Christian Religion,* which have been newly translated into English by F.L. Battles and edited with introduction and notes by John T. McNeill, 2 vols. (Philadelphia, Westminster Press, 1960).

A very useful bibliography of the Reformation is now being published under the auspices of La commission internationale d'histoire ecclésiastique comparée au sein du comité internationale des sciences historiques, entitled *Bibliographie de la réforme 1450–1648* (Leiden, E.J. Brill, 1960 ff.). Small collections of documents containing important creeds have been made by H.S. Bettenson, entitled *Documents of the Christian Church* (N.Y., Oxford Univ. Press, 1956); also B.J. Kidd has made a useful collection in *Documents Illustrative of the Continental Reformation* (Oxford, Clarendon Press, 1911).

The Catholic Reformation is now beginning to receive from Roman Catholic scholars equally as close a scrutiny as that given to the Reformation by Protestant scholars. This renewed interest centers around the Council of Trent and has been greatly aided by H. Jedin, *A History of the Council of Trent* (N.Y., Thomas Nelson & Sons, 1957–   ), tr. by Dom Ernest Graf. Four volumes are planned.

F. Modern Christendom

With the breakup of Western Christendom and the rise of nationalism, traditions become so multiple that it would encumber this chapter far beyond its allotted space to attempt to list denominational and church histories of the ongoing church of our times. It must suffice to refer the reader to an excellent one-volume survey by James Hastings Nichols, *History of Christianity, 1650–1950: Secularization of the West* (N.Y., Ronald Press, 1956) and to *A Bibliographical Guide to the History of Christianity* (*op. cit.*). There are, however, some excellent journals which specialize in the field of historical research and contain reviews of all significant publications; among them may be singled out three semi-annuals: *Revue de l'histoire des religions* (Paris, 1880–   ), published at the Collège de France; *Archiv für Reformationsgeschichte* (Berlin, 1903–   ), published under the auspices of the Verein für Reformationsgeschichte and the American Society for Reformation Research; and *The Journal of Ecclesiastical History* (1950–   ), published at the University of London.

The important quarterlies are *The Catholic Historical Review* (Washington, 1915–   ), the official organ of the American Catholic Association, and *Church History* (Pennsylvania, 1932–   ), published by the American Society of Church History.

XII. CHRISTIANITY AND OTHER RELIGIONS

With the clash of Occidental and Oriental cultures in our modern world, Christianity has become acutely conscious of rival non-Christian religious traditions. The question of what the church's attitude towards these other higher religions should be has produced a large library of lively literature both of a philosophic and polemical nature. F.S.C. Northrop in *The Meeting of East and West* (N.Y., Macmillan, 1946) speculates about a possible synthesis of Occidental and Oriental cultures and sees in the rich culture of Mexico the beginnings of such a synthesis. In *Civilization on Trial* (*op. cit.*), A.J. Toynbee makes the prediction that the impact of Western civilization on its contemporary civilizations in the second half of the twentieth century "was the first step towards the unification of mankind." In *Christianity among the Religions of the World* (N.Y., Charles Scribner's Sons, 1957) he is less the prophet and more the analyst and feels that if Christianity is to play its part in reconciling the diverse cultures of the world, it must be purged both of its exclusiveness and of its Western accretions.

Toynbee's critical attitude towards Western culture has not gone unchallenged. Dr. Douglas Jerrold in *The Lie about the West* (London, J.M. Dent & Sons, 1954) asserts that Toynbee (particularly in *The World and the West* [London, Oxford Univ. Press, 1953]) has made Christianity a false religion; for, if it is true, it must be unique.

Another of Toynbee's critics is H. Kraemer, who in *World Cultures and World Religions* (Philadelphia, Westminster Press, 1960) takes "issue with almost every aspect" of the former's idea of religion; nevertheless, he agrees that "the religion is the deepest in the total meeting of the Orient and the Occident." Furthermore, he gives Toynbee credit for hammering home the undeniable fact that "Late modern Western technology has brought all the living higher religions over the world into closer contact with one another than ever before." His objection to Toynbee's analysis and to the syncretists is that they write from a humanist rather than a Christian viewpoint. W.E. Hocking's *The Coming World Civilization* (N.Y., Harper & Brothers, 1956) probably comes under Kraemer's rebuke, but Hocking maintains that if we take some lessons from the East we will only be moving nearer "to the spirit of an earlier Christianity." Still one of the most profound and provocative twentieth-century discussions of this issue is in Nathan Söderblom's Gifford Lectures for 1931, *The Living God* (London, Oxford Univ. Press, 1933), which, together with Rudolf Otto's *The Idea of the Holy,* tr. by J.W. Harvey (N.Y., Oxford Univ. Press, 1923), gave a new direction to the study of Christianity as a religion.

Besides the problem involved in the meeting of Eastern and Western cultures, Christianity faces the challenge of living in a Western secularized society which can no longer be regarded as motivated by Christian ideals. John Baillie has pointed out in *What Is Christian Civilization?* (*op. cit.*) that "the Christian can never offer more than a qualified loyalty or attachment to an earthly civilization"; nevertheless, he feels that Christians must strive for a Christian community and to retain a "conception of a Christian civilization" which "it is still our duty to export"—a theme dealt with in greater detail by E. Brunner in *Christianity and Civilization,* 2 vols. (London, James Nisbet, 1948–49). Brunner deals with the problem raised by the secularization of all aspects of life and asks the question, "What are the chances of a Christian civilization in our age?" to which he gives no certain answer. He has, however, intensified a debate about two cities, the spiritual and the secular, that reaches back to Augustine, if not to the beginnings of Christianity itself.

XIII

Islām

Charles J. Adams

I. THE NAME

Approximately one-seventh of the world's population profess a faith and a religious involvement to which they give the name "Islām." Unlike the names of other major religions, most of which were invented by outsiders to designate faiths different from their own, the name "Islām" has an integral relation to the experience of those who claim it. Its origins lie in the very beginning of the Islamic adventure in history; the Prophet Muḥammad employed this word both to characterize his own response to the Almighty Being who had called him and to describe that to which he was summoning his fellow Arabs. The community that traces its spiritual ancestry from Muḥammad continues to use the same term today, as it has for the past 1300 years, as the name for its faith. Evidently, therefore, the name expresses something fundamental in the religious experience of Muslims (Arabic for those who make or do Islām).

Morphologically "Islām" is a verbal noun, the infinitive of a verb meaning "to accept," "to submit," or perhaps "to surrender." It is sometimes translated as "acceptance" or "surrender" but better as "submission;" in contemporary theological language the word that most nearly renders its sense is "commitment." The verbal quality of the word should be emphasized; by its very form it conveys a feeling of action and ongoingness, not of something that is once and for all finished and static. Hence, rather than "commitment" it might still better be translated as "committing" in order to underline the continued renewal and repetition of man's obeisance to his Creator that it implies. In its most basic meaning Islām is the name of a relationship between men and their Sovereign Lord in which men self-consciously and reverently commit, submit, or surrender themselves anew with each moment to the highest reality they are capable of apprehending. One who thoughtfully and with awareness declares, "I am a Muslim," has uttered a profoundly religious statement. Although the declaration has obvious sociological connotations, it does much more than indicate membership in a certain community. The essentially religious nature of the declaration becomes clear when the Arabic word "Muslim" is translated, so that the statement says, "I am one who commits himself to God."

The specific form "Islām" so far as anyone knows, was not used in the speech of pre-Islamic Arabia but the related verb form "aslama" was commonly employed in commercial dealings among the rich traders of Makkah to signify the acceptance of the conditions of a contract. One of the achievements of Muhammad is to have invested this common root word with profound new meanings, to have transformed it from a mundane business term into an expression that sums up the meaning and purpose of human existence. The history of the term and its meaning are discussed in H. Ringgren, *Islam, aslama, and Muslim* (Uppsala, C.W.K. Gleerup, 1949).

A different approach to the term was taken in chap. I of *The Spiritual Background of Early Islam* (Leiden, E.J. Brill, 1972) by M.M. Bravmann who investigates this and related forms from the same root word in the pre-Islamic poetry. Bravmann shows that the root played a role in the vocabulary of bravery of the proud and boastful pre-Islamic Arab warriors for whom it meant "defiance of death " "readiness to defy death," or "self-sacrifice," in short to stake one's all for something that he passionately valued. The relation between this meaning of the word and its religious sense is not difficult to discern.

By far the most thoughtful and provocative consideration of the changes rung on this key term may be read in chap. IV of Wilfred Cantwell Smith's *The Meaning and End of Religion* (N.Y., Macmillan, 1963). In footnotes 105 and 107 to this chapter, pp. 289–99, is found a brief bibliography of other writings on the subject. In his analysis Smith illustrates the process by which this originally religious word was transmuted and debased into becoming the name of an abstraction, a system of thought and practice—in other words how it came to be considered the name of a "religion." As a result for most modern men, including Muslims, the word has lost its implications of a personal act of faith and is used as though

"Islām" were an entity in its own right, having an independent reality separable from the inner state of the men of faith who call themselves Muslims. Such a manner of conceiving Islām is not only inadequate; it is even obstructive of the understanding of Muslim religiousness. The central thesis of Smith's work, which is of great importance for every student of religion, holds that the essentialist notion of "a religion" is useless, even positively harmful, and should be abandoned for a more historical mode of thought which recognizes the living nature of men's religious traditions and their basis in the profound experience of faith. His views, however, have drawn sharp criticism; as an example see I.R. al-Fārūqī, "Essence of Religious Experience in Islām," in *Numen*, XX (1973), 186–201.

II. THE PRE–ISLAMIC BACKGROUND

If the rise of Islām is to be understood properly, the community must be seen against the background from which it emerged. The Prophet Muhammad lived, preached, and established his community among the Arabs of the Arabian Peninsula in the early years of the seventh century A.D. For millenniums before the inhabitants of the interior of the peninsula, for the most part Bedouin, had led a relatively isolated and protected existence behind their desert barriers though they had been in contact with the higher civilizations bordering the deserts. Around the fringes of the peninsula itself, most notably in the south, several higher civilizations had risen and fallen. Unfortunately it is difficult to reconstruct the history of pre-Islamic Arabia in any detail; until recently governments of the states in the peninsula have been reluctant to permit foreign scholars to enter their territories for the purposes of archeological work, and there have been no nationals of these states with proper training for such study. The situation now, however, is more promising; in the past few years a number of expeditions have been permitted (Belgian, Danish and American). Further, a major center of study of ancient Arabia has existed for some time at the University of Louvain. Perhaps more promising still is the creation of a group of highly trained archeologists among the people of the region, individuals who may be relied upon to pursue the ancient history of the area with skill and devotion.

A summary of modern knowledge of pre-Islamic Arabian history is presented in a readable and succinct way in Part I of Philip K. Hitti, *History of the Arabs*, 8th rev. ed. (London, Macmillan, 1964). As the title indicates, the book surveys the whole of Arab history. Hitti's is the best known and by far the most usable of the one-volume histories of the Arabs available in the market. Its chief virtues lie in Hitti's command of the sources, the felicitousness of his presentation, the meticulous accuracy of detail, and an excellent index. The writer's love for his own people shines through on every page; the volume is an extended effort to present the beauty, achievements, and glory of Arab civilization to the English reader by the man who, as much as any single individual, is responsible for the firm place that Arab and Islamic studies now enjoy in North American universities. The work has been criticized, however, for its close dependence upon its sources and for its preference of detailed factual treatment above broad interpretations. Of quite a different type is the small but incisive volume by Bernard Lewis, *The Arabs in History* (London, N.Y., Hutchinson's University Library, 1950); Lewis sets out to analyze the great trends of Arab development and to interpret the role of the Arabs in the regions where they have lived as well as their role in the history of the world as a whole. Pre-Islamic Arab history is considered with emphasis upon the relationship between the "days of ignorance" and the cultural flowering that followed the rise of Islām.

Recent scholarship, stimulated by the new access to the peninsula, has produced a growing body of material on the history of pre-Islamic Arabia. The ancient civilizations of the south are treated in a lavishly produced and illustrated volume by Brian Doe, *Southern Arabia* (London, Thames & Hudson, 1971). Franz Altheim and Ruth Stiehl have assembled a massive work that concentrates on the relations between the ancient Arabs and the classical world; it is called *Die Araber in der alten Welt,* 5 vols. (Berlin, de Gruyter, 1964–68), volume III deals with the religion of the area in ancient times. Other important work on the subject has come from the pen of Hermann von Wissman of Tübingen; his *Zur Geschichte und Landeskunde von alt Südarabien* (Wien, Hermann Böhlaus, 1964) and *Beiträge zur historischen Geographie des vorislamischen Südarabien,* written in conjunction with Maria Höfner (Mainz, Akademie der Wissenschaft und der Literatur in Kommission bei Franz Steiner, Wiesbaden, 1953) may be cited as examples. Among the older literature, the three volumes of A.P. Caussin de Perceval, *Essai sur l'histoire des arabes avant l'Islamisme* (Paris, Didot, 1847–48) are useful as an attempt to write a comprehensive history. There is a more up-to-date work of wide scope from the pen of Maxime Rodinson, his *L'Arabie avant l'Islam* (Paris, Encyclopédie de la Pléiade, 1957). Readers who may wish a broad but less detailed introduction will find the work by DeLacy O'Leary of value; it is called *Arabia before Muhammad* (London, Kegan Paul, Trench, Trübner, 1927).

Specifically, Islām arose in the western coastal region of Arabia known as the Ḥijāz, in the city of Makkah. In an effort to establish the background of the rise of Islām in depth, the Belgian scholar Henri Lammens devoted several careful studies to this region. His *Le Berceau de l'Islam,* vol. I (Rome, Sumptibus Pontificii Instituti Biblici, 1914), discusses its geography and climate, something of its history, and the religious and social customs of its inhabitants. The treatment extends into the Islamic period and illuminates the activities of the Prophet. A companion article describes life in Makkah at a slightly later period, "La Mecque à la veille de l'Hegire," in *Mélanges de la faculté orientale de l'Université St. Joseph de Beyrouth*, IX (1924), 240–54. One of the most helpful reconstructions of life in Makkah and the changes effected through Muḥammad is the insightful article of Eric R. Wolf, "The Social Organization of Mecca and the Origins of Islam," *Southwestern Journal of Anthropology,* VII (1951), 329–56. Having shown the dislocations in Makkan life consequent upon the development of a mercantile economy in the city and the disparity between the theories of social organization on the one hand and the realities of power and social control on the other, Wolf is able to demonstrate the significance of Muḥammad's innovations with great precision and clarity. The emphasis upon social and economic factors in the city and their relevance to the rise of Islām has been taken up and carried further by scholars such as Montgomery Watt, Maxime Rodinson (see below), and M.J. Kister. The most important writings of Kister on this subject are the two detailed articles, "Mecca and Tamīm (Aspects of Their Relations)," *Journal of the Economic and Social History of the Orient,* VIII (1965), 113–63; and "Some Reports Concerning Mecca from Jahiliyya to Islam," in the same journal, XV (1972), 61–93. The outcome of these studies is to make Muḥammad and the situation he faced understandable in human terms. On Makkah, as on many other subjects, there are authoritative and useful articles in the various editions of *The Encyclopaedia of Islām* (see Appendix I); for example see "Makkah," "Arabia," "Ka'bah," and others.

Muḥammad's success in winning acceptance of a new world view was due in large part to his ability to build upon while at the same time modifying the traditional ways of life of his people. Many of the values and customs of pre-Islamic Arabia, in somewhat changed form, continued to be observed among the members of Muḥammad's community; they were, however, invested with new meanings as they were taken up into the grand moral order of Islām. Perhaps the most influential writing on pre-Islamic Arabia and its outlook in the history of Western scholarship is vol. I of Ignaz Goldziher's famous *Muhammedanische Studien,* now available in English translation by S.M. Stern, ed., as *Muslim Studies,* 2 vols. (London, George Allen and Unwin, 1967–71); the first two chapters and the first two notes at the end of the volume are of particular importance. Discussing the concept "Jāhilīyah", which is the usual designation for the pre-Islamic era of Arab history, Goldziher argued that the essential meaning of the word was not "ignorance", as a literal translation might indicate, but rather "barbarism." His findings are corroborated and advanced in the sociological study of Bichr Farès, *L'Honneur chez les arabes avant l'Islam* (Paris, Adrien-Maisonneuve, 1932), which traces elements of seeming excessiveness in Arab behavior to an underlying concern for reputation or the image that a man and his tribe project to the world. The most incisive study of the relation of pre-Islamic values and understandings of the end of man to the great themes of Muḥammad's preaching is found in Toshihiko Izutsu's *The Structure of the Ethical Terms in the Koran* (Tokyo, Keio Institute of Philological Studies, 1959). Izutsu, like Farès, draws most of his information on the world view of the Jāhilīyah from the pre-Islamic poetry. For a more general background on the customs and mores of Arabian life, *Kinship and Marriage in Early Arabia* by W. Robertson Smith (Cambridge, Cambridge Univ. Press, 1885) provides an excellent introduction.

Specifically on the subject of religion, W. Robertson Smith's *Religion of the Semites* (Cambridge, 1889; N.Y., Meridian Books, 1956) is the classic study. Its central thesis, that sacrifice among the ancient Semites was a type of communion with deity, has long since been rejected, but in other respects it is a masterly survey and analysis of the evidence of Semitic religion. Particularly interesting is the discussion of certain pagan practices, such as the cult of the Kaʻbah, that were carried over into Islām, albeit infused with a new meaning. Mention should also be made of Julius Wellhausen, *Reste arabischen Heidenthums,* 2nd. ed. (Berlin and Leipzig, W. de Gruyter, 1927), an old but authoritative work. More recently much new work has been done on the religious life of the pagan Arabs, none of it unfortunately in English. Toufic Fahd has written on *La Divination arabe* (Leiden, E.J. Brill, 1966), treating not only pre-Islamic divinatory practices but continuing the analysis into the mediaeval Islamic era. His work on this subject turned up a wealth of information on ancient Arab religion enabling the composition of a second work, *Le Panthéon de l'Arabie centrale à la veille de l'hégire* (Beirut, Institut Français d'Archéologie; Paris, Geuthner, 1968). Joseph Chelhod, who shares the phenomenologically oriented approach of Fahd, has written on *Le Sacrifice chez les arabes* (Paris, Presses universitaires de France, 1955) and *Les structures du sacré chez les arabes* (Paris, Maisonneuve et Larose, 1964). The best summary statement of recent scholarly discoveries concerning ancient Arabian religion is still G. Ryckmans, *Les Religions arabes préislamiques* (Louvain, Bibliothèque du Muséon, 1951), vol. XXVI. Specifically for South Arabia there are works by A. Jamme, his *Le Panthéon sud-arabe préislamique d'après les sources épigraphiques* (Louvain, Universitas Catholica Louvaniensis, 1947) and "La Religion sud-arabe préislamique," in M. Brillant and R. Aigrain, eds., *Histoire des religions,* IV (1953), 239–307. One of the literary sources on pre-Islamic religion dating from early Islamic times, a work by Ibn al-Kalbī, is available in the English translation of Nabīh Amīn Fāris as *The Book of Idols* (Princeton, Princeton Univ. Press, 1952).

When all of the works recommended here have been read, however, the religious background of the rise of Islām will still not have been adequately sketched. It cannot be too strongly emphasized that the Islamic community is the heir of the entire previous religious tradition of the ancient Near East, and to be studied properly it should be set into the context of this developing tradition. For both theological and historical reasons it is customary in scholarship to deal with Islām as a discrete entity, as though it had no integral relation to what preceded it. The consequence has been many failures of understanding. The scholar who has reflected most deeply on this matter is the late Marshall G.S. Hodgson whose views can be read in an article "Islam and Image" found in *History of Religions,* III, 2 (Winter, 1964) 220–60, and in vol. I of his monumental *The Venture of Islam* (Chicago, Univ. of Chicago Press, 1974). A bibliographical guide to ancient Near Eastern religion is given elsewhere in this volume.

The principal cultural monument of the Bedouin of pre-Islamic Arabia and the best source of information about them is a body of poetry originally preserved in an oral tradition before being committed to writing in Islamic times. Eloquence was, and still is, among the most respected accomplishments of the Arabs, and an important factor in the success of Muḥammad was no doubt the impact of the sonorous phrases of the *Qur'ān* upon a people accustomed to revere force and felicity of verbal expression. Even today for Arabic speaking people the poetry of pre-Islamic Arabia has the status of "a model of unapproachable excellence" (R.A. Nicholson); its influence on literary standards throughout Islamic history is incalculable. The best book on this ancient literature is Sir Charles Lyall, *Translations of Ancient Arabian Poetry* (London and Edinburgh, 1885; London, Williams and Norgate, 1930). The most famous poems of all, the seven *Mu'allaqāt* or "Suspended Ones" are translated and studied by A.J. Arberry, in *The Seven Odes* (London, George Allen and Unwin, 1957); the last chapter of this work reviews the controversy over the authenticity of the pre-Islamic poetry. Another collection of ancient poetry, *The Mufaḍḍalīyāt*, was edited, translated and annotated by Lyall in 3 vols. (Oxford, Clarendon Press, 1918–21; vol. III, Leiden, 1924). The poetry is set into historical context and related to the evolution of Arabic literature by Reynold A. Nicholson in chaps. I to III of *A Literary History of the Arabs* (London, 1907; Cambridge, Cambridge Univ. Press, 1953). Nicholson's book is one of the classics in the Islamics field; it is a treasure house of careful and appreciative scholarship whose treatment of pre-Islamic literature and history is only one of its many merits. No serious student of Islām can neglect so fundamental a cultural expression as the literatures of the Muslim peoples. Nicholson's magnificent volume is not only an excellent introduction to Arabic literature but also a sensitive historical study of the connection between literature and other facets of Arab development in their always changing relationships.

III. THE PROPHET

The central figure of Islamic history is Muḥammad ibn 'Abdullāh who was born into a prominent Makkan family about A.D. 570 (the precise date is unknown). According to Muslim historians, when he was 40 years old—some say 43—a divine commission to serve as prophet to his people was laid upon him. Thereupon, the series of revelations collected in the *Qur'ān* began to come to him, and he assumed the at first highly unpopular role of religious teacher, reformer, and preacher. In a little more than twenty years, by his death in 632, not only had he won a large following and established a state based on commitment to God and his Chosen Prophet, but he had united virtually the whole of Arabia under his rule, something that no one in previous history had been able to accomplish.

Muslim piety, as may be expected, has lavished generous attention upon the Prophet. His contemporaries fastened upon his sayings and actions, remembered them, and passed them on in a living oral tradition, later to become a written one. As the number of stories about the Prophet increased and reflection upon his character became more intense, Muḥammad rapidly began to assume the characteristics of a superhuman creature, sinless, and capable of performing miracles. The tendency throughout Muslim history has been toward an always greater idealization, even romanticization, of the Prophet. The trend culminates in the modernist biographies of Muḥammad that portray him as the great hero of all history, the most profound thinker ever to have lived, and the perfect exemplar of all the virtues. This development testifies to the continuing and renewed significance of Muḥammad for Islamic faith; for those who wish to understand the meaning of the Prophet to Muslims, it is of little significance that the claims he made for himself are much more modest than those of his followers.

In contrast to Muslim biographers, Western students of the Prophet have often been unsympathetic. Some scholars have gone to the extreme of explaining Muḥammad's strange trancelike states while receiving revelations as due to epilepsy, and even Sprenger (see below) has diagnosed him as an hysteric. Others have outspokenly condemned Muḥammad on moral grounds for certain of his actions. Virtually all Western scholarship, almost without stopping to consider, considers Muḥammad and his teaching to be the results of historical and personality factors rather than of divine activity. Such elements in Western writings about the Prophet shock and offend Muslim sensibilities and are in no small part responsible for the defensive and apologetic tone of much contemporary Muslim literature. In defense of the Westerners it may be said that their motives in studying the Prophet necessarily differ from those of Muslims; as critical scholars they can hardly be expected to view the Prophet in the light in which the eyes of faith see him. Although much that Western scholars write may seem disrespectful to a reverent Muslim, their work has resulted in a greatly expanded and more sure understanding of Muḥammad's ilfe.

One of the knottiest of methodological problems in connection with Muhammad arises in relation to the use of the *Qur'ān* as a source for the Prophet's biography. There is no serious doubt among even the most skeptical scholars—and it goes without need for emphasis that Muslims concur —that the *Qur'ān* is genuinely Muhammadan. The weight of critical study supports the conclusion that the *Qur'ān's* pages offer a reliable record of the proclamations which the Prophet attributed to a divine source. When seen against the background of the untrustworthiness of so much of the material bearing on Muḥammad's life, the *Qur'ān* seems to offer especially valuable resources to the biographer. Almost universally, non-Muslim writers have recognized and employed these resources; and though the usefulness of the *Qur'ān* as biographical material is dependent upon establishing the chronology of its contents, for critical scholars it has seemed to offer the one uncorrupted fountainhead of information about Muḥammad. The methodological problem becomes apparent when it is recognized that use of the *Qur'ān* for biographical information on Muhammad involves the assumption that the book is in some sense the product and outcome of Muhammad's personality in interaction with factors in his environment. The view of history and historical causation held by most scholars demands such as assumption; any other stand would be unintelligible.

To the pious Muslim, however, this assumption is wholly unacceptable. For those of Muslim faith the *Qur'ān* is an eternal book whose author is God, not Muḥammad, and which is, therefore, in no respect subject to forces of historical conditioning. Since the personality of Muhammad played no part in the formation of the *Qur'ān,* the Holy Book cannot provide a key to that personality or its development.

Furthermore—and this is the vital issue—it is often wounding to the religious sensibilities of a Muslim to suggest that the *Qur'ān* can or should be a source for the study of Muḥammad's life. The outside observer must be aware of this fact and take measures to come to terms with it if he is not to offend his Muslim friends and if his understanding of Muslim religiousness is to be a faithful reflection of the experience in the hearts of Muslims. From one perspective the determination of the events of Muḥammad's life and the analysis of their underlying causes and relationships may appear to be purely "objective" and "scientific" questions, but any attempt to deal with them brings one inevitably into confrontation with the content of Muslim faith and with Muslims as persons. Ultimately, all religious studies appear to have an extra dimension of personal involvement, and this involvement makes extraordinary and peculiarly sharp demands of the student of religion.

(415)

A. Muslim biographies of the Prophet

The earliest sources for the life of the Prophet go back to the oral tradition of his sayings and doings that sprang from the circle of his immediate companions. Among the pagan Arabs there was an established and much enjoyed custom of reciting the exploits of the past, especially the deeds of great heroes. Gradually, as the Prophet gained more esteem and the influence of his community spread, the tales of dead and living heroes were replaced by tales of the Prophet. At first the stories with greatest appeal seem to have been those of his *maghāzī* or military campaigns. In the first generations after Muḥammad's death these stories began to be collected, and there arose what is known as the *maghāzī* literature. As the earliest material concerning the Prophet outside the *Qur'ān,* it is one of the most promising sources of information about him. Very little of this literature has survived, however, and only two small portions of it are available in Western languages. One of them, a fragment of a lost book by Mūsā ibn 'Uqbah of the third generation after Muḥammad, is translated by Alfred Guillaume in his *The Life of Muhammad* (London, Oxford Univ. Press, 1955) xliii–xlvii. The other example is an abridged translation of al-Wāqidī's *maghāzī* book by Julius Wellhausen: *Muḥammad in Medina* (Berlin, G. Reimer, 1882). The Arabic original of this work has been republished in a new edition by Marsden Jones under the title *The Kitāb al-Maghāzī of al-Wāqidī,* 3 vols. (Oxford Univ. Press, 1966). al-Wāqidī who lived between 797 and 874, is one of the two basic sources for the life of Muḥammad, both because of his own book and because of his influence on a prominent disciple, Ibn Sa'd, who also set down the life of the Prophet, his companions, and successors in a famous book, *Kitāb al-Ṭabaqāt al-Kabīr.* The portions dealing with Muḥammad's life are available in a translation by S. Moinul Haq and H.K. Ghazanfar (Karachi, Pakistan Historical Society, 1967) under the above title.

The first systematic effort to compile a biography of Muḥammad is attributed to Ibn Isḥāq who was born (85 A.H.) and grew up in Madīnah, where he had ample opportunity to collect the stories of the Prophet current among its populace. These stories he set down as he received them, with a bare minimum of editorial comment, to form a connected narrative in three parts. Although Ibn Isḥāq's biography is the fundamental source on Muḥammad's life for the early Muslim historians, it has come down to us independently only in a shortened, edited form. One, Ibn Hishām, of the generation after Ibn Isḥāq, edited the latter's text in accord with certain principles which he explains in his Preface. Ibn Hishām's work has been translated by Alfred Guillaume in the volume cited just above, and it is by all odds the most important single early source for Muḥammad's life. Something of Ibn Isḥāq has also been preserved in the writings of historians who employed his book as source material, notably al-Ṭabarī, the foremost historian of the early Islamic era. al-Ṭabarī's version of the

Prophet's life in an abridged translation from Persian by M. Herman Zotenburg is available in *Chronique de Tabari* (Paris, G.P. Maisonneuve, 1957), vols. I–III. A much later biography, which was for a long time the only one known in the West, is that by Abū al-Fidā, tr. by Noël Desvergers along with other texts in *Classiques de l'islamologie* (Algiers, La Maison des Livres, 1950).

After the initial surge of interest in the biography of Muḥammad, little advance was made in the subject for many centuries. This is not to say that no biographies were written or that the role of the Prophet in Muslim thought and piety became any less. The reasons lay rather in the fact that no significant body of source materials remained unexploited, and in the nature of Arab historical writing later historians were content to reproduce what their predecessors had written. The exception to this generalization belongs rather to the history of piety and dogma than to the tradition of biographies of the Prophet; it is the Ṣūfī or mystical versions of Muḥammad's life. When mysticism began to develop among Muslims, its exponents were quick to find sanction for both their practice and belief in the example of Muḥammad. In course of time the mystical trend of piety created a veritable cult of the Prophet that has been of enormous importance among all levels of Muslims. The only English example of a Ṣūfī approach to Muḥammad known to this writer is the poem *Mevlid Sharif* of Sulayman Chelebi, tr. by F. Lyman MacCallum (London, John Murray, 1943). This, however, is a particularly excellent example and, even in translation, a moving one.

In quite recent times, since about 1875, Muslim interest in the biography of Muḥammad has reawakened; there have been more biographies of the Prophet in the past seventy-five years than in perhaps the entire previous span of Islamic history. The causes of this effusion are clearly attributable to the deep stirrings of self-consciousness and vitality affecting the Muslim world in our day. Many of these biographies are reactions against what Muslims consider to be calumnies of the Prophet by orientalists, missionaries, and others; almost all evidence the crisis of cultural and religious identification that is perhaps the fundamental element in contemporary Muslim thought. Because their purpose and tone are avowedly apologetic and argumentative, the majority have little worth as sober historical work: their value lies rather in what they tell us of the contemporary meaning of Muḥammad in Muslim hearts and minds. Probably the best known work of this kind is *The Spirit of Islam* by Sayyid Amīr ʿAlī (London, Christopher's, rev. ed., 1922, and many others). Other representative works are Hafiz Ghulam Sarwar, *Muhammad the Holy Prophet,* 3rd imp. (Lahore, Ashraf, 1949) and Khwaja Kamal-ud-Din, *The Ideal Prophet* (Woking, Basheer Muslim Library, 1925). The most widely read and influential biography in an Islamic language is doubtless Muḥammad Ḥusayn Haykal's *Ḥayāt Muḥammad* (*The Life of Muḥammad*), (Cairo,

Maktabah al-Nahḍah al-Miṣrīyah, 5th imp., 1952), which has had many printings and whose English translation is awaiting publication. There is a monographic study of this biography called *A Modern Arabic Biography of Muḥammad* by Antonie Wessels (Leiden, E.J. Brill, 1972).

B. Western biographies

The lives of Muḥammad in the early nineteenth century tended on the whole to accept as authentic the version of the Prophet's biography presented in the source materials then available. About the middle of the century the works of Ibn Saʿd, al-Ṭabarī, and, above all, Ibn Hishām, became known in Europe, and new biographies based on examination of this variety of sources rapidly displaced the older ones which had drawn their information from Abū al-Fidā, who in his turn depended upon the relatively late historian Ibn al-Athīr. The new state of knowledge of the sources is reflected in Sir William Muir, *The Life of Mohammad* (1861, rev. ed., Edinburgh, John Grant, 1912), which has introductory chapters discussing sources and the early history of Arabia. Unfortunately, these chapters were omitted from the second and subsequent editions. There is a similar focus on sources in A. Sprenger's *Das Leben und die Lehre des Mohammad,* 3 vols. (Berlin, Verlagsbuchhandlung, 1861–65). The appearance of these two writings marks the birth of serious biographical work on Muḥammad.

As in other aspects of Islamic studies, the appearance of Ignaz Goldziher's *Muhammedanische Studien* and other work on early Muslim traditional material wrought a revolution in approaches to the biography of the Prophet. Goldziher demonstrated that many of the early traditional sayings attributed to the Prophet, or stories about him, are the product of contending sects and viewpoints within the Muslim community, each one eager to claim the authority of Muḥammad for its own peculiar stand. Muslim collectors of tradition themselves recognize and deplore the wholesale fabrication of traditions, particularly of prophetic sayings, in the early period. As a result the entire body of traditional material falls under the shadow of doubt as regards its historical reliability. Since Goldziher, biographers of Muḥammad have been compelled to subject their source materials to a critical sifting. One group of Western scholars has drawn the radical conclusion that the tradition is not to be used at all. These men hold that the *Qur'ān* alone is reliable as a biographical source on Muhammad. This view is most strongly expressed by Henri Lammens. See his "Qoran et tradition, comment fut composée la vie de Mahomet," *Recherches des sciences religieuses,* I (1910), 26–51, and "L'Âge de Mahomet et la chronologie de la Sīrā," *Journal asiatique,* 10th series, XVII (1911), 209–50.

More recent work on Muḥammad is typified by the books of W. Montgomery Watt who, while duly aware of the pitfalls awaiting the incautious, is more inclined than many to rely on traditional materials. His chief works are *Muḥammad at Mecca* (Oxford, Clarendon Press, 1953) and *Muḥammad at Medina* (Oxford, Clarendon Press, 1956). These two are abridged in a short but useful volume, *Muḥammad: Prophet and Statesman* (London, Oxford Univ. Press, 1961). Watt's writings on the Prophet are notable for the meticulous care with which he has traced the alliances and tribal relationships that account for the Prophet's success in consummating his control over Arabia, the broadly sympathetic treatment of Muḥammad's personality, and the author's conviction that religious developments are accompanied by, related to, and in part determined by economic and social developments. The third of these—the central thesis of his work—has led to another volume *Islam and the Integration of Society* (London, Routledge and Kegan Paul, 1961), in which he explores the relations of religion and society in later phases of Islamic history. There is a somewhat similar emphasis upon the social and economic factors in Muḥammad's situation and the relevance of the Islamic ideology to them in a provocative book by Maxime Rodinson, *Mohammed,* tr. by Anne Carter (London, Allen Lane, Penguin Press, 1971).

Watt's work, however, has been subjected to severe and biting criticism by R.B. Serjeant; see his review in *Bulletin of the School of Oriental and African Studies,* XXI, 1 (1958). Serjeant contends that there is no direct evidence to support the argument that Makkah was suffering serious upheaval because of changes in the social and economic pattern; on the contrary he holds that tribal law and custom continued to prevail there in Muḥammad's time. It is the failure to understand tribal life in Arabia that has, in his opinion, vitiated the contributions of many scholars, including Watt. Serjeant sees a much greater place for the insights and methods of the ethnologist and the folklorist than the traditional type of philologically oriented scholar has afforded to them. His views are developed in a series of writings that offer a great insight into many heretofore unresolvable problems in the Prophet's life. Especially important are "Ḥaram and Hawtah, the Sacred Enclave in Arabia," in 'Abd al-Rahmān Badawī, ed., *Ilā Tāhā Ḥusayn* (Cairo, 1962), 41–58; "The 'Constitution of Medina,' " *Islamic Quarterly,* VIII (1964), 3–16; and *Saiyids of Hadramawt* (London, School of Oriental and African Studies, 1957).

The work of the Swedish scholar Tör Andrae must also be mentioned. His *Mohamed the Man and His Faith,* tr. by Theophil Menzil (N.Y., Barnes and Noble, 1934; latest ed., Harper Torchbooks, 1960), is readable and sympathetic to Muḥammad but has been replaced by later work. Andrae emphasizes the similarity of much in Muḥammad to Monophysite Christianity and stresses especially the eschatological side of the Prophet's teaching. A second book, *Die Person Muhammeds in Lehre und Glauben seiner Gemeinde,* Archives d'Études Orientales XVI (Stockholm, J.A. Lundell, 1918 and repr.), is the fundamental work of its kind. It is not a biography of the Prophet but rather a study of the changing roles and conceptions of the Prophet in Muslim piety. The development of Muḥammad's significance is presented from the perspective of a comparative method that gives full range to Andrae's knowledge of the history of religions as well as his interest in religious psychology. The Muḥammad of faith is a very different figure from the Muḥammad of history, and it is essential for students of the religious life of Muslims to know how different groups of Muslims at different times have responded to and appropriated the Prophet.

Among scholarly works on Muḥammad perhaps the sanest and best-balanced is Frants Buhl's full treatment in *Das Leben Muḥammeds,* tr. by H.H. Schaeder, 2nd ed. (Heidelberg, Quelle & Meyer, 1955). The views of this Danish scholar are summarized in his article "Muḥammad" in *Shorter Encyclopaedia of Islam.*

Many special problems in connection with Muḥammad have intrigued scholarly interest, one of the most important being the sources of his ideas and teachings. Much of nineteenth-century scholarship was preoccupied with tracing out the historical antecedents of movements, ideas, institutions, and so forth, and Muḥammad did not escape attention from this perspective. At first the tendency was to emphasize the Prophet's dependence on Judaism. The case for the Jewish background of Islām is best stated by C.C. Torrey in *The Jewish Foundation of Islam* (N.Y., Jewish Institute of Religion Press, 1933). Abraham I. Katsh also has written a volume, *Judaism in Islam* (N.Y., Bloch, 1954), to show the "Biblical and Talmudic backgrounds of the Koran and its Commentaries." Since the work of Tör Andrae, mentioned above, and his *Der Ursprung des Islams und das Christentum* (Uppsala, Kyrohist, Söreningen, 1926), the majority of students has come to believe the major influence upon the Prophet to have been Syrian Christianity rather than Judaism. Richard Bell's *The Origin of Islam in Its Christian Environment* (London, Macmillan, 1926) also examines the relations of Muḥammad's thought to Christianity.

Finally, attention may be called to several works that survey the state of scholarship on Muḥammad and early Islām. The incisive study by Régis Blachère, *Le Problème de Mahomet* (Paris, Presses universitaires de France, 1952), demonstrates that Muḥammad is not the well-known figure he is often said to be. On the contrary, at many crucial points our sources are entirely silent, and at others their reliability and the method of their use are so much in doubt that little can be said with certainty. The fullest and most useful treatment of studies on the early period is Maxime Rodinson, "Bilan des études Mohammadiennes," *Revue historique,* CCXXIX (1963), 169–220. There will be special interest for students of religion in the article by James E. Royster, "The Study of Muḥammad; A Survey of Approaches from the Perspective of the History and Phenomenology of Religion," *Muslim World,* LXII (1972), 49–70.

IV. THE *QUR'ĀN*

As central as the Prophet's person has become for Muslims, there is another factor in the Islamic scheme of things with which he is indissolubly linked and to which in an important sense he is subordinate. This other factor is the *Qur'ān*, the divine book containing God's message of mercy, guidance, and warning for mankind that came through the Prophet's agency. When Muslims affirm that Muḥammad is the Prophet of God, the meaning is that he, like others in the past, was chosen as the human means for the delivery of a divine message to the people of his time and, through them, to all succeeding generations everywhere. There is little doubt that in Muḥammad's own eyes his message was of more importance than his person, though he insisted upon a close relationship between the two (as, for example, in the dictum that obedience to God implies obedience to His Prophet). The basis of the Prophet's claim on the believers lay in his acting in the name of God and not in his peculiar personal characteristics. The fact of massive significance was that God had spoken through his Prophet, renewing the guidance already offered through former prophets, but corrupted and spurned by contumacious men. In renewing His revelation through Muḥammad, this time God also undertook to preserve it against loss or distortion for all time to come. The *Qur'ān* is thus a final and definitive expression of the divine will for the guidance of men and, as such, the foundation upon which the entire Islamic structure rests, even its view of the Prophet.

Muslims consider the *Qur'ān* to be the very words of God himself, delivered to Muḥammad piecemeal by an angelic messenger, usually said to be Gabriel, at intervals after the prophetic call. The developed Muslim theology of classical times holds the *Qur'ān* to be eternal and uncreated, always to have existed alongside God as an eternal manifestation of the divine will. The book that men possess, bound between covers and written on paper, is a partial reproduction of that eternal original known to Islamic thought as the "well preserved Tablet" or the "Mother of the Book".

Many features of Islamic faith and practice have their explanation in the conviction that the *Qur'ān* contains the very speech of God. For instance, this conviction lies at the base of the resistance to translating the *Qur'ān* that until recently was all but universal among Muslims. A.L. Tibawi has reviewed the variety of Muslim opinion in history about the translation problem in the *Muslim World*, LII, 1 (1962) 4 ff., "Is the *Qur'ān* Translatable?" This conviction is also the motivation for the great reverence and affection shown the *Qur'ān*. Millions of Muslims have committed the entire book to memory, including many who do not understand the sense of the Arabic but who cherish the divine words for their very sound. Most important of all, the conviction is the justification for the *Qur'ān's* place as supreme and undisputed authority in both Muslim law and theology.

A. Translations

The *Qur'ān* is expressed in Arabic that is strikingly forceful, epigrammatic, and vivid. Though it does not exemplify the canons of formal Arabic poetry, it has many of the qualities of poetry, including a strong rhythm and elements of rhyme. The style of its expression so affected the Arabs—who, it must be remembered, revere beauty of expression as a cardinal accomplishment—that the classical Islamic proof for the divine origin of the *Qur'ān* has been its inimitability as literature. To translate such a book is a monumental and somewhat daring undertaking, and it should come as no surprise that the attempt has often been less than successful. In the Prefaces to two renderings of the *Qur'ān* by A.J. Arberry, his complete *The Koran Interpreted,* 2 vols. (London, George Allen & Unwin, 1955), and his selection *The Holy Koran* (London, George Allen & Unwin, 1953, Ethical and Religious Classes East and West, No. 9), there are excellent discussions of both the history of *Qur'ān* translations into English and of the problems encountered in translating.

The older translators of the *Qur'ān*, recognizing its significance as a scripture, tended to render it into language resembling the King James Bible. Such a style sacrifices the force of the Arabic original, and these translations are heavy and dull. Otherwise, some of the older translations are excellent, notably that by E.H. Palmer for the *Sacred Books of the East,* vols. VI and IX, which is still widely admired. J.M. Rodwell's translation, *The Koran* (London, J.M. Dent and Sons, 1909), Everyman's Series, is perhaps as widely used, though its chapters have been rearranged in sequence to reflect the translator's view of Qur'ānic chronology. The rendition by George Sale, *The Koran* (Philadelphia, 1855, and several reprints), the earliest to be widely known in the English-speaking world, can also be recommended.

The best of recent translations is that by A.J. Arberry, mentioned above. Arberry has made a detailed study of the rhythm patterns of the *Qur'ān* along lines that no previous scholar has pursued, seeking in this way to discover the secret of the *Qur'ān's* unique drawing power and force. He has been boldly experimental in devising verse forms to express these patterns. The result is a translation with great variety that makes the *Qur'ān* come to life for the English reader with something of the freshness and power of the original. Arberry's literary gifts are matched by formidable erudition; in addition to being beautiful and graceful, the translation also follows the findings of critical scholarship on the meaning and content of the *Qur'ān*.

Two other translations may be mentioned since they are readily available and often seen. One, by an English convert to Islām, Marmaduke Pickthall, *The Meaning of the Glorious Koran* (Hyderabad, 1938; N.Y., Mentor, 1953), was prepared after consultation with eminent Muslim scholars and reference to the standard commentaries on the Holy Book. Just as Arberry's rendition or the more recent German one by Rudi Paret, *Der Koran* (Stuttgart, etc., W. Kohlhammer Verlag, 1971), reflect critical Western understanding of the *Qur'ān,* Pickthall's translation shows the standard Sunnī Muslim interpretation of the text. *The Koran,* tr. by N.J. Dawood (Middlesex, Penguin Books, rev. ed., 1959), has been prepared to exhibit the *Qur'ān's* literary quality. Dawood has also rearranged the chapters, in this case to create a literary effect. His translation is pleasing and readable and has some notes based on classical authorities.

B. Commentaries on the *Qur'ān*

In a sense the entire body of Islamic religious writing might be considered as an extended commentary on the *Qur'ān*. There is also, however, a specific literature that aims at expounding and elucidating the Holy Book, a literature that is extensive and that has been of great historical importance in the development of Muslim religious thought. For all its importance, however, there is real difficulty in making use of the *tafsīr* literature, as it is called (from *fassara,* meaning to explain, expound or to comment upon), for one who does not know the Muslim languages. Very little of *tafsīr* has been translated, because these works are often long and technical, and but few of them were originally written in Western languages. Among the *tafsīrs* most respected and used by Sunnī Muslims is that by al-Bayḍāwī, a thirteenth-century scholar and controversialist. Parts of it exist in translation in Eric F.F. Bishop, *Chrestomathia Baidawiana* (Glasgow, Jackson, Son, 1957); D.S. Margoliouth, *Chrestomathia Baidawiana* (London, Luzac, 1894); and A.F.L. Beeston, *Baiḍāwī's Commentary on Sūrah 12 of the Qur'ān* (Oxford, Clarendon Press, 1963). Each of these volumes translates the commentary on one chapter of the *Qur'ān;* and though they were prepared primarily as aids for students of Arabic, they may and should be studied for their substance as well. There are also several modern works of commentary on the *Qur'ān* in English written by Indian Muslims. The one that most deserves to be called a *tafsīr* in the traditional sense is that by Muḥammad ʿAlī, *The Holy Qurʾān,* 4th rev. ed. (Lahore, Ahmadiyyah Anjuman Ishāʿat Islām, 1951). Quite similar in character is A. Yūsuf ʿAlī's *The Holy Quran, Text, Translation and Commentary,* 3rd ed. (Lahore, Ashraf, 1938). Either of these works will serve to introduce the reader to the nature of *tafsīr,* though they are hardly substitutes for the classical works. Another useful way of affording the non-orientalist some taste of the classical *tafsīrs* is adopted by a Swiss scholar, Helmut Gätje, whose *Koran und Koranexegese* (Zürich & Stuttgart, Artemis Verlag, 1971) is a selection of translated passages from different commentaries arranged to show the differences among their authors in the interpretation of certain verses or doctrines. Unfortunately, there is no similar work available in English.

Not only has *tafsīr* failed to attract translators; it has also inspired but little attention from historians and analysts. The paucity of literature may perhaps be attributed to the difficulty of the subject and the voluminousness of the source materials. There is but one major work on *tafsīr* in Western languages, and that in German. It is the monumental study by Ignaz Goldziher, *Die Richtungen der islamischen Koranauslegung,* 2nd ed. (Leiden, E.J. Brill, 1952). Baron Carra de Vaux also surveys the development of commentaries on the *Qurʾān* in vol. III of *Les Penseurs de l'Islam,* chap. xi (Paris, Geuthner, 1932), but his sketch is not of the quality of Goldziher's masterly work. Attention may also be called to a study of al-Ṭabarī, mentioned above as a basic source for the life of the Prophet, whose *tafsīr* is the best known and most important of all the classical commentaries. His work is described by O. Loth in vol. XXXV of *Zeitschrift der deutschen Morgenländischen Gesellschaft* (1881) "Ṭabarī's Korankommentar." There are also several technical studies of *tafsīr* especially in the earlier periods. The important contributors are Harris Birkeland and Nabia Abbott. Birkeland's views are found in three studies: *The Lord Guideth* (Oslo, H. Aschenhoug, 1956); *Old Muslim Opposition against Interpretation of the Koran* (Oslo, Jacob Dybwad, 1955); and *Muslim Interpretation of Surah 107* (Oslo, H. Aschenhoug, 1958). Miss Abbott's work is reported in vol. II of her *Studies in Arabic Papyrii* (Chicago, Univ. of Chicago Press, 1967).

Those who may be interested in modern expressions of *Qurʾān* exegesis are more fortunate than students of the classical period. A Dutch scholar, J.M.S. Baljon, has supplemented Goldziher's history by the study of several contemporary *tafsīr* writers in his *Modern Muslim Koran Interpretation 1880–1960* (Leiden, E.J. Brill, 1961). There is a detailed analysis of tendencies in early twentieth-century Egypt in J. Jomier, *Le Commentaire coranique du Manār* (Paris, G.P. Maisonneuve, 1954). Jomier is concerned with the group of Muslim modernists surrounding Rashīd Riḍā who founded the periodical *al Manār* as the vehicle for spreading his ideas. This book may also be read as a study of one important phase of modern

Muslim development among the Arabs, namely, the trend toward reappropriation of the fundamental sources of Muslim piety. The astonishing vitality of the *tafsīr* tradition and its continuing relevance in Muslim religious life are convincingly demonstrated in *The Interpretation of the Koran in Modern Egypt* by J.J.G. Jansen (Leiden, E.J. Brill, 1974), who surveys the considerable number of *tafsīrs* produced in the land of the Nile in recent years and analyzes the trends which they exhibit.

C. Critical works on the *Qur'ān*

The issues that have preoccupied Western students of the *Qur'ān* are principally four: (1) its origin and chronology, (2) the process by which it attained its present form, (3) the history of the standard *Qur'ān* text, and (4) the historical sources of its teaching. From the standpoint of Western scholarship—though decidedly not for Muslims—the latter is equivalent to the sources of Muḥammad's ideas.

The foundation stone of Western Qur'ānic studies was laid in the nineteenth century in the epoch-making work of Theodor Nöldeke, *Geschichte des Qorans,* 2 vols., best known in its 2nd rev. ed. prepared by Friedrich Schwally (Leipzig, Dieterich, 1909). In the 1930s a third volume dealing with the history of the *Qur'ān* text was added to the work by G. Bergsträsser and O. Pretzl, and the whole has now been reprinted in a readily available single-volume edition (Hildesheim, Georg Olms, 1961).

Nöldeke's first volume, entitled *Concerning the Origin of the Qur'ān,* is largely an attempt to establish the chronological sequence of the materials collected in the *Qur'ān.* He has distinguished four periods in Muḥammad's life, during each of which the revelations to the Prophet show identifying marks, and classified the chapters of the *Qur'ān* accordingly. The Scottish scholar Richard Bell also took up this problem and devoted a major effort to a "higher criticism" of the *Qur'ān.* Bell advanced beyond Nöldeke by dividing the individual chapters of the *Qur'ān* into what he considered to be their component parts and then rearranging the whole in chronological order. The results, worked out in meticulous detail, may be seen in his *The Qur'ān,* translated with a critical rearrangement of the Surahs, 2 vols. (Edinburgh, T. & T. Clark, 1937–39), and the short companion work *Introduction to the Qur'ān* (Edinburgh, Edinburgh Univ. Press, 1953). The latter has been completely revised and enlarged by W. Montgomery Watt and published as No. 8 of the Islamic Surveys series, bearing the title *Bell's Introduction to the Qur'ān* (Edinburgh, Edinburgh Univ. Press, 1970); the volume is an excellent and comprehensive guide to the Muslim Holy Book that is easily accessible.

Another wide-ranging introduction to the Islamic scripture that can be commended is Bishop Kenneth Cragg's *The Event of the Qur'ān* (London,

George Allen & Unwin, 1971). Here as elsewhere in his writings Cragg strives to elicit and bring home the religious quality of Islamic life. His attention is directed to the significance of the *Qur'ān* as one of the crucial events in Islamic experience, and in pursuing his theme he discusses all the many issues that have attracted critical scholars. Cragg's scholarship is notable for the beauty with which it is presented; he writes in a carefully crafted, lush, often poetic language that makes his books a joy to read.

The most readable summary of the state of scholarship respecting the *Qur'ān* as well as the best introduction to the problems arising from it is vol. 1 of Régis Blachère, ed. and tr., *Le Coran,* 3 vols. (Paris, G.P. Maisonneuve, 1947–51); the other two volumes are a translation of the text. Blachère is capable of clarity and great simplicity in his writing without sacrificing a sound treatment of the subject matter, and he is nowhere better than here. Information on Qur'ānic scholarship was brought up to date and treated in more technical fashion in Arthur Jeffery's "The Present Status of Qur'ānic Studies" in *Report on Current Research on the Middle East* (Washington, D.C., Spring, 1957), 1 ff. Before his death Jeffery was perhaps the leading student of textual problems in the *Qur'ān,* and his grasp of past accomplishments as well as future scholarly requirements will satisfy the most exacting specialist. Prior to World War II Jeffery worked with a group of German scholars to prepare a critical text of the *Qur'ān* based on the surviving manuscripts from early times; the nature of his concerns can be seen in *Materials for the History of the Text of the Qur'ān, the Old Codices* (Leiden, E.J. Brill, 1937). Unfortunately, the war brought an end to this promising project when the manuscript collection was destroyed in Allied bombing raids.

Those who require a succinct but scholarly introduction to the *Qur'ān* should consult the article "al-Kur'ān" in *Shorter Encyclopaedia of Islam.*

D. Analyses of the contents of the *Qur'ān*

The *Qur'ān's* teachings have been studied from a number of different points of view. Recently a fruitful new line has been opened up by the application of techniques of linguistic analysis to the text of the *Qur'ān.* A Japanese Arabist, Toshihiko Izutsu, has employed these methods to produce some of the most illuminating studies of fundamental Qur'ānic concepts ever made. His work is a revelation of the peculiarly Qur'ānic force and meaning of such common but important terms as "faith," "unbelief," "good," and "evil." The first of his studies was called *The Structure of the Ethical Terms in the Koran* (Tokyo, Keio Institute of Philological Studies, 1959); a much revised version of this book was published in 1966 as *Ethico-Religious Concepts in the Qur'ān* (Montreal, McGill Univ. Press). Using the same approach Izutsu has also studied *God and*

Man in the Koran (Tokyo, Keio Institute of Cultural and Linguistic Studies, 1964). Another work with a similar but less sophisticated method is Daud Rahbar's *God of Justice* (Leiden, E.J. Brill, 1960). By grouping together and studying the contexts in which some of the basic epithets applied to God occur, he has sought to penetrate through the historical accumulation of pious interpretations to lay bare the significance of the *Qur'ān* for Muḥammad's contemporaries. His conclusion is evidenced in the title.

One of the most attractive studies of the content of the *Qur'ān* ever penned is to be had in Kenneth Cragg's *The Mind of the Qur'ān* (London, George Allen & Unwin, 1973), a companion work to his *The Event of the Qur'ān*. The volume is a series of religious essays turning upon the principal terms in the Qur'ānic vocabulary. Their purpose is both to show the significance of the *Qur'ān* in the minds of the people who apprehend and affirm it as true as well as to illustrate the nature and thrust of Muḥammad's challenge to Arab paganism. Underlying the study is a concern for inter-religious communication, and every word demonstrates the personal involvement of its author with the religious life of those about whom he writes.

Of a somewhat different kind are two volumes on the *Qur'ān* by W. Montgomery Watt and Rudi Paret. Watt has provided a *Companion to the Qur'ān* (London, George Allen & Unwin, 1967), to be used in conjunction with Arberry's translation. Both Watt's work and Paret's somewhat resemble a traditional Muslim *tafsīr*; they proceed verse by verse through the text of the *Qur'ān* explaining difficult words or phrases, offering comments or otherwise illuminating the reader's understanding. Paret's volume, *Der Koran: Kommentar und Konkordanz* (Stuttgart, W. Kohlhammer, 1971), also cites the scholarly literature bearing on the points discussed and in this way provides an invaluable and highly convenient bibliographical resource for the serious student. Paret aims to achieve an explicitly historical understanding of the *Qur'ān,* to make clear what Muḥammad meant to say in a particular circumstance or milieu but not to trace the subsequent development of Qur'ānic ideas. Paret's commentary, the product of many years of careful study of the *Qur'ān,* is the highwater mark of modern Western *Qur'ān* interpretation.

Among writings that are helpful in understanding what the *Qur'ān* has to say are three others that can be especially recommended. In a thick French volume, *Le Koran analysé* (Paris, Maisonneuve, 1878), Jules La Beaume has grouped together all of the Qur'ānic passages dealing with such subjects as Muḥammad, the Bible, cultic practice, law, and so forth, making it easy for the inquirer to locate the material that may bear on a particular subject. *The Social Laws of the Qoran* (London, Williams Norgate, 1925) by Robert Roberts performs a similar function for Qur'ānic teachings on such matters as marriage and divorce, inheritance, the treatment of slaves, and commercial relations. Arthur Jeffery, mentioned above, has composed a small volume expounding the concept of "Scripture" as it is used in connection with the *Qur'ān*. Several of the major religious communities of the world possess scriptures which they revere as sacrosanct, but the significance of these sacred writings differs for each, the Muslims having an especially strong tie with the "Book." Jeffery has endeavored to make clear the unique features of the Muslim conception of Scripture, and this has led him inevitably into a broad consideration of many aspects of *Qur'ān* teaching. The work in question is *The Qur'ān as Scripture* (N.Y., Moore, 1952).

The literature about the *Qur'ān* in Western languages is enormous in extent; it exists in both monographic form and in articles scattered through the pages of journals and other collective works. The latter can be located by consulting J.D. Pearson's *Index Islamicus* (see below). As an indication of the richness of the monographic works, the following few examples of books published since World War II must suffice: Thomas O'Shaughnessy, *The Development of the Meaning of Spirit in the Koran, The Koranic Concept of the Word of God* and *Muḥammad's Thoughts on Death,* the first two published in Rome by Pont. Institutum Orientalium Studiorum in 1953 and 1948 respectively, and the latter in Leiden by E.J. Brill in 1969; Y. Moubarac, *Abraham dans le Coran* (Paris, J. Vrin, 1958); and S.H. al-Shammā', *The Ethical System underlying the Qur'ān* (Tübingen, Hopfer, 1959). Further information and comment on recent works are available in Willem Bijlefeld, "Some recent contributions to Qur'ānic Studies; Selected Publications in English, French and German, 1964–73," *The Muslim World,* LXIV, 2, 3, and 4 (1974).

V. ḤADĪTH

Among the sciences cultivated by Muslims one of the foremost in importance is the science of *ḥadīth,* which is concerned with the reports from the early days of the sayings, actions, and approbations of Muḥammad. Above, mention was made of the interest manifested among the early Muslims in every action and word of the Prophet and of the fact that zealous efforts were made to collect and preserve the enormous body of material relative to him. This material has been the building blocks not only of the prophetic biography but, as well, of the greater part of *Qur'ān* commentary and Islamic law, even of theology. Considered from the standpoint of its function, as opposed to the theory about it, the tradition of the Prophet has perhaps played an even greater role in Islamic history than the *Qur'ān* itself, since it is principally in the light of the tradition that the *Qur'ān* is viewed and understood. There were some in the earliest generations who explicitly acknowledged the primacy of the tradition as a religious authority, although later Muslim thought tended to subordinate it, at least in theory, to the Book of God. The great eighteenth-century Indian thinker Shāh Walīyullāh of Delhi characterized the science of prophetic traditions as "the base and crown of the assured sciences, the basis and foundation of the religious arts . . . a lamp in the darkness, the sign-post of guidance . . . a shining full moon. He who submits to it and understands it fully is surely sound and rightly guided and is brought to great good."

A. Collections

In the third Islamic century earnest efforts began to be made to collect the corpus of prophetic tradition in systematic fashion and to develop a critical machinery for distinguishing its genuine elements from spurious ones. The work of the collectors was spurred on the one hand by the great reverence for the Prophet's precept and example and on the other by revulsion against a wholesale tendency to fabricate prophetic sayings in justification of novel ideas and practices or partisan views. The more important of the collections of prophetic sayings that resulted are known as *al-Sittah al-Ṣaḥīḥ* or the Six Sound Books. By far the best known are the collection of al-Bukhārī and Muslim, though the others are widely used. These books are the chief resource of Muslims when they endeavor to discover the guidance offered by prophetic example on any point of belief or practice, but they are by no means the only resource. Other less well known collections of tradition exist in abundance and are extensively cited.

The only one of the *Ṣaḥīḥ* books readily available to Westerners is that of al-Bukhārī. It has been partially translated into English by Muḥammad Asad, whose ambition was to make the whole available to English readers. He was successful, however, in producing only one of eight projected volumes, and that one (no. 5) deals with the life of the Prophet and his companions; *Ṣaḥīḥ al-Bukhārī* (Lahore, Arafat Publications, 1938). In French there is a complete translation with notes and index prepared by O. Houdas and W. Marçais, published under the title *Les Traditions islamiques,* 3 vols. (Paris, Imprimerie nationale, 1903–14). Probably the most useful gateway to the literature of tradition will be one of the collections of selected sayings of Muḥammad; for example, *Selections from Muhammadan Traditions,* tr. by William Goldsack (Madras, Christian Literature Society for India, 1923), which is based on a well-known Arabic book combining the Six Sound Books with some other minor authorities. The traditions in Goldsack's selection are arranged under subject headings that facilitate locating materials relevant to a particular area of interest. Reading is made easier by elimination of the long chains of transmission that occupy so much of the space in traditional Muslim collections of *ḥadīth*. The original work from which Goldsack's selection was drawn, *Mishkāt al-maṣābīḥ,* has been published in four volumes of English translation (vol. I, Lahore, 1960) by James Robson who also provides a concise and learned introduction that sketches the background and development of *ḥadīth* generally as well as giving information about the work concerned. Another broadly based anthology is Mīrzā Abū'l-Faḍl's *Sayings of the Prophet Muḥammad* (Allahabad, Reform Society, 1924). A compendium of al-Bukhārī's *ḥadīth* book is available in Muḥammad ʿAlī, *A Manual of Hadith,* 2nd ed. (Lahore, Ahmadiyyah Anjuman Ishāʿat Islām, n.d.). None of these books constitutes easy reading, but in view of the fundamental importance of *ḥadīth* in Muslim thought their perusal will amply repay the reader.

B. Critical works

The fundamental critical study of the *ḥadīth* literature is vol. II of Ignaz Goldziher's *Muslim Studies* (Chicago, Aldine-Atherton, 1971), ed. by S.M. Stern, whose first part is entitled "On the Development of the Ḥadīth." The original German volumes, called *Muhammedanische Studien,* from which the translation was prepared, were published in Halle in 1890 and proved to be epoch-making in the development of Islamic studies. With an erudition and critical acumen that have seldom been matched, Goldziher lays bare the fundamental concepts, the historical development, and the significance of the *ḥadīth* in early Islamic history. While he concludes that much of the *ḥadīth* is not what it claims to be and cannot be relied upon for the information it purports to offer concerning Muḥammad, he demonstrates at the same time the unique and invaluable merits of the *ḥadīth,* even spurious *ḥadīth,* as a key to intellectual, religious, and political tendencies in the first two Islamic centuries. The serious student will find Goldziher's work indispensable. The themes of Goldziher's magisterial study were presented also in an excellent volume by the British Arabist Alfred Guillaume, *The Traditions of Islam* (Oxford, Clarendon Press, 1924), which in the days before the present translation existed was the only good English treatment of the subject.

The work of Goldziher was so solidly based in scholarship and so convincing in its argument that for many years it went without serious challenge. There were many, especially Muslim authors, who found his thesis about the *ḥadīth* unpalatable on theological grounds but none who could meet him effectively with firm historical evidence. In 1967, however, Fuat Sezgin began to publish his *Geschichte des arabischen Schrifttums* (Lei-

. den, E.J. Brill), and in vol. I he reopens the question of the authenticity of the *hadīth,* criticizing Goldziher for the first time in terms that compel attention. Sezgin points to a contradiction in Goldziher's analysis of the history of the science of *hadīth*. Whereas Goldziher believed the recording of *hadīth* not to have begun until some time in the second Islamic century, at the same time he acknowledged the existence of written collections of prophetic sayings in the hands of prominent Muslims at a very early time. Sezgin argues that Goldziher's confusion arose from the failure to understand some of the evidence available to him, in particular, the significance of the technical terms employed in *hadīth* narration. The proper analysis of these terms allows us to see that written records of *hadīth* go much farther back than Goldziher had thought, thus removing some of the suspicion about the authenticity of the *hadīth*. Another contribution to a more adequate understanding of this issue is made by Nabia Abbott in vol. II of her awesomely learned *Studies in Arabic Literary Papyri* (Chicago, Univ. of Chicago Press, 1957–   ; Oriental Institute Publications, no. 76). Miss Abbott does not address herself specifically to the authenticity of the *hadīth,* but one of the results of her studies is to show that written collections of traditional material existed in the early second Islamic century. To date, however, no one has succeeded in demonstrating that such collections existed in the first century. Those who may be interested in a learned Muslim contribution to the debate about *hadīth* should consult Fazlur Rahman, *Islamic Methodology in History* (Karachi, Central Institute of Islamic Research, 1965).

Discussions about the authenticity, but more important about the authoritativeness, of the *hadīth* have been one of the preoccupations of Muslim thought in the past 100 years. Because the medieval Islamic systems of law and theology drew so heavily from *hadīth* materials, it was perhaps inevitable that the continuing value of *hadīth* should be brought into question when the medieval system as a whole began to be criticized by modernizing reformers. Some insight into the nature of these debates, which are carried on in the various Muslim languages, can be had from the published doctoral thesis of G.H.A. Juynboll, *The Authenticity of the Tradition Literature* (Leiden, E.J. Brill, 1969) and from Charles J. Adams, "The Authority of *Hadīth* in the Eyes of Some Modern Muslims," in *Islamic Studies, Essays presented to Niyazi Berkes* (Leiden, E.J. Brill, 1976), 27–49.

Attention should also be called to an important reference work that provides a useful tool to the research scholar. It is *Concordance de la tradition musulmane,* a comprehensive concordance of the *hadīth* literature which makes its content readily accessible. This massive work was prepared by A.J. Wensinck in cooperation with other European scholars and has been published in fascicule form from Leiden since 1933.

C. Works by Muslims

Just as in the case of the primary foundation of Islām, the *Qur'ān*, the *ḥadīth* have brought into being an enormous literature. There is, in fact, an entire group of sciences related to the study of *ḥadīth*, concerned with such matters as the classification of *ḥadīth* according to their reliability and the investigation of the chains of transmission through which individual *ḥadīth* have come. Very little of this literature has been translated, since it is of interest only to specialists. It may be sampled, however, in J. Robson's *An Introduction to the Science of Tradition* (London, Royal Asiatic Society of Great Britain and Ireland, 1953), and in Raimund Köbert's edition and translation of a work by Ibn Fūrak under the title *Bayān Muškil al-Aḥadīt des ibn Fūrak* (Rome, Pontificium Institutum Biblicum, 1941). The latter is an attempt to offer acceptable explanations of *ḥadīth* that pose difficulties for the theological views cherished in the Ash'arīyah school of Sunnī Muslims.

VI. KALĀM

There is in common use among Muslims no word that corresponds strictly to the English term "theology," although the Arabic word *kalām* is often so translated. Etymologically, this word signifies discussion or speech; but in its technical use as the name of one of the traditional Islamic religious sciences, it refers to the systematic statement of a religious belief or the reasoned argument supporting it. A detailed analysis of the term and its historical development is available in the article "Kalām" in *Shorter Encyclopedia of Islām*.

Throughout the greater part of their history Muslims have shown no great interest in the kind of activity associated with *kalām*. *Kalām* was one of the sciences that developed and flowered in the second and third Islamic centuries, after the early conquests had been consolidated and the great 'Abbāsī empire had reached its creative peak. It was, thus, not one of the earliest concerns of the community, which is hardly surprising since the Arabs had no tradition of refined intellectual inquiry in pre-Islamic days. Nor, once it had developed, did *kalām* long continue to occupy the minds and hearts of Muslims. For a variety of reasons that cannot be sketched here the religious commitment of the community rapidly led it away from the somewhat arid doctrinal expositions of the learned into a preoccupation on the one hand with practical matters of the religious law and on the other with mysticism. This long-range development of the Muslim religious drive is studied and analyzed by H.A.R. Gibb in a brilliant essay entitled "The Structure of Religious Thought in Islam," most easily accessible in the volume edited by S.J. Shaw and W.R. Polk, *Studies on the Civilization of Islam* (Boston, Beacon Press, 1962). In our own day it is extremely difficult, often impossible, to elicit from Muslims a serious response to speculative theological questions; and this indifference poses a most bewildering puzzle for Westerners, who have been taught by their own religious tradition to put such speculation at the center of religious concern. Clearly, to understand that the Muslim's faith does not center in theology, and, beyond this, to understand the reasons therefor, is to make a major advance toward penetrating the Islamic view of the world.

The factors stimulating the growth of *kalām* when it did make its appearance were in the main two: internal tensions within the community, particularly over political issues, and the confrontation in such centers as Damascus and Baṣrah with sophisticated and articulate polemicists of different religious persuasions, possessed of the resources of Hellenistic thought, and ready to attack the ill-formulated doctrines of the young Islamic community. The circumstances of its genesis gave to the *kalām* the air of apologetics which it has always borne. Partly for reasons of piety and partly for reasons of self-defense the Muslims found themselves compelled to give a precise statement of the major tenets of their faith. The earliest development is treated in detail by W. Montgomery Watt in *Free Will and Predestination in Early Islam* (London, Luzac, 1948); the book carries the treatment of its theme—the first major subject of theological dispute among Muslims—well into the period when *kalām* had achieved its major development. The old volume by Duncan Black MacDonald, *Development of Muslim Theology, Jurisprudence and Constitutional Theory* (N.Y., Charles Scribner's Sons, 1903), is still a useful sketch of the history. The fundamental study of *kalām* is *Introduction à la théologie musulmane,* by Louis Gardet and M.M. Anawati (Paris, J. Vrin, 1948). The volume has the subtitle "Essai de théologie comparée," and represents the efforts of its authors to come to terms with the great issues of Muslim theological thought through comparisons with Christian thought, as a precondition for a "dialogue" between Muslims and Christians. The authors are both Catholic theologians, thoroughly trained in scholastic thought, and their approach to *kalām* reflects their scholastic orientation. A list of basic works on the subject must also include A.J. Wensinck, *The Muslim Creed* (Cambridge, Cambridge Univ. Press, 1932), a careful study of great erudition that in addition to delineation and discussion of the principal themes of early Muslim religious thought offers translations, analyses and comparisons of several basic documents from the early period. Serious readers will also wish to use the work of A.S. Tritton, *Muslim Theology* (London, Luzac, 1947), a mine of careful scholarship but stylistically difficult. W. Montgomery Watt has done a rapid survey of the development of *kalām* in *Islamic Philosophy and Theology,* Islamic Surveys I

(Edinburgh, Edinburgh Univ. Press, 1962); despite the title the volume, in fact, has little to say about philosophy. Of much more weight and importance is Watt's mature reflection on his years of work in the field, *The Formative Period of Islamic Thought* (Edinburgh, University Press, 1973), where an attempt is made to draw together the many strands of Muslim intellectual and religious endeavor in the first three centuries into a coherent picture. Watt believes that scholarly understanding of Muslim religious life has to some extent been misled by the biases of the Muslim heresiographers from whose works most of our knowledge of the earlier periods is drawn. He tries, therefore, to get behind the heresiographers for a fresh grappling with the events of the early development. One of the heresiographers of whom Watt speaks is al-Shahrastānī whose *Kitāb al-milal wa-l-nihal* is basic source material for the study of early Islām. The parts of this famous book dealing with Islamic sects have been translated into English by A.K. Kazi and J.G. Flynn and published as three articles in *Abr-Nahrain*, VIII, 37–68; IX, 81–107; and X, 49–75. The articles are entitled "The Mu'tazilites," "The Jabarites and the Ṣifātīya," and "The Khārijites and the Murji'ites," respectively. A similar work by 'Abd al-Qāhir al-Baghdādī is translated under the title *Moslem Schisms and Sects* by K.C. Seelye (N.Y., AMS Press, 1966). Much the same ground of early thought and controversy is covered by Henri Laoust in *Les Schismes dans l'Islam* (Paris, Payot, 1965). A book that may be strongly recommended to those approaching the study of Islamic theology for the first time is Francis E. Peters, *Allah's Commonwealth* (N.Y., Simon and Schuster, 1973) which integrates the development of thought among the Muslims with the political evolution of the community up to A.D. 1100. Although the work is a history in the broad sense, Professor Peters is clearly most interested in the development of thought which he treats with great clarity. His volume offers a most happy combination of sound scholarship and felicitous expression.

There are many specialized works having to do with *kalām* that might be commended. The late J.W. Sweetman embarked upon an ambitious period by period comparison of Islamic and Christian thought to show the historical interrelationships between their respective developments; only part of the massive projected work appeared in print as *Islam and Christian Theology* (London, Lutterworth Press, 1945), vols. I and II of Part I, and vol. I of Part II; vol. II of Part II appeared in 1967. There is an informative and sympathetic study of Aḥmad ibn Ḥanbal, a central figure of the religious ferment and controversy of early 'Abbāsī times, in Walter M. Patton, *Aḥmad ibn Ḥanbal and the Mihna* (Leiden, E.J. Brill, 1897). Ibn Ḥanbal was perhaps the finest representatitve of pious traditionalism in his day, and his influence has been perpetuated among earnest followers who stretch in an unbroken chain down to the Wahhābīs of Arabia in our own time. The later history of his school was studied by Ignaz Goldziher in another of his masterly books, *Die Ẓâhiriten, ihr Lehrsystem und ihre Geschichte* (Leipzig, Otto Schulze, 1884). More light on the school may be had from Henri Laoust's studies of Ibn Taymīyah, the thirteenth century controversialist, his most important book being *Essai sur les doctrines sociales et politiques de Takī-d-Dīn Aḥmad b. Taimīya* (Cairo, Imprimerie de l'Institut français d'archéologie orientale, 1939). The best of recent scholarship on the nature and development of *kalām* may be seen in the pages of Josef van Ess, *Die Erkenntnislehre des 'Adudaddīn al-īcī* (Wiesbaden, Franz Steiner, 1966); van Ess is a scholar of formidable learning and great productivity who has made a number of important contributions to text publication and analysis for the early period. Another kind of specialized work on *kalām* explores particular themes in Islamic theological thought; as examples one may cite Michel Allard, *Le Problème des attributs divins dans la doctrine d'al-Aš'arī et de ses premiers grands disciples* (Beirut, Institut de Lettres Orientales, 1965); and Louis Gardet, *Dieu et la destinée de l'homme* (Paris, J. Vrin, 1967), the first of a promised two-volume study of major doctrines of Islamic theology. Another work falling into this category is Toshihiko Izutsu's *The Concept of Belief in Islamic Theology* (Tokyo, Keio Institute of Cultural and Linguistic Studies; Yokohama, Yurindo, 1965) where Izutsu employs a semantic analytic method to clarify the role of *īmān* in Islamic theological thought.

The group in Islamic history probably most responsible for the emergence of *kalām* and for the direction which its development eventually took is known as the Mu'tazilah. For a short time the Mu'tazilah enjoyed the patronage of the 'Abbāsī rulers in Baghdad, during which their views became the official creed of the state. In due course, however, they were rejected by the majority of the community and disappeared, to be known only from the works of their opponents; but the vigor of their intellectual probing had served to provoke other thinkers to work out the position that the great majority of Sunnī Muslims have since held. In spite of their historical importance, there is no full-length work on this group that may be unqualifiedly recommended; the old work by Heinrich Steiner, *Die Mu'taziliten, oder die Freidenker im Islām* (Leipzig, S. Hirzel, 1865) is outdated. The basic writings about them in English are H.S. Nyberg's two articles in *Shorter Encyclopedia of Islam,* "al-Mu'tazilah" and "al-Naẓẓām." There is also available a work that studies the philosophical foundations of Mu'tazilī thought by Albert N. Nader, *Le Système philosophique des Mu'tazila* (Beirut, Éditions les lettres orientales, 1956). The same author has translated the first authentic Mu'tazilī treatise to be known to scholarship (published in Arabic in Cairo, 1925, by H.S. Nyberg), *Kitāb al-intiṣār,* by al-Khayyāt (Beirut, Éditions les lettres orientales, 1957). Al-Khayyāt wrote his book to defend the Mu'tazilah against allegations of a deserter from the sect. In the 1950s *al-Mughnī,* by an important

Mu'tazilī author, Qāḍī 'Abd al-Jabbār, was discovered in the Yemen; the text has now been published in Cairo. George F. Hourani has translated some portions of the work and analyzed them in *Islamic Rationalism: the Ethics of 'Abd al-Jabbār* (Oxford, Clarendon Press, 1971). There is a specialized study by Richard Frank devoted to the man who is reputed as the founder of Mu'tazilī dogmatics in *The Metaphysics of Created Being according to Abū l-Hudhayl al-'Allāf* (Istanbul, Nederlands Historisch-Archaeologisch Institut, 1966), which can be recommended also for its wide-ranging inquiry into the nature and purposes of the *kalām* generally. Frank also has a fine article on the same man entitled "The Divine Attributes according to the Teaching of Abū al-Hudhayl al-'Allāf," in *Le Muséon,* 82 (1969), 451–506.

The task of introducing material on *kalām* would be incomplete without pointing the reader to some of the original writings of Muslim thinkers. We are fortunate to possess a full translation by Walter Klein of the basic theological work of Abū al-Ḥasan al-Ash'arī, *al-Ibānah 'an uṣūl al-diyānah* (New Haven, American Oriental Society, 1940). al-Ash'arī, who was a Mu'tazilah in his youth, in later age underwent a conversion that transformed him into a spokesman for the traditional position of the community—with the difference, however, that he began to employ a highly developed *kalām* to support and expound his views. Ash'arism, as his position is often called, has affected most subsequent creedal statements of Sunnī Muslims and is the variety of theological position usually referred to when people speak (wrongly) of "orthodox" Islām. A theological treatise in the same tradition which is widely studied in traditional Muslim schools even today is al-Taftazānī's *Commentary on the Creed of Islam* (N.Y., Columbia Univ. Press, 1950), tr. by E.E. Elder. The work is doubly interesting since al-Taftazānī, who lived in the fourteenth century, belonged to a theological school different from that of the man upon whose creed he was commenting. Both this volume and the preceding one cited have introductions of much value for reconstructing the history of religious thought among the Muslims. Some additional works by al-Ash'arī as well as biographical information about him from other Arabic sources are translated by Richard J. MacCarthy in *The Theology of al-Ash'arī* (Beirut, Imprimerie catholique, 1953). There is a biographical study of this key figure in Islamic theological development by W. Spitta, *Zur Geschichte Abu'l-Hasan al-As'arî's* (Leipzig, J.C. Hinrichs, 1876), old but the best available. Mention should also be made of the translation of the *Kitāb nihāyat al-iqdām fī 'ilm al-kalām* of the twelfth-century thinker al-Shahrastānī done by Alfred Guillaume (London, Oxford Univ. Press, 1934). This volume concentrates discussion on a single problem confronting the practitioners of *kalām*—that of the "eternity of the world"—illustrating the refinement and subtlety of the scholastic method employed by these thinkers. A portion of al-Ghazālī's *Brief Treatise on the Creed* (al-Iqtiṣād fī-l-iʿtiqād) is translated by Abdu-r-Rahman Abu Zayd in *Al-Ghazali on Divine Predicates and Their Properties* (Lahore, Sh. Muḥammad Ashraf, 1970). Finally attention may be called to the translations of works in the *kalām* tradition included in Arthur Jeffery, *Reader on Islam* ('s Gravenhage, Mouton, 1962).

VII. *FALSAFAH*

During the era when the Muʿtazilah, using the tools of Hellenistic thought, began to forge their religious system, compelling the traditionists of the community to adopt the same tools for the defense of their views, another group, even more thoroughly Hellenized, made its appearance among the Muslims. They came to be known as philosophers, or *falāsifah*, the very name indicating their close dependence upon the heritage of Hellenistic philosophy (*falsafah*) with which they were widely acquainted through the efforts of a number of translators. These men occupied themselves with the speculative problems of Greek philosophy as presented in the Neo-Platonic commentators on Aristotle and Plato, but in spite of their predominantly Greek mode of thought, they were Muslims, living in a Muslim society as inheritors of the Islamic tradition. The necessity of accommodating these two elements, the Greek and the Islamic, posed the characteristic problem of the Muslim philosophers.

The task of wedding Hellenistic thought and traditional Muslim faith proved far from easy; the philosophers were soon in conflict with the traditionalists of the community. In their own eyes the *falāsifah* were keeping faith with the religion of their ancestors when they endeavored to grasp and express its insights by the use of Greek concepts. Even when the rigor of their thought led them flatly to reject convictions held in the community at large, such as creation *ex nihilo* or the resurrection of the body, they believed their stand to be a truer appropriation of the revelation given through the Prophet than the traditional one. For the majority of the community, however, things appeared otherwise; they could see no clear benefit from the activities of the philosophers and much to make them suspicious. The *falāsifah*, who were never more than a small intellectual élite, were subject to harsh attacks and bitter calumny. In the end the majority Sunnī Muslim community repudiated them; their philosophizing did not become an integral part of the developing common Sunnī religious mind but remained something apart, alien and suspect. Serious philosophical speculation of a Peripatetic or Neo-Platonic variety ceased among Sunnī Muslims in the Western Islamic regions in early medieval times, and for centuries the philosophers' works were ignored in traditional Sunnī schools of religious learning, except as instances of deviation from the way of the "people of tradition and of the community." The last truly great philosopher in the Islamic West was Ibn Rushd (Averroës), the Spanish thinker who died in 1198. In the Islamic East, however, philosophical speculation took a different tack and has continued to flourish down to our own day.

Only in very recent times have the *falāsifah* of the classical Islamic period enjoyed a revival of their fame. Modern Muslims recognize in the philosophers' towering intellects a resource of strength and energy which they wish to appropriate for themselves. At the same time, the philosophers stand as concrete evidence of the Muslim mind's ability to comprehend, digest, and contribute to the most subtle intellectual discussions, while remaining consciously fixed upon its Islamic roots. Much of modern writing about the *falāsifah* ignores the traditional Sunnī rejection of them, but it has served to remind Muslims of the work of the great men of the past.

Although the *falāsifah* have not played a basic role in traditional Sunnī religious thought, they are nevertheless important for the student of the Islamic tradition. The methods and concepts of their speculative philosophy, if not its content, were an important element in molding the *kalām,* and their transmission of Neo-Platonic ideas doubtless affected mystical theology and theory among the Muslims. Furthermore, they constitute a basic link in the transmission of the philosophic thought of antiquity to later times; the medieval philosophers of Europe gained their knowledge of Aristotle through the Arabic language works and translations of the Muslims and shaped much of their thought against the anvil of the massive Muslim philosophical erudition. Most important of all, the early philosophers demonstrate the tenacity of the Islamic ideal for life in the world and its capacity for meeting the challenges posed to it. Properly understood, the *falāsifah* should be seen as defenders and advocates of the Islamic ideal, not as deviators from it. Their historical function was to turn to the service of the Muslims a weapon (Greek thought) that might well have destroyed the very bases of classical and medieval Islamic society.

In the past twenty-five years scholarship has opened new perspectives on the history of philosophical thought in Islam by demonstrating the existence in the eastern Islamic regions, particularly Iran, of a lively tradition of speculation that had previously been ignored, even unknown. The discovery of a coherent, powerful and influential chain of thought stretching down to the twentieth century has forced a re-evaluation of the history of Islamic philosophy. No longer is it possible to hold that philosophical activity died among Muslims in medieval times, and no longer is it tenable to identify "Islamic" philosophy with the Peripatetic and Neo-Platonic tendencies of the classical period, that is, with the Islamic philosophical heritage important for the history of Western thought. Instead, it is now recognized that the same period which witnessed the demise of Ibn Rushd also saw the emergence of a different type of philosophy—albeit one that was still deeply in debt to Greek thought—whose principal figures were Shihāb al-Dīn Yaḥyā Suhrawardī and Muḥīyu al-Dīn ibn al-'Arabī. This philosophy was strongly colored with mysticism, insisting that insight into the nature of reality implies and cannot be achieved without a personal illuminative "vision" of the realms of the spirit. Philosophy of this type had its greatest flowering in Safavid Iran where the towering figure of the age was Mullā Ṣadrā Shīrāzī whose many heirs and disciples sustain the most vigorous philosophical activity to be seen in the Muslim world today.

A. Introductions

The best single sketch of the progress of Muslim philosophy up to medieval times, including the phase of translation of Hellenistic works from Syriac and Greek into Arabic, may be read in T.J. deBoer's *The History of Philosophy in Islam,* tr. E.R. Jones (London, Luzac, 1903; repub. 1961). This book is not a good, or even an adequate, treatment of the subject; it has gained the recommendation given it here by the default of any serious rival. The same ground is covered by R. Walzer in "Islamic Philosophy," in vol. II of *History of Philosophy Eastern and Western* (London, George Allen & Unwin, 1953), reprinted in a volume of Walzer's works that includes other and more detailed studies of the Muslim philosophical heritage: *Greek into Arabic,* Oriental Studies I (Oxford, Bruno Cassirer, 1962). The foundation for understanding the mystical illuminationist philosophy of the eastern Islamic world is laid by Henry Corbin in *Histoire de la philosophie islamique* (Paris, Éditions Gallimard, 1964); unfortunately only one part of a projected three has been published, that one dealing with the period from the origins to the death of Ibn Rushd. One who wishes to follow the history of this "oriental" line of speculation further should consult others of Corbin's numerous writings and text editions. This French scholar, almost alone, is responsible for Western knowledge of post-Averroëan thought in the eastern Islamic lands. Especially important is. his four volume study *En Islam Iranien* (Paris, Éditions Gallimard, 1971–72), the distillation of more than twenty years of pioneering scholarship. Corbin has traced the teachings of the major schools and individuals who have contributed to the tradition of philosophy in Islamic Iran, demonstrating the close relationship among philosophy, mysticism and Twelver Shi'ism. These volumes are now in process of translation into English at McGill University for publication beginning in 1976. The most extensive study of the contribution of Muslim thinkers to scientific ideas is found in the pages of George Sarton's *Introduction to the History of Science,* 4 vols. (Baltimore, Williams and Wilkins, 1927–48). Any of the above books will provide orientation for a reader willing to pursue his inquiries into more specialized works; regrettably, however, an adequate English-language survey of the development of philosophy among Muslims yet remains to be written.

Two specialized studies devoted to the difficulty of reconciling traditional Islām with Greek thought are worthy of special mention. A.J. Arberry takes up this matter, which he calls "the scholastic problem," in *Revelation and Reason in Islam* (London, George Allen & Unwin; N.Y., Macmillan, 1957), ranging beyond the circle of philosophy proper to consider "the scholastic problem" in mystical and theological contexts, as well. The doctrine of prophecy held by the Muslim philosophers is studied by Fazl al-Raḥman in *Prophecy in Islam* (London, George Allen & Unwin, 1958), a sharply focused work that shows how a fundamental Islamic teaching was adapted to the system of the philosophers.

B. Specialized works and translations

The most productive approach to Islamic philosophy lies in the use of specialized studies of individual thinkers and the translations of their work. Many such studies, too numerous to cite, are available in a variety of languages. DeLacy O'Leary's *Arabic Thought and Its Place in History* (London, Routledge & Kegan Paul, 1922) is especially good for its survey of the transmission of Hellenistic thought to the Arabs. On the early philosopher, al-Fārābī, there is an old work by M. Steinschneider, *al-Fārābī, des arabischen Philosophen Leben und Schriften* (St. Petersburg, 1869), and a second study in German by F. Dieterici, *al-Fārābī's philosophische Abhandlungen, aus dem Arabischen übersetzt* (Leiden, 1892). The Egyptian savant, Ibrahim Madkour, has written to describe *La Place d'al-Farabi dans l'école philosophique musulmane* (Paris, Adrien-Maisonneuve, 1934). On Ibn Sīnā, perhaps the most creative mind among the *falāsifah,* there is a wealth of material. His autobiography and some other writings are translated by A.J. Arberry in *Avicenna on Theology* (London, John Murray, 1951). Soheil M. Afnān's study called *Avicenna: His Life and Works* (London, George Allen & Unwin, 1958) sets the great thinker in the historical context of political events and the prevailing intellectual atmosphere. Henry Corbin has studied the esoteric and mystical side of Ibn Sīnā's thought in *Avicenna and the Visionary Recital,* tr. by W. Trask (N.Y., Pantheon Books, 1960), and Louis Gardet has worked to make clear *La Pensée religieuse d'Avicenne (Ibn Sīnā)* (Paris, J. Vrin, 1951). The well-known works of A.M. Goichon illuminate the content of Ibn Sīnā's thought; the more important of them are *Lexique de la langue philosophique d'Ibn Sīnā (Avicenna)* (Paris, Desclée de Brouwer, 1938); *La Philosophie d'Avicenne et son influence en Europe médiévale,* 2nd rev. ed. (Paris, Adrien-Maisonneuve, 1951); and *La Dis-*

tinction de l'essence et de l'existence d'après Ibn Sīnā (Avicenna) (Paris, Desclée de Brouwer, 1937). Bibliographical guidance on this important thinker may be gained from G.C. Anawati, *Essai de bibliographie avicennienne* (Cairo, Arab League, 1950) and Y. Mahdavi, *Bibliographie d'Ibn Sīnā* (Teheran, Univ. of Teheran Publication No. 206, 1954).

The Muslim thinker who has attracted the greatest attention in the West is doubtless al-Ghazālī (d. 1111), though it is the mystical rather than the philosophical facet of his activity that has been of the most interest. The autobiography of this remarkable man—a source of insight into his times as well as his inner life—is available in a beautiful translation by W. Montgomery Watt, *The Faith and Practice of al-Ghazali* (London, George Allen & Unwin, 1953); the same writer has a full-scale study of al-Ghazālī's intellectual and spiritual development in his *Muslim Intellectual* (Edinburgh, University Press, 1963). Al-Ghazālī's chief claim to be considered part of the philosophical tradition of Islām rests upon his famous *Incoherence of the Philosophers,* where he mounts a scathing attack upon these "heretics" of the community, especially Ibn Sīnā and al-Fārābī, for their teachings that the world is eternal, that God cannot know particulars, and that there is no resurrection from the dead. The treatise is available in an excellent translation by Ṣabīḥ Aḥmad Kamālī, *al-Ghazali's Tahafut al-Falasifah* (Lahore, Pakistan Philosophical Congress, 1958). Al-Ghazālī's polemic is also reproduced by Ibn Rushd who penned a reply which he called *The Incoherence of the Incoherence;* it is translated by Simon Van den Bergh, *Averroes' Tahāfut al-Tahāfut* (London, Luzac, 1954).

One of the greatest of Muslim minds, who stands in close relation with the *falāsifah,* if not in their direct line, was the North African, Ibn Khaldūn (d. 1406). Ibn Khaldūn's peculiar concern, sparked by his frustration in active political life, was the application of the principles of philosophy to history in such a way that the meanings of history might become clear. The incomparably best reconstruction of the life, thought, and circumstances of this thinker is Muḥsin Mahdī's *Ibn Khaldūn's Philosophy of History* (London, George Allen & Unwin, 1957). Mahdī has sought to present Ibn Khaldūn according to his own intentions and, thus, to rescue him from the obfuscating effects of contemporary writing that would make him a precursor of modern sociology or a proto-Marxist. Part of the introduction to Ibn Khaldūn's universal history, his major work, has been translated by Franz Rosenthal as *The Muqaddimah,* 3 vols. (London, Routledge & Kegan Paul, 1958).

Readers who wish to carry their study of Muslim philosophical thought further will find value in referring to bibliographies in this field. An extensive bibliography that takes into account secondary works, analyses, and periodical materials as well as primary sources may be had in P.J. de Menasce, *Arabische Philosophie*, Bibliographische Einführungen in das

Studium der Philosophie, no. 6 (Bern, 1948). Somewhat more up-to-date is R. Walzer, "A Survey of Works on Medieval Philosophy, 1945–52. Part I: Medieval Islamic Philosophy," in *Philosophical Quarterly,* 3 (April, 1953), 175–81. The best source for the illuminationist philosophy of the later period is found in the notes and bibliographies of Corbin's many works.

VIII. ISLAMIC INSTITUTIONS

A. *Sharī'ah*

There is no subject more important for the student of Islām than what is usually called Islamic "law." It is widely agreed that one major element in the Islamic commitment—for many it is the predominant one—lies in a practical concern to live according to a divinely ordained pattern made known in the guidance given through the Prophet. Accordingly, Muslims have been vitally interested to work out and systematize rules of conduct that reflect the divine guidance. Historically this concern produced a class of jurists whose business it was to elucidate the implications of the revelation of the *Qur'ān,* the example of Muḥammad, and the practice of the early community. In time their labors resulted not only in systematic compilations of legal rules touching many different spheres of life but also in the emergence of an elaborate structure of jurisprudential theory. Islamic "law" is the creation of the jurists, but it is also an expression of some of the most deeply felt religious instincts of the community and a characteristic Islamic concern.

Even so, there are few facets of Muslim religiosity more difficult to comprehend than the "law." Its study is confused on the one hand by the persistence of a time-hallowed theory about the origin of the "law" that obscures its historical development, and on the other by the failure to evolve a satisfactory methodology for studying the "law." The word "law" itself contributes to the confusion by fostering the concept of a principle laid down and enforced by sovereign authority, usually the state. In the Islamic instance such a concept is not relevant, for Islamic "law" implies no institution, either governmental or ecclesiastical, that can be said to have sovereignty or that is clearly charged with the sanctions of enforcement. With but few exceptions, the rules in Muslim "law" books refer to persons, conceived as individually responsible to God. Furthermore, the scope of the "law" is very wide; it contains rules bearing on spheres of life that are elsewhere considered to fall outside the province of law (such as, for example, religious belief and religious practice and even personal hygiene and dress). An adequate grasp of this mass of diversified rules is extraordinarily difficult to achieve.

For a long time no trustworthy or adequate introduction to Islamic "law" was to be found within the compass of a single volume. This lack has been remedied, however, by the appearance of Joseph Schacht's *An Introduction to Islamic Law* (Oxford, Clarendon Press, 1964), which traces the development of Muslim legal thinking through its various stages. The same field is traversed also by Noel Coulson in his *A History of Islamic Law* (Edinburgh, University Press, 1964). On the whole Coulson's study follows and confirms the earlier pioneering work of Schacht (see below), differing in some details, but is more readable and, perhaps, more appropriate to launch one's study of the "law." Other worthwhile introductory reading materials are Schacht's articles, "Islamic Law," in vol. VIII of *Encyclopaedia of the Social Sciences,* 344–49, and "Sharī'a," in *Shorter Encyclopaedia of Islām,* 524–29. Goldziher's article, "Fiqh," pp. 102–07 of the latter encyclopaedia is also of basic importance.

The late Joseph Schacht was unquestionably the leading student of Islamic law of his generation. His special concern was to uncover the historical processes leading to the view of "law" held by the schools that appeared in the third Islamic century. Once these schools had consolidated their position and articulated a systematic theory of jurisprudence that traced the specific rules of "law" back to certain *uṣūl,* or sources, the tendency among Muslims was to accept the jurisprudential theory as an accurate description of the actual historical formation of the "law". In his *Origins of Muhammedan Jurisprudence* (Oxford, Clarendon Press, 1950), which is the bench-mark of all modern work in this field, Schacht demonstrates that the theory of the "sources of law" is itself the product of historical evolution, especially of the influence of the great jurist, al-Shāfi'ī (d. 820). Schacht also has many other writings on both the history of Islamic "law" and its modern evolution which may be pursued with profit. There are, for example, two of his articles in a large symposium volume, *Law in the Middle East* (Washington, D.C., Middle East Institute, 1955), ed. by M. Khadduri and H. Liebesny.

One of the treatises of al-Shāfi'ī upon which Schacht's work relies heavily is translated by Majid Khadduri in *Islamic Jurisprudence, Shāfi'ī's Risālah* (Baltimore, Johns Hopkins Press, 1961). For those who do not read Arabic it offers one of the few basic works in Islamic "law" to have found its way into an European language.

For insight into the substantive concerns of Islamic "law" and the methods adopted by jurists in approaching them, there is obviously no substitute for firsthand acquaintance with books that Muslims consider authoritative in this area. A variety of manuals of "law" in European languages faithfully reproduce the normative teachings of the Muslim "law" schools in systematic fashion. These books present the "law" from a lawyer's point of view, as it were, giving the detailed rules, with exceptions and special applications, that govern matters such as marriage, inheritance, divorce, and many others. Asaf A.A. Fyzee has prepared such a manual to cover "that portion of the Islamic Civil Law which is applied in India to Muslims as a personal law" in *Outlines of Muhammadan Law*, 2nd ed. (London, Oxford Univ. Press, 1955). One of the oldest manuals of law and perhaps the most widely used is Th.W. Juynboll's *Handbuch des islämischen Gesetzes* (Leiden, E.J. Brill, 1910); its purpose is to present the teachings of the school of al-Shāfiʿī. Comparisons with manuals presenting the teachings of the other three schools that, along with al-Shāfiʿī's, have been recognized as authoritative will enable one to judge the basic agreement as well as the detailed differences among them. The "law" according to the school of Mālik ibn Anas, followed by most Muslims in North Africa, is set out by G.H. Bousquet in his *Précis de droit musulman,* 2 vols., 2nd rev. ed. (Algiers, Maison des Livres, 1950). Henri Laoust, who has done so much otherwise to illuminate the influence of Ahmad ibn Ḥanbal, has also devoted a volume to his school of "law," *Le Précis de droit d'Ibn Qudāma* (Beirut, Institut Français de Damas, 1950). A comprehensive compendium of the "law" as it is interpreted in the school of Abū Ḥanīfah is available in Sir Charles Hamilton's translation of the *Hedaya* of the Central Asian lawyer, al-Marghinānī, 2nd rev. ed. (Lahore, New Book, 1957). Abdul Rahim has attempted to compare the four schools in reasonably brief compass in *The Principles of Muhammadan Jurisprudence* (London, Luzac, 1911). There is a superb piece of comparative work on the problem of inheritance under Islamic "law" by Noel Coulson in *Succession in the Muslim Family* (Cambridge, Cambridge Univ. Press, 1971). Inheritance is the most complicated and difficult matter treated by the classical Islamic jurists. In a masterly survey Coulson has brought together the opinions of the four traditional Sunnī schools and compared these with the changes in the law of inheritance now occurring in the various Muslim lands in response to forces of modernization.

Like every other legal system in history, Islamic "law" has given birth to certain characteristic judicial institutions. There have been several different types of courts in the Muslim world, each with distinctive functions and each presided over by a distinctive type of judge having special qualifications or jurisdiction. The nature of these judicial institutions is treated at length in the magisterial work of Émile Tyan, *Histoire de l'organization judiciaire en pays d'Islam*, 2 vols., 2nd rev. ed. (Leiden, E.J. Brill, 1960), which must be considered the basic writing on the subject. There is a briefer treatment in chapter VII of Reuben Levy's *The Social Structure of Islam*, 2nd rev. ed. (Cambridge, Cambridge Univ. Press, 1957), which contains other material important for understanding the "law." For the nature of judicial institutions in the Ottoman Empire on the eve of modern times, there is an analysis by H.A.R. Gibb and Harold Bowen in part II of vol. I of their *Islamic Society and the West* (London, Oxford

Univ. Press, 1957). A full-scale work on the judicial institutions of the Mughal Empire of India is to be had in M.B. Ahmad, *The Administration of Justice in Medieval India* (Karachi, Manager of Publications, 1951).

With the advent of strong European influence in the Muslim world, there began a tendency to modify, to move away from, or to replace the rules and institutions of traditional Islamic "law." In a number of countries the trend has led to outright displacement of Islamic "law" by systems of jurisprudence based on European models, while in others the traditional "law" was retained only in the area of personal law. The most important student of these new developments is J.N.D. Anderson, who offers a general survey of the modern situation in *Islamic Law in the Modern World* (N.Y., New York Univ. Press, 1959). All of Anderson's writings on this subject cannot be listed, but note should be made of *Islamic Law in Africa* (London, Her Majesty's Stationery Office, 1954); the series, "Recent Developments in Shari'a Law," *The Muslim World,* XL, 4 (1950) to XLII, 4 (1952); and "Law Reform in the Middle East," *International Affairs,* XXXII, 1 (1956), 43–51. A more recent treatment for certain of the Islamic countries appears in *The Law of the Near and Middle East* (Albany, State Univ. of N.Y. Press, 1974), ed. by Herbert Liebesny. For the reaction of Muslim minds to the situation of traditional "law" in the modern world, the *Report of the Marriage and Family Law Commission* appointed by the Government of Pakistan, with a dissenting note by a conservative *'ālim* (Karachi, 1956), offers an interesting practical example. The theoretical issues of adapting the "law" to new situations as they appeared to one of the most acute Muslim intellects of our age are set out in chap. VI of Sir Muḥammad Iqbal's *The Reconstruction of Religious Thought in Islam* (Lahore, Ashraf, rep. 1954).

As a final reference on the "law," attention is called to Coulson's study of some of the problems and polarities exhibited in the development of Islamic "law" in his Haskell Lectures at the University of Chicago published as *Conflicts and Tensions in Islamic Jurisprudence* (Chicago, Univ. of Chicago Press, 1969).

B. The state

Although the primary sources of Islamic "law," the *Qur'ān* and the tradition of the Prophet, do not explicitly detail the constitution of a state, Muslims believe these sources to have teachings relevant for the organization and conduct of society in general. In this field, as in others, they have attempted to work out the implications of basic teachings and so to form a political theory. Characteristically, discussions in this area center upon the caliphate, the institution evolved by the community for its own government after the death of the Prophet. In all Muslim discussion of government and the state, however, there is a certain ambiguity; while some arrangements for a ruling institution are held to be necessary to insure order in the world, there is also a profound suspicion of rulers and association with them. Pious Muslims of many persuasions have concurred in recommending obedience to constituted authority while also warning the faithful against the religious and moral dangers of direct involvement in the affairs of state. S.D. Goitein's article "Attitudes towards Government in Islam and Judaism," in *Studies in Islamic History and Institutions* (Leiden, E.J. Brill, 1966), offers some insights into this tension in Islamic thought.

An excellent brief presentation of the basic concepts in traditional Islamic political thinking is to be had in Sir Hamilton Gibb's article "Constitutional Organization," in *Law in the Middle East (op. cit.)*, pp. 3–27. Louis Gardet has essayed a full-scale treatment of Islamic political philosophy as it is implied in some of the fundamental teachings of Islamic "law" and in the historical practice of the Muslim community. Taking his cue from St. Augustine's *City of God*, he entitles his description of the Islamic ideal *La Cité musulmane, vie sociale et politique* (Paris, J. Vrin, 1954); this book is indispensable for the serious student. Majid Khadduri's investigation of *War and Peace in the Law of Islam* (Baltimore, Johns Hopkins Press, 1955) pushes beyond the narrow limit of its subject to expound the general principles of the ideal Muslim society, its nature and purpose, and its relation with other societies. The book makes wide use of original source materials and has the rare virtue of being written with great clarity of organization and expression. The classic English work on the institution of the caliphate is Sir Thomas Arnold, *The Caliphate* (Oxford, Clarendon Press, 1924). From a Muslim pen comes the lengthy volume of A. Sanhoury, *Le Califat* (Paris, Geuthner, 1926) in which he discusses the central political institution of the early Islamic world according to both theory and practice. Émile Tyan also deals with the caliphate in vol. I of his *Institutions du droit public Musulman,* 2 vols. (Paris, Recueil Sirey, 1954 & 1956).

Perhaps the most important—at all events, the best known—exposition of the caliphate in a classical Islamic source is the book of al-Māwardī (d. 1058), *al-Aḥkām al-sulṭānīyah,* tr. by E. Fagnan as *Les Status gouvernementaux* (Algiers, Adolphe Jourdan, 1915). In some twenty chapters a great variety of questions, ranging from the necessity of there being a leader for the community to the administration of pious bequests and the conduct of the holy war, have been treated in the light of Qur'ānic teaching, prophetic example, and the prior practice of pious men. Al-Māwardī's book was, thus, an attempt to describe a norm for the state sanctioned by religion, and his views are important material for the scholars who have written on the subject. H.A.R. Gibb has supplied some of the historical background for al-Māwardī's book as well as an analysis of it in an essay "al-Mawardi's Theory of the Caliphate" in *Studies on the Civilization of Islam*. A dissenting opinion on al-Māwardī's purpose and significance is argued by Donald P. Little in "A New Look at al-Aḥkām al-Sulṭāniyya," *The Muslim World*, LXIV, 1 (1974), 1–15.

In addition to work of the type of al-Māwardī's, the Muslims have also produced practical manuals of statecraft that reflect the actual problems and conditions of rule rather than the ideal. The best known of its kind was prepared by the famous Saljūq wazīr, Niẓām al-Mulk, for his master the Sulṭān Malikshāh, and translated by Hubert Darke as *The Book of Government, or, Rules for Kings* (London, Routledge & Kegan Paul, 1960). This book may be read both to ascertain the approach to practical problems of one of the most astute and powerful men of his time and as a source of information for the disturbed conditions of life in the 'Abbāsī empire in the years after its flowering. Two other works of the same genre are also available in fine translations. The first is al-Ghazālī's *Book of Counsel for Kings (Naṣīḥat al-Mulūk),* tr. by F.R.C. Bagley (London, Oxford Univ. Press, 1964), and the other *A Mirror for Princes,* The Qābūs Nāma, by Kai Kā'ūs ibn Iskandar, tr. by Reuben Levy (London, Cresset Press, 1951).

Muslims have also given a certain amount of attention to the state from a purely philosophical point of view. Among the early philosophers in the East al-Fārābī is most notable for his concern with the state and may be considered the real originator of philosophical interest in the matter among the Arabs. He was strongly influenced by Plato's *Republic* and devoted several of his writings to the elaboration of very similar views. These may be sampled in English in D.M. Dunlop's translation, *Fuṣūl al-Madanī or Aphorisms of the Statesman* (Cambridge, Cambridge Univ. Press, 1961), and in French in the translations of R.P. Jaussen, Y. Karam, and J. Chlala, *Idées des habitants de la Cité Verueuse* (Cairo, L'Institut français d'archéologie orientale, 1949). The views of the famous al-Ghazālī are analyzed by Henri Laoust in *La Politique d'Gazālī* (Paris, Paul Geuthner, 1970). In the Western Islamic regions the principal thinker in this area was unquestionably Ibn Khaldūn, some guide to whose works is offered above.

We may conclude this section on the state by recommending to the reader an ambitious volume by Erwin I.J. Rosenthal in which the effort is made to survey both the history of "constitutional" thought among Muslims and the progression of philosophical speculation in respect to the state. It is the first conspectus of Muslim political thought on such a large scale and, while less successful than it might be, constitutes an important resource. The volume is called *Political Thought in Medieval Islam* (Cambridge, Cambridge Univ. Press, 1958).

C. Cultus and worship

The overt practices and observances made obligatory for all Muslims are commonly spoken of as the "Pillars of Islām." They are five in number: confession of faith, prayer, alms giving, fasting in the month of Ramadhān, and pilgrimage to the holy shrine at Makkah. Some authorities add a sixth duty to this list, that of participating in the holy war. The detailed rules for performance of these obligations may be read in any standard compendium of Islamic "law." For Western readers there are brief discussions of them in Reuben Levy, *The Social Structure of Islam* (Cambridge, Cambridge Univ. Press, 1957) and Henri Lammens, *Islam, Beliefs and Institutions,* tr. by E. Denison Ross (London, Methuen, 1929). E.E. Calverly describes the daily prayers of Muslims in meticulous detail in his book *Worship in Islam* (London, Luzac, 1945; rev. ed. 1957), which includes a translation of the "Book of Worship" from al-Ghazālī's *magnum opus, The Revivification of the Religious Sciences.* On the pilgrimage there is a full-length volume by Gaudefroy-Demombynes, *Le Pèlerinage à la Mekke* (Paris, Geuthner, 1923) that offers an abundance of historical material about the holy shrine, the *Ka'bah,* as well as minute consideration of the varied rites performed by the pilgrim. As for many other things the most useful source on the pillars is the *Shorter Encyclopaedia of Islām* where the following articles should be consulted: "Ṣalāt," "Zakāt," "Ḥadjdj," "Ṣawm," and "Masdjid."

The overt expressions of religious life in the Muslim community are by no means comprehended in these five pillars, however; Muslims also cherish a variety of other practices, festivals and the like that have great religious value. The devotional formulae and prayers, other than the prescribed ritual prayers, in use in different countries have been collected and presented with great sensitivity by Constance Padwick in her *Muslim Devotions* (London, Society for Promoting Christian Knowledge, 1961). Miss Padwick's book is a convincing refutation of the frequently expressed view that ordinary Muslims lack either a sense of their own sinfulness and creaturehood or an appreciation of the warmth, love, and nearness of God. The more important Muslim festivals are described in the slim volume by G.E. von Grunebaum, *Muhammadan Festivals* (N.Y., Henry Schuman, 1951). The religious perceptions of the greater mass of Muslims, who like ordinary people everywhere know little of the learned tradition of the community, are treated in a variety of works on what may be called "popular religion." Duncan Black MacDonald's *The Religious Attitude and Life in Islam* (Chicago, Univ. of Chicago Press, 1909), which deals with this subject, is one of the fundamental works in the entire field of Islamics and should be read in conjunction with more systematic expressions of Islamic faith in the *kalām* tradition. From the same older generation of scholars there is a similar work of Max Horten called *Die religiöse Gedankenwelt des Volkes im heutigen Islam* (Halle, N. Niemeyer, 1917–18). More recently two folklore specialists, Rudolf Kriss and Hubert Kriss-Heinrich, have done a major study of the Islamic countries around the Mediterranean basin. Their work, called *Volksglaube im Bereich des Islams,* 2 vols. (Wiesbaden, Otto Harrassowitz, 1960 and 1962), treats such matters as pilgrimage, saint worship, oaths, magical formulae, and the use of amulets, especially in the Arab region. E. Dermenghem also illuminates the religion of common people in his study of *Le Culte des saints dans l'Islam maghrébin* (Paris, Gallimard, 1955). A description of the beliefs and rites connected with death in the Arab countries is set out by H. Granqvist in *Muslim Death and Burials* (Helsinki, Societas Scientiarium Fennica, 1965). The popular beliefs and practices discussed in these works are of vital importance for the student who wishes to know how Islām is actually experienced and lived.

IX. THE SHĪ'AH

The Muslims of the world may be divided into two great groups, usually called the *Sunnīs* and the *Shī'ah,* each with a number of subgroups. The term *"Sunnī"* may be translated as "followers of the traditional way or *sunnah* of the community" and clearly has a normative import for those who claim to be *Sunnī. Shī'ah* on the other hand means "partisan," having originated as the name for the supporters of the claims of 'Alī (the cousin and son-in-law of the Prophet) to the leadership of the community after Muḥammad's death. In explanations of the differences between the two groups, the analogy of relations between the Catholic and Protestant branches of Christianity has often been suggested, with Catholics representing the *Sunnīs* and Protestants the *Shī'ah*. The analogy is misleading for a number of reasons, not least because it suggests that the *Shī'ah* were an offshoot from an already firmly established tradition and because it encourages the conception, implicit in the terms themselves, that the *Shī'ah* are heterodox. In fact the *Shī'ah* as a religious group developed out of the same complex and many-faceted situation in the early days of the Muslim community from which the crystallization of beliefs and institutions we call *Sunnī* Islām also emerged. The roots of the *Shī'ah* go as deeply into Muslim history as do those of persons who appropriate the title "the people of tradition and the community," as *Sunnīs* like to style themselves. Furthermore, in a number of respects the *Shī'ah* have influenced and contributed to *Sunnī* Islām profoundly so that the gap between the two is by no means so great as many treatments of the subject would suggest.

One result of considering the *Shī'ah* heterodox has been a relative neglect of their contribution to Islamic history by Western scholars, who for the most part look upon the *Sunnīs* as the main line of Islamic development. Students of Muslim faith, therefore, experience some difficulty in regard to materials bearing on the *Shī'ah,* and in many areas there is nothing available but the original sources in Persian and Arabic. The deficiency is in process of being remedied, but much remains to be done.

The best English introduction to the history, thought, institutions, literature, and other facets of the *Shī'ah* is the book by the long-time missionary to Persia, Dwight M. Donaldson, *The Shī'ite Religion* (London, Luzac, 1933). Donaldson reproduces considerable portions of the traditional material about the lives of the *Shī'ah Imāms* and quotes liberally from accepted *Shī'ah* authorities in his exposition of the central doctrines; the strength of his book lies in the abundance of material rather than in his interpretive efforts. He also gives attention to the great shrines of the *Shī'ah* in 'Irāq and Persia and describes the rites associated with pilgrimages to them. Another missionary, John N. Hollister, has written *The Shi'a of India* (London, Luzac, 1953) in which he gives a history of the group in India and describes the several unique communities of *Shī'ah* origin that have grown up in the subcontinent. Hollister also sketches the origins, history, and characteristics of this large group of Muslims; relative to Donaldson's work his book has the advantage of treating the more radical *Shī'ah* sects as well as the moderate ones. The books of both men have excellent and extensive bibliographies. As an introduction to the religious system of the *Shī'ah,* vol. IV of E.G. Browne's *A Literary History of Persia* (Cambridge, Cambridge Univ. Press, 1951–53), p. 354 ff., can be recommended. This volume and its three companions are to Persian history and literature what Reynold Nicholson's literary history is to the Arabs. Browne was among the greatest of British orientalists, and these indispensable volumes amply exhibit the sensitivity, critical acumen, grace of style, and learning which made him great. There is also an exposition of Shī'ism by one of the most revered religious teachers in present-day Iran, 'Allāmah Sayyid Muḥammad Ḥusayn Ṭabāṭabā'ī; the book offers an authoritative account of *Shī'ah* faith, doctrine, practice, and history as they are seen by an authentic representative of the community's tradition. Entitled *Sh'ite Islam* (Albany, State Univ. of N.Y. Press, 1974), this work was translated by Seyyed Hossein Nasr.

In European languages there is a much greater abundance of useful material on the *Shī'ah* than may be had in English. R. Strothmann's old book, *Die Zwölfer-Schī'a* (Leipzig, Harrassowitz, 1926) is a study of two important *Shī'ah* religious personalities from Mongol times, the famous Naṣīr al-Dīn al-Ṭūsī and Radī al-Dīn Tā'ūsī. Al-Ṭūsī's book on ethics is given a superb translation by G. Michael Wickens, *The Nasirean Ethics* (London, Allen & Unwin, 1964).

Strothmann, who devoted much of his scholarly career to the *Shī'ah* is, perhaps, most notable for his contributions to knowledge of the sect called the Zaydīyah on which he has several works. The theological position of this group, and especially its relation to the views of the Mu'tazilah, are investigated by Wilferd Madelung in his *Der Imām al-Qāsim ibn Ibrāhīm und die Glaubenslehre der Zaiditen* (Berlin, Walter de Gruyter, 1965). In May of 1968 a colloquium was held at the University of Strasbourg where eighteen specialists, including most of the leading scholars of Europe, presented papers. These proceedings are published as *Le Shī'isme imâmite,* ed. by Toufic Fahd (Paris, Presses universitaires de France, 1970); the volume is an excellent means of surveying the present state of scholarship on the *Shī'ah*. There is a readable and straightforward account of the religious aspects of Shī'ism in Alessandro Bausani's *Persia Religiosa* (Milano, "Il Saggiatore," 1959), which recounts the religious history of Iran from the Zoroastrians to the rise of Bahā'ism. By far the most prolific scholar of *Shī'ah* matters, however, is the indefatigable Henry Corbin who has numerous publications in this area. Fortunately, there is an excellent summation of his views in the four volumes of *En Islam Iranien (op. cit.).* Corbin is interested primarily in one aspect of *Shī'ah* experience, its esoteric or illuminative, mystical side, and he tends to neglect other facets of Shi'ism such as, for example, the "law." His work, however, is the most comprehensive and penetrating study of *Shī'ah* esoterism that has been done.

For original statements of *Shī'ah* theology from authoritative writers, there are two short treatises available in translations. One is the well-known book with the curious title *The Eleventh Chapter,* tr. by William Miller, *al-Bābu'l-Hādī 'Ashar* (London, Royal Asiatic Society of Great Britain and Ireland, 1928; rep. 1958). The author of this treatise was 'Allāmah al-Ḥillī, a prominent theologian who lived during the period of Mongol supremacy. The original short statement, almost creedal in form, is accompanied by a commentary. The other writing of the same type is a treatise on religious doctrine by one of the most highly respected of all *Shī'ah* doctors, Ibn Bābawayhī (d. 991). It has been translated by Asaf A.A. Fyzee, *A Shī'ite Creed* (London, Oxford Univ. Press, 1942). The works of both Ibn Bābawayhī and al-Ḥillī reflect the religious position of the moderate branch of the *Shī'ah*, the so-called Twelvers. A similar writing exhibiting the convictions of the radical wing has been translated by W. Ivanow as *Kalami Pir* (Bombay, Islamic Research Association, 1935). Although the date of *Kalami Pir* is late and its authorship impossible to ascertain precisely, it is, nevertheless, an accurate statement of Ismā'īlī theology belonging to the same genre as Ivanow's translation of *A Fatimi Creed* (Bombay, 1936). Quite a different expression of *Shī'ah* faith may be read in James Merrick's translation of vol. II of al-Majlisī's *Ḥayātu-l-Qulūb,* published as *The Life and Religion of Mohammad* (Boston, Phillips, Samson, 1850). One of the bitter charges *Shī'ah* Muslims level against the *Sunnīs* is that of having suppressed or distorted information about the Prophet's preference for ʿAlī, his son-in-law, and, especially, about the specific appointment of ʿAlī as the Prophet's successor. Al-Majlisī gives the story of the Prophet's life as recounted in *Shīʿah* sources and avails himself of every opportunity to put forward the *Shīʿah* case, in many instances citing and refuting recognized *Sunnī* authorities.

The cause of the radical *Shīʿah* has been much better served by scholarship than that of the moderates. No small part of the credit for the advancing state of knowledge in this field goes to the efforts of a single man, the Russian scholar, W. Ivanow. Ivanow has worked diligently to make translations of important Ismāʿīlī writings available and to unravel the incredibly complex and often distorted history of various *Shīʿah* groups. His publications are too numerous to list completely, but we may take note of the following in addition to those already mentioned: *Studies in Early Persian Ismailism* (Bombay, Ismaili Society, 1955); *Brief Survey of the Evolution of Ismailism* (Leiden, E.J. Brill, 1952); *On the Recognition of the Imam* (Bombay, Ismaili Society, 1947); and *Ibn al-Qaddah (The Alleged Founder of Ismailism)*, 2nd rev. ed. (Bombay, Ismaili Society, 1947). The late Marshall G.S. Hodgson also pursued significant studies on the radical *Shīʿah*. His published doctoral dissertation, *The Order of Assassins* ('s Gravenhage, Mouton, 1955) is in a class by itself for mastery of the sources and critical sifting of them. His is also the most authoritative piece on the early history of the Druze, another group having its origin in radical *Shīʿism,* "al-Darazī and Ḥamza in the Origin of the Druze Religion," *Journal of the American Oriental Society,* LXXXII, 1 (1962), 5–20. In a very condensed work that was also originally a doctoral thesis, *The Origins of Ismāʿīlism* (Cambridge, W. Heffer & Sons, 1940), Bernard Lewis has endeavored to distinguish the many strands in the historical background of the Ismāʿīlīs. True to the tradition of British Orientalism, Lewis enumerates his original sources and assesses their value. His work is as useful, therefore, for the orientation to Ismāʿīlī studies it provides as for the conclusions it reaches.

As a parallel development to their tendency to differ from *Sunnī* Islām in theological matters, in authoritative collections of traditions, and so on, the *Shīʿah* have also evolved a jurisprudence and system of "law" peculiarly their own. In basic principle the chief point of difference lies in the authority which the *Shīʿah* ascribe to the *Imāms* or divinely appointed successors to ʿAlī as leaders of the community. In detail the differences are not nearly so great as one might expect, it being readily apparent that *Shīʿah* and *Sunnī* "law" share a common Islamic origin and point of view. There is a manual of *Shīʿah* "law" available in translation by Neil B.E. Baillie, *A Digest of Moohummudan Law,* vol. 2 *Imameea* (Lahore, Premier Book House, 1957). Asaf A.A. Fyzee, because of his own background as both a lawyer and a *Shīʿah,* has evinced particular interest in this subject. Among his articles the following may be noted: "Ismaʿili Law and

Its Founder", *Islamic Culture,* IX (1935), 107–12; and "Qadi an-Nu'man, the Fatimid Jurist and Author", *Journal of the Royal Asiatic Society* (1934), 1–32. In a longer work he has studied *The Isma'ili Law of Wills* (Bombay, 1933).

X. ṢŪFISM

In the experience of the Prophet and in the *Qur'ān* elements of a distinctly mystical nature are to be found. The presence of these elements provided both the ground and much of the material for the early development of a mystical tradition within the Muslim community. In the Islamic context mysticism is usually called Ṣūfism, or *taṣawwuf*, the etymology of the word being traceable to the rough robes of wool (*ṣūf* in Arabic) that were the identifying badges of the mystics. As the name suggests, the first stage of development was marked by ascetic practices, but there soon emerged an active quest for the experiences of intimate closeness to God that are the climax of genuine mysticism. Eventually an elaborate system of mystical thought and theory also came to be articulated.

Within four hundred years of Muḥammad's death the principal features of the Ṣūfī approach to life were clearly established, and from at least the fifth Islamic century, if not earlier, Ṣūfism tended increasingly to occupy the central place in the religious life of the great majority of Muslims. Its hold on the religious consciousness was strengthened precisely in the degree that other expressions of Islamic faith lost vitality. During medieval times there grew up organized mystical brotherhoods or orders, each with a hierarchy of saints who formed its spiritual ancestry and each with a peculiar discipline and ritual form. In many cases, these brotherhoods came into close association with craft and chivalrous organizations and thus served among the fundamentally important formative forces in medieval Islamic society. In the premodern era, however, Ṣūfism began to evidence serious corruption and degeneration that have caused modernist reform movements to adopt a negative attitude toward the mystical aspect of the Islamic heritage.

For something more than five centuries Ṣūfism dominated Muslim religious life, and any effort to trace the many lines in the historical development of Muslim faith must, therefore, give it a major place. Although for the first time since its origins Ṣūfism is on the wane among some classes of Muslims, in thousands of hearts in many different parts of the world the great *Ṣūfī* concerns are yet alive. Particularly among those classes not strongly affected by education of a Western type, religion is suffused with *Ṣūfī* ideas, stories of the *Ṣūfī* saints, pilgrimages to the tombs of saints, and the like. Of such areas as Sindh or the Northwest Frontier of Pākistān, and many others, it is no exaggeration to say that Ṣūfism continues to be, as it has been for centuries, their true religious commitment.

For all of its importance, the history of Ṣūfism was relatively late in being written and still lacks the definitive treatment for which one would hope. Among the early students in the field was the incomparable Goldziher, whose chapter "Asketismus und Ṣūfismus" in his *Vorlesungen über den Islam*, 2nd rev. ed. (Heidelberg, Carl Winter, 1910), established the historical progression from asceticism to mysticism among the early Muslims. The sketch of Ṣūfism that may be recommended as an initiation to the subject is Reynold Nicholson's *The Mystics of Islam* (London, G. Bell & Sons, 1914), which in spite of its age is a work of fundamental importance. There is a brief history of Muslim mysticism by A.J. Arberry in his *Sufism* (London, George Allen & Unwin, 1950). Like Nicholson, who was his teacher, Arberry devoted a major portion of his scholarly career to Ṣūfī studies; this slim volume reflects his wide acquaintance with textual materials and the principal scholarly trends in the field. The work will provide an orientation for the beginning student while at the same time attracting the more advanced scholar to taste its richness of erudition. In 1975 there appeared a full-scale introduction to Ṣūfism by Annemarie Schimmel, her *Mystical Dimensions of Islam* (Chapel Hill, Univ. of North Carolina Press), which is the broadest, most useful and most authoritative general treatment now available. The work is distinguished by its extensive references to Ṣūfī writings, especially poetry, in all of the principal Islamic regions. Its treatment extends to literatures, figures, and movements, such as those of the Indian sub-continent or Afghanistan, which are not covered by other general studies on Ṣūfism. M.M. Anawati and Louis Gardet have also published a major study of Ṣūfism offering a sketch of the historical development in its first part, supplemented by close analysis of Ṣūfī experiences and methods in the remaining three parts: *Mystique musulmane* (Paris, J. Vrin, 1961). One attractive feature of the book is the generous citation and translation of texts in support of its analyses.

The two greatest names in the study of Muslim mysticism are probably those of Reynold Nicholson and Louis Massignon. Both have been unusually productive scholars, and both have responded to the loftier reaches of the Muslim spirit in a fashion that brought personal involvement with the objects of their study. Massignon's principal contribution consists of two works. One is a study of the great personality, al-Ḥusayn ibn Manṣūr al-Ḥallāj, *La passion d'al-Ḥallāj* (Paris, Geuthner 1922); it not only illuminates the spirituality of this commanding figure but touches upon virtually every other aspect of Ṣūfism and, indeed, of the entire religious life of the early Muslim community. Massignon sees al-Ḥallāj as the climax and culmination of the early developments in Muslim spirituality, the crowning figure of the entire Ṣūfī tradition, after whom there was only falling away and decline from the heights attained. The second work, *Essai sur les origines du lexique technique de la mystique musulmane* (Paris, Geuthner, 1922), is a study of the technical vocabulary of the Ṣūfīs, which Massignon holds to be the essential foundation for all scientific work in the field; his view has exerted a decisive influence on the method pursued by later scholars in Europe. From the analysis, which traces the basic terms back to purely Muslim sources, Massignon gained support for his conviction that the origins of Ṣūfism lie within the dynamics of Islam itself; he has argued this point of view strongly against others who have sought Christian, Neo-Platonic, Indian or other roots of the Ṣūfī tradition.

Reynold Nicholson is distinguished both for his analytical studies on the Ṣūfīs and for his superb translations of some of their most compelling writings. It is rare that the mastery of technical scholarship and literary ability are wedded in one man as they were in Nicholson. His principal analytical works are *Studies in Islamic Mysticism* (Cambridge, Cambridge Univ. Press, 1921) and *The Idea of Personality in Ṣūfism* (Cambridge, Cambridge Univ. Press, 1923). The pinnacle of his achievement as a translator was attained in his rendering of the *Mathnawī* (London, Luzac, 1925–40) of Jalāl al-Dīn al-Rūmī, who perhaps deserves to be ranked as the greatest mystical poet of all times. There is a selection of translations of Rūmī's poetry from the *Mathnawī* and other sources in the little volume *Rūmī, Poet and Mystic* (London, George Allen & Unwin, 1950). Of a quite different nature but fundamentally important for the history of Ṣūfism is his translation of the *Kashf al-Maḥjūb of al-Hujwīrī* (d. 1064) (London, Luzac, 1911). Al-Hujwīrī's Persian treatise, which belongs to the period when Ṣūfism had just reached its full development, traces the spiritual ancestry of various Ṣūfī schools and expounds many of the principal Ṣūfī doctrines.

There are, of course, a number of other valuable writings on this attractive subject. Margaret Smith has contributed both a book of selections, *Readings from the Mystics of Islam* (London, Luzac, 1950) and a full-scale study of an early woman mystic, *Rabi'a, Poet and Mystic* (Cambridge, Cambridge Univ. Press, 1928). Her *Studies in Early Mysticism in the Near and Middle East* (N.Y., Macmillan, 1931) is an extended argument for the Christian backgrounds of Ṣūfism. The best presently available study of the Ṣūfī brotherhoods is J. Spencer Trimingham's *The Sufi Orders in Islam* (London, Oxford Univ. Press, 1970), a very broad-ranging inquiry into all aspects of Ṣūfī experience which deserves to be classified among the basic literature in the field. It is packed with information on a neglected aspect of Ṣūfī studies, and offers one of the fullest bibliographies on the subject to be had. Mention should also be made of the extensive bibliography in Annemarie Schimmel's *Mystical Dimensions (op. cit.)*. The French volume *Les Confréries religieuses musulmanes* by O. Depont and X. Coppolani (Algiers, Adolphe Jourdan, 1897) concentrates its attention on the orders of North Africa. One of the brother-hoods prominent in Turkey is subjected to searching probing in John K. Birge's *The Bektashi Order of Dervishes* (London, Luzac, 1937); this order is particularly interesting for its relationship with the Ottoman government, many of whose servants were Bektashis, and the clear dependence upon *Shī'ah* concepts and practices that it exhibits.

There are many studies on individual mystics or mystical writings that might be cited here. These along with text editions constitute the growing edge of *Ṣūfī* studies, providing the indispensable basis on which further more general work may proceed. For example, the most important mo-nistic thinker among the *Ṣūfīs*, Ibn al-'Arabī, who exercised a dominating influence on mystical thought after the fourteenth century, is the subject of several major works. A.E. Affifi has dealt with him in *The Mystical Philosophy of Muḥyid Dīn Ibnul 'Arabī* (Cambridge, Cambridge Univ. Press, 1939). Toshihiko Izutsu offers a refreshingly clear analysis of this difficult mentality in vol. I of his *A Comparative Study of the Key Philo-sophical Concepts in Sufism and Taoism* (Tokyo, Keio Institute of Cul-tural and Linguistic Studies, 1966–67). Henry Corbin has also studied Ibn al-'Arabī at length in *Creative Imagination in the Sufism of Ibn 'Arabi* (London, Routledge & Kegan Paul, 1970); a comparison of this volume with Izutsu's treatment of the same figure is instructive about the influence of a scholar's background and preconceptions on his view of a subject. Other outstanding examples of works of this kind would include books by Hellmut Ritter and Fritz Meier. Ritter has carried out a penetrating study of the Persian mystical poet Farīd al-Dīn al-'Aṭṭār in his *Das Meer der Seele* (Leiden, E.J. Brill, 1955), while Meier has studied Najm al-Dīn Kubrā in *Die fawā'ih al-ğamāl wa fawātiḥ al-ğalāl des Naǧmuddīn al-Kubrā* (Wiesbaden, Franz Steiner, 1957). Some insight into the contem-porary reality of *Ṣūfī* experience is afforded in the pages of Martin Ling's *A Moslem Saint of the Twentieth Century* (London, Allen & Unwin, 1961).

The great Muslims mystics, like similarly minded men of other traditions, have held that true knowledge of the mystic verity may be gained only by him who joins in the quest for union with God, who oversteps mere intellectual contemplation to a direct experience or taste (*dhawq*) of the divine nature. Those who view the mystics from the outside can, perhaps, hope for no more than a distant and indistinct hint of the ineffable ex-perience which is the goal of the *Ṣūfī's* quest. Surely, however, the best source for the earnest student who wishes to understand the *Ṣūfīs* is the *Ṣūfīs'* own descriptions of the way and its goal. There are many transla-tions of *Ṣūfī* writings, some already mentioned, and the number grows with each year. For example, in addition to translations of Persian mystical poetry already cited, there are *Selected Poems from the Divān-i Shams i Tabrīz* (Cambridge, Cambridge Univ. Press, 1952) and *Tales of Mystic*

Meaning (N.Y., Frederick A. Stokes, 1931), both rendered by Reynold Nicholson and both presenting the works of Jalāl al-Dīn al-Rūmī. A.J. Arberry has added to the literature of Rūmī in English with his *Tales from the Masnavi* (London, George Allen & Unwin, 1961) and *Discourses of Rūmī* (London, John Murray, 1961). The same team of scholars, teacher and student, who are largely responsible for the British tradition of *Ṣūfī* studies, have given similar service for other greats of the mystical tradition. Nicholson has translated a collection of mystical odes with commentary from the most difficult of *Ṣūfī* masters, Ibn al-ʿArabī, *The Tarjumān al-Ashwāq* (London, Royal Asiatic Society, 1911). From Arberry's pen comes *The Poem of the Way* (London, Emery Walker, 1952) of Ibn al-Fāriḍ, whose mystical longings, in company with those of many others, centered on the figure of the Prophet. His translations of a book by Abū Bakr al-Kalābadhī, *The Doctrine of The Ṣūfīs* (Cambridge, Cambridge Univ. Press, 1935) and of works by al-Niffarī, *The Mawāqif and Mukhātabāt of Muḥammad ibn ʿAbdi'l-Jabbār al-Niffarī* (London, Luzac, 1935) are important contributions to the knowledge of *Ṣūfī* theology. Arberry has also provided an example of *Ṣūfī* hagiographical literature in a translation of episodes from the famous *Tadhkirat al-Awliyāʾ* of Farīd al-Dīn al-ʿAṭṭār under the title *Muslim Saints and Mystics* (London, Routledge & Kegan Paul, 1966).

The Muslim saint who is usually given credit for having reconciled the concerns of the mystics with the tenets of *Sunnī* Islām and for having won acceptance of *Ṣūfism* by the community at large is the great al-Ghazālī. The flavor of his mystical thought may be experienced in a little book taking its title from a famous verse in the *Qurʾān, Mishkāt al-Anwār,* tr. by W.H.T. Gairdner (London, Royal Asiatic Society, 1924).

As a final source from the abundant literature on Ṣūfism, the small book by Margaret Smith, *The Ṣūfī Path of Love* (London, Luzac, 1954) may be strongly recommended. This anthology draws its materials both from the *Ṣūfīs* themselves and from their many interpreters. In six chapters, made up of an elaborate fabric of quotations, it traces the nature of Ṣūfism and the principal doctrines of its devotees. The bibliography and acknowledgments are a guide to the treasurehouse of *Ṣūfī* materials in English.

XI. THE MODERN PERIOD

As demanding as the study of the historical development of a religious community may be, the task of assessing what is happening to it in the living present is infinitely more difficult. The student must attempt to understand forces and actions whose consequences have not yet been worked out fully and to come to terms with constantly changing situations.

Men are too much involved in the historical stream of their own times to be able to view it easily from a detached and comprehensive perspective. It should not be surprising, therefore, that there are few among the numerous publications on the modern period that contribute substantially and profoundly to understanding the contemporary Muslim mind. Yet there is no more vital aspect of Islamic studies than the effort to chart the spiritual currents flowing in Muslim hearts; the effort is as important for the Western peoples, whose lives daily become more closely linked with those of Muslims, as for the Muslims themselves. If it be at all true that the future of the human race depends upon the ability of men of different cultures, faiths, and nations to learn to live in accord, the attempt to comprehend the spiritual travail of the modern Muslim community is one of the urgent enterprises of our time.

The place to begin one's reading on the modern Islamic period is H.A.R. Gibb's *Modern Trends in Islam* (Chicago, Univ. of Chicago Press, 1947); the book is a gem of succinct and lucid analysis. Its great virtue is exhibited in the author's ability to set the central concerns of Islamic modernism against the background of the entire historical tradition of Islamic thought and experience. Gibb was the leading English-speaking Arabist of his generation, and he employed his vast knowledge to elucidate the tensions of Muslim religious thought in the modern age, the efforts to resolve these tensions, and the successes and failures attained. In tribute one writer professes himself to consider all subsequent studies of the subject as mere "footnotes" to Gibb's masterly analysis.

A second fundamental general study of modern Islamic developments is Wilfred Cantwell Smith's *Islam in Modern History* (Princeton, Princeton Univ. Press, 1957). Smith's work is characterized by his keen sense of personal involvement with Muslims and his awareness of a moral obligation to speak of Islām in a fashion that is both scholarly and acceptable to the sensitive Muslim mind. The book is, therefore, as much an effort to enter into discussion with Muslims about their situation in the modern world as it is an attempt to inform outsiders of the nature of that situation. *Islam in Modern History* is somewhat broader in scope and more detailed than Gibb's compact work since it treats areas with which Gibb did not deal.

One of the most fruitful ways of approaching modern Islamic developments lies in studying specific Muslim countries or groups; the cause of scholarship has been better served with respect to specialized works than with respect to more general ones. On Turkey, for example, there is the two-part study of H.A.R. Gibb and Harold Bowen, *Islamic Society and the West,* vol. I (London, Oxford Univ. Press, Part I, 1950; Part II, 1957), which systematically describes Turkish society (including the Arab provinces) in the eighteenth century as a foundation for assessing Western impact on the society. The importance of sketching carefully the background against which modern developments have occurred is undeniable, and it is unfortunate that the work of Gibb and Bowen was abandoned after the appearance of only one of several projected volumes. Among the best work now available on Turkey is *The Emergence of Modern Turkey* by Bernard Lewis (London, Oxford Univ. Press, 1961). More limited in scope but distinguished for its penetrating insight is *The Genesis of Young Ottoman Thought* by Şerif Mardin (Princeton, Princeton Univ. Press, 1962). The most ambitious and successful study of modern Turkish trends yet achieved is Niyazi Berkes, *The Development of Secularism in Turkey* (Montreal, McGill Univ. Press, 1964). Written from the perspective of one personally involved with the events he describes, yet with consummate scholarship and knowledge of things Turkish, the book is a classic in its field.

For the background to the modern period in the Arab countries there is the remarkable memoir of Edward Lane, *Manners and Customs of the Modern Egyptians* (in many editions, e.g., London, Dent; N.Y., Dutton, 1954), a delightful as well as a useful book. Lane was an engineer who lived in Egypt during the early part of the nineteenth century; he both wrote about his experiences there and used his considerable drafting ability to illustrate what he saw. More relevant to modern stirrings is George Antonius' *The Arab Awakening* (London, Hamish Hamilton, 1938, and several reprints), a book that is famous. Antonius was concerned with the political struggle of the Arabs to free themselves from the Turks and later from the encroachments of European imperialism, but he also sketches the intellectual ferment and the effect of new forces released in Arab society from the latter part of the nineteenth century onward. On the religious side, the most profound and best-informed study of Muslim modernism among the Arabs is Charles C. Adams, *Islam and Modernism in Egypt* (London, Oxford Univ. Press, 1933). Adams devotes the major portion of his attention to the work of two men, Jamāl al-Dīn al-Afghānī and Muḥammad 'Abduh, and the movements which they inspired. Both men are looked upon throughout the Muslim world as heroes of recent history, and their influence, especially that of 'Abduh, has been enormous. There is a detailed study of the religious opinions held among the disciples of 'Abduh in J. Jomier's *Le Commentaire coranique du Manār*, mentioned above. Undoubtedly the most admired work on the modern Arabs is *Arabic Thought in the Liberal Age, 1798–1939* by Albert Hourani (London, Oxford Univ. Press, 1962). Hourani studies the modern intellectual development of the Arabs, including Christians as well as Muslims, but he has at many points to deal with the modern Arab's understanding of Islām. The book is learned and perceptive, presents its material in a lively, engaging style, and is altogether the best summation of Arab thought in recent times to be had. A somewhat similar study with many of the same virtues, but dealing with only one country, is Nadav Safran's *Egypt in Search of Political Community* (Cambridge, Harvard Univ. Press, 1961).

The serious study of the recent religious history of Muslim India was begun by Wilfred Cantwell Smith's *Modern Islam in India* (London, Victor Gollancz, 1946). The volume is a vigorous and uncompromising Marxist analysis of movements and trends in the subcontinent from the latter third of the nineteenth century until the eve of Partition. Although Smith's enthusiasm for Marxism led him to some excesses, he assembled an unequalled body of information on modern Indian Islām. Until recently his book was the only serious connected account of modern developments in India in the English language; it has provoked responses and criticisms too numerous to mention. More recently, Muslims in the subcontinent have turned to writing the history of their own community, largely under the stimulus of the political controversies that brought about Partition. The book by Ishtiaq Husayn Qurayshi, *The Muslim Community of the Indo-Pakistan Subcontinent (610–1947)* ('s Gravenhage, Mouton, 1962) is a scholarly and serious attempt to present the history of Muslim India in a way that justifies the existence of Pakistan. An Indian view of the same history is set out in Muḥammad Mujīb, *The Indian Muslims* (Montreal, McGill Univ. Press, 1967), which is perhaps the most rewarding study of the community in the subcontinent ever to have been penned. Although it amounts to an *apologia* by a Muslim who preferred remaining in India after the separation of Pakistan, the book is not partisan and offers some penetrating insights into the earlier history of the Muslims. Another scholar of exceptional sensitivity and ability, as well as productivity, is 'Azīz Aḥmad who has many writings on Muslim India. His views of the principal elements in the modern situation are summed up in *Islamic Modernism in India and Pakistan* (London, Oxford Univ. Press, 1967).

Although Indonesia is the largest Muslim country of the world in terms of population, there has been a dearth of English literature dealing with Islām in the island republic. The situation is now improving, but the Dutch language continues to be of great importance for students of Indonesian affairs, especially for work in history. The quality of scholarly work pursued by Dutch professors and colonial officials may be seen in the famous volumes, *The Achenese,* tr. by A.W.S. O'Sullivan (Leiden, E.J. Brill, 1906), by C. Snouck Hurgronje, one of the fathers of Islamic studies as they are known today. On modern developments in Indonesia there are several works that may be recommended. There is a broad treatment of the numerous religious and related political movements of the country in a most valuable book by Deliar Noer, *The Modernist Muslim Movement in Indonesia,* 1900–1942 (Singapore, Oxford Univ. Press, 1937). One of these movements is given a very careful and detailed consideration by Howard M. Federspiel in his *Persatuan Islam* (Ithaca, Modern Indonesia

Project, 1970). Much attention has also been focussed on the Japanese occupation of the Indonesian Islands and the policy which the conquerors pursued in relation to Islamic groups there. Harry J. Benda has a book, *The Crescent and the Rising Sun* (The Hague, van Hoeve, 1958); and C.A.O. van Nieuwenhuijze also treats the subject in *Aspects of Islam in Post-Colonial Indonesia* (The Hague, van Hoeve, 1958). In order to fulfill their purposes both authors found it necessary to trace trends and tendencies in Indonesian Islām during the colonial period, and the latter went on to treat the more important concepts and movements of the post-war period. In another work the late Professor Benda has essayed a more comprehensive picture of Islamic development in Indonesia. The work in question is his *Continuity and Change in Indonesian Islam* (New Haven, Yale Univ. Press, 1965). Of quite a different type is Clifford Geertz's detailed study of religion in a village in Java in all its facets, those that are clearly Muslim as well as those that are not. This ethnographical study, *The Religion of Java* (Glencoe, Free Press, 1960), gives a picture of the meaning of their Islamic faith for one group of villagers. Also to be highly recommended is Geertz' slim volume of lectures, *Islam Observed* (Chicago, Univ. of Chicago Press, 1971), where a most imaginative effort is made to compare the spirit or ethos of Islām in Indonesia with that of Morocco. The book illustrates in dramatic and admirable fashion the colors which Islamic commitment may assume under the influence of the varying cultural environments where it has taken root.

The best source for knowledge of contemporary Muslim thought is undoubtedly, as in all other fields, the writings of Muslims themselves. Several influential works are readily available, and their perusal will afford the reader a glimpse into the workings of the modern Muslim mind. The most important of Muhammad 'Abduh's treatises, in which all the major emphases of his thought emerge, has been translated by B. Michel and Moustapha Abdel Razik as *Rissalat al Tawhid, Exposé de la religion musulmane* (Paris, Geuthner, 1925). This small book is one of the formative documents for the modernist Muslim mentality and deserves the closest study. A collection of essays of the Turkish sociologist, Ziya Gökalp, whose ideas played an important role in the emergence of modern Turkey and the accommodation of "Turkish Culture, Islam and contemporary civilization" has been translated by Niyazi Berkes as *Turkish Nationalism and Western Civilization* (London, George Allen & Unwin, 1959). The most engaging and able exposition of the modernist understanding of Islamic faith is a lengthy book by Muhammad 'Alī called *The Religion of Islam* (Lahore, Ahmadiyyah Anjuman Ishā'at Islam, 1950). Muhammad 'Alī himself was a member of the dissident Aḥmadīyah sect, but the interpretation of Islamic faith he presents is all but universal among the educated and Westernized classes of Muslims both in his native India and elsewhere. The best known and most widely read expression of modernism in English is probably Sayyid Amīr 'Alī's *The Spirit of Islam,* mentioned above in connection with the Prophet.

Among the many attempts to study the meaning of Islamic faith in the twentieth century one of the intellectually most impressive is Sir Muḥammad Iqbāl, *The Reconstruction of Religious Thought in Islam* (Lahore, Ashraf, 1951). Iqbāl was foremost among contemporary Muslims in his grasp of the significance of recent developments in philosophy and scientific thought, and he was almost alone in having appreciated the radical necessity these developments pose for rethinking the very foundations of religious knowledge. The famous six lectures are thus essays in philosophy of religion, a field of thought that, for all its importance, has produced little of value in the Muslim community of this century.

In more recent times French-trained North African intellectuals have taken up this task of re-interpreting Islam to the modern age on a profound level. Of special importance are the philosopher, Muḥammad 'Azīz Laḥbābī, whose views are best perused in his *Le Personnalisme musulmane* (Paris, Presses universitaires de France, 1967) and the Marxist thinker, 'Abdallāh al-'Arwī (Laroui) who argues vigorously for a re-interpretation of the Islamic philosophy of history in *La Crise des intellectuels arabes; traditionalisme ou historicisme?* (Paris, Maspero, 1974).

FOR TEACHERS

It remains now only to offer suggestions about materials that may be given to beginning students for the study of Islām.

By far the most successful single volume introduction to the Muslim tradition is H.A.R. Gibb, *Mohammedanism* (N.Y. & London, 1949; rep. 1950); it is superior to its competitors in virtually every respect: in the material it comprehends, in the skillfully woven interpretation of Islamic development it offers, and in the clear, elegant style that makes it a joy to read. By emphasizing historical development, the book avoids mere narrative or description, offering something to both the beginner and the more advanced student. The latter especially will perceive more of depth and insight with each rereading of its pages. In 1955 this splendid volume was reprinted by the New American Library of New York in an inexpensive paperback edition.

To set the background for the study of Islām, the teacher may find it useful to put into student hands a broader range of materials than those dealing only with religion. For a general survey of the Middle East, the heartland of Islām, and a description of geography and society in the area there is nothing to excel Carleton Coon's *Caravan* (N.Y., Holt, 1951) which is both readable and authoritative. A variety of atlases are available providing the key to much information on the Islamic world through maps. Among older atlases R. Roolvink, *Historical Atlas of the Muslim Peoples* (Amsterdam, 1957) and Harry W. Hazard, *Atlas of Islamic History,* 2nd rev. ed. (Princeton, Princeton Univ. Press, 1952) are both worthy of mention. In 1974 a lavishly produced and most attractive *Historical Atlas of the Religions of the World,* ed. by I.R. al-Fārūqī and David E. Sopher made its appearance (N.Y. & London, Macmillan); it combines text with maps and should prove to have wide use in the teaching of comparative religions.

For the study of Islamic history and an introduction to Islamic civilization on a broad scale there are also excellent studies. Perhaps the most useful and readable for the period up to 1100 A.D. is F.E. Peter's *Allāh's Commonwealth,* mentioned previously. This book is especially good as a supplementary source for a course in religion because of its special concern with the development of Islamic thought and the author's ability for clear exposition. For the later period G.E. von Grunebaum's *Mediaeval Islam* (Chicago, Univ. of Chicago Press, 1953, and rep.) can be highly recommended. This is a superb work of scholarship, erudite and profound but beautifully and clearly written. No finer or more polished portrayal of medieval Muslim society exists in any European language. The most far-reaching and impressive effort to set out the major themes and the development of Islamic culture in a single work, including the pre-modern and modern periods, is the three posthumous volumes of Marshall G.S. Hodgson, *The Venture of Islam* (N.Y. & London, Univ. of Chicago Press, 1974). These volumes are not easy reading even for the established scholar, but they offer an integrated attempt to interpret Islamic culture based upon massive learning. Hodgson was the finest native born North American scholar of his generation to work in the Islamics field, and his untimely death at age 48 was an unmitigated tragedy for all who are concerned with Islamics.

One of the best types of literature for student use is the anthology that allows the Islamic tradition to speak for itself, and several good books of this kind, giving representative pieces of Muslim writing, are available. One of the best of these is *The Islamic World,* ed. by Wm. H. McNeill and Marilyn R. Waldman (N.Y., Oxford Univ. Press, 1973). This book like that of John A. Williams, ed., *Islam* (N.Y., George Braziller, 1961, and rep.), combines a carefully chosen cross-section of readings, religious and otherwise, with short introductions to the selections. Williams has a similar volume, more substantial in content, called *Themes of Islamic Civilization* (Berkeley, Univ. of California Press, 1971). The late Arthur Jeffery, ed., did two works of this kind: *Islam, Muhammad and his Religion* (N.Y., Liberal Arts Press, 1958) and *A Reader on Islam* ('s Gravenhage, Mouton, 1962); the latter is the most ambitious such effort in English and is especially useful for more serious students of religion. The anthology that may lay claim to the prize for attractiveness is *Muhammad's People,* ed. by Eric Schroeder (Portland, Bond Wheelwright, 1955), in which a wide range of abstracts from the Arabic literature of the first five Islamic centuries is translated and combined in mosaic fashion. Religious writings are included, but the collection also comprehends history, poetry, literature, even finance, to give a picture of Islamic life that is at once authentic and captivating.

No mention has been made in this essay of works on Islamic art, though the subject is one of great importance and fascination. Only one book may be mentioned, but it is an extraordinary work of authoritative scholarship as well as great beauty. The reference is to *The World of Islam* by Ernst J. Grube (London, Paul Hamlyn, 1966) which contains 105 color photographs and many others in monochrome depicting the masterpieces of Islamic art. No teacher could do more to enliven the imagination of students than to acquaint them with this superbly produced book.

The last book we shall recommend is one prepared especially with the needs of students in mind. It is Kenneth Morgan, ed., *Islam—The Straight Path* (N.Y., Ronald Press, 1958). The essays in this volume were all written by eminent Muslim scholars under Professor Morgan's able guidance. While the work is not altogether successful, it represents an earnest effort by men thoroughly versed in things Islamic to lay bare for the Western student the spiritual tradition that has nourished them.

APPENDIX

I. Reference books

The indispensable reference source for the student of Islām is *The Encyclopaedia of Islām,* ed. by M. Th. Houtsma et al. (Leiden, E.J. Brill, 1913–38), four volumes and a Supplement. The *Encyclopaedia* has articles on a wide variety of subjects, all pitched at the highest of scholarly standards, and all written by specialists with particular qualifications for the work undertaken. At the time of its publication the *Encyclopaedia* was, in effect, a compendium of the state of Western knowledge about the Islamic world. Among its numerous virtues is the inclusion of a bibliography at the end of each article citing the most significant literature on the subject discussed. These bibliographies not only survey the European literature of relevance but give, as well, the principal primary and secondary works in Oriental languages. Their value to a serious student can scarcely be overstated.

The *Encyclopaedia* is currently in process of revision and republication under the title *The Encyclopaedia of Islām, New Edition,* ed. by H.A.R. Gibb and J.H. Kramers et al. (Leiden, E.J. Brill, 1960–   ). To date the first three volumes and several fascicules of vol. IV have appeared; new fascicules continue to appear at a slow rate. When completed, the *New Edition* will not only have been revised to reflect the current state of knowledge more truly but will have been considerably expanded to include a number of subjects not treated in the original edition.

During preparations for launching the *New Edition* its editors brought out a shorter work that includes only articles having to do with religion, many of which are revised and enlarged versions of articles in the original edition. This volume is called *Shorter Encyclopaedia of Islām*, ed. by H.A.R. Gibb and J.H. Kramers et al. (Leiden, E.J. Brill, 1953). Persons without a knowledge of Arabic may sometimes find this work and the other editions of the *Encyclopaedia* somewhat difficult to use in pursuing a particular topic because the titles of articles are often given in the appropriate Arabic word. The article on the mosque, for example, will be found under its Arabic term, *Masdjid*. The difficulty is minor, however, when measured against the enormous usefulness of these various versions of the *Encyclopaedia*.

Older in date and on a much smaller scale, but still useful, is Thomas Patrick Hughes, *A Dictionary of Islam* (London, W.H. Allen, 1895). Like the *Encyclopaedia*, this volume has articles on a variety of subjects that concern the Muslim's faith, but the articles are shorter, and far fewer subjects are covered.

II. Periodicals

The following is a select list of periodicals devoted in whole or in part to articles on aspects of Islām.

Arabica
Ars Islamica
IBLA, Institute des belles lettres arabes
International Journal of Middle Eastern Studies   (IJMES)
Der Islām
Islamic Culture   (IC)
Islamic Quarterly   (IQ)
Journal of the American Oriental Society   (JAOS)
Journal of Near Eastern Studies   (JNES)   Formerly *American Journal of Semitic Languages and Literatures.*
Journal of the Royal Asiatic Society   (JRAS)
Middle Eastern Affairs   (MEA)
Middle East Journal   (MEJ)   This journal has a monthly survey of periodical literature that is particularly useful for keeping abreast of current work.
Muslim World   (MW)   Formerly *Moslem World.*   The pages of this journal from its inception to date constitute the best single source for modern developments in all of the Muslim world.
Numen
Oriente Moderno   (OM)   One of the useful features of this Italian journal is its full chronology of events in the Near and Middle East. It is often a convenient way for following a development through its various stages day by day.
Revue des études islamiques   (REI)
Revue de l'histoire des religions   (RHR)
Rivista degli studi orientali   (RSO)
Studia Islamica   (SI)
Die Welt des Islams   (IW)

III. Bibliographical aids

Islamicists enjoy a considerable advantage over their colleagues in other fields in the possession of a tool that opens the rich periodical literature on their subject to them: *Index Islamicus 1906–1955,* compiled by J.D. Pearson and Julia F. Ashton (Cambridge, W. Heffer & Sons, 1958; rep., 1961), together with four supplements that advance the coverage through 1974. A fifth supplement that will combine the four previous ones with new material is in process of preparation. This magnificent piece of work, directed by the Librarian of the School of Oriental and African Studies in London, catalogues periodical articles and some other materials under subject headings. *Index Islamicus 1906–1955* gives a complete cataloguing of articles pertaining to Islām in 510 European-language periodicals, 120 Festschriften, and 70 proceedings of congresses and other bodies. The supplements enlarge the scope to take in publications omitted from the first volume in addition to bringing the catalogue up to date. There are doubtless omissions in the list of periodicals surveyed, but the student with these volumes at his disposal may survey the vast bulk of periodical literature on a given subject at a glance. Supplements to *Index Islamicus* will continue to be issued from time to time. The compilers have also brought a similar index of periodical materials in Arabic to an advanced stage of preparation and have projected plans for similar indices of materials in Persian and Urdu.

There are two important surveys of Arabic language materials pertinent to the study of Islām; both are mines of bio-bibliographical information. The first is Carl Brockelmann, *Geschichte der arabischen Litteratur,* best known in its 2nd rev. ed. (Leiden, E.J. Brill), vol. I published in 1943 and vol. II in 1949. There are also three supplements to the original edition, published in 1937, 1938, and 1942 respectively. Brockelmann's *GAL* is the basic reference work on Arabic literature of all kinds. Originally begun as a project to correct and repair the omissions in *GAL, Die Geschichte des arabischen Schrifttums,* 4 vols. (Leiden, E.J. Brill, 1967–74), by Fuat Sezgin has become an original work in its own right that supplements and partially replaces Brockelmann. Both are fundamental reference materials.

There are also available several excellent bibliographies of Islamic studies. The best guide to the history of Islām is Jean Sauvaget's *Introduction to the History of the Muslim East,* rev. by Claude Cahen (Berkeley & Los Angeles, Univ. of California Press, 1965). The most up-to-date major bibliography available is *Middle East and Islam,* ed. by Derek Hopwood and Diana Grimwood-Jones (Zug & London, Inter Documentation, 1972). The old work of Giuseppe Gabrieli, *Manuale di Bibliografia Musulmana* (Rome, 1916), is still most useful for its guidance in nineteenth-century literature and its meticulous attention to detail; reportedly it is to be republished in revised form. C.L. Geddes has prepared *An Analytical Guide to the Bibliographies on Islam, Muhammad, and the Qur'ān* (Denver, American Institute of Islamic Studies, 1973). The last resource to be mentioned is the major project sponsored by the Council for Intercultural Studies and Programs of the University of the State of New York/State Education Department. The project, which is nearing consummation, will result in a volume to be entitled *Resources for the Study of Asian Philosophies and Religions*; it will include an extensive and carefully annotated bibliography, "Guide to Islamic Religion," ed. by David Ede.

Appendix

The History of the History
of Religions

Charles H. Long

The following words are found at the beginning of Joachim Wach's post-humous work, *The Comparative Study of Religions* (N.Y., Columbia Univ. Press, 1958):

> This present century will not come to an end without having seen the establishment of a unified science whose elements are still dispersed, a science which the preceding centuries did not have, which is not yet even defined, and which perhaps for the first time, will be named science of religion.

This quotation is taken from Eugène Burnouf's, *La Science des religions* (Paris, 3rd ed., 1870). Behind this statement lies a long pre- and proto-history of the study of religions in the Western world. The prehistory extends from the classical Greeks through the periods of Western Christendom and its theologians to the Enlightenment. The Enlightenment forms the watershed; the protohistory dates from the Enlightenment until the late nineteenth century when the discipline of the History of Religions appears.

The classical period was concerned with the problem of myth and the fabulations of the poets. What status ought one to assign to these utterances? Plato designated the myth as *pseudos,* a lie, and in Xenophanes we observe a critique of Homer and Hesiod. Positions such as these, as well as those of Prodicus, Epicurus and Aristotle form one of the bases for the Western critique of religion and myth, and thus one is not surprised to see these critiques occurring again and again in the course of Western history.

The early Christian theologians, both the Greek and Latin Fathers, used their knowledge of pagan religions to refute and criticize these religions from the point of view of the Christian revelation. They were equally on guard against the syncretism of pagan with Christian notions and practices. The early Church, though directly concerned with a doctrine of God and the praxis of the Christian community, was aware that syncretism might well occur through linguistic and ritual forms of behavior. See Hugo Rahner's suggestive work, *Greek Myth and Christian Mystery* (N.Y., Harper & Row, 1963). Given the geographical context of early Christianity, the lands of its expansion, the culture of classical Greece, situated as they were around the Mediterranean Sea, one would expect many and varied relationships among the religions and cultures of this area over time. We thus find a discussion of Manichaeism in Augustine's *Confessions,* while St. Thomas' *Summa* presupposes a background of ancient Greek philosophy translated by Muslims and taken over by medieval Christians. See De Lacy O'Leary's, *Arabic Thought and Its Place in History* (London, Routledge & Kegan Paul, 1958).

The two situations most evocative of theories on the nature of religion have been those where rival religious systems confronted one another directly and those of crisis and breakdown within an established religious community. As an example of the first, one might cite the encounter of Christianity with Hellenistic religions in the early years of its history or its struggle with Islam in medieval times. The second type is exemplified in the radical reexamination of basic Christian theological themes after the Cartesian revolution in philosophy and the rise of rationalism in Europe. Though the motives of the explanations of religion that grew out of such situations, as well as their modes of conception, were theological and polemical, nevertheless, these explanations constitute rudimentary theories of the origin and nature of religion. Theories of this type clearly are not, however, the real ancestors of the "history of religions," for they fall very short of the ideal of disinterested scientific observation. They may be called prescientific theories and therefore we have designated them as prehistoric in their relationship to the discipline. Properly, they belong to the history of religious apologetics within whatever tradition they may be developed and not to the history, in the strict sense, of the scientific study of religions.

The most thorough treatment of this period in relationship to the development of the history of religions as a discipline is to be found in H. Pinard de la Boullaye's *L'Étude comparée des religions,* 2 vols. (Paris, Gabriel Beauchesne, 1929). The discussion of the very early period is

contained in volume one entitled, *Son histoire dans le monde occidental.*
For a similar study of the history and understanding of myth and mythology see Jan de Vries' *Forschungsgechichte der Mythologie* (Freiburg/
München, Karl Aber, 1961). De Vries has also written an excellent com-
pact history of the history of religions, *The Study of Religion, A Historical
Approach* (N.Y., Harcourt Brace & World, 1967). The most exhaustive
study in English, rivalling Boullaye's work, but omitting the Greek and
Christian theological orientations, is Jacques Waardenburg, *Classical Approaches to the Study of Religion,* 2 vols. (The Hague, Mouton, 1973).
Volume one contains a history of the discipline since the time of F. Max
Müller; it also includes excerpts from the methodological writings of
prominent historians of religions and scholars in cognate disciplines. Volume two contains a very complete bibliography for the sources of the discipline in the world of Western scholarship since the time of F. Max Müller.

Properly speaking, the discipline of the history of religions is a child of
the Enlightenment. The Enlightenment describes that intellectual period in
the modern West wherein the basis for scientific methodologies in the
natural and human sciences were formed. For an authoritative analytical
view of the Enlightenment see Ernst Cassirer, *The Philosophy of the Enlightenment* (Princeton, Princeton Univ. Press, 1959), and for a detailed
account of these intellectual currents as they are related to religion see
Frank Manuel, *The Eighteenth Century Confronts the Gods* (Cambridge,
Harvard Univ. Press, 1959).

Ernst Cassirer in the text mentioned above makes the following statement regarding the distinctive character of the Enlightenment,

> But in eighteenth century thought the intellectual center of gravity
> changes its position. The various fields of knowledge—natural science,
> history, law, politics, art—gradually withdraw from the domination and
> tutelage of traditional metaphysics and theology. They no longer look
> to the concept of God for their justification and legitimation; the various
> sciences themselves now determine that concept on the basis of their
> specific form. The relations between the concept of God and the con-
> cepts of truth, morality, law are by no means abandoned, but their
> direction changes. *An exchange of index symbols takes place as it were.
> That which formerly had established other concepts, now moves into
> the position of that which is to be established, and that which hitherto had
> justified other concepts, now finds itself in the position of a concept
> which requires justification* (p. 159, italics added).

The special quality of the Enlightenment as a "watershed" of modern
thought is revealed by this characteristic. The meaning of meaning must
from this point on be established through a rational epistemology. *Homo
sapiens* now becomes the locus of all knowledge; the epitome of this position is found in the Kantian Critiques. Not all Enlightenment thinkers were
rationalists, but all made rationality the norm for the discussion of epis-

temological questions. The other side of the Enlightenment defined those who attempted to establish other than rational grounds for the basis of knowledge, but even here the appeal was not to revelation but to forms of the human consciousness (the will, emotion, imagination, and so forth), that were equal to or even more sensitive and intuitive than the rational consciousness.

In this latter category we place those called the romantics. Jan de Vries in *The Study of Religion . . .* , defines three kinds of romantics. First are the philosophical romantics such as Johann Gottfried von Herder—see his *Reflections on the Philosophy of the History of Mankind* (Chicago, Univ. of Chicago Press, 1968)—and Friedrich Schelling—see *The Ages of the World* (N.Y., Columbia Univ. Press, 1942). Second are the symbolists, represented by a scholar such as Friedrich Creuzer; see his *Symbolik und Mythologie der alten Völker, besonders der Greichen* (Leipzig & Darmstadt, Heyer und Leske, 1819–23). A portion of this work is translated in Burton Feldman and Robert D. Richardson's *The Rise of Modern Mythology 1680–1860* (Bloomington, Indiana Univ. Press, 1972). Third are the romantic historians, the most important of whom was Carl Otfried Müller whose major work was *Prolegomena zu einer wissenschaftlichen Mythologie* (Göttingen, Vandenhoeck & Ruprecht, 1825). A section of this work in English translation appears in the above volume by Feldman and Richardson.

Thus rationalism, understood as a search for the internal laws of nature and human consciousness, and romanticism which tended to found these laws upon the willful, imaginative consciousness of man formed the philosophical background of the first historian of religions, Friedrich Max Müller. Müller was born in 1823 in Dessau, Germany, where he received his early education. In 1841 he enrolled at the University of Leipzig where he studied classical languages, psychology, and anthropology. Müller chose Sanskrit as his major subject and studied with Hermann Brockhaus, obtaining his doctorate in 1843. He then studied comparative philology at Berlin with Franz Bopp and philosophy with Friedrich Schelling. He spent a year in Paris studying with the Sanskritist Eugène Burnouf.

Müller went to England in 1846 and to Oxford in 1848. He became Professor of Comparative Philology in 1848 but retired from active duty in 1875 to edit *The Sacred Books of the East*. Müller's most important works for the student of the history of the history of religions are *Natural Religion* (London, Longmans, 1881), *Introduction to the Science of Religion* (London, Longmans, 1873), and *Lectures on the Origin and Growth of Language* (London, Longmans, 1878). The importance of Müller's work lies not so much in the theories that he put forth; hardly any of them were ever widely accepted in the scholarly community. His notion that religion resulted from a "disease of language," did not give any specific valuation to religion itself, and it was a highly speculative and unprovable theory about language. What is important about Müller is that he made the first systematic and integrative attempt to understand the nature of religion in a scientific manner. He was also influential in convincing the popular mind that such a possibility existed. While this influence may have led to excesses and aberrations of scholarship, such may be the price of innovation. See Richard Dorson, *The British Folklorist: A History* (London, Routledge & Kegan Paul, 1968), for an understanding of Müller's influence upon folkloristic proponents of "meteorological mythology." The fact that this same ground defined the arena of debate between Andrew Lang and Müller may be salutary.

> This first stage of study was characterized by a genuine enthusiasm, a sincere desire to understand other religions, and a measure of speculative interest. . . . Language study, history, and philosophy were blended during this era while theology receded. The term "science of religion" (*Religionswissenschaft*) was used to denote the emancipation of the new discipline from the philosophy of religion and especially theology.
> Joachim Wach, *The Comparative Study of Religions* (p. 3).

The interest in the newly conceived "science of religions" found concrete expression in the establishment of chairs of the history of religions in several European universities. The first was founded in Geneva in 1873, and in the next few years four chairs were established in Dutch universities. A chair was established at the Collège de France in 1878. Two of the Dutch chairs were first occupied by two scholars whom Wach notes as prominent in the second phase of the discipline. See Joachim Wach, "On Teaching History of Religions" in *Pro Regno Pro Sanctuario* (Uitgever and Nijkerk, G.F. Callenbach, 1950), 525–32.

Cornelius P. Tiele was appointed to the chair of history of religions at Leiden in 1877, and Chantepie de la Saussaye assumed the chair at Amsterdam in 1878. Chantepie's importance lies in his delineation of the historical and philosophical distinctions within the history of religion. This enabled him to suggest a morphology of religions which was both historical and philosophically based. See his *Manual of the Science of Religion* (London & N.Y., Longmans, Green, 1891). C.P. Tiele goes even further in a more direct manner towards establishing the integrity of the discipline on historical and philosophical grounds. See his *Elements of the Science of Religion,* 2 vols. (Edinburgh and London, W. Blackwood and Sons, 1898). According to Wach the next phase of the history of the discipline is defined by the Religionsgeschichtlicheschule. He seems to discern a fourth phase in the work of Nathan Söderblom and Rudolf Otto.

If the possibility of a science of religions had been established by Friedrich Max Müller, and if some of the elements of that science had been established by the scholars of the second phase, the Religionsgeschichtlicheschule represents the first reintegrative attempt in the new science. This school made a lasting impact on the historical study of religion, but it failed to become a normative synthesis for the history of religions probably for two reasons. First of all its historical data were primarily those of the biblical tradition, and secondly new philosophical problems concerning the very nature of historical knowledge had been raised by Wilhelm Dilthey.

It is well to remember that within the same generation of the publication of Friedrich Max Müller's *Science of Religion,* E.B. Tylor had published the first scientific work in the new discipline of anthropology. Ethnological and anthropological reports, knowledge from archeological excavations and new theoretical assumptions regarding the nature of religion from the point of view of psychology, neo-positivistism, and political theory were *en vogue.* For the history of German ethnology see Robert Heine-Geldern "One Hundred Years of Ethnological Theory in the German-Speaking Countries: Some Milestones," *Current Anthropology,* V, 5 (December, 1964). The members of the Religionsgeschichtlicheschule paid hardly any attention to these issues.

If indeed Joachim Wach saw the beginnings of a fourth phase in the history of the discipline in the work of Nathan Söderblom and Rudolf Otto, it is precisely because their work was carried out in the midst of the aforementioned problems. Already in Nathan Söderblom we see the problem of historical origins of religion correlated with the origin of belief in God in the human consciousness. See "Holiness" in the *Encyclopaedia of Religion and Ethics,* 1913. This way of stating the problem placed the discipline in direct contact with the discussions emmanating from anthropologists and folklorists. It furthermore revealed an awareness of the kinds of issues raised by Wilhelm Dilthey's critique of historical reason. For Dilthey see *Wilhelm Dilthey. An Introduction* (London, Routledge & Kegan Paul, 1949) by H.A. Hodges; and *The Essence of Philosophy* (Chapel Hill, Univ. of North Carolina Press, 1954) by Wilhelm Dilthey. The best discussion of Dilthey's philosophy is *The Philosophy of Wilhelm Dilthey* (London, Routledge & Kegan Paul, 1952) by H.A. Hodges.

Rudolf Otto's study *The Idea of the Holy* (London, Oxford Univ. Press, 2nd ed., 1958) constitutes the first systematic attempt to come to terms with the irreducible nature of the religious experience and its expressions. In the case of both Söderblom and Otto the tendency is to render objectively that subjective form of human consciousness which in its constitutive nature gives rise to the religious experience and its expression. A certain high point is reached in the work of Otto. Subsequently the history of religions emphasized hermeneutical theories. We have only to look at the work of Otto's student Joachim Wach who published the outstanding work on the history of hermeneutical theory, *Das Verstehen: Grundzüge einer Geschichte der hermeneutischen Theorie im 19. Jahrhundert,* 3 vols. (Tübingen, Mohr, 1926–1933). Throughout his life Wach continued to stress two central issues, the importance of hermeneutics and the sociology of religion. In the latter case he shows his indebtedness to both Wilhelm Dilthey and Max Weber.

In the work of G. Van der Leeuw we see an apparent transition from the emphasis on religious experience as found in Otto and Wach to an emphasis on the modes and forms of expression. *Religion in Essence and Manifestation* 2 vols., (N.Y. & Evanston, Harper & Row, 1963). In this work we have chapters entitled "Sacred Environment. Sacred Stones and Trees," "Representation. The King," "Conduct and Celebration," etc. I said that this was an *apparent* transition, for underlying all of these representations is a theory of religion founded upon an epistemological basis for the religious experience.

With the exception of Friedrich Max Müller the "founding father" of the discipline, all of the prominent scholars who referred to themselves as practitioners of the science of religions have been theologians and historians of religion. This may have occurred because theologians wish to protect the meaning of religion as a *sui generis* human experience and expression from the deteriorating reductionism of rationalistic philosophies and neo-positivistic theories of man and society. This may account for the subjective and epistemological emphases in their methodologies.

Mircea Eliade reports:

The year 1912 was a significant date in the history of the scientific study of religion. Émile Durkheim published his *Formes élémentaires de la vie religieuse* and Wilhelm Schmidt finished the first volume of his monumental work, *Ursprung der Gottesidee,* which was to be completed only after forty years, with Vols. XI and XII appearing posthumously in 1954–55. Also in 1912, Raffaele Pettazzoni brought out his first important monograph, *La religione primitiva in Sardegna,* and C.G. Jung his *Wandlungen und Symbole der Libido.* Sigmund Freud was correcting the proofs of *Totem und Tabu,* to be issued in book form the following year.   "The History of Religions in Retrospect: 1912–1962," *The Journal of Bible and Religion,* XXX, 2 (April, 1963), 98–109.

Eliade goes on to say that these works coming as they did from sociology, ethnology, psychology, and history were destined to play a profound role in the history of the history of religions. And even more significantly, with the exception of Pettazzoni, none of the authors was an historian of religion. Though Söderblom, Wach and Van der Leeuw wrote after this period and were quite aware of the meaning of these works, it is questionable whether they understood the long-term structural effect that these studies had on the history of religions. A. Eustace Haydon deals with the impact of these kinds of studies in two articles in the *Journal of Religion.* The first one is "From Comparative Religions to History of Religions," II, 6 (November, 1922), 577–87; the other is an excellent comprehensive article, "Twenty-five Years of History of Religions," VI, 1 (January, 1926), 17–

40. In a sense the publication of these works meant that the discipline of history of religions could no longer be safeguarded by epistemological theories of religious experience. If the discipline was to become a true science, it must conceive of itself in an objective mode. A similar methodological change occurred in the study of language with the movement from historical-philology to linguistics. Furthermore the relationship of historians of religions to their colleagues in cognate disciplines must define a moment of methodological awareness. This does not mean that historians of religion must adopt the methods and procedures of their colleagues, but it does mean that methodological imperialism from either side must be eliminated.

During most of the history of the discipline two major issues have been at the fore of methodological considerations; they are the origin of religion and/or primitive religions. See Mircea Eliade's "The Quest for the 'Origins' of Religion," *History of Religions. An International Journal for Comparative Historical Studies,* IV, 1 (Summer, 1964), 154–69. Even though several works devoted to religions of the civilizational type had appeared by 1925, hardly any of these works became the basis for a more general methodological understanding of the nature of religion as have the works dealing with primitive religions. Charles J. Adams alludes to this characteristic of methodology in the history of religion when he says that:

> During the nineteenth century there were students of religion who consciously held to the theory that the so-called primitive religions were purer and more genuine representations of the human religious drive than the more complex traditions. They reasoned to this conclusion, as everyone knows, from the assumption that the "primitive" religions were closer and more faithful to the original "simple" religious responses of our earliest ancestors. As everyone also knows, this theory has long since been given up as untenable. . . . I wish only to call attention to one of its consequences, that it has resulted in difficulties for those with interests outside the primitive or ancient fields. "The History of Religions and the Study of Islam," in *The History of Religions. Essays on the Problem of Understanding,* ed. by J.M. Kitagawa, M. Eliade, and C.H. Long (Chicago, Univ. of Chicago Press, 1967), 184–85.

Georges Dumézil's study of the religious traditions of the Indo-Europeans may provide a methodological bridge between the predominance of methodologies deriving from the primitive and ancient traditions and methodological positions which must emphasize the historical, sociological, and textual forms of religious expression. For a discussion of Dumézil's theories and a complete bibliography see C. Scott Littleton's *The New Comparative Mythology. An Anthropological Assessment of the Theories of Georges Dumézil* (Berkeley & Los Angeles, Univ. of California Press, 1966).

A clue for this methodological change may already be seen in Joachim Wach's *Sociology of Religion* (Chicago, Univ. of Chicago Press, 1944). Wach does not reduce religion to society, but he provides us with a thorough discussion of a sociological expression of religion. If indeed as Dumézil has remarked, "It is under the sign of *logos* rather than *mana* that we do our work," the history of religions as a discipline must strive for a methodological orientation which will be able to do justice to the various kinds of religious phenomena without undergoing *religious* reductionism. Though this overall methodological position has not been enunciated, it is clear that the discipline is now well established and that its practitioners are aware of its problems. It is hoped that Burnouf's prophecy might be fulfilled by the end of this century.

Index of Authors, Compilers, Translators, and Editors

Note: All names in this index have been treated like Western names for purposes of alphabetization, i.e., the last element in the name is taken as a surname and treated accordingly.

Index of Subjects